Ibn Ashur
Treatise on *Maqāṣid al-Shariʿah*

IBN ASHUR

Treatise on Maqāṣid al-Sharīʿah

MUHAMMAD AL-TAHIR IBN ASHUR

Translated from the Arabic and Annotated by
MOHAMED EL-TAHIR EL-MESAWI

THE INTERNATIONAL INSTITUTE OF ISLAMIC THOUGHT
LONDON • WASHINGTON

THE INTERNATIONAL INSTITUTE OF ISLAMIC THOUGHT
P.O. BOX 669, HERNDON, VA 20172, USA
WWW.IIIT.ORG

LONDON OFFICE
P.O. BOX 126, RICHMOND, SURREY TW9 2UD, UK
WWW.IIITUK.COM

ISBN 1–56564–422–0 paperback
ISBN 1–56564–423–9 hardback

Typesetting and cover design by Shiraz Khan
Printed by Biddles Ltd, King's Lynn, UK

CONTENTS

FOREWORD

Of knowledge, we have none, save what
You have taught us. (The Qur'an 2:32)

The International Institute of Islamic Thought (IIIT) has great pleasure in presenting this scholarly work on the topic of *Maqāṣid al-Shariʿah*. The author of the work, Shaikh Muhammad al-Tahir ibn Ashur, is the most renowned Zaytuna Imam and one of the great Islamic scholars of the 20th century.

The publication of the English translation of Shaikh Ibn Ashur's *Treatise on Maqāṣid al Shariʿah** is a breakthrough in the studies on Islamic law in the English language.

In this book, Ibn Ashur proposed *Maqāṣid* as a methodology for the renewal of the theory of the Islamic law, which has not undergone any serious development since the era of the great imams, starting with al-Shāfiʿī in the second/eighth century and ending with al-Shāṭibī in the eighth/fourteenth century. Ibn Ashur's methodology takes a centrist position between two contemporary extremes, namely, 'neo-literalism', which ignores rationales and valid re-interpretations of the Islamic rulings for the sake of literal traditional views, and 'neo-rationalism', which ignores the religious and cultural identity of Muslims in its quest for 'modernization' and 'rationality'. *Maqāṣid* of the Islamic law highlights rationales, purposes and common good in the Islamic rulings and stresses their importance, while basing itself on the Islamic scripts and observing the Islamic faith.

* It was a challenging effort to render the term *Maqāṣid* in English. We chose to leave it as it is in the book's title. However, throughout the book, it was translated as: goals, objectives, higher objectives, principles, intents, purposes, and ends, depending on context. A glossary of the more common terms is included at the end of this book.

Ibn Ashur also addressed the sensitive topic of the intents/*Maqāṣid* of Prophet Muhammad (*ṢAAS*)* behind his actions and decisions. He introduced criteria to differentiate between the Prophetic traditions that were meant to be part of the Islamic law, and the Prophetic actions/sayings that were meant to be for the sake of specific purposes such as political leadership, court judgment, friendly advice, and conflict resolution, etc. But Ibn Ashur's most significant contribution in this book has been the development of new *Maqāṣid* by coining contemporary terminology that were never formulated in traditional *uṣūl al-fiqh*. For example, Ibn Ashur developed the theory of the 'preservation of lineage' into 'the preservation of the family system', the 'protection of true belief' into 'freedom of beliefs', etc. He also introduced the concepts of 'orderliness', 'natural disposition', 'freedom', 'rights', 'civility', and 'equality' as *Maqāṣid* in their own right, and upon which the whole Islamic law is based. This development opens great opportunities for the Islamic law to address current and real challenges for Muslim societies and Muslim minorities.

The IIIT, established in 1981, has served as a major center to facilitate sincere and serious scholarly efforts based on Islamic vision, values and principles. Its programs of research, seminars and conferences during the last twenty four years have resulted in the publication of more than two hundred and fifty titles in English and Arabic, many of which have been translated into several other languages. IIIT has given especial attention to the topic of *Maqāṣid* and has published several books and theses in Arabic and English on the topic, the latest of which is *Imam al-Shāṭibī's Theory of the Higher Objectives and Intents of Islamic Law* by Ahmad al-Raysuni (published in English by the IIIT in 2005).

We would like to express our thanks to the editorial and production team at the IIIT London Office who labored tirelessly to check and ensure the accuracy of the translation, the references cited, as well as revising some of the complex and difficult passages; they include, Sylvia Hunt, Maryam Mahmood, Shiraz Khan, and Fouzia Butt.

---

* *(ṢAAS) – Ṣallā Allāhu ʿalayhi wa sallam*. May the peace and blessings of God be upon him. Said whenever the name of Prophet Muhammad is mentioned.

We would also like to express our thanks to the translator of the work, Mohamed El-Tahir El-Mesawi, who, throughout the various stages of production, cooperated closely with the editorial team. His extensive notes added valuable and useful contemporary and scholarly dimensions to Shaikh Ibn Ashur's masterpiece on *Maqāṣid*.

ANAS S. AL-SHAIKH-ALI
Academic Advisor
IIIT London Office, UK

GASSER AUDA
PhD Programme
University of Wales, Lampeter, UK

Ramadan 1427
September 2006

Muhammad al-Tahir Ibn Ashur

(1879–1973)

Muhammad al-Tahir ibn Ashur was born in Tunis in 1879 to an affluent family of high social standing. Originally of Andalusian origin dedication to the pursuit of knowledge seems to have been a continuous and established tradition throughout the successive generations of the family's ancestors.

Although Ibn Ashur's father is not mentioned by Tunisian biographers as one of the *ʿulamā'* elite of his time, his paternal grandfather, Muhammad al-Tahir ibn Ashur (1815–1868) is usually referred to as one of the finest and most authoritative scholars of his time. Ibn Ashur, however, was born into the household of his maternal grandfather, the eminent scholar and statesman, Shaikh Muḥammad al-ʿAzīz Bū ʿAttūr (1825–1907), one of the foremost collaborators of the renowned statesman Khayr al-Dīn Pasha (1822–1889) during his reform efforts of the 1860s and 1870s, before French colonial occupation. The young Ibn Ashur thus entered a family milieu that was at once familiar and, to a reasonable extent, aligned with the reformist movement that had been germinating in Tunisia for decades.

In 1892 Ibn Ashur entered the Zaytūna (a formal educational establishment, like al-Azhar in Cairo) and arrangements were made for the appointment of his future teachers. An eminent senior professor was chosen for this task. As their biographical data clearly show, almost all the teachers appointed for the young Ibn Ashur were reform-minded *ʿulamā'* involved in the 1860s–70s reform attempts led by Khayr al-Dīn.

During these year Ibn Ashur achieved a number of high level qualifications, which he considered merely formal requisites to consolidate his scholarly capacity and prove his personal worth. His real aim was general presence amongst the Zaytūna's permanent teaching staff and particularly close contact with its authoritative professors, notably his foremost teachers, ʿUmar ibn al-Shaikh (1826–1911)and Sālim Bū Hājib (1828–1924). It was a valuable opportunity for it allowed him to deepen and broaden the scope and nature of his knowledge in a manner more specialized and focused than general formal classes would have made possible.

This type of extensive contact study was also crucial in qualifying Ibn Ashur to earn what is known in classical Islamic scholarship as an *ijāzah*, an attestation by a prominent scholar(s) that a student has mastered a specific branch of knowledge and become a reliable authority in it. Nevertheless, whatever formal training Ibn Ashur might have received and whatever the influence of his teachers, personal dedication and natural talent always played an equally essential role in developing his excellent academic and scholastic abilities as well as mastery of an amazingly wide range of disciplines. Ibn Ashur quickly rose to various prominent positions and in 1927 was promoted to the office of chief judge and within a few years (1932), named Shaikh al-Islam, an illustrious post which conferred upon him the highest scholarly rank and authority in the country.

Despite his administrative duties and teaching commitments at the Zaytūna and elsewhere, Ibn Ashur was a prolific writer and author publishing many articles and works. He was an almost regular contributer to most of the leading journals and magazines published in Tunisia as well as others published in Egypt and Syria.

The long and varied list of his works include *Tafsīr al-Taḥrīr wa al-Tanwīr* (a fifteen-volume commentary on the Qur'an), *Kashf al- Mughaṭṭā* (a commentary on the *Muwaṭṭa'* of Mālik ibn Anas), *al-Naẓar al-Fasīḥ* (a commentary on *al-Jāmiʿ al-Ṣaḥīḥ* of Muḥammad ibn Ismāʿīl al-Bukhārī), *Alaysa al-Ṣubḥ bi-Qarīb* (an historical and critical study of Islamic education accompanied by a project for reforming it), *Uṣūl al-Niẓām al-Ijtimāʿī fī al-Islām* (a study of the principles and enduring values of the Islamic socio-political system), *Ḥāshiyat al-Tawḍīḥ wa al-Taṣḥīḥ* (a critical and elaborate commentary on *Sharḥ Tanqīḥ al-Fuṣūl*, a treatise on *uṣūl al-fiqh* by the Mālikī jurist Shihāb al-Dīn al-

Qarāfī) and *Maqāṣid al-Shariʿah al-Islāmiyyah* the translation of which is provided in this publication.

This latter work on the higher objectives of the Shariʿah was first published in 1946 in Tunis. It was the outcome of a deep and serious study of the possible ways and means for revitalizing Islamic jurisprudence. The issue had become a major concern for the author as early as 1903 when he met Shaikh Muhammad Abdu, the spokesman for modern Islamic reformism in Egypt and the Arab world, during his visit to Tunisia. The meeting sealed Ibn Ashur's alignment with the spirit of the Islamic reform movement and shortly thereafter he began to publish articles on the need for reforming Islamic education (in terms of content, method and administration etc.) laying special emphasis on the place that *maqāṣid al-Shariʿah* should occupy in the teaching and study of Islamic jurisprudence. Indeed interest in the subject had been growing since *al-Muwāfaqāt,* the work of Abū Isḥāq al-Shāṭibī (d. 790/1388) was first published in Tunis in 1883.

Ibn Ashur's work on *Maqāṣid al-Shariʿah* is a pioneering study of the Shariʿah's higher objectives and it is not known whether any modern jurist prior to Ibn Ashur has made any attempt to develop a comprehensive and systematic study of its different aspects. The work stands as a testament to his deeply cherished objective of establishing *maqāṣid al-Shariʿah* as an independent discipline in its own right, under the title *ʿIlm Maqāṣid al-Shariʿah*.

Ibn Ashur worked tirelessly to the end, never laying down his pen nor losing the great pleasure that reading and research afforded him until he breathed his last on 13 Rajab 1393 (12 August 1973) at the venerable age of ninety-four. He left behind him a wealth of long and detailed experience in public and administrative life as well as a rich legacy of diverse and scholarly publications and articles absolutely unmatched in nineteenth and twentieth century Tunisia, many of which still await critical study and publication today.

Author's Preface

ALL PRAISE BE TO GOD FOR GUIDING US TO HIS LAW AND WAY, and for inspiring us with the means of realizing His higher objectives (*maqāṣid*) and outlining systematic argumentation to establish them. May the blessings of God be upon our Prophet Muhammad *(ṢAAS)*, through whom God has laid the solid foundations for reform. May His Mercy be upon the Prophet's Companions and the members of his household, luminaries of Islam and jewels in its crown, and upon the leading scholars through whom divine knowledge has radiated following the advent of Islam.

I intend in this book to develop some important discourses on the *maqāṣid* of the Islamic Shariʿah and to illustrate them and argue for their affirmation. The objective of these discourses is that those seeking to study and understand the religion of Islam will take them as a guide and frame of reference when faced with differences of opinion and change in time. I also intend these discourses to be a means of minimizing disagreement between the jurists of the different areas of Islam. My purpose is, moreover, to train the jurists' followers, when facing such a situation, to be just in preferring one opinion over another, so that fanaticism is rejected and truth accepted. Likewise, the aim of this book is twofold. It consists of assisting Muslims with a healing legislation for their contingent interests when new cases (*nawāzil*) emerge and matters become complicated, and of providing them with a decisive opinion in the face of conflicting arguments by different juristic schools (*madhāhib*) and the competing views of their respective scholars. My awareness of the difficulties confronting the contending jurists in their argumentation and reasoning concerning Shariʿah-related matters prompted me to devote my attention to this subject. The case of the jurists is unlike that of the scholars of the rational sciences. The latter base their logical and philosophical reasoning on necessary evidence, or on established observation or taken-for-granted postulates that force all contestants to stop arguing, thus resolving all points of dispute between them.

In contrast, the jurists do not in their juridical reasoning draw on necessary and categorical (*ḍarūriyyah*) evidence or on evidence bordering need, that the obstinate is forced to yield and the confused is guided. In my opinion, the scholars of the Shariʿah have a stronger right to such compelling reasoning, and the Hereafter is better than this worldly life.

One might believe that the propositions and rules (*masā'il*) of the science of *uṣūl al-fiqh* are sufficient to guide anyone seeking the above-mentioned objective. However, when one masters *uṣūl al-fiqh*, one will certainly realize that most of its propositions are contested among scholars, whose differences over the basic principles (*uṣūl*) continue owing to their disagreement on applied legal rulings (*furūʿ*). In other words, this situation exists because the general rules and universal principles of *uṣūl al-fiqh* were derived from the particular qualities of those rulings. This is because the systematic compilation (*tadwīn*) of the science of *uṣūl al-fiqh* was completed only nearly two centuries after the codification of fiqh (moral law). It has to be mentioned, furthermore, that a number of jurists were weak in matters of *uṣūl*, and thus they engaged in the field of fiqh with inadequate knowledge. In fact, when new cases requiring original legal rulings presented themselves, only a few jurists could make use of the general rules and universal principles of jurisprudence laid down in *uṣūl al-fiqh*. Accordingly, *uṣūl al-fiqh* has never been the final arbiter whose verdict is accepted by those disagreeing on matters of fiqh. Bringing the jurists to one unified opinion or at least reducing their differences of opinion thus proved difficult, if not impossible.

In addition, most of the propositions and inquiries of *uṣūl al-fiqh* hardly serve the purpose of expounding the underlying wisdom (*ḥikmah*) and establishing the goals of the Shariʿah. Rather, they revolve around the deduction of provisions (*aḥkām*) from the literal expressions and words (*alfāẓ*) of the Lawgiver by means of methodological rules enabling the person knowing them to derive positive legal rulings from those expressions, or to extract certain attributes and qualities (*awṣāf*) suggested by them. These qualities and attributes would then be considered a means of legislation. Hence, many new cases would be subsumed under one particular expression of analogical deduction on the basis that all these cases have in common the attribute that is thought to be the intended meaning of the words of the Lawgiver, which is called the *ʿillah* (*ratio legis*).

To express this point more clearly, those methodological rules would enable whoever is conversant with them to argue for the sake of detailed legal rulings (*furūʿ*) derived by the jurists before the founding of the science of *uṣūl al-fiqh*. Therefore, thanks to those rules, the rulings become acceptable to those practising them from among the followers of the different juristic schools (*madhāhib*). In brief, the most important purpose those methods can serve is to explicate the meanings of the texts of the Shariʿah under their different conditions of isolation (*infirād*), association (*ijtimāʿ*), or separation (*iftirāq*), so as to allow the person skilled in them to reach almost the same understanding as that of a native Arabic speaker. Those methods include issues concerning the requisites and different connotations of words such as being general (*ʿumūm*), absolute and unrestricted (*iṭlāq*), explicit (*naṣṣ*), apparent (*ẓuhūr*), real meaning (*ḥaqīqah*), and the opposites of all these. They also include questions of the conflict of legal proofs (*taʿāruḍ al-'adillah*), such as specification (*takhṣīṣ*), qualification (*taqyīd*), interpretation (*ta'wīl*), reconciliation (*jamʿ*), preponderance (*tarjīḥ*), etc.

All this deals with the Shariʿah dispositions (*taṣārīf*) in isolation from any consideration of its universal wisdom (*ḥikmah*) and the general and particular goals of its commands and rulings. Scholars of *uṣūl al-fiqh* have thus confined their inquiries to the external and literal aspects of the Shariʿah and to the meanings readily conveyed by its letter, that is, the underlying causes (*ʿilal*) of analogy-based rules. Then again one might come across many important rules concerning the *maqāṣid* of the Shariʿah in advanced works of fiqh, none of which could be found in *uṣūl* works. These *maqāṣid*-related rules, however, deal only with the particular higher objectives of the various types of the Shariʿah prescriptions (*mashrūʿāt*) at the beginning of the respective sections of fiqh-compendia, not with the general objectives (*maqāṣid ʿāmmah*) of legislation.

Furthermore, there are hidden insights in the discourses dealing with some of the propositions of *uṣūl al-fiqh*, or in its unnoticed sections. These sections are either unstudied or deemed tedious; and when dealt with, it is at the end of the books on *uṣūl*. When authors reach them, it is with weariness that they write them down, if ever, and only the most patient and persevering students will manage to read them. Therefore, these insights have always remained scarce and forgotten, although they are worthy of being included in the constituent elements of the discipline dealing with the higher objectives of the Shariʿah (*ʿilm maqāṣid al-Shariʿah*). These insights can be found in the discussions of the notions of suitability (*munāsabah*) and imagination (*ikhālah*) in the inquiries into the methods of identifying and confirming the underlying cause (*masālik al-ʿillah*). They are also to be found in the discussions on textually unregulated benefits (*maṣāliḥ mursalah*), the multiple contiguous narrations (*tawātur*), matters of necessary knowledge (*maʿlūm bi al-ḍarūrah*), and interpreting unrestricted terms (*muṭlaq*) as qualified ones (*muqayyad*), whether there is similarity or difference between the motive (*mūjib*) and the requisite (*mūjab*). In the introductory part of his book *al-Burhān*, Imām al-Ḥaramayn al-Juwaynī[1] apologized for including what was not categorical in the study of *uṣūl* matters. He wrote:

> It might be objected that the detailed discussion of isolated traditions (*akhbār āḥād*) and the varieties of analogical deduction (*aqyisah*) is not found except in the *uṣūl* works, though they are not categorical (*qawāṭiʿ*). Our answer is that the task of the legal theorist (*uṣūlī*) is to establish the necessity (*wujūb*) of acting upon these proofs in general. Yet, it remains necessary to mention such details in order to clarify the intended meaning (*madlūl*) and connect it with its indicant (*dalīl*).[2]

However, this answer is unconvincing, for we do not find that scholars have included in *uṣūl al-fiqh* only those categorical rules and principles (*uṣūl qawāṭi*ᶜ) which can halt any contestant who goes against their requisites, as they have done in respect of the fundamentals of belief (*uṣūl al-dīn*). In fact, we find only a few categorical principles, such as the necessary universals (*kulliyyāt ḍarūriyyah*), consisting of the preservation of religion (*ḥifẓ al-dīn*), the preservation of life (*ḥifẓ al-nafs*), the preservation of intellect (*ḥifẓ al-ᶜaql*), the preservation of progeny (*ḥifẓ al-nasl*), the preservation of property (*ḥifẓ al-māl*) and the preservation of honor (*ḥifẓ al-ᶜirḍ*). Apart from these, all the principles of jurisprudence are conjectural and probable (*maẓnūnah*).

Abū ᶜAbd Allāh al-Māzarī[3] realized this problem in the course of his commentary on al-Juwaynī's discussion in his *al-Burhān* concerning the proofs of legal commands (*'adillat al-aḥkām*) as consisting of "the unequivocal (*naṣṣ*) texts of the Qur'an, the unequivocal texts of *mutawātir* traditions (Sunnah) and consensus (ijmaᶜ)."[4] Thus, al-Māzarī wrote:

> The formulations of legal theorists (*uṣūliyyūn*) differ in this regard. Some of them do not accept this qualification (by using the restrictive term "unequivocal") and simply refer to the texts of the Qur'an, the Sunnah (that is, they mention them without qualifying them as unequivocal) and consensus. When they are asked if they also mean texts of probabilistic connotations (*ẓawāhir*) and isolated reports (*akhbār āḥād*), their answer is that they mean by that statement what they are certain is intended by the Book [that is, the Qur'an]. They say this although we, so they argue, may not be completely certain that a particular instance of general applicability (ᶜ*umūm*) is intended by it. They also say the same concerning isolated reports, that we may not be sure that a specific report is part of the corpus of the Sunnah. Others do not use this qualification to remove the ambiguity. Yet, a third group of scholars maintain that anything indicating a command (*ḥukm*) is a legal proof, even if it is merely conjectural (*maẓnūnah*), and this does not require any qualification.[5]

According to Qarāfī's[6] commentary on *al-Maḥṣūl* [of Fakhr al-Dīn al-Rāzī],[7] when dealing with commands (*amr*) and prohibitions (*nahy*) in the second issue of expressions (*lafẓ*), al-Abyārī[8] said in his commentary on *al-Burhān*:

> The propositions of *uṣūl* are categorical, allowing for no conjecture (*ẓann*). They derive from categorical evidential ground that is not to be found in books. This means that whoever is thoroughly cognizant with the juridical cases (*aqḍiyah*) and debates of the Prophet's Companions and their edicts (*fatāwā*), and is familiar with the sources of the Shariʿah and their provenance, will attain certain knowledge of what constitutes the principles of jurisprudence (*qawāʿid al-uṣūl*); and whoever falls short of this will gain nothing except mere conjecture.[9]

This is also non-productive, for what we are concerned with here is evaluating the status of the actual propositions of *uṣūl al-fiqh* not what might be experienced by certain scholars of the Shariʿah. Moreover, in Qarāfī's commentary on al-Rāzī's *Maḥṣūl* in the second chapter dealing with the premises, it is mentioned that Abū al-Ḥusayn al-Baṣrī[10] said in his *Sharḥ al-ʿUmad* that adoption and imitation (*taqlīd*) are not permissible in matters of *uṣūl al-fiqh*, just as not every *mujtahid* in this respect is right; there is rather just one *mujtahid* whose opinion is correct. Furthermore, he who is wrong in matters of *uṣūl al-fiqh* commits a sin, which is different from fiqh matters. To this Qarāfī retorted by maintaining that there are in *uṣūl al-fiqh* certain propositions that have a weak basis, such as implicit consensus (*ijmāʿ sukūtī*), anyone contesting them will in fact contest conjecture, not certainty. That person should not, therefore, be accused of sin. This is similar to our position concerning the fundamentals of faith (*uṣūl al-dīn*), for we do not consider sinful anyone asserting that accidents continue to exist for more than one moment (*al-ʿaraḍ yabqā zamānayn*)[11] or rejecting the idea of a vacuum *khalā'*)[12] and other issues which are not important elements of the fundamentals of religion; this is because they are mere supplements to the discipline dealing with *uṣūl al-dīn*.[13] In the first premise of his book *al-Muwāfaqāt* Abū Isḥāq al-Shāṭibī[14] also attempted to demonstrate that the principles of jurisprudence are categorical, although his effort was unsuccessful.[15]

In my opinion, the reason for disagreement between the scholars of *uṣūl al-fiqh* over reducing legal indicants (*'adillah*) to what is categorical stemmed from the confusion arising from the status of legal indicants for they were actually familiar with them and their desire to make *uṣūl al-fiqh* as categorical and certain as the textually established foundations of faith (*uṣūl al-dīn al-samʿiyyah*). As they embarked on this task and collected the rules and propositions of *uṣūl al-fiqh* and systematized them, they realized that only very few of them were categorical. Indeed, the number was so small that it was hardly worth including them in the propositions of *uṣūl al-fiqh*. How could it have been otherwise, when there are differences of opinion among scholars over most of the propositions of *uṣūl al-fiqh*?

Likewise, if we want to lay down definitive and categorical principles for the understanding of the Shariʿah, we need to return to the traditionally accepted propositions of *uṣūl al-fiqh* and reformulate them. We should critically evaluate them, rid them of the alien elements that crept into them, and supplement them with the results of thorough comprehension and careful thought. Then, we need to reformulate the whole and classify it as an independent discipline called "science of the higher objectives of the Shariʿah" (*ʿilm maqāṣid al-Shariʿah*). In other words, we should leave the discipline of *uṣūl al-fiqh* as it is, a source from which the methods of formulating legal argumentation could be derived. As for those elements of it which fall within the purview of our purpose of systematizing the study of *maqāṣid al-Shariʿah*, we should incorporate them as part of the foundational principles of this noble discipline: *ʿilm maqāṣid al-Shariʿah*.

We ought therefore to state that *uṣūl al-fiqh* must be categorical, in the sense that scholars have the right to include in its propositions only what is categorical, either by being a matter of necessary and self-evident truth (*ḍarūrah*) or as the result of compelling sound reflection. This issue has always been a matter of debate, and the protagonists' attempts to come up with satisfactory solutions to it are abundant in the lessons of Hadith studies during the month of Ramadan.[16]

Some Muslim scholars have indeed made felicitous statements that have become cogent and definitive rules for engaging in jurisprudence. However, their diffusion and submersion in the course of reasoning over particular juristic issues (*juz'iyyāt*) have made them difficult to access by whoever wants to benefit from them when need be. These insights include maxims such as: "there is no harm nor return of harm"[17] and the statement by ʿUmar ibn ʿAbd al-ʿAzīz that "people incur as many court cases as the iniquity they perpetrate."[18]They also include statements as Mālik's saying in *Muwaṭṭa'* that "God's religion is based on easiness."[19] To the same category belongs Mālik's comment on the Prophetic tradition according to which God's Apostle *(ṢAAS)* said: "Do not ask for a woman in marriage when another Muslim has already done so."[20] According to Mālik, this tradition means that "when a man has asked for a woman in marriage, and she has inclined to him... It does not mean that when a man has asked for a woman in marriage and his proposal is acceptable to her and she does not incline to him that no one else can ask her for marriage. That is a door to misery for people."[21]

These were joined by some peerless scholars who also, I believe, had a strong desire to pursue such a course, like the Shāfiʿī, ʿIzz al-Dīn ibn ʿAbd al-Salām,[22] in his *Qawāʿid* and the Mālikī, Shihāb al-Dīn Aḥmad ibn Idrīs al-Qarāfī, in his book *al-Furūq*. These two scholars specifically tried more than once to lay the foundations for the discipline of the higher objectives of the Shariʿah. However, the genius who applied himself to systematizing this discipline is the Mālikī jurist Abū Isḥāq Ibrāhīm ibn Mūsā al-Shāṭibī. He devoted the second volume of his book *ʿUnwān al-Taʿrīf bi-Uṣūl al-Taklīf fī Uṣūl al-Fiqh*, to its explanation[23] and entitled it *Kitāb al-Maqāṣid* [Book of the Higher Objectives of the Shariʿah]. However, in dealing with its methodological precepts, he fell into the trap of longwinded and confused analysis. He also omitted some crucial aspects of the Shariʿah's higher objectives and thus failed to reach the target that he had set himself. None the less, he made a great contribution. I for my part, follow in his footsteps, not neglecting what he has contributed.

However, I do not intend merely to quote or to summarize what he said.

Moreover, my aim in this book is confined to the study of the objectives of Islam concerning the laws and rules governing civil transactions (*muʿāmalāt*) and manners (*ādāb*). These laws, I think, deserve to be exclusively called the Shariʿah, for they reflect that aspect to which Islam has paid great attention in specifying and identifying the various levels of benefit (*maṣāliḥ*) and harm (*mafāsid*) and the criteria for assessing them. This aspect is also a clear manifestation of the greatness of the Islamic Shariʿah in comparison with other religious teachings (*sharāiʿ*), civil laws, and social policies whose aim is to preserve the order of the world and reform human society.[24]

Therefore, when I use the term legislation (*tashrīʿ*), my terminology is specific to what constitutes the general law of society, and I do not mean by it all prescribed matters in an absolute sense. Thus, the recommended (*mandūb*) and the repugnant (*makrūh*) are not intended in my discourse. In this connection, I think that the commands and rules pertaining to the devotional acts of worship (*ʿibādāt*) should appropriately be called 'religiousness' (*diyānah*).[25] As such, they comprise different inner meanings concerned with managing and refining the soul and reforming the individual who constitutes society. For this reason, we have given it a technical term: the order of Muslim society. I have devoted a book to this subject by the title *Uṣūl Niẓām al-Mujtamaʿ fī al-Islām* [Basis of the Order of Human Society in Islam].[26]

None the less, dealing with the issue of *maqāṣid* in this specific way has faced us with some difficulty when seeking support from the works of early scholars, owing to the scarcity of helpful relevant material in the discourses of the scholars of fiqh, *uṣūl al-fiqh* and *jadal* (juristic polemics). The reason is that they confined most of their polemics, legal argumentation, and inquiries concerning causation and rationalisation (*taʿlīl*) to questions of devotional acts of worship and to a few instances of the lawful and unlawful relating to contracts of sale. These limited topics are not of much help to someone seeking to discover the inner wisdom and underlying purposes of the rules and commands regulating civil dealings and transactions (*muʿāmalāt*).

They may be appropriate for legal theorists in illustrating their precepts and rules, for polemicists in conducting their debates, or for jurists in developing the premises of the first chapters of their (fiqh) treatises, when they are still enthusiastic and not yet wearied or bored. These topics, however, remain inappropriate for someone who wants to comprehend the rules of *muʿāmalāt*.

For this reason, I took the trouble of providing examples of *muʿāmalāt* dealings, which my reflection led me to discover or which I came across in my readings. Nevertheless, sometimes I have been compelled to use examples of matters of "religiousness" (*diyānah*) and devotional acts of worship (*ʿibādāt*). This is because in these examples there are some hints and clues to one or other general objective of the Lawgiver, or there are associated with them some insights expressed by the luminaries of the Shariʿah in detecting the intent of the Lawgiver.

I have divided this book into three parts. The first part is concerned with establishing the existence of the Shariʿah's higher objectives and proving the need of the jurist to know them, the categories of these goals and the methods of identifying and confirming them. The second part examines the universal or general objectives of legislation. Finally, the third part deals with the particular objectives of the different types of dealings, designated *abwāb fiqh al-muʿāmalāt* in the literature of applied jurisprudence (fiqh).

PART I

Establishing *Maqāṣid al-Sharī*ʿ*ah*

I

Prefatory Note

Nobody would contest that the provisions and ordinances of any divine law (Shariᶜah) instituted for humankind aim at certain objectives intended by God (SWT)*, the Wise Lawgiver. It is proven beyond any dispute that God does not act in vain, as is plainly shown in His fashioning of the creation. Thus, we are informed in the Qur'an: "For [thus it is:] We have not created the heavens and the earth and all that is between them in mere idle play. None of this have We created without [an inner] truth: but most of them do not understand it" (44:38–39), and, "Did you, then, think that We created you in mere idle play, and that you would not have to return to Us...?" (23:115). Moreover, one of the most important qualities of human beings is their God-given disposition for, and acceptability of, civilization, whose greatest manifestation is the making of laws to regulate their lives.

God sent messengers and revealed laws (*sharā'iᶜ*) only for the purpose of establishing human order. As He says:

> Indeed, [even afore-time] did We send forth Our apostles with all evidence of [this] truth; and through them We bestowed revelation from on high, and [thus gave you] a balance [wherewith to weigh right and wrong], so that men might behave with equity. (57:25)

* (SWT) – *Subḥānahu wa Taᶜālā*: May He be praised and may His transcendence be affirmed. Said when referring to God.

The Islamic Shariʿah is the greatest and most upright of all laws, as indicated by the Qur'an: "Behold, the only [true] religion in the sight of God is Islam" (3:19). This is expressed by the use of the grammatical form denoting both exclusivity and intensity.

Hence, when we find that God has described the revealed Books preceding the Qur'an as books of guidance and called them "religion" (*dīn*), as in this verse: "O followers of the Gospel! Do not overstep the bounds [of truth] in your religion" (4:171), referring to Moses' law, and when He says: "In matters of religion, He has ordained for you that which He had enjoined upon Noah – and into which We gave thee [O Muhammad] insight through revelation – as well as that which We had enjoined upon Abraham, and Moses, and Jesus: Steadfastly uphold the religion, and do not break up your unity therein" (42:13), and when we find that He calls what is mentioned here *sharāʾiʿ*, as in the following verse: "Unto every one of you is appointed a [different] law and way of life. And if God had so willed, He could surely have made you all one single community" (5:48); when we find, on the other hand, that God describes the Qur'an as the best of all of them, then we know for certain that the Qur'an is the best and most exalted of all guidance.

In this connection, God says [about the Torah]: "Verily, it is We who have bestowed from on high the Torah, wherein there was guidance and light" (5:44), after which He says [about the Gospel]: "And We caused Jesus, son of Mary, to follow in the footsteps of those [earlier prophets], confirming the truth of whatever there still remained of the Torah, and as a guidance and admonition unto the God-conscious" (5:46). Thus, God attributes two properties to the Qur'an: its confirmation of the truth of earlier revelations, that is, the laws brought by the Torah and the Gospel that have not been abrogated by the Qur'anic Revelation; and its guidance over previous revelations concerning those laws in the Torah and the Gospel that it has abrogated as well as the fundamentals of the Shariʿah that it has introduced.

Accordingly, the Qur'an is superior in the sense that it bears witness to the truth and reveals alterations of previous revelations. All divine laws, and particularly the Islamic Shariʿah, have come down for the benefit of humankind both now and in the future. By "the future" we are not referring to matters of the Hereafter, for divine laws do not determine how people should behave in the afterlife. Instead, God has made people's status in the Hereafter the result of their conduct in this world. What we rather mean is that some provisions (*aḥkām*) of the Shariʿah, such as the prohibitions of drinking or selling wine, may seem to entail hardship and harm to those under obligation and that the latter are thus made to forsake some benefits. However, when we reflect on these provisions, we discover their real benefits in relation to the ultimate consequences of things.

From an inductive examination (*istiqrāʾ*) of numerous indicants in the Qur'an and the authentic Prophetic traditions, we can with certainty draw the compelling conclusion that the rules of the Islamic Shariʿah are based on inner reasons (*ḥikam*) and causes (*asbāb*) that devolve upon the universal goodness and benefit of both society and individuals, as we shall see below. Our aim here is to prove that the Shariʿah in general has intended higher objectives, although we leave the elaboration of those goals to its appropriate place. In the Introduction to the section on *Maqāṣid al-Shariʿah* of his book *ʿUnwān al-Taʿrīf*, Abū Ishāq al-Shāṭibī mentioned a number of textual indicants to this effect.[1] Of them only the following are appropriate and productive.

In conclusion to the verse instituting ritual ablution, God says, "God does not want to impose any hardship on you, but wants to make you pure, and to bestow upon you the full measure of His blessings, so that you might have cause to be grateful" (5:6).

On a different occasion, He says "For in [the law of] just retribution, O you who are endowed with insight, there is life for you, so that you might remain conscious of God" (2:179). To these indicants we can add many others, such as the following verses. Concluding the prohibition of the consumption of alcohol and gambling, God says, "By means of intoxicants and gambling, Satan seeks only to sow enmity and hatred among you" (5:91). In other contexts, we read, "This will make it more likely that you will not deviate from the right course" (4:3), "and God does not love corruption" (2:205).

Other examples will be mentioned in the next discourse on the methods of establishing *Maqāṣid al-Shariʿah*, and also in the third part of this book which is devoted to a detailed exposition of the specific higher objectives of the Shariʿah in the different spheres of legislation.

2

The Jurists' Need to Know *Maqāṣid al-Shariʿah*

The disposition of the *mujtahid* to comprehend the Shariʿah takes five modes:

1. The first mode is to understand its expressions (*aqwāl*) and grasp the meanings (*madlūlāt*) of those expressions in accordance with the language use and legal polysemy (*naql sharʿī*),[1] by applying the linguistic rules governing juristic argumentation. Most of this has been taken care of in the discipline of *uṣūl al-fiqh*.

2. The second mode is to search for anything that clashes with the indicants (*'adillah*) advanced by the *mujtahid* and in respect of which he has exhausted all possible effort to discover their meanings. The purpose of this search is to make sure that those indicants are free from anything nullifying their connotations or requiring their invalidation (*ilghā'*) or emendation and refinement (*tanqīḥ*).[2] When he is certain that an indicant (*dalīl*) is free from any contradiction, he applies it. If, on the contrary, he finds a counter-indicant (*muʿāriḍ*), then his task is to see how to reconcile the two and apply them together or to decide the superiority of one to the other.

3. The third mode is to give, by means of analogy, that whose rule (*ḥukm*) has not been given in the texts of the Lawgiver the same rule of that which has been mentioned therein, once the effective

causes of the Shariʿah legislative rules have been known by any of the methods of identification and confirmation of the *ratio legis* laid down in *uṣūl al-fiqh*.

4. The fourth mode is to give a specific rule to a certain act or event whose rule has not been provided by the textual indicants of the Shariʿah as known to the *mujtahids*, nor is there an equivalent to which it can be connected by analogical deduction.[3]

5. The fifth mode is to accept some textually established rules of the Shariʿah simply as someone who does not know their causes or the inner wisdom of the Shariʿah in enacting them. Here, the *mujtahid* acknowledges his incapacity to comprehend the Lawgiver's wisdom in prescribing such rules, and belittles his knowledge in relation to the vastness of the Shariʿah. He then considers this kind of provisions as merely devotional.

Thus, the jurist needs to know *Maqāṣid al-Shariʿah* on all these levels. His need for that knowledge on the fourth level is quite obvious. This, in fact, ensures the continuity of the rules of the Islamic Shariʿah throughout the ages and generations following the age of Revelation until the end of the world. It is in this context that Mālik, may God have mercy on him, established the authoritativeness of the principle of *maṣāliḥ mursalah* or textually unspecified benefits.[4] It is also in this context that the scholars of jurisprudence ascertained the consideration of the necessities (*kulliyyāt ḍarūriyyah*), and appended them with the needs (*ḥājiyyāt*) and embellishments (*taḥsīniyyāt*). All this is called *munāsib*[5] (suitable), as established in *uṣūl al-fiqh* in the context of the discussion on the methods of the identification and confirmation of the *ratio legis*.

It is again in this context that rationalists (*ahl al-ra'y*) resorted to independent opinion (*ra'y*) and juristic preference (*istiḥsān*),[6] but were faced by the vociferous opposition of the traditionists (*ʿulamā' al-athar*). The latter were aware of indicants from traditions and past practices containing the rules (*aḥkām*) of the situations and cases that had escaped the attention of the rationalists, as was the case with Mālik who rejected the opinion of Shurayḥ[7] concerning the invalidity of public endowment (*ḥabs*).[8] Scholars combining the knowledge of traditions (*āthār*) with rational thinking and reasoning (*naẓar*) also protested against the views of the speculative jurists regarding the issues which conflicted with the Shariʿah's objectives as established by inductive inference. It is in this context that Mālik opposed the views of the Predecessors (*Salaf*) who had maintained that the buyer and seller have the right to withdraw from their sale agreement before parting company (*khiyār al-majlis fī al-bayʿ*).[9] Thus, he said in *Muwaṭṭa'*: "In our view, this has no specific limit, nor is there any established practice supporting it."[10] His followers explained that what he meant is that the time of agreement (*majlis*) cannot be accurately defined and that this contradicts the purpose of the Shariʿah regarding creation of contracts.[11]

We now need to examine the first three modes. The jurist needs to know the *maqāṣid* in the first mode in order to decide, for example, whether a given word, or expression, has undergone legal polysemy (*naql sharʿī*). As for the second mode, his need for that knowledge is more pressing for the following reason. The motive compelling the jurist to think about the existence of counter-indicant and then to search for it in its likely sources, intensifies and weakens in proportion to what strikes him – while examining the indicant before him – as to the inappropriateness of the indicant to be intended by the Lawgiver without any modification. His search for a counter-indicant therefore intensifies in proportion to the degree of his doubt concerning the sufficiency of the available indicant to yield the Shariʿah ruling on the case in hand. By the same token, his conviction about the end of his search, upon not finding any counter-indicant, is proportionate to the extent of the doubt that has assailed him. This can be illustrated by the following authentic tradition. ʿAbd Allāh ibn ʿUmar heard the following report by ʿĀ'ishah:

> God's Apostle said to her: "Do you know that when your people [the Quraysh] re-built the Kaʿbah, they reduced it from its original foundation laid by Abraham as they ran short of money?" She said, "O God's Apostle! Why don't you rebuild it on its original foundation laid by Abraham?" He replied, "Were it not for the fact that your people are

> close to the pre-Islamic period of ignorance [that is, they have recently become Muslims], I would have done so." Upon hearing this, ʿAbd Allāh (ibn ʿUmar) stated: "ʿĀ'ishah must have heard this from God's Apostle for, in my opinion, God's Apostle had not placed his hand over the two corners of the Kaʿbah opposite *al-ḥijr* only because the Kaʿbah was not rebuilt on its original foundations laid by Abraham."[12]

Therefore, we learn from what he said that the evidence that had reached him concerning the practice of the Prophet, namely, not placing his hands on the two corners, perplexed him. He thought that there was a reason implied by that evidence (*mūjib*) that he did not know. When he heard ʿĀ'ishah's report, he realized that what she had reported was that reason, and this reassured him.

Similarly, the jurist's conviction, in case of the existence of a counter-indicant, is fast or slow in tandem with the degree of his doubt about whether or not the counter-indicant suits the purpose of the Shariʿah. Does one not see that when Abū Mūsā al-Ashʿarī[13] sought permission, three times, to enter ʿUmar ibn al-Khaṭṭāb's house and as the latter did not answer him, he simply left. Then, ʿUmar sent after him. When he came back, ʿUmar reproached him for leaving, upon which Abū Mūsā mentioned that he had heard from God's Apostle that if a person requests permission to enter, and upon the third request is not granted such permission, he should leave. However, ʿUmar asked him to provide evidence for his statement and pressed him so much that Abū Mūsā had to look for one of the *Anṣār* (Supporters of the Prophet in Madinah) to testify that God's Apostle had indeed said so. The elders of the *Anṣār* told him: "By God, only the youngest person will go with you [as a witness]," and Saʿīd al-Khudrī[14] was the youngest of them. When Abū Saʿīd testified to ʿUmar that the Prophet had said so, ʿUmar was satisfied and realized, furthermore, that many of the *Anṣār* also knew about this. ʿUmar acted in that way because he had a great doubt that the counter-indicant could consist in qualifying the principle of asking permission three times, upon which one should leave if permission is not given upon the third time, since there is in Abū Mūsā's report a clarification of the ambiguity in the verse in which God says "Do not enter it until you are given leave" (24:28).[15] On the contrary, when ʿUmar was in doubt about collecting the poll-tax (*jizyah*) from the Magians (Majūs) and ʿAbd al-Raḥmān ibn ʿAwf informed him that he had heard God's Apostle saying: "Follow the same way (sunnah) with them as you follow with the People of the Book (*Ahl al-Kitāb*),"[16] ʿUmar accepted his testimony and did not require him to provide evidence for his statement. This was because he did not entertain any serious doubt concerning the existence of counter-evidence, which was not the case regarding Abū Mūsā's seeking of permission.

In respect of the third mode, the jurist's need to know the *maqāṣid* is because deduction by analogy depends on the affirmation of underlying causes (*ʿilal*), which may require the knowledge of *Maqāṣid al-Shariʿah*,[17] for example, suitability (*munāsabah*), that is, the extraction and specification of the *ratio legis* (*takhrīj al-manāṭ*), the emendation and refinement of the *ratio legis* (*tanqīḥ al-manāṭ*), and the invalidation of difference (*ilghā' al-fāriq*).[18] Clearly, when the scholars stipulated that the *ratio legis* (*ʿillah*) must be a defining element for some deeper wisdom, they were also referring us to inference of the different aspects of *sharʿī* rationales, which are themselves among the Shariʿah objectives.

Furthermore, jurists need to know the higher objectives of the Shariʿah as criteria for the acceptance of Prophetic Traditions and for the consideration of the opinions of jurists from among the Companions and early scholars, and also in the different ways of juristic reasoning and argumentation. One has to remember that ʿUmar refused to accept the report of Fāṭimah bint Qays regarding the maintenance of a woman in her waiting period.[19] ʿĀ'ishah also rejected the report of Ibn ʿUmar, stating that a deceased person is punished because of his family's weeping over him,[20] and recited as evidence for her view the Qur'anic verse in which God says: "And no bearer of burdens shall be made to bear another's burden" (6:164).

As for the fifth mode, the jurists need to have that knowledge because, the greater their awareness – and therefore their understanding – of the Shariʿah objectives, the fewer the cases of *taʿabbudī* which produce perplexity, they will face.

Having said this, it should be mentioned that not every *mukallaf* (legally competent and responsible person) is required to know *Maqāṣid al-Shariᶜah*, for this is a subtle kind of knowledge. The duty of lay people is to learn the ordinances of Shariᶜah and accept them without being required to know their purposes (*maqāṣid*), for they do not possess the capacity and skill to identify and apply them accurately in their proper context. Ordinary people should be introduced to the knowledge of the *maqāṣid* gradually in tandem with the increase of their studies of the various Islamic disciplines. This is to avoid their incorrect application of the *maqāṣid* that they are taught, with undesirable results, thus defeating the true purpose of this knowledge. It is the duty of the learned to comprehend these *maqāṣid*; as we have already mentioned, scholars vary in this according to their intelligence and interest.

3

Methods of Establishing *Maqāṣid al-Shariᶜah*

I assume that what I have mentioned previously should convince you that the Shariᶜah has higher objectives in its legislation by virtue of evidence and proofs, the grasp of which will satisfy, though in general terms, the purpose at hand. You may be now looking forward to knowing the methods by which we can establish the specific higher objectives of the Shariᶜah in the different spheres of Islamic legislation. You may also look forward to knowing how we can reason and affirm a particular goal in a way that would make it, once established, a subject of agreement among the students of jurisprudence, both those who have inferred it and those who are merely informed of it. Once this objective is achieved, it would be a means for reaching accord in the understanding of the *mujtahids* and conciliation among the antagonists among the followers (*muqallidīn*) of the different legal schools.

You should know that our approach does not consist of establishing the various *Maqāṣid al-Shariᶜah* on the basis of the conventional proofs, with which we are familiar in *uṣūl al-fiqh*. Neither does our approach draw on the methods used in the discussions about evidence of specific juristic issues or on those concerning issues of juristic disagreement (*khilāf*). This is because certainty (*qaṭᶜ*) or high probability bordering on certainty (*ẓann qarīb*) in those proofs is rare or even nonexistent. The reason is the following. Even though these proofs are derived from the Qur'an, whose text is definitively established by contiguous multiple transmission (*mutawātir*), most of the Qur'anic indicants belong, however, to the category of literal connotations that are probabilistic rather than definitive and categorical. None the less, there are in the Qur'an certain indicants pertaining to *Maqāṣid al-Shariʿah* that are close to explicit texts (*nuṣūṣ*) – we shall mention them in our discussion of the second method. On the other hand, these proofs are derived from the traditions (sunnah), all of which consist of isolated reports (*akhbār āḥād*) and, hence, do not yield certainty or high probability.

This is why the Qur'an was at the disposal of all the *mujtahids* and yet they disagreed upon the rules and provisions they derived from it, even though some of its indicants might be more obvious than others. For instance, God says, "unless it be that they forego their claim or he in whose hand is the marriage-tie" (2:237). Stated Mālik in *Muwaṭṭa'*: "He being the father of a virgin daughter or the master of a female slave,"[1] that is because the father and the master are the ones who effect the marriage contract of those under their guardianship, according to Mālik. Al-Shāfiʿī, on the other hand, understood this to be a reference to the husband, and maintained that the verse meant that the husband has a hold over marriage, and it is in his power to dissolve it by divorce.[2]

Likewise, I shall outline the methods for analyzing and substantiating *Maqāṣid al-Shariʿah* based on what I have concluded after profound reflection and drawing also on my consultation of the views of the most authoritative scholars. The utmost guiding principle for the jurist in this respect must be to abide by objectivity and justice and shun bias and fanaticism to a prejudgment, to a past ijtihad opinion, or to the view of a great scholar or teacher. In respect of this kind of knowledge (that is, *maqāṣid*), the jurist should avoid imitating a student of Ibn ʿArafah, who said about his teacher: "I never disagreed with him in his life, and I will not differ with him now that he is dead."[3] Therefore, when evidence has been established concerning a Shariʿah objective, all contenders must show fairness and discard all weak possibilities of opinion.

The first method, which is also the most important, consists of the thematic inference (*istiqrā'*) of *Maqāṣid al-Shariʿah* that lie behind its various dispositions and measures (*taṣarrufāt*) and it includes two types.

(1) The first type, the greater of the two, is to conduct an exhaustive examination of the provisions and commands, whose effective causes are known. This study will, in fact, result in an inductive inference of the rationales affirmed by the methods of identification and confirmation of the *ratio legis*. It is by the induction of rationales that we acquire a ready knowledge of *Maqāṣid al-Shariʿah*.

When we conduct an inductive survey of numerous causes, which share the quality of being defining elements for one underlying wisdom (*ḥikmah*), we can infer from them one specific objective and ascertain that it is an intended purpose of the Shariʿah (*maqṣad sharʿī*), just as we draw one universal concept (*mafhūm kullī*) from the examination of particulars (*juz'iyyāt*) by applying the rules of induction as established in logic.

Example: We know the *ratio legis* (*ʿillah*) of the prohibition of *muzābanah* (that is, buying something whose number, weight, or measure is unknown with something whose number, weight or measure is known) which is established by means of allusion (*maslak al-īmā'*) in the authentic tradition that God's Apostle said to the person who asked him about the sale of dried dates in exchange for fresh dates: "'Do ripe dates diminish in size when they become dry?' When he was told that they did, he forbade that."[4] Then we know that the reason for the prohibition of *muzābanah* is ignorance of the quantity of one of the two items exchanged in the transaction, that is, fresh dates which are exchanged for dried dates. Similarly, if we know of the prohibition of *bayʿ al-juzāf bi al-makīl* (that is, buying or selling something whose number, weight, or measure is unknown with something whose number, weight, or measure is known), and further know that the cause of this prohibition is ignorance of the amount of one of the two items transacted by derivation of the *ratio legis*; and if we know the unlawfulness of deceit (*ghubn*) in sales, and realize that the rationale is to banish cheating from among the Ummah, by virtue of the explicit statement of God's Messenger, in which he told the man who told him that he was always being cheated in sales: "When you enter a transaction say, 'No trickery!'";[5]

when we know all these causes, we can then infer from them one single goal which is the abolition of ambiguity (*gharar*) and substantial risk (*khaṭar*) in transactions. There remains, therefore, no disagreement that any exchange entailing risk or ambiguity in the price, the commodity, or the time of the transaction is void.

Second example: We know the prohibition of asking for a woman in marriage when another man has already done so, and the prohibition of bidding against another when he has concluded a deal with a customer,[6] and we know that the underlying reason (*ʿillah*) of all these prohibitions lies in the alienation which results from striving to deprive others of a benefit that they seek. When we know all that, we infer from it a specific objective that consists in maintaining and promoting brotherhood among Muslims. Accordingly, we use this objective to establish the negation of prohibition in proposing marriage after another proposal or in making a deal with a customer after another deal, if the first person who proposed marriage and the first person who made a deal has changed his mind.

(2) The second type consists in examining the numerous textual proofs of Shariʿah commands and rules (*aḥkām*) that have a common *ratio legis*. Then, we can infer with certainty that this *ratio legis* represents an objective that is intended by the Lawgiver.

Example: The *ratio legis* of the prohibition of selling foodstuff before their receipt is to encourage the circulation and availability of foodstuff in the market. The *ratio legis* of the prohibition of the sale of one kind of foodstuff on credit in exchange for another kind, when considered in absolute terms as maintained by the majority of scholars, is to avoid the foodstuff remaining in someone's debt and, therefore, does not circulate in the market. The prohibition of hoarding foodstuff as established by the Prophet's Saying narrated by Muslim from Maʿmar that: "He who hoards is a sinner,"[7] has as *ratio legis* the prevention of the shortage of foodstuffs in the market. From the examination of such instances, we can infer that the circulation and availability of foodstuff and the facilitation of access to it is one of the higher objectives of the Shariʿah. Then, we take this objective and make it a principal rule (*aṣl*), on the basis of which we assert that the circulation and availability of foodstuff take place in certain forms of transactions and its shortage happens owing to certain other forms of transactions, since people never stop buying and selling, and if we exclude the latter forms of exchange, there is no fear of scarcity of foodstuff. This is why we maintain that partnerships, the resale at the original stated price (*tawliyah*) and cancellation (*iqālah*) in foodstuff is permissible before its receipt. Of the same kind of inductive inference is the examination of the repeated commands to free slaves, which means that realizing and promoting freedom is one of the higher objectives of the Shariʿah.

The second method consists of the Qur'anic textual proofs whose connotations are clear. Their clarity is such that, according to the Arabic usage, it is very unlikely that their meaning is something other than what is apparent (*ẓāhir*). No one will, therefore, doubt the intended meaning of such indicants except those who easily give way to insignificant doubt. Is it not clear that we are quite certain that the meaning of the phrase "Fasting is prescribed (*kutiba*) for you" (2:183) is that God has made the fast obligatory? If someone were to say that the apparent meaning of this expression is that fasting is written on paper, that person would be absolutely wrong. Because the text of the Qur'an is established beyond any doubt (*qaṭʿī*) by continual multiple transmission (*mutawātir*), there is certainty in attributing its content to the Lawgiver. Nevertheless, because the meaning of its verses might be conjectural and speculative (*ẓannī*), it is required for our purpose that their signification be clear so that it would preclude the possibility of the existence of another meaning.

Thus, once certainty of the text (*qaṭʿiyat al-matn*) is conjoined with the high probability of signification (*quwwat ẓann al-dalālah*), we can infer from it a Shariʿah objective that shall remove disagreement when debating juristic matters. This can be illustrated by the following verses: "and God does not love corruption" (2:205); "O you who believe! Do not devour one another's possessions wrongfully" (4:29); "And no bearer of burdens shall be made to bear another's burden" (6:164); "By means of intoxicants and gambling, Satan seeks only to sow enmity and hatred among you" (5:91), "God wills that you should have ease, and does not will you to suffer hardship" (2:185); "and has laid no hardship on you in [anything that pertains to] religion" (22:78); in each of these Qur'anic verses there is an explicit indication of, or allusion to, a specific objective.

The third method is through the contiguously transmitted traditions (*sunnah mutawātirah*). Its instances fall in two different kinds.

(1) One consists of recurrent reports centered on a specific theme (*mutawātir maʿnawī*). It includes those acts of the Prophet which were witnessed by most of his Companions in such a way that they all immediately acquired the conclusive knowledge in an equal manner of a certain legislation (*tashrīʿ*) sanctioning those acts. To this category belong all religious matters of which a knowledge is necessary (*maʿlūm min al-dīn bi al-ḍarūrah*) as well as those matters of prescribed religious practice (*ʿamal sharʿī*) that are almost known to be necessary in Islam, such as the legality and sanctioning of continual charity (*ṣadaqah jāriyah*) called public endowment (*ḥabs*). This is the type of action meant by Mālik when he heard of Shurayḥ's rejection of the lawfulness of public endowment by declaring that there was no such thing when it comes to God's prescriptions. Mālik said on this occasion:

> May God's mercy be on Shurayḥ! He said what he said while remaining in his hometown [that is, Kūfah,] and he never visited Madinah to see the legacy of the most eminent people from among the wives of the Prophet *(ṢAAS)*, his Companions and the Successors (*tābiʿūn*), and the properties they have left as public endowments [without any objection from anyone].[8] And here are the endowments of God's Messenger *(ṢAAS)*, consisting of seven walled gardens. A person should judge only that which he knows about.[9]

Instances of this kind of knowledge are quite abundant in the area of devotional worship, such as the fact that the sermon of the two *ʿĪds* follows the performance of prayer.

(2) The second kind is thematically recurrent practice (*tawātur ʿamalī*) occurring to certain of the Companions, thanks to their

repeated observation of the acts of God's Apostle in such a way that they could infer, accordingly, a particular higher objective of the Shariᶜah. It is reported in *Ṣaḥīḥ al-Bukhārī* from al-Azraq ibn Qays who said:

> We were at al-Ahwāz [fighting the al-Ḥarūriyah tribe]. When I was on the bank of a river, a man was praying while holding the reins of his animal in his hands. The animal was struggling and he was following the animal. (Shuᶜbah, a sub-narrator, said that the man was Abū Barzah al-Aslamī). A man from the Khawārij said, "O God! Deal harshly with this shaikh." When the shaikh [Abū Barzah] had finished his prayer, he said, "I heard your remark. Certainly, I participated with God's Apostle in six or seven or eight battles and saw his leniency, and certainly, I would rather hold onto my animal than let it return to its stable, for it would cause me much trouble."[10]

Likewise, from his observation of the conduct of God's Apostle this Companion concluded that easiness and leniency were among the intended *Maqāṣid al-Shariᶜah*, and saw that abandoning the prayer to retrieve his horse and then returning to finish the prayer was better than continuing with his prayer with the prospective hardship of returning home on foot. Thus, for Abū Barzah, this higher objective of the Shariᶜah was so highly probable that it bordered certainty. However, for others to whom his report was related, it was only probable, since it was accepted from him on the basis of emulation and trust.

At the end of the third volume of his book *al-Muwāfaqāt*, which he devoted to discussing *Maqāṣid al-Shariᶜah* under the subtitle *Kitāb al-Maqāṣid*, al-Shāṭibī made important points that I think should be included here. He wrote:

> How can what is intended (*maqṣūd*) by the Lawgiver be distinguished from what is not intended? By means of rational division (*taqsīm ᶜaqlī*), there are three possible ways to do so. The first is to say that the intended purpose of the Lawgiver (*maqṣad al-Shāriᶜ*) is hidden from us unless it is expressed by a text whose meaning is explicit (*naṣṣ*). The gist of this

position is to consider only the apparent meaning (*ẓāhir*) of the texts in an absolute sense. This is the opinion of the Zahirites,[11] who confine the possible sources of knowing the intended purposes of the Lawgiver to the apparent meanings of the texts (*ẓawāhir*). The second way is that the intended purpose of the Lawgiver is neither in the apparent meanings of the texts nor in their implications, that it is rather something beyond all that, and that this applies to the entirety of the Shariʿah in such a way that none of its apparent meanings (*ẓawāhir*) can be relied upon to determine the intended purposes of the Lawgiver. All those seeking to suspend and abolish the Shariʿah, especially the Bāṭinīs (*al-bāṭiniyyah*),[12] have held this view. The third way is to reconcile the previous two approaches in a manner that neither the deeper meaning of the texts is excluded nor is the opposite [that is, the literal and apparent meaning] violated. In this way the Shariʿah runs according to one single coherent pattern free from any discrepancy or contradiction. This is the position adhered to by most scholars.

Thereupon, we can say that the intent of the Lawgiver can be known in various ways. The first one consists merely of initial, declarative commands and prohibitions (*amr wa nahy ibtidā'ī taṣrīḥī*). If the command is such because it requires action, then the Lawgiver intends the performance of the act in conjunction with it, and so is the case with prohibition in requiring abstention from an action. The second way is to consider the underlying causes (*ʿilal*) of commands and prohibitions, such as procreation being the rationale of marriage, and using the commodity sold and benefiting from its price as the rationale of selling and buying. The last is that in instituting the commands (*aḥkām*), the Lawgiver has primary and secondary objectives. Some of these are explicitly stated (*manṣūṣ*), some merely alluded to, while others are to be inferred from the texts. We therefore conclude from this that whatever is not clearly stated but can be arrived at from induction, is intended by the Lawgiver.[13]

4

Evaluation of the Predecessors' Methods

This topic could be counted as one of the ways for establishing *Maqāṣid al-Shariʿah*. Nevertheless, I do not consider it so, for I do not take as authoritative all the views held by the Predecessors.[1] This is because in some of these opinions the respective authors do not explicitly state that they had in view a particular higher objective of the Shariʿah when formulating their views. In other opinions, there might be such an explicit statement, or something close to it. Yet, this cannot in itself be considered an authoritative legal proof, since it is merely a personal opinion with regard to understanding a particular higher objective of the Shariʿah.

None the less, the fact remains that the statements of the Predecessors generally bear clear evidence of the necessity of considering *Maqāṣid al-Shariʿah*. The abundance of their statements in this respect is also an indication that they used to search for *Maqāṣid al-Shariʿah* in its legislative pronouncements by inductive inference. To illustrate this, I have chosen to provide numerous examples that clearly show how much attention the Predecessors had paid to this important subject. This will enable the reader to realize also that the most accurate *mujtahids*, and the most accurate ijtihad-based opinions of each *mujtahid* depend on the depth and thoroughness of their efforts to search for *Maqāṣid al-Shariʿah*. We shall explain this in the course of the remaining chapters of this first part of the present work.[2]

First Example:

> Jābir ibn ᶜAbd Allāh reported from Abū Hurayrah and Rāfiᶜ ibn Khadīj that God's Apostle said, "Whoever has land should cultivate it himself or give it to his fellow Muslim brother, but if the brother refuses it then he should keep it (uncultivated)."[3] When ᶜAbd Allāh ibn ᶜUmar knew of this report, he went to Rāfiᶜ ibn Khadīj and said to him, "You know that we used to rent our farms in the lifetime of God's Apostle *(ṢAAS)* for the yield of the banks of the watercourses (*arbiᶜā'*)[4] and for a certain quantity of figs."[5] Nāfiᶜ said, "Ibn ᶜUmar *(RAA)** used to rent his farms in the time of God's Apostle *(ṢAAS)*, and in the times of Abū Bakr, ᶜUmar, ᶜUthmān, and in the early days of Muᶜāwiyah's reign. Then, Ibn ᶜUmar was afraid that the Prophet had forbidden it, and he had no knowledge of it, so he gave up renting his land."[6]

Ṭāwūs narrated that Ibn ᶜAbbās mentioned that the Prophet did not forbid renting the land. Rather, he said, "One had better give the land to one's fellow muslim brother gratis rather than charge a certain amount for it."[7] Thus, he understood this tradition as an encouragement and an act of moral perfection.

Bukhārī adopted the latter view and devoted to this question a section in his *Ṣaḥīḥ* that he entitled, "Chapter on the Mutual Help of the Companions of the Prophet, Blessings and Peace be Upon Him." He also narrated the tradition reported by Rāfiᶜ ibn Khadīj from his uncle, Ẓuhayr ibn Rāfiᶜ, who said,

> "God's Apostle *(ṢAAS)* forbade us to do something out of mercy for us." I said, "Whatever God's Apostle *(ṢAAS)* said is right." He said, "God's Apostle *(ṢAAS)* once called and asked me, 'What are you doing with your farms?' I replied, 'We let them on the basis that we receive the yield produced at the banks of the watercourses for the rent, or rent them for some *awsaq*[8] of barley and dates.' He said, 'Do not do so, but cultivate (the land) yourselves or let it be cultivated by others gratis, or leave it uncultivated.' Rāfiᶜ said, 'I hear and obey'."[9]

---

* *(RAA) – Raḍiya Allāhu ᶜAnhu.* May Allah be pleased with him. Said whenever a Companion of the Prophet Muhammad is mentioned by name.

Under the heading of this chapter, Bukhārī, as is his usual practice and as (according to the scholars) a reflection of his wit and deep understanding, mentioned that this refers to helping others, and this is neither obligatory nor does it constitute proper grounds for a court judgment.

In his *Muwaṭṭa'*, Mālik ibn Anas explained the prohibition of *muḥāqalah* as being the interdiction of buying unharvested wheat in exchange for threshed wheat and renting land in exchange for wheat.[10] Said Ibn Shihāb:[11] "I asked Saʿīd ibn al-Musayyab,[12] 'What about renting for dinārs and dirhams?' He replied, 'There is no harm in it'."[13] Bukhārī also reported that al-Layth ibn Saʿd[14] said: "If those who have the ability to distinguish what is lawful from what is unlawful looked into what has been forbidden concerning this matter, they would not permit it, for it is surrounded with dangers."[15] In this manner, al-Layth understood this prohibition as referring to the leasing which might lead to a forbidden sale and thus followed a course of considering the different proofs together. Also, in the "Book of Battles" of *Ṣaḥīḥ al-Bukhārī*, al-Zuhrī reported from Sālim from Rāfiʿ ibn Khadīj that God's Messenger had prohibited the leasing of fields for cultivation. Al-Zuhrī asked Sālim: "Do you lease them yourself?" He said: "Yes, indeed Rāfiʿ is hard on himself."[16]

It seems that Rāfiʿ was forced to reinterpret the report that he had narrated, owing to the Companions' constant rejection of his view. In the "Book of Agriculture" in *Ṣaḥīḥ al-Bukhārī*, it is reported that Rāfiʿ ibn Khadīj said:

> We worked on farms more than anybody else in Madinah. We used to rent the land on the basis that the yield of a specific portion of it was to be given to the landlord. Sometimes the vegetation of that portion was affected by blights, etc., while the rest remained safe and vice versa, so the Prophet *(ṢAAS)* forbade this practice. At that time gold and silver were not used [for renting the land].[17]

Hence, he understood the reason for this prohibition to be the risk entailed in the contracts that his people used to conclude.

Second Example: In the chapter "The Delegation of the Yemen" (*Wafd al-Yaman*), Bukhārī narrated that Khabbāb ibn al-Aratt went to visit ᶜAbd Allāh ibn Masᶜūd. When the latter saw him wearing a gold ring, he exclaimed: "Hasn't the time come yet for throwing it away?" Khabbāb replied: "You will not see me wearing it after today" and he threw it away.[18] The scholars explained that Khabbāb was of the opinion that the Prophet's prohibition (*nahy*) on wearing gold rings was meant as absolving (*tanzīh*) not as an absolute interdiction (*taḥrīm*). This is why Ibn Masᶜūd spoke to him about taking the gold ring off, and kept insisting until Khabbāb agreed to take it off to please his friend. Ibn Masᶜūd's request was not made in a tone that might suggest an attempt to change something evil (*taghyīr al-munkar*).

Third Example: Mālik narrated in *Muwaṭṭa'* the hadith stating: "Both parties in a business transaction have the right of withdrawal as long as they have not separated, except in the transaction called *khiyār*," [*khiyār* is the right of withdrawal in a business transaction] then he commented by saying: "There is no specified limit nor any matter which applied in this case according to us,"[19] that is, determining the time of 'not parting company', to which Mālik did not adhere in his juristic doctrines. The explanation of this position is that this stipulation contradicts the Lawgiver's purpose in the creation of contracts. Therefore, what is meant by parting company, according to Mālik, is the parting of the buyer and seller with their words, which is none other than the utterance of the formula of buying and selling (*ṣīghat al-bayᶜ*).

Fourth Example: Abū Isḥāq al-Shāṭibī mentioned in the second discourse in the Book of Proofs (*Kitāb al-'Adillah*), quoting Ibn al-ᶜArabī:[20] "Is it permissible to act on a solitary report when it clashes with one of the established rules of the Shariᶜah? Abū Ḥanīfah was of the opinion that it is not permissible, while al-Shāfiᶜī maintained that it is. Mālik's well-known view, which is also the most reliable position, is that if another rule supports such a report, then one can act upon it and if there is no supporting rule then one should discard it. Moreover, Mālik rejected the report about the cattle whose milk is kept in their udders for days (*muṣarrāt*)[21] because he found it in conflict with the established rules (*uṣūl*), such as the rule that "The benefit of a thing is a return for the liability for loss from that thing" (*al-kharāj bi al-ḍamān*).[22] A person has to compensate the like, or value, of what he has damaged; he does not have to compensate with something different, whether it is food or goods.[23]

Fifth Example: Mālik reported in *Muwaṭṭa'* regarding the question of covering the face of a person who is in a state of *iḥrām* (ritual consecration in Hajj) that ʿAbd Allāh ibn ʿUmar shrouded his son, Wāqid ibn ʿAbd Allāh, who died at al-Juḥfah while in *iḥrām*, and he covered his head and face and said: "If we had not been in *iḥrām*, we would have perfumed him ourselves." Mālik commented: "A man can only do things while he is alive. When he is dead, his actions stop."[24]

Mālik was alluding to the fact that when a person dies in a state of *iḥrām*, perfume can be applied to him if someone who is not in a state of *iḥrām*, and who can touch perfume, happens to be available. Then, he alluded to the explanation of the Prophetic tradition narrated by Bukhārī about the person whose neck was broken, while he was in a state of *iḥrām*, by his camel. God's Apostle said: "Do not apply perfume to him."[25] It seems that the narrator of this tradition understood this prohibition was for the sake of the deceased person, when in fact it was because of the living people who were present, or else it was a specific injunction concerning this particular case. This narrator's understanding is rejected because it contradicts the established rules of the Shariʿah, not because there are other reports contradicting it, for no other report has been narrated to this effect.

5

Insufficiency of the Literal Methodology without Knowledge of Higher Objectives

Never has speech in any human language, nor any of its genres and styles in a particular language, been sufficient by itself to indicate the intent (*maqṣad*) of the speaker in such a way that would preclude any possibility of doubt about the signification (*dalālah*) of his words. I mean the kind of signification referred to as explicit expression (*naṣṣ*) that is unequivocal in denoting one particular meaning to the exclusion of others.[1] However, the meanings of words in different languages, and the meanings of the different types of speech in the same language, vary greatly in the degree of doubt and probability (*iḥtimāl*) arising in the mind about the purport (*murād*) of that speech. Some types of speech are more open to interpretation than others, just as speech authors differ in their capacity to articulate in an unequivocal way the meanings they intend by the words they use. Hence, some speakers are described as fluent or eloquent.

Similarly, in so far as their understanding of its import is concerned, the share of listeners to a speech also varies according to their understanding and practice of the idioms of that speech and the styles of those who belong to the same category as the author of that speech. Likewise, neither speakers nor listeners can afford to ignore certain features that surround a speech act, namely the context, the capacity (*maqām*) from which that act flows as well as its background information. All these elements consolidate one another in such a way as would exclude some possibilities of interpretation that might occur to the listener's mind concerning the speaker's intention. This is the reason why the speaker's direct words to his listeners express his intention more clearly than when they are conveyed by another person. Likewise, a speech conveyed to others in writing is more open to different interpretations than a speech conveyed verbatim, let alone speech that is addressed directly. This is because a written speech loses the connotations of context and the features of both the speaker and the conveyor, despite the fact that it is more accurate for it is less subject to distortion, omission, or having its meaning expressed in different words when the conveyor fails to retain the original words of the speaker.

As a result, some scholars fall into unending errors when they focus all their attention on words and confine the process of deriving the rules (*aḥkām*) of the Shariᶜah to squeezing the words so as to extract their meaning, believing this to be the proper and only course. They continue to examine words and analyze them, hoping to extract their core and essence. Thus, they neglect and fail to take stock of the context of the speech act, which consists, as we have already mentioned, of contextual evidences (*qarā'in*), speech conventions (*iṣṭilāḥāt*), and general context. It is obvious that the context of legislation (*maqām al-tashrīᶜ*) is so sensitive that taking these elements into consideration to comprehend the legislative purport of speech cannot be overemphasized.

Jurists differ clearly in paying attention to these considerations. However, none of them can dispense with a thorough examination of the Prophet's acts and dispositions (*taṣarrufāt*) or with extracting the underlying causes of the *aḥkām*. During the time of the *Tābiᶜūn* (Successors to the Companions) and their Successors, jurists would travel to Madinah in search of firsthand knowledge of the legacy and practice of the Prophet as well as of his Companions and those *Tābiᶜūn* who kept company with them. This would provide them with information that would enable them to discard many probable meanings in the signification of words and terms (*alfāẓ*) and enlighten them on the derivation of the proper causes of the *aḥkām* in accordance with the inner wisdom and underlying purposes of the Shariᶜah.

In this respect, we can clearly see the inadequate position of the Ẓāhirīs and some traditionalists, who confined the understanding of the Shariʿah to transmitted reports. It is here also that we can realize the inaccuracy and unsoundness of the statement attributed to al-Shāfiʿī, in which he is reported to have said: "If a tradition (*khabar*) from God's Apostle is proven authentic, then that is my adopted position,"[2] for such a statement cannot be uttered by a scholar who has attained the level of *mujtahid.*

Moreover, evidence from al-Shāfiʿī's juristic doctrines compels us to believe that this statement is either wrongly attributed to him or has been distorted, unless he means by authenticity the perfect signification based on the considerations that we have explained, and provided it is free from opposition from what we have warned against.

Accordingly, al-Shāfiʿī's statement can be interpreted as follows: When you examine my juristic views, you should know that they are based on an authentic tradition.[3]

The same applies to what al-Shāṭibī has reported in *al-Iʿtiṣām* from Aḥmad ibn Ḥanbal as saying: "The weak hadith is better than anological reasoning (*qiyās*)."[4] This is also unsound for the following reason. If a weak tradition is as open to error as *qiyās*, it is furthermore open to the possibility of forgery and fabrication. This likelihood has greater impact in removing confidence in weak reports than the likelihood of error in analogical reasoning. This is why we are certain that the previous statement is a distortion of what Aḥmad ibn Ḥanbal really said.

How pertinent, indeed, was Bukhārī when he devoted one section in *Kitāb al-Iʿtiṣām* of his *Ṣaḥīḥ*, which he entitled: "Chapter on what the Prophet *(ṢAAS)* has mentioned and encouraged the people of knowledge to agree on, and on what the two Holy Precincts, Makkah and Madinah, are in consensus about, and on the place where the Prophet prayed, the pulpit and the grave." Then he narrated the report of ʿĀṣim who said: "I asked Anas ibn Mālik: 'Did you ever hear the Prophet saying: "There is no alliance (*ḥilf*) in Islam"? Anas replied: 'The Prophet brokered an alliance between the Quraysh and the *Anṣār* in my house, which is in Madinah.'"[5] By this

Anas was in fact referring to the invalidity of the report by Umm Salamah, Jubayr ibn Muṭʿim and Ibn ʿAbbās in this regard.[6]

This is enough to show to what extent consideration should be given to the opinions of the Companions in those juristic matters depending on transmission and practice. Thus, when faced with different probabilities of interpretation, they used to seek clarification from God's Messenger just as they used to observe those circumstances which would give them insight into the Lawgiver's intent.

6

The Prophet's Intent of Legislation

An essential skill for the seeker of *Maqāṣid al-Sharīʿah* is to distinguish the different intents of the words and actions of the Prophet. The Prophet had many qualities deserving to be references for the statements and actions that have ensued from him. Scholars seeking *Maqāṣid al-Sharīʿah* need to determine the quality on which a statement or action of the Prophet was based. The first person to be aware of this distinction and put it into practice was the eminent scholar, Shihāb al-Dīn Aḥmad ibn Idrīs al-Qarāfī, in his book *Anwār al-Burūq fī Anwā' al-Furūq.*[1] He devoted to this question a whole section called "The Thirty-Sixth Distinction between the Rule of the Conduct of God's Messenger (*ṢAAS*) as Judge (*qaḍā'*), the Rule of his Conduct as Deliverer of Legal Edicts (*fatāwā*) – which are none other than conveyance and propagation (*tablīgh*) [of what was revealed to him] – and the Rule of his Conduct as Head of State (*imāmah*)." Then he said:

> God's Messenger *(ṢAAS)* is the supreme imam, the most judicious judge and the most learned jurisconsult (mufti). He is the leader of all leaders, the judge of all judges and the foremost scholar of all scholars. We cannot think of any religious function (*manṣab dīnī*) without thinking of him as its perfect model and prototype. None the less, most of his actions and conduct (*taṣarrufāt*) flow from his capacity as conveyor and propagator (*tablīgh*) by virtue of his predominant capacity of

Apostleship (*waṣf al-risālah*). Thus his actions and conduct include various capacities. There is first the type of actions and conduct flowing from his capacity as conveyor and propagator of Revelation and promulgator of fatwas [religious-legal edicts], and this is a matter of unanimous agreement. Scholars would agree that this type belongs to his capacity as judge and they would agree that it flows from his quality as head of state. There is also what would be a point of disagreement, owing to the possibility of combining two or more qualities, for which reason scholars would differ in such a way that some of them would give precedence to one capacity, whereas others would give it to another.

Again, his actions and conduct in the abovementioned capacities have different consequences in the Shariʿah. Thus, everything he said or did by way of transmission and conveyance is a binding general rule (*ḥukm ʿāmm*) for all until the Day of Resurrection. If it consists of prescriptions, each one should personally abide by them, and the same applies to what is permissible (*mubāḥ*). If it consists of prohibitions, everyone is also personally duty bound to avoid them. As for what the Prophet *(ṢAAS)* did in his capacity as the supreme political leader, no one can imitate it without the explicit permission of the head of state. This is because the reason for the Prophet's conduct depended on his capacity as head of state rather than as conveyor and transmitter (*muballigh*) of Revelation. Similarly, it is not permissible to engage in anything that the Prophet did by virtue of his capacity as judge without the explicit verdict of a court judge, because the reason for acting in his capacity as judge requires that.

These are the differences between the three reference rules, and they are verified by four cases. The first case comprises the following instances: the dispatching of armies, the allocation and spending of the wealth of the Treasury (*bayt al-māl*) in its proper departments and its collection from the correct sources, the appointment of governors and the distribution of booties. We should know that anything God's Messenger *(ṢAAS)* did in relation to all of these kinds of actions was done in his capacity as head of the state, not in any other capacity. We should also know that whatever he did when arbitrating between any two people in matters of property claims or partnerships entailing physical participation by partners (*aḥkām al-abdān*), etc. with evidences, oaths, retractions, etc. – was done in his capacity as judge rather than as head of the state. By the same token, anything in which he engaged concerning devotional matters of worship (*ʿibādāt*) – whether in words, deeds or as answers to questions on religious matters – was done in his capacity as deliverer of edicts (*fatāwā*) and conveyor of the Divine Message. There is no ambiguity in these instances.

The remaining three cases present instances of ambiguity and indecision. They are as follows: The second case consists of such things like the Saying of the Prophet *(ṢAAS)*: "He who cultivates land that does not belong to anybody has a greater right to it."[2] Scholars disagreed on the purport of this statement. Did the Prophet *(ṢAAS)* make this statement in his capacity as conveyor and transmitter of Revelation and deliverer of religious edicts, so that anyone can cultivate barren land, even without the permission of the head of state, as maintained by al-Shāfiʿī and Mālik? Or, was it an expression of his capacity as head of state and, therefore, no one can cultivate a barren land without the permission of the head of state, as maintained by Abū Ḥanīfah?[3]

The third case consists of such things as the statement of God's Messenger *(ṢAAS)* to Hind bint ʿUtbah, the wife of Abū Sufyān. When she told him: "O God's Apostle! Abū Sufyān is a miser and he does not provide sufficiently for me and our children, unless I take it from him without his knowledge." he said to her: "Take for your needs what is just and reasonable."[4] Scholars have also differed regarding the connotation of this statement. Did the Prophet *(ṢAAS)* make it in his capacity as conveyor and transmitter of revelation and deliverer of religious edicts? Therefore, is it permissible for anyone who claims what is rightfully his, or the equivalent of what is rightfully his, to take it without the knowledge of his rival? Or was it made in his capacity as judge and, hence, it is not permissible for anyone to take what is rightfully his, or the equivalent of what is rightfully his, without a judicial verdict?

The fourth case consists of such things as the statement of God's

Messenger *(ṢAAS)*: "Whoever has killed an enemy [in a battle] and has evidence of his action, can claim [the enemy's] possessions [that is, the property of the deceased such as clothes, arms, horse, etc.]."[5] Again, scholars have conflicting views regarding this statement. Was it a statement made by the Prophet *(ṢAAS)* in his capacity as head of the state and, therefore, the killer does not deserve the spoils of the slain enemy unless the head of state permits him? Al-Shāfiʿī was of the view that the Prophet *(ṢAAS)* made this statement in his capacity as conveyor and transmitter of Revelation and deliverer of religious edicts and, which means that the killer is not required to seek the permission of the head of state to take his victim's spoils.[6]

This is the gist of Qarāfī's view. To what he said we must add that God's Messenger had qualities and was in different positions which required him to act in specific ways or make specific statements. It is, therefore, our duty to be aware of the situation and take it into account when seeking enlightenment to help us solve the multitude of problems that have always troubled many people and caused much confusion. The Companions used to make a clear distinction between the commands of God's Messenger that ensued from his position as legislator (*maqām al-tashrīʿ*) and those that did not. When they were not sure about a certain matter, they sought clarification about it.

It is related in an authentic tradition that Barīrah was the wife of Mughīth, a slave, at the time when her masters freed her. When she became mistress of her own destiny by manumission (*ʿitq*), she divorced her husband because she loathed him. Yet, Mughīth, who loved her very much, approached the Messenger of God about this divorce. When the Prophet spoke to her about returning to her divorced husband, Barīrah said: "O God's Apostle! Do you order me to do so?" He said, "No, I only intercede for him." She said, "I am not in need of him."[7] She thus refused to return to her husband, and neither God's Messenger nor the Companions criticized her for that.

It is reported in *Ṣaḥīḥ al-Bukhārī* from Jābir ibn ʿAbd Allāh that his father ʿAbd Allāh ibn ʿAmrū ibn Ḥarām died, leaving behind him a debt. Then, Jābir requested the Prophet to speak with his father's creditors so that they might waive some of his debt. When the Prophet asked them about it, they refused to cancel any part of the debt. Jābir said: "When God's Messenger asked them about the matter, their enmity was roused against me." However, the Muslims did not criticize them for that. Similar examples of this kind are mentioned below.

None the less, in their discussion of issues relating to the Prophetic traditions, scholars of *uṣūl al-fiqh* have shown that those actions of God's Messenger that emanate from his natural disposition (*jibillī*) are not part of legislation. This is because they took into account those positions of the Prophet that are the result of his natural constitution (*khilqah*) and which have nothing to do with legislation or instruction. Yet, these scholars have displayed much hesitation about those actions which are likely to be due to either natural disposition or legislation, such as going on the pilgrimage mounted on a she-camel. Some scholars may be mistaken regarding certain aspects of the Prophet's conduct and, hence, hasten to take them as grounds for analogical reasoning (*qiyās*), before knowing accurately their underlying causes.

For the time being I have identified twelve different capacities in respect of which statements or actions would ensue from God's Messenger. Qarāfī mentioned some of them. They include legislation (*tashrīᶜ*), issuing edicts (fatwa), adjudication (*qaḍā'*), political leadership of the state (*imārah*), guidance (*hady*), conciliation (*ṣulḥ*), advice to those seeking his opinion (*ishārah*), counselling (*naṣīḥah*), spiritual uplifting of people (*takmīl al-nufūs*), teaching high and lofty truths (*taᶜlīm al-ḥaqā'iq al-ᶜāliyah*), disciplining (*ta'dīb*) and non-instructive ordinary statements (*tajarrud ᶜan al-irshād*).

1. The capacity as legislator is the predominant and most distinctive characteristic of God's Messenger, for that is why God sent him, as indicated in the Qur'an: "And Muhammad is only an Apostle" (3:144). Evidence that the Prophet was invested with the power of legislation is abundant and manifest. One instance of this is his sermon at the farewell pilgrimage (*ḥajjat al-wadāᶜ*), during which he appointed certain people to repeat what he said

so that others could hear his words.[8] Another indication is his statement: "Learn your rituals from me [by seeing me performing them], for I do not know whether I will be performing Hajj after this Hajj of mine,"[9] and his saying after concluding the same sermon: "Let those present inform those who are absent."[10]

2. The capacity of issuing edicts has signs such as the report mentioned in *Muwaṭṭa'* and the authentic collections of Bukhārī and Muslim on the authority of ʿAbd Allāh ibn ʿAmrū and Ibn ʿAbbās that, during the farewell pilgrimage, the Prophet stopped for people at Minā, and they asked him about different matters, while he was still mounted on his she-camel. A man came and said to him: "I sacrificed before throwing the stones." He advised: "Throw, and don't worry." Then another came and said: "I shaved before sacrificing", and the Prophet answered him: "Sacrifice, and don't worry." He was not asked about anything that one would, out of ignorance or forgetfulness, do after or before without his saying, "Do it, and don't worry."[11]

3. The capacity of judgeship refers to what emanates from the Prophet when settling disputes between people, such as his statement: "Hold the water, O Zubayr, until it reaches the base of the tree and then release it,"[12] and his settlement of the quarrel between a man from Ḥaḍramawt and a man from Kindah regarding a disputed piece of land, as mentioned in the *Ṣaḥīḥ* collection of Muslim.[13] Any action of the Prophet performed without the presence of adversaries is not classified as an instance of judgeship, as is the case in the report of Hind bint ʿUtbah mentioned above.

   One of the indicators of the capacity of judgeship is the explicit statement of the adversary: "judge between us" or the Prophet's statement: "I will certainly judge between you." An example of this is the report mentioned in *Muwaṭṭa'* from Zayd ibn Khālid al-Juhanī, who said:

> A Bedouin who came to the Prophet with his adversary said: "O Messenger of God, judge between us by the Book of God." His adversary, who was wiser than he, said: "Yes, Messenger of God, judge between us by the Book of God, and allow me to speak." Then, each one of them made his case. God's Messenger said: "I will assuredly judge between you according to what God has revealed in His Book..."[14]

> The eminent scholar, Muḥammad ibn Faraj ibn al-Ṭallāʿ al-Qurṭubī,[15] compiled and examined most of the cases of judgeship made by the Prophet in an interesting book. Another sign is his statement to Ḥabībah bint Sahl al-Anṣārī – the wife of Thābit ibn Qays – when she complained to him that she did not love her husband and that she wanted to divorce him: "Will you give him back his walled garden?" She said: "I have all that he has given to me." Then, the Prophet said to Thābit: "Take it from her." And so he took his walled garden and divorced her.[16]

All these three capacities are clearly evidence of legislation. However, they are distinguished from one another for determining the categories of the Shariʿah rules belonging to them. Moreover, issuing fatwas and administering justice (*qaḍā'*) are both examples of the application of legislation. In most cases, they consist of equating the applied rule (*ḥukm taṭbīqī*) with the general legislative rule (*ḥukm tashrīʿī*) in such a way that the [new] issue constitutes a particular part (*juz'īy*) of the original Shariʿah rule, just as a minor premise necessarily follows a major one in syllogism. They may also be due to a relationship of generality in one respect and particularity in another (*ʿumūm wa khuṣūṣ wajhī*) between a universal law and the ruling given to a particular case. Likewise, it might happen that some accident (*ʿāriḍ*) occurs to the action of the person seeking a fatwa, thus requiring the inclusion of that action under a specific rule, not because the action itself falls under that rule. It is thus similar to the syllogism whereby one proposition entails another by means of an ambiguous term (known as fallacy of equivocation).

An instance of this with regard to fatwas is the prohibition on depositing raisin juice (*nabīdh*) in dry gourds, jars varnished in green, asphalt or tar.[17] This prohibition was imposed because of external factors causing the fast fermentation in the Hijaz of raisin juice into wine. The rule should not be understood as a ban on putting raisin juice in, for example, varnished containers for people living in cold areas. Anyone maintaining that opinion would surely expose the Shariʿah to mockery. The same applies to instances of the administration of justice, such as the judgment of God's Messenger whereby he gave a neighbour the right of pre-emption (*shufʿah*). This should be understood on the basis that the narrator of the report saw a neighbour who had been given the right of pre-emption, but did not know that this neighbour was a co-owner.[18]

4. As for the capacity of supreme leadership of state, most of its instances cannot be confused with those pertaining to the capacity of legislation, except in such situations as would happen during wartime and which may admit particular applicability, such as the prohibition of eating donkey meat in the battle of Khaybar. The Companions disagreed on this issue. Was the prohibition of God's Messenger to eat the flesh of donkeys, and his command to spill the pots in which it was cooked, a proscriptive legislation entailing an absolute prohibition of consuming donkey meat? Or did it ensue from his capacity as supreme leader in the interest of the army, since their mounts in that battle were donkeys?[19]

   Another example is the permission to cultivate barren lands, and we have already seen Qarāfī's exposition of this issue. A further instance consists of the Prophet's statement at the battle of Ḥunayn: "Whoever has killed an enemy and has evidence of his actions, can claim the enemy's possessions (*salab*) [that is, the possessions of the deceased such as clothes, arms, horse, etc.]." Mālik understood it as stemming from the Prophet's capacity as supreme political leader (Imam). He, therefore, maintained that no one was allowed to claim the effects of the dead person without the permission of the sovereign (or Imam),[20] which is a special kind of bonus (*nafl*) that is different from the fifth share (*khums*) which falls within the jurisdiction of the army commander. This was also the view of Abū Ḥanīfah. However, al-Shāfiʿī, Abū Thawr, and Dāwūd maintained that this does not depend on the Imam's permission; it is rather the warrior's right. Thus, they saw this Prophetic statement as stemming from the Prophet's capacity as the issuer of fatwas and conveyor of the Divine Message.[21]

5. The capacity of guidance and instruction is more general than that of legislation.[22] This is due to the fact that God's Messenger may command and prohibit while his intention is not decisiveness, but rather the indication of different ways to goodness and righteousness. Thus, words arousing people's interest to follow the way of the Afterlife or describing the eternal bliss that people will enjoy in Paradise as well as most recommended matters (*mandūbāt*) flow from this capacity of guidance and instruction. Therefore, what I particularly mean by guidance and instruction here is those directives inviting people to hold on to good morality, manners of good company, and right belief. It is reported in an authentic tradition which was narrated by Abū Dharr that God's Messenger said:

> Your slaves are your brethren, upon whom God has given you authority. So, if one has one's brethren under one's control, one should feed them with the like of what one eats and clothe them with the like of what one wears. You should not ask them to do things beyond their capacity, and if you do so, help them [with their hard job].

> The narrator [al-Maʿrūr ibn Suwayd] said: "At al-Rabadhah I met Abū Dharr, who was wearing a cloak, and his slave, too, was wearing a similar one. I asked the reason for it. He replied, 'I scolded a slave by calling his mother bad names.' The Prophet said to me, 'O Abū Dharr! Did you abuse him by calling his mother bad names? You still have some characteristics of the age of pagan ignorance (*Jāhiliyyah*). Your slaves are your brethren ...'"[23]

6. The capacity of conciliation between people differs from that of judgeship. An example is the action of God's Messenger when al-Zubayr and Ḥumayd, a man from the *Anṣār*, quarrelled about a watercourse in al-Ḥarrah,[24] known as *Shirāj al-Ḥarrah*, which both of them used for irrigation.

 The Prophet said to Zubayr: "O Zubayr! Irrigate [your garden] first, and then let the water flow to your neighbour." The *Anṣārī* became angry and said, "O God's Apostle! Is it because he is your cousin?" On that the countenance of God's Apostle changed and he said [to al-Zubayr], "Irrigate [your garden] and then withhold the water till it reaches the walls [surrounding the palms]." ʿUrwah ibn Zubayr commented: "Before that, God's Apostle had given a generous judgment benefiting al-Zubayr and the *Anṣārī*, but when the *Anṣārī* irritated God's Apostle he gave al-Zubayr his full right according to the evident law." Al-Zubayr said: "By God! I think the following verse was revealed concerning that case: 'But no, by your Lord, they can have no faith until they make you judge in all disputes between them' (4:65)."[25]

 A similar example is that of Kaʿb ibn Mālik when he demanded repayment of a debt from ʿAbd Allāh ibn Abī Ḥadrad, and their voices grew very loud in the mosque. The Messenger of God passed by them and said: "O Kaʿb!" beckoning with his hand as if intending to say, "Deduct half of the debt" (out of kindness). Kaʿb agreed and so he took half of what Ibn Abī Ḥadrad owed him and remitted the other half.[26]

7. Concerning the capacity of giving advice to those seeking it, mention can be made of the advice given by God's Messenger to someone who sought it. It is reported in *Muwaṭṭa'* that ʿUmar ibn al-Khaṭṭāb had given someone a horse to carry him in the way of God, and the man neglected it. ʿUmar wished to buy the horse from the man, thinking that he would sell it cheaply. When he asked the Prophet about it, he told him: "Do not buy it, even if he gives it to you for one dirham, for someone who

takes back his *ṣadaqah* is like a dog swallowing its own vomit."[27]

This is an instance whereby God's Messenger advised ʿUmar, and there is no other report suggesting that God's Messenger did prohibit publicly such an action. This is why there is disagreement among scholars over their understanding of this prohibition. The majority of scholars understood it as an interdiction meant to absolve (*nahy tanzīh*) the person concerned so that one would not take back what he had given in charity for God's sake. This is the understanding of Mālik as stated in *Muwaṭṭa'*[28] and *al-Mudawwanah*,[29] for he was convinced that had the above-mentioned sale taken place, it would have been valid. Ibn al-Mawwāz,[30] on the other hand, understood it to be a prohibition implying absolute unlawfulness (*nahy taḥrīm*). However, he did not say that the sale would be considered invalid, even though in truth such a sale would be invalid if the prohibition was categorical.[31] This is because the rule in the Malikite School is that interdiction entails invalidity unless there is proof to the contrary.

The report concerning Barīrah – when her masters wanted to sell her, provided her *walā'* [clientage, people who have lost families etc. and who have been adopted by others to be taken care of by them] be to them and ʿĀ'ishah wanted to buy her [in order to free her] but rejected that condition – should, in my opinion, be understood on the same lines. ʿĀ'ishah informed God's Messenger as if she wanted to seek his advice. He told her: "There is no harm if you stipulate *walā'* for yourself." In another version, he is reported to have said to her: "Take her and stipulate that *walā'* is yours, for *walā'* is for the one who manumits." So ʿĀ'ishah did that and then God's Messenger stood up in front of the people and said: "What is wrong with people who make conditions which are not in the Book of God? Any condition that is not in the Book of God is invalid even if it is a hundred conditions. The decree of God is truer and the conditions of God are firmer and the *walā'* belongs only to the one who sets free."[32] If his statement to ʿĀ'ishah was a legislative rule or legal edict, the condition would be binding and this would contradict his saying in the sermon that "the *walā'* belongs only to the one who sets free." However, it was merely an indication of a legal entitlement that the Prophet made to ʿĀ'ishah, which would enable her to obtain the right as a means to satisfy her desire to buy Barīrah and then free her.[33]

This is a possible interpretation of this tradition that God has inspired in me, and by which all the difficulties that puzzled scholars in the understanding of this hadith can be removed.[34]

It was in a similar manner that Zayd ibn Thābit understood the prohibition of God's Messenger to sell fruit before it is ripe. It is reported in *Ṣaḥīḥ al-Bukhārī* from Zayd that people in the lifetime of God's Apostle used to trade in fruit. When they harvested their dates and the purchasers came to receive their due, the buyers would say, "The dates have gone rotten; they are blighted with disease, they are afflicted with the *qushām* [a disease which causes the fruits to fall before ripening]." God's Apostle said: "Do not sell the fruits before their benefit is evident." Zayd commented that the Prophet said this "by way of advice, for they quarrelled too much."[35]

8. As for counselling (*naṣīḥah*), mention can be made of the tradition narrated in *Muwaṭṭa'* and the hadith collections of Bukhārī and Muslim on the authority of al-Nuʿmān ibn Bashīr that his father Bashīr ibn Saʿd gave one of his slaves to his son, al-Nuʿmān, to the exclusion of his other children. So his wife, ʿAmrah bint Rawāḥah, al-Nuʿmān's mother, said: "I will not be pleased [with this act] until you make God's Apostle a witness to it". Then Bashīr went and informed God's Messenger of what had happened. The Prophet asked him: "Have you done the same with all your sons?" He said: "No." Thereupon, the Prophet said: "Do not call me as a witness to injustice." In

another version, he said: "Would it please you that they [your children] should all behave virtuously towards you?" Al-Nuʿmān said: "Yes." He [the Prophet] said: "Then do not do it."[36]

Mālik, Abū Ḥanīfah, and al-Shāfiʿī were of the opinion that God's Messenger prevented Bashīr from doing so out of consideration for his kinship ties and kindness to his children and did not mean to sanction the prohibition or abolition of gifts. Accordingly, Mālik maintained that it is lawful for a man to give part of his wealth to some of his children to the exclusion of others.[37] The only ground for their view is that since this prohibition was not widely known from the Prophet, we therefore can infer that it came by way of counsel and advice for the benefit and protection of the family, not as a categorical proscription. This understanding is supported by the fact that, in a different version of the same tradition, the Prophet is reported to have said to al-Nuʿmān that: "No, find someone else to be your witness."[38]

On the other hand, Ṭūwūs, Isḥāq ibn Rāhawayh, Aḥmad ibn Ḥanbal, Sufyān al-Thawrī, and Dāwūd ibn ʿAlī were of the opinion that making such a gift was categorically prohibited, thus confining themselves to the outward purport of the prohibitive form (*nahy*) without delving into its real purpose.[39]

A similar example is reported in *Ṣaḥīḥ Muslim* that Fāṭimah bint Qays mentioned to God's Messenger that both Muʿāwiyah ibn Abī Sufyān and Abū Jahm had proposed to her. The Prophet said to her: "Abū Jahm never puts his stick down, whereas Muʿāwiyah is a mere wandering pauper."[40] This statement does not imply that it is not permissible for a woman to marry a poor man. It simply means that Fāṭimah bint Qays sought the advice of the Messenger of God, who advised what was best for her.

9. As for the capacity of encouraging people to follow the best

forms of conduct, numerous examples of the commands and prohibitions of God's Messenger can be found, whose aim was to perfect the character of his Companions and encourage them to follow the course befitting their high standing in Islam, such that it would be extremely hard for the entire Muslim community to follow, were it required to do. I have found many of this type of the Prophet's acts, and I have noticed that, owing to their ignorance and negligence of this aspect of his conduct, some scholars made many juristic errors and seriously misunderstood the interpretation of many legal proofs from the Sunnah.

By coming upon this, I have been relieved of much confusion and perplexity concerning such issues. Indeed, the Prophet was specifically the legislator for his Companions. He drove them to assume the most perfect of states by strengthening the bonds of Islamic brotherhood in its utmost forms, shunning the glitter of this lower world and delving deep into the teachings of the religion so as to understand it. This is because they were being prepared to be the bearers and disseminators of Islam. God has praised them in *Sūrah al-Fatḥ* (29) by saying: "Muhammad is God's Apostle; and those who are [truly] with him are firm and unyielding towards all deniers of the truth, [yet] full of mercy toward one another." This meaning is also expressed in a number of sayings by the Prophet, such as: "My Companions are like the stars,"[41] "Do not abuse my Companions, for if any one of you spent gold equal to *Uḥud* (in God's Cause) it would not be equal to a *mudda* or even half a *mudda*[42] spent by one of them."[43] Therefore, when Saʿd ibn Abī Waqqāṣ fell ill in Makkah upon its conquest, the Prophet said: "O Allah! support my Companions in their emigration, and do not drive them back to where they came from. But the unfortunate one is Saʿd ibn Khawlah," thus expressing sorrow that Saʿd had died in Makkah.[44] He said so because he wanted perfection for them in life and death, even though the death of an emigrant in Makkah did not diminish the reward of his migration in any way.

These are many examples of this capacity. It is reported in *Ṣaḥīḥ al-Bukhārī* that al-Barā' ibn ʿĀzib said: "God's Messenger commanded us to practice seven things and prohibited us from practicing seven. He commanded us to visit the sick, to walk behind funeral processions, to pray for someone upon sneezing, to approve of someone's oath, to help the oppressed person, to spread the greeting of peace, and to accept the invitation of the invitee. On the other hand, he prohibited us from wearing gold rings, using silver utensils, using red saddlecloth made of cotton (*mītharah*), wearing Egyptian clothes with silky extensions (*qasiyyah*), clothes made of thick silk (*istabraq*), thin silk (*dībāj*), or normal silk (*ḥarīr*)."[45] Likewise, he mentioned together different commanded and prohibited practices of varying degrees. Some of them are known to be obligatory (such as helping anyone who is wronged), or forbidden (such as drinking from a silver utensil), while others are known to be not obligatory (such as praying for the person who sneezes or obliging someone who makes an oath) or not categorically forbidden (such as using red saddlecloth made of cotton, Egyptian clothes with silky extensions).

The Prophet prohibited the abovementioned practices only to raise his Companions above showing signs of pretension, pride, and ostentation by wearing striking colors, such as red. This interpretation removes many difficulties in understanding the reasons behind the prohibition of some of the practices mentioned previously, which those who commented on this hadith failed to grasp. Such an understanding is further confirmed by the report narrated by Abū Dāwūd from ʿAlī ibn Abī Ṭālib, who said: "God's Apostle *(ṢAAS)* forbade me to use gold rings, to wear silk clothes and clothes dyed with saffron, and to recite the Qur'an while I am in *rukūʿ* and *sujūd* [bowing and prostration in prayer]. I am not saying he forbade you these things,"[46] meaning that some of the things mentioned here were not forbidden to the entire Muslim community, but only to ʿAlī.

Another example is the report by Abū Rāfiᶜ that God's Messenger said: "A neighbor has a greater right to the property next door,"[47] that is, to buy it if his neighbor sells it. The Prophet's intent in this statement was to drive his Companions to show more compassion and brotherhood towards one another. The neighbor was therefore given pre-emption in consideration of his proximity. If it had not been for the expression "has a greater right" (*aḥaqqu*), we would have understood the saying as mere encouragement. However, on considering the expression "has a greater right" we realized that a neighbor from among the Companions was given pre-emption over the property of his neighbor, when it was offered for sale. There is, therefore, no contradiction between the above tradition and the report of Jābir that God's Messenger said: "Pre-emption relates to what is not allotted. There is no pre-emption when borders are drawn and walkways traced."[48]

Similarly, the report mentioned in *Muwaṭṭa'* and in the authentic collections of Bukhārī and Muslim on the authority of Abū Hurayrah that God's Messenger said: "No one should prevent his neighbour from fixing a wooden peg in his wall." Then Abū Hurayrah said: "Why do I see you turning away from it? By God! I shall keep on at you about it."[49] Here, Abū Hurayrah understood this saying to be a binding legislation, whereas Mālik understood it as a form of encouragement (*targhīb*). Thus, Mālik maintained that the judge could not force someone to give priority of pre-emption to the neighbor, for that would contravene the rule stipulating the exclusive right of the owner to dispose of his property without interference from anyone else.[50]

It is also in this way that we should understand the report of Rāfiᶜ ibn Khadīj, who said: "God's Messenger forbade us to do a thing which was a source of help to us." Rāfiᶜ said: "What God's Messenger said is the truth." Then he added: "God's Messenger summoned me and said: 'What are you doing with your farms?' I said: 'We let them on the basis that we receive the yield produced at the banks of the watercourses for the rent, or rent them for some barley and dates.' He said: 'Do not do so, but cultivate the land yourselves or let it be cultivated by others gratis, or keep it uncultivated.'" Rāfiʿ said: "I said: 'We hear and obey.'"[51] Most scholars understood from this tradition that the Messenger of God commanded his Companions here to help one another. This is why al-Bukhārī included this tradition under the heading: "Chapter: The Companions of the Prophet used to share the yields and fruits of their farms with one another gratis."

10. As far as the capacity of teaching lofty notions and higher truths is concerned, this pertained to the high ranks of God's Messenger and his closest Companions. An example of it is the report of Abū Dharr, who said: "My beloved said to me: 'O Abū Dharr! Do you see [the mountain of] *Uḥud*?' I said: 'I do!' He said: 'I do not wish that I have the like of *Uḥud* in gold to spend all except for three pieces of gold'."[52] Abū Dharr thought that this was a general command applying to the entire Muslim community, and he therefore warned against accumulating wealth. As we shall see, ʿUthmān, may God be pleased with him, rejected his understanding.[53]

11. As for the capacity of disciplining people (*ta'dīb*), it should be carefully considered, for statements flowing from it might be couched as hyperboles aimed at provoking awe and fear. The jurist ought therefore to distinguish between what is appropriate to be specifically intended as legislation and what is appropriate to be specifically meant as a rebuke and threat, but which none the less falls under legislation by genre, that is, by a general consideration of the idea of disciplining.

    This can be illustrated by the Tradition reported in Mālik's *Muwaṭṭa'* and the hadith collections of al-Bukhārī and Muslim on the authority of Abū Hurayrah that God's Messenger said:

By Him in Whose Hand my self is! I had in mind to order firewood to be collected, then order the prayer to be called, and to appoint a man to lead the people in the prayer, and then come up behind certain men and burn their houses down about them! By Him in Whose Hand my self is! If one of them knew that he would find a meaty bone or two good legs of meat, he would be present at the *ʿIshāʾ* prayer.[54]

There is no question that God's Messenger was really going to burn the houses of Muslims because of their failing to attend the *ʿIshāʾ* prayer in congregation. His statement was rather made in the context of browbeating for the sake of discipline or, alternatively, because God had informed him that those men were hypocrites and, hence, gave him permission to destroy them if so he wished.

Another example is the Tradition narrated in *Ṣaḥīḥ al-Bukhārī* from Abū Shurayḥ who said: "God's Messenger said: 'By God! He does not believe! By God! He does not believe!' It was said, 'Who is that, O Messenger of God?' He said: 'The one whose neighbour does not feel safe from his evil.'"[55] Here, the statement is formulated in a threatening manner regarding anyone who causes harm to his neighbour, to the extent that it is feared he would not be among the believers. What is really meant, however, is that such a person is not a true believer.

12. As for the capacity of non-instruction (*tajarrud ʿan al-irshād*), it is not concerned with legislation, religiosity, the education of souls, and the sound management of the social order of the community. It rather concerns those actions emanating from innate human nature (*jibillah*) or the requirements of material life.

This is something that cannot be mistaken, for God's Messenger performed actions in relation to his family affairs and the earning of a living, which were not intended as legislation nor as an example to be emulated. Moreover, it is established in the discipline of *uṣūl al-fiqh* that the Muslim community is not required to emulate those actions of God's Messenger flowing from his innate nature as a human being, but rather each individual should follow the course that suits his condition. Such deeds include the way in which he ate, wore his clothes, lay down, walked, mounted his beast, and so on. This is so regardless of whether these things are unrelated to the Shariʿah prescriptions, such as walking in the street or riding a beast on a journey, or are related to them, such as riding a she-camel when performing the pilgrimage, and placing the hands on the prayermat before the knees when prostrating in prayer, according to those who – like Abū Ḥanīfah – maintain that God's Messenger did so when he was old and quite stout.

Another example is the report that the Prophet stopped on the farewell pilgrimage at al-Muḥaṣṣab – a hill overlooking a watercourse in Banū Kinānah, also called al-Abṭaḥ[56] – where he performed the *Ẓuhr, ʿAṣr, Maghrib,* and *ʿIshā'* prayers. Then he lay down for a short while before embarking for Makkah, with all those who were with him, to perform the farewell circumambulation (*ṭawāf al-wadāʿ*). Now, Ibn ʿUmar used to stop at this same place during the season of pilgrimage and considered that doing so was part of the Prophet's Sunnah [to be emulated]. However, it is narrated in Bukhārī's *Ṣaḥīḥ* from ʿĀ'ishah that she said: "Camping at al-Abṭaḥ is not one of the ceremonies of hajj, but was simply a place where the Prophet *(ṢAAS)* used to camp so that it might be easier for him to leave for Madinah."[57] She meant that that area was vast and could accommodate a large number of people. This was also the opinion of Ibn ʿAbbās and Mālik ibn Anas. A similar example of actions stemming from this capacity is the report concerning lying down on the right side after performing the Dawn prayer (*Fajr*).[58] Similarly, it is mentioned in the report about the battle of Badr that God's Messenger reached the water before the Quraysh. He went to where the water was closer to Badr and camped there with the army.

Al-Ḥubāb ibn Mundhir asked him: "O Messenger of God, this place where we are now – has God revealed it to you, that we should neither advance nor retreat from it, or is it a matter of opinion and war strategy?" He said: "It is a matter of opinion and war strategy." There-upon al-Ḥubāb said: "This is not the place to halt, but take us, O Messenger of God, to one of the large wells which is nearest the enemy, whose abundance which I know is full. Then, we fill the other wells with earth, so that we can have access to water, whereas they cannot." God's Messenger said: "Indeed, it is good advice that you have given."[59]

It is reported in *Jāmiᶜ al-ᶜUtbiyyah*,[60] the narration of Ibn al-Qāsim, that Mālik said:

The Messenger of God *(ṢAAS)* passed by some gardens where he saw people were pollinating palmtrees. He said to them: "It may perhaps be better for you if you do not do that." People then abandoned pollination (*liqāḥ*) that year. However, since the palmtrees did not bear good dates, they complained to God's Messenger *(ṢAAS)* who said to them: "I am a human being. If there is any use in it, then they should do it."

Abū al-Walīd ibn Rushd said in *al-Bayān wa al-Taḥṣīl*:

This tradition was narrated in different versions. In one version the Prophet is reported to have said: "I do not think this is of any use; if they leave it, the trees will yield fruit all the same." In another version he said: "I do not think pollination makes any difference." Then, people abandoned pollination and, as a consequence, the palmtrees did not yield dates. When God's Messenger was informed of this, he said: "I am not a planter, nor an owner of palmtrees; keep on pollinating your trees."[61]

After all, the jurist ought to examine thoroughly the circumstances and scrutinize the circumstantial evidence (*qarā'in*) of the various actions of the Prophet. Among the contextual indications pertaining to legislation is the Prophet's concern about having his words conveyed to the general public, his commitment to act upon what he said, and the notification of the legal command and its formulation in universal propositions, such as in his statements: "No bequest shall be made for an inheritor",[62] and "the *walā'* belongs only to the one who manumits." Amongst the signs of non-legislation is the lack of keenness to perform an act, as in the statement of the Prophet during his last illness:

> "Bring writing materials so that I can dictate what will preserve you from error after me." Ibn ʿAbbās said: "Those present disagreed. Some said the Book of God was sufficient, while others insisted on giving him paper so that he could dictate, and others said that they should not argue in front of the Prophet. When he saw their squabbling, he said: 'Leave me. I am better in the state [than the one in which you are engaged]'."[63]

You should also know that the capacity which is most specific to God's Messenger is that of legislation, because that was God's primary objective in sending him to humankind. Indeed, God has stated in the Qur'an that legislation was the Prophet's exclusive quality: "Muhammad is only an Apostle" (3:144). For this reason, we should consider the statements and deeds that ensued from God's Apostle relating to the general condition of the Muslim community to be a matter of legislation, unless there is circumstantial evidence to the contrary. Muslim jurists have unanimously agreed on the legislative value of the report concerning Saʿd ibn Abī Waqqāṣ, who sought permission from the Prophet to bequeath some of his wealth. The Prophet told him: "[Bequeath] a third, and a third is a lot." They considered bequests exceeding one third invalid, unless the other inheritors approved of it.

Thus, the scholars did not understand this tradition as emanating from the Prophet by way of mere suggestion or advice, despite the existence of co-textual evidence permitting that, namely the Prophet's words to Saʿd: "Leaving your heirs rich is better than leaving them poor to beg from people."[64] It gives the impression that this was something specific to Saʿd and his heirs, owing to their extreme poverty. They did so although this episode happened only between God's Messenger and Saʿd, and even though the Prophet himself did not act upon this tradition, nor was it reported from him by any other Companion except Saʿd. This would imply that a jurist can allow bequests exceeding a third for someone whose heirs are rich – a view that none of the scholars has advocated – or for someone who does not have heirs – as has been attributed by Ibn Ḥazm in *al-Muḥallā* to some scholars like Ibn Masʿūd, ʿUbaydah al-Salamānī and others, which is at variance with the majority view of scholars.[65]

7

Certain and Probable *Maqāṣid al-Shariʿah*

In their search for *Maqāṣid al-Shariʿah*, scholars ought to think carefully and take their time before venturing to affirm a Shariʿah objective. They must avoid partiality and hastiness, for the determination of a Shariʿah objective – be it universal or particular – can have many ramifications in the legal proofs and rulings ensuing from it during juristic deduction (*istinbāṭ*). Errors, therefore, have very grave consequences. Scholars should never determine any Shariʿah objective before undertaking a comprehensive thematic study of the dispositions (*taṣarrufāt*) of the Shariʿah concerning the genre of teachings chosen for the legislative purpose, and before consulting the works of the scholars of Islamic jurisprudence, to gain enlightenment and understanding from their profound experience of the subject. In this way, they will certainly acquire the ability to deduce from the texts the intentions of the Lawgiver.

However, despite these efforts, they will still realize that what they have learnt concerning the identification of a Shariʿah objective varies in certainty. This is because the strength of conviction that something constitutes a higher objective of the Shariʿah varies according to the existence and availability of indicants and proofs. This is not merely the result of the jurist's mental exertions and indefatigable inquiry. Rather, the quantity of indicants and evidence varies for the different types of legislation according to the amount of time available during the legislation, and the circumstances of the

Muslim community at the time of Revelation. Clearly, there are more detailed textual proofs from the Lawgiver concerning questions of manners (*ādāb*) and devotional acts of worship (*ʿibādāt*) than social dealings (*muʿāmalāt*) and emergent cases (*nawāzil*). This is because most instances of legislation before the migration to Madinah were confined to the former two types to the exclusion of the third. At the beginning, people were more ignorant in their lives and culture of God and His attributes, the history and character of the Apostles, the Last Day, and the devotional acts of worship than of dealing fairly with one another.

Accordingly, the knowledge acquired by the seeker of the Shariʿah objectives might be certain (*qaṭʿī*), highly probable, thus bordering on certainty (*ẓann qarīb mina al-qaṭīʿ*), or merely conjectural (*ẓann*). Mere conjectural or weak knowledge is discounted. However, if jurists can reach only weak conjecture, then they must accept it as a mere hypothesis and a possible starting point for jurists after them, as taught by God's Messenger, who said: "Some of those to whom knowledge is conveyed may comprehend it better than those who have conveyed it."[1]

It is most important that jurists identify a number of definitive higher objectives (*maqāṣid qaṭʿiyyah*) as a frame of reference and ultimate criteria in fiqh and juristic polemics. Indeed, some polemicists among *uṣūl* scholars attempted to lay down some categorical rules (*uṣūl qaṭʿiyyah*) for fiqh and juristic reasoning. As a result, they succeeded in leaving to posterity some judicious statements. However, their attempts to explain how to attain that objective fell into confusion. To my knowledge, the first to have made such an attempt was Imam al-Ḥaramayn al-Juwaynī in his book *al-Burhān*. Explaining the meaning of the principles of jurisprudence (*uṣūl al-fiqh*), he said: "They consist of the categorical proofs in the technical usage of the scholars of jurisprudence."[2] Clearly, what he means here are the categorical, transmitted proofs (*'adilla samʿiyyah*), for it is impossible to have non-transmitted, categorical proofs except in questions of the fundamentals of faith (*uṣūl al-dīn*). Then he continued: "And its subdivisions are: the explicit text (*naṣṣ*) of the Qur'an, the explicit text of the Sunnah and ijmaʿ (juridical consensus)."[3]

In his commentary on *al-Burhān*, al-Māzarī said:

> The author has made a qualification with regard to the first two proof sources (i.e. the Qur'an and the Prophet's traditions) but not in respect of ijmaʿ for two reasons. The first reason is that the consensus he refers to is that which is known as authoritative (*ḥujjah*). The second is that the conditions required for ijmaʿ to be authoritative are so many that it is impossible to delimit them except by detailing the issues and expanding the discussion over many chapters.[4]

Al-Juwaynī then added:

> If someone were to say: "but the details of solitary reports (*akhbār āḥād*) and varieties of analogy (*aqyisah*) are available only in the principles of jurisprudence and these are not certain", we would answer that all that is required from the legal theorist (*uṣūlī*) is to show what is categorical as far as the need for acting upon it is concerned. However, it is necessary to mention them to clarify the purport (*madlūl*) and connect it to the proof.[5]

Hence, according to al-Juwaynī, what is definitive about these conjectural matters is that they constitute legal proofs that must be used as a whole, not in their particular details.

In his discussion of the first question about "words" (*lafẓ*) in the chapter on "commands" (*awāmir*) in his commentary on *al-Maḥṣūl* of Imam al-Rāzī, Shihāb al-Dīn al-Qarāfī wrote:

> Al-Abyārī said in his commentary on *al-Burhān*: "The propositions of the science of *uṣūl* are certain, probability and conjecture (*ẓann*) being insufficient therein. Their evidence (*mudrak*) is certain, but it does not consist of what is mentioned in the books. Rather, what is meant by the scholars' statement that 'they are certain' is that whoever undertakes a thorough examination of the cases judged by the Companions, may God be pleased with them, and is familiar with their debates, edicts, and is aware of the levels and categories of the textual indicants of the Shariʿah, can realize the categorical nature of the rules of *uṣūl al-fiqh*.

> Anyone falling short of this will reach only mere conjecture. The scholars have posited the texts of apparent meanings (*ẓawāhir*) in their books simply to trace the source of evidence (*aṣl al-mudrak*), not by virtue of considering them the basis of definitive evidence. There is therefore no contradiction in affirming that these propositions are categorical, whereas the texts provide only probable meanings."[6]

In the introduction to his book *al-Muwāfaqāt*, Abū Isḥāq al-Shāṭibī also suggested a different approach to prove that the principles of jurisprudence (*uṣūl al-fiqh*) are definitive. However, only the following statement is sound and productive:

> The proof for this [that is, the definitive nature of the rules of *uṣūl*] is that they are all traceable to the Shariʿah universals (*kulliyyāt*), and anything of this kind is definitive (that is, when we are sure that something specific stems from those universals). I mean by the universals the indispensable (*ḍarūriyyāt*) and the needs (*ḥājiyyyāt*).[7]

He then went on to support this assertion mostly using weak, casuistic, and rhetorical premises.

What these scholars had to say has already been mentioned at the beginning of this book – and that is all our ancestors have left to posterity regarding this point. Their views are mentioned here to further enlighten our understanding, so that we realize that it is possible to arrive at definitive, or almost definitive, rules, even if there are very few of them. None the less, we are not committed in Islamic legislation to certainty (*qaṭʿ*), or to anything bordering on certainty all throughout, since this realm allows for probability and conjecture. My aim here is to formulate a set of definitive rules as a frame of reference in case of disagreement or obstinacy. What ensues from such rules will constitute what we have called *ʿIlm Maqāṣid al-Shariʿah*, which is something different from the discipline of *uṣūl al-fiqh*.

The probable and conjectural objectives can easily be attained by an incomplete induction of the rules of the Shariʿah, for such a quick survey would enable us to acquire some familiarity with the conventions and usage (*iṣṭilāḥ*) of the Lawgiver and what He considers in legislation. In this connection, ʿIzz al-Dīn ibn ʿAbd al-Salām, in his book *al-Qawāʿid*, said in conjunction with his inquiry on contractual exchanges (*muʿāwaḍāt*) conflicting with the rules of analogical deduction:

> An instance of this [type of knowledge] is the case of a person who frequents an intelligent, wise person, and understands everything he likes and dislikes under all circumstances. If such a person comes across an instance of benefit (*maṣlaḥah*) or harm (*mafsadah*) about which he does not know the specific opinion of his companion, he can decide for the instance of benefit and shun the instance of harm, simply by judging on the basis of his overall knowledge of his companion's attitude and habits that he would opt for that specific benefit and avoid that specific harm.[8]

An example of definitive Shariʿah objectives is what can be derived from those Qur'anic indicants which occur so frequently that they cannot be mere metaphors or hyperboles, such as "facilitation" (*taysīr*). God has said: "God wills that you shall have ease, and does not want you to suffer hardship" (2:185). The emphasis expressed by the sentence "and does not want you to suffer hardship" after the phrase "God wills that you shall have ease" makes the connotation of this verse close to that of explicit and unambiguous meaning.

To this we can add the following verses: "and [He] has laid no hardship on you in [anything that pertains to] religion" (22:78); "O our Sustainer! Do not lay upon us a burden such as that which you do lay upon those who lived before us! O our Sustainer! Make us not bear burdens which we have no strength to bear!" (2:286); "God is aware that you would have deprived yourselves of this right,[9] and so He has turned unto you in His mercy and removed this hardship from you. Now, then, you may lie with them skin to skin, and avail yourselves of that which God has ordained for you"[10] (2:187); and "God wants to lighten your burdens" (4:28). We may also add a number of traditions, according to which the Prophet is reported to have said: "I was sent to people with the lenient, tolerant, True Religion (*ḥanīfiyyah samḥah*);"[11] "Do [good] deeds that are within your capacity,"[12] "This religion is very easy and entails no hardship."[13] His instruction to Muʿādh and Abū Mūsā al-Ashʿarī when he sent them to the Yemen: "Facilitate things for the people and do not make things difficult for them. Be kind and lenient [both of you] with the people, and do not be hard on them and give the people good tidings and do not reject them,"[14] and also his saying: "You have been sent to make things easy and not to make them difficult."[15]

Therefore, a thematic inference (*istiqrā'*) is sufficient for scholars to assert that making things easy (*taysīr*) is one of the higher objectives of the Shariʿah. All the indicants examined on the basis of inductive survey are both recurrent and general, just as they are all certain in their attribution to the Lawgiver, since they are found in the Qur'an, whose text is definitive.

The probable objectives bordering on certainty consist of what al-Shāṭibī mentioned in conjunction with the second question, in the first part of the "Book of Proofs" (*Kitāb al-'Adillah*):

> A probable (*ẓannī*) proof may be traced to a definitive principle such as the saying of God's Messenger *(ṢAAS)*: "No harm should be sustained or incurred upon others," for this statement stems from a definitive general principle, according to which harm must be removed. This is because the prohibition of subjecting oneself to harm (*ḍarar*) or causing it to others (*ḍirār*) is widely expressed throughout the sources of the Shariʿah, in both particular cases and universal general rules, as in God's saying, Exalted is He, "But do not retain them against their will in order to hurt [them]: for he who does so sins indeed against himself" (2:231), "[Hence,] let the women [who are undergoing a waiting-period] live in the same manner as you live yourselves, in accordance with your means; and do not harass them with a view to making their lives a misery" (65:6), and, "Neither shall a mother be made to suffer because of her child, nor, because of his child, he who has begotten it" (2:233).
>
> Of the same kind is the prohibition of aggression against human life, property, and dignity, and the proscription of usurpation, oppression, and anything causing harm to one's own self or to others. This includes all sorts of offence against people's lives, minds, progeny and property.

All this is so general and inclusive in the Shariʿah that it is beyond any dispute or doubt.[16]

Now, even though quite numerous, all the proofs mentioned by al-Shāṭibī are of particular connotation (*juz'ī*). The only proof that is of universal bearing – that is, the Prophet's statement that "No harm should be sustained or incurred upon others" – is an isolated report. Its attribution to the Lawgiver is not definitive (*qaṭʿī*), since non-*mutawātir* traditions are not certain in their textual content (*matn*). This is something I have already pointed out in the inquiry concerning "The Methods of Affirming *Maqāṣid al-Shariʿah*".

You should also know that the degrees of probability and conjecture (*ẓann*) in understanding *Maqāṣid al-Shariʿah* depend on the varying levels of the thematic survey of its sources, and this, in turn, depends on the indicants available to the investigating jurists as well as on the strength and clarity of their signification. For example, it is clear that the objective of the Shariʿah in prohibiting intoxicants is the preservation of the human mind from corruption. This is why there is no disagreement among the *mujtahids* over the prohibition of anything that might cause intoxication. However, the prohibition of intoxicants is an indication that blocking the means to the corruption of the human mind is intended by the Shariʿah so that we can infer from this the prohibition of consuming small quantities of wine or fermented date juice (*nabīdh*) that do not necessarily cause intoxication, is a subtle meaning not readily realized. That is why scholars disagreed over whether the prohibition of intoxicants extends to fermented date juice and small quantities of wine. Those jurists for whom this was highly probable understood this prohibition to include all three instances, and advocated the imposition of categorical punishment (*ḥadd*) on anyone consuming fermented date juice and intoxicants, whether in small or large quantity, and upheld this act to be a blemish in a person's moral character. On the other hand, the jurists who distinguished between consuming alcohol and fermented date juice dealt with the question differently. Nevertheless, the possibility of the existence of contradicting proof (*muʿāriḍāt*), to the jurist's evidence based on thematic inference, clearly affects the level of his doubt, as taught in philosophy (*ʿilm al-ḥikmah*).[17] This is because under such circumstances, the available evidence for a Shariʿah objective is quite clear, and very little, if anything, is excluded from it. However, when the thematic induction is inaccurate and the possibility of opposing evidence persists, the likelihood of attaining that objective decreases accordingly.

8

Rationalised & Non-Rationalised Shariʿah Injunctions

The method developed by the jurists for reasoning and argumentation in fiqh and *uṣūl al-fiqh* has forced them to confine their reasoning to the literal wording (*alfāẓ*) of the Qur'an, the Prophet's Sayings and acts as well as his silence, and to consensus (ijmaʿ). Those statements, nevertheless, might denote universal rules and provisions (*aḥkām kulliyyah*), such as God's saying: "O you who believe! Be true to your covenants" (5:1), and "God wants you to have ease, and does not want you to suffer hardship" (2:185). Other examples are the Sayings of God's Messenger: "If a large amount of anything causes intoxication, a small amount of it is prohibited,"[1] and: "No harm should be borne by or caused to others." They may also denote particular rules, which applies to most cases, as in the Prophet's Saying: "O Zubayr! Irrigate [your garden] first, and then let the water flow to your neighbor."

The jurists derived from these statements various specific rulings (*furūʿ*) either by establishing the effective cause (*taḥqīq al-manāṭ*)[2] of the universal rules, since what are derived are specific applications of those universal propositions, or by analogical deduction (*qiyās*) in specific rules. The derived rules resemble those specific rules in one characteristic, (*waṣf*), that has been implied by the latter rules as their basis. This is notwithstanding the disparity between the associated instances regarding the varying clarity of their shared characteristic, a disparity that results from the difference in the methods for establishing the *ratio legis* (*masālik al-ʿillah*). The jurists then turned to the category of commands established in the Shariʿah in which the intent of the Lawgiver remained beyond the reach of the *mujtahid*, and they considered them merely devotional (*taʿabbudī*). In such a situation the *mujtahid* admits the limitation of his own knowledge in relation to the vastness of the Shariʿah after exerting all possible effort and failing to discover the specific intent of the Lawgiver. Therefore, the *mujtahid* concludes that the Shariʿah requires us simply to submit to God's commands as part of our faith, for it did not explain their purpose according to his understanding.

Bukhārī narrated from Abū al-Zinād that he said: "Traditions and different aspects of truth often contradict what people think, yet Muslims have no choice but to accept them. Likewise, we find that a woman, after finishing her menstruation, has to make up any missed days of fasting but she does not have to make up missed prayers."[3] It is also narrated in *Muwaṭṭa'* that ʿUmar ibn Khaṭṭāb said: "It is strange that one can inherit from the paternal aunt yet she herself cannot inherit."[4]

Hence, according to the jurists, the Shariʿah commands are of two kinds: rationalised (*muʿllal*) and devotional (*taʿabbudī*). The *mujtahids* differ in affirming the latter kind. However, we have found that the jurists who dealt with the question of analogical deduction (*qiyās*) and rationalised (*taʿlīl*) almost all agreed on classifying the Shariʿah commands into three categories:

1. A category that is necessarily rationalised, and this includes those commands whose underlying causes are stipulated or alluded to in the textual sources of the Shariʿah, or something of this kind.
2. A category of commands that are purely devotional, which includes all those commands whose underlying causes are beyond human grasp.
3. A category that stands midway between categories 1 and 2. It includes all those commands whose underlying causes are covert but which the jurists can arrive at by rational inference, though they might disagree on the inferred causes.

Instances of the third category include the prohibition of stipulated excess (*ribā al-faḍl*) in the six types of commodities,[5] and the absolute prohibition of leasing land, according to the Companions and their followers. They maintained that this is absolutely prohibited. In affirming reasons of this kind, one runs the risk of error and misinterpretation of the teachings of Islam. To avoid this danger, the Zāhirīs were inclined to consider only the apparent meanings (*ẓawāhir*) of Shariʿah texts and rejected *qiyās*. As a result of an exaggerated adherence to analogical reasoning, disagreement among jurists took different forms, so much so that some of them rejected the authenticity of the transmission chains of many traditions.

Yet, it is true that many jurists who advocated, as one of their methodological rules, adherence to the apparent purport (*ẓāhir*) of the Lawgiver's expressions, or to the type of *ratio legis* (*waṣf*) specified at the time of the Revelation, could not avoid falling into what resembled the Zāhirī position of confining the Shariʿah commands to the devotional category.

An example of this is some jurists' misinterpretation of the Qur'anic verse (4:92) on murder requiring retaliation (*qawad*). They based their understanding on the Tradition according to which God's Messenger is reported to have said: "Everything may be accepted as a mistake except the sword."[6] In my view, this is due to their taking into account the characteristic (*waṣf*) of the instrument, namely, the sword, which was mainly used for murder at the time when the rule on just retribution (*qiṣāṣ*) was revealed. Then, any sharp instrument was subjoined to the sword by analogy based on the original property. Subsequently, strangulation causing death, burning with fire, and slaughtering with a reed were also subjoined by analogy. Agreements, however, ended at this point. There was disagreement over just retribution for murder, in which a heavy hard rock is thrown from above onto the victim, the case where the victim is murdered by hitting his head with a nail, or by being drowned with his hands tied, or by being starved for days, etc. The only reason for this disagreement was that the jurists took into account the literal wording or the specific ground rather than the real purpose (*maqṣad*) of the rule.

Now, if one looks at the methodological principles of the Ẓāhirīs, one finds that they almost deny that the Shariʿah associates its commands with any deeper wisdom (*ḥikmah*). This is because they rejected deduction by analogy and the consideration of deeper meanings (*maʿānī*) and, therefore, stopped at the level of the apparent meanings (*ẓawāhir*) of the texts. This also explains why their argumentation and polemics do not go beyond the letter of the Traditions and the actions of God's Messenger and his Companions. This attitude is clearly manifested in Ibn Hazm's book *al-Iʿrāb ʿan al-Ḥayrah wa al-Iltibās al-Wāqiʿayn fī Madhāhib Ahl al-Ra'y wa al-Qiyās*, for this was the axis of his debates with the proponents of deduction by analogy.[7]

Indeed, by following this course, the Ẓāhirīs ran the risk of suspending the Shariʿah commands concerning the situations and cases about which the Lawgiver has mentioned no specific rules. This is a dangerous attitude, for there is the real risk that one who wavers about this issue might eventually deny the relevance and applicability of the Islamic Shariʿah at every time and in every place. In conjunction with his discussion of the Tradition concerning the splitting of the Muslim community in his book *al-ʿĀriḍah*, Abū Bakr ibn al-ʿArabī aptly summarized the Ẓāhirī's position in poetry:

> They (the Ẓāhirīs) said: *ẓawāhir* are a rule that we must
> not depart from to any kind of opinion or reflection
> [We say:] *ẓawāhir* are limited in number and occurrence:
> how then can they provide rules for people's changing condition?[8]

Once the jurists are certain that a command is purely devotional, they are duty bound to preserve its form (*ṣūrah*) and not alter it by extending, or losing sight of, its original devotional character. This can be seen in the case of reduction and adjustment in inheritance (*ʿawl*)[9] when the shares of inheritance exceed the estate. It is known that the shares of inheritance have been established by an explicit and unambiguous Qur'anic text and accepted by the Muslim community as a command of devotional character, for God has ordained it in the following verse: "You know not whether your parents or your children are nearest to you in benefit" (4:11). It is, therefore, not up to anyone to increase or decrease any share of inheritance on the basis of the extent of the heirs' benefit, goodness, or kinship. When, during the reign of ʿUmar, Muslims faced a case where the shares of those entitled for inheritance exceeded the inherited property, ʿUmar did not hesitate to consult the Companions and resort to independent opinion (*ra'y*) and rationalisation (*taʿlīl*) regarding the shares of inheritance, using the method of adjustment (*ʿawl*). The case was as follows: a woman died and left behind her husband, her mother and her full sister.

Al-ʿAbbās or ʿAlī ibn Abī Ṭālib suggested the following solution: If a man dies in debt to seven people – owing one dinar to each person – but has left only six dinars, the money left by him will be divided into seven equal shares and all seven people lose a portion of what is due to them. ʿUmar and those who were present among the Prophet's Companions approved this solution.[10] Here, we see that the Companions preserved the devotional aspect of the rule in giving each person the same share and in not neglecting any inheriting party. However, they did not consider it in the amount of each share of inheritance because this proved impossible, and so they had to apply rationalisation in this particular case.

Nevertheless, ʿAbd Allāh ibn ʿAbbās had a different view. He used to argue that had ʿUmar preferred those whom God has preferred and relegated those whom God has relegated, he would not have applied reduction and adjustment to inheritance. Accordingly, Ibn ʿAbbās upheld the view that the sister is the one who loses in this particular instance because her priority is less than that of the husband and mother, since it is possible for her to shift from being a heir entitled to an obligatory share to being an agnate or universal heir (*ʿaṣabah*),[11] that is, with the daughters.[12] Thus, Ibn ʿAbbās refused to apply rationalisation. Nor did he accept that the shares of the mother and husband be decreased, stipulating instead that the sister take whatever was left of the inheritance (the residue) – which amounted to nothing in this instance. Here, instead of resorting to rationalisation, he applied some kind of cogency by means of equivalence (*tanẓīr*).

In fact, the scholars of Islamic jurisprudence should not have accepted the existence of devotional commands in the legislation of human dealings and transactions (*muᶜāmalāt*). Instead, they should have insured that what was asserted to be devotional rather consists of rules based on subtle and hidden reasons. Many of the rules concerning transactions that some jurists interpreted as merely devotional have been the cause of numerous difficulties for Muslims in their dealings. Indeed, the Muslim community has suffered severely because of this, whereas God says: "and [He] has laid no hardship on you in [anything that pertains to] religion" (22:78).

Therefore, jurists must scrutinize and analyze carefully those Traditions that might suggest rules whose reasons and objectives are hidden. If they cannot find a way to construe a specific Shariᶜah objective, they should search all the different versions of those traditions to discover why some narrators erroneously assumed that the rules listed in their reports were devoid of any wisdom or objective. The jurists ought also to consider the overall situation of the Muslim community when those Traditions were spelled out. An example of this are the reports of Rāfiᶜ ibn Khadīj and of Anas ibn Mālik that the Messenger of God prohibited the leasing of agricultural land (*muḥāqalah*). According to Ibn ᶜAbbās, "The Prophet did not forbid that, but said: 'One had better give the land to one's fellow muslim brother gratis rather than charge a certain amount for it.'"[13]

On the other hand, Mālik, Ibn Shihāb and Ibn al-Musayyab followed the understanding of Abū Saᶜīd al-Khudrī, who maintained that God's Messenger prohibited *muḥāqalah*, that is, the leasing of agricultural lands in exchange for barley. This is why Mālik mentioned this Tradition, together with others in *Muwaṭṭa'*, under the heading of "*al-muzābanah wa al-muḥāqalah*"; he did not understand *muḥāqalah* to mean anything except this.[14]

Some Companions and leading jurists took into consideration the instance in which the prohibition was imposed, namely, the report of Rāfiᶜ ibn Khadīj in *Ṣaḥīḥ al-Bukhārī*, who said:

> We worked on farms more than anybody else in Madinah. We used to rent the land on the basis that the yield of a specific delimited portion of

> it was to be given to the landlord. Sometimes the crop of that portion was affected by blight, etc., whereas the rest remained safe, and vice versa, so the Prophet forbade this practice. At that time gold and silver were not used (for renting the land).

In another version, it is narrated that "One of those portions might yield something and the other might not."[15] It is for this reason that al-Layth ibn Saʿd said: "If those who are capable of distinguishing what is legal from what is illegal looked into what has been forbidden concerning this matter, they would not permit it, for it is surrounded with uncertainty and risk."[16]

You should also know that Abū Isḥāq al-Shāṭibī in the eighteenth and nineteenth propositions of the fourth type in *Kitāb al-Maqāṣid* dealt at length with "devotionality" (*taʿabbud*) and rationalisation (*taʿlīl*),[17] although most of what he mentioned is inaccurate and unfocused. I have deliberately omitted it because of its length and ambiguity. Readers can consult his work and reflect upon what he said, if they so wish, and compare it with what I have discussed here.

In sum, we can say that we are certain that all the Shariʿah commands embody the Lawgiver's purposes, which consist of underlying reasons, benefits, and interests. It is, therefore, the duty of the scholars of the Shariʿah to search for the reasons and objectives of legislation, both the overt and the covert. Some underlying reasons might be hidden, and people's minds vary in perceiving and detecting them. Now, if some or all the scholars of a given period fail to discover some of these objectives, this does not necessarily mean that the scholars who come after them will also fail.

However, those who fail to discover them should call upon their peers for further discussion, directly or in writing, so that they can determine the volume of legal rules that can be derived from the Lawgiver's discourse. If they do so and still fail to discover the Lawgiver's intent [in a specific rule], then they must not exceed what is reported concerning that rule, nor infer derivative cases resembling it, or use deduction by analogy on its basis. They should deduct from such a rule neither an attribute (*waṣf*) nor a general rule (*ḍābiṭ*), because the differences in those cases that do not allow for deduction by analogy are unclear when one does not know the underlying reason for the rule in question.

Moreover, some differences have an effect while some others do not. However, if it is permitted to affirm the existence of devotional rules that are devoid of any rationally detectable reasons, or whose underlying reasons cannot be detected, it should not include financial and economic dealings or criminal matters. In fact, I do not think that these areas should be covered by devotional commands, and the jurists must infer underlying reasons for them. It is for this reason that Mālik, Abū Ḥanīfah, and al-Shāfiʿī, resorting to analogy based on the six types, were assertive in discovering an underlying cause due to the prohibition of non-equivalent usury therein. Yet, they all inferred an underlying cause that served as a general rule, but failed to present us with a specific reason.[18]

PART II

On The General Objectives of Islamic Legislation

9

The Determinant Characteristic of *Maqāṣid al-Shariʿah*

The general objectives of Islamic legislation consist of the deeper meanings (*maʿānī*) and inner aspects of wisdom (*ḥikam*) considered by the Lawgiver (*Shāriʿ*) in all or most of the areas and circumstances of legislation (*aḥwāl al-tashrīʿ*). They are not confined to a particular type of the Shariʿah commands. Thus, they include the general characteristics of the Shariʿah, its general purpose and whatever notions contemplated by the legislation. They also include certain meanings and notions that are present in many, though not all, of the Shariʿah commands.

Maqāṣid al-Shariʿah are of two kinds: real ideas (*maʿānī ḥaqīqiyyah*)[1] and universal conventional ideas (*maʿānī ʿurfiyyah ʿāmmah*). Both kinds must be certain, evident, regular, and constant. Real ideas are those notions which are true in themselves so that sound minds can perceive their conformity or incompatibility with what is good (*maṣlaḥah*) – that is, they entail a universal benefit or harm – independently of any prior knowledge of any custom or law. Examples are that justice is useful, or that aggression against peoples' lives is harmful, or that punishing the aggressor is useful for society. Qualifying the minds as sound is meant to exclude the perceptions of abnormal minds, such as the love of aggression and injustice in the age of *Jāhiliyyah* as expressed by al-Shamaydhar al-Ḥārithī,[2] one of the poets of the *Ḥamāsah*, who had great pride in himself and his tribe:

We are not like those whom you used to strike with swords
So that we accept oppression and injustice or resort to a judge.
Nay, the verdict of the sword shall reign supreme on you,
And only when the sword is satisfied will we be satisfied.[3]

And as boasted by Sawwār ibn al-Muḍarrab al-Saʿdī who said:[4]

I have always been a brother of wars:
If I am not the injurer, I am the shield against the injurer.[5]

The universal conventional ideas consist of time-tested notions that are familiar to the general public and acceptable to them, owing to their conformity with the public good. Examples are believing that benevolence is something with which people should treat one another, or that punishing criminals will deter them from reoffending and others from committing crimes, and that acquitting them will lead to the opposite of these two aspects of deterrence, or that rubbish should be removed.

For both categories of ideas I have stipulated the properties of certainty (*thubūt*), evidence (*ẓuhūr*), consistency (*inḍibāṭ*), and regularity (*iṭṭirād*). By certainty I mean that these ideas are a matter of definitive knowledge or of high probability bordering on certainty. By evidence I mean that they are so clear that the jurists will not disagree over their meaning and that most of them will not confuse them with anything else owing to some similarity. This can be illustrated by the preservation of lineal identity (*ḥifẓ al-nasab*), that is, the purpose of the Shariʿah in instituting marriage. This is so clear that it cannot be confounded with its preservation through love-companionship (*mukhādanah*) or "adherence" (*ilāṭah*), whereby a female prostitute would attribute her conceived embryo to a specific man among those who had had sexual intercourse with her.

By consistency I mean that the interpretation of these ideas has precise limits that it does not exceed nor fails to meet. Its precision distinguishes it so that when it is taken as an objective of the Shariʿah, it is not subject to doubt.

An example of this is considering the protection of the intellect (*ḥifẓ al-ʿaql*) to the extent of distinguishing rationally sound people from those who are not, the intended objective of the Shariʿah in the sanctioning of discretionary punishment (*taʿzīr*)[6] by flogging for intoxication. By regularity, I mean that the interpretation of these ideas does not change according to the circumstances of places, peoples, or ages, such as being Muslim, and financial capacity as conditions for suitability in marriage – known as competence (*kafā'ah*) – according to the view of Mālik and some other jurists, in contrast to similarity in wealth or tribal descent.[7]

Some notions might oscillate between good (*maṣlaḥah*) at certain times and harm (*mafsadah*) at others, thus lacking constancy, and therefore cannot be absolutely accepted or rejected as Shariʿah objectives. Instead, they must be referred to the scholars and rulers of the Muslim community, who have the authority of abolition and compulsion (*ahl al-ḥall wa al-ʿaqd*) and are entrusted with promoting its interests, so that they determine the appropriate characteristic (*waṣf*) that should be considered in certain circumstances rather than others. An example is warfare. It might be harmful if it is waged to break the unity of the community, whereas it can be useful for protecting its sovereignty and defending it against its enemies. Thus, we read in the Qur'an:

> It is but the recompense of those who make war on God and His Apostle, and endeavour to spread corruption on earth, that they are slain in great numbers, or crucified in great numbers, or have, as the result of their perversity, their hands and feet cut off in great numbers, or are being [entirely] banished from [the face of] the earth: such is their ignominy in this world. (5:33)

Their waging of war – known as *ḥirābah* – is considered a reason for their punishment, for their action brings about corruption. God also enjoins us: "If two groups of believers fall to fighting, make peace between them" (49:9); thus teaching us that this fighting is evil; God orders the rest of the community to reconcile the quarrelling parties and put an end to their strife. Then, God Almighty says: "but then, if one of the two [groups] continues acting wrongfully toward the other, fight the one that is acting wrongfully until he reverts to God's commandments" (49:9), which is an order that war should be waged to reach a conciliation. God also says: "Fight, then, in God's cause" (2:244) and many other similar verses.[8]

Once such notions are established with their stipulated conditions, we must be sure that they constitute Shariᶜah objectives. If evidence has been furnished that the Shariᶜah has posited certain conventions or customs for consideration as part of its objectives for realizing some universal good or avoiding some universal harm, then jurists should examine them carefully. Examples are that breast feeding is a reason for the prohibition of marrying one's foster sibling, the relationship being regarded in the same way as lineage (*nasab*),[9] or that the Qurayshite descent is one of the conditions for the post of caliph.[10] If the Lawgiver is considered to have intended their application as a mere possibility, then the jurists must confirm them as particular cases closely linked to the general principles and should not venture to extend them beyond their specific and proper context.

However, if it is probable that they constitute invariably intended Shariᶜah objectives, the jurists can take them as general rules that can be extended beyond the specific context in which they were enacted. Examples are considering masculinity a condition for judiciary tenures and political rule – according to some scholars – based on the universal custom prevailing in the world at their time, or considering adoption an appropriate action with all the legal effects of real affiliations at the dawn of Islam before the abrogating Qur'anic verse "[As for your adopted children,] call them by their [real] fathers' names: this is more equitable in the sight of God" (33:5).

It therefore follows that *Maqāṣid al-Shariᶜah* consist of real ideas that have their own external existence. To them are attached mentally posited ideas (*maᶜānī iᶜtibāriyyah*)[11] that have some measure of reality creating the link. They also include established general conventional ideas (*maᶜānī ᶜurfiyyah*) that are supported by closely linked customary notions.

Illusions (*wahmiyyāt*) consist of notions created by the imagination without any basis in the reality of the external world, such as the unfounded belief (*tawahhum*) by many people that there is something fearful or repulsive about a human corpse when one is alone with it. This kind of perception consists of both active (*fiʿl*) and passive (*infiʿāl*) aspects, for we find that the mind acts and is influenced [by its own act] at the same time. It invents the idea and then perceives it [and is influenced by it]. In a similar category are the fancies of the imagination (*takhayyulāt*). They consist of ideas created by the imagination (*quwwat al-khayāl*) and helped by illusion with the combination of various sensible images stored in the memory, such as the prohibition of some kind of fish [i.e. capybara or water hog] just because in Arabic it is called 'sea pig' (*khinzīr baḥrī*).[12] None of these ideas is appropriate for *Maqāṣid al-Shariʿah*, for God said to His Apostle: "... for, behold, that in which you believe is self-evident truth" (27:79), meaning that it is truth free from all sorts of falsehood and corruption.

From a thorough examination of the Shariʿah, we have found that it rejects illusions and fancies of the imagination. Therefore, basing its commands on illusions is unacceptable to the Shariʿah except in need, which means that fancies of the imagination cannot be included as part of *Maqāṣid al-Shariʿah*. It is narrated in *Muwaṭṭa'* that the Prophet saw a man driving a camel which he was going to sacrifice, and he told him to ride it. The man refused to ride the camel and said: "Messenger of God, it is an animal that I am going to sacrifice," and he replied: "Ride it, woe to you," two or three times.[13]

It is also reported that ʿAbd Allāh ibn ʿUmar shrouded his son Wāqid ibn ʿAbd Allāh, who had died at al-Juḥfah while in *iḥrām*, and he veiled his head and face and said, "If we had not been in *iḥrām*, we ourselves would have perfumed him." Mālik commented: "A man can do things only while he is alive. When he is dead, his actions stop."[14] This comment was meant to highlight the abrogation of the tradition, according to which the Prophet said, concerning a man who had died because his she-camel had broken his neck while he was in *iḥrām*, "Do not shroud his face, and do not perfume him, for he will be resurrected on the Day of Rising in a state of *talbiyah*."[15] Some jurists said that this was due to some secret quality that God knew was specifically present in that particular person.[16] In my view, the real reason was to prevent the people enshrouding him from touching perfume, which means that the prohibition was for the sake of the living people rather than the dead person. Thus, depriving the latter of perfume was made a reason for his resurrection in a state of *talbiyah* as a means to show the importance of the Hajj. Accordingly, the Shariʿah abolished the rules of adoption that had existed during the period of *Jāhiliyyah* and the early years of Islam, because adoption is not based on any reality. Therefore, whenever jurists are faced with the impression that an imaginary or illusionary idea is the basis of a Shariʿah command, they should think carefully to discard that illusion and discover the real meaning underneath, which has been associated with something imaginary in such a way that it has been hidden from the sight of the general public, which is usually inclined to follow fancies and illusions.

This can be illustrated by the prohibition of washing the body of a martyred person while fighting in God's cause. In this respect, the Prophet is reported to have said: "He will be resurrected on the Day of Rising and his blood will be gushing forth, with the color of blood and the smell of musk".[17] Many people might think that the reason for not washing the martyr is to keep his blood in his veins so that he will be resurrected with it on the Day of Rising. The truth is far from this, for if he were washed out of ignorance, forgetfulness or even intentionally, this would not cancel his virtue, and God might create in his wounds a blood that would gush forth, testifying for him on the Day of Resurrection.

Accordingly, the reason for this recommendation is that people are so busy during the fighting that they cannot spare time for washing the martyr. Since God knew that the fighters would be heartbroken upon seeing their bleeding wounds and knowing that they would be buried in that state if they were killed, and since He knew that this would also break the hearts of their relatives and next of kin, He compensated them with a great virtue. Hence, there is a reversal of the cause, that is to say, the cause is the effect while the effect is the cause. Similarly, the command to cover one's private parts while performing prayer alone is actually meant to emphasize that one should not take lightly good customs and manners as a means of strengthening magnanimity and habituating people to it.

There might be some commands of the Shariʿah that are based on certain things (*maʿānī*) for which we cannot find any interpretation, save that they are imaginary notions, such as facing the *Qiblah* in prayer, or substituting *tayammum*[18] for ablution, or kissing the Black Stone during the pilgrimage. These things must be acceptable as they are and considered part of the devotional category in which the Shariʿah objective is beyond our grasp, or should be understood as explained below. Other commands might be contingent on an interpretation that would exclude them from mere imaginary or illusionary notions, such as ritual impurity. We should therefore examine these commands as carefully as possible. This topic is covered in greater detail in Part III, "*Maqāṣid al-Shariʿah*: The Human Context."

You should know that imaginary things, though they are not appropriate as objectives of legislation, might be useful for achieving certain Shariʿah objectives. They can be used for inviting to Islam (*daʿwah*) or to arouse people's interest (*targhīb*) or fear (*tarhīb*), such as in the Qur'anic verse: "Would any of you like to eat the flesh of his dead brother? Nay, you would loathe it" (49:12) or the Prophet's Saying: "Someone who takes back his charity (*ṣadaqah*) is like a dog swallowing its own vomit."

Likewise, jurists must differentiate between the two categories, and should not try to derive juristic rules from such exhortations – for this is a sign of sheer ignorance. Otherwise, the case would be like that of someone who would think that a fasting person would break his fast by backbiting against another person because he would have eaten his flesh! Fantasies (*wahmiyyāt*) are thus only rarely considered to realize a Shariʿah objective as a last resort. It might be that what we have mentioned concerning *tayammum* and facing the *Qiblah* stems from this. So, examine it.

10

Grounding of *Maqāṣid al-Sharīʿah* on *Fiṭrah*

God says in the Qur'an:

> And so, set thy face steadfastly towards the [one ever-true] religion, turning away from all that is false (*ḥanīfan*), in accordance with the natural disposition which God has instilled into man (*fiṭrat Allāh*): [for,] not to allow any change to corrupt what God has created. (30:30)

What is meant by "religion" (*dīn*) is Islam, for the verse is addressed to the Prophet Muhammad, who is thus ordained to set his face towards the religion with which he was sent. That Muslims are all included in this verse is a matter of agreement among all Qur'an commentators.

To set his face towards this religion means to commit himself to it and take it seriously. The word "face" refers to all the self, and the face has been singled out because it includes most of a human's senses and means of perception. As for the expression "set towards (*ḥanīfan*)", which means "inclination" (*mayl*), it is a circumstantial phrase (*ḥāl*) for the term "face". What is meant by inclination here is turning away from all kinds of polytheism toward the religion of Islam, as is stated in another verse where God says: "and shun every word that is untrue, inclining (*ḥunafā'*) towards God, [and] turning away from all that is false" (22:30–31).

Now, to continue our syntactical analysis of the verse, we find that the expression *fiṭrat Allāh* is a noun in the accusative, since it is an appositive of *ḥanīfan* – itself a circumstantial phrase for *dīn*. Accordingly, *fiṭrah* here is a second circumstantial phrase for *dīn*. Therefore, the meaning of the verse can be expressed in the following way: "And so, set your face steadfastly to the straight and true religion, which is the natural disposition of man". Likewise, *dīn* refers to the entirety of religion as both articles of faith and rules of conduct (*aḥkām*).

Therefore, confining the meaning of *dīn* to the articles of faith, as done by some Qur'an commentators like Fakhr al-Dīn al-Rāzī and al-Bayḍāwī,[1] is mere compliance with the apparent meaning implied by the sequence of the preceding verses from that which states: "God creates [man] in the first instance, and then brings him forth anew: and, in the end, unto Him you will be brought back" (30:11).[2] This misunderstanding is due to the fact that those verses are apparently meant to condemn polytheism and invalidate the beliefs of polytheists and atheists. In addition, those commentators thought that the particle "And so" (*fā'*) connecting the verse (that is, "And so, set thy face...") to those before it is that which connotes subdivision (*tafrīʿ*). However, both interpretations are unsound.

Firstly, the sequence and context of the previous verses do not entail breaking down the generic noun *dīn*, which means all that people use to express their religiousness, as indicated by the Tradition according to which the Prophet is reported to have said: "That is the Archangel Gabriel, he came to teach you your religion."[3] In this connection, the scholars of *uṣūl al-fiqh* have pointed out that if we find in the Qur'an a statement dealing with a specific subject, and it is followed by a general term including that specific subject and others for a specific affinity or correspondence (*munāsabah*), then that term should not be confined to some parts of its meaning to the exclusion of the others on the grounds of the context and sequence.[4]

Secondly, it is clear that the particle connecting the verse in question to what precedes it denotes eloquence (*fā' al-faṣīḥah*) rather than subdivision (*tafrīʿ*). This type of connotation suggests the existence of an implicit term when the particle is used after a statement meant to demonstrate something intended by the speaker following the elaboration of its premises and proofs. Then, what follows the particle "And so" (*fā'*) comes as the conclusion in syllogism. Accordingly, the meaning of the verse would be: "If you have known the proofs confirming monotheism and invalidating polytheism that We have expounded to people, then set your face, that is, set yourself to Islam, which is the natural disposition (*fiṭrah*)." The definite article added to *dīn* therefore denotes familiarity (*taʿrīf al-ʿahd*), meaning what the Prophet knew in both the articles of faith and the body of legal rules and commands (Shariʿah) that had been revealed to him. This is similar to the following verse:

> In matters of faith, He has ordained for you that which He had enjoined upon Noah – and into which We have given you [O Muhammad] insight by Revelation – as well as that which We had enjoined upon Abraham, and Moses, and Jesus: Steadfastly uphold the [true] faith, and do not break up your unity therein. (42:13)

It follows that what is meant by *fiṭrah* in the verse is the totality of religion, including its fundamentals of faith and the rules of conduct. Thus it was understood by Ibn ʿAṭiyyah[5] and al-Zamakhsharī.[6] Ibn ʿAṭiyyah said:

> People disagreed on the meaning of *fiṭrah* here. Makkī[7] and others mentioned all that this term can apply to, and not all that [they said] is sound. Therefore, what is acceptable in the understanding of this term is that it refers to the natural disposition (*khilqah*) and condition (*hay'ah*) in the child by which he is destined and prepared to know the Creation of God – Exalted is He – and to reason from it the existence of his Lord and know His laws and believe in Him.[8]

In his turn, al-Zamakhsharī said in his *al-Kashshāf*: "The meaning [of the verse] is that [God] has created them predisposed to accept monotheism and the religion of Islam."[9]

Having said this, we must now explain how Islam is equivalent to *fiṭrah*, for no one, to my knowledge, has done so proficiently. *Fiṭrah* is the natural disposition (*khilqah*) and order (*niẓām*) that God has instilled in every created being. Thus, the *fiṭrah* of human beings is the inward (*bāṭin*) and outward (*ẓāhir*) condition in which human beings have been created, that is, in both intellect and body. Thus, walking on one's feet is an aspect of the human being's physical disposition (*fiṭrah jasadiyyah*), whereas attempting to hold things with one's feet is incongruous with that nature. Similarly, relating effects to their causes and drawing conclusions from their proper premises are part of a human being's intellectual and mental disposition (*fiṭrah ʿaqliyyah*), whereas drawing conclusions from causes that are not real – known in the science of reasoning as invalidity of argument (*fasād al-waḍʿ*) – contradicts that intellectual disposition. Affirming that the things we see in the external world are realities in themselves is also part of a human being's intellectual disposition. On the other hand, the Sophists' denial of these realities runs counter to that disposition. Likewise, the description of Islam as the *fiṭrah* means that it is congruent with man's natural disposition, since Islam consists of beliefs (*ʿaqā'id*) and legislations (*tashrīʿāt*) that are all rational matters or matters that accord with what is perceived and confirmed by reason.[10]

Abū ʿAlī ibn Sīnā (Avicenna)[11] expounded the meaning of *fiṭrah* in his book *al-Najāt*. He said:

> The meaning of *fiṭrah* can be explained as follows. Let a person imagine that he has come into being in this world at once with full intelligence. However, he neither knew any thought, nor adopted any faith, nor mixed with any people, nor experienced any politics. Yet, he observed the sensible (*maḥsūsāt*) from which he derived images (*khayālāt*). Let him then imagine something and doubt it. If he could doubt it, this means that *fiṭrah* does not confirm the doubted thing; if he cannot doubt it, this means that *fiṭrah* requires it. Nevertheless, not all that is required by man's *fiṭrah* is true (*ṣādiq*); only those things that are confirmed by the faculty called intellect (*ʿaql*) are true.
>
> As for humankind's mental *fiṭrah* (*fiṭrat al-dhihn*) in general, it might be false (*kādhibah*), and this falsehood pertains to matters that are not

> themselves perceived by the senses (*maḥsūsāt*) but constitute first principles to that which is sensible. Thus, genuine *fiṭrah* (*fiṭrah ṣādiqah*) consists of primary propositions (*muqaddimāt*) and widely-known and praiseworthy notions (*ārā' mashhūrah maḥmūdah*), whose acceptance has been necessitated either by people's universal consent (*shahādat al-kull*), such as the goodness of justice, or by the testimony of the majority of them, or by that of the knowledgeable and virtuous amongst them. Widespread ideas (*dhā'iʿāt*) as such do not belong to what is consented (*taṣdīq*) by the *fiṭrah*, and therefore widespread ideas that are neither primary intelligibles (*awwalī ʿaqlī*) nor imaginary notions (*wahmī*)[12] are not matters of the *fiṭrah*. They are rather established in the minds as a result of custom fixed in childhood or because they are required for peaceful coexistence and courteous behavior that are necessary for humankind. They might also originate in general human morality, such as modesty and friendship, or result from accumulated observation. Furthermore, it might be that the notion in itself requires a subtle condition to be classified as absolutely true, yet that condition is unheeded and the notion is taken in absolute terms.[13]

Ibn Sīnā has indeed excellently articulated the meaning of *fiṭrah* and pertinently cautioned against confusing it with false perceptions deeply rooted in the minds owing to the particular experience of human beings, such as age-long bad habits perpetrated by wrong-headed people. He clearly states that it is the scholars and sages – that is, people of sound reason – who should undertake the task of distinguishing between what is and is not relevant to the true meaning of *fiṭrah*. It is they who have the power to articulate the true meaning of *fiṭrah* and distinguish it from all kinds of wrong perceptions and passions that might creep into it. However, if people are faced with the difficulty of establishing a subtle aspect of *fiṭrah* or one that is so intermingled with other things that they run the risk of being overwhelmed by their own desires by believing what is not entailed by *fiṭrah* to be so, then they must take time to consider it carefully and consult the works of excellent and reputable scholars known for the probity and soundness of their thought.

It should have become clear from the above that humankind's

psychological nature (*fiṭrah nafsiyyah*) consists of the state in which God has created the human species free from all kinds of frivolity and bad habits. This is what is meant by the phrase in the verse quoted above: "the natural disposition which God (*fiṭrat Allāh*) has instilled into man" (30:30). Therefore, humankind is endowed with the capacity for acquiring virtues (*faḍā'il*), and acting according to them as confirmed by God in the Qur'an: "Verily, We create man in the best of moulds, and thereafter We reduce him to the lowest of the low (*asfali sāfilīn*) – excepting only such as attain to faith and do good works" (95:4–6).

There is no doubt that what is meant by the expression "the best of moulds (*aḥsan taqwīm*)" here is the valuation of the intellect, which is the principle of right beliefs and good deeds, while the phrase "the lowest of the low (*asfal sāfilīn*)" refers to humankind's propensity to acquire bad qualities (*radhā'il*) from false beliefs and evil deeds. Therefore, this moulds has nothing to do with the human being's physical form (*ṣūrah*). This is because the human physical form does not degenerate. It is also because the exclusion (*istithnā'*) in the phrase "excepting only such as attain to faith and do good works" precludes any possibility that the general term in the verse refers to the outward form. Moreover, righteous believers are not privileged with having beautiful physical forms to the exclusion of others.[14]

Accordingly, the fundamentals of *fiṭrah* (*uṣūl fiṭriyyah*) consist of what God has instilled in human beings, whom He has created for the purpose of inhabiting the world. They are therefore suited to the orderly functioning of the world in the most appropriate manner. Hence, they correspond to the teachings of Islam that God has willed for putting the world to rights and removing disorder from it. The Qur'anic description of Islam as *fiṭrat Allāh* likewise means that its fundamentals (*uṣūl*) originate in man's natural disposition. To those fundamentals are subjoined principles and sub-principles belonging to the widespread and universally accepted virtues that Islam came to confirm and enhance, for they constitute part of the good manners deeply rooted in human life and emanating from good purposes free from harmful effects. When left on its own, *fiṭrah* may not attest to such manners or to their opposites. However, when they happened, they proved agreeable to it and it therefore accepted them in such a way that they became firmly established in it. Likewise, they are attributable to the fundamentals of *fiṭrah*.

Modesty and decency (*ḥayā'*) and impudence (*waqāḥah*) are examples of such manners. When their practice does not reach the level of causing harm, these two qualities are the same in the testimony of *fiṭrah*, so much so that some philosophers, such as Diogenes[15] in ancient Greece, were known for their impudence and insolence. However, we find that decency and modesty as a value has been so much cherished by people that it has become a solidly established custom in human society and thus the ground for so many useful things for the good of both the individual and society. That is why Islam considered it one of its mottos. It is reported in an authentic tradition that the Prophet, passed one day by one of the *Anṣār* who was chiding his fellow muslim brother for his modesty. The Prophet told him: "Leave him alone, modesty is part of faith."[16] Likewise, it is found that people rejected certain ideas of wisdom and shunned their authors only because of the latter's harsh and hard character. Hence, God says in the Qur'an: "And it was by God's Grace that you [O Muhammad] dealt gently with your followers: for if you had been harsh and hard of heart, they would indeed have broken away from you" (3:159).

It is clear from this discussion that only real ideas (*ḥaqā'iq*) and mentally posited notions (*iʿtibāriyyāt*) in human intellectual perception flow from the *fiṭrah*. Illusions (*wahmiyyāt*) and imagination (*takhayyulāt*) do not constitute part of that *fiṭrah*, for they do not obtain in the things engrained in the intellect. However, they consist of things that have occurred in the *fiṭrah* so frequently that they have become closely linked to human beings and thus they have acquired a status that is almost similar to innate natural things (*fiṭriyyāt*). Because such things have occurred in the *fiṭrah* owing to the misuse of reason and misunderstanding of cause and effect, we find that rational people are agreed on *ḥaqā'iq* and *iʿtibāriyyāt* rather than *wahmiyyāt* and *takhayyulāt*. Indeed, we find that the strength of the latter increases in proportion to the weakness of the minds, and that people of sound minds are immune to their hold. It follows from this that the Shariᶜah calls its followers to safeguard the *fiṭrah* and preserve the acts flowing from it, to restore those aspects of it that have been obliterated, and to cleanse it from all that has crept into it. Likewise, marriage and nursing (*irḍāᶜ*) are matters of the *fiṭrah*, whose evidence is furnished by the human constitution itself; cooperation and good manners of companionship are also matters of the *fiṭrah* for they are required for cooperation to insure human survival. By the same token, protecting people's lives and safeguarding their lineal identity (*nasab*) constitute an aspect of the *fiṭrah*. Moreover, true civilization is a manifestation of the *fiṭrah*, for it is the expression of the movement of the human intellect that is itself part of the *fiṭrah*.

Similarly, the various branches of good knowledge are also a matter of the *fiṭrah*, for they result from the interaction and exchange between human minds. So too are the different kinds of scientific and technical inventions, for they flow from people's thinking – and it is an aspect of the *fiṭrah* that people love to see what emanates from their natural constitution manifested in the external world.[17]

Now, when we carefully examine the all-purpose principle (*maqṣad ᶜāmm*) of Islamic legislation, which will be discussed below, we find that it only promotes the preservation of the *fiṭrah* and prevents its violation and corruption. Thus, anything leading to its violation would be forbidden and avoided in the Shariᶜah, whereas anything leading to its restoration and preservation would be ordained by it. Whatever stands at a lower level in relation to these two limits would be either forbidden or required in general terms, while anything that does not affect it in any way is permissible.

When the requirements (*muqtaḍayāt*) of the *fiṭrah* are found to conflict with one another and there is no way of reconciling them, then priority must be given to what is stronger and more significant for the preservation of the *fiṭrah*. Thus, in Islam, killing a human soul is considered the gravest sin next to polytheism (*shirk*),[18] and monastic asceticism is disapproved.[19] Moreover castration of human beings is considered one of the gravest crimes,[20] just as making use of the human being in a way that destroys or incapacitates him is not allowed, such as torturing a slave[21] – this of course differently from the use of animals, although it is not allowed to torture an animal, or to kill an animal (except for consumption).[22]

It thus becomes crystal clear that resorting to established custom in legal judgment flows from the meaning of the *fiṭrah*, for it is a precondition that when used for this purpose, custom must not contravene the established rules of the Shariʿah, but should relate to the principle of permissibility (*ibāḥah*). As we have already seen, anything conforming to this principle is a matter of the *fiṭrah*, either because the *fiṭrah* does not reject it and therefore people would like to acquire it, or because it is acceptable to the *fiṭrah* – and this does not require further argument.

11

Magnanimity of the Shariʿah

Magnanimity (*samāḥah*) is the ease in dealing with one another in moderation. Standing midway between sternness (*taḍyīq*) and indulgence (*tasāhul*), *samāḥah* derives its meaning from the ideal of moderation, justice, and temperance. It is a concept which our sage masters have praised highly in their comparative analysis of the various – noble and ignoble – qualities of human souls and minds. They are agreed that, being the middlemost position between the two extremes of excessiveness (*ifrāṭ*) and negligence (*tafrīṭ*), moderateness constitutes the backbone of all virtuous qualities. The extremes are the outcome of following vain desires against which God has warned us on many occasions. Thus, God says: "and do not follow vain desire, lest it lead you astray from the path of God" (38:26); "O Followers of the Gospel! Do not overstep the bounds [of truth] in your religious beliefs, and do not say of God anything but the truth" (4:171), "O Followers of the Gospel! Do not overstep the bounds [of truth] in you religious beliefs; and do not follow the errant views of people who have gone astray aforetime"(5:77); "But as for monastic asceticism – We did not enjoin it upon them: they invented it themselves out of desire for God's goodly acceptance" (57:27).

Although the last two verses refer primarily to the followers of previous revelations (*Ahl al-Kitāb*), they are meant as an exhortation for the Muslim community to avoid what provoked God's wrath with earlier peoples and led to their downfall. In this connection, the

Prophet said concerning the Jews: "If [in the first instance] they sacrificed any cow chosen by themselves, they would have fulfilled their duty; but they made it complicated for themselves, and so God made it complicated for them."[1]

Moderation between the two extremes of excessiveness and negligence is the spring of all human perfection. Hence, God has described the Muslim community or its first generations in the following way: "And thus We have willed you to be a community of the middle way, so that [with your lives] you might bear witness to the truth before all mankind" (2:143). In this connection, Abū Saʿīd al-Khudrī narrated from the Prophet that the meaning of "the middle way" in the verse is balance, that is, between excessiveness and negligence.[2]

The Qur'an commentators have affirmed this understanding in their interpretation of that verse,[3] and of the following verse: "Said the most right-minded among them (*awsaṭuhum*)..." (68:28), that is, the most knowledgeable and just among them.[4] The Follower Muṭarrif ibn ʿAbd Allāh ibn al-Shikhkhīr al-Tabiʿī[5] is reported to have said: "The best of affairs is their middle way."[6] Some scholars have reported this statement as a Prophetic Tradition. However, its chain of transmission is weak, though it is quoted quite often.[7]

Likewise, *samāḥah* is commendable easiness in matters in which people tend toward sternness. That *samāḥah* is commendable means that it does not result in harm or corruption. It is thus narrated in an authentic Tradition on the authority of Jābir ibn ʿAbd Allāh that the Prophet said: "May God's mercy be on him who is lenient in his buying, selling, and in demanding back his money."[8] Similar to this is the report by Abū Hurayrah.[9]

Characterizing Islam as magnanimous is confirmed by the Qur'an and the Sunnah. God says: "God wants you to have ease, and does not want you to suffer" (2:185); "... and [He] has laid no hardship on you in [anything that pertains to] religion" (22:78); "God does not want to impose any hardship on you" (5:6); "O our Sustainer! Do not lay upon us a burden like that which you laid upon those who lived before us! O our Sustainer! Do not make us bear burdens which we have no strength to bear!" (2:286).

It is reported in an authentic Tradition from Ibn ᶜAbbās that the Prophet said: "The most beloved religion to God is magnanimous *ḥanīfiyyah*."[10] By this he means that Islam is the best of all religions, because it is the magnanimous *ḥanāfiyyah*, thus ascertaining that magnanimity is a major attribute of Islam. It is also reported on the authority of Abū Hurayrah that the Prophet said: "The religion [of Islam] is very easy, and whoever overburdens himself in his religion will not be able to continue in that way,"[11] meaning that Islam will always prevail. In another Tradition, he is reported to have said: "I was sent to people with the lenient, tolerant, True Religion (*ḥanīfiyyah samḥah*)."[12] Though in its wording this Tradition is weak from the point of view of its chain of transmission, it concurs with the earlier one as far as its meaning is concerned. At any rate, the thematic analysis of the sources of the Shariᶜah has proven that magnanimity and ease constitute an integral part of the objectives of Islam.

It is also reported by Bukhārī and others that the Prophet sent Abū Mūsā al-Ashᶜarī and Muᶜādh ibn Jabal to the Yemen and told them: "Facilitate things for the people and do not make things difficult for them; give the people good tidings and do not reject them."[13] In another Tradition, God's Apostle is again reported to have said: "You have been sent to make things easy (for the people) and you have not been sent to make things difficult for them."[14] In a Tradition attributed to ᶜĀ'ishah, she is reported to have said: "Whenever the Prophet was given an option between two things, he used to select the easier of the two as long as it was not sinful."[15] By "sin" (*ithm*) is meant what the Shariᶜah has prohibited. In this respect, al-Shāṭibī stated on many occasions in a chapter dealing with legal impediments (*mawāniᶜ*): "Evidence concerning the removal of hardship from this community is established beyond any doubt."[16] To substantiate this, he cited many of the Traditions we have already mentioned.

Then, I would say: the underlying wisdom of magnanimity in the Shariᶜah is that God has made Islam the religion of the *fiṭrah* and matters of the *fiṭrah* pertain to humankind's constitution and inborn disposition. Since matters of the *fiṭrah* are rooted in the human souls, people easily accept them. Similarly, it is an aspect of the *fiṭrah* to avoid hardship and sternness, in which respect God has said: "God wants to lighten your burdens: for man has been created weak" (4:28). Thus, God willed the Islamic Shariʿah to be universal and eternal. This necessitated that its implementation should be easy, and easiness required freedom from sternness. Accordingly, by its unfailing magnanimity, the Shariʿah has been suitable for and acceptable to all human beings, because it brings comfort to both the individual and society.

In fact, magnanimity has manifested its great importance in the spread and unbroken historical continuity of the Shariʿah. And this provides further evidence that ease is a matter of the *fiṭrah*, for it is part of human nature to love ease and comfort. For this reason, God expressed His dislike of the polytheists' alteration of the creation by attributing it to Satan. Thus, the verse in the Qur'an: "... and I [Satan] shall command them – and they will cut off the ears of the cattle [in idolatrous sacrifice]; and I shall command them – and they will corrupt God's creation" (4:119). Of course, alteration is unacceptable when it is done for no useful purpose (*maṣlaḥah*), but if it is done for some purpose that is acceptable to the *fiṭrah*, such as circumcision, cutting the nails,[17] or cutting one's hair during the hajj, then it is praiseworthy.

12

The General Objectives of Islamic Legislation

From a comprehensive thematic analysis of the textual sources of the Shariʿah pertaining to the objectives of legislation, we can draw the following conclusions. Both its general rules and specific proofs indicate that the all-purpose principle (*maqṣad ʿāmm*) of Islamic legislation is to preserve the social order of the community and insure its healthy progress by promoting the well-being and righteousness (*ṣalāḥ*) of that which prevails in it, namely, the human species. The well-being and virtue of human beings consist of the soundness of their intellect, the righteousness of their deeds as well as the goodness of the things of the world where they live that are put at their disposal.

God says concerning the prophet Shuʿayb and in praise of him: "I desire no more than to set things to rights (*iṣlāḥ*) in so far as it lies within my power; but the achievement of my aim depends on God alone" (11:88). From this verse we come to know that God ordained that prophet to set things to rights inasmuch as it was within his capacity. Again we read in the Qur'an: "And Moses said to his brother Aaron: 'Take my place among my people; and act righteously, and do not follow the path of the spreaders of corruption'" (7:142). We also read: "Behold, Pharaoh exalted himself in the land and divided people into castes. One group of them he deemed utterly low; he would slaughter their sons and spare [only] their women: for, behold, he was one of those who spread corruption [on earth]"

(28:4). The preceding two verses clearly indicate that the qualities attributed to Pharaoh are all a matter of corruption that is blameworthy, and that Moses was sent to deliver the children of Israel from Pharaoh's corruption. From this we realize that what is meant by corruption is not disbelief (*kufr*), but evil deeds on earth, for the Israelites did not actually follow Pharaoh in his disbelief.

God says concerning Shuʿayb's law to the people of Madyan:[1] "Give, therefore, full measure and weight [in all your dealings], and do not deprive people of what is rightfully theirs; and do not spread corruption on earth after it has been so well ordered" (7:85). In another verse we read: "[And Moses said:] 'Eat and drink the sustenance provided by God, and do not act wickedly on earth by spreading corruption'" (2:60). We also read concerning the prophet Ṣāliḥ, who was sent to the people of Thamūd:[2] "...and do not act wickedly on earth by spreading corruption" (7:74). Addressing the Muslim community, God says: "Call unto your Sustainer humbly, and in the secrecy of your hearts. Verily, He does not love those who transgress the bounds of what is right: hence, do not spread corruption on earth after it has been so well ordered" (7:55–56). And referring to the behavior of some people, He says: "But whenever he prevails, he goes about the earth, spreading corruption and destroying [man's] tilth and progeny: and God does not love corruption" (2:205). Again, He says: "[Ask them:] 'Would you, after having turned away [from God's commandment, prefer to revert to your old ways, and] spread corruption on earth, and [once again] cut asunder your ties of kinship?'" (47:22).

These are all-round explicit textual proofs confirming the fact that the overall objective of the Shariʿah is to set things to rights (*ṣalāḥ*) and remove corruption (*fasād*) in all kinds of human activity. There are also in the Qur'an many verses in which setting things to rights has been mentioned in exhortation and praise, whereas spreading corruption has been mentioned in warnings and criticism. I have not quoted these verses because they do not state clearly that setting things to right and corruption relate to human deeds, although it is likely that they refer to belief (*imān*) and disbelief.

Similar to what has been mentioned are textual proofs suggesting (*īmā'*)[3], that righteousness and well-being in this world are great favors that God bestows upon the righteous (*ṣāliḥīn*) people as their reward. Thus, God says in the Qur'an, "And, indeed, after having exhorted [man], We laid it down in all the books of divine wisdom that My righteous servants shall inherit the earth: herein, behold, there is a message for people who [truly] worship God" (21:105–106). He also addresses the Muslims and says, "God has promised those of you who have attained faith and do righteous deeds that, of a certainty, He will cause them to accede to power on earth, even as He caused [some of] those who lived before them to accede to it" (24:55).

Again, He says in the form of a promise, "As for anyone – be it man or woman – who does righteous deeds, and is a believer withal – him shall We most certainly cause to live a good life" (16:97). Reminding the children of Israel of the blessings that He bestowed upon them by freeing them from their worldly bondage, God says, "And, Lo, Moses said to his people: 'O my people! Remember the blessings which God bestowed upon you when He raised up prophets among you, and made you your own masters'" (5:20). Had righteousness and well-being in this world not been intended by the Lawgiver, He would not have mentioned it as a favor for the righteous among His servants.

Accordingly, we should realize that the righteousness intended and praised by the Lawgiver is not confined to righteousness of belief and acts of ritual worship, as some people might wrongly believe. Rather, what is meant by righteousness is setting things to rights in people's worldly condition and social affairs, as indicated by the following verse: "But whenever he prevails, he goes about the earth, spreading corruption and destroying [people's] tilth and progeny: and God does not love corruption" (2:205). Indeed this verse clearly indicates that what is meant by the corruption warned against here is that affecting the things of this world. It equally indicates that it should not be understood that the One Who created this world and instituted in it the laws of its preservation and existence did so in mere idle play. Hence, He says, "Did you, then, think that We created you in mere idle play, and that you would not have to return to Us?" (23:115).

If He had not intended the orderly running of the world, He would not have ordained punitive laws to deter people from perpetrating corruption nor permitted them to enjoy the beautiful and good things of life. Thus, He has ordained just retribution for the killing of human souls and mutilation of people's organs. He has also ordained value compensation for destroyed property and punishment for destroying villages or drowning commodities. In order to set people's dealings with one another to rights, the Shariʿah has established a system of rights and entitlements (*niẓām al-ḥaqq*) that is certainly meant to remove corruption.[4] This is explicitly mentioned in the following verse: "But if the truth were in accord with their own likes and dislikes, the heavens and the earth would surely have fallen into ruin, and all that lives in them [would long ago have perished]" (23:71). Likewise, the Shariʿah has considered what is right and antithetical to corruption.

From the totality of these and other similar indicants, we can attain categorical knowledge that the Shariʿah aims at the acquisition of what is good and beneficial (*jalb al-maṣāliḥ*) and the rejection of what is evil and harmful (*dar' al-mafāsid*). We can consider this as a fundamental universal rule of the Shariʿah. Thus, it is firmly established that the all-purpose principle of the Shariʿah is to achieve righteousness and goodness (*ṣalāḥ*) in the world and remove corruption from it. This can happen only by setting humankind's affairs to rights and removing the corruption that it produces. That is, since the human being is the predominant creature (*muhaymin*) in this world, its righteousness and the orderly functioning of its affairs depends on the righteousness and virtue of the human beings. Accordingly, we find that Islam has dealt with setting to rights the condition of humankind by tackling the affairs of both the individual and the community. Likewise, it started its call by reforming matters pertaining to faith and belief, for it is right belief that constitutes the foundation of sound and correct human thinking that leads the mind to proper reflection on the affairs of the world. Then, Islam addressed itself to purifying the human psyche and uplifting the human soul, since it is the inner person that actually motivates one to righteous deeds, as indicated in the Prophet's saying: "Beware!

There is in the body a piece of flesh (*muḍghah*), if it becomes good (reformed), the whole body becomes good, but if it is spoilt, the whole body is spoilt, and that is the heart."[5] As some philosophers have said: "man consists of an intellect that is served by the organs."[6] Thereupon, Islam concerned itself with reforming human deeds by instituting detailed legislation for the various aspects of human activities.

Human beings have a natural propensity for perfection. However their actual achievement of perfection develops only gradually in tandem with their spiritual purification and moral uplifting. Indeed, we have in the gradual development of Islamic legislation from the beginning of the Prophet's call to the post-Hijrah period a sufficient guide concerning the strategy of the Sharīʿah for achieving its desired reform (*iṣlāḥ*). In fact, all that we have already discussed has been expressed by the Tradition reported by Muslim on the authority of Abū ʿAmrah al-Thaqafī, who said: "I asked: 'O Messenger of God, tell me about Islam something which might remove from me the necessity of my asking anybody after you.' He [the Prophet] said: 'Say: I affirm my faith in God, and then remain steadfast to it.'"[7]

It is not our purpose in this book to deal with the question of global reform (*iṣlāḥ ʿāmm*). Therefore, we shall refrain from discussing matters pertaining to the reform of belief, spirituality, morality, and devotional acts of worship,[8] and focus instead on the specific aspects of reform pertaining to the public affairs of the Muslims in the rules and laws regulating civil and social dealings (*muʿāmalāt madaniyyah*). This is what is known in Islamic jurisprudence as the attainment of what is good and beneficial (*jalb al-maṣlaḥah*) and rejection of the evil and harmful (*dar' al-mafsadah*).

13

The Meaning of *Maṣlaḥah* and *Mafsadah*

As its name indicates, *maṣlaḥah* means the utmost righteousness and goodness (*ṣalāḥ*). For this, it has been expressed in the morphological form *mafʿalah* connoting the place in which there is intensity of the meaning from which this form is derived, which is here an allegorical place. It likewise appears to me that *maṣlaḥah* can be defined as being an "attribute of the act (*fiʿl*) whereby righteousness and goodness (*ṣalāḥ*) takes place, that is to say utility and benefit (*nafʿ*), always or mostly for the public or individuals." By "always" I refer to the *maṣlaḥah* that is absolute and regular, while by "mostly" I mean the *maṣlaḥah* that is predominant in most of the cases. As for the expression "for the public or individuals," it means *maṣlaḥah* is of two kinds, as will be explained later.

In his commentary on the *Mukhtaṣar* of Ibn al-Ḥājib,[1] ʿAḍud al-Dīn al-Ījī[2] defined *maṣlaḥah* as being "pleasure and its means."[3] Then, he defined it in his book *al-Mawāqif* as being what is agreeable to humankind's nature and purpose (*gharaḍ*).[4] Al-Shāṭibī also defined it in his book *ʿUnwān al-Taʿrīf* as that which produces a benefit for people at the collective or individual level and is acceptable to the human beings because of its importance for their lives.[5] This definition is inaccurate, though it is the closest to ours.[6] As for *mafsadah*, it is the opposite of *maṣlaḥah*,[7] meaning that it is an attribute of the act whereby corruption or harm happens always or mostly to the public or to individuals.

From the previous definition, it appears that *maṣlaḥah* is of two kinds: public and private. Public interest (*maṣlaḥah ʿāmmah*) consists of what is beneficial and useful for the whole or most of the community, and does not concern individuals only in so far as they are members of the whole. An instance of such *maṣlahah* is the safeguarding of everything of economic value (*mutamawwilāt*) from destruction by flood or fire, etc. This kind of security procedure attracts the interest of anyone desiring to make use of it so that he or she can obtain it by following the legitimate means specified by the Shariʿah. Corrupting or destroying it will deprive people of their benefit. This category of *maṣlaḥah* constitutes the subject matter of most of the Qur'anic legislation and most of what pertains to collective obligations (*furūḍ al-kifāyah*), such as the pursuit of religious and other kinds of knowledge that will strengthen the ummah, and the defence of Muslim lands and people against aggressors.

Private interest (*maṣlaḥah khāṣṣah*) consists of anything that benefits the individuals. It is concerned with the righteousness and goodness of the individuals' acts as a means to the righteousness and well-being of the whole society to which they belong. Thus, the primary concern here is with the interest of the individuals rather than that of the general public, which is regarded only secondarily. Part of the Qur'anic legislation and most of that of the Sunnah are concerned with this category of *maṣlaḥah*. An instance of this is the protection of the private property of mentally incompetent people (*safīh*) from squandering by placing them under interdiction (*ḥajr*) during the period of their incompetence.[8] This measure is taken for the benefit of the proprietors so that they will make use of it when they recover, or that of their inheritors after them. It does not concern the general public. The scholars should therefore think carefully to discover the hidden and subtle aspects of *maṣlaḥah*, for they will undoubtedly realize that most of them consider the general interest and welfare of the Ummah and community or that of the order of the world.

For example, the payment of blood money (*diyyah*) for accidental homicide has been prescribed for one's next of kin and tribe[9] though, apparently, there is no benefit for them.[10] It rather benefits the killer, who will keep his wealth. However, if the matter were confined to the private interest of the killer, it would instead look more reasonable that the killer's interest should be relinquished to relieve his next of kin from the harm of burdening them with the payment of the blood money.

Yet, careful consideration shows that this prescription aims to achieve a more general and important objective consisting of consolation (*muwāsāt*) in times of hardship so that it becomes a norm in society, whereby people shoulder one another's burdens in great calamities. It thus constitutes a benefit so that they can face whatever future misfortunes befall them, as God said in the Qur'an, "And do not forget [that you are to act with] grace towards one another" (2:237). This objective, of course, is in addition to the fact that the collective payment of the blood money is meant to bring satisfaction to the relatives of the killed person and to remove from their hearts any resentment and hatred that might push them to harm the killer, for their delight with the large amount of the blood money would compensate their loss. If the killer were to bear the burden of blood money alone, he might not be able to afford it or might be made destitute. Therefore, a threefold purpose is achieved, consisting of security, consolation, and mercy.

To preserve the well-being and order of the world, the Shariʿah has surrounded the vital and invariable interests of human beings with permanent means of protection even in situations where there is apparently no benefit, whichever way one looks at it. An example is the case of an ignorant, poor, and senile person racked with disease, from whom no benefit can be expected. The life of such a person is sanctified and must be protected for the sake of preserving human life. This is because the well-being of society and preservation of the order of the world depend on the sanctity and protection of human souls under all circumstances. At the same time, the Shariʿah teaches patience and forbearance in the face of severe calamities that might befall some people. In this way, it aims at preventing indifference and selfishness from permeating people's minds in dealing with human life and to protect the vulnerable from people's varying and conflicting considerations that might lead to breaching and undermining the order of the world. By insisting on the protection of human life and emphasizing its sanctity, the Shariʿah envisages safeguarding human beings from being subjugated to people's vagaries as well as from their own whims and vain desires. It thus aims at protecting the order of the world from being easily undermined at its human foundations.[11]

Now, to formulate a clear-cut definition by which a characteristic of action would determine whether the action should be considered a *maṣlaḥah* or *mafsadah* is a delicate matter requiring very careful and precise expression. However, establishing their meaning is not difficult and can easily be achieved by careful thought and sound observation. This is because pure benefit and utility (*nafʿ khāliṣ*) and absolute harm (*ḍurr khāliṣ*), though they do exist, are rare in comparison with mixed benefits and harms. For this, ʿIzz al-Dīn ibn ʿAbd al-Salām said in the third chapter of his *Qawāʿid*:

> You should know that pure benefits rarely exist, for it is only by hard work and self-exertion that people's benefits, such as food and shelter, can be attained. When these benefits are achieved, they are mixed with certain harms and evils that contaminate them.[12]

He also said:

> You should know that giving preponderance to the acquisition of what is most beneficial over what is only beneficial and to the removal of what is most harmful over what is simply harmful is deeply rooted in the nature of human beings... Only someone ignorant of the worth of what is most beneficial or a heedless miserable person who is unaware of the variation between the two levels will give preponderance to what is simply beneficial over what is most beneficial.[13]

In the same vein, al-Shāṭibī said in the fifth discourse at the beginning of the 'Book of *Maqāṣid*' [*Kitāb al-Maqāṣid*] in his *Muwāfaqāt*:

> The *maṣāliḥ* and *mafāsid* pertaining to worldly life should rather be understood in accordance with what is predominant (*mā ghalab*). If the

prevalent aspect is that of *maṣlaḥah*, then this constitutes what is conventionally known as *maṣlaḥah*; and if the opposite prevails, then this is what is conventionally understood as *mafsadah*. Accordingly, actions including both aspects of *maṣlaḥah* and *mafsadah* are usually judged according to the predominant aspect. When the first aspect prevails in the action, the latter is desired and is therefore considered a *maṣlaḥah*. If, on the contrary, it is the second aspect that prevails, the action is avoided and is therefore considered a *mafsadah* in accordance with the accepted norm in its similarities.[14]

However, their statements must not make you believe that pure utility and absolute harm do not exist. Cooperation between two persons, for example, is beneficial to both of them and does not entail any harm, while setting ablaze someone's property is absolutely harmful. However, we are not bound to consider the two aspects solely intra-individual dealings between two or more persons, for if we examine the matter at the personal level of the individual's actions we can multiply its instances. Yet, even at the first level, some measure of harm might be tolerated by the person affected by it and is thus negligible and reduced to nil. This can be illustrated by the harm that might affect a person from handing over something from the ground to a mounted person. Though this action is undoubtedly a pure benefit to the mounted person, it does not however cause any harm to the other. It seems that ʿIzz al-Dīn ibn ʿAbd al-Salām believed this type of *maṣlaḥah* to be very scarce, because he regarded it in terms of the dealings between just two persons. Both he and al-Shāṭibī were on the margin of identifying the criteria according to which an action can be considered a *maṣlaḥah* or *mafsadah*, but they failed to pinpoint them. Therefore, I would say that those criteria should consist of the following five things:

1. The benefit or harm must be definite and regular. Enjoying the breathing of fresh air, or exposing oneself to sunlight or swimming in cold sea or river water on an extremely hot day are examples of definite benefit entailing no harm for others. Similarly, setting fire to certain agricultural crops simply to destroy them,

without knowing their owner and not for revenge, as was the case with Nero,[15] who burnt the city of Rome in 64 AC, is definitely an absolute harm.

2. The harm or benefit must be so prevalent and evident that rational and wise people would readily acknowledge it, so that they are not challenged by its opposite when subjected to careful consideration. This constitutes most of the varieties of *maṣlaḥah* and *mafsadah* as envisaged by the Islamic legislation and is what ʿIzz al-Dīn and al-Shāṭibī had in mind. An example of this is the rescuing of a drowning person. This is a *maṣlahah*, despite the harm that might consequently afflict to the rescuer by suffering from exhaustion, hypothermia or even illness. However, this harm is negligible in comparison with the benefit of the action of rescuing a drowned person. Instances of this type of *maṣlahah* and *mafsadah* are indeed innumerable.

3. The characteristics of the action must be of a type that cannot be replaced with something else, either in creating a benefit or incurring harm. For instance, the consumption of intoxicants creates obvious harm, including the corruption of minds, disputes, and waste of property. It also produces evident benefits, such as loss of fear, causing a distress to be forgotten. However, we find that the harm resulting from this action is irremediable, whereas its benefits can be obtained by other means, such as inspiring people to perform good deeds by goodly exhortation and enjoyable poetry. It should be mentioned that the purpose of this third type is to indicate a degree of utility (*nafʿ*) or harm (*ḍurr*) that is lower than the second type and higher than the fourth one.[16]

4. One of the two aspects of benefit and harm, though equivalent to its opposite, must be corroborated by something of its genus that makes it outweigh the other aspect. For example, fining a vandal the value of the property that he has intentionally destroyed produces both benefit for the owner of that property and harm for the vandal, and thus there is equivalence between them. However,

the aspect of benefit is further supported by the notion of justice and equity, whose priority is acknowledged by every person of wisdom and sound reason.

5. One of the two aspects of benefit and harm must be definite and certain, whereas the other is indefinite and uncertain. An example is the harm resulting from asking for the hand of a woman in marriage when someone else has done so, or bidding against another person at a sale. Both of these actions are reported to have been forbidden by the Prophet as narrated in *Muwaṭṭa'* on the authority of Abū Hurayrah.[17] The harm is indefinite and uncertain and not everyone may be aware of it if it is considered simply a marriage proposal or a bid without the inclination and mutual satisfaction of the parties concerned. Therefore, if we apply the apparent meaning of the Tradition, this would mean that it is forbidden to propose to a woman when another man has already asked her for marriage but no agreement between them has been reached. It would also mean that it is forbidden to bid for a commodity when someone else has done so but the price offered did not satisfy the owner. No doubt, such understanding will only result in great harm for both the woman and the owner of the commodity as well as for everyone wishing to propose to that woman or buy that commodity. This is why Mālik said, after narrating the Tradition concerning marriage proposals (*khiṭbah*):

> The explanation of the statement of the Messenger of God according to what we think – and God knows best – is that when a man has asked for the hand of a woman in marriage, she is attracted to him, they have agreed on a dowry and are mutually satisfied (with the arrangement), and she has made any conditions for herself, it is forbidden for another man to ask for that woman in marriage. It does not mean that when a man has asked for a woman in marriage and his suit is not acceptable to her and she is not attracted to him, no one else can ask her for marriage. That is a door to misery for people.[18]

After mentioning, in a chapter on 'What is Forbidden in Haggling and Similar Transactions', the Tradition in which the Prophet is reported to have said, "Do not let one of you bid against the other," Mālik also said:

The explanation of the words of God's Messenger, may God bless him and grant him peace, according to what we think – and God knows best – is that it is forbidden for a man to offer a price higher than that offered by his fellow muslim brother when the seller has inclined to the bargainer, has made conditions about the weight of the gold, and has declared himself not liable for faults and such things by which it is recognized that the seller wants to make a transaction with the bargainer. This is what he forbade, and God knows best... If people were to abandon haggling when the first person starts to haggle, an unreal price might be accepted and the disapproved would enter into the sale of goods.[19]

In this connection, ᶜIzz al-Dīn ibn ᶜAbd al-Salām said under the subtitle 'A Rule for knowing what is good (*ṣāliḥ*) and what is evil (*fāsid*)':

The goods (*maṣāliḥ*) and evils (*mafāsid*) of this world and their means are known by necessity, experience, custom, and careful conjecture. If any of that is ambiguous, its meaning should be sought from its proper proofs. Anyone seeking to know how to distinguish between the *maṣāliḥ* and the *mafāsid* and which outweighs the other, must submit it to the test of reason on the assumption that the Shariᶜah has not mentioned it. Let him then build the *aḥkām* on it; he will discover that almost none of them violates the rules of the Shariᶜah except the prescriptions and proscriptions that God imposed on His servants as merely devotional matters without revealing to them the relevant aspects of *maṣlaḥah* or *mafsadah*.[20]

He also said in the third chapter of his *Qawāᶜid*:

Acquiring pure benefit for oneself and for others and warding off absolute harm from oneself and from others are both praiseworthy and good, and so too is preferring to acquire outweighing benefit over avoiding outweighed harm. Similarly, preferring to avoid outweighing harm over the acquisition of outweighed benefit is both praiseworthy and good. There is usually unanimous agreement on this by people of wisdom and sound reason. When disagreement sometimes arises in this respect, it often stems from the difference over the equivalence or preponderance of the aspects of benefit or harm.[21]

In conjunction with the twenty-first example of the 'exchanges (*muʿāwaḍāt*) deviating from the rules of analogy (*qiyās*)', he also said the following:

Anyone examining carefully the objectives of the Shariʿah concerning the acquisition of *maṣāliḥ* and prevention of *mafāsid* will certainly realize the following. From the totality of those objectives a strong belief and firm knowledge (*ʿirfān*) can be attained with regard to the necessity of realizing this particular benefit or avoiding that particular harm, even if no relevant specific text, consensus, or analogy is found. This is what the proper understanding of the spirit of the *Sharʿ* rather necessitates. This knowledge can be likened to the case of someone who is so familiar with a person that he knows very well what that person likes and dislikes in every respect. When faced with a particular case of benefit or harm on which he does not know his companion's exact opinion, this person will be able to decide that the former would prefer that particular benefit and prevent that particular harm, based on his familiarity with his general ways and habits... This is obvious with regard to pure good and absolute evil. However, the problem arises when one does not know which of two types of benefit or harm outweighs the other, or whether a benefit outweighs a harm, or a harm outweighs a benefit, or does not altogether know what constitutes a benefit or harm. There are varieties of *maṣlaḥah* that are perceived only by people of sound understanding and upright nature, those capable of distinguishing between subtle differences in benefit and harm and differentiating their outweighing aspects from those which are outweighed. People vary in this respect inasmuch as they differ on those different aspects; thus it might happen that the most learned and skilled scholar omits what the less learned and skilled would discover, though this happens only rarely.[22]

To clarify this further, ʿIzz al-Dīn mentioned, in a chapter on 'The Simultaneous Occurrence (*ijtimāʿ*) of *Maṣāliḥ* and *Mafāsid*,' many instances of which only the following are most appropriate and productive. Preventing an [excessively] sick person from making a bequest of more that one third of his property is bad and harmful for him, but it is beneficial and good for his heirs and, therefore, priority has been given to the right of his heirs in the two thirds of his property. Laying hands on someone's property is harmful to the owner and, therefore, liability for damage has been prescribed. Yet, this has not been considered with respect to judges in case they give wrong verdicts and consequently no fine (*ghurm*) is imposed on them thus priority being given to the *maṣlaḥah* of encouraging judges to carry out their task over the *mafsadah* affecting the wrongly sentenced person.[23]

Ṣalāḥ might also be called good (*khayr*) and *mafsadah* evil (*sharr*), as in the tradition of Ḥudhayfah ibn al-Yamān: "People used to ask the Messenger of God (may peace be upon him) about the good things (*khayr*), but I used to ask him about bad things (*sharr*), fearing lest they overwhelm me;"[24] and as in the statement of Abū Bakr to ʿUmar concerning the collection of the Qur'an: "By God, that is something good,"[25] meaning collecting it in a *muṣḥaf* [book form].

It follows from this discussion that the legislation covering the perception of *maṣāliḥ* does not incur any *mafsadah*, and the legislation concerning the prevention of *mafāsid* does not result in the omission of any *maṣlaḥah*. Rather, all Islamic legislation aims at the awareness of *maṣlaḥah*. It can be seen from this that *maṣlaḥah* does not simply consist of what is certainly acceptable, nor does *mafsadah* consist of what is absolutely unacceptable. This is because the insignificant aspect of *mafsadah* does not in any way affect the order of the world in the presence of overwhelming *maṣlaḥah*. This is equally true of the insignificant aspect of *maṣlaḥah* in relation to overwhelming *mafsadah*. Likewise, when the effect of a certain cause has been neutralized by another, counteracting cause, then the neutralized cause becomes insignificant.

Accordingly, there is between the meaning of *maṣlaḥah* and *mafsadah* and what has been mentioned a relationship of generality in one respect and specificity in another (*ʿumūm wa khuṣūṣ wajhī*). This is why the Qur'an has affirmed that consuming wine and gambling can produce some benefit when it says: "In both there is great evil as well as some benefit for man" (2:219). This benefit is not, however, a real *maṣlaḥah*, for if it were so, the consumption of wine and gambling should have been made permissible or obligatory. We have already stated concerning the question of *fiṭrah* what should be remembered here, so one needs to consult it!

It must be realized that absolute and preponderant *mafsadah* outweighing *maṣlaḥah* varies clearly regarding its genus. This variation can be seen in the impact of actions producing *mafāsid* in undermining the Shariʿah objectives concerning the universal fundamentals (*kulliyyāt daruriyyah*), or the general needs (*kulliyyāt ḥājiyyah*), or some aspects of the complementary matters that are close to the general needs. It can also be seen in the degrees of the harmful and inimical effect of those types of *mafsadah* on the general condition of the community. This depends on their level of occurrence, their management, or their duration, according to the varying ages and circumstances.

All prohibitions concern *mafāsid*. Though the Shariʿah stated these *mafāsid* in synoptic categories, jurists subsequently explained them in detail. Thus, mention has been made in the Shariʿah of shameful deeds (*fawāḥish*) and grave sins (*kabā'ir*): "Those who avoid the [truly] grave sins and shameful deeds" (53:32), and of sinning (*ithm*) and transgression (*baghy*): "Say: 'Verily, my Sustainer has forbidden only shameful deeds, be they open or secret, and [every kind of] sinning, and unjustified envy...'" (7:33). Prohibitions have also been described as consisting of some that are greater than others:

> They will ask thee about fighting in the sacred month. Say: "Fighting in it is an awesome thing; but turning men away from the path of God and

denying Him, and [turning them away from] the Inviolable House of Worship and expelling its people therefrom – [all this] is yet more awesome in the sight of God, since oppression is more awesome than killing." (2:217)

A number of authentic traditions have stated, in a hierarchical order, the gravest of sins or answers to questions about what constitutes the gravest sins.[26]

Moreover, on certain occasions the Qur'an has mentioned corruption unqualified and on others qualified as being a grave sin: "He [Pharaoh] was one of those who spread corruption [on earth]" (28:4); "Oh, verily, it is they, they who are spreading corruption" (2:12); "and [they] brought about great corruption therein" (89:12).

It was thus in accordance with the consideration of the relevant degrees of evil (*mafāsid*) that the Companions made the punishment of same-sex fornication equivalent to that of adultery. This is because they found the evil of the former greater and the excuse of its perpetrators weaker.[27] In the same vein, ʿAlī ibn Abī Ṭālib considered the punishment for the consumption of wine the same as the *ḥadd* punishment for slander, because he saw that drunkenness most likely results in slander. Moreover we find this consideration clearly manifested in the juristic dispositions and opinions of the Companions and subsequent generations of scholars in matters related to the different types of punishment and pardon. Thus, the punishment for armed robbery and brigandage (*ḥirābah*)[28] has been made far more severe than that for assassination (*ghīlah*) to set an example without hope of a pardon, "Save for such [of them] as repent ere you [O believers] become more powerful than they…" (5:34). Likewise, the Shariʿah accepts no pardon by the parents or associates (*awliyā'*) of the killed person in the case of assassination. In the same way, punishment for theft has been made less severe than that for assassination, and that for embezzlement less severe than that of theft, and so too is the case with usurpation. In this connection, some jurists coined certain terms for some categories of *mafāsid* that are neither numerous nor regular and constant. Likewise, the Shāfiʿīs came up with the categories of prohibited, reprehended (*makrūh*) and 'deviation from the more appropriate' (*khilāf al-awlā*), while the *ḥanafīs* came up with the categories of prohibition (*taḥrīm*), prohibitive reprehension (*karāhat al-taḥrīm*), and exonerative apprehension (*karāhat al-tanzīh*).[29]

14

The Pursuit of *Maṣāliḥ* in the Shariᶜah

With all its variants, *maṣlaḥah* is of two main kinds. One kind consists of obvious benefits (*ḥaẓẓ ẓāhir*) for human beings. These benefits are so ingrained in people's innate disposition (*jibillah*) that they are inherently driven to pursue and acquire them because they are acceptable to them. The other kind consists of benefits that are less obvious. I have defined one kind as obvious to contrast it with the other kind that contains in its variants many benefits that people do not readily perceive.

Instances of obvious benefits include the consumption of food to survive, wearing clothes, and associating with the opposite sex. Less obvious benefits are, for example, the paving and widening of roads and the provision of night security guards. These and similar activities do not produce immediate obvious benefits for a particular person. Generally speaking, people do not appreciate the benefits provided for them by public services while the latter are available. However, when these services are not available, people realize their benefits. Indeed, some individuals might live for a long time without making use of certain public services, such as a chronically ill person in relation to the paving and widening of roads.

Both kinds of *maṣlaḥah* have certain characteristics for which the Lawgiver has taken them into account. Thus, it is not the concern of the Lawgiver to order people to pursue the *maṣlaḥah* of obvious benefits for the Shariᶜah has been satisfied with humankind's natural impulses so that it is unnecessary to lay down specific rules for its achievement. The Shariʿah is more concerned to remove the obstacles to achieving the obvious benefits, such as preventing aggression against people to steal their food and clothes, or regulate marriage to remove obstacles to procreation such as preventing women from marrying. We find that contracts of sale and marriage are included in the category of the permissible (*ibāḥah*), although they constitute two important aspects of *maṣlaḥah* requiring them to be given the value of what is obligatory (*wujūb*).

In contrast, the *maṣlaḥah* of the less obvious benefits has been handled positively by Islamic legislation, which has prescribed it and enacted specific penalties for abandoning and violating it. Part of it has been prescribed for individuals and part for the community as a whole, depending on the respective aspects of *maṣlaḥah*. Thus, activities whose benefits can be achieved only when carried out by everyone, such as the protection of life (*ḥifẓ al-nafs*), have been made the personal obligation of every individual.

On the other hand, actions whose benefits can be achieved when carried out by an individual or a group of individuals, such as rescuing a drowning person or extinguishing a fire that is destroying homes, have been considered a matter of collective obligation (*kifāyah*). Instances of this also include maintaining wives and children, helping the needy, hosting strangers, and, appointing officers to take care of the public affairs of the community.

Some variants of the obvious benefits may be subsumed under the less obvious owing to certain corrupting influences that might affect people's innate disposition as a result of depraved habits and teaching. These influences might distort their innate disposition, such as the whims and illusions affecting some individuals and making them abstain from food. It is thus reported that during the pre-Islamic era of pagan ignorance (*Jāhiliyyah*) a man sat to eat his lunch near a pond. While swallowing the food he saw his reflection in the water, and was so disgusted by it that he vowed not to eat any more food until he died of hunger. This certainly indicates a psychological disorder. It also occurred to some Arab tribes to bury their newborn girls alive for fear of poverty or their bringing dishonor on the tribe if they were taken hostage when grown up. Similarly, the poet, al-Maʿarrī,[1] abstained from marriage to avoid having a descendant whose ultimate end would be death! If what is attributed to him is true, he would have made his will to have the following verse written on his grave:

This is what my father inflicted upon me
And I myself have not harmed any body.[2]

Similar abnormalities are found in certain people who abandon working to earn their living out of laziness, or to some ascetics who devote themselves totally to living as hermits, thus neglecting other aspects of *maṣlaḥah*.

Therefore, those upholding the Shariʿah and those in a position to explain its legislative rules ought to take a firm stand to prevent these deviations and discrepancies by teaching and guidance that will eradicate them and expose superficial ideas and corruption. This is in accordance with what God has said in the Qur'an: "Say: 'Who is there to forbid the beauty which God has brought forth for His creatures, and the good things from among the means of sustenance?'" (7:32); "Hence, do not kill your children for fear of poverty: it is We who shall provide sustenance for them as well as for you. Verily, killing them is a great sin" (17:31). It is also reported in a Tradition that the Prophet said to ʿAbd Allāh ibn ʿAmr ibn al-ʿĀṣ: "I have been informed that you pray all night and fast during the day!" ʿAbd Allāh said, "I answered: '(Yes) I do.'" The Prophet then said: "If you do so, your eyesight will become weak and you will become weak. There is no doubt that your body has a right over you, and your family has a right over you. So fast (for some days) and do not fast (for some days), and pray for some time and then sleep."[3]

When abnormalities are confined to the person committing them, moral exhortation and proper education are the means to dealing with them. If, on the contrary, they infringe upon others and cause harm to them either by word or action, such as calling people to follow these fancies, punishment is the remedy. Accordingly, it is the duty of the ruler (*walī al-amr*) to compel those abandoning work to work in order to provide for their families and to deport those inviting others to their innovations and fancies, as ʿUmar did when he deported Ṣubaygh from Basra.[4] ʿUmar also compelled traders hoarding food to sell what people needed of the various provisions, as narrated in the *Muwaṭṭa'*,[5] although selling and buying is in principle permissible, since its permissibility is rooted in people's natural impulse for acquisition and the pursuit of profit. Thus, it is the difference of purpose that is taken into consideration in the course of action.

That is how the Shariʿah operates its strategy for protecting the different kinds of *maṣāliḥ* by using both tolerance and restraint, depending on its evaluation of people's behavior with respect to the two categories of *maṣlaḥah* discussed above. Accordingly, every person is free to exert his/her personal rights on others. People can forgo them if they wish, because the fact that they are entitled to them and others are required to fulfill them makes it most likely that they would persist in pursuing them. Thus, the Shariʿah leaves people to their natural impulses, namely, those of self-love and competition for acquisition, for which reason forgoing one's rights can only be for a good purpose. However, if this behavior exceeds all reasonable measures owing to some deficiency in a person's natural impulses, then it is a case of legal incompetence and the person will be put under guardianship.

However, forsaking personal rights that are not related to others is valid in an absolute sense. Accordingly, donations and grants have been legalized and so too has the Shariʿah validated a pardon for crimes that are not capital offenses and the cancellation of debts if it is done for a good purpose. None the less, if, owing to a deficiency in one's natural impulses, one forgoes one's rights in a way that would result in *mafsadah*, then it is a case of legal incompetence, and preferring *mafsadah* is a clear sign of that deficiency in a person's natural impulses. Is it not apparent that a person can allow a surgeon to remove one of his organs if the surgeon deems it the only way to treat an illness, although the benefit from this treatment might be merely conjectural (*ẓannī*)? One can also sacrifice one's life for the sake of defending one's nation and country provided the conditions and requirements for it are properly observed. Nevertheless, one cannot permit the removal of one's organ for no reason. This is what concerns the type of *maṣlaḥah* consisting of obvious benefits. As far as the type consisting of less obvious benefits is concerned, no one is permitted to forgo one's right because that right is associated with that of others.

To sum up, it can be said that the Shariʿah always protects the underrated *maṣlaḥah*, whether public or private, as a means to safeguarding both public and private rights that are affected either by the whims of others or by the whims of the person himself. When conflict arises between two different aspects of *maṣlaḥah*, preference is given to the greater and more important of them. Likewise, just retribution has outweighed the immunity of the killer against whom the retribution is implemented. This is because the benefit of just retribution is far greater. It helps to realize a threefold objective: to console and satisfy the relatives of the victim, thus preventing revenge and counter-revenge, to deter would-be murderers from committing homicide, and to purge society of an evil person. If the relatives and those taking care of the interests of the victim (*awliyā'*) forgo the right to just retribution, the greatest benefit will thus have been relinquished while two benefits will still be preserved. One can be realized by the impossibilities of total pardon and the other by the rehabilitation of the criminal by prison and other kinds of punishment. Just retribution can be waived by a pardon except in the cases of assassination and armed robbery, because the gravity of these crimes outweighs greatly the benefit of safeguarding the life of a person whose evil is so manifest that he/she is considered beyond redemption.

For the same reason, sacrificing one's life for the sake of defending one's nation and country has been considered a lawful purpose. Thus, the Prophet commanded Ṭalḥah ibn ʿUbayd Allāh[6] when he stood defending the Prophet with sword and arrows during the Battle of Uḥud until his hand was injured, for the survival of the Prophet was then indispensable for the survival of the whole Muslim community. This was clearly expressed by Abū Ṭalḥah himself, who said to the Prophet: "Do not expose yourself to the enemy lest an arrow reach you, my neck is before your neck."[7]

From the above discussion, it becomes clear how we should deal with the various aspects of *maṣāliḥ* when we are unable to realize them all at the same time and how we should deal with the various aspects of *mafāsid* when it is impossible to prevent them all. In this connection, al-ʿIzz ibn ʿAbd al-Salām has shown in his book *al-Qawāʿid* that preferring the outweighing over the outweighed *maṣlaḥah* is the norm of the Shariʿah, whereas priority must be given to removing the outweighing over the outweighed *mafsadah*. When there is equivalence in all respects, the rule then is to leave the matter to choice.[8]

I should add here that an example illustrating the question of choice has been mentioned in books of *uṣūl al-fiqh*, which consists of the case of a person falling onto a crowd of injured people. If he hits any of them he will kill him, and if he falls he will also kill anyone on whom he might step. Jurists upheld two different views. Some said that this person must remain on the injured person on whom he has first fallen, while others said that it was his decision.[9] The question of choice is clearer regarding the dispositions of rulers in the case of conflicting *maṣāliḥ*, such as widening a road between two mountains leading to a specific place by narrowing another road leading to a different place.

It is worth mentioning that one should resort to choice only when every possible effort has been made to search for any evidence for preferring (*tarjīḥ*) one *maṣlaḥah* over another and none has been found. Needless to say, scholars may differ over the methods used in the search, which implies that the jurist ought to be careful and accurate in dealing with these matters. Preference can be decided in various ways. One can compare the impact of one *maṣlaḥah* with another, such as giving priority to salvaging faith and belief over deeds, or the preservation of life over the protection of property, or what the Lawgiver has made obligatory over what He has simply advised, or the principal rule (*aṣl*) over its ramifications (*farʿ*).

Moreover, one of the subtle ways of preference that is difficult to realize, though its effects are apparent in people's dealings, that is (*muʿāmalāt*), is to give priority to one *maṣlaḥah* over its equivalent by considering the principal rule. This can be demonstrated by the following example. In many areas of commerce, it so happens that when someone follows a particular trade, it will affect someone else in the same line of business. In this situation, the interest of the second person lies in the pursuit of that business, while the interest of the first lies in having it abandoned by his/her counterpart. Their interests are thus equivalent and, hence, cannot be reconciled. Here, the Shariᶜah has resorted to preference based on the rule that people are in principle free to choose and pursue what they like and, therefore, it is the person's decision to continue or relinquish the pursuit of such business. Accordingly, the Shariᶜah has permitted anyone to trade in any kind of commodity, even though someone else might be doing the same business prior to, or contemporaneously with, him. Consequently, if one intends by such an act to harm others, one's intention will, of course, be sinful, although it will not be legally forbidden.[10]

In conclusion, the Shariᶜah seeks to realize its objectives in respect of the whole community without causing difficulty and hardship, by reconciling as much as possible the different aspects of the purposes intended by its prescriptions and laws. It thus ascends by the community from the lower to the higher levels of those objectives inasmuch as the circumstances can allow. Otherwise, it will descend from the most difficult to what follows it in such wise that it might suspend some of the most important goals. What has already been mentioned in our discussion of *fiṭrah* can provide us with the basis for linking the Shariᶜah rules (*aḥkām*) concerning the conflict of *maṣāliḥ* and *mafāsid* to the question of the preservation or undermining of human nature. One should not fail to realize this in cases of such conflict, so one should give it one's attention.

15

Categories of *Maṣlaḥah* Intended by Islamic Legislation

We have shown in the last two chapters that the all-purpose principle (*al-maqṣad al-ʿāmm*) of the Shariʿah aims at preserving the order of the world and regulating the conduct of human beings in it by preventing them from inflicting corruption and destruction upon one another. This objective can be achieved only by acquiring what is good and beneficial (*maṣāliḥ*) and warding off what is evil and harmful (*mafāsid*) as far as the meaning of *maṣlaḥah* and *mafsadah* can be understood. I must now provide examples and analogies (*naẓā'ir*) for the kinds of *maṣāliḥ* that the Shariʿah considers and the *mafāsid* that it avoids, so that students of the study of *maqāṣid* can learn how to discover the intent of the Lawgiver and, then, follow His way in dealing with the different kinds of *maṣāliḥ* and *mafāsid* in both acquisition and rejection depending on the circumstances of the community.

It is important to acquire this skill because *maṣāliḥ* are so numerous and vary so much in their impact on the righteousness and well-being of the whole community. They also vary in their contingencies, which might consist of factors that either totally or partly corroborate or nullify their effects. Since *maṣāliḥ* are so numerous and diffuse, only those which we know for certain were included by the Shariʿah are taken into consideration. Likewise, it has been part of the objectives of the Shariʿah to abolish many things that people of sound reason have at certain times considered good and beneficial (*maṣāliḥ*), and to establish instead other *maṣāliḥ* outweighing them.

Undoubtedly, the purpose of the Lawgiver can consist only of *maṣlaḥah*, although this does not in any way mean all kinds of *maṣlaḥah*.

Therefore, students of Islamic legislation must know well the varieties and manifestations of *maṣāliḥ* in themselves and in relation to the contingencies and circumstances, affecting them. They must also probe the terms and underlying reasons considered by the Shariʿah in their parallels and analogies, whether by recognition and sanctioning or rejection and invalidation. This exercise will serve as a guide and a model to be followed. The reason for insisting on this is as follows. When faced with pressing new issues and unprecedented problems, scholars should not aspire to find in the textually enacted rules of the Shariʿah (*aḥkām manṣūṣah*) some precedents as a basis for reasoning by analogy, let alone specific texts in which they can seek refuge. Likewise, when the community is faced with new demands and issues and people rush to the scholars, seeking their definitive opinion on what they should do, they would rather find brilliant minds capable of incisive thought, not dim-witted and sluggish individuals.

CRITERIA OF THE CLASSIFICATION OF *MAṢLAḤAH*

Maṣāliḥ can be classified according to three different criteria. Firstly, they can be divided into three kinds, according to their impact on and necessity for the existence of the community: *ḍarūriyyah*, *ḥājiyyah*, and *taḥsīniyyah*.[1] Secondly, with regard to their relationship with the totality of the community or its groups and individuals, they can be divided into particular (*juz'iyyah*) and universal (*kulliyyah*) *maṣāliḥ*. Thirdly, they can be divided into certain (*qaṭʿiyyah*), probable (*ẓanniyyah*), and illusionary (*wahmiyyah*), according to the evidence supporting their importance for the existence of both the community and individuals.

MAṢLAḤAH ACCORDING TO ITS IMPACT AND NECESSITY

The first classification of *maṣāliḥ* into what is indispensable, needed, and complementary, presents us with three levels. The indispensable *maṣāliḥ* (*ḍarūriyyah*) are things whose realization is essential for the community both collectively and individually. The social order of the community will not function properly if there is any defect in these *maṣāliḥ*. Indeed, any defect and loss in them will result in the corruption and disintegration of the whole community. I do not mean by this its total destruction and extinction, for that is a fate that even the most idolatrous and barbaric peoples are spared. Rather, I mean that the community will degenerate into bestiality, thus failing to live up to what the Lawgiver wanted it to be. Yet, some forms of degeneration might lead to the long-term disappearance of the community either because of mutual destruction among its members or by falling under the domination of enemies if it is the target of hostile nations. That was the situation of the Arabs during the era of pagan ignorance (*Jāhiliyyah*)[2], as pointed out in the Qur'an: "and [remember how, when] you were on the brink of a fiery abyss, He saved you from it" (3:103).

Al-Ghazālī in his book *al-Mustaṣfā*, Ibn al-Ḥājib, al-Qarāfī, and al-Shāṭibī described the *ḍarūrī* category as consisting of the preservation and safeguarding (*ḥifẓ*) of religion (*dīn*), life (*nufūs*), intellect (*ʿuqūl*), property (*amwāl*), and lineage (*ansāb*).[3] Qarāfī mentioned that some jurists added the preservation of honor (*ʿirḍ*), and this has been attributed in some Shāfiʿite sources to Najm al-Dīn al-Ṭūfī.[4]

Thus, al-Ghazālī said:

> Preventing the loss of these five fundamentals (*uṣūl*) and protecting them can never be neglected in any religious community (*millah*) or legal system (Shariʿah) that is meant for the good and well-being (*ṣalāḥ*) of human beings... and this would be a consideration of a *maṣlaḥah* that we know by necessity was intended by the Shariʿah, not on the basis of one single proof or one particular rule, but on multiple proofs that are beyond enumeration.[5]

Al-Shāṭibī also said:

> The knowledge of these indispensables (*ḍarūriyyāt*) is definitive, and

> the certainty of this knowledge does not depend on one specific or single proof. The knowledge that these [five universals] are congruent with the purpose of the Shariʿah rather flows from multiple proofs that are not confined to one particular sort (*bāb*) [of the Shariʿah teachings]. Similarly, concerning *tawātur maʿnawī* (thematic recurrent reports), where there is no question of one single report yielding certain knowledge in isolation, here too there is no question of one particular proof constituting the basis of our necessary knowledge of the five universals. This is because all individual proofs are conjectural when considered separately. Thus, for example, when we look at the protection of the human soul (*ḥifẓ al-nafs*), we find that it is forbidden to kill it, that killing has been associated with polytheism in addition to being considered a cause for just retribution (*qiṣāṣ*), that one must allay one's hunger even by eating carrion when facing the danger of death, then we know for sure that killing is categorically prohibited. Once the universal principle is established, it will operate as a general proof under which all the particulars (*juz'iyyāt*) carrying that general meaning (*ʿumūm*) will be subsumed.[6]

Some *uṣūl* scholars have noticed that these fundamental universals have been indicated in the following Qur'anic verse in which God says:

> O Prophet! Whenever believing women come to you to pledge their allegiance to you, [pledging] that [henceforth] they will not ascribe divinity, in any way, to anyone but God, will not steal, will not commit adultery, will not kill their children, and will not indulge in slander, falsely devising it out of nothingness, and would not disobey you in anything [that you declarest to be] right – then accept their pledge of allegiance, and pray to God to forgive them their [past] sins: for behold, God is much-Forgiving, a Dispenser of Grace. (60:12)[7]

The implication of this verse for the present discussion is that there is nothing specific for believing women in what is stated in the verse. In fact, as reported in *Ṣaḥīḥ al-Bukhārī*, the Prophet used to take pledge from believing men on exactly the same terms as believing women.[8]

According to Shāṭibī, the preservation of these fundamental universals is achieved in two different ways: (1) by establishing and strengthening them; and (2) by averting all harm that might affect them.[9] In my view, the preservation of these fundamental universals means to maintain them in relation to all individuals and *afortiori* in relation to the whole community. Likewise, the preservation of religion means to salvage the faith of every individual Muslim from being affected by anything that might undermine and confuse his or her beliefs and distort his or her behavior based on them. As for the community as a whole, the maintaining of religion means to prevent anything that might violate and destroy its fundamentals, which includes defending Muslim land and sovereignty and preserving the means of Islamic learning and education among the present and future generations of the Muslim community.

The preservation of human souls (*hifẓ al-nufūs*) means to protect human lives from being ruined either individually or collectively. This is because that society or the human world (*ʿālam*)[10] comprises the individuals of the human species and every single soul has its specific characteristics that are essential for the existence and survival of the human world. I do not mean by this the protection of human life merely by just retribution (*qiṣāṣ*), as has been upheld by the jurists. On the contrary, we find that just retribution is the weakest means for protecting human souls, because it consists of only a partial remedy for the loss. Thus, the most important way to protect human life is to prevent harm and ruin before they happen, such as combating and eradicating epidemics. For this reason, ʿUmar ibn al-Khaṭṭāb did not allow the Muslim army to enter Syria when the plague struck the city of Amuas.[11]

By human souls, we mean all the souls that are respected and immune in the sight of the Shariʿah and that have been defined in Islamic jurisprudence as immune lives (*maʿṣūmat al-dam*). Therefore, we find that the punishment for a married man who has committed adultery is stoning to death, even though the preservation of lineal identity (*ḥifẓ al-nasab*) is less important than the preservation of life. Of similar reckoning is the protection of certain organs in the human body, the injury to which has been equated to killing. Even if the injury is unintentional, the victim is left severely disabled, and therefore the Shariʿah has prescribed full blood money.

The preservation of the intellect means the protection of people's minds from being affected by anything putting them in disorder. This is because any disorder of the intellect leads to serious corruption consisting of improper and perverted human conduct. Thus, any defect affecting the mind of an individual leads to partial corruption and evil, while any defect affecting the minds of large groups or of the entire community results in total and devastating evil. Therefore, it is obligatory to prevent people from consuming alcohol and from becoming drunk and to prevent the spread of this practice throughout the community, as well as the spread of all kinds of intoxicating substances corrupting the minds, such as hashish, opium, morphine, cocaine, heroine and all such drugs, the consumption of which has increased markedly during the fourteenth century AH [nineteenth century AC].

The preservation of property means protecting the wealth of the community from being ruined and from shifting to the hands of others without compensation. It also means protecting the different constituents of that wealth which is valued in the Shariʿah from being destroyed for no return. [For this definition to be correct,] it is not necessary to exclude certain returns from consideration, such as the payment of a return for the postponement of debts known as *ribā al-Jāhiliyyah* (usury of the pre-Islamic period of pagan ignorance), the forsaking of compensation for guarantee, credit-worthiness (*jāh*) or loan. Nor is it necessary to exclude from consideration the protection of property from being transferred from one person to another within the community without the consent of its owner, for all this belongs to the category of *ḥājī* rather than *ḍarūrī*. Furthermore, the preservation of private wealth leads eventually to the preservation of the community's wealth, because the preservation of the whole is achieved by preserving its constituent parts.

The preservation of lineage, which is also called preservation of progeny (*nasl*), is a term that scholars have used without clarifying its meaning. I shall therefore elaborate on it here. If it is interpreted as preventing the breakdown and cessation (*taʿṭīl*) of procreation, then it is evident that it belongs to the *ḍarūrī* category, for it is by procreation that the individuals of the human species are replaced. Thus, if progeny in this sense is stopped, this will lead to the decline and disappearance of the species, as Lot said to his people: "Must you indeed approach men [with lust], and thus go against the way [of nature] (*wa taqṭaʿūna al-sabīl*)? – and must you commit these shameful deeds in your open assemblies?" (29:29), according to one interpretation.[12] In this sense, there should not be any doubt about considering it among the fundamental universals, for it is in fact equivalent to the protection of human souls. Thus, for example, the males of the community must be prevented from emasculation and the females from continuous celibacy, etc. Similarly, females must, normally, be prevented from hysterectomy and tubal ligation[13], which deprive them of the organs necessary for conception and birth, and from abortion, which is becoming widespread.

However, if preservation of lineage is understood to mean the preservation of descent or lineal identity (*nasab*), for which specific rules of marriage have been instituted and adultery prohibited with a categorical punishment (*ḥadd*) set for committing it, it is then unclear how to consider it among the fundamental universals. In fact, there is no imperative reason for the community to know that X is the offspring of Y. Rather, what is necessary is the existence of the individuals of the species and the proper management of their affairs. Nevertheless, this situation produces great evil that can be explained as follows. Uncertainty about the offspring's relationship to their parents (*aṣl*) destroys the latter's natural innate inclination (*mayl jibillī*) to protect their children, look after them and insure their survival and balanced physical and mental growth by upbringing, education, and provision until they reach maturity and self-reliance. Similarly, this uncertainty removes from the offspring the feeling of gratitude and filial devotion towards their parents, that feeling which makes the children take care of them when they reach old age. However, this harm does not reach the level of necessity, for the mothers' care of the children can still satisfy part of what is meant by procreation.

Accordingly, understanding the preservation of lineage in this latter sense by disentangling its various aspects reveals that it belongs to the *ḥājī* category. However, because neglecting these aspects results in the harmful consequences of the undermining of the social order and family breakdown, our scholars included it among the fundamental universals owing to the severe punishment for adultery and the strong abomination of secret marriage and marriage without a guardian (*walīy*) and witnesses. We shall explain this later when we discuss the objectives of the family system, which concerns the protection of children's rights. In contrast, it is not correct to consider the preservation of honor (*ᶜirḍ*) as indispensable. The truth is that it belongs to the *ḥājī* category. What led some scholars, like Tāj al-Dīn al-Subkī in his *Jamᶜ al-Jawāmiᶜ*,[14] to include it in the category of *ḍarūrī* is their consideration of the severity of the *ḥadd* punishment prescribed by the Shariᶜah for slander. We do not, however, see any necessary correlation between what is indispensable and that whose violation incurs the *ḥadd* penalty. This was most likely the reason why al-Ghazālī and Ibn al-Ḥājib did not classify the preservation of honor in the *ḍarūrī* category. This kind of *ḍarūrī* is rarely dealt with in the Shariᶜah because human beings have taken care of it by themselves from time immemorial and it has thus become deeply ingrained in their nature. No civilized human society can be found that does not care about it. Indeed, the only area where legal systems (*sharā'iᶜ*) really excel one another in this regard is the ways and means that they devise for dealing with it.

Let us now move on to the category of *ḥājī*. It consists of what is needed by the community for the achievement of its interests and the proper functioning of its affairs. If it is neglected, the social order will not actually collapse but will not function well. Likewise, it is not on the level of what is indispensable (*ḍarūrī*). According to al-Shāṭibī, it consists of what is needed to attain comfort and alleviate hardship. If it is neglected, human subjects (*mukallafīn*) will suffer distress and hardship. None the less, the harm resulting from neglecting it cannot be equated with that relating to the fundamental universals.[15] As instances of the *ḥājī* category, the *uṣūl* scholars mentioned contracts of sale, leasing, speculative partnership (*qirāḍ*) and sharecropping (*musāqāh*).[16] In fact, most of the the permissible (*mubāḥ*) social transactions (*muʿāmalāt*) appear to belong to this category. Accordingly, it includes legal marriage. In addition, the preservation of lineal identity, that is, the attribution of children to their real parents, is needed for both the children and the parents: for the children to secure the satisfaction of their needs and their proper upbringing, and for the parents to enhance kinship and protect the family.

The protection of honor, which means the protection of people's honor from being offended and tarnished, belongs to the category of *ḥājī*, so that people refrain from offending one another by even the slightest means, such as speech. Parts of the *ḥājī* stand as supplements to the *ḍarūrī*, such as blocking the means to evil practices, and appointing judges and establishing a police force for the enforcement and implementation of the Shariʿah rules. Furthermore, there are certain aspects of the *ḥājī* that may belong to the category of *ḍarūrī*, though they are not on the level of imperative need (*ḍarūrah*), as we have already pointed out in the previous examples. Thus, some of the rules pertaining to marriage are not a matter of *ḍarūrī* but of *ḥājī*, such as the requirement of a guardian (*walīy*) and a public announcement (*shuhrah*). Also, some rules relating to sales do not belong to the *ḥājī*, such as the prohibition of deferred sales (*buyūʿ al-ājāl*) as a blocking of means, the prohibition of usury, or the prohibition of receiving remuneration for providing a guarantee or mediation. Many of those rules actually complement the preservation of property and do not constitute part of its essence.

The importance given by the Shariʿah to the *ḥājī* almost equals its concern about the *ḍarūrī*. That is why it has prescribed some categorical penalties for violating some of its kinds, such as the *ḥadd* punishment for slander.[17] Below that, the matter is open for *mujtahid* scholars to exert their minds, for which reason we find them disagreeing over the punishment for consuming a small quantity of intoxicants and the prohibition of temporary marriage (*nikāḥ al-mutʿah*).[18]

The category of *maṣāliḥ taḥsīniyyah*, (beautifiers, luxuries), in my view, comprises what leads to the perfection of the community's condition and social order so that it leads a peaceful life and acquires the splendour and beauty of human society in the sight of other nations.

In this way, the Muslim community will become an attractive model for others to belong to it or to seek friendship with it. Indeed, good manners and mores play an important role in this regard, whether they are universal, such as covering one's private parts, or specific to certain nations, such as observing the customs of *fiṭrah*[19] and growing a beard. In short, the *maṣāliḥ taḥsīniyyah* are part of restoring to people their fine and lofty sensibilities.

In this respect, al-Ghazālī said:

> They function as embellishing elements facilitating the achievement of virtues and fine ways in manners and dealings...[20]

To the *taḥsīnī* category belongs blocking the means to evil,[21] which is better than waiting to fall in it.

These are the categories of *maṣāliḥ* examined from the standpoint of their impact on the existence and survival of the community. From their examination and analysis of the various dispositions of the Shariʿah in its rules and prescriptions, scholars have found that they all revolve around these three categories. Only rarely would the Shariʿah abandon anything of them so long as it finds the appropriate and possible means to attaining it and it does not conflict with something else overweighing it, whether in realizing a greater benefit or preventing a greater evil.

THE NOTION OF *MAṢLAḤAH MURSALAH*

By elaborating on these categories, our aim is not just to discover that the Shariʿah has observed them in enunciating its rules and commands, which is mere juristic knowledge. That is part of the task of the jurists (*fuqahā'*) and is, therefore, less important in the discipline of the Shariʿah objectives (*ʿilm maqāṣid al-Sharīʿah*). Nor is our aim just to learn how to apply analogy by referring new cases to the established precedents of those *maṣāliḥ*, which is also the purpose of the jurists. Rather, our aim is to familiarize ourselves with as many forms of the varieties of *maṣāliḥ* intended by the Shariʿah as possible, so that we gain a full knowledge of their universal genres (*ṣuwar kulliyyah*). Thus, whenever we are faced with new cases and emergent issues which did not exist during the time of Revelation and which have no equivalent in the precedents whose rules have been established in the Shariʿah sources, we will know how to classify and judge them according to the relevant rules (*aḥkām*). We will then be confident that we have formulated valid Shariʿah judgments.

This constitutes what is known as *maṣāliḥ mursalah*. The reason for this description is that the Shariʿah has left this kind of *maṣāliḥ* textually unqualified. Likewise, there is no specific legislation for it, nor is there a similar precedent on whose rule could be based an analogy. It is thus unrestricted like an untethered horse. However, there should be no hesitation about its soundness as a reference principle for the following reason. We confirm [in the discipline of *uṣūl al-fiqh*] the validity (*ḥujjiyyah*) of analogy that consists of basing a case having no textual rule in the Shariʿah on another case whose rule has been codified according to the common extracted *ratio legis* (*ʿillah mustanbaṭah*). It is valid even though the *ratio legis* relates mostly to a partial and conjectural *maṣlaḥah* owing to the scarcity of cases of textually expressed effective cause (*ʿillah manṣūṣah*). If we do so, then it would be more appropriate and, indeed, more consonant with logical syllogism and juristic argument to accept the authority of reasoning by analogy for the validity of a new universal good (*maṣlaḥah kulliyyah*) for the community. Although the case is not covered by specific legislation, it falls into a universal category whose acceptability by the Shariʿah has been established from a thorough search of its textual proofs that yields certain knowledge or a strong likelihood bordering on certainty.

I am indeed extremely astonished how Imam al-Ḥaramayn al-Juwaynī, with his vast knowledge and perceptive mind, could hesitate on this issue! As for al-Ghazālī, he vacillated, sometimes moving forward to the right position of confirming the validity of the *maṣāliḥ mursalah*, and sometimes taking the position of al-Juwaynī, for he hesitated about the scope of *maṣlaḥah*. Reproducing al-Juwaynī's words in *al-Burhān* and al-Ghazālī's in *al-Mustaṣfā* will only be superfluous.[22]

In contrast to them, I would say the following. Scholars familiar with the Shariʿah dispositions and habit (*taṣārīf*) and indicants must not disagree on one important fact. It is a Shariʿah imperative to seek to achieve what is beneficial (*maṣāliḥ*) and avoid what is harmful (*mafāsid*) for the community under all circumstances, especially when faced with unprecedented problems and pressing adversity. A true scholar must not simply wait to deal with *maṣāliḥ* covered by specific Shariʿah legislation or relevant analogous precedents. Indeed, how could a scholar argue that, before going into details, one must first consider the genus of the new *maṣāliḥ*, because the Lawgiver would certainly have assessed the genera (*ajnās*) of their analogs even though the latter might have been lesser than the former in their ensuing benefit? I cannot imagine that a scholar, having considered the matter carefully, could have any doubt on the following fact. To analyze the genera of new *maṣāliḥ* based on syllogism by relating them to the genera of their counterparts established during the time of Revelation or agreed upon by the early authoritative Islamic scholars, is far more acceptable than just judging their particulars (*juz'iyyāt al-maṣāliḥ*) on partial analogy (*qiyās juz'ī*), be they private or public.

This is because the particulars of *maṣāliḥ* are subject to probability and uncertainty on three accounts: (1) the evidence supporting the different types of appropriate analogy; (2) the identification of the common properties, known as effective causes (*ʿilal*), taken as the basis for analogy with their precedents; and (3) the degree of accuracy of the established similarity between the original and new cases.

In contrast, the evidence for the genera of *maṣāliḥ* is derived from the thematic inductive study of the Shariʿah, which yields certainty or strong likelihood bordering on certainty. Moreover, the attributes of wisdom [that is, *maṣāliḥ*] are self-subsistent predicates that do not require establishing the similarity of a new case (*farʿ*) with an established original case (*aṣl*). Though they vary in their degree of clarity, these attributes are obvious to perceptive minds, and therefore it is unnecessary to resort to inference (*istinbāṭ*) and its means.

Therefore, are not these *maṣāliḥ* worthy of being assessed according to the genera of their equivalents established by inductive thematic inference from the Shariʿah dispositions? If some of these *maṣāliḥ* are so clear that they do not conflict with other *maṣāliḥ* and do not contain any *mafāsid*, learned scholars of the Shariʿah should not hesitate to follow them. If, however, they are contradicted by other *maṣāliḥ* or mixed with some *mafāsid*, they should then be assessed according to the appropriate rules discussed in the previous chapter. In fact, this requires greater independent judgment (ijtihad) that varies according to the importance of both the *maṣāliḥ* that are followed and the *maṣāliḥ* or *mafāsid* conflicting with them as well as the degree of certainty concerning their weight and their strength. Therefore, they will be matched with the genera of their equivalents that are inductively proven to be intended by the Lawgiver, either by preferring outweighing to outweighed *maṣāliḥ* or by considering their public and private character. Anyone objecting seriously to the realization of these *maṣāliḥ* will run the risk of appearing to support the opponents to reasoning by analogy.

Nevertheless, if one considers the circumstances surrounding the realization of *maṣāliḥ* and rejection of *mafāsid*, one will find wide variation. For instance, the circumstances of administering justice regarding people's private and public rights – which is the essence of civilization in peacetime – differ greatly from those of achieving *maṣāliḥ* by implementing specific military strategies and political measures in wartime, and anticipation of confrontation with the enemy. This is because, in wartime, there is no room for profound reflection and relaxed consideration of the instances of particular (*juz'iyyāt*) *maṣāliḥ*. This is a time of distress or recovery from it that requires quick action to attain a benefit or prevent an evil, depending on the circumstances, and regardless of any particular harm that might be tolerated or benefits that might be overlooked. Yet, one will always realize the evident difference between the situation where we are on the defensive against the attacking enemy and where we are on the offensive regarding the time available for deep reflection and weighing of the various *maṣāliḥ*.

The cases of unanimous agreement (ijmaʿ) by the community's Predecessors from the time of the Companions and the Successors were, except for matters of necessary religious knowledge (*maʿlūm mina al-dīn bi al-ḍarūrah*) mostly based on the principle of *maṣlaḥah mursalah*, whether it was universal and certain or simply prevalent. Their agreement was drawn from their ijtihad based on conjectural proofs approximating certainty. It was seldom founded on textual evidence from the Qur'an and the Sunnah. It was for this reason that consensus was considered a third proof source after the Qur'an and the Sunnah, for its textual basis was not exactly determined. Otherwise, if it was based exclusively on the textual indicants of the Qur'an and the Sunnah, it should rather be an extension of them and not a counterpart.

One example of this is the collection of the Qur'an in the *muṣḥaf* decreed by Abū Bakr upon a suggestion by ʿUmar that was approved by the rest of the Companions. Bukhārī reported on the authority of Zayd ibn Thābit,[23] who said:

> Abū Bakr called me on the occasion of the slaughter of the people of Yamāmah[24] and ʿUmar was with him. Abū Bakr said: "ʿUmar came to me and said that the slaughter on the day of Yamāmah claimed the lives of so many of the Qur'an readers and he feared that further deaths elsewhere might cause the loss of many parts of the Qur'an, so he suggested that we compile the Qur'an. I [Abū Bakr] said to ʿUmar: 'How can we do something that the Prophet did not do?' ʿUmar said: 'It is, by God, good.' And he kept arguing with me until God opened my heart to it. You are a young intelligent man; we do not have the slightest suspicion concerning your honesty since you wrote the Revelations at the dictation of the Prophet *(ṢAAS)*. Take it upon yourself, therefore, to compile the Qur'an." I [Zayd] said: "How would you do something not done by God's Messenger?" Abū Bakr replied: "By God, it is good."[25]

From ʿUmar's statement "By God, it is good (*khayr*)" and the opening of Abū Bakr's heart to his suggestion, we know that it pertained to *maṣāliḥ*, because the word *khayr* refers to what is beneficial for the community. The statement of both Abū Bakr and Zayd that it was "something not done by the Prophet *(ṢAAS)*" indicates that it was a *maṣlaḥah mursalah* which was not confirmed by any particular evidence, and yet the Companions agreed unanimously after considering it.

In the same category was their consensus during the time of ʿUmar on the punishment of eighty lashes for consuming intoxicants, which was followed by later caliphs and judges; the introduction of the office (*dīwān*) for the administration of bonuses and pensions;[26] ʿUmar's abstention from dividing the rural areas (*sawād*)[27] of Iraq among the soldiers, thus leaving them as a reserve for facing future misfortunes that might happen to the Muslim community; the recording and collection of the Traditions of God's Messenger during the time of ʿUmar ibn ʿAbd al-ʿAzīz. To these can be added: ʿUmar ibn ʿAbd al-ʿAzīz's statement: "People face court cases inasmuch as they cause corruption,"[28] which many scholars of Islam, such as Mālik ibn Anas, took as a juridical norm. To this category also belongs the introduction by the scholars of Islam of such things as the pleading procedures, fixation of terms, cross-examination of witnesses, imprisonment of persons abstaining to answer court questions, court oath for a person proving by evidence to have some right over a deceased or absent person, etc.

PUBLIC AND PRIVATE *MAṢLAḤAH*

Let us now move on to the second classification of *maṣāliḥ* according to whether they concern the whole community, some of its groups, or only individuals. Based on this criterion, *maṣāliḥ* are classified into universal (*kulliyyah*) and particular (*juz'iyyah*). In juristic terminology, *maṣlaḥah kulliyyah* means that which equally concerns the whole community, very large numbers of its individuals or one whole country. By *maṣlaḥah juz'iyyah* is meant anything other than that.

Instances of universal *maṣlaḥah* pertaining to the whole Muslim community are scarce. They include the protection of Muslim sovereignty and land; the reuniting of the community; ensuring the existence and continuity of the religion of Islam; protecting the two sanctuaries of Makkah and Madinah from falling into the hands of non-Muslims; guarding the Qur'an from disappearance or distortion owing to a reduction in the numbers of its transmitters or the loss of its books (*maṣāḥif*); safeguarding the Sunnah from the addition of forgeries; and anything whose goodness or evil affects the whole community and every one of its members. Some varieties of the *ḍarūrī* and *ḥājī* categories that concern the whole community also belong to the universal *maṣlaḥah*.

The *maṣlaḥah* and *mafsadah* affecting large groups, consist of the *ḍarūriyyāt*, *ḥājiyyāt*, and *taḥsīniyyāt*, relating to regions, tribes, and countries according to their needs. Examples are judicial legislations for settling disputes, treaties concluded by Muslim rulers with the rulers of other nations to guarantee the security of Muslim traders in non-Muslim lands and ensure their safety while sailing through seas controlled by non-Muslims; pacts signed with non-Muslims traders using Muslim sea-ports and trading in Muslim countries to pay a certain percentage of the value of their sales as customs tax. On the other hand, private *maṣlaḥah* concerns the interest of individuals or small number of individuals. It consists of various kinds and degrees and it has been covered by the rules and commands regulating the different types of transactions.

MAṢLAḤAH ACCORDING TO EVIDENCE

Maṣlaḥah based on the verification of the necessary realization of its benefits or the avoidance of its harm is classified into three types: categorical, probable, and illusionary. A categorical *maṣlaḥah* has been established on explicit textual proofs that preclude any interpretation, such as God's saying in the Qur'an: "Hence, pilgrimage to the Temple is a duty owed to God by all who are able to undertake it" (3:97). It also consists of what multiple proofs have concurrently denoted, based on the inductive inference from the Shariʿah sources, such as the fundamental universals mentioned previously. Furthermore, it includes whatever reason has proven the need for realizing or avoiding it owing to its great benefit or great harm for the community, such as fighting those who refused to pay the zakah during Abū Bakr's caliphate.

Conjectural *maṣlaḥah*, on the other hand, consists of what reason has established only as likelihood, such as keeping watchdogs in urban homes in times of fear and insecurity. In the city of Kairouan,

Shaikh Abū Muḥammad ibn Abī Zayd[29] kept a watchdog in his house. When he was told that Mālik ibn Anas disliked the keeping of watchdogs in urban areas,[30] he answered: "Had Mālik lived in an age like ours, he would have put a lion at the gate of his house."[31] It also includes what has been founded on a speculative Shariʿah textual proof, such as the hadith, "A judge must not pass judgment when in a state of anger."[32]

Illusionary *maṣlaḥah*, is what appears to create benefit, but, when subjected to investigation, it is revealed to be harmful. This is due either to the covertness of its evil, such as the consumption of narcotic drugs like opium, hashish, cocaine and heroin – their consumers might find them agreeable, though they gain no real benefit from them, or that its benefit is outweighed by its evil, as God Almighty has indicated in the Qur'an: "They will ask you about intoxicants and gambling. Say: 'In both there is great evil as well as some benefit for man; but the evil that they cause is greater than the benefit that they bring'" (2:219).

This is the quintessence of what can be said about *maṣāliḥ* as considered by the Shariʿah. Our elaboration on this subject is of great importance and interest for the seekers of the knowledge [of *maqāṣid*]. It teaches them that comprehending the idea of *maṣāliḥ* is the clearest and most straightforward way for the jurists in dealing with the affairs of the community and solving its difficulties when there is confusion over which line to follow. It also shows them that if they do not follow this clear path, they might prevent Islam from being a universal and eternal religion, thus "travelling in a most dreadful valley where only God can save him [or them]."[33]

In addition to the above, there is classification of *maṣlaḥah* according to whether it is intended in the act (*qaṣd*) or is merely consequential upon the act (*ma'āl*). This classification requires jurists to be especially adept and skillful. The reason is that the fundamentals of *maṣāliḥ* and *mafāsid* are barely concealed from people of sound reason. The legislative context of the Shariʿah regarding the realization of the one and the avoidance of the other is clear and adherence to it is easy, and so too scholars' agreement on them is not difficult. In contrast, subtle *maṣāliḥ* and *mafāsid* and their effects as well as the means for realizing the former and preventing the latter, are all a cause of much perplexity and confusion. Here, scholars' perception varies in terms of pertinence or inadvertence and acceptance or negligence. It is a realm where tricks (*ḥiyal*) and proper means come into play, and where attention to and neglect of reasons and purposes compete. It is here also that the variation between different legal systems (*sharā'iᶜ*) has manifested itself and it is here that the Islamic Shariᶜah has proven its universal and permanent relevance. This is clarified in chapters 22 and 23 on manipulation and the prohibition of evasive legal means (*sadd al-dharā'iᶜ*).

16

Universality of the Islamic Shariʿah

It is a necessary part of Islamic knowledge that the Shariʿah came as a universal law requiring the adherence of all human beings. Since it is the last revealed law, it is inevitably applicable to the whole of humankind everywhere on earth until the end of the world. The supporting evidence is so abundant in the Qur'an and the Sunnah that it amounts to a thematic recurrence (*tawātur maʿnawī*) yielding certainty. Thus for example, God says, "Now [as for you, O Muhammad,] We have not sent you otherwise than to mankind at large" (34:28), "Say [O Muhammad]: 'O mankind! Verily, I am an Apostle to all of you'" (7:158). In an authentic Tradition, the Prophet is reported to have said: "I have been given five things no one before me was given", and he counted among them: "An apostle used to be sent specifically to his own people, while I have been sent to all of mankind."[1] Accordingly, the universality of the Shariʿah does not need to be elaborated upon here, for our purpose is not to prove it for those who reject it, but to rather deal with what follows from it.

Since God willed by His fathomless wisdom that Islam be the last religion revealed to humankind, it was necessary that it should be grounded in a universal attribute shared by all human beings, which is rooted in their psyche, and with which their sound minds are familiar, namely, the attribute of *fiṭrah*. In this way, the injunctions and rules (*aḥkām*) of the Shariʿah would be accepted happily and eagerly by thinking people who understand their meaning and their purpose and therefore always submit to them without question. In other words, this arrangement allows the more highly educated individuals to extend the established general principles of the Shariʿah and work out its details, while those who are less educated will also accept it willingly and obey its commands.

Since it was not possible that the transmitter of the Shariʿah be a group of apostles from the different races and tribes of humankind – for such plurality would impede good management – God chose to send a Prophet from amongst the Arabs, an individual of the human race itself, as He says in the Qur'an:

> Yet whenever [God's] guidance came to them [through a prophet,] nothing has ever kept people from believing [in him] save their objection: "Would God have sent a [mere] mortal man as His apostle?" Say: "If angels were walking about on earth as their natural abode, We would indeed have sent down to them an angel out of heaven as Our apostle." (17:94–95)

Indeed, there is a fathomless wisdom in God's choice of a man from among the Arabs to convey the message of Islam. It is not our purpose here to explain in detail those aspects which we have been able to discern, and God says in this respect: "[But] God knows best upon whom to bestow His message" (6:124).

Nevertheless, we would like to say the following. Since the Prophet was from the Arabs, it was necessary that he should speak the Arabic tongue. This required that the Arabs be the first ones to receive the Shariʿah from him. Likewise, the Arabs were the transmitters of the Islamic Shariʿah to all those to whom it is addressed, including their own selves. God chose them for this mission because, at the time of the Qur'anic Revelation, they were distinguished by four characteristics that had never in history been combined in a single nation. These characteristics consisted of fine minds, strong memories, simplicity and naturalness of civilization and legislation, and aloofness from association with other nations of the world.

Their fine minds enabled them to understand the message of Islam and grasp its teachings, while their strong memories meant that they were qualified to preserve it and not become confused in transmitting it. The simpleness of Arab society made them open to absorbing its teachings easily, for they were the closest to the original human nature (*fiṭrah*) and were not followers of any well-established religious law which they would firmly uphold.[2] Finally, their isolation meant that the Arabs were prepared to mix and associate openly with other nations with whom they had no hostilities. In contrast to the Persians in relation to the Byzantines and the Copts in relation to the Israelites, their hostilities were only among their tribes. Yet, no importance should be attached to the battles that broke out between Arab tribes and the Persians and Byzantines such as that of Dhī Qār and Ḥalīmah,[3] for they were rare incidents. Moreover, in such incidents, the Arabs were actually fighting on behalf of either the Persians or Byzantines, and thus the hostilities of those for whom they were directly fighting overshadowed their own hostilities with these two nations.

One of the most important aspects of the universality of the Shariʿah is that its rules and commands should apply equally to all human beings as much as possible, because uniformity in this area is crucial for the realization of social unity of the community. Thanks to this wisdom and particularity, God based the Shariʿah on an inner wisdom (*ḥikam*) and underlying causes (*ʿilal*) that can be perceived by the mind and which do not change according to nations and custom. Accordingly, scholars of Islam in every era have agreed, except some whose disagreement is insignificant, that it is the duty of the scholars of the community to consider the purposes of the commands and rules of the Shariʿah and to derive rulings from them. To support their position, they have cited the following two verses: "Remain, then, conscious of God as best as you can" (64:16); "Learn a lesson (*iʿtabirū*), then, O you who are endowed with insight" (59:2). These are, however, mere rhetorical proofs. Therefore, we would rather adhere in this respect to consensus and to the established practice of the Companions and scholars of the community throughout the ages.

This universality of the Shariʿah has been expressed in many verses of the Qur'an, such as "God wills that you shall have ease, and does not will you to suffer hardship" (2:185), "and God does not love corruption" (2:205), "We bestowed Revelation from on high, and [thus gave you] a balance [on which to weigh right and wrong,] so that men might behave with equity" (57:25); "for, in [the law of] just retribution, O you who are endowed with insight, there is life for you, so you might remain conscious of God" (2:179). In the Prophetic Traditions, it has been expressed as general rules such as the Prophet's Sayings: "No doubt! Your blood, your properties, and your honor are inviolable to one another like the sanctity of this day of yours, in this (sacred) town (Makkah) of yours, in this month of yours;"[4] "If a large amount of anything causes intoxication, a small amount of it is prohibited;"[5] and "There is no injury nor return of injury." Similarly, most of the ambiguous (*mujmalāt*) and unrestricted (*muṭlaqāt*) expressions in the Qur'an are intended to convey general and absolute meanings. However, jurists gave themselves unnecessary trouble by seeking to clarify the ambiguous and qualify the unrestricted by interpreting what is unrestricted in one place in terms of what is qualified in another, even though they might not belong to the same category. For this purpose, they developed a number of methods.[6]

This happened even during the time of the Companions. When he was in Kufah, ʿAbd Allāh ibn Masʿūd understood that the Qur'anic statement "and the mothers of your wives" (4:23) meant that contracting a marriage with the mother does not make her daughter forbidden unless the husband has consummated the marriage with the mother. Ibn Masʿūd understood this absolute phrase in this way by referring it to the following qualified expression in the same verse: "and your step-daughters – who are your foster-children – born of your wives with whom you have consummated your marriage; but if you have not consummated your marriage, you will incur no sin [by marrying their daughters]" (4:23). When he returned to Madinah, he was informed that the established tradition was to interpret the phrase "and the mothers of your wives" in its absolute meaning without any restriction or qualification. It is indeed surprising that scholars of *uṣūl al-fiqh* elaborated on interpreting unrestricted statements as qualified ones, even though the rule is that the generalization of a *ḥukm* should be restricted to its genus. The legislative rules (*tashrīʿāt*) covering the particulars, of individual cases are equally open to generalization and particularization. Perhaps it was for this type of rule that the Prophet forbade the people to write down, when he said: "Do not take down anything from me, and anyone who has taken down anything from me, except the Qur'an, should efface it,"[7] lest particular cases be taken as universal rules.

Therefore, the Companions needed special permission from the Prophet when Abū Shāh wanted them to write down for him what the Prophet had said concerning the boundaries of the Makkan sanctuary (*Ḥaram*). Then, he told them: "Write it for Abū Shāh."[8] That is why we find much disagreement amongst the scholars over juristic arguments relying on particular cases and isolated reports when they contradict the general rules, that is, literal universals (*kulliyyāt lafẓiyyah*) and inductive thematic universals (*kulliyyāt maʿnawiyyah*), or with *qiyās*, or with the established practice of the people of Madinah (*ʿamal ahl al-Madinah*), according to well-known doctrines in *uṣūl al-fiqh*.[9]

Accordingly, giving a special consideration to the mores and customs of different peoples refutes claims of a binding and universal legislation. This objective is accommodated in the legislative default of permissibility, on the basis of which each human group can enjoy living according to its customs. Nevertheless, since the basis of permissibility is that what is permissible does not contain an indispensable *maṣlaḥah* or a serious *mafsadah*, then this principle must be applied to mores and customs. If the customs and mores comprise an indispensable or necessary *maṣlaḥah* affecting the whole community or a *mafsadah* that is considerable for its followers, then they must be subsumed under the universal legislative rules of obligation or prohibition.

Therefore, we find that Islamic legislation did not concern itself with determining what kinds of dress, house, or mount people should use. For example, it did not require people to ride camels when travelling, nor did it prevent the people of Egypt and Iraq from riding donkeys, or the people of India and the Turks from using bullocks as means of transportation. This is why Muslims have not needed any evidence allowing them to use wheels, carts, or trains. The same principles apply to the different kinds of food that do not contain anything unlawful, so that only someone who is ignorant of their composition or unaware of the methodology of Islamic legislation will ask about these matters.

Accordingly, we can ascertain that noone has the right to impose the customs and mores of a particular people on them or on other people as 'legislation'. Of course, Islamic legislation takes into account such customs and mores so long as their followers have not altered them. This is because people's adherence to those customs and mores and the latter's continuance as part of their lives endow them with the status of default terms and conditions (*shurūṭ*) between them. Likewise, when, in their transactions, nothing different is stipulated, people are then bound by their customs and mores.

This is what Mālik ibn Anas meant when he maintained that a husband cannot force his wife, who is an [Arabic] woman of high lineage, to breastfeed her child, if this is accepted as an established custom among her people, thus enjoying the status of terms and conditions. He understood God's saying: "And the mothers may nurse their children for two whole years" (2:233) to be applicable to women who do not enjoy this status, or to determine the period of nursing, though not to make nursing itself obligatory.[10]

This method of interpreting customs and mores has removed much confusion and many perplexing difficulties that faced the scholars in understanding the reasons why the Shariᶜah prohibited many practices in which no aspect of *mafsadah* could be perceived. One example of this is the prohibition for women to add hair extensions (*waṣl al-shaᶜr*), to create a gap between the two front teeth, or to tattoo themselves, as mentioned in the Tradition narrated by ᶜAbd Allāh ibn Masᶜūd that the Prophet said: "God has cursed those women who add hair extensions, practice tattooing and those who have themselves tattooed, those who reshape their eyebrows, and those who create a space between their teeth artificially to look beautiful, and hence changing the features created by God."[11] One is at risk of straying in understanding the implication of this Tradition, for the practices mentioned are no different from any other allowed beautifying practices such as make-up and henna; and yet, one is astonished at the strong tone in which the prohibition of those practices has been expressed.

Nevertheless, the correct meaning of this, in my view, and I do not know of anyone who stated this clearly, is that the practices mentioned in the hadith were, according to the Arabic traditions of the time, indications of a woman's lack of chastity. Therefore, the prohibition of these practices was actually aimed at preventing promiscuity or the violation of the woman's honor when people associate her with such traits. Similarly, we read the following verse in the Qur'an: "O Prophet! Tell your wives and your daughters, as well as [other] believing women, that they should draw over themselves some of their outer garments [when in public]: this will be more conducive to their being recognized [as decent women] and not annoyed" (33:59). This is a legislation that took into consideration an Arab tradition, and therefore it does not necessarily apply to people whose women do not wear this style of dress.[12]

Therefore, careful consideration of these matters and a thorough search for the legislative reasons relating to their genera enlighten us on an important issue. It shows us the difference in the Shariʿah particulars (*juz'iyyāt*) between what is and is not appropriate to be taken as a reference rule (*aṣl*) for judging its analogs according to *qiyās*, for matters of Islamic legislation are not based on a single pattern.

It might also be appropriate to count as one aspect of the universality of the Shariʿah the fact that many matters have been delegated to the ijtihad of its scholars. They are matters for which there is no textual evidence specifying the relevant rules or determining the intent of narrators in reporting them. Thus, it is reported that the Prophet said: "God has set up boundaries, so do not transgress them; He kept silent on certain things out of mercy on you rather than forgetfulness, do not ask about them."[13] To this category belongs what we mentioned previously regarding the Prophet's prohibition on the Companions from writing down anything except the Qur'an, so that universal and permanent legislation would not be confused with temporary and particular cases.

The Companions used to emulate the Prophet's deeds and judicial verdicts, though no specific texts were reported that required their continuity. These deeds and verdicts would have enlightened them on many aspects of what was right, because their circumstances were very similar to those prevailing during the Prophet's time. That is why ᶜUmar ibn ᶜAbd al-ᶜAzīz, during his governorship or tenure of the Caliphate, asked Abū Bakr ibn Muḥammad ibn ᶜAmr ibn Ḥazm[14] to write down the transmitted Traditions of the Prophet.[15] I assume that he wanted those Traditions to provide a guiding light for the scholars of the community in understanding the objectives of the Shariᶜah. This is especially true when time is too short to allow a more careful consideration of the fundamental rules and essential proofs of the Shariᶜah to derive new rulings from them, although they would possibly reanimate the provisions of those particular instances in similar circumstances. As ᶜUmar ibn ᶜAbd al-ᶜAzīz said: "People face court cases inasmuch as they cause corruption."

An example of specification and determination is the scholars' preoccupation with gathering and studying the legacy of the rightly guided caliphs (*al-khulafā' al-rāshidūn*) in determining the exact punishments they applied to some crimes, and fixed amounts of poll tax (*jizyah*), land tax (*kharāj*), blood money, and compensation for injuries (*urūsh*). However, some of those amounts were subject to a reduction in both value and circulation, which meant that they became inadequate as an accepted indemnity.

Of the same kind is the Mālikī jurists' fixation of *mawāqīt*[16] of hajj, etc. This also includes what the jurists of the different schools fixed concerning the words and statements of divorce and oaths, though some of these expressions are no longer in use, and even when they are used, they have no clear and definite meaning. These specifications should be seen only as examples for consideration as inspiring models.

In short, the universality of the Shariᶜah and its inclusion of all humankind throughout the ages is a subject of unanimous agreement among Muslim scholars. In addition, they unanimously agreed on its suitability for human beings in all times and places. However, Muslim scholars did not show how that suitability is manifested. In my opinion, the suitability of the Shariʿah for humankind can be said to assume two different modes.

(1) The first mode is that the fundamental rules (*uṣūl*), universal principles (*kulliyyāt*), commands and injunctions (*aḥkām*) of the Shariʿah are applicable to all circumstances without any difficulty or hardship. The evidence is the way in which scholars of the Ummah have interpreted many of the textual proofs of those commands and rules to insure their flexible application. Of course, each Shariʿah scholar participates in the interpretation. When their contributions are combined, we will have an abundant wealth of sound interpretation of the apparent meanings (*ẓawāhir*) of the Shariʿah that makes its commands and rules suitably applicable to human beings under their different conditions.

An example of this is the prohibition of the renting of land. Mālik and most of the jurists interpreted the rule as promoting piety and encouraging Muslims to assist one another without implying categorical proscription of the practice and invalidating contracts concerning it.[17] Another example is the prohibition of gaining a benefit from giving loans to others. Some Ḥanafī jurists took this prohibition to be confined to what is not a matter of need (*ḍarūrah*), for which reason they sanctioned the sale of *wafā'*[18] in the vineyards of Bukhārā.

(2) The second mode consists of the fact that the situations of all peoples and nations throughout the ages have been receptive to the teachings of Islam without any difficulty or hardship. This is evidenced by the transformation that Islam has brought about in the daily lives of the Arabs, the Persians, the Copts of Egypt, the Berbers, the Tartars, the people of India, the Chinese, and the Turks, without these peoples facing any difficulty or hardship in discarding their age-old bad habits or being compelled to forsake their established good customs.

These two modes of the Shariʿah suitability are interconnected and thus complement each other. They have been expressed implicitly in the following Qur'anic verse: "and [God] has laid no hardship on you in [anything that pertains to] religion" (22:78).[19] Accordingly, the suitability of the Shariʿah should in no way be understood to mean that all human beings are required to follow the customs and manners of a particular people or nation, such as the Arabs during the time of Revelation. Nor should it mean that other nations are bound to follow the special rulings and specific cases that conferred certain benefits on those who lived during the time of Revelation, whether or not they could be appropriate. This is to avoid the suitability of the Shariᶜah being blemished by any difficulty or contradicting what is indispensable for human beings. Some might understand the underlying wisdom of the suitability of the Shariᶜah to mean that human beings would live by it and implement its teachings in all ages without running the risk of perdition or distress. However, if this is the meaning of suitability, then it cannot in any way be considered a distinctive characteristic of the Islamic Shariᶜah. This is because we do not find in the laws of humankind any provisions intended to lead human beings into destruction or anarchy when they are forced to abide by them. Otherwise, every nation could claim the characteristic of universality and eternity for its law.

Therefore, it follows from this that the meaning of the suitability of the Islamic Shariᶜah for every time and place must be understood in a different manner as follows. Its commands and injunctions (*aḥkām*) consist of universal principles and meanings comprising wisdom and benefits (*maṣāliḥ*), which can be projected into various rulings that are diverse in form but unified in purpose. That is why the fundamental sources of Islamic legislation avoided detailing and determination [at the time of Revelation].

In this respect, we read in the Qur'an concerning the punishment of those who indulge in immorality: "And punish [thus] both of the guilty parties" (4:16). No mention of 'flogging' or 'stoning' has been made here. Similarly, Muslims are discouraged in the Qur'an and Sunnah from indulgence in asking about the Shariᶜah commands. Thus, we read in the following verses:

> O you who have attained to faith! Do not ask about matters which, if they were to be made manifest to you [in terms of law], might cause you hardship; for, if you ask about them while the Qur'an is being revealed, they might [indeed] be made manifest to you [as laws]. God has

absolved [you from any obligation] in this respect: for God is Much-Forgiving, Forbearing. People before your time have indeed asked such questions – and in result thereof have come to deny the truth. (5:101–102).

In an authentic Tradition, it is stated that, "He (that is, God) kept silent on certain things out of mercy on you rather than forgetfulness, so do not ask about them."[20] In another tradition, it is said, "The most sinful person among the Muslims is the one who asked about something which had not been prohibited, but was prohibited because of his asking."[21]

The Prophet forbade Muslims to write down anything other than the Qur'an. The reason was that he used to make statements and deal with people in different ways that were the result of particular circumstances, which narrators might believe to be of universal and permanent bearing. One instance of this is the Tradition according to which "God's Apostle gave pre-emption (*shufʿah*) to the neighborhood."[22] Our scholars have maintained that this report bears no authoritative evidence because it was probably restricted to the case of a specific neighbor; who happened to be a partner and a neighbor at the same time. However, the narrator thought the case was judged on the basis of neighborhood.[23] It is also reported that Mālik ibn Anas disliked the supposition of cases of fiqh, for he used to say to anyone asking about hypothetical cases: "Leave them alone until they take place."[24]

However, since the Qur'an was revealed on different occasions and addressed different situations, and since its purpose was to guide the community in various ways, and because inimitability (*iʿjāz*) was intended to be one of its essential characteristics, we find that it comprises various modes of legislation. It contains permanent general and universal forms of legislation. It also contains legislation as particular rules dealing with specific real cases, thus serving as examples for understanding the fundamental universal rules. Likewise, there are in the Qur'an particular legislative rules that are equivalent to the particulars of the Sunnah, such as God's saying: "As for the adulteress and the adulterer – flog each of them with a hundred stripes"

(24:2); and "And for those women whose ill-conduct you have reason to fear, admonish them [first]; then leave them alone in bed; then chastise them" (4:34)*. And there is in it abrogated legislation. Yet, most of the Qur'anic legislation belongs to the universal permanent type.

The Sunnah was collected and classified by the scholars from the generation of the Companions and their successors. The motives for its collection and classification were different, as were the criteria for the acceptance of reports. It mostly consists of particular legislative provisions, because it dealt with individual cases (*qaḍāyā aʿyān*). However, it contains manifest general legislative rules that are an appropriate basis for universal permanent legislation.

Consequently, it is inevitable that *mujtahid* scholars examine Islamic legislation in both its universal and particular forms. It is their duty to make every effort to distinguish in the Qur'an and Sunnah between these two modes and classify the texts of the Shariʿah correctly. This is indeed a great task to which our ancient scholars contributed their very best and produced relevant insights.

---

* For a discussion of a new interpretation of this *ayah* see: AbdulHamid AbuSulayman, *Marital Discord: Recapturing the Full Islamic Spirit of Human Dignity* (London: IIIT, 2003). [Translator].

17

Equality in the Shariʿah

One of the most important consequences of the universality of the Shariʿah, whose consideration depends on the proper understanding of its meaning and its different modes and manifestations, is the question of the meaning and nature of equality in the community, how Shariʿah achieves it amongst its members, and how much it is taken into account. This is because Muslims are equal members of the Muslim community according to God's decree: "All believers are but brethren" (49:10). Brotherhood implies universal equality, according to which all Muslims are entitled to the same rights accorded them by the Shariʿah without any discrimination in all matters that do not allow for variation between Muslims. Knowing that Muslims are equal owing to their common created nature and their unity of religion, we can ascertain that they are worthy of being equal under the Shariʿah law, regardless of their level of power. Thus, neither the strength of the powerful raises them above others in the sight of the Shariʿah, nor does the humility of the weak bar them from equal treatment by it.

Likewise, because Islam is fundamentally the religion of nature (*dīn al-fiṭrah*), anything in which the primal human nature (*fiṭrah*) attests to equality between human beings is treated by Islamic legislation accordingly. However, the Shariʿah also avoids imposing equality and similarity on anything in which the primal human nature confirms variation. Variation is left to be dealt with by the social and civil systems according to the politics of Islam rather than by its fundamental legislative rules. Concerning equality, God says:

> O you who have attained to faith! Be ever steadfast in upholding equity, bearing witness to the truth for the sake of God, even though it be against your own selves or your parents and kinsfolk. Whether the person concerned be rich or poor, God's claim takes precedence over [the claims of] either of them. (4:135)

As far as difference is concerned, He says: "Not equal are those of you who spent and fought [in God's cause] before the Victory [and those who did not do so]: they are of a higher rank than those who would spend and fight [only] after it" (57:10).

Under Islamic legislation, equality in society stems from the equality of human beings in their inborn nature and in all related matters, in which variation [between individuals] has no implications for the well-being and virtue of society (*ṣalāḥ al-ʿālam*). Thus, human beings are the same in respect of their humanity: "All of you are children of Adam."[1] They are also equal in their right to live in this world because of their primal nature, and no differences in color, anatomy, race, or place can affect that equality. This basic equality insures their equality in the fundamentals of Islamic legislation, such as the right to existence, expressed by the terms "protection of life" and "protection of progeny", and to the means of life, expressed by the term "protection of property". Among the foremost means of life to which human beings are equally entitled is the right to live on the land that they have acquired or where they were born and brought up. They are also equally entitled to the means of living a proper and good life known as the "protection of intellect" and "protection of honor". Above all is the right of belonging to the religious community (*jāmiʿah dīniyyah*), expressed by the phrase "protection of religion". The way to achieving these rights have been mentioned and further discussion follows in order of their importance.

It thus becomes clear that human beings in the Shariʿah are equal with regard to what is indispensable (*ḍarūrī*) and neccessary (*ḥājī*). There is no distinction between them in the *ḍarūrī*, and seldom do we find differences between them concerning the *ḥājī*, such as depriving the slave of the legal capacity (*ahliyyah*) to act freely in his property except with the permission of his master. Only when there are valid reasons preventing equality (*mawāniʿ*) do differences between human beings arise.

Accordingly, equality in Islamic legislation is a fundamental principle that operates unfailingly except in situations where there are valid *mawāniʿ*. This means that, to establish the equality of individuals or groups in Islamic legislation, we are not required to search for its underlying reasons (*mūjib*); it is sufficient to insure that nothing contravenes equality. That is why the scholars of the Ummah insisted that the Qur'anic discourse in the masculine form include women as well.[2] Moreover, to apply the Shariʿah injunctions to women, there is no need to change the discourse of the Qur'an and Sunnah from the masculine to the feminine form, nor vice versa. It is reported in *Ṣaḥīḥ al-Bukhārī* on the authority of ʿUbādah ibn al-Ṣāmit that he said: "While we were with the Prophet *(ṢAAS)*, he said, 'Will you swear to me the pledge of allegiance that you will not worship anything besides God, will not commit illegal sexual intercourse, and will not steal?' Then he recited the verse concerning the women."[3] The rule governing the acts issuing from God's Apostle is that they are legislated for the whole community on equal terms, unless it is proven that something is specific to him.

IMPEDIMENTS TO EQUALITY

Impediments (*mawāniʿ*) to equality consist of incidents (*ʿawāriḍ*) which, when they occur, necessitate the suspension or abolition of equality because of certain predominant *maṣlaḥah* or *mafsadah* resulting from its implementation. I mean by *ʿawāriḍ* considerations arising from the circumstances of the application of equality in certain cases so that adherence to equality either does not produce the desired good that might rather lie in its opposite, or it results in greater or total evil. Designating such impediments as *ʿawāriḍ* does not mean that they are necessarily temporary, for they might be permanent or frequent. They are described as *ʿawāriḍ* because they hinder the implementation of a primary rule in the Shariᶜah. Likewise, those impediments are considered accidental owing to their effect in suspending a fundamental principle, since, as we have already shown, equality is the norm in Islamic legislation.

Taking into account these incidents and their effect of suspending equality is subject to the following rule. They must be restricted to the purpose for which they are appropriate to suspend equality and be assessed in accordance with the extent of their occurrence, permanence, or prevalence. For example, in a meritocracy, the excellent and the less excellent are not given the same amount of rewards, although this unequal treatment does not affect their equality in other rights. Therefore, the criteria for evaluating the extent to which those obstacles could remove equality between human beings stem from either a careful rational consideration (*maᶜnā*) requiring the suspension, or the rules of codified law. Thus, ascertaining the inequality between someone who is knowledgeable in a specific branch of knowledge and someone who is not is due to the reason for suspending their equality.

Moreover, the inequality of certain rights between Muslims and non-Muslims living under Islamic rule (*ahl al-dhimmah*), such as the competency to occupy religious posts, is also based on a specific rationality. This is because correctness of belief is among the fundamentals of Islam, which means that the unsoundness of the faith of non-Muslims implies their deficiency in the sight of the Shariᶜah to be entrusted with the control of Muslim religious affairs. Furthermore, it is difficult to anticipate and measure the effect of their conduct on the Muslim community if they are given authority over Muslim religious affairs. Accordingly, Muslim scholars agreed on preventing non-Muslims from holding certain official posts.

Determining the inequality between non-Muslims and Muslims in certain rules of transactions (*muᶜāmalāt*), is covered by the rules of codified law, which is a matter of the particular details (*furūᶜ*) of the Shariᶜah. It depends on the judgment of the jurists and their understanding of Islamic teachings. One example of this is the inequality between non-Muslims and Muslim relatives concerning inheritance by Muslim relatives, which is a matter of agreement between the scholars.[4] Another example is the inequality between Muslims and non-Muslims in the implementation of just retribution against the former for the sake of the latter,[5] and the acceptance of a non-Muslim's testimony, which are matters of disagreement amongst scholars.[6] All these matters are referred to the rules governing the codification of the applied Shariʿah rulings (*furūʿ*), which constitutes part of the jurists' task.

The equality between non-Muslims and Muslims in most of the rights in secular transactions (*muʿāmalāt*) has been clearly established by the Prophet in the following Saying: "They are entitled to the same rights as we are, and they shoulder the same responsibilities as we do."[7] It is moreover grounded in our knowledge that equality of the subjects of the same government is a fundamental principle (*aṣl*) that does not need any further justification. However, God's Apostle made the above statement only to indicate that this principle is firmly established. Some obstacles to equality are not obstacles in the real sense. They rather consist of situations where the grounds for equality do not exist. An example is the inequality between any member of the Muslim community and the Prophet's Companions concerning the merits and virtues of Companionship, for he or she has missed the privilege of combining seeing and accompanying the Prophet with believing in him as God's Apostle.

Furthermore, the obstacles preventing equality in certain areas of the Shariʿah can be divided into four categories: inborn and natural (*jibilliyyah*), legal (*sharʿiyyah*), social (*ijtimāʿiyyah*), and political (*siyāsiyyah*). These considerations might be permanent or temporary, major or minor. The natural, legal, and social considerations relate to moral conduct, the respect of others' rights, and the orderly and ethical management of the affairs of the Muslim community. Political considerations aim at protecting Islamic political power from being undermined.

Permanent natural obstacles of equality include the inequality of man and woman in certain areas, in which woman is by nature weaker than man, such as army command and the office of the Sovereign (*khilāfah*) according to all scholars,[8] and the office of judgeship in the majority view of scholars.[9] They also include inequality of man and woman in the right of custody over young children.[10] Next to the natural impediments to equality come considerations that are closely linked to them, which stem from original human nature, such as the inequality of man and woman whereby the woman is not required to support her husband financially since it has become an established custom that generally it is the man who should maintain the family. This custom is a manifestation of man's inborn disposition enabling him to bear the pain of hard work in earning and accumulating wealth.

There are also certain acquired qualities that are the result of both original human nature and personal endeavor. These acquired qualities are important in molding a person's inborn character, and only those who possess their proper means will attain them in such a way that they will be reflected in perfecting their perception and thinking. This is manifested in the differences in people's minds and talents concerning their capacity to comprehend hidden truths and subtle meanings. Thus, a person who is knowledgeable cannot be regarded in the same way as someone who is not in all matters in which difference of intellectual perception and comprehension is decisive. Examples of this inequality include the capacity to interpret the Shariʿah and to comprehend those aspects of it that are the subject of subtle derivation and reasoning. They also include the capacity to understand the Shariʿah injunctions concerning different situations and apply them properly to their relevant subjects, such as distinguishing between complicated cases, detecting the tricks used by litigants in court cases, and determining the integrity (*ʿadālah*) of court witnesses. That is why priority is given to those who have attained the level of ijtihad over those who have not in the eligibility to assume judgeship, thus preventing their equality with scholars of lower ranks. The same principle is applied to those who are closer to the level of ijtihad and those who are not.

It is, therefore, the duty of both jurists and rulers to take into account those obstacles and realize their scope and the extent to which they have become deeply rooted in human life. Then, once this is done, they must consider their effects on equality accordingly. They must also differentiate in those obstacles to freedom between what is only remotely related to the human being's innate disposition (*jibillah*) – thus being susceptible to removal by the existence of its opposite causes – and what is unclear in its relationship with it. They should be careful of the first category of obstacles to avoid formulating permanent Shariʿah rulings for them, whereas they should disregard the second category unless experience has proven them to be worthy of consideration.

Legal impediments, consist of circumstances whose impact on equality has been recognized by Islamic legislation. Indeed, real and just legislation can be based only on wisdom and sound reasons that might be manifest or hidden. This means that the Shariʿah is the reference and guide in specifying these impediments and determining their effects by taking into account specific legislative rules whose implementation overrides the realization of equality. These legislative rules are based on the Shariʿah fundamental universals, such as the protection of lineage (*ḥifẓ al-ansāb*) preventing the equality of men and women concerning polygamy. If polyandry were allowed, the safeguarding of lineage could not be achieved. These principles can also be known by inference from the particulars of the Shariʿah, such as the requirement of the testimony of two women specifically in financial and commercial matters.[11]

Social obstacles of equality are mostly based on what is considered to be the general good for society. Some might have a rational basis, whereas others might be the result of deeply rooted conventions in people's lives. An instance of the rational kind is the inequality of the ignorant person and the knowledgeable in their capacity to manage the public affairs and interests of the community. [Historically] the other kind [was] illustrated by the inequality of slaves and freemen in the acceptance of their testimony. Yet, we find that most of the social obstacles of equality are always open to ijtihad, and it is seldom that the Shariʿah has established hard and fast rules regarding them.

Political obstacles stem from the general conditions affecting the political life of the community. They might require the suspension of the principle of equality between certain groups or individuals or under particular circumstances, for the sake of a specific interest deemed of a higher value for the Islamic state. One of their features is that they are mostly subject to temporary consideration. An example of permanent consideration is the restriction of the *imamate* to the tribe of Quraysh,[12] whereas the Prophet's statement on the day of the conquest of Makkah (*al-Fatḥ*): "Who enters the house of Abū Sufyān, he is safe"[13] is obviously of temporary purport.

18

Freedom in the Shariʿah

It has already been established that equality is one of the objectives of the Shariʿah. It necessarily follows that equality of the community's members in freely conducting their personal affairs constitutes one of the primary goals of the Shariʿah. This is what is meant by "freedom." The Arabic term *ḥurriyyah* has been used to denote two meanings, one deriving from the other.

(1) The first meaning is the opposite of slavery. It refers to the original ability of all rational and mature people to handle their affairs themselves without depending on the consent of someone else. By the phrases "original" and "by himself", I mean to exclude the conduct of the legally incompetent (*sufahā*') in handling their property, the conduct of the husband and wife concerning marital rights, and the conduct of two contracting parties in accordance with the terms of the contract. These matters have been excluded from this first meaning of freedom because the conduct of each one of these categories of people depends on the consent of someone else. This dependence is not original. It is something conventional to which one binds oneself by a contract. However, in the final analysis, it constitutes a voluntary act whereby a person puts restrictions on one's personal freedom for one's own interest. As mentioned previously, this meaning of *ḥurriyyah* is the opposite of slavery. Accordingly, slavery means the inability of people to act by themselves except with the permission of their masters.

Slavery itself emerged as a result of hegemony and domination in ancient times when force was the sole arbiter in human affairs. Captivity in wars and invasions was one of the most prominent manifestations and products of slavery. During their captivity, prisoners used to undergo various kinds of oppression. However, if their captors decided to spare their lives, they would be enslaved and thus would act only according to the will of their masters. Enslavement was considered transferable from one hand to another. Likewise, the captors of prisoners of war might hand them over to others who might be hostile toward them so that they would either kill them or subject them to forced labor. They might also sell their prisoners to benefit from their price and thus they would become slaves to their buyers.

(2) The second meaning of the term *ḥurriyyah* derives from the first by metaphorical usage. It denotes one's ability to act freely and handle one's affairs as one likes, without opposition from anyone. This is the opposite of having one's hands tied or being unable to act freely. Having one's hands tied describes a person who, owing to powerlessness, poverty, lack of protection, or pressing need, is driven into a situation similar to that of a slave, in which he or she is subject to the will of someone else in all his or her dealings. One is thus deprived of all sense of self-respect and condemned to accept humiliation.

These two meanings of freedom have been intended by the Shariʿah, for both stem from *fiṭrah* and reflect the notion of equality that constitutes, as shown earlier, one of the essential objectives of the Shariʿah. It was in this light that ʿUmar ibn al-Khaṭṭāb exclaimed: "On what grounds do you enslave people whose mothers have born them free?"[1] – meaning that being free is something inherent to man's inborn nature.

The usage of the first meaning in the Shariʿah is common and well established. One of the maxims of Islamic jurisprudence states: "The Lawgiver aspires for freedom."[2] This has been inferred from various dispositions of the Shariʿah indicating that one of its main objectives is to abolish slavery and promote freedom for all. However, the diligence of the Shariʿah in considering public and shared interests and safeguarding the social order prevented it from freeing the slaves and abolishing the factors of slavery all at once, although this would have served its purpose. This was because the institution of slavery constituted an essential element of human societies at the advent of Islam. Thus, male slaves were workers on the farms, servants in the household, gardeners, and shepherds, while female slaves were like spouses to their owners, and worked as maids in their households and nurses for their children. Furthermore, slaves were one of the most important categories constituting the basis of the family and socio-economic system of peoples and nations at that time. Had Islam sought to transform that order in a radical way, this would have led to the breakdown of human civilization in such a manner that it would have been difficult to restore it. This was the main reason why the Shariʿah refrained from any abrupt abolition of the existing slavery system.[3]

The Shariʿah's abstention from totally abolishing the causes of enslavement – especially prisoners of war – and preventing their renewal, can be explained as follows: For a long time before the coming of Islam, it had been an established tradition that nations would enslave and make use of the groups and individuals taken prisoner in wartimes. Likewise, one of the great objectives of the strategy adopted by Islam was to put an end to the excessive aggression of the dominant nations, restore justice to the weak, and help them take revenge on their aggressors. Spreading its message and enhancing its authority in the world were the means employed by Islam to achieve this objective. However, if the powerful nations at that time dominating the world were to feel secure from falling as prisoners of war into the hands of the rising Muslim power (and enslavement was the consequence of war which those nations feared and disliked most) they – the Arabs and others – would not have wavered for a moment in rejecting the message of Islam. They would have relied on their strength and large numbers to maintain their dominance and independence.[4] In this respect, Ṣafwān ibn Umayyah[5] said: "To be subjugated by a man from the Quraysh [his tribe] is better for me than to be subjugated by a man from the Hawāzin."[6] In the same vein, the pre-Islamic Arab poet, al-Nābighah,[7] said:

I am always watching out so that I will not be subjugated,
Nor will my women be humiliated until they die noble and free.[8]

Likewise, in pursuing its objectives, Islam aimed at striking a balance between spreading freedom and preserving the order of the world by promoting the means to freedom over those of slavery. Thus, it combated the causes of slavery by reducing their number and tackling what remained of them in various specific ways. Hence, the Shariʿah abolished many factors leading to slavery except prisoners of war. For instance, it abolished voluntary enslavement, where one would sell oneself, or the eldest of the family selling some of its members, a practice that had been sanctioned by many laws of the world. It also abolished slavery as a punishment for committing an offense, whereby the offender would be sentenced to become a slave to the person against whom the offense had been committed. This has been described by the Qur'an in relation to the situation that had prevailed in Egypt:

> [The brothers] replied: "Its requital? He in whose camel-pack [the cup] is found, shall be [enslaved as] in requital! Thus do we [ourselves] requite the wrong doers." Thereupon [they were brought before Joseph to be searched; and] he began with the bags of his half-brothers before the bag of his brother [Benjamin]: and in the end he brought forth the drinking-cup out of his brother's bag. (12:75–76)

In addition, Islam abolished enslavement in payment of debt, a practice that was part of the Roman law[9] and Solon's law[10] that had preceded it in Greece.[11] It also categorically forbade enslavement during times of oppression and internal strife between Muslims. It abolished the enslavement of wayfarers, another common practice, such as the caravan that enslaved Joseph when they found him.[12]

Furthermore, Islam approached slavery as it actually existed or as it might exist in the future and deal with it by adopting two methods. One aimed at eliminating altogether the harmful results of slavery by multiplying the means of its abolition. The other method consisted of alleviating the effects of existing slavery by reforming the behavior of slave masters, that was mostly oppressive.[13] As an aid to the abolition of slavery, Islam allocated a certain proportion of the zakah to buying slaves and freeing them, as clearly stated in the Qur'an: "... and for the freeing of human beings from bondage" (2:177). It also made the manumission of slaves one of the options of obligatory compensation for manslaughter,[14] intentional breaking of the fast in the month of Ramadan,[15] injurious comparison (*ẓihār*),[16] and the breaking of oaths.[17] In the same spirit, Islam directed slave owners to write out deeds of freedom for those in their possession if the latter so wished. Thus, the Qur'an says to this effect: "And if any of those whom you rightfully possess desire [to obtain] a deed of freedom, write it out for them" (24:33). Whether this verse implies an order or merely a recommendation is a matter over which scholars have differed. Hence, as directed by the Prophet, if someone manumits his share in a slave, the share of his partner shall be assessed and he shall pay its value so that the shared slave becomes totally free. Thus, he said: "Whoever manumits a slave owned by two masters, should manumit him completely (not partially) if he is rich, after having his price evaluated."[18]

Similarly, if a female slave gives birth as a result of sexual relationship with her master, she acquires the status of a free woman, and her master cannot sell her, or give her away to someone else, or even force her to do any hard work. After his death, she must be manumitted by using his wealth.[19]

In a similar vein, Islam aroused people's interest and encouraged them to manumit slaves. Thus, God Almighty says in the Qur'an: "But he would not try to ascend the steep uphill road... And what could make you conceive what it is, that steep uphill road? [It is] the freeing of a human being from bondage" (90:11–13). Islam's encouragement of the manumission of those slaves who were expensive and beloved by their masters is even stronger. In this respect, Abū Dharr narrated: "I asked the Prophet, 'What is the best deed?' He replied, 'To believe in God and to fight for His Cause.' I then asked, 'What is the best kind of manumission (of slaves)?' He replied, 'The manumission of the most expensive slave and the most beloved by his master'."[20]

In another Tradition, the Messenger of God is reported to have said: "He who has a slave-girl and educates and treats her nicely and then manumits and marries her, will gain a double reward."[21] In my view, one important aspect of the wisdom behind this Prophetic insistence on the emancipation of slaves is that these people must not remain in bondage, for this would deprive society from fully benefiting from their talents and that freeing them is better for them.

To the other method belongs the prohibition of overburdening slaves with too much or heavy work and the obligation to provide them with food and clothing. Thus, it is reported that the Prophet said:

> Your slaves are your brethren, upon whom God has given you authority. So, if one has one's brethren under one's control, one should feed them with the like of what one eats and clothe them with the like of what one wears. You should not overburden them with what they cannot bear, and if you do so, help them [with their hard work].[22]

Islam also forbade beating slaves for no reason; should someone torture his slave, the latter must be freed.[23] In the same spirit of promoting good treatment of slaves, the Prophet said: "One should not say, my slave (*ᶜabdī*), or my girl-slave (*amatī*), but should say, my boy (*fatāy*), my girl (*fatātī*), and my young man (*ghulāmī*)."[24]

From a thematic analysis of these and similar teachings and dispositions, we ascertain that it is an objective of the Shariᶜah to promote and spread freedom in the first meaning mentioned above. As for the second meaning, it has many forms and manifestations that constitute an integral part of the intended objectives of Islam. These forms and manifestations relate to the fundamental principles governing people concerning their beliefs, opinions, and speech as well as conduct and acts. All this can be subsumed under a universal rule by virtue of which all those living under the authority of the Islamic state must be able to act freely and deal with whatever matters the Shariᶜah has allowed them to dispose of without fearing anyone. All these matters are governed by definite rules and limits established by the Shariᶜah and noone can force people to abide by something else.

For this reason, God has strongly condemned those people who would try to do so:

> Say: "Who is there to forbid the beauty which God has brought forth for His creatures, and the good things from among the means of sustenance?" Say: "They are [lawful] in the life of this world unto all who have attained to faith – to be theirs alone on Resurrection Day." Thus clearly do We spell out these messages to people of [innate] knowledge! Say: "Verily, my Sustainer has forbidden only shameful deeds, be they open or secret, and [every kind of] sinning, and unjustified envy, and the ascribing of divinity to anything beside Him – since He has never bestowed any warrant for that from on high – and the attributing to God anything of which you have no knowledge." (7:32–33)

The phrase "and the attributing to God anything of which you have no knowledge" includes the prohibition of the permissible things queried at the beginning of this passage in the form of disapproving interrogation (*istifhām inkārī*).

Likewise, Islam has established freedom of beliefs. Islam refuted all wrong beliefs which perverse people forced upon their followers without knowledge, without any guidance, and without any enlightening revelation, and also called for finding conclusive proofs for any proclaimed true faith. Furthermore, while Islam has confirmed the freedom of belief by ordering its followers to call others to God's path with wisdom and goodly exhortation and by arguing with them in the most kindly manner (16:126), it has also forbidden coercion in matters of faith (2:256). I have discussed this point in some detail in my book *Uṣūl al-Niẓām al-Ijtimāʿī fī al-Islām*.[25] Were it not because freedom of belief is one of the fundamentals of the Shariʿah, the punishment for the miscreant who conceals unbelief and shows belief would not have been such that his repentance should not be accepted by God, for he has no excuse in doing so.

Freedom of expression (*ḥurriyat al-aqwāl*) consists of showing one's beliefs and views within what it is allowed by the Shariʿah. God has ordained part of what belongs to this type of freedom in the following verse:

> In this way God makes clear His messages to you, so that you might find guidance, and that there might grow out of you a community [of people] who invite to all that is good, and enjoin the doing of what is right and forbid the doing of what is wrong: and it is they, they who shall attain to a happy state. (3:103–104)

It has also been expressed in the following Tradition, in which the Prophet is reported to have said:

> He who amongst you sees something abominable should modify it with the help of his hand; and if he has not strength enough to do it, then he should do it with his tongue, and if he has not strength enough to do it, (even) then he should (abhor it) from his heart, and that is the least of faith.[26]

Freedom of expression also includes the freedom to pursue knowledge (*taʿallum*), to instruct others (*taʿlīm*), to produce intellectual works, and to publish one's views. This aspect of freedom was best manifested during the first three centuries of Muslim history, when scholars could announce their views and doctrines and argue for them openly without this causing any animosity. Indeed, this was an embodiment of the Prophet's Saying in which he stated: "May God brighten a man who hears a tradition from us, learns it by heart and passes it on to others. Many a bearer of knowledge conveys it to one who is more versed than he is; and many a bearer of knowledge is not versed in it."[27]

It was in this spirit that Mālik ibn Anas rejected a suggestion by the Abbasid caliph Abū Jaʿfar al-Manṣūr to enforce his juristic doctrines as the law of the land. The caliph is reported to have said to him:

> "I have decided to copy your book [that is, *Muwaṭṭa'*], send one copy of it to each of the regions of the caliphate, and order [the people] to abide by it and not leave it to anything else." Mālik replied: "O leader of the faithful, do not do so, for people have already learnt certain views and known certain traditions, and the inhabitants of each region have

adhered to one or the other of the different opinions of the Companions of God's Apostle and others according to which their religious practice has been shaped. Preventing them from that will be hard, so leave people to their practice and to what they have chosen for themselves."[28]

Were it not for the consideration of freedom expression, confessions, contracts, obligations, divorce pronouncements, and wills would have no legal effect. That is why these actions are ineffective once it is established that they have taken place under coercion.

Freedom of action (*ḥurriyat al-aʿmāl*) refers to one's management of one's personal and others' affairs. The kind of freedom relating to one's personal affairs consists of applying oneself to, and enjoying, all that is permissible (*mubāḥ*). Permissibility (*ibāḥah*) is the widest domain where human freedom to act is mostly manifested. No one has the authority to prevent human beings from enjoying what is permissible, for none is kinder to them than God. By the permissible is meant all that is allowed in the Shariʿah even if it is expressed in general terms (*ʿumūm*), including the abominable (*makrūh*).

The permissible includes, for example, the pursuit of any kind of lawful profession, settling in any permitted places, and benefiting from all natural resources such as water and pasture. It also includes disposing of one's property and earnings in any lawful way, choosing any type of food, dress, or accommodation one likes, and fulfilling any lawful desires. That is why a wife can deal freely with her property without her husband's consent, notwithstanding the disagreement among the jurists over the extent of her freedom in doing so.[29]

Freedom of action that affects others is lawful so far as it does not cause harm to them. This kind of freedom combines a twofold objective of the Shariʿah, namely, the freedom to act that does not go beyond the actor and the freedom to act that affects someone else's freedom to act, without however causing harm to him or her. Harm might consist of suspending someone's right or destroying it altogether. This requires the offender to compensate for the damage caused, as has been expounded by the jurists. For this reason, a person can be prevented from an act that would result in the violation of someone else's freedom, for this is a form of injustice. When one has carried out an act that has harmed another person, one is responsible for that harm and must rectify it as far as possible. If the damage is such that it cannot be rectified by financial compensation, then recourse must be had to deterrent punishment.

To freedom of action that affects others' freedom of action belong also the obligations – that is, contracts and agreements – into which people enter voluntarily for certain benefits which they envisage will be the result. Committing oneself in this way is a manifestation of the exercise of one's freedom to act whereby one agrees to grant certain rights to someone else. This has been the subject of detailed juristic discussion in relation to contracts and the distinction between those that are binding simply by the verbal creation of agreement and those that become binding only after entering into execution of the matter contracted upon.

Furthermore, the Shariʿah has placed certain obligations upon its followers, according to which their freedom to act is restricted for their own good (*ṣalāḥ*), both now and in the future. These obligations include the fulfillment of what relates to the public good (*maṣāliḥ ʿāmmah*), such as implementing collective obligations (*furūḍ al-kifāyāt*), or realizing the good of those whose well-being the Shariʿah has made the duty of specific persons, like providing for one's relatives. If people transgress the limits of their freedom in this respect, they will have to be stopped at the limits of the Shariʿah by liability, such as compensation for negligence, or by punishment without acceptance of repentance, as in armed robbery (*ḥarābah*), or after inducing them to repent, as in the case of apostasy (*riddah*). Examples illustrating this are abundant.

You should know that the violation of freedom is one of the gravest forms of injustice and wrongdoing (*ẓulm*). Therefore, the realization and determination of the extent of people's freedom in the sight of the Shariʿah must be the responsibility of judges who are invested with the power to settle disputes between the people. That is why if a victim revenges himself on the offender, this would be considered an aggression for which he deserves to be reprimanded. Thus, God says in the Qur'an:

> And do not take any human being's life – [the life] which God has willed to be sacred – otherwise than in [the pursuit of] justice. Hence, if anyone has been slain wrongfully, We have empowered the defender of his rights [to exact a just retribution]; but even so, let him not exceed the bounds of equity in [retributive] killing. [And as for him who has been slain wrongfully –] behold, he is indeed succoured [by God]! (17:33)

That is also why ʿUmar ibn al-Khaṭṭāb considered taking one's revenge a kind of enslavement as in the case of the son of ʿAmrū ibn al-ʿĀṣ. When ʿAmrū's son slapped someone for having trodden on his dress, and the person complained about it to the caliph, ʿUmar made his famous statement: "On what grounds do you enslave people whose mothers have born them free?" True, the son of ʿAmrū was unintentionally hurt by having his dress trodden upon in such a way that it might have been dirtied or torn. However, when he undertook to revenge himself on his offender, he went too far and treated the person who had offended him as if he were his slave. Yet, ʿUmar did not content himself with simply making this statement, for he also authorized that person to take revenge on the son of ʿAmrū ibn al-ʿĀṣ.[30] Imprisoning a person falls exclusively under the jurisdiction of judges, and no one else can imprison anyone else, for this is a grave violation of people's freedom, and this also applies to expulsion.

Accordingly, in many of its dispositions the Shariʿah has guarded freedom to act by blocking all means leading to its violation, such as forbidding compulsory authorization (*wakālah)* whereby the debtor would delegate his or her creditor in sale, etc., at the date of maturity of the debt.[31] In a similar vein, the Shariʿah has also prohibited all kinds of terms imposed by capital owners on the workers undertaking commenda (*qirāḍ*),[32] land-tenancy (*muzāraʿah*), *mughārasah*, sharecropping (*musāqāh*), etc., as we shall explain in conjunction with our discussion of the specific objectives of the Shariʿah – some of which has been mentioned in chapter 24.

19

Alteration and Confirmation Objectives in the Shariᶜah

It might be strongly believed by many scholars, without a thorough investigation of the different modes of Islamic legislation, that the Shariᶜah came exclusively to change the condition of human beings. The truth, however, is that Islamic legislation has adopted a double method consisting of both alteration and confirmation.

One method consists of removing decadence and declaring its corruption. This method has been highlighted in the following Qur'anic verses, in which God says:

> God is near to those who have faith, taking them out of deep darkness into light. (2:257)

> Now there has come to you from God a light, and a clear Divine writ, through which He shows to all that seek His goodly acceptance the paths leading to salvation and, by His Grace, brings them out of the depths of darkness into the light and guides them onto a straight way. (5:15–16)

Alteration might mean further restriction (*shiddah)* with human welfare in mind. It may also result in leniency (*takhfīf)* to put an end to extremism (*ghuluw*). An example of confirmation is the reduction of the waiting period of the widow from one year to only four months and ten days.[1] There is no benefit in the waiting period for anyone except the protection of the lineal identity (*ḥifẓ al-nasab*) of the deceased husband if the woman is pregnant, and this period is sufficient to confirm her pregnancy. Similarly, the period of mourning one's husband. During the age of pagan ignorance (*Jāhiliyyah*), a widow was forced to wear only the scruffiest clothes and stay in a very miserable shack without washing or perfuming herself for a whole year. When Islam came, it abolished all that by banning colored dress (except black), perfume, and eye makeup (kohl) for only four months and ten days.

One aspect of wise and purposeful change in human affairs is taking care to implement it without deviation, for indulgence threatens to undermine it from both sides. If it is a change toward restriction, people might seek to evade it; whereas if it is a change towards alleviation, they might wrongly believe that this is a reason not to abide by it. That was why, when a woman came to God's Apostle and asked him whether her widowed daughter, whose eyes were troubling her, could apply some kohl on them, he did not allow that and said, "No" two or three times. Then he said, "It is only four months and ten days. In the *Jāhiliyyah*, none of you threw away the piece of dung until a year had passed." In this connection, Zaynab bint Abū Salamah[2] said,

> In the *Jāhiliyyah* when a woman's husband died, she would go into a small tent and dress in the worst clothing. She did not touch perfume or anything until a year had passed. Then an animal was brought to her – a donkey, a sheep, or a bird – and she would break her waiting-period (*ʿiddah*) by rubbing her body against it (*taftaḍḍu*). Rarely did she break her waiting period with anything (by rubbing herself against it) but that it died. Then she would come out and be given a piece of dung. She would throw it away and then return to using whatever she wished of perfume or whatever.[3]

The other method consists of confirming good practices that have been followed by human beings. They are what the Qur'an has defined as *maʿrūf* in the following verse: "those who shall follow the [last] Apostle, the unlettered Prophet whom they shall find described in the Torah that is with them, and [later on] in the Gospel: [the Prophet] who will enjoin upon them the doing of what is right (*maʿrūf*)" (7:157).[4] Indeed, if one examines carefully the things that humankind has adopted since time immemorial and upon which human civilization has been founded, one will discover that they consist mostly of good practices inherited from the advice of parents, instructors, educators, prophets, sages, and just rulers so that they have become deeply rooted in human life and psychology. They include practices like rescuing the distressed, repelling aggressors, defending one's tribe and city, assembling on feast days, marriage, caring for children, and inheritance.

None the less, these virtues and righteous things are not spread equally amongst tribes and nations, which made it necessary for the universal Shariʿah to deal with them by evaluating them (*ḥukm*) as an obligation (*wujūb*), a recommendation (*nadb*), and permissibility (*ibāḥah*), and specifying the relevant definition. Likewise, taking into consideration the differences between tribes and nations is one of the most important aims of any universal law, as indicated by the Tradition reported by Mālik, Bukhārī, and Muslim, in which the Prophet said: "I intended to forbid a couple's intercourse while the woman is pregnant (*ghīlah*) but I noticed that the Byzantines and Persians do that without it causing any harm to their children."[5] Similarly, the Shariʿah pays special attention to the differences between human beings in their readiness to abandon good practices when tempted by the bad practices resulting from people's desires, since keeping to those virtues requires a certain effort. For this, we find that the Shariʿah encourages people to marry and requires them to provide financial support for their relatives.

What is mostly needed is the affirmation of the legislative rule of permissibility (*ibāḥah*) to put an end to the excessiveness of extremists by encouraging them to follow what is normal and acceptable to the majority of reasonable and good people. Thus, God says in the Qur'an: "and make lawful to them the good things of life (*ṭayyibāt*)" (7:157).[6] Though human beings have always enjoyed the good things of life, some nations and tribes deviated, however, from the general norm by denying themselves many kinds of good and lawful things. This attitude was spread amongst some Arab tribes, such as Banū Salīm who forbade themselves to eat the flesh of lizards (*ḍabb*), asserting that it was a metamorphosed Jew. Another example was that many Arabs banned women from eating the born-alive offspring of *baḥīrah* and *sā'ibah*,[7] which were reserved exclusively for men, as described by the Qur'an in the following verse: "And they say, 'All that is in the wombs of such-and-such cattle is reserved for our males and forbidden to our women; but if it be stillborn, then both may have their share of it'" (6:139). Hence, the Qur'an states: "Say: 'Who is there to forbid the beauty which God has brought forth for His creatures, and the good things from among the means of sustenance?'" then it says in the same verse: "Say: 'They are [lawful] in the life of this world to all who have attained faith – to be theirs alone on Resurrection Day'"(7:32); it continues "Say: 'Verily, my Sustainer has forbidden only shameful deeds, be they open or secret...'" (7:33).

Confirmation also requires removing any illusions that people might have, under which they are led to believe that good deeds are evil when unrighteous persons do them. That was why Ḥakīm ibn Hiẓām asked the Prophet the following question:

> "O God's Apostle! What do you think about my good deeds which I used to do during the period of ignorance [before embracing Islam] like keeping good relations with my kith and kin, manumitting slaves, and giving alms, etc. Shall I receive the reward for that?" God's Apostle said, "You have embraced Islam with all those good deeds which you did."[8]

God has said in the Qur'an: "Today, all the good things of life have been made lawful to you. And the food of those who were vouchsafed revelation previously is lawful to you" (5:5). Likewise, of the types of sexual relationships (*ankiḥah)* between a man and a woman, Islam sanctioned only the public marriage and barred anything outside it, such as prostitution, wife-lending (*istibḍāʿ*), and adultery (*sifāḥ*).[9]

Sanctioning, however, does not require a verbal declaration. As we have already seen, the need for verbal declaration in this mode of Islamic legislation arises only when it is necessary, such as removing a misunderstanding, answering an inquiry, or exhorting others to action. Except for these and similar reasons, the silence of the Lawgiver (*sukūt al-Shāriʿ*) is considered to indicate the confirmation of what people are doing. Therefore, permissibility is the foremost rule of the Shariʿah because its subject matter comprises innumerable varieties. This has been established by inductive inference from the Prophet's statements and actions and is further corroborated by a Tradition narrated by al-Dāraquṭnī and others on the authority of Abū Thaʿlabah al-Khushanī, according to which the Prophet is reported to have said:

> God has prescribed obligations, so do not omit them; He has set up boundaries, so do not transgress them; He has forbidden certain things, so do not violate them; and He has kept silent on certain things out of mercy on you rather than forgetfulness, so do not ask about them.[10]

Therefore, the Prophet did not like persistant questioning about matters that have not been mentioned in the Shariʿah, for asking unnecessary questions about unambiguous things is mere idle play. Thus, the Qur'an says: "O you who have attained to faith! Do not ask about matters which, if they were to be made manifest to you [in terms of law], might cause you hardship" (5:101). Yet, from the Lawgiver's silence indicating confirmation are excluded those matters covered by rules other than permissibility, which have been established by reason, in other words, *qiyās* in all its variations.

Alteration and confirmation here are not applicable exclusively to the specific conditions of the Arabs, but to the whole of humankind. This is because humankind has never lacked good practices that are the result of divine laws or good advice or sound minds. Thus, the Arabs were inheritors of the *ḥanīfiyyah*, the Jews were heirs of the great Law of Moses, and the Christians were inheritors of both the Mosaic Law and the teachings of Jesus. The whole of humankind had inherited much of ancient good laws, such as those of the Egyptians, the Greeks, and the Romans, and were following many good practices and values emanating from sound human nature (*fiṭrah salīmah*), such as considering the killing of the human soul a crime. Accordingly, alteration and confirmation in Islamic legislation might, as mostly happens, correspond to the conditions of certain nations to the exclusion of others, such as the prohibition of usury and the prescription of dower (*mahr*) and blood money (*diyyah*). They might also correspond to the conditions of all nations, such as the proscription of intoxicants, the abolition of bequests for one's heirs, bequests of more than one-third of one's property for non-inheritors, and the sanctioning of the marriages of those who embraced Islam.

One important aspect of the mercy of the Shariʿah is that it has left the different nations to their inherited customs and ways as long as they do not result in evil. As narrated in *Muwaṭṭa'*, the Prophet is reported to have said: "Any house or land that has been divided in the *Jāhiliyyah*, it is according to the division of the *Jāhiliyyah*. Any house or land that has not been divided before the coming of Islam, is divided according to Islam."[11] On the day of the conquest (*Fatḥ*) of Makkah, the Prophet said: "But has ʿAqīl left for us any house to lodge in?,"[12] meaning that ʿAqīl ibn Abī Ṭālib had re-leased them according to the rules of the *Jāhiliyyah*, so the Prophet did not want to revoke what he had done when Makkah was conquered.

20

Shariᶜah is About Essences and Real Attributes, Not Names and Forms

What we have learnt from the previous discussions, especially in chapters 18 and 19 as well as in chapter 12, will now enable us easily to realize the following. The purpose of the Shariᶜah in all its rules and injunctions is to associate the genera[1] of those rules and injunctions with states, attributes, and actions in human conduct, both individually and collectively. This association is based on the essential meanings (*maᶜānī*) of those states, attributes, and actions resulting in righteousness and benefit or unrighteousness and harm, be they strong or weak. Likewise you should beware of the wrong belief that some rules and injunctions are linked merely to the names of things or to their external forms without consideration of the essential meanings intended by the Shariᶜah (*maᶜānī sharᶜiyyah*), thus falling into grave error in fiqh.

One should therefore avoid imitating some jurists who forbade the consumption of the porpoise, which some people call sea swine, because they considered it as swine, as they say.[2] One should also shun some jurists who forbade the simultaneous marriage of two men and two women on the basis that this practice is what is known as *shighār*,[3] simply by looking at its apparent form resembling that of *shighār:* a man married a woman under his guardianship to another man for a given dower, while the other man married a woman under his guardianship to the first man for a given dower (that was or was not equal to that of the first woman). Such jurists failed to realize the real reason and proper attribute for which the Shariʿah has forbidden the *shighār* marriage.

Thus, it is the jurist's duty to examine carefully the original names of things and the variations taken into account during the time of Revelation. They constitute an appropriate way to know the contemporary circumstances observed by the Shariʿah so that we can be guided by that knowledge to the attribute considered by the Lawgiver as a basis for the *ḥukm*. We shall elaborate on this point in the discussion of the characteristics of precision (*ḍabṭ*) and determination (*taḥdīd*) in Islamic legislation. It is in this context that some jurists fell in many errors, such as issuing the legal opinion (fatwa) upholding the death penalty for charlatans because they call them sorcerers, thus totally ignoring the real meaning of sorcery for which the Lawgiver enunciated the death penalty for its practitioners.[4] Likewise, when discussing sorcery or if asked about it, jurists ought to explain and distinguish carefully its real properties and essence. They should not hasten to issue legal verdicts based merely on the name sorcery (*siḥr*), thus deciding that the sorcerer must be put to death and his repentance cannot be accepted, for this is indeed very grave.

Equally mistaken were other jurists who issued the fatwa proclaiming the prohibition of the smoking of tobacco, which became known in the early twelfth [eighteenth] century under the name of *ḥashīsh*. Those jurists thought that tobacco was the same as the drug hemp used by hashish addicts. Equally erroneous was the fatwa issued by some juristic scholars prohibiting the consumption of the Yemenite beans known as coffee when it was discovered at the beginning of the tenth/sixteenth century, because of its name, *qahwah*, which means wine in Arabic, although *qahwah* when applied applied to the beans, was actually a corruption of the non-Arabic [French] word *café*.

Therefore, jurists have always sought to distinguish the attributes taken into account by the Lawgiver from those that are merely associated with them but have nothing to do with the purpose of the Lawgiver. They call these associated attributes co-present properties (*awṣāf ṭardiyyah*), even though they might constitute a dominant aspect of the real meaning (*ḥaqīqah sharʿiyyah*) intended by the

Shariᶜah, such as that which takes place in the wilderness in the case of armed robbery and brigandage (*ḥirābah*). Although it might be true that armed robbery mostly takes place in the countryside and wilderness, it is not what the Lawgiver has intended. Accordingly, adept jurists decided on the penalty (*ḥadd)* for armed robbery for criminals using arms and frightening the public in urban areas.

Therefore, Islamic legal terms (*asmā' sharᶜiyyah*) should be interpreted only according to the meanings intended by the Lawgiver concerning practices designated by those terms when Islamic terminology was established. When the designated practice changes, then the term has no value in itself. This is why Mālikī jurists held the view that legal forms expressing voluntary donations (*tabarruᶜāt)* might interchange. Thus, *ᶜumrā muᶜaqqabah*[5] becomes endowment; endowment with conditions of sale becomes life-grant (*ᶜumrā*), a charity with the right of the donor to buy it back turns into a gift, and donation subject to the donor until his death is transferred into testament, even though it might be called endowment, gift, or life-grant (*ᶜumrā*).[6] They also stated that if the guardian of a woman said to a man, "I donate to you such and such as a dower," this would be an expression of marriage, even though he has called it gift (*hibah*).

Indeed, the Prophet warned severely and disapprovingly that some of his community would consume intoxicants and call them by another name.[7] Likewise, just as the alteration of names has no effect in legalizing what is forbidden, so too it has no effect in terms of prohibiting what is lawful. More generally, names in themselves cannot be the reasons for the Shariᶜah injunctions. Rather, they identify practices with specific attributes on which the injunctions are based. Accordingly, it is those attributes which are important. An example is the Prophet's ban on preparing non-alcoholic drinks in containers such as *ḥantam* (water-skins), *dubbā'* (green jars), and *muzaffat* (jug smeared with pitch),[8] because drinks in those containers ferment rapidly, not because of their names.

21

Analogical Reasoning Based on Effective Causes and Medium and High Shariʿah Objectives

I do not consider anyone doubting that the Shariʿah injunctions are open to analogical reasoning (*qiyās*) to be capable of deep thinking and to have a sound understanding of the Shariʿah. I consider them only passive recipients and memorizers of transmitted particular juridical rules without realizing the unifying aspects between those of them that have been subsumed under the same rules. Indeed, I can only imagine that they are utterly confused when seeking rules governing the practices for which no specific guidance can be found in the transmitted traditions.

However, it will not be too long before they realize their urgent need for *qiyās*; and if they examine their thinking, they will find that they have based it on analogical reasoning.

In fact, the inductive study of the Shariʿah in all its different dispositions (*taṣarrufāt*) has convinced the scholars of the Ummah that it did not treat multiple particular cases and details equally by subsuming them under one general rule (*jins ḥukm*) except where it covered common specific attributes. Consequently, it has become an established practice amongst them from the time of the Companions and the Successors to evaluate certain things in terms of others. That is, scholars apply the Shariʿah-given rules governing the earlier practices to the later practices, based on the attributes (*awṣāf*) considered the reasons for the legislation and taken into account bythe Lawgiver in enacting the Shariʿah injunctions. If those attributes are secondary and readily understood (*qarībah)*, we call them effective causes (*ʿilal*), such as intoxication (*iskār*); if they are fundamental universals, we call them medium objectives (*maqāṣid qarībah*), such as the protection of the intellect (*ḥifẓ al-ʿaql*); and if they are sublime universals, then we call them high or ultimate objectives (*maqāṣid ʿāliyyah*), which are of two kinds: *maṣlaḥah* and *mafsadah* – all this has already been discussed.

In legislation (*tashrīʿ*) and elaboration (*tafrīʿ*) of the rules of the Shariʿah, the jurists resorted to reasoning by analogy on the basis of analogs (*naẓā'ir*) and particulars (*juz'iyyāt*) rather than searching for the mediate fundamental universals and the two ultimate and sublime objectives, that is, *maṣlaḥah* and *mafsadah*, for two reasons. (1) They found the signification of analogs with regard to each other closer to the meaning which the Lawgiver has explicitly mentioned or alluded to as being intended by Him, or which they felt there was a strong likelihood that the Lawgiver had specifically considered it in giving analogs the same rule (*ḥukm*). This is because the signification of analogs concerning the meaning intended by the Lawgiver is precise and clear and is further accompanied by its example. One of our expert scholars stated that adducing parables and analogs by scholars was crucial to bringing to light subtle meanings and uncovering hidden truths.[1] Parables and analogs thus spare jurists the effort of searching for the deeper meanings and their higher genera (*ajnās ʿāliyyah*). (2) Furthermore, thanks to their clear explanation, parables and analogs enable *mujtahids* to move to the meaning present in the analogs whose rule (*ḥukm*) is not known and thereby subsume them under the rule governing their medium universals and then under their generic universals. It will not then be difficult for the *mujtahids* to do this, since the three levels (*marātib*)[2] of the objectives of the Shariʿah rules and commands will be manifest to them.

In fact, it has always been an aspect of rational argumentation (*istidlāl*) amongst philosophers and mathematicians to gain an understanding of subtle and lofty meanings by easily understood examples. So too, I consider the jurists should follow this method, for it is the most appropriate for people of higher perception. Having known this, you can now certainly accept that the principle rule is that all the Shariʿah rules and commands allow for reasoning by analogy so long as the underlying meaning intended by the Lawgiver has been confirmed. Accordingly, those which do not fit in this category must be considered to be very few.

The leading scholars of Islamic jurisprudence disagreed over the applicability of analogy to categorical penalties (*ḥudūd*), expiations (*kaffārah*), and exemptions (*rukhaṣ*) as well as causes, conditions, and impediments.[3] It is also due to this that they agreed on the inapplicability of *qiyās* to matters of ritual worship (*ʿibādāt*).[4] Likewise, Abū Bakr and ʿUmar equated the paternal grandmother with the maternal grandmother in inheritance, whereby Abū Bakr divided the sixth between them. It is reported in *Muwaṭṭa'* that "Two grandmothers came to Abū Bakr al-Ṣiddīq, and he wanted to give the sixth to the maternal grandmother. A man from the *Anṣār* said, 'What? Are you omitting the one from whom he would inherit if she died while he was alive?' Abū Bakr divided the sixth between them."[5] That was reasoning by analogy of the superior (*faḥwā)* brought to Abū Bakr's attention by the *Anṣārī's* words, while the division of the sixth between the two grandmothers is a recognition of the property grounding the rule (*taḥqīq manāṭ*). This is always the case whenever there is plurality of heirs but no text allows the increase of shares. It is also reported in *Muwaṭṭa'*:

> A paternal grandmother came to ʿUmar ibn al-Khaṭṭāb and asked him for her inheritance. He said to her: "You have nothing in God's Book, and what has been decided is only for other than you [that is, what was decided by Abū Bakr, based on the Prophet's practice as also reported in *Muwaṭṭa'* by al-Mughīrah ibn Shuʿbah and Muḥammad ibn Maslamah]. I am not one to add to the fixed shares other than that sixth. If there are two of you together, it is between you. If either of you is left alone with it, it is hers."[6]

Thus, ʿUmar applied reasoning by analogy in the division of the sixth between the two grandmothers, although he refrained from applying it by increasing the prescribed share in the case of plurality of heirs to make it one-third, thus taking as a basis for *qiyās* the brothers from the mother's side.

22

Manipulation to Make the Unlawful Appear Lawful

The term manipulation (*taḥayyul*) means to give a lawful appearance to a practice that is prohibited by the Shariᶜah, or to represent an action disapproved of by the Shariᶜah as though it were acceptable, to avoid being blamed for it. Thus, manipulation in the Shariᶜah context relates to practices whose prohibition is canonical (*sharᶜī*) and the prohibiting authority is the Lawgiver.

However, manipulation does not include seeking to perform a lawful act in a different way or by providing its means. Rather, this can be called management (*tadbīr*), or eagerness (*ḥirṣ*) or devoutness (*waraᶜ*).

An example of management is the case of a man who, falling in love with a woman, seeks to marry her so that he can live with her in a lawful manner. An instance of eagerness is the case of Abū Bakrah, who, entering the mosque for prayer while the Prophet had already bowed for *rukūᶜ* and fearing to miss the *rakᶜah* and desiring to be in the first row to receive its favors, bowed and moved forward in a state of prostration until he reached the first row. Then, the Prophet said to him: "May God increase your love for the good. But do not do it again."[1]

Devoutness can be illustrated by asking someone to wake you up for the dawn (*ṣubḥ*) prayer lest you fear being overcome by sleep. Thus did the Prophet on the way back from Khaybar. When he stopped for a rest toward the end of the night, he asked Bilāl to stay awake to keep watch for the *ṣubḥ* prayer, yet Bilāl himself was overcome by sleep, as reported in *Muwaṭṭa'*.[2]

Manipulation can also be verbal. An example is someone who, under the threat of death, is forced to utter blasphemous or illicit words, although coercion allows him to do so, according to the following Qur'anic verse: "As for anyone who denies God after having once attained faith – and this, to be sure, does not apply to one who does it under duress, while his heart remains true to his faith" (16:106). Another form of verbal manipulation is the use, by someone who fears persecution, of expressions whose meaning is unclear to the public. For example, when the great traditionalist, Abū ʿAbd Allāh al-Bukhārī, was questioned about the issue of the 'creation' of the Qur'an (*khalq al-Qur'an*), his answer was: "Our speech is part of our acts, and our acts are created."

However, this is not the meaning of the manipulation that we are examining here. Nor does our discussion include the use of manipulation in transactions to trap people in certain legal corollaries of which they are unaware. This is known as deceit (*taghrīr*), such as when one of two litigants resorts to reconciliation as a means to obtaining confession or concession from his or her counterpart. Therefore, the definition of manipulation in the terminology of the Shariʿah scholars is that given at the beginning of this chapter. Hence, Abū Isḥāq al-Shāṭibī, in the tenth proposition of the second section of *Kitāb al-Maqāṣid* in his book *ʿUnwān al-Taʿrīf*, explained it as follows.

> God has prescribed certain things and proscribed others absolutely without giving specific reasons (*asbāb*), such as the prescription of prayer and fasting (...) and the proscription of adultery and usury. He has also prescribed certain things and proscribed others for specific reasons, such as the prescription of zakah and expiations (*kaffārāt*), and the prohibition of a divorced woman [marrying before the end of her waiting period] and the use of items usurped or stolen. Thus, if the human agent (*mukallaf*) manages to evade his obligations or practice what is forbidden by such means as to make the obligatory appear optional and the forbidden lawful, then such conduct (*tasabbub*) is called manipulation (*taḥayyul*).[3]

Al-Shāṭibī, adduced a number of examples for analysis. This is also what Bukhārī meant in the chapter entitled *Kitāb al-Ḥiyal* [Book of Manipulation], of his Hadith collection. Here he cited the Prophetic Traditions abolishing stratagems (*ḥiyal*) and classified them, in the manner of the jurists, according to the different actions of the human agents (*taṣarrufāt al-mukallafīn*).[4] There is no doubt that stratagems in this sense are forbidden. In the second section of *Kitāb al-Maqāṣid* of *ᶜUnwan al-Taᶜrīf*, al-Shāṭibī wrote:

The Twelfth Proposition: since it has been established that the Shariᶜah injunctions (*aḥkām*) are instituted for the welfare (*maṣāliḥ*) of human beings, human acts are judged accordingly, for this constitutes the Lawgiver's purpose concerning them. If the act, both outwardly and inwardly (that is, in its benefit and inner wisdom), conforms to the original rule of legitimacy, then there is no problem. However, if its outward form conforms with the rules of the Shariᶜah, but it violates their inner wisdom and purpose, then it is invalid. This is because acts in the Shariᶜah (that is, which are meant to be performed according to its rules) are not an end in themselves (that is, are not meant merely for their appearance). They are meant for something beyond that, which consists of the inner meanings attributed to them, that is, the *maṣāliḥ* for which they have been prescribed. Therefore, any acts performed contrary to these conditions are contradicting the prescriptions of the Shariᶜah (*mashrūᶜāt*).[5]

In the second proposition of the same section, he said:

The Lawgiver's intent pertaining to the human agent (*mukallaf*) is that the latter's intent in the execution of prescribed acts must conform to His [that is, the Lawgiver's] intent in legislation (*tashrīᶜ*). This is clearly evidenced by the very institution (*waḍᶜ*) of the Shariᶜah itself, for we have already shown that it has been instituted for the well-being (*maṣāliḥ*) of humankind.[6]

In the third proposition of that section, he said:

> The Shariʿah prescriptions and proscriptions have been instituted exclusively for the realization of *maṣāliḥ* and the avoidance of *mafāsid*. If they are violated, then the associated acts will not achieve what is good or avoid what is evil.7

What al-Shāṭibī said can be summarized as follows. All prescribed acts are contingent on specific causes (*asbāb*), which have been classified as such only because they reflect the inner wisdom and underlying *maṣāliḥ* particularly associated with them by the Lawgiver. He has made those causes indicators of that wisdom and its relevant *maṣāliḥ*. Accordingly, if the act is stripped of that wisdom, its performance will then be devoid of its original purpose. For example, fighting might assume the same form and be carried out by similar means; however, it might be due to different causes and done for different purposes. It might be legitimate, such as fighting for the sake of God or fighting against a group of Muslims acting wrongly against another group, which are governed by different rules. It might also be illegitimate, such as fighting for the sake of booty or fame, as indicated by the Prophetic Tradition: "[God will] tell him [that is, the fighter] [on Judgment Day]: 'You fought so that you might be called a "brave warrior". And you were called so.'"8

Having considered carefully the different stratagems used to evade the Shariʿah injunctions and how they lead to the partial or total omission of the Shariʿah objectives we have found that manipulation does not follow one single pattern. Our thorough examination of the Shariʿah sources has enabled us to classify stratagems into five categories.

(1) There are stratagems resulting in the total omission of a Shariʿah objective (*maqṣad*) without replacing it with another. They consist of manipulation so as to create an obstacle (*māniʿ*) that will prevent the realization of a purpose prescribed by the Shariʿah. It thus consists of using an act as an impediment rather than the means to fulfilling the purpose intended by the Shariʿah. There should be no doubt that this category of stratagems is blameworthy and, therefore, illegal and that its user must be treated with the opposite of

his/her intention once it is known. Evidence to this effect is so abundant in the Qur'an and Sunnah that it yields certainty. Abū ᶜAbd Allāh al-Bukhārī mentioned it frequently in *Kitāb al-Ḥiyal* of his *Ṣaḥīḥ*, and so did al-Shāṭibī in Section 11 of *Kitāb al-Maqāṣid* in his *al-Muwāfaqāt*, although some of his citations are questionable.[9]

An example of this type of manipulation is the case of someone who donates his wealth one day before the end of the lunar year to avoid paying the zakah due on it, and then takes it back from the person to whom it was donated. Another example is that of someone consuming intoxicating substances to become drunk at prayer time and is therefore unable to pray. Of the same type are many kinds of credit sales used as means of practicing usury.

(2) There are stratagems used to omit a lawful practice to shift to another thing that is also lawful. That is, these stratagems consist of the use of the act as a means to something allowed, for it is something intended by the Lawgiver that the effect should follow from its cause.

This can be illustrated by the case of an irrevocably divorced woman (*mabtūtah*) proposing herself for marriage whereas her real intention is to make *khul*ᶜ[10] from her would-be new husband or provoke him to divorce her after consummating the marriage with him, so that it becomes lawful for her first husband to remarry her. Thus, marriage is used as a means to discharge herself from irrevocable divorce. Hence, when she marries the second man, her intended purpose is achieved lawfully. Another example is to employ one's accumulated money in trade lest it be decreased by zakah. By doing so, one is actually using the money in another lawful way. This results in spending the money on buying commercial goods, and this in turn leads to the reduction in saving to below the required level for zakah (*niṣāb*), thus qualifying for exemption from the zakah imposed on gold and silver coins (*naqdayn*).[11] Nevertheless, the advantage of this practice has shifted from benefiting the poor, to whom the zakah could have been paid, to benefiting the wider public thanks to its circulation in economic activity. Similarly, zakah is transferred to the merchandise in the person's charge.

Of the same category is to shift from the cause of a prescribed act to the cause of another equally prescribed act, in which respect the human agent is free to choose either of them. Upon realizing that one of them is more difficult for him than the other, he then chooses the easier of the two. An instance of this is the case of a person whose money has reached the *niṣāb* towards the end of the lunar year in the month of Dhū al-Ḥijjah. Then, this person decides to perform the hajj and spends his money on this lawful purpose so that the total falls below the *niṣāb*. When the end of the year comes, he has no money liable for zakah.

Generally speaking, this category of stratagems is lawful. Here, in fact, the agent omits one Shariʿah rule only to move to another, and forgoes one Shariʿah objective just to realize another, regardless of the differences between particular cases and examples.

(3) This category consists of stratagems employed to omit something prescribed by the Shariʿah in such a way as to move to another prescribed practice that is easier for the agent than what is omitted. An example is the wearing of leather socks (*khuffayn*) to avoid washing one's feet in ablution, thus shifting to wiping (*masḥ*).[12] Similarly, wearing leather socks is employed in its causality as a cause (*sabab*) rather than impediment (*māniʿ*) to wiping.

Another example is that of someone who, owing to the month of Ramadan coinciding with the hot season or because of forgetfulness, decides to go on a journey to avoid fasting in the heat and then compensate for it at a more suitable time. This is seeking license (*tarakhkhuṣ*) when facing hardship in performing the omitted rule (*ḥukm*), which is yet higher than legal exemption (*rukhṣah*) consisting of a total suspension of the original rule.

(4) This category consists of stratagems used in acts that do not contain important meanings intended by the Lawgiver. Resorting to this type of manipulation might lead to achieving certain objectives resembling those of the Lawgiver. Of this type are stratagems used in oaths that do not affect the rights of others, such as swearing not to enter the house or not to wear a specific dress. The Shariʿah rule is

that expiation (*kaffārah)* is obligatory for someone who swears an oath and then breaks it. The purpose is to venerate the name of God, Whom one has made witness to observing the oath. If one finds it hard to do so and seeks to be discharged from the oath in a manner that resembles observing it, then the purpose of revering God's name will be fulfilled. In this connection, Judge Abū Bakr ibn al-ʿArabī mentioned the following story in his book *al-ʿAwāṣim*. He said,

> I saw Imām Abū Bakr Fakhr al-Islām al-Shāshī[13] sitting in the court of the public gate of the caliphate palace. A man came to him and said: "I have sworn not to wear this dress." The Imām cut a piece the size of a digit from the man's dress, and then told him: "Now you can wear it and you are not guilty of breaking your oath."[14]

Scholars have a wide scope for ijtihad regarding the various details of this category of stratagems, and that is why there is much disagreement amongst them on this specific issue. Thus, Mālik's view is that such a person is duty bound to fulfill his oath, otherwise he is guilty of breaking it. In contrast, al-Shāshī was a Shāfiʿī jurist, and maybe he issued the fatwa reported by Ibn al-ʿArabī for someone whom he knew would not make expiation for breaking his oath, or someone whom he knew could not afford to feed the poor or manumit a slave. It might also be that he knew the man was either unable to fast or found fasting too difficult, such as people doing hard physical work. Therefore, he resorted to this fatwa as a means to preserving the sanctity of the oath in the mind of the inquirer. In a similar vein, some Ḥanafī jurists, when asked about someone's swearing not to enter the house, would advise the inquirer to climb through the window or the skylight.

(5) There are stratagems that do not contravene the Lawgiver's intent or that might even help in the realization of His purpose. Nevertheless, they do entail the loss of someone else's right or create another kind of harm. This category can be illustrated by the lengthening of the waiting-period of a divorced woman when divorce had no specific limit at the early period of Islam.

Mālik narrated in *Muwaṭṭa'* through two different chains of transmission the following:

> It used to be that a man would divorce his wife and then return to her before her waiting-period (*ʿiddah*) was over, and that was acceptable, even if he divorced her a thousand times. The man went to his wife and then divorced her and when the end of her waiting-period was in sight, he took her back and then divorced her and said, "No! By God, I will not go to you and you will never be able to marry again." God, Exalted is He, sent down, "A divorce may be [revoked] twice, whereupon the marriage must either be resumed in fairness or dissolved in a goodly manner" (2:229); and "But do not retain them against their will in order to hurt [them]: for he who does so sins indeed against himself. And do not take [these] messages of God in a frivolous spirit" (2:231).[15]

God is referring to pre-Islamic divorce customs, which were meant to harm the wife and, hence, He limited divorce to three times only. The same purpose, though, has been preserved. Of the same type is the example of a man marrying an irrevocably divorced woman (*mabtūtah*) with the intention of making it lawful for the man who divorced her to remarry her. Apparently, such an act conforms to the Shariʿah rules and fulfills the Lawgiver's purpose that consists of encouraging the husband to take back his divorced wife (*rajʿah*) provided she has married another man. However, in a Tradition reported on the authority of ʿAbd Allāh ibn Masʿūd by al-Tirmidhī who confirmed its authenticity, the Prophet cursed the person who behaved in this way.[16]

Admitting the authenticity of this tradition, the Prophet's strong condemnation of this act might, in my opinion, be due to either or both of the following two reasons. First, it might indicate that one lacks a sense of honor, for the real purpose of marriage is companionship, and, accordingly, a man should not make his wife available to others. It might also be a form of temporary marriage (*nikāḥ al-mutʿah*) according to the view forbidding this kind of contract.

Each of these two reasons thus constitutes part of the effective cause. In fact, scholars have disagreed on whether or not it is lawful for a man to take back his irrevocably divorced wife by this kind of marriage.

This question, however, requires further reflection, since its evil aspect concerns the *muḥallil* not the *muḥallal*,[17] unless the abolition of this kind of marriage is meant to treat its practitioner with the opposite of his improper purpose in manipulating the law. In this connection, the Prophet is reported to have said: "One should not prevent others from watering their animals with the surplus of his water in order to prevent them from benefiting from the surplus of grass."[18] Withholding a surplus water owned by someone is lawful because it is an exercise of one's freedom in dealing with one's property, according to our view[19] that charity is not obligatory. However, since it has been used as a means of depriving other people of benefiting from the surplus of grass, withholding a surplus of water was forbidden, as herdsmen do not take their livestock to places where there is no water.

The same applies to the abolition of verbal stratagems in oaths which are meant to deprive people of their rights; hence, oaths are interpreted according to the adjured person's intention.

Once these categories of stratagems are established, those who wish to take them up with open minds and without bias will certainly realize that the proofs usually adduced to support legal manipulation consist of practices that have not been properly scrutinized. It will not then be difficult for them to apply those proofs to their proper contexts and trace their nuances. Accordingly, what has been transmitted in this respect as part of the Islamic Shariʿah can easily be resolved. For example, acts that were given provisions varying from the established rules governing their analogs (*naẓā'ir*) are so either because they happened at the beginning of Revelation and therefore the Prophet exempted them, or because they concerned specific situations.

To the former category belongs what has been narrated in Mālik's *Muwaṭṭa'* and Muslim's *Ṣaḥīḥ* regarding the abolition of adoption in Islam.

The latter category comprises what is in the Tradition concerning a man whom the Prophet married to a woman who had entrusted herself to the Prophet [so that he might contract her marriage with anyone at his discretion]. The man said: "I have nothing for her dower." Then, God's Apostle told the man: "Go, I have married her to you for the part of the Qur'an which you know."[20] There is no doubt that this was a specific case, which was given a form resembling that of marriage and dower to preserve as much as possible the sanctity of the dower according to one interpretation of the expression "for the part of the Qur'an which you know" in the Prophet's statement.

We should not expatiate on the content of earlier revelations. This is because the available details of those laws are insufficient for us to ascertain the extent to which the known forms of what we call stratagems differ from the rest of the provisions of that legislation. For example, the Qur'anic story of the prophet Ayyūb (Job): "[And finally We told him;] 'Now take in your hand a small bunch of grass, and strike her with it, and you will not break your oath'" (38:44), has been interpreted as follows. Ayyūb swore an oath that he would punish his wife for her blasphemy with a hundred stripes. However, when his anger was spent, he felt pity for her, which means that he wavered about fulfilling his oath. Then, God ordained him to strike her with a bunch of grass. It is likely that this was a special provision instituted by God for him as one of two possible ways of fulfilling such an oath, just as God has given us provision for the expiation of broken oaths. It might also be a special permission that God gave to the apostle, for God can allow His apostles whatever He wills for they are preserved from making light of God's name.

Nor do we need to discuss the Qur'anic story of the prophet Yūsuf (Joseph): "In this way did We contrive for Joseph [the attainment of his heart's desire]: under the King's law, he would [otherwise] have been unable to detain his brother, had not God so willed" (12:76). If this was manipulation, it was meant to achieve a benefit that no revered Divine law had forbidden. Clearly, the phrase "under the King's law" refers to the Pharaoh; hence, the attribution of the law to that king indicates that it was not a Divine law.[21]

23

Prohibition of Evasive Legal Means

In the terminology of Muslim jurists, the compound noun *sadd al-dharā'iᶜ* is used to refer to the nullification (*ibṭāl*) of those acts which would result in considerable harm, though they are not evil in themselves. According to al-Māzarī in his commentary on ᶜAbd al-Wahhāb al-Baghdādī's[1] *al-Talqīn*, "The blocking of means (*sadd al-dharīᶜah*) is the prohibition of what is lawful so that it is not used as a means to what is unlawful."[2] This practice is closely related to manipulation (*taḥayyul*). However, stratagems are those acts carried out by some people independently to evade certain obligations by using means that are also lawful in the Shariᶜah, so that their behavior apparently conforms to the Shariᶜah rules. However, the term *dharīᶜah* used here refers to what leads to evil in most circumstances, whether or not human agents intended it. Likewise, means (*dharā'iᶜ*) and stratagems (*ḥiyal*) vary in two respects: in generality (*ᶜumūm*) and specificity (*khuṣūṣ*) on the one hand, and intention and non-intention on the other. Furthermore, stratagems and means differ in another respect. Whereas stratagems refer exclusively to what leads to the omission of a Shariᶜah objective, means (*dharā'iᶜ*) might or might not produce the same result.

That good practices might lead to evil consequences is, you should know, well known in much of human behavior. Indeed, it might even happen that such consequences only take place when a process reaches its state of perfection. For example, the perfect state of fire, consisting of combustion from which people actually benefit, is achieved by the destructive manifestation of the flames. Accordingly, the Shariʿah resorts to the blocking of means whenever the likelihood of evil consequences outweighs the original good of the act. Hence, the means that must be blocked are those acts whose evil consequences prevail over their original good. In Section 94 of his book *al-Furūq*, Qarāfī divided the means leading to evil consequences into three categories:

1. Means in respect of which there is unanimous agreement between the jurists that they should not be blocked, such as preventing the cultivation of grapevines for fear that wine would be made out of them and preventing the construction of terraced houses for fear of adultery.

2. Means on the blocking of which there is unanimous agreement amongst the jurists, such as digging a well on a public footpath without a fence.

3. Means on the blocking of which there is disagreement amongst the jurists, such as deferred sales (*buyūʿ al-ājāl*).[3]

Qarāfī did not, however, discuss the question of why some of those means must be counted rather than others. In my view, the answer is that the Shariʿah aims at striking a balance between the inherent good of the act that is used as a means and its possible evil consequences. Thus, the question falls under the rule governing the conflict of *maṣāliḥ* and *mafāsid*, which we discussed in conjunction with the all-purpose principle of legislation in chapter 12. Accordingly, the means that are prohibited consist of things whose evil consequences prevail over their original good, like the digging of wells on roads without a fence. However, those practices whose original good prevails over their evil consequences, such as the cultivation of grapevines, are not forbidden. Nevertheless, regardless of the consequences of those means, society's need of them and that their consequences might or might not be achieved by other means have a great impact on blocking certain means rather than others.

Yet, this should not lead to the belief that the society's need of those means stems from their absolute need (*ḍarūrah*) for its existence. What is meant here is that if the act, which is used as the means, has been forbidden, numerous people will face hardship. For example, although society can dispense with grapes, burdening the people with that deprivation is contrary to the magnanimity (*samāḥah*) of the Shariʿah. For this reason, the permissibility of cultivating grapevines has been given priority over the possible result of making wine from grapes. In contrast, if the construction of terraced houses is forbidden, this will cause very serious harm that is almost intolerable; thus it belongs to what is greatly needed (*ḥājī*) by society. Although the possible evil consequences of adultery are far greater than those resulting from the consumption of wine, they are extremely unlikely.

Thus, the principle of blocking the means has an important legislative purpose in mind. This purpose has been confirmed by inductive inference from the various dispositions of the Shariʿah in its detailed rules, its ways of dealing with the different nations of the world, and the strategy it established to achieve its objectives. Therefore, it manifests itself at three different levels. Careful analysis of human behavior, from the view of a means to evil consequences, shows that it falls into two main categories:

1. The first category consists of acts that are undoubtedly means to evil consequences. Evil is one of their constant properties. In other words, it constitutes an integral part of their essence. The scrutiny of this type is one of the fundamental principles of the Shariʿah and is the basis of numerous textually enunciated provisions (*aḥkām manṣūṣah*) of the Shariʿah, such as the prohibition of intoxicants.

2. The second category consists of acts that might or might not lead to evil consequences. The likelihood of evil varies from high to low. This category is also the subject of textually enacted legislation, such as the prohibition of selling foodstuff before one has taken full possession of it.[4] Certain varieties of this type did not happen during the Prophet's time but afterwards, which is why

jurists have differed in their judgment of them vacillating between sanction and prohibition. Their indecision is due to the fact that the evil consequences of those varieties might be manifest or covert, frequent or infrequent, temporary or permanent, and opposed or not by what necessitates the avoidance of evil.

Likewise, whereas the first category is the basis (*aṣl*) for reasoning by analogy (*qiyās*) in this respect, the second category is an area where *qiyās* might be evident (*jalī*) or concealed (*khafī*),[5] depending on how the jurist succeeds in establishing the relevance of the act in question to the original case (*aṣl*). Moreover, the consideration of those means (*dharā'iʿ*) is thus revealed to belong to the preservation of good (*ḥifẓ al-maṣāliḥ*) and the prevention of evil (*dar' al-mafāsid*). To this category belongs the contracts of deferred sales that take various forms. Mālik ibn Anas disapproved of these contracts and forbade them on the basis that people frequently use them as means to legalize usurious transactions, which are evil in themselves.[6] In his view, people's intention to enter into these contracts led to their propagation, and so they resulted in the evil (*mafsadah*) of usury, which was forbidden. That was why Mālik was inclined here to take suspicion into consideration, for people's intentions have no impact on the nature of legislation. The decision would have been different, had it not been because when these transactions prevail, people seeking to legitimize what has been forbidden to them would purposely pursue the evil consequences.

This is an important aspect of Mālik's thought that none has properly understood. In fact, as pointed out by Qarāfī, it has been so misunderstood that some able jurists said: "Since the prohibition of these transactions is due to suspicion, those which are created by people of merit and religious piety should not be prohibited."[7] Far from it! People's intentions have no influence on changing Divine legislation. However, they have been taken as an indication of their persistence in legalizing the unlawful. Do you not see that intention has no consideration outside such circumstances?

For instance, if a person, who used to deal in usurious transactions during the time of pagan ignorance (*Jāhiliyyah*), converted his usurious dealings into buying-in-advance (*salam*) transactions when he embraced Islam, his practice would not be considered unlawful. The reason is that even though he replaced his usury-incurred profits with those based on *salam*, his transactions were thus free of the evil (*mafsadah*) of usurious dealings, which were prohibited. Moreover, his practice had fulfilled a good purpose (*maṣlaḥah*), for which *salam* was allowed. And since, as we have shown previously, the Shariᶜah is not vindictive, it is not its purpose to deprive such a person of his profits earned in a lawful manner simply because of his intention.

Thus, it becomes clear that the consideration of blocking the means is open to both restriction and relaxation according to the level of people's self-discipline, as we will see in our discussion of the concept of *wāziᶜ* in chapter 27. If the term *sadd al-dharā'iᶜ* had not been used specifically to designate blocking the means of evil as shown earlier, we would have liked to say the following. As correctly stated by Qarāfī in his *Tanqīḥ al-Fuṣūl*, just as the Shariᶜah has blocked certain means, it has also allowed others.[8]

Yet, since we have followed the jurists' terminology in this respect, we should not, however, omit to draw the reader's attention to the following point. The Shariᶜah has concerned itself with the means to what is good and allowed them by subsuming them under the rule of what is obligatory, even when their formal appearance might entail their prohibition or mere permissibility. This is known in *uṣūl al-fiqh* under the dictum "that which is a means to something obligatory is also obligatory" and in fiqh as precaution (*iḥtiyāṭ*). Do you not see that fighting for the sake of God in its form is an evil practice, since it results in the loss of lives and property? However, it is one of the great obligations because it is a means to protecting the security of the Muslim community. If people relinquish fighting altogether, the loss will be far greater. This particular case falls under the rule according to which human acts are divided into means (*wasā'il*) and ends (*maqāṣid*), which will be discussed in Part III of this book [chapter 32]. Therefore, one should be careful not to confuse these two issues.

One more thing must be pointed out here concerning the understanding of the Shariᶜah and practice of ijtihad. It is the distinction between excessiveness (*ghuluw*) and the blocking of means. Indeed, this is a subtle distinction, for while the question of the blocking of means arises whenever there is evil, excessiveness means the indulgence in subjoining a permissible practice to what is obligatory or forbidden. Excessiveness includes also performing some Shariʿah prescriptions in a more difficult way than what is actually required, on the pretext of fearing to fall short of the Lawgiver's purpose. This attitude has been described in the Sunnah as exaggeration (*taʿammuq*)[9] and hair-splitting (*tanaṭṭuʿ*).[10]

Excessiveness thus exists at different levels. It may be clarified as devoutness (*waraʿ*),[11] whether individually by committing oneself to some difficult practices or by compelling others to accept hardship. Other degrees of excessiveness may belong to blameworthy evil-whispering (*waswasah*). Here, indeed, jurists and jurisconsults are faced with a serious challenge. They ought to avoid the pitfall of excessiveness and be careful what measures they prescribe for the people.

24

Precision and Determination in Islamic Legislation

I have already shown that one of the most important characteristics of the Shariʿah is associating its ordinances with specific meanings. To that I should add the following. Since the Shariʿah has intended its ordinances to be easily implemented by the people under all circumstances, it has also included precision *(ḍabṭ)* and determination *(taḥdīd)* so that its meanings are clearly understood. Likewise, it has established those attributes as indicators (*amārāt*) to the scholars of the meanings underlying the legislation. For ordinary people, it has used clear-cut terms (*ḥudūd*) and precise measures (*ḍawābiṭ*) encompassing those meanings that might be beyond their grasp. These terms and measures are a suitable guide for scholars when the deeper meanings implied by those attributes are unclear. They are also necessary for non-scholars to increase their understanding of the deeper meanings and ambiguous attributes intended by the legislation and encapsulated by those terms and measures. Therefore, knowledge of all that has been mentioned is indispensable to anyone seeking to know *Maqāṣid al-Shariʿah*.

This is, indeed, a subtle point that has escaped the attention of many jurists. Mālik highlighted this in a statement in *Muwaṭṭa'* concerning the transaction called *khiyār al-majlis*.[1] He mentioned the Tradition narrated by ʿAbd Allāh ibn ʿUmar, in which the Prophet is reported to have said: "Both parties in a business transaction have the right of withdrawal as long as they have not separated, except in the transaction called *khiyār* (choice)." Then he made the following comment: "There is no specified limit nor any matter which applied in this case according to us." He meant that it was difficult to rely on this report as a basis for legislation on the transaction called *khiyār*, since there is no specification in it of the *majlis* nor is there any practice to clarify it. Moreover, the *majlis* is undetermined, for both parties might be on board ship or in a vehicle, etc.

Therefore, when applying *qiyās*, the jurists focus their whole attention on the evident and regular attributes as the basis of the Shariʿah ordinances and provisions. None the less, they also explicitly acknowledge that the existence of those attributes indicates the underlying meaning that may be called wisdom (*ḥikmah*), *maṣlaḥah* or *mafasdah*. Anyhow, the Shariʿah categorically avoids imprecision in its provisions and ordinances, for this is a characteristic of the rule of pagan ignorance (*Jāhiliyyah*), against which God has warned us in the following verse: "Do they, perchance, desire [to be ruled by] the law of pagan ignorance?" (5:50).[2]

Under that regime, the management of people's affairs was based on mere impressions arising from circumstances, such as, for example, divorce and *rajʿah*,[3] which had no specific terms or limits. It was a practice that the Qur'an clearly condemned in the following verse: "But do not retain them [that is, women] against their will to hurt [them]: for he who does so sins indeed against himself" (2:231). The same is also true of the division of inheritance. In this respect, Judge Ismāʿīl ibn Isḥāq[4] mentioned that people in the age of pagan ignorance never gave wives and daughters the inheritance rights that Islam has given them, nor did they have any definite rules of inheritance that could be observed. The same applies to polygamy and the confirmation of lineal attribution (*luḥūq al-nasab*).

Only very few instances can be excluded from this general state of affairs, such as the amount of blood money for both members of the elite (*khāṣṣah*) and the general public (*ʿāmmah*). Thus, the amount of blood money for an ordinary person used to be one hundred camels, whereas that of an aristocrat was double or even more which they called *takāyul*.[5] When Islam came with its Divine provisions and rules, it totally abolished the chaos in all aspects of life by exclusively adopting a method of precision and of determination. Therefore, the Shariʿah has ordained its followers to abide by its terms and limits (*ḥudūd*). Hence, if a person performs the noon prayer (*ẓuhr*) before midday, it will not be valid. From a thorough survey of the ways and means used by the Shariʿah to achieve precise determination, I have found that they include six methods.

1. The first method is to define essences and meanings clearly in order to prevent any confusion. Thus, each meaning is explained in detail, together with its properties and effects, such as specifying the levels of kinship that qualify for inheritance or the prohibition of unmarriageable kin. Only these considerations are taken into account, barring all other irregular and indefinite considerations, like love, friendship, benefit, or adoption, whatever their degrees. The Qur'an says: "As for your parents and your children – you know not which of them is more deserving of benefit from you: [therefore this] ordinance from God. Verily, God is All-Knowing, Wise"(4:11), "so, too, has He never made your adopted sons [truly] your sons: these are but [figures of] speech uttered by your mouths – whereas God speaks the [absolute] truth: and it is He alone who can show [you] the right path." (33:4). It is also reported in an authentic Tradition that when the Prophet asked Abū Bakr for ʿĀ'ishah's hand in marriage, Abū Bakr said: "But I am your brother!" The Prophet said, "You are my brother in God's religion and His Book, but she [ʿĀ'ishah] is lawful for me to marry."[6] This category also includes the link between the consumption of wine and slight drunkenness, regardless of whether the wine is made from grapes or dates.

   The phrase "to prevent any confusion" can be explained as follows. Confusion is present for the clear-sighted jurist experienced in distinguishing the properties of legal essences (*māhiyyāt sharʿiyyah*), although some people might be confused over certain essences sharing similar properties. This is illustrated by the following Qur'anic verse: "for they say, 'Buying and selling is but a kind of usury' – the while God has made buying and selling lawful and usury unlawful" (2:275). Selling and usury might look the same at first sight, for both of them consist of financial transactions meant for profit, especially when selling includes deferment. Therefore, God indicated by the expression "the while God has made buying and selling lawful and usury unlawful" that He allowed one and prohibited the other only because of their different essences and properties. Thus, selling consists of a transaction between two parties entailing an exchange by both sides, whereas usury is a transaction affecting only one party, that is the lender to satisfy the need of the borrower. As a result of this distinction, seeking profit has been allowed for the parties engaged in selling, whereas it has been forbidden in loan contracts to seek any profit. The alternative to usury is that either one should lend money simply for the sake of fulfilling someone else's need or keep one's money.

2. The second method consists of mere correspondence between the name and the named, such as associating the canonical punishment (*ḥadd*) for the consumption of intoxicants with one single drink of wine. This is because if the punishment was made conditional upon the actual effect of the intoxicant (*iskār*), it would be subject to much irregularity and indeterminacy. Susceptibility to intoxication varies greatly from one person to another, thus resulting in difficulty and confusion in implementing the penalty.

   On the other hand, if the punishment was applicable only to the utmost degree of drunkeness, that is, overwhelming intoxication, serious harm would result before that state was reached. This equally applies to linking the validity of selling fruits to reddening and of dates to yellowness.[7] It is also true of making the payment of the rest of the dower conditional upon the consumation of the marriage with the wife[8] and making contracts binding by the offer and acceptance formula uttered by the different parties.

3. The third method consists of specifying amounts (*taqdīr*), such as specifying the minimum level (*niṣāb*) of cereals and money, etc. for liability to pay zakah, limiting the number of wives in polygamy, setting a limit for divorce, determining the value of stolen goods for the implementation of the theft penalty (*ḥadd*) according to the juristic view upholding the minimum scale (*niṣāb*) for this crime,[9] fixing the minimum amount of dower,[10] and determining a maximum distance of 12 miles between the home of the infant's guardian and that of the nurse according to Mālikī jurists.

4. The fourth method is timing, such as the elapsing of one year for the payment of zakah on money and property, the rise of Pleiades for the zakah on cattle, four months for forswearing one's wife (*īlā'*),[11] one year for the revocation of marriage in the case of certain defects,[12] two months for the inability to provide maintenance for one's wife,[13] four months and ten days for the waiting-period of a widow, and the elapsing of one year for the prescription of the right of pre-emption.

   Some of our scholars maintained the view of not giving credence to a woman in her waiting-period (*muʿtaddah*) if she asserts that it is less than forty-four days. Indeed, Ibn al-ʿArabī held that a waiting-term of less than three months should not be accepted, a view that became the rule of thumb amongst the people of *Ifrīqiyyah* (Tunisia) out of concern for precision.

5. The fifth method is to specify the properties determining the meaning of the things contracted upon, such as specifying the kind of work in hire and requiring a dower and a guardian for a valid marriage to distinguish it from adultery.[14]

6. The sixth method consists of inclusion (*iḥāṭah*) and determination. Examples are the requirement for the cultivation of a wasteland (*iḥyā' al-mawāt*) is that it should be so far from the village or city that the latter's 'smoke cannot be seen from it';

the prohibition of logging in the sanctum of Makkah (*ḥaram*); and the stipulation that property should be kept in a safe place (*ḥirz)* to differentiate theft from pilferage (*khilsah*).[15]

25

Rigor and Mercy in Enforcing and Observing Islamic Legislation

The topics discussed so far shall be sufficient to help you realize that one of the objectives of the Shariʿah is that its legislation must be implemented in the community and that all its members must abide by it. This is because its intended benefits cannot be achieved without implementation and observance of its rules. Thus, the community's submission to the Shariʿah is a great objective, and the utmost motive for its observance and implementation is that it is God's Word to humankind. Abiding by its rules is therefore a matter of faith, to which Muslims commit themselves willingly, because by this they please their Lord and Sustainer, and they seek His Mercy and the granting of success in this world and salvation in the Hereafter. Hence, we read the following in the Qur'an, "Now there has come to you from God a light, and a clear Divine writ, through which God shows to all that seek His goodly acceptance the paths leading to salvation and, by His Grace, brings them out of the depths of darkness into the light and guides them onto a straight way" (5:15–16).

Accordingly, all the Shariʿah ordinances (*aḥkām sharʿiyyah*) conveyed by the Prophet were revealed to him. The Shariʿah scholars from the generation of the Companions onward have always sought that their juridical views and doctrines be derived from, and grounded in, its fundamental sources as enshrined in the Qur'an and Sunnah. That is why we find them in many instances levelling strong criticism against people who resort to mere speculative opinion (*ra'y*) without the basis of any evidence from the Qur'an or Sunnah. To achieve its objective mentioned above, the Shariʿah adopted two techniques that have been applied equally. One is the application of strictness (*ḥazm*) and determination in the implementation of its rules. The other is the application of ease and mercy in a way that would not lead to the omission of its objectives.

STRICTNESS AND DETERMINATION

The Shariʿah has paved the way for it by means of exhortation and instilling fear. Thus, we read in the Qur'an God's statement: "These are the bounds set by God; do not, then, transgress them: for they who transgress the bounds set by God – it is they, they who are evildoers!" (2:229), etc. In an authentic Tradition, the Prophet is reported to have said: "If somebody innovates a practice which is not in harmony with the principles of our religion, then it is rejected."[1] It is also reported regarding the manumission of Barīrah that the Prophet addressed the people and said:

> What is wrong with the people who make conditions which are not in the Book of God? Any condition that is not in the Book of God is invalid even if it is a hundred conditions. The decree of God is truer and the conditions of God are firmer, and the clientage (*walā'*) belongs only to the manumitter.[2]

From such teachings has originated in Islamic jurisprudence the rule according to which "the legally inexistent is the same as the really inexistent,"[3] which has many ramifications and many applications (*furūʿ*). Of similar provenance is the rule stating that "prohibitions (*nahy*) entail vitiation (*fasād*),"[4] which is an established rule in both *uṣūl al-fiqh* and fiqh. These rules aim at preventing people from ignoring the objectives of the Shariʿah, for such an attitude will ultimately lead to its total suspension.

For this reason, the Shariʿah pays great attention to the implementation of its rules and provisions, even when it is clear that none of its objectives would be violated. This is illustrated by the prohibition of a bequest (*waṣiyyah*) to the heirs even by less than one-third of one's property, although the Shariʿah has permitted bequests to non-heirs, which makes devoting one-third in bequests to one's heirs seem more justifiable. Nevertheless, this has been forbidden solely for preserving the purpose of inheritance, namely, the specification of inviolable definite shares, thus abolishing the practice of the era of pagan ignorance. Hence, bequests to heirs has been absolutely forbidden, whereas it has been permitted to bequeath upto one-third of the property to non-heirs.

To achieve fully the objective of applying strictness and determination, the Shariʿah has required the institution of trustworthy and powerful individuals whose task should be to implement its provisions and rules in society by both desire and fear, that is, by exhortation and the use of force. This has been alluded to in the following verse:

> Indeed, [even afore time] did We send forth Our apostles with all evidence of [this] truth; and through them We bestowed revelation from on high, and [thus gave you] a balance [wherewith to weigh right and wrong], so that men might behave with equity (*qisṭ*); and We bestowed [upon you] from on high [the ability to make use of] iron, in which there is awesome power as well as [a source of] benefits for man. (57:25)[5]

Therefore, the Prophet executed the *ḥudūd* penalties and appointed governors and magistrates in distant areas, and this became an established practice of his. As ʿUthmān ibn ʿAffān, said: "God deters by the state power (*sulṭān*) what may not be restrained by exhortations of the Qur'an."[6]

Accordingly, it is one of the fundamental principles of the Islamic system of governance to appoint caliphs, rulers, magistrates, and consultants (*ahl al-shūrā*) in *iftā'*, police and *ḥisbah* as well as deputies in each of these offices. The purpose of all these offices is to implement the Shariʿah provisions and rules concerning the rights of the community and those of private individuals. According to Qarāfī in his book *al-Furūq*, for each of these offices a number of personal, mental, and practical qualities and conditions are required of the appointees so that the tasks entrusted to them will be fulfilled correctly.7

EASE AND MERCY

This technique can be explained as follows. As has already been shown, the Islamic Shariʿah is characterized by the ease of its acceptability by human beings because, far from being hard and vindictive, it is a natural and magnanimous law. Likewise, it uses all possible means of ease and mercy to encourage people to pursue what is good for them by implementing its rules, for legislation will have no purpose if it is not implemented. This characteristic of ease has three aspects in the Shariʿah.

1. Its rules and ordinances are grounded in ease (*taysīr*) out of consideration of the general circumstances of human beings. Thus, God says in the Qur'an: "it is He Who has elected you [to carry His message], and has laid no hardship on you in [anything that pertains to] religion" (22:78), and He also says: "God wills that you shall have ease, and does not will you to suffer hardship" (2:185), etc.

2. Under certain circumstances that might face the whole of society or individuals, the Shariʿah changes its rules and provisions from strictness and restriction to ease and indulgence, thus attenuating what might bear hardship and difficulty. To this effect, God says in the Qur'an:

   And why should you not eat of that over which God's name has been pronounced, seeing that He has so clearly spelled out to you what He has forbidden you [to eat] unless you are compelled [to do so]? (6:119);

   He has forbidden to you only carrion, and blood, and the flesh of swine, and that over which any name other than God's has been invoked; but if one is driven by necessity – neither coveting it nor exceeding his immediate need – no sin shall be upon him: for, behold, God is Much-Forgiving, a Dispenser of Grace. (2:173)

For this reason, it has become one of the fundamental principles of Islamic jurisprudence that "Hardship calls for ease"[8] – and this pertains to the question of license (*rukhṣah*).

3. The Sharīʿah has not left its addressees any excuse justifying their failure to abide by its rules, for it is grounded in profound wisdom and sound rationality and characterized by precision and determination. Thus, God says in the Qur'an:

Do they, perchance, desire [to be ruled by] the law of pagan ignorance? But for people who have inner certainty, who could be a better lawgiver than God? (5:50);

[Say: "Our life takes its] hue from God (*ṣibghat Allāh*)! And who could give a better hue [to life] than God, if we but truly worship Him?" (2:138)

26

Public and Individual License

Since we have already come across the question of license (*rukhṣah*), we must deal with this topic more clearly and in greater detail. In fact, I have found that the jurists have omitted certain aspects of license. Of course, they are agreed that license consists in changing an act prescribed for an individual or a community from strictness and difficulty to ease and indulgence owing to some compelling circumstances requiring the Shariʿah to forgo its purpose of realizing a benefit or removing an evil. The relaxation is achieved by tolerating an evil act that is originally forbidden. They illustrated this meaning of license by the permission for the person under need to eat carrion. In this connection, Shāṭibī has shown that while *ʿazīmah* pertains to the principle of original obligation (*taklīf*) as such, *rukhṣah* emanates from the rule of attenuation (*takhfīf*), and that both constitute categorical general and permanent rules of the Shariʿah.[1]

I have noticed, though, that the jurists have discussed license and illustrated it only with regard to individuals under circumstances of need.[2] Nevertheless, when we examine the topic carefully and find that license stems from hardship (*ḥaraj*) and need (*ḍarūrah*), then clearly we should consider it at both individual and community level. Accordingly, we have found that need is usually general and permanent, and this constitutes the basis of universal legislation on practices belonging to general categories of acts that were originally forbidden, such as *salam*,[3] fruit-sharecropping (*mughārasah*),[4] and general sharecropping (*musāqāh*).[5]

Despite the harm resulting from these practices and the likelihood that they might result in financial loss requiring their prohibition, they have been allowed because of society's great need of them. Thus, they are subsumed under the *ḥājī* category, as mentioned by Shāṭibī in his discussion of *rukhṣah* and *ʿazīmah*.[6] Hence, they belong to what is permanently permissible. We have also found that there are instances of individual and temporary necessity that have been expounded by the Qur'an and Sunnah, as illustrated by the following verse: "but if one is driven by necessity – neither coveting it nor exceeding his immediate need – no sin shall be upon him" (2:173). The jurists confined themselves to this kind when they discussed the issue of necessity.

However, midway between these two types of necessity, is a third, which has been neglected. It consists of a permanent general necessity whereby the whole community or most of it might be in a situation which would require the permissibility of a prohibited act to achieve a specific objective. An example is preserving the safety of a community whose temporary and general circumstances are variable. There is no doubt that the consideration of this kind of necessity when it occurs is more important than individual requirements. Therefore, the rules governing the circumstances in which that general necessity arises need to be modified.

There are not many cases of this kind. An example is permanent renting (*kirā' mu'abbad*), whose lawfulness was approved in a fatwa issued towards the end of the ninth [fifteenth] century by some Andalusian jurists, such as Ibn Sirāj[7] and Ibn Manẓūr,[8] concerning *waqf* land. People lost interest in renting *waqf* land for the cultivation of cereals, owing to the hard work and high cost that it entailed, for it was left lying fallow for long periods. They were equally discouraged from renting it for growing fruit trees or building owing to the short leases.

For these reasons, and also because developers and gardeners would be unwilling to demolish the buildings that they had erected on that land or uproot the trees that they had grown on it, Ibn Sirāj and Ibn Manẓūr issued a fatwa allowing the permanent lease of *waqf* land. In their view, this practice would not cause any harm, since the land would not cease to exist.[9] The tenth [sixteenth-century] jurist, Nāṣir al-Dīn al-Laqqānī,[10] followed them in Egypt by issuing a fatwa allowing the hoarding (*iḥkār*)[11] of *waqf* property. These fatwas became the basis of popular practice in Morocco and Tunisia and took different forms. A similar judgment was the basis of the fatwa issued by the Ḥanafī scholars of Bukhārā concerning the permissibility of *bayʿ al-wafā'* for grapes due to the farmers' need for money to spend on the cultivation of their vineyards before they bore fruit; hence, they had to borrow that money.

It might happen that greater forms of necessity occur that require special attention to give them appropriate rulings. In the section dealing with the exceptions to the general rules governing exchanges in his book *al-Qawāʿid al-Kubrā*, ʿIzz al-Dīn ibn ʿAbd al-Salām explained this point as follows:

> If the unlawful overwhelms the world to the extent that nothing lawful can be found, it is permissible to use of it what will satisfy people's needs. That license, however, must not be restricted to the level of necessity, for this would lead to the weakening of Muslims and the domination of infidels and rebellious people over the land of Islam. It would also cause the collapse of crafts (*ḥiraf*) and businesses (*ṣanā'iʿ*) indispensable for achieving people's welfare... However, people must not indulge in the use of unlawful money in the way they would with what is lawful; they must rather limit themselves to what is really needed. This can be illustrated by the following example. Suppose there is a property whose owner is unknown [at present] but who might be known in the future. Of course, if there is no chance of knowing him/her, this case cannot be imagined, for the property would be transferred to the public treasury. It is allowed to use such property only before being able to know the owner, because public interest is as important as personal necessity. In fact, if a person is driven by necessity to take someone else's property by force, he is allowed to do so. Indeed, he must do so if he fears the danger of death because of hunger, heat, or cold. And if this is permitted to save one soul, how would it be in respect of the survival of numerous souls?[12]

This is a situation that has been considered by the *mujtahid* scholars in their various dispositions to derive the Shariʿah rulings with varying degrees of success. In fact, we might find the same jurist approximating to the truth or moving away from it in dealing with this issue owing to various factors, such as the conflict of evidences, etc.

27

Wāziᶜ: Its Meaning and Varieties

We are now returning to the topic of enforcement and observance of the Shariᶜah, after the discussion of license. So, we must now show how the Shariᶜah has used, in respect of the observance and implementation of its legislative rules (*tashrīᶜ*) by human beings, the different kinds of restraint (*wāziᶜ*) that prevent people from ignoring its limits.

First, it invokes inborn self-restraint (*wāziᶜ jibillī*). This type of *wāziᶜ* is considered sufficient so that the Shariᶜah did not have to elaborate on its legislation. Human beings instinctively seek certain benefits or avoid certain evils. Examples are eating food, wearing clothes, and protecting one's wife and children.

Likewise, we do not, for instance, find in the Shariᶜah commandments regarding the protection of wives, because this is part of a man's inborn disposition (*jibillah*) and the very existence of a marital relationship is sufficient to stimulate husbands to protect their wives.[1] Similarly, we seldom find the Shariᶜah commanding people to protect their children, except in some specific circumstances in which the Arabs neglected them, such as burying baby daughters alive (*wa'd*). Thus, the Qur'an says in this regard: "Hence, do not kill your children for fear of poverty: it is We who shall provide sustenance for them as well as for you. Verily, killing them is a great sin" (17:31).[2]

For this reason, in dealing with serious matters in respect of which it fears a lack of the religio-spiritual self-restraint (*wāziᶜ dīnī*), it is characteristic of the Shariᶜah to depict them in such a way as to make them look like human instinct. Similarly, it has dealt with the prohibition of marrying one's mother-in-law or one's stepdaughter. By likening the step-parents of the husband and wife to their natural parents, the Shariᶜah has attached the relationship by marriage (*ṣihr*) to lineage (*nasab*) as a means of transforming self-restraint against committing adultery with one's stepdaughter or mother-in-law into something similar to human instinct. Hence, God says in the Qur'an:

> Forbidden to you are your mothers, your daughters, your sisters, your aunts paternal and maternal, a brother's daughters, a sister's daughters; your foster-mothers, your foster-sisters; your mothers-in-law; and your step-daughters – who are your foster children – born of your wives with whom you have consummated your marriage; but if you have not consummated your marriage, you will incur no sin [by marrying their daughters]; and [forbidden to you are] the spouses of the sons who have sprung from your loins; and [you are forbidden] to have two sisters [as your wives] at the same time but what is past is past: for, behold, God is indeed Much-Forgiving, a Dispenser of Grace. (4:23)

Commenting on this verse, Fakhr al-Dīn al-Rāzī said:

> If a man marries a woman, and then his father and son are not allowed in her presence and the woman's mother and daughter are not allowed in the man's presence, the woman will thus be like a prisoner in her own home and many of the benefits of the two spouses will consequently be suspended. However, if that association is permitted without inviolable boundaries (*ḥurmah*), it might happen that some would incline to each other. If the man then marries his mother-in-law or stepdaughter, this will result in severe alienation between her and them, for resentment of relatives is most hurtful for a person,[3] thus leading to separation and divorce. However, when the proscription on the basis of relationship by marriage is sanctioned, this will put an end to any covetous inclinations and that evil will be prevented, thus protecting the marital relationship between the spouses against any harm.

> Therefore, it is clear that the purpose of this proscription is to safeguard and strengthen the relationship between the husband and wife.[4]

To al-Rāzī's words we can add that it is the Lawgiver's intent to transform the adultery that might ensue from intimate association into a taboo by resorting to the instinctive restraint rather than the religio-spiritual ban; because it is impossible to have recourse to the blocking of means in social intercourse, as he himself has shown.

In fact, it is not difficult to transform religio-spiritual self-restraint into a natural instinct by warnings of punishment and repeatedly and strongly condemning all types of undesirable behavior. Many practices that appear to be instinctive have been only the result of religious teachings, such as covering one's private parts and the prohibition of incest. We might also find certain lawful things that people avoid simply because they have been disdained. Thus, the people of the age of pagan ignorance (*Jāhiliyyah*) allowed the son to marry the wife of his deceased father, though they considered it a loathsome marriage (*nikāḥ al-maqt*). In this connection, it is related that someone told Abū ʿAlī al-Jubbā'ī:[5] "You consider that *nabīdh* [wine] is not forbidden but you personally do not drink it!" He said: "Because debauched people drink it, it has become disgusting."

Whenever they want to emphasize the blocking of means to evil consequences, the jurists follow this established norm of the Shariʿah. Thus, Mālik ibn Anas, while not considering live pigs to be impure (*najis*), maintained that wine is impure in itself, though he was aware that God only forbade drinking it. He did not, for example, forbid staining one's body with it. Mālik inferred from recurrent evidence in the Sunnah that it is a categorical objective of the Shariʿah to make people abstain from consuming intoxicants. However, this was not an easy objective to achieve owing to people's deep love of wine as a result of the widespread glorification of its attractions by drinkers. Therefore, the Sunnah aimed at strengthening the religio-spiritual self-restraint to prevent people from consuming it. So it resorted to implanting in people's minds the sense of the impurity of wine and considered it among filthy things (*najāsāt*). Likewise, it has become a popular proverb in Tunisia that, whenever people want to describe someone's abhorrence of something, they say: "He said about it what Mālik had said about wine." Of similar purport is the Tradition in which the Prophet is reported to have said: "The bad example is not for us. He who takes back his gift is like a dog that swallows back its vomit."[6]

Nevertheless, the implementation of most of the Shariʿah commands and provisions depends on religio-spiritual self-restraint; that is, the power of true faith consisting of both hope (*rajā'*) and fear (*khawf*). For this reason, the execution of the prescriptions and proscriptions of the Shariʿah has been entrusted to the religiousness of those to whom they are addressed. Thus, God says in the Qur'an:

> And the divorced women shall undergo, without remarrying, a waiting-period of three monthly courses: for it is not lawful for them to conceal what God may have created in their wombs, if they believe in God and the Last Day (2:228);

> But you will incur no sin if you give a hint of [an intended] marriage offer to [any of] these women, or if you conceive such an intention without making it obvious: [for] God knows that you intend to ask them in marriage. Do not, however, plight your troth with them in secret, but speak only in a decent manner; and do not proceed with tying the marriage-knot before the ordained [term of waiting] has come to its end. And know that God knows what is in your minds, and therefore remain conscious of Him; and know, too, that God is Much-Forgiving, Forbearing. (2:235)

In fact, there are numerous Qur'anic verses and Prophetic Traditions that emphasize this aspect, which it is beyond our purpose to adduce here.

However, when the religio-spiritual self-restraint weakens at a specific time or amongst a specific group of people or under certain circumstances in which it is believed that the motive driving human beings to violate the Shariʿah rules is stronger for most individuals than the religio-spiritual self-restraint, then state control (*wāziʿ sulṭānī*) is the next recourse. The implementation of those rules is then entrusted to the external force of political authority; as ʿUthmān ibn ʿAffān put it, "God deters by the authority of the state what may not be restrained by exhortations of the Qur'an."[7] Because of this, the Andalusian scholar Ibn ʿAṭiyyah[8] was of the view that the opinion of executors of his time concerning orphans' maturity should not be accepted unless it is confirmed by a judge.[9] He likewise did not consider them to be worthy of the trust required by the Shariʿah as expressed in the following verse: "And test the orphans [in your charge] until they reach a marriageable age, then, if you find them to be mature of mind, hand over to them their possessions; and do not consume them by wasteful spending, and in haste, ere they grow up" (4:6).

Subsequent Mālikī jurists approved this view. In the same vein, Ibn al-ʿArabī maintained that a divorced woman's assertion of the completion of her waiting-period should not be accepted if the period is less than forty-five days,[10] owing to the weakening of women's religiousness in his time. He upheld this position although the Qur'an has clearly entrusted the matter to their faith and honesty by saying: "for it is not lawful for them to conceal what God may have created in their wombs, if they believe in God and the Last Day" (2:228). Ibn al-ʿArabī's view became the basis for the fatwa and judicial practice amongst later Mālikī jurists, as has been mentioned by [Abū Abd Allāh al-Fulālī al-Siljimāsī] the author of *al-ʿAmaliyyāt al-ʿAmmah*.

Accordingly, when doubts arise concerning the trustworthiness of anyone to whom the Shariʿah has entrusted the implementation of certain rights, it is appropriate to transfer control to the state authorities (*sulṭān*).

Consequently, it is the duty of the jurists to determine the situations where people entrusted with the implementation of the Shariʿah rules could be deprived of their authority once there is evidence of the weakening of people's self-restraint, the shallowness of their religiousness, or the spread of ignorance amongst them. Indeed, the textual sources of the Shariʿah do allow for that possibility, for most of the Qur'anic discourse on these matters is written in the plural form. Since its discourse is clearly addressed to individuals as well as to the Muslim community as a whole, we can take it as an indication of the need for establishing a special group, that is, rulers (*awliyāʾ al-umūr*), to be entrusted with the power of implementing the laws of the Shariʿah. Therefore, ʿUmar ibn al-Khaṭṭāb introduced *ḥisbah*[11] as a different institution from the judiciary. The reason is that there are certain rights whose protection and promotion constitute an objective of the Shariʿah. However, when they are violated, it will not result in harming a specific person who will take the matter to the court, or it might be that the victim is not in a position to defend his/her rights.

Now, it should be known that religio-spiritual self-restraint is always taken into account even when the other two types of *wāziʿ* are used. In fact, the restraining force of the state (*wāziʿ sulṭānī*) is an application of the *wāziʿ dīnī*, whereas self-restraint (*wāziʿ jibillī*) is a prelude to it. Accordingly, what matters most in the sight of the Shariʿah is religio-spiritual self-restraint, whether it is the result of voluntary submission or external compulsion. Therefore, it is the responsibility of the rulers to salvage spiritual-religious self-restraint and protect it from being neglected and undermined. When it is feared that it is neglected or misused, then the authority of the state must be invoked to strengthen it.

28

The Merciful Nature of the Shariᶜah

It has been conclusively established in our detailed discussion of the magnanimity of the Shariᶜah and its dissociation from hardship that the Shariᶜah does not seek to burden human beings. One of the characteristics of the Shariᶜah is that it is a practical law seeking the realization of its objectives for both the community and private individuals. Therefore, it is most important that its objectives should be achievable, which can happen only by applying leniency. Accordingly, I consider that avoiding sheer vindictiveness in legislation is a major characteristic of the Law of Islam.

Thus, it has been mentioned in the Qur'an that God had imposed some punitive laws on certain nations:

> So, then, for wickedness committed by those who followed Judaism did We deny to them certain of the good things of life which [earlier] had been allowed to them;[1] [We did this] for their having so often turned away from the path of God, [for] their taking usury although it had been forbidden to them, and their wrongful devouring of other people's possessions. And for those of them who [continue to] deny the truth, We have prepared grievous suffering. (4:160–161)

There is here clear indication that the prohibition of certain good things for the Israelites was a punishment for them owing to their indulgence in disobeying the Divine law revealed to them.

Likewise, when Islam authorises a practice or relaxes its legislation, it actually runs according to its manifest characteristic of magnanimity. And when it applies restrictions or modifies a rule from permissibility to prohibition, etc., it in fact considers the good of the people and their gradual progress on the path of reform in a gentle manner. Accordingly, Islam intended the prohibition of intoxicants from the beginning of the Prophet's mission. However, it was silent about it for a certain period so that intoxicants were allowed, and then forbidden during prayer time. This was a gradual preparation for its complete prohibition.[2]

Therefore, deterrents (*zawājir*), sanctions, and categorical penalties (*ḥudūd)* can be seen only as aiming to reform the condition of human beings by using necessary measures to attain what is beneficial for them, neither more nor less. This is because if what is less is sufficient to achieve their good, the Shariʿah would not have exceeded it. Similarly, if the penalties established by the Shariʿah transgress the limits of required punishment, its purpose would be sheer vindictiveness rather than reform. This is why most of the Shariʿah penalties are corporal, meant to cause physical pain; for this type of pain is felt by everyone. In contrast, financial penalties are not common in the Shariʿah, except as compensation for injury (*ghurm al-ḍarar*).[3]

Thus, if offenses are committed for which there is no specific penalty established by the Shariʿah and whose motive is the love to accumulate more wealth, then it is very likely that the *mujtahid* will impose a financial penalty, such as confiscation. An example is when ʿUmar ibn al-Khaṭṭāb ordered that Ruwayshid al-Thaqafī's house be reduced to ashes as a punishment because he was using it as a tavern in which he used to gather drinking companions to drink intoxicating liquors. Likewise, Yaḥyā al-Laythī[4] reported that Mālik's opinion was to torch the wine merchant's house.[5] It is also stated in *al-Wāḍiḥah* that Mālik held the view that any house used as a shelter for people of debauchery must be confiscated and sold.[6] However, Ibn al-Qāsim's[7] position is contrary to that of Mālik on both issues.[8]

Of the penalties oscillating between vindictiveness and ordinary punishment regarding the motive of the offense, is the juristic view maintaining the absolute and permanent prohibition of a woman to the man who has consummated the marriage with her while still in her waiting period (*ʿiddah*). ʿUmar ibn al-Khaṭṭāb's adjudication was based on this view, and it was maintained by Mālik.[9] However, some scholars of Islamic jurisprudence were of the view that the marriage contract should be annulled, although they did not uphold the view of permanent proscription – which is more acceptable.[10] Therefore, some Mālikī jurists, when judging this kind of case, preffered to impose an annullment without making it an absolute and permanent proscription. The reason is that maybe their affair will run properly according to the view that does not uphold the permanency (*ta'bīd)* of prohibition. Of the same kind is the question of a man eloping with a married woman.[11]

This cannot be disputed on the basis of what has been reported in *Ṣaḥīḥ al-Bukhārī* on the authority of Abū Hurayrah that when the Prophet knew that some of

> the Companions were practising *wiṣāl* (continuous fasting), he forbade them to do so. So, one of the Muslims said to him, "But you practice *wiṣāl*, O God's Apostle!" The Prophet replied, "Who amongst you is similar to me? My Lord gives me food and drink during my sleep." So, when the people refused to stop *wiṣāl*, the Prophet fasted day and night continuously along with them for a day and then another day. Then they saw the crescent moon (of the month of Shawwāl). The Prophet said to them (angrily), "If it (the crescent) had not appeared, I would have made you fast for a longer period." That was a punishment for them when they refused to stop practicing continuous fasting.[12]

This specific act of the Prophet was not, however, meant as universal legislation, but a measure for educating his Companions. Thus it was a kind of advice to his Companions, not a general legislative rule.

29

The Shariʿah's Aim in Avoiding Elaboration at the Time of Revelation

Inductive thematic inference from the Prophet's sayings and acts and consideration of the universality and permanence of the Shariʿah clearly show that one of the main objectives of the Shariʿah is to base its injunctions (*aḥkām*) on different attributes necessitating them and to vary those injunctions accordingly. Otherwise, if the Shariʿah were temporary, thus being confined to a specific people or age, one might then assert that its rules are fixed, for they are applicable to a fixed period. Once that period is ended, God will address people with a new revelation abrogating the earlier laws. However, since the Islamic Shariʿah is universal and eternal and changing circumstances is a very obvious aspect of the permanent Divine law (Sunnah) in the creation, the fixing of the Shariʿah injunctions while the causes necessitating them (*mūjib*) are subject to alteration implies admitting what contravenes the Lawgiver's purpose in basing the Shariʿah rules on specific causes. Likewise, either of the two acts is absurd or utterly stubborn in denying the change in those causes. This is, in most cases, belied by observation yielding certainty or high probability. Whatever the case, this amounts to considering that the Shariʿah rules are meant for themselves rather than depending on the causes necessitating (*mūjibāt*) them.

We need here to adduce more instances of the Prophet's sayings and deeds to inspire the seeker of truth with confidence, for deniers may be numerous and observers blind. In a Tradition narrated by

Mālik, Bukhārī, and Muslim on the authority of ʿĀṣim ibn ʿAdiyy al-Anṣārī regarding *liʿān*,[1] it is reported that ʿUmaymir al-ʿAjlānī came to ʿĀṣim and said to him,

> "O ʿĀṣim! Suppose a man saw another man [having sexual intercourse] with his wife, would he kill him, whereupon people would kill him; or what should he do? Please, O ʿĀṣim, ask about this on my behalf." ʿĀṣim asked God's Apostle about it. The Prophet *(ṢAAS)* disliked being asked these questions (*masāʾil*) and considered it disgraceful.[2]

That is, the Prophet disliked being questioned not only about this particular matter, but also about all hypothetical matters, which is implied by ʿĀṣim's use of the plural *masāʾil.*

In another Tradition narrated by Bukhārī on the authority of Saʿd ibn Abī Waqqāṣ, the Prophet is reported to have said: "The most sinful person among the Muslims is the one who asked about something which had not been prohibited, but was prohibited because of his asking."[3] In an authentic hadith concerning night prayer during the month of Ramadan (*tarāwīḥ*), ʿĀʾishah said:

> God's Apostle went out in the middle of the night and prayed in the mosque and some men prayed behind him. In the morning, the people spoke about it and then a large number of them gathered and prayed behind him (on the second night). The next morning the people again talked about it and on the third night the mosque was filled with a large number of people. God's Apostle came out and the people prayed behind him. On the fourth night the Mosque was overwhelmed with people and could not accommodate them, but the Prophet came out [only] for the morning prayer. When the morning prayer was finished, he recited *tashahhud* and [addressing the people] said, "Your presence was not hidden from me, but I was afraid lest the night prayer (*qiyām*) should be enjoined on you and you might not be able to continue with it."[4]

More illuminating for our purpose is the Tradition reported by

Abū Thaʿlabah al-Khushanī that the Prophet said: "God has set boundaries, so do not transgress them; He kept silent on certain things out of mercy for you rather than forgetfulness, do not ask about them."[5] Thus, Ibn ʿAbbās said: "I have not seen better than Muhammad's Companions, they only asked him fifteen questions, all of which are [mentioned] in the Qur'an."[6]

To prevent the spread of forgery of the Prophet's Sayings and to discourage many of the students of jurisprudence from relying on certain acts emanating from him regarding particular cases or on some of his Sayings that are of doubtful transmission or unspecified origin, ʿUmar ibn al-Khaṭṭāb, as mentioned by Abū Bakr ibn al-ʿArabī in his book *al-ʿAwāṣim*, used to forbid people to say "God's Apostle said" and did not allow them to propagate the Traditions unnecessarily, even if they were forgotten. There is indeed a wonderful wisdom behind this policy, for God has already and clearly mentioned what is prescribed and forbidden in His Book and warned people against raising unnecessary questions. Thus, He says:

> O you who have attained faith! Do not ask about matters which, if they were to be made manifest to you [in terms of law], might cause you hardship; for, if you ask about them while the Qur'an is being revealed, they might [indeed] be made manifest to you [as laws]. God has absolved [you from any obligation] in this respect: for God is Much-Forgiving, Forbearing. People before your time have indeed asked such questions – and as a result, have come to deny the truth. (5:101–102)

Then, Ibn al-ʿArabī said: "The Companions agreed on the compilation of the Qur'an so that it is not lost and left the Traditions to flow according to the appearance of new cases (*nawāzil*). And when some people amongst the Companions indulged in the transmission of Prophetic Traditions, ʿUmar deterred them from that."[7]

I wish to add the following. I have examined the details of the Shariʿah at the time of the Prophet and found that most of them concern matters of ritual worship (*ʿibādāt*). Indeed, if you look at the compilations of the Traditions, you will certainly realize that the chapters concerning ritual worship are far longer than those on social transactions (*muʿāmalāt*). The reason is that acts of ritual worship concern the realization of unchanging purposes, whose permanence and uniform obligation on people throughout the ages do not result in any harm except in very rare situations that are dealt with by the rule of license (*rukhṣah*). In contrast, social transactions require explanation according to the changes in circumstances and eras. Therefore, binding people with fixed and uniform rules entails great difficulty and inconvenience for many sections of the community. Accordingly, analogical reasoning operates very rarely in matters of ritual worship in contrast with social transactions where it operates on a very wide scale. Because of this, we find that in the Qur'an the commands regarding transactions are mostly framed in general and universal terms, to an extent that when God provided the detailed rules of inheritance,[8] the Prophet said: "God Himself has undertaken the division of inheritance."[9]

The Shariʿah's explanation of transactions has a twofold purpose. Sometimes its aim is to bind people with a permanent and universal rule, such as the prohibition of usury (*ribā*); at other times, its aim is to formulate judgments between people, whereby the particular judicial decision constitutes an implementation of a universal legislative rule. These are two aspects that require much attention to realize the difference between them. Therefore, the leading scholars of *uṣūl al-fiqh* said that matters for which the Lawgiver has provided no specific rules should be dealt with according to the following rule: "Anything beneficial is in principle permissible, and anything harmful is in principle forbidden."[10]

Nevertheless, since we have considered the blocking of means to be one of the fundamental rules of Islamic legislation, and since this rule operates under specific circumstances, it should therefore be the duty of the *mujtahids* to consider when such means must be blocked and when they can be left open. They must do that by realizing the extent and duration of the accidental harm resulting from the act, thus requiring its interdiction. Once that accidental (*ʿāriḍ*) harm has ceased the act must be subsumed under the original (*dhātī*) rule given to it by the Shariʿah.[11]

30

The Shariʿah's Aim in Building a Solid and Stable Social Order

That the main objective of the Shariʿah is to establish a strong community with a stable social system and promote the orderly functioning of its affairs by achieving its welfare and preventing evil is so obvious that not the slightest doubt about it should arise in the mind of any thinking person. All Muslim jurists and Shariʿah scholars realized this regarding the welfare of individuals, although they failed to demonstrate it for the welfare of the community as a whole. Nevertheless, none of them will deny that if the welfare of individuals and the proper management of their affairs is intended by the Shariʿah, then the same applied to the community as a whole is even more important. Is it not true that the righteousness of the parts is the way to achieving the righteousness of the whole? Is it not true that a sound whole can be comprised only of sound parts, just as good spears can only be made of strong wood? Therefore, if it is supposed that the aggregate of righteous individuals will be a corrupt whole, this means that such righteousness can only vanish like a candle in the wind.

Therefore, God has reminded Muslims as well as other righteous communities of the favors that He bestowed upon them by establishing them on the earth and made their conditions good. Thus, He says: "God has promised those of you who have attained faith and do righteous deeds that, of a certainty, He will cause them to accede to power on earth, even as He caused [some of] those who lived before them to accede to it" (24:55); "As for anyone – be it man or woman – who does righteous deeds, and is a believer withal – him shall We most certainly cause to live a good life" (16:97). Addressing the early Muslims, He says: "And remember the blessings which God has bestowed upon you: how, when you were enemies, He brought your hearts together, so that with His blessing you became brethren" (3:103). He also said: "However, all honour belongs to God, and [thus] to His Apostle and those who believe [in God]: but of this the Hypocrites are not aware" (63:8). Accordingly, we need to imagine the Muslim community as one individual Muslim and subject its conditions to the rules of the Shariʿah just as we do for individuals. This will certainly provide us with clear insight into how Islamic legislative rules should apply to the public affairs of the community.

One of the most important things that must never be forgotten when considering the general social conditions of the community in light of the Shariʿah is the notion of license. The jurists, however, confined themselves to discussing and illustrating it only with regard to the individuals. They ignored the fact that the whole community might also face social hardships thus requiring the implementation of this principle as we have already explained in chapter 26 on *rukhṣah*. It must be pointed out that the blocking of means and the consideration of textually unregulated interest (*maṣlaḥah mursalah*) are no less important than the rule of license. It is one of the essential characteristics of these two notions that they concern the whole of the community and rarely apply to individuals.[1]

31

The Necessity of Ijtihad

Owing to what has been mentioned in the previous chapter, the Muslim community is always in need of far-sighted scholars with a thorough understanding of the Shariʿah and a firm grasp of its objectives as well as a comprehensive awareness of people's needs. Their duty is thus to provide Shariʿah-inspired solutions to the community's problems to cure it of all types of disease and salvage its strength and honor. In fact, God has guided us to this by commanding us to reflect on the Shariʿah indicants and proofs and to make every effort to discover His intent. This is inferred from numerous Qur'anic verses and authentic Prophetic Traditions.

Indeed, God has criticized many communities for accepting only the superficial meanings of matters and failing to think more carefully about them and search for deeper meanings. Thus, in His criticism of the children of Israel, He said:

> And lo! We accepted your solemn pledge that you would not shed one another's blood, and would not drive one another from your homelands – whereupon you acknowledged it; and you bear witness to it [even now]. And yet, it is you who slay one another and drive some of your own people from their homelands, aiding one another against them in sin and hatred; but if they come to you as captives, you ransom them – although the very [act of] driving them away has been made unlawful to you!" (2: 84–85).

The purport of the verse is that the solemn pledge was accepted from them not for abstaining from taking ransom from their own people, whom they treat as captives, for this cannot be imagined to happen for no reason. Rather, it was that they should not drive them out of their homes, for this might happen as a result of anger and as a form of punishment. However, they disobeyed God's command, expelled some of their people, treated them as enemies, fought them, and took them as prisoners of war to be released only upon paying a ransom.

Likewise, God reprimanded them for this because imposing a ransom on some of their own people implies that they considered them aliens in their own homeland so that they were required to ransom themselves if they were to be allowed to settle in their homes.[1] Similarly, God reprimanded those people who would ask for fixed and detailed rules for everything, as stated by the Qur'an in the story of the cow.[2] We have already discussed this issue in chapter 29.

Accordingly, ijtihad is a collective obligation (*farḍ kifāyah*) on the Muslim community according to the needs and circumstances of its different peoples and countries. The whole Muslim community is therefore sinful by failing to fulfill this obligation when its means and instruments are available.[3] *Uṣūl al-fiqh* scholars have agreed that the duty of ijtihad is implied by God's command in the following verses: "Remain, then, conscious of God as best as you can, and listen [to Him], and pay heed" (64:16); "Learn a lesson, then, O you who are endowed with insight" (59:2).[4] In his book *al-Tanqīḥ*, Shihāb al-Dīn al-Qarāfī sought refuge with God from the cessation of ijtihad.[5]

The negative impact of failing to exercise ijtihad is clearly visible in those aspects of Muslim life that have changed since the time of the great *mujtahid* scholars as well as in those new aspects which have no precedent. It is also apparent where the new circumstances of life require Muslims to act in unison, which cannot be achieved with the different juristic doctrines existing today. Muslims are now in need of scholars capable of assessing the different schools followed by the people and deciding which of them should be given priority so that the community can act in unison. On all these levels there is an urgent need for a thorough study and discussion of the

Shariᶜah to determine its primary and secondary objectives as well as the adaptability or rigidity of the doctrines of the early *mujtahids*.

It is sufficient to highlight a few instances of the issue that require special treatment. They include the sale of food (*bayᶜ al-ṭaᶜām*), settlement of accounts (*muqāṣṣah*), deferred sales (*buyūᶜ al-ājāl*), sharecropping, and pre-emption in what is liable to division. Many of these issues are subject to restriction in the juristic literature.

The first step that should be taken toward this crucial intellectual and scholarly objective is to form a specialist body of eminent Shariᶜah scholars from all the juristic schools (*madhāhib*) in the Muslim countries.[6] The task of these scholars must be to study and discuss the vital needs of the Ummah so as to produce agreed upon resolutions on how the Muslim community should act in their respect. Then, they ought to convey their resolutions to all Muslim countries, and I do not have any serious doubt that Muslims will abide by their recommendations.

Another duty of the members of this suggested body is to identify the Shariᶜah scholars around the world who have attained or nearly attained the level of ijtihad. Once this is done, Muslim scholars must choose the best qualified among themselves to take the leading role in exercising ijtihad. In electing this group of scholars, special attention must be given to the following matter. Besides knowledge, this group of scholars must combine integrity and observance of the Shariᶜah in their personal lives so that the Ummah has full confidence in their scholarly erudition and there will be no suspicion concerning the truthfulness and soundness of their recommendations.

PART III

Maqāṣid al-Sharīʿah: Human Dealings (*Muʿāmalāt*)

Ends and Means in
Transactions

This topic is a prerequisite for examining the rules of the Shariʿah on human conduct and social interaction. Its aim is to distinguish between what constitutes an end (*maqṣad*), to which the Shariʿah gives priority in affirmation for both realization and prevention, from what is only a means, which takes second place because it depends on something else. This is an important subject with which early scholars did not, however, deal satisfactorily. They confined themselves to *sadd al-dharāʾiʿ*, in which they designated the *dharīʿah* as the means and that which the *dharīʿah* is used for as the end (*maqṣad*). Since we have already dealt with *sadd al-dharāʾiʿ*, our purpose is to examine the question of means (*wasāʾil*) and ends (*maqāṣid*) more profoundly. Thus, I have not come across anyone who considered this topic beyond the blocking of means, except what was mentioned in ʿIzz al-Dīn ibn ʿAbd al-Salām's *Qawāʿid* and Qarāfī's "Fifty-Eighth *Farq*" of his book *al-Furūq*. I shall therefore combine their statements, for neither is sufficient on its own.

CLASSIFICATION OF *MAṢĀLIḤ* AND *MAFĀSID*
AS ENDS AND MEANS

The subject-matter of the Shariʿah rules falls into two categories: ends (*maqāṣid*) and means (*wasāʾil*). Ends consist of *maṣāliḥ* and *mafāsid* in themselves, whereas means consist of the ways and methods leading to them. The means to the best ends are the best means, the means to the worst ends are the worst means, and there are others somewhere in between.[1] Means are thus classified according to the levels of *maṣāliḥ* and *mafāsid*. Fortunate is the person whom God guides in comprehending the levels of *maṣāliḥ*, thus being capable of placing them in order of excellence. However, scholars might differ on the order of certain *maṣāliḥ*, thus disagreeing on what should be given priority of realization and what should not when realizing them together proves impossible. So also fortunate is the one who is guided in comprehending the order of *mafāsid*, thus knowing how to avoid the worst of them by tolerating the least in a conflict. Scholars here might also differ on the order of *mafāsid* and therefore on what must be avoided and what can be tolerated when avoiding them all at the same time is impossible. The Shariʿah abounds with instances of what we have mentioned.[2]

Furthermore, in a chapter on the degrees of *maṣāliḥ* in his book *Qawāʿid*, ʿIzz al-Dīn ibn ʿAbd al-Salām said:

> And he [the Prophet] mentioned in the hadith[3] jihad after *īmān* because its value does not lie in itself but as a means. Then, he added: "There is no doubt that appointing judges and rulers is a means to the realization of *maṣāliḥ*, while appointing aides to the judges is a means to the means (*wasā'il al-wasā'il*)... Similarly, bearing witness is a means to testimony before the court and testimony is a means to adjudging, while adjudging serves as a means to realizing *maṣāliḥ* and avoiding *mafāsid*.[4]

It is clear from what Ibn ʿAbd al-Salām and Qarāfī said about ends and means that they limited themselves to the question of *maṣāliḥ* and *mafāsid*. Nevertheless, we aim to discuss it further and the jurist's need of it is indeed greater. Although they might look similar in their classification according to what is designated in fiqh and *uṣūl al-fiqh* as the categories of legal command (*ḥukm sharʿī*),[5] the rules on human conduct, both righteous and evil, vary, depending on whether they are ends or means, in the view of the Lawgiver or that of humankind. Therefore, we need to elaborate on these two levels of human conduct.

1. ENDS (*MAQĀṢID*)

Ends consist of the types of conduct that are intended for their own sake, and which human beings strive to achieve by various means or with which they are compelled to comply with in obedience. They are divided into two kinds: actions based on the purposes of the Lawgiver (*maqāṣid al-Shāriᶜ*) and those based on the purposes of human beings (*maqāṣid al-nās*).[6] By now you must have a clearer idea of the purposes of the Lawgiver, for it is not too long since you have been introduced to them, since they have been elaborated in the first and second parts of this book.

In Part III we need to deal with the knowledge of *maqāṣid al-Shariᶜah* concerning the different spheres of human transactions (*muᶜāmalāt*). These objectives consist of the methods (*kayfiyyāt*) intended by the Lawgiver for realizing the useful purposes of the human beings or preserving their public interests (*maṣālih ᶜāmmah*) relating to their private conduct. The aim here is to prevent people's pursuit of their personal interests from leading to the undermining of their established public interests, owing to carelessness, whimsical errors, and vain desires. It includes any sensible measures considered in the institution of the Shariᶜah rules governing human conduct, such as the documentation (*tawthīq*) of credit in a mortgage contract, the establishment of the family in a marriage contract, and the removal of permanent harm in the legality of divorce.

The objectives of human actions include all the purposes (*maᶜānī*) for which they enter into contracts, execute transactions, fine each other, sue one another in courts, or accept reconciliation, etc. These purposes are also divided into two categories. The first category, which is the most important and widespread, consists of actions that most or all sensible people have agreed upon because they found them suitable for the proper functioning of their social lives, such as sales, hire and loans. It also includes the rules governing those acts that are an essential part of them, such as distribution (*tawzīᶜ*) in hire, deferment in *salam* sales, and the prohibition of the leasing of endowment property. Knowledge of this category of acts can be obtained from historical inference from the social conditions of humankind.

The second category, which is less important and less widespread, consists of objectives pursued by a specific group of people or individuals because they are particularly suitable for their circumstances. This category can be illustrated by life-gift (*ʿumrā*) and advance sale (*ʿāriyyah*).[7] Another example is permanent rent (*kirā' mu'abbad*), known as *inzāl* and *nuṣbah* in the renting of commercial premises in Tunisia, as *ḥikr* in Egypt, and as *jilsah* in Morocco. Mortgaging of the yield of special endowment (*waqf khāṣṣ*)[8] in the Jerid oasis of Tunisia and *bayʿ al-wafā'* in the vineyards of Bukhārā are further examples. The means of recognizing this category of acts can be signs (*amārah*), contextual evidence (*qarīnah*), or emergent need (*ḥājah ṭāri'ah*).

RIGHTS OF GOD AND RIGHTS OF INDIVIDUALS

The above two categories of objectives are again divided into the rights of God (*ḥuqūq Allāh*) and the rights of human beings (*ḥuqūq al-ʿibād*).[9] Here, the rights of God do not refer to the apparent meaning connoted by their attribution to God, in the sense that they constitute His personal rights. This is because the rights of God in this sense pertain to the realm of faith (*īmān*) and devotional acts of worship as expressed in the following hadith and verse. It is narrated on the authority of Muʿādh ibn Jabal that the Messenger of God said: "Muʿādh, do you know the rights of God over mankind (*ʿibād*)?" He [Muʿādh] said: "God and His Apostle know best." He [the Messenger of God] said: "That God alone should be worshiped and nothing should be associated with Him."[10] In the Qur'an, we read: "And I [God] have not created the invisible beings and men to any end other than that they may [know and] worship Me. [But withal,] no sustenance do I ever demand of them, nor do I demand that they feed Me" (51:56-57).

The rights of God in the previous sense are not, therefore, what we mean here. This term means firstly a set of rights belonging to the community as a whole, by means of which a universal benefit is realized. Secondly, it refers to the rights of people who are incapable of self-protection. The rights of God thus consist of those for which

God has prescribed obligatory protection and therefore people must be compelled to observe them. The nature of these rights is such that no one is allowed to ignore them, because they serve as a means of preserving the universal and ultimate objectives of the Shariʿah. They also serve to prevent the people's action in pursuit of their personal or public interest from leading to the undermining of those very objectives. Similarly, they serve to safeguard the rights of the weak who might not be able to do so. An example of the rights of God is those embodied in the public treasury (*bayt al-māl*). Another example is the rights of minors and the custody of children who have no guardians.

On the other hand, the rights of human beings, which constitute most of the Shariʿah rules, refer to the actions that people perform to acquire what is suitable and useful for them and the prevention of what is harmful, that is provided that it does not result in the undermining of a public interest (*maṣlaḥah ʿāmmah*) or the causing of a general harm (*mafsadah ʿāmmah*), or the undermining of an individual's interest or the causing of harm to him/her.

The rights of God and the rights of human beings might be interrelated. In certain cases, it is the rights of God that prevail; in others, the rights of human beings might prevail when those of God cannot be rectified. Just punishment for slander (*qadhf*) and rape are examples of the former. An instance of the latter is the right of the victim of a murderer to forgive the culprit before dying, since the right to life for which killing has been absolutely forbidden cannot here be rectified, thus giving priority to the individual's right. However, God's right in this case is not totally ignored, for the forgiven murderer must still be punished by one hundred lashes and one year of imprisonment.[11]

2. MEANS (*WASĀ'IL*)

The term *wasā'il* refers to the rules (*aḥkām*) instituted by the Lawgiver as a means to the realization of interim objectives [constituting means to the final objectives]. They are thus not intended for their own sake, but as means to achieving something else in the most appropriate manner. Without them, the purpose of the Shariʿah might be totally missed or not fully achieved. For example, the requirement in marriage of announcement and attestation by witnesses is not a superficial formality, but is required as a means of removing from marriage any resemblance to adultery and living in sin. Similarly, possession (*ḥawz*) of the property in a mortgage contract (*rahn*) is not required for itself but to fulfill the principle of the pledge and ensure the security of the debt, so that the mortgagee (*rāhin*) does not pledge it with another creditor, thus forgoing the first mortgage.[12]

Like ends, means are also divided into what pertains to the rights of God and what pertains to the rights of human beings. For instance, the prohibition of bribing rulers and government officers falls under a right of God that is not meant for its own sake. Its aim is to guarantee that rights are granted to those of the litigants to whom they are due as well as to ensure that those in authority can perform their duty. Also, prompt fulfillment (*tanjīz*) of gifts (*ʿaṭāyā*) is, in our [Mālikīs'] view, a means to their completion, lest an impediment (*māniʿ*) prevent it. This stipulation is part of the rights of God and aims at preventing the use of bequests as means of abolishing an inheritance or making a bequest for more than a third of the estate. Similarly, considering contracts binding either by conclusion or by beginning to fulfill them is meant to avoid their revocation. Therefore, this is a right of God intended for the realization of the Shariʿah objective of preventing disputes between people.

Means include the causes (*asbāb*) indicating the Shariʿah rules (*aḥkām*), the conditions (*shurūṭ*) necessary for their implementation, and the absence of impediments (*mawāniʿ*). They also include anything of import, such as the formulas of contracts and the pronouncements of the creators of endowment (*wāqifīn*) in that they are a means of knowing the intentions of the contracting parties and the conditions stipulated by the *waqf* creators. It has already become clear that means are secondary to ends. That is why it has become one of the maxims of Islamic jurisprudence that if an objective is nullified, then so is its means.[13]

An appropriate example is the invalidation of marriage by a sick man. Its revocation is a means of protecting the rights of heirs.

However, if the marriage is not revoked until the sick man has recovered, Mālik is reported to have upheld the view that it should not then be rescinded.[14]

A similar example is the termination of a divorced woman's right of custody over her child if she marries someone other than the child's father.[15] However, if the child's father has not claimed the child from the mother and the latter has been divorced from her second husband, the child must not be separated from her. This rule is meant to protect the child from loss. That is, since this purpose has been abolished by the mother's divorce from the second husband, the means for it is also annulled.

This also applies to using certain formulas of contracts in a context that is different from their original usage provided they are associated with this that which would clarify the new meaning, such as using the word "give" in a marriage contract, when it is associated with "dower," etc. Of the same kind is the opposition between the words used by the *waqf* creator and his real intent, provided there is evidence to his intent other than his words. Accordingly, jurists have stated that if meanings are clear and sound, words should not matter much.

It might happen that there is a plurality of means of achieving the same objective. Here, the Shariʿah considers the best of them and prescribes it for the pursuit of that objective, so that it is achieved efficiently. This is, indeed, a vast domain manifesting the breadth and far-sightedness of the Shariʿah in dealing with the question of *maṣāliḥ* and testifying to its accuracy and its lack of extremism and negligence.

Yet, no one, to my knowledge, has drawn attention to this important aspect. I suppose, though, that the leading *mujtahids* were aware of it in their juristic reasoning.

Therefore, a thorough examination of the various methods followed by the Shariʿah in considering this aspect must be one of the major aims of *mujtahid* scholars and jurists concerned with elaborating the fundamental rules of the Shariʿah and deriving its rulings and expounding its rationales. It must also be the special concern of judges and rulers, whose task is to implement the Shariʿah. It is, indeed, a manifold and far-reaching principle. If we assume the existence of a plurality of means leading to the same goal that are equivalent in all respects, then the position of the Shariʿah is to treat them evenly and leave the choice for the human agent (*mukallaf*) to opt for any of them, since, as already mentioned, means are not meant for their own sake. One example of this can be found in the following Qur'anic command:

> And as for those of your women who become guilty of immoral conduct, call four of you who have witnessed their guilt; and if they bear witness to it, confine the guilty women to their homes until death takes them away or God opens for them a way [by repentance]. (4:15)

This command is addressed to the community as a whole, and its purpose is that the punishment of such a woman by confinement should be implemented. Whether this punishment is carried out by the woman's guardian, her husband, or by a court judge makes no difference. However, if, owing to the prevailing circumstances, the authority of the guardian or the husband is weakened, this task becomes the specific duty of court judges, for this is a more effective means of applying the penalty.

This discussion concerns the means required for realizing the Shariʿah objectives, that is, the means constituting the subject-matter of the different categories of obligations (*aḥkām taklīfiyyah*). No importance should be attached to the variation in means in achieving objectives once causation and effect have occurred.

That is why most jurists have adopted a unified rule (*ḥukm*) regarding the *ḥadd* punishment for the consumption of grape wine and date *nabīdh* or any other intoxicant, in both affirmation and negation, for there is no difference between these kinds of drinks in their inebriating effect.

That is also why the rule of just retribution (*qiṣāṣ*) has been instituted for intentional killing by an instrument designed to cause death when it is used on a person. It does not matter whether the instrument causes death immediately or needs to be used repeatedly to bring about its effect.

Accordingly, the rule of just retribution applies equally, regardless of whether the killing has been carried out with a sword or a firearm, or other instrument or method etc.

33

Specification of the Principles and Categories of Rights in the Shariʿah

Specifying the principles of entitlement (*uṣūl al-istiḥqāq*) is the best and most solid basis for legislating on people's transactions. It fulfills two important objectives that are the basis for granting rights to those entitled to them. Laying down such principles consolidates and clarifies rights in the minds of judges and rulers and establishes them in the hearts of litigants. Thus, when judgments are decided in accordance with them, no one will be inclined to reject them. As will be shown in chapter 39 one of the objectives of the Shariʿah is to eradicate the causes of conflict between people. It will be seen from that discussion how the specification of the principles underlying people's entitlement to the different kinds of rights is the crucial factor in achieving that objective. It will also be seen that removing the causes of conflict is both the cause and purpose of the Shariʿah objective discussed here.

The term "rights" refers to the ways human beings make use of, and benefit from, what God has created for them in the world in which He has placed them, as has been stated by the Qur'an: "He it is Who has created for you all that is on earth, and has applied His design to the heavens and fashioned them into seven heavens; and He alone has full knowledge of everything" (2:29).[1] Expressed in a general fashion requiring further elaboration, this Qur'anic text stipulates explicitly that all the bounties of the world are the right of humankind. If the resources available on earth were sufficient to satisfy readily the needs and desires of all human beings under all circumstances and in every age, then people should not need any specification of their rights in making use of them. However, people's needs and desires may not be equal to the resources available (whether in time or under certain circumstances). This might be either because resources are less than the need and desire for them or because some of them are more pleasant and better than others, for which reason people will usually swarm in pursuit of only that which is more attractive. Obviously, this creates competition over scarce resources, which might cause conflict, resulting in the powerful usurping the rights of the weak. This conflict might ultimately lead to the mutual exhaustion of the powerful, in their fight for the resources, and the extermination of the helpless who "cannot bring forth any strength and have not been shown the right way."[2]

Therefore it has been a major objective of the Shariʿah to specify the different kinds of rights according to the categories of people entitled to them, to determine the priority of some people over others in certain rights, and to demonstrate the ways people should share the benefits of resources that are to be shared. In so doing, it has followed a just and natural (*fiṭrī*) course in which no human being feels any alienation or injustice. While avoiding recourse to chance or compulsion, the Shariʿah has adopted an approach grounded in both justice and persuasion, in respect of which fair-minded people do not feel embarrassed or wronged. With its threads firmly knit and its ambit solidly established, the Shariʿah has required human beings to abide by a scale of rights whose criteria are clearly defined to make them more easily accessible.

The thrust of the rules governing the specification of rights can be traced to two basic principles: inborn constitution (*takwīn*) and preponderance (*tarjīḥ*). *Takwīn* means that the very existence of human beings is the basis of certain inalienable rights that are linked to them in their creation. This constitutes the fundamental and universal category of rights. *Tarjīḥ*, on the other hand, consists of giving preference to one individual or group of individuals over another in certain rights that were originally open to exploitation by many. The way to establish this preference is either reason that testifies to the priority of one over the other or an authority (*ḥujjah*) that is accepted by the general public. Where no support is found in reason or authority, one may turn to preferential criteria based on established conventions (*murajjiḥāt iṣṭilāḥiyyah waḍʿiyyah*), such as precedence in acquisition due to old age, which is precedence in existence. If it is proven on the basis of these preferential criteria that the contenders are equal in certain rights, then recourse might be made to casting lots, which belongs to the rule of chance. Recourse might also be made to dividing the disputed right between its contenders, thus being satisfied with a partial benefit to each of them.

CATEGORIES OF RIGHTS

From our thorough examination of the different kinds of rights we can classify them into nine categories according to the strength of the underlying reason for them.

(1) The first category consists of original rights to which people are entitled by their inborn constitution (*takwīn*) and innate disposition (*jibillah*). This category concerns one's fundamental right to utilise (*taṣarruf*) of one's body and organs, as well as senses, such as thinking, eating, sleeping, hearing, etc. It also includes one's right to what ensues from oneself, such as a woman's right to the children that she bears as long as they do not know what their rights are or insofar as the Shariʿah has not given them specific rights. When the children reach the age of discrimination and become capable of distinguishing for themselves what is beneficial from what is harmful, their mother's right to possess them decreases and the decision becomes theirs in proportion to their power of discrimination. It is for this reason that prophet Ibrāhīm (Abraham) addressed his son Ismāʿīl (Ishmael), who was a discerning child, in the following manner: "O my dear son! I have seen in a dream that I should sacrifice you: consider, you, what would be your view!" (37:102), thus leaving him the choice of allowing prophet Ibrāhīm or not to sacrifice him.

To this category belongs also one's right to anything originating from a resource to which one has an already established right, such as one's right to the offspring of one's cattle, or the fruits produced by one's trees, or the minerals in one's land. Since the right to the roots (*uṣūl*) of these resources is established by a category of rights that is lower than the present one, it follows that one's right to what results from those roots is greater.

(2) The second category is closely linked to the first, though it differs in some respects. It requires an element of convention that is the result of either the social order on the legal system of the community. It can be illustrated by the father's right to his children, whom the Law (*Sharᶜ*), in view of their specific relationship to him, considers his offspring for the following reasons. Owing to the man's exclusive relationship with the woman in marriage and his maintenance and protection of her, and considering also her undoubted chastity, the Shariᶜah prescribes that her conception during that period must be attributed to him. Accordingly, it considers the husband to be the legitimate father of the child resulting from that conception and rejects any assertion denying the child's lineal attribution to the man to whom its mother is married (*ṣāḥib ᶜiṣmat ummih*). Only the husband has the possible right of disowning the child if it is proven definitively that it is not his.

In the pre-Islamic times of pagan ignorance (*Jāhiliyyah*), people followed different methods of confirming lineal identity (*nasab*). For instance, if an unmarried woman conceived as a result of fornication, they used to accept her confession that she became pregnant by so-and-so, one of her lovers. They would also resort to the opinion of physiognomists and diviners to support her confession. There was even greater variation in the means of confirming the fathers of children born to adulterous female slaves.

(3) The third category consists of situations where many people are originally entitled to a resource on an equal footing. However, some of them have made a physical effort or acted in advance to acquire that resource before others, such as logging, stripping tree leaves [for forage] (*ikhtibāṭ*), hunting, extracting water from the ground, installing water-mills on rivers, laying fishnets inshore etc.

(4) The fourth category, which is lower than the previous one, consists of acquiring resources by sheer dominance and use of force.

Though this was the norm during the anarchic and barbarous stages of human history, prevailing even over the third category, we have intentionally included it here, for most of its content is condemned by both the Shariʿah and sound reason. It includes such things as fighting for the acquisition of land, plundering cattle, taking captives to enslave them, etc. At its advent, however, Islam did confirm people's ownership of whatever they had already acquired in that way.

It is narrated in *Muwaṭṭa'* that when ʿUmar ibn al-Khaṭṭāb appointed his client (*mawlā*) Hunay' for the administration of the *ḥimā*,[3] he told him:

> By God, these people think that I have been unjust to them. This is their land, they fought for it in the pre-Islamic period of ignorance (*Jāhiliyyah*) and they embraced Islam (willingly) while it was in their possession. By Him in Whose Hand my life is! Were it not for the animals (in my custody) which I give to be ridden for striving in God's Cause, I would not have turned even a span of their land into a *ḥimā*.[4]

To this category also belongs what the Shariʿah has approved regarding public rather than private rights, such as the right to the spoils of war. Though originally constituting public property belonging to all members of the community, these spoils may become the particular rights of certain individuals [i.e. the fighters] either by the rule of distribution or as a gift from the army leader.

(5) The fifth category consists of rights resulting from antecedence that is not accompanied by any effort to obtain them. It includes the occupation of market-places by non-shop-owner merchants and customers, seats in mosques, extracting water from streams and rivers and any water that is not the exclusive property of a specific person. Another example is found items (*iltiqāṭ, luqaṭah*), which have elaborate rules in Islam in contrast to other laws.

(6) The sixth category consists of rights acquired on the basis of priority over others who are also entitled to the same thing, owing to the impossibility of enabling all of them to make use of it. The mother's right of custody over her young children rather than the father when they are separated is a typical example of this category. While

living together as husband and wife, this right belongs to the father and mother at the same time. When they are divorced, it becomes difficult to have it undertaken by both of them; hence, the mother is given priority over the father. Another instance of this category of rights is delegating superintendence over the property of young children to the father rather than the mother. This is on account of the father's better management, though the mother's right to the children is greater since it belongs to the first category of rights explained above.

This category is manifested in different forms and by numerous instances, such as guardianships (*wilāyāt*). Rights belonging to this category are determined according to the priority of one party over the other(s). In this connection, Judge Abū Muḥammad ʿAbd al-Wahhāb of Baghdad maintained in his book *al-Ishrāf* – the chapter on *īlā'* – that rights are considered in relation to those to whom they are due. Thus, the four-month grace period is the right of the husband and no account is to be taken of the wife's status, whether she is a free woman or a slave.[5]

(7) The seventh category includes the right to a resource acquired by offering a satisfactory substitute for it to its original owner, whose right to it has been established on the basis of any of the previous categories. This category consists of the exchange of whatever is available for exchange, as we shall explain below. As already mentioned, ʿUmar said to Hunay':

> This is their land, they fought for it in the pre-Islamic period of ignorance (*Jāhiliyyah*) and they embraced Islam (willingly) while it was in their possession. By Him in Whose Hand my life is! Were it not for the animals (in my custody) which I give to be ridden for striving in God's Cause, I would not have turned even a span of their land into a *ḥimā*.

In human civilization, this category constitutes the most encompassing way to the acquisition of rights.

(8) The eighth category consists of rights acquired by transferring them from their original holders to their closest relatives who also have the strongest claim to the holders' inheritance after their death.

Different customs (*ʿawāʾid*) and laws (*sharāʾiʿ*) each follow different methods for determining this kinship.

However, Islam is the most just of all laws in dealing with this, for it has based inheritance rights on true natural (*aṣliyyah*) and acquired accidental (*ʿaraḍiyyah*) kinship ties, regardless of any considerations of affection or its opposite, as we shall see below. Thus, God says in the Qur'an: "As for your parents and your children – you know not which of them is more deserving of benefit from you: [therefore this] ordinance from God. Verily, God is All-Knowing, Wise" (4:11).[6]

Taking family ties as the governing principle in this respect, the Shariʿah has made descent (*nasab*), relationship by marriage (*zawjiyyah*) and relationship by contract or clientage (*walāʾ*) the only grounds for inheritance. Each of these grounds has specific limits that must not be violated. In default of such grounds, the property of the deceased person becomes a property with no specific owner, thus reverting to its original status, that is as a public property of the whole community.

Islam has founded its approach to the question of inheritance on the principal consideration of *fiṭrah*. Likewise, it has not excluded from it female relatives who used to inherit nothing from the property of their deceased relatives in most of the ancient nations. Moreover, it has calculated this in a balanced and just manner, as we shall see in our discussion of kinship ties. On the other hand, Islam has confined inheritance rights to purely economic and financial property in contrast with the dominant practice of the period of pagan ignorance, whereby the children and brothers of a deceased man could inherit even his spouse.

(9) The ninth category, which is the lowest and least important, consists of chance and coincidence without any attempt at acquisition. Scholars have differed on validating it. Therefore, cases in this category are acceptable according to the views of only a few scholars. Examples are drawing lots in the partition of property and goods (*qismah*), according to Mālik ibn Anas,[7] casting lots for the *adhan*, as reported in a Prophetic tradition;[8] treating the elderly with respect as stated in the report concerning Ḥuwayyiṣah and Muḥayyiṣah;[9]

and being situated to the right of the cup-bearer for the priority of drinking, as narrated by Ibn ʿAbbās.[10]

ADMONITIONS

(1) Rights might be the entitlement of one person, which constitutes the most personal and specific manner of making use of it. They might also be the entitlement of a specified group, such as a number of partners sharing the use of a house or piece of land. They might be the entitlement of an unspecified group, such as the rights of people sharing a common attribute, like soldiers, poor people, students and scholars, the common grazing of tribes, and the public rights of all members of the community, like their right to the public treasury. If some of the group sharing a particular right require to be given their share separately, their request must be fulfilled, for this is the rule governing whatever is liable to distribution.

Some variants of this kind of rights can be managed by resorting to the appointment of trustees to look after the use of the shared right. This will be discussed in conjunction with the objective of the Shariʿah regarding the institution of judges and rulers (*ḥukkām*).

(2) Depriving people of certain rights to which they are proven ineligible is an intended objective of the Shariʿah, which might obtain in one of the categories of rights explained above, such as stripping a person of a right to which he or she is not entitled by nature. An example is the exclusion of women from the obligation to fight in God's cause, as mentioned in the Prophetic tradition explaining the Qur'anic verse:[11]

> Hence, do not covet the bounties which God has bestowed more abundantly on some of you than on others. Men shall have a benefit from what they earn, and women shall have a benefit from what they earn. Ask, therefore, God [to give you] out of His bounty: behold, God has indeed full knowledge of everything. (4:32)

Scholars have varying views of these cases, like preventing a woman from being a judge.[12]

Depriving someone of certain rights may be for the sake of giving priority to one of the parties entitled to it over the rest, as demonstrated in the sixth category. It may also be because someone else's right has been established by one of the ways explained in the third and fourth categories. To this also belongs depriving the insane of their right to manage their property on their own, which is the result of a disorder in their natural capacity to handle their affairs properly. Similarly, it applies to preventing the legally incompetent from handling their property. In both these examples, account must be taken of the rights of the properties' owners, who are incapable of protecting them as well as the rights of their families and heirs.

(3) No person should be deprived of his or her rights except for the sake of a general interest, such as requisitioning land for common grazing (*ḥimā*) or as a base for military forces defending the community. Similarly, a right can be taken from its owner only as compensation for someone else's right that has been used by that person, such as the sale by a judge of the landed property of an indebted person [to pay back the debt], or for the sake of an outweighing right like pre-emption.

34

Maqāṣid al-Shariʿah: Family

The consolidation and proper functioning of the family constitute the foundation of human civilization and the integrating factor of society's order. Therefore, it has been one of the objectives of all laws in the world to take special care of the family by laying down specific rules for its formation and proper functioning. In fact, establishing the family was one of the earliest concerns of civilized human beings in the process of laying down the underpinnings of civilization, toward which they were guided by Divine inspiration. Its purpose was to protect descendants (*ansāb*) from doubt about their lineal identity (*intisāb*), that is, that a man confirms the attribution of his children to himself, as we have already pointed out in chapter 15.

Thus, it has always been the aim of the different systems of law (*sharā'iʿ*) to take care of the founding principle of the family unit, namely the association between the human male and female expressed by the term marriage (*zawāj, nikāḥ*). This is because this bond is the root from which stems human procreation and spreads the notion of kinship (*qarābah*), including both descendants (*furūʿ*) and ascendants (*uṣūl*). This also required the regulation of the in-law relationship (*ṣihr*), that soon manifested its crucial significance for the formation of clans, tribes, and nations. The marriage bond likewise gave rise to motherhood (*umūmah*), fatherhood (*ubuwwah*), and filiations (*bunuwwah*), and from the latter sprang the relationship of brotherhood (*ukhuwwah*) and other more distant kinship ties.

From the combination of the marriage bond with those of lineal and kinship ties emerged the bond of the in-law relationship (*ṣihr*).

Overriding all truthful laws, the Islamic Shariᶜah has instituted the most just, most sound and most sublime rules for the regulation and functioning of the family. Undoubtedly, the most important principle underlying any legislation for the family should consist in consolidating the bonds of marriage, kinship, and in-law relationship and elucidating the ways of dissolving these three bonds if they are liable to dissolution.

THE MARRIAGE BOND

It has been the will of the Originator of the cosmos to ensure the survival and continuation of humankind and the different forms of life. For this purpose, He has made the law (*nāmūs*) of procreation an essential aspect of their governing order. As part of that law, He has endowed mankind and species with a natural impulse propelling individuals to pursue that objective spontaneously, without external incitement or compulsion, to ensure the fulfillment of that law at all times and under all circumstances. This natural impulse consists of the inner inclination of the males of each species toward its females and vice versa.

However, God has endowed the human species with the distinctive sense of discovering and recognizing the meaning and value of virtue and dignity and distinguishing them from whatever good qualities or evil deeds that might surround them. He has thus instilled in human beings the power of reason, which considers acts in terms of their ends and concomitants, and which pursues what is most essential, no matter how. Nevertheless, while sexual desire between the males and females of animal species is satisfied instinctively, human beings, soon after their creation realized the motives and ends as well as concomitants pertaining to the sexual act. They found in the combination of all the senses of love and affection, tenderness and mercy, cooperation and procreation, complementarity and unity, the grounds paving the way for the formation of family units, households, and the establishment of kinship ties, tribes, peoples and nations. Throughout all this they discerned and discovered various notions of good, righteousness, knowledge, and civility.

Likewise, humans have been inspired with the sense that the sexual impulse in their species is not the same as in that of animals, which are aware only of the driving force of desire. They thus came to know that the purpose of their Creator in endowing them with this impulse is in fact more sublime than in the animal species. Accordingly, thanks to the advice of their guides and assistance of their likes, human beings started ennobling this impulse, giving it a shape other than its primitive form at the beginning of Creation. For, indeed, the virtues and noble ends that have resulted from this impulse have made its primitive instinctive root quite insignificant. Hence, the sexual impulse in humankind has acquired its value and significance by virtue of the nobility of its effect.

This important development has been clearly described in the following verse of the Qur'an in which God states:

> It is He who has created you [all] out of one living entity, and out of it brought into being its mate, so that man might incline [with love] towards woman. And so, when he has embraced her, she conceives [what at first is] a light burden, and continues to bear it. Then, when she grows heavy [with child], they both call unto God, their Sustainer, "If You have indeed granted us a sound [child], we shall most certainly be among the grateful!" (7:189)

So, consider the phrases "out of it", "might incline [with love] towards woman", "they both call unto God, their Sustainer", "If You have indeed granted us a sound [child]" and "we shall most certainly be among the grateful." All of these phrases are a clear indication of Divine guidance regarding the sexual impulse and the realization of its virtues and righteous consequences.

Yet, the driving desire of sex can also become vicious and is therefore condemned whenever it is accompanied by evil and repulsive effects, such as those of adultery, prostitution, female infanticide (*wa'd*), licentiousness, and profligacy. The evil of such practices was, however, overlooked during the period of pagan ignorance, just like many other abominable habits and practices. Thus, Bukhārī reported in his *Ṣaḥīḥ* that ʿĀ'ishah, the wife of the Prophet, told ʿUrwah ibn al-Zubayr:

> There were four types of marriage (*nikāḥ*) during the pre-Islamic period of pagan ignorance. One type was similar to that of the present day, that is, a man used to ask somebody else for the hand of a girl under his guardianship or for his daughter's hand, and give her a dower (*mahr*) and then marry her. The second type was that a man would say to his wife after she had become clear from her period, "Send for so-and-so and have sexual relations with him." Her husband would then keep away from her and would never sleep with her till she became pregnant by the other man with whom she was sleeping. When her pregnancy became evident, her husband would sleep with her if he wished. Her husband did so [that is, let his wife sleep with some other man] so that he might have a child of noble lineage. That marriage was called wife-lending (*istibḍāʿ*).
>
> The third type of marriage was when a group of fewer than ten men would gather and visit a woman, and all of them would have sexual relations with her. If she became pregnant and gave birth to a child and some days had passed after her delivery, she would send for all of them – and none would refuse to come. When they had all gathered before her, she would say to them, "You all know what you have done, and now I have given birth to a child. So, it is your child, O so-and-so!" naming whoever she liked, and her child would follow him and he could not refuse to take him.
>
> The fourth type of marriage was when many men would visit a woman and she would never refuse anyone who came to her. Those were the prostitutes, who used to have flags at their doors as signs, and he who wished would have sexual intercourse with them. If any of them became pregnant and delivered a child, all those men would be gathered for her. They would call the *qā'ifs* [that is, people skilled in recognizing the likeness of a child to its father] to them and they would let the child follow the man [whom they recognized as his father]. The

woman would let him belong to him and be called his son. The man could not reject any of that.

However, when Muhammad, *(ṢAAS)*, was sent with the Truth, he abolished all the types of marriage observed in the pre-Islamic period of ignorance except the type that people recognize today.[1]

In her report, ʿĀ'ishah mentioned only what used to be a common and open practice. She did not mention fornication and the keeping of mistresses, which have been pointed out in the following Qur'anic verse:

> And [lawful to you are], in wedlock, women from among those who believe [in this Divine writ], and, in wedlock, women from among those who have been vouchsafed revelation before your time – provided that you give them their dowers, taking them in honest wedlock, not in fornication, nor as secret mistresses. (5:5)

The Qur'an, however, has mentioned only fornication (*sifāḥ*) and the keeping of mistresses (*mukhādanah*)[2] because the practices stated in ʿĀ'ishah's report were permitted during the pre-Islamic times of pagan ignorance and then Islam forbade them. However, the secret practices, that is, fornication and the keeping of mistresses, were not actually allowed even during that period, for men used to prevent the women and girls under their guardianship from indulging in them, as expressed by the poet Umrū' al-Qays[3] in the following verse:

> Slipping past packs of watchmen to reach her,
> with a whole tribe hankering after my blood,
> eager every man-jack to slay me.[4]

Another poet, a slave of the Banū al-Ḥasḥās tribe,[5] also said:

> They are the tribe's women, if their people knew of [what
> We did with them], a great disaster would happen because of them.[6]

In addition, the Arabs used to have another semi-secret sexual relationship called *ḍimād* or *ḍimd*. At times of economic difficulty, a married woman would take a lover who would maintain her financially when her husband was unable to do so. This could happen with the knowledge of the husband himself. The non-Arabs used to have other forms of illegal sexual relationships.

Therefore, it has been one of the most important objectives of the Shariʿah to give special attention to marriage, because it constitutes the basic principle of the family. Likewise, it severely restricted the sexual relationship between man and woman to the marital bond to the exclusion of all other types of relationship mentioned in ʿĀ'ishah's report. The essence of marriage thus consists of the exclusive relationship of a man with one or more women, who are the depository of his offspring (*qarārat al-nasl*) so that this exclusivity ensures the true attribution of her or their offspring to him. From time immemorial, this exclusive relationship between man and woman has always been surrounded by practices that would prevent a woman from falling into a situation that might lead to the confusion of lineage. This restraint originates mainly from a woman's personal chastity that is the result of her upbringing, education, and religiousness. It also originates from her husband's protection of her as well as from the supervision of her neighborhood, which is like a mirror for the husband. Therefore, it was not the purpose of the Shariʿah to rescind those marriages contracted during the time of pagan ignorance, for they had been done in the spirit of those virtuous considerations. This is because in Islam it is not required for the validity of the marriage contract that the parties concerned should observe in it the Shariʿah-legal provision of intention (*niyyah*), for intention does not have any effect in strengthening those considerations emanating from the virtues of manhood and sense of honor.

However, the Shariʿah has bestowed upon the marriage bond a much deeper sense of nobleness and solemnity that it never had before. It likewise considered it the fountainhead of all those virtues. In fact, by casting it in the context of a religious purpose, the Shariʿah has placed marriage in a more sanctified rank, elevating it above the satisfaction of sexual desire. This is clearly indicated in the following Qur'anic verse in which God says: "And among His wonders is this: He creates for you mates out of your own kind, so that you might incline toward them, and He engenders love and tenderness between you: in this, behold, there are messages indeed for people who think" (30:21).[7]

The above discussion makes it crystal clear that the contractual form required for the formation of the marriage bond in the most appropriate manner is incidental to the essence of marriage. This form has emanated from the keen concern to ensure the consent of the woman and her relatives vis-à-vis her association with the man and the latter's genuine intention to share his life with, and be faithful to, her. Otherwise, marriage in the early days of human history used to take place simply by the inclination of the man and woman toward each other and by mutual seduction and consent, so that each would feel comfortable with the other. Likewise, their affairs would run through a course of intimacy and harmony, thus building the family and ensuring the survival and protection of progeny.

Our thorough analysis of the material consisting of the primary and secondary rules regulating marriage, and from which the Shariʿah objectives pertaining to this institution can be inferred, has enabled us to trace two fundamental principles. The first principle aims at establishing a clear-cut distinction between the specific form of the marriage bond and all other possible forms of association between man and woman. The second principle consists of ensuring that marriage is not contracted on a temporary basis.[8]

The importance and scope of the first principle must now have become clear from what has been said so far. In it, the Shariʿah has required adherence to what has been explained in ʿĀ'ishah's report in highlighting the essential difference between marriage and other forms of abominable association of man and woman, resulting in doubt concerning lineal identity (*nasab*). This is achieved by imposing three main conditions. The first is that a guardian of the woman must contract her marriage to her future husband, be it a particular (*khāṣṣ*) or general (*ʿāmm*) guardian – the general guardian being a court judge where the woman has no guardian who is a blood relative. The aim is to ensure that she has not inclined to the man on her own without the knowledge of her immediate family and other relatives.[9]

This constitutes the first aspect of the difference between marriage, on the one hand, and adultery, cohabitation, prostitution and wife-lending (*istibḍāʿ*) on the other. The wisdom behind this is that, generally speaking, guardians would not accept the latter kinds of association between man and woman. More importantly, when a guardian undertakes the contracting of the marriage of the woman under his guardianship, this predisposes him to protect her and makes his relatives, friends, associates, and neighbors also ready to assist him in achieving that. This has been agreed by jurists of all regions and has become the basis of issuing fatwas. The requirement of a guardian in the marriage contract is the majority view of Muslim jurists, with the exception of Abū Ḥanīfah, who stipulated it only for the marriage of the young, the insane, and slaves.[10]

The second condition is that the marriage contract must include a dower (*mahr*) given by the husband to the wife. Dower has become an emblem of marriage, for it is a vestige of old human practices whereby marriage was considered an act of ownership, in which the wife was regarded as a slave. None the less, dower in Islam is not a substitute for the husband's exclusive relationship and sexual intercourse (*buḍʿ*) with the wife, as expressed by certain jurists as an approximate comparison. If it were a substitute, the amount of the benefit that it would compensate should have been taken into account. This should, in turn, have required that another sum of money must be paid by the husband when it is clear that the previous sum has already been exhausted by the benefits that he has enjoyed during the time he has spent with his wife, just as in a contract of hire (*ijārah*).

Indeed, if dowry is given for the woman, how could she be required to return it upon divorce when God has said: "But if you desire to give up a wife and take another in her stead, do not take away anything of what you have given the first one, however much it may have been. Would you, perchance, take it away by slandering her and thus committing a manifest sin?" (4:20) It is thus a pure gift and a symbol of marriage, distinguishing it from fornication and cohabitation. That is why God has called it a gift in the following verse: "And give unto women their marriage portions in the spirit of a gift" (4:4).

As for calling it by the word wage (*ajr*) in the following verse:

> And [lawful to you are], in wedlock, women from among those who believe [in this Divine writ], and, in wedlock, women from among those who have been vouchsafed revelation before your time – provided that you give them their dowers (*ujūr*),[11] taking them in honest wedlock, not in fornication, nor as cohabitation. (5:5)

This is not meant in its apparent connotation and, therefore, calls for interpretation. This is why the type of marriage known as *shighār* has been prohibited, owing to its lack of dower. From the legal point of view, marriage has taken the form of contract owing to the existence of the offer-and-acceptance formula and dower, which is only incidental to it. For this reason, our scholars said: "marriage contracts are based on virtue and quality (*mukāramah*), while sales are based on measure and quantity (*mukāyasah*)."[12]

I do not, however, mean that the Shariʿah has totally ignored the woman's benefit ensuing from the dower. I only mean that this is not of primary importance in the sight of the Shariʿah. Otherwise, I fully realize that a woman's beauty and virtuous qualities are a blessing that God has bestowed on her and authorized her to make use of in relation to the man's desire to take her as his wife. Accordingly, it is a woman's right that her dower should be commensurate with her nobility and value, for her beauty and good character constitute one of the means of gaining her living. That is why neither the executor (*waṣīy*) nor the judge or ruler is allowed to give the orphan girl under his guardianship in marriage with a dower less than that which she deserves (*mahr al-mithl*). Thus, God says: "And if you have reason to fear that you might not act equitably towards orphans, then marry from among [other] women such as are lawful to you – [even] two, or three, or four" (4:3). The meaning of the apodosis entailed by the conditional clause in this verse has been elucidated in the following tradition.

ʿUrwah ibn al-Zubayr narrated that when he asked ʿĀ'ishah about the meaning of this verse, she said,

> O son of my sister! An orphan girl used to be under the care of a guardian with whom she shared property. Her guardian, being attracted by her wealth and beauty, would intend to marry her without giving her a just *mahr*, that is, the same *mahr* as any other person might give her [in case he married her]. So those guardians were forbidden to do that unless they did justice to their female wards and gave them the highest *mahr* that their peers might receive. God ordered them to marry women of their choice other than those orphan girls.

ʿĀ'ishah added,

> The people asked God's Apostle his instructions after the revelation of this verse whereupon God revealed: "And they will ask you to enlighten them about the laws concerning women. Say: 'God [Himself] enlightens you about the laws concerning them' – for [His will is shown] in what is being conveyed unto you in this Divine writ about orphan women [in your charge],[13] to whom – because you yourselves may be desirous of marrying them – you do not give that which has been ordained for them..."(4:127)

ʿĀ'ishah further said,

> And God's statement: "you yourselves may be desirous of marrying them" refers to a man's refraining from marrying an orphan girl [under his guardianship] when she is lacking in property and beauty. Therefore, they were forbidden to marry those orphan girls for whose wealth and beauty they had a desire unless with justice, and that was because they would refrain from marrying them if they were lacking in property and beauty.[14]

From this we learn that a woman's benefiting from the dower and making use of her God-given talents and qualities as a means for earning money is not totally disregarded in the Shariʿah. Indeed, if it were so, it would be harmful to the woman. This is why God has said in this respect, "to fear that you might not act equitably toward orphans," meaning that is, to fear to act not in fairness, thus calling it injustice.

The third condition is a public declaration (*shuhrah*). The reason for this condition is that keeping marriage secret brings it closer to adultery and prevents people from honoring and protecting it. It also raises doubt regarding the lineal identity (*nasab*) of its offspring and exposes the woman's chastity to suspicion and makes it defective in the sight of the people. Certainly, there can be some reasons for hiding it from people, such as the jealousy of another wife in a polygamous marriage. However, this might be overlooked if other conditions pertaining to the validity of marriage have been satisfied, such as its being attested by two witnesses and known by a large number of people.

It has been maintained by some jurists that a marriage whose witnesses have agreed to keep it totally concealed from others is in fact a secret marriage, even if their number is as big as the crowd filling a mosque. Although this view is disputed, what is most likely is that total secrecy in marriage has a nullifying effect. Hiding it from some people is not seriously prejudicial. None the less, something remains to be investigated. That is, whether the documentation of marriage and registration of the attestation of the witnesses in such a way that would preclude the possibility of its denial can replace the public declaration in realizing most of the wisdom it contemplates. This is indeed an issue that calls for further ijtihad.

Thus, the public declaration of marriage aims at achieving two main objectives. Firstly, it makes the husband more concerned about taking care of his wife. Since he knows that people are aware of his exclusive relationship with her, anything raising suspicion about her character is disgraceful to him personally. Secondly, the declaration and publicity of marriage commands more respect for the woman from the people and prevents other men from any covetous inclination toward her, as she is covert and inaccessible to them by being married (*muḥṣanah*).[15]

That is why the Qur'an has considered marriage a kind of moral protection (*iḥṣān*). Hence it has considered husbands moral protectors (*muḥṣinīn*), whereas it has described the wives as being morally protected (*muḥṣanāt*), using for this the *nomen patientis* form.

Likewise, we read verses such as the following:

> And [lawful to you are], in wedlock, women from among those who believe [in this Divine writ], and, in wedlock, women from among those who have been vouchsafed revelation before your time – provided that you give them their dowers, taking them in honest wedlock (*muḥṣinīn*), not in fornication, nor as cohabitation. (5:5)

> Marry them, then, with their people's leave, and give them their dowers in an equitable manner – they being women who give themselves in honest wedlock (*muḥṣanāt*). (4:25)

Moreover, the Qur'an describes wives as women who have become protected, as in the following expression: "... and when they are married (*fa'idhā uḥṣinna*)" (4:25), using the subjective form, which implies that they are protected by their husbands.[16]

The second principle underlying the rules governing marriage is that concluding the marriage contract on a temporary basis likens it to hire and tenancy contracts. Consequently, it strips marriage of the sense of nobility and sanctity emanating from the sincere intention of each spouse to be a mate and consort to the other so long as their conjugal relationship and lives run properly. Under such temporary circumstances, they will be concerned to do only what will help them to preserve it for a limited period. This is because whenever something is temporary, thus being limited to a certain time, it creates in the minds the eagerness of awaiting its deadline and the concern about preparing for its eventual replacement. Likewise, the wife will be merely preoccupied with either looking forward to another man, promising him and awakening his desire for her or taking advantage of the husband's wealth as much as possible.

This throws both the husband and wife into a state of psychological disorder that prevents them from being dedicated to each other. Undoubtedly, this situation results in the weakening of the sense of moral fortification and chastity (*ḥaṣānah*) mentioned above. This is why temporary marriage (*nikāḥ al-mutʿah*) was allowed in the early days of Islam and then abolished at Khaybar.[17] The majority of scholars are of the view that it is an invalid marriage and that if that type of marriage has been contracted, it must be rescinded. Some jurists, however, have deviated from this general position and allowed it either in absolute terms, a view attributed to the Zaydites,[18] or only in the case of a journey [keeping one away from one's wife]. It seems those holding the permissibility of temporary marriage had in mind the rule tolerating the commission of the lesser of two evils (*irtikāb akhaff al-ḍararayn*) to avoid falling into the evil of adultery. This view has been widely attributed to Ibn ʿAbbās.[19]

Having firmly established the sense of the sacredness and solemnity of the marriage bond, the Shariʿah has prescribed upon the husbands to live in good companionship with their wives and to take great care of them. Accordingly, it has considered any harm resulting from the failure to do so a sufficient reason for the dissolution of the marriage bond through divorce by a court judge once such harm has been confirmed. Thus, we read the following verses in the Qur'an:

> And consort with your wives in a goodly manner; for if you dislike them, it may well be that you dislike something which God might yet make a source of abundant good. (4:19)

> And for those women whose ill-will you have reason to fear, admonish them [first]; then leave them alone in bed; then chastise them; and if thereupon they pay you heed, do not seek to harm them. Behold, God is indeed Most High, Great. (4:34)

> And if a woman has reason to fear ill-treatment from her husband, or that he might turn away from her, it shall not be wrong for the two to set things to rights between themselves: for peace is best, and selfishness is ever-present in human souls. (4:128)

I believe the limit to the number of wives that a man can have at the same time as only four has taken into consideration the husband's capacity to observe justice and consort with his wives in a goodly manner. This is clearly implied in the following extract from the Qur'an: "but if you have reason to fear that you might not be able to treat them with equal fairness, then [only] one – or [from among] those whom you rightly possess. This will make it more likely that you will not deviate from the right course" (4:3). Likewise, the duty of the husband to maintain (*infāq*) his wife, even if she is rich, aims at actualizing the marriage bond, while considering marriage a ground for inheritance [between spouses] aims at consolidating that bond.

THE LINEAGE (*NASAB*) AND KINSHIP (*QARĀBAH*) BONDS

The kinship bond is an outgrowth of the filial relationship (*bunuwwah*) and parenthood (*ubuwwah*), for it is the sexual intercourse between the males and females that is at the origin of descent (*nasl*). However, the descent that is respected by the Shariʿah is that originating from sexual intercourse within a marital contract excluding any doubt about its lineal identity (*nasab*). From a relevant and thorough examination of the Shariʿah, we have learnt that the Shariʿah aims at establishing a genuine lineal identity that can be achieved only within marriage, whose characteristics we have already explained.

However, the Shariʿah did accept what ensued from prevailing conventions other than marriage (like prostitution, wife-lending, etc.) that had been used for confirming lineal identity (*ithbāt al-nasab*) before Islam, because people of the period of pagan ignorance (*Jāhiliyyah*) had trusted them in this regard. The reason was that the validity of lineage before the institution of the Islamic rules of marriage was entrusted to people's natural propensity to reject attributing to himself or herself someone who was not of their descent. The offspring of the different forms of sexual relationship known during the period of pagan ignorance constituted rare cases that were mixed with the prevailing authentic descent and, thus, people trusted them as a means of confirming lineal identity. Therefore, further detailed investigation into this topic would be so difficult and impractical that it would be a waste of time and only cause trouble and disorder. Furthermore, it would be an excuse for people to vilify one another and shed doubt on one another's lineal identity, especially since people's lineal identities (*ansāb*) before the advent of Islam had been established during times lacking in accuracy and righteousness. For all these reasons, the Shariʿah concerned itself with abolishing only those forms of sexual relationship that are prone to uncertainty so that people do not revert to them.

In addition to marriage as a valid basis for establishing lineage, sexual intercourse with one's female slave (*tasarrī*) has also been accepted as a valid means of lineal identity, so that the child borne by the female slave is attributed to her master. The reason is that when the master takes his female slave in an intimate and covetous relationship, he becomes much more concerned about her character and chastity than about that of ordinary maidens owing to both natural and social motives. Thus, when she bears a child, she becomes what is known as the child's mother (*umm walad*), whose status is dealt with under specific juristic rules in Islamic jurisprudence.[20] However, the Shariʿah did not allow freemen to marry female slaves unless they could not afford to marry free women or they feared falling into the evil [of adultery]. This is because the situation comprises two kinds of mastery over the slave woman, namely, that of her master and that of her husband, in which case her chastity (*ḥaṣānah*) is defective owing to her being possessed by a master. This gives her a status similar to that of a woman married to more than one man at the same time. In contrast, a male slave is allowed under the Shariʿah to marry a female slave, for a free woman does not usually agree to marry a slave. Nevertheless, as already mentioned, a free man is allowed to marry a female slave in a case of necessity.

Likewise, by attributing children to their real fathers, the preservation of lineal identity (*ḥifẓ al-nasab*) undoubtedly endows the offspring with a deep sense of filial devotion and obedience to their parents just as it instills in the parents a profound feeling of affection and compassion for their offspring. This is a real and deeply rooted element of human nature; it is in no way a figment of the imagination.

The great concern of the Shariʿah about the protection of lineal identity and its confirmation beyond the slightest doubt stems from a profound consideration of an important psychological aspect of God's mystery in His fashioning of human beings. Its obvious and more immediate objective is to stabilize and enhance the establishment of the family and prevent all causes of disputes resulting from deep-rooted human jealousy or the parents' doubt about their offspring's lineage and vice versa. To the marital bond has been added that of breastfeeding, whereby the wetnurse has been considered a real mother and the foster brother a real brother as stated in the following Qur'anic verse and Prophetic Tradition enumerating the women one is not allowed to marry: "and your milk-mothers, and your milk-sisters" (4:23); "What is forbidden (*ḥarām*) by blood relationship (*nasab*) is forbidden by fosterage (*raḍāʿ*)."[21]

From the solemnity and sanctity of the kinship bond has emerged the sense of shrouding it in inviolability and veneration in such a way that the Shariʿah has declared the unlawfulness of marriage by lineage, namely the prohibition of marriage between ascendants (*uṣūl*) and descendants (*furūʿ*). The reason is that full kinship (*qarābah tāmmah*) is regarded with both honor and sublime affection free from all kinds of obscene feeling or erotic desire. That is why marriage with the enumerated next-of-kin women has been forbidden.

Of course, the reason for the ban varies according to the categories of women with whom marriage has been prohibited. Thus, Fakhr al-Dīn al-Rāzī had the following to say about those women in the lineage (*nasab*) category:

> As a reason for the prohibition of marrying one's mother, scholars have mentioned that sexual intercourse with her constitutes a sort of humiliation from which people usually recoil. It is therefore a practice from which mothers must be excluded and protected. The same applies to the other categories.[22]

In my view, this can be formulated more precisely as follows. Since one important and pervading aspect of the purpose of marriage consists of sexual pleasure, it is natural that the relationship between the husband and wife should not be burdened with the sense of shyness and chastity. This, undoubtedly, runs counter to what is required by kinship as respect and honor on one side and decency and modesty on both sides. This is clearly applicable to a man's ascendants and descendants as well as their counterparts such as paternal and maternal aunts. The prohibition of marriage between brothers and sisters aims at endowing them with a sense of mutual respect.

Turning now to the prohibitions based on the marital relationship (*ṣihr*), we find that some of them, like that of marrying one's stepmother or stepdaughter – even if her daughter has passed away – once the marriage has been consummated with the mother, are because they have been annexed to lineage. Other prohibitions are meant to prevent any kind of discord that might lead to severing the ties of kinship, the strengthening of which is one of the Shariᶜah's objectives. Accordingly, it is forbidden to marry two sisters at the same time or to marry a woman and her maternal or paternal aunt at the same time.[23]

The reason for the prohibition based on fosterage (*raḍāᶜ*), is that the Shariᶜah has given the bond of wet-nursing the same status as that of lineage according to the Prophet's Saying: "What is forbidden (*ḥarām*) by blood relationship (*nasab*) is forbidden by fosterage." The prohibition based on someone else's right are self-evident and do not need justification. For example, Mālik's prohibition of some cases of polygamy due to the harm that the first wife incurs. Furthermore, there are prohibitions based on the difference of religion, whereby a Muslim is not allowed to marry someone embracing a faith that is not based on Divine revelation.[24] The reason is that there is a basic difference between Islam and non-revealed religious faiths, which is not true of revelation-based religions.

Some marriage prohibitions are based on what is totally God's right. For instance, an irrevocably divorced woman is banned from remarrying the man who has divorced her if she has not married another man and the marriage has not been consummated.

Since women are the depository of descent (*qarārat al-nasl*), the Shariᶜah has forbidden a woman to be the wife of more than one man at the same time (*taʿddud azwāj*), whereas it has permitted a man to have more than one wife up to a specific limit and under certain conditions.

The considerations observed during the age of pagan ignorance for the preservation of the purity and legitimacy of descent and the precise rules and regulations set up by Islam for achieving this purpose stem from a very profound and noble concern about the protection of the rights of offspring from being violated as well as preventing perverted upbringing and education as a consequence of the lack of proper guardianship and care.

The Shariʿah strengthens the kinship bond further with additional measures, such as making it one's duty to provide financial maintenance (*nafaqah*) for one's children and parents.[25] They also include, according to some scholars, the obligation to provide maintenance for one's grandparents and grandchildren.[26] These measures include, for example, considering kinship in general the grounds for inheritance[27] as well as the command to be kind and respectful toward one's parents and next of kin. These measures have no parallels in earlier religious laws. To this also belongs the immunity from blame for eating at the homes of one's relatives without invitation or permission, as stated in the following Qur'anic verse:

> and neither [does blame attach] to yourselves for eating [whatever is offered to you by others, whether it be food obtained] from your [children's] houses, or your fathers' houses, or your mothers' houses, or your brothers' houses, or your sisters' houses, or your paternal uncles' houses, or your paternal aunts' houses, or your maternal aunts' houses. (24:61)

A similar measure is the rule concerning a woman's display of her charms, as in the following verse:

> And tell the believing women to lower their gaze and to be mindful of their chastity, and not to display their charms [in public] beyond what may [decently] be apparent thereof; hence, let them draw their head-coverings over their bosoms. And let them not display [more of] their

> charms to any but their husbands, their fathers, their husbands' fathers, their sons, their husbands' sons, their brothers, their brothers' sons, or their sisters' sons. (24:31)

Thus the Qur'an has mentioned the close male relatives together with the husbands. This principle can be applied equally to the females belonging to the categories enumerated in the verse, such as the mother-in-law in relation to her daughter's husband and the brother's daughter in relation to her uncle. One of the rights based on the lineage bond is inheritance, with which we shall be dealing in chapter 36.

RELATIONSHIP BY MARRIAGE (*ĀṢIRAT AL-ṢIHR*)

This relationship stems from the combination of lineage and marriage, as stated by God in the following verse: "And He it is Who out of this [very] water has created man, and has endowed him with [the consciousness of] descent (*nasaban*) and relationship by marriage (*ṣihrā*)" (25:54). It also grows from the sense of respect and honor, on which the love for one's relatives is based, as has already been mentioned. Likewise, the relationship by marriage (*ṣihr*) is established by those whose kinship is formed on the basis of the marriage bond, such as stepdaughters, sisters-in-law, the wife's paternal and maternal aunts and the mother-in-law. It is also formed from the marriage with those belonging to the kinship bond, such as the daughter-in-law and the mother-in-law.

As it came into being, the relationship by marriage developed into two kinds: close (*qarīb*) and distant (*baʿīd*). That is why marriage is forbidden between the mother-in-law or the sister-in-law and the husband, similarly, between the father-in-law or the brother-in-law and the wife. The reason for these prohibitions is the combination of the unlawfulness stemming from both the kinship relationship of those who are forbidden to the wife or the husband and their relationship by marriage with the husband or the wife.

The Shariʿah has also forbidden marriage between the mother-in-law and the son and the daughter-in-law and the father. The purpose of this is not merely to preserve the ties of affection between the forbidden person and the person who is the cause of the prohibition. This is because we find that, with the exception of the ban on marrying two sisters at the same time,[28] the prohibition based on the relationship by marriage (*ṣihr*) continues even after the death of the person who is the cause thereof. This is the result of a close relationship by marriage (*ṣihr qarīb*). The distant relationship by marriage (*ṣihr baʿīd*) consists of various degrees. Some of those degrees are grounds for the prohibition of conjoining, such as two sisters, or a woman and her paternal and maternal aunts, whereas others do not fall into this category because the bond is so weak.

THE WAYS OF DISSOLVING THREE BONDS

Whenever it is proven that any of these bonds is corrupt and collapsing or that it cannot be maintained properly, the Shariʿah has established a specific way for its dissolution. Our aim here is to explain how this is done. It is worth noting that the methods laid down are based on the general purpose of the creation and annulment (*fusūkh*) of contracts, even though the lineage (*nasab*) bond and relationship by marriage (*ṣihr*) are not contracts and the contractual form of marriage is only incidental and has no meaning in itself. As already pointed out, marriage has been raised to a higher status than ordinary contracts, for which reason it has become an established juridical maxim that "marriage contracts are based on quality and nobleness (*mukāramah*), whereas sales are based on measure and quantity (*mukāyasah*)."

The dissolution of the marriage bond takes place either through divorce by the husband or a court judge or through rescission. The purpose of dissolution is to prevent a greater harm by tolerating a lesser one whenever it has become difficult for the husband and wife to live in marital harmony and there is fear of disorder in their personal lives that threatens to embarrass the whole family. Hence, as indicated by the Qur'an, divorce has been allowed as a last resort to put an end to these evils:

> A divorce may be [revoked] twice, whereupon the marriage must either be resumed in fairness or dissolved in a goodly manner. And it is not lawful for you to take back anything of what you have ever given to your wives unless both [partners] have cause to fear that they may not be able to keep within the bounds set by God: hence, if you have cause to fear that the two may not be able to keep within the bounds set by God, there shall be no sin upon either of them for what the wife may give up [to her husband] in order to free herself. These are the bounds set by God; do not, then, transgress them: for they who transgress the bounds set by God – it is they, they who are evildoers! (2:229)

Of the two spouses, the authority of divorce has been given to the man because he is mostly more concerned about keeping his wife, more attached to her, and more clear-sighted concerning the well-being of the family. Yet, the woman has been given the right to obtain a divorce either by self-redemption (*khulʿ*) or by taking the matter to the court in the case of harm. Moreover, the Shariʿah has established measures for protecting the woman against the weak-mindedness and uncouthness of certain men or certain tribes or certain ages as well as against easy recourse by the husband to divorce as a result of following his immediate and temporary lusts and desires. Thus, she has been given the right to stipulate in the marriage contract that the authority of her divorce should be in her hands, that her husband's marriage to a second wife must depend on her consent and that, if the husband causes her any harm or damage, then it is up to her to decide what could be done, etc. To this effect, it has been narrated that the Prophet said: "From among all the conditions which you have to fulfill, the conditions which make it legal for you to have sexual relations [that is, the marriage contract] have the greatest right to be fulfilled."[29]

In this connection, Saʿīd ibn al-Musayyab was of the view that any supplementary condition to the marriage contract was absolutely invalid, that is, whether it constituted part of the contract itself or was just appended to it.[30] Mālik ibn Anas, on the other hand, held the view that if the condition was part of the marriage contract, it was invalid. However, if it is stipulated voluntarily by the husband after the marriage contract has been concluded, then it is binding for two reasons: (1) one is bound by the decision to which one has committed oneself; and (2) this is apparently implied by the above-mentioned hadith.[31] This is indeed a weak point of view. For, how can the matter be on the part of the husband while the Prophet has called it "conditions that have the greatest right to be fulfilled"? Furthermore, if it is simply a matter of volunteering, it is rather more appropriate that it should not be binding for the man for whom such a condition has been stipulated. This is only absurd, for no other reason would commit the woman to marriage!

Divorce by a court judge or rescission, has been legalized as a means of preventing harm when the marriage does not take place according to the rules enunciated by the Shariʿah.

Let us now look at the dissolution of the lineal bond (*āṣirat al-nasab*). This depends on the filial bond (*bunuwwah*), because, as we have already seen, the latter is the real root of lineage (*nasab*). Linked to it are the ties of fatherhood, motherhood, and the other kinship ramifications. This means that when the filial bond is confirmed, the rest follow suit and, equally, if it is negated, they too are negated. Indeed, using the word dissolution to designate the abolition of the lineal bond entails a considerable degree of tolerance, for it is not the demolition of a solid construction, but a realization of the untruth of what was believed to be a lineal bond. Established lineage, however, can be neither dissolved nor revoked.

Thus qualified, the dissolution of the lineal bond is effected in two different ways. One is by imprecation (*liʿān*), while the other is by proving the descent of a person from a father other than the man to whom he attributes himself or people attribute him. The rules of imprecation have been specified in Islamic jurisprudence. In this connection, the Prophet abolished the denial of lineal identity based on the dissimilarity of the child from the father, for this is not a valid reason,[32] notwithstanding the fact that the Arabs and many other nations erroneously relied on it when deciding people's lineal identity out of sheer ignorance.

The second method was established in the Shariʿah by the abolition of adoption (as practiced by the Arabs before Islam) according to God's statement in the following verse: "[As for your adopted children,] call them by their [real] fathers' names: this is more equitable in the sight of God; and if you know not who their fathers were, [call them] your brethren in faith and your friends" (33:5). Thus, Islam referred people to what they actually knew concerning the confirmation of adopted children's lineal identity by calling them by their real fathers' names, such as Zayd ibn Ḥārithah, who used to be called Zayd ibn Muḥammad, and Sālim the adopted son of Abū Ḥudhayfah, who used to be called Sālim ibn Abī Ḥudhayfah.[33] This became a universal and eternal truth that whenever there is mistaken lineal attribution, it must be corrected and the true lineal identity established by either clear evidence or indisputable ownership.

However, in the second method, the Shariʿah has allowed the attributed child to defend his or her lineal identity. Accordingly, our scholars have stated that there should be no incapacitation with regard to establishing one's lineal identity.

Lastly, the dissolution of the relationship by marriage is contingent upon that of its root according to juristic details. Thus, certain aspects of this bond admit of absolute dissolution, such as in the case of the woman's sister and paternal and maternal aunts when her marriage with a man is dissolved by death or divorce. In other aspects, it admits of no dissolution, such as in the case of the wife's mother, the father's wife, the son's daughter and the stepdaughters.

35

Maqāṣid al-Shariʿah: Financial Transactions (1)

THE STATUS OF WEALTH ACCORDING TO THE SHARIʿAH

A Shariʿah whose aim is to preserve the human social order and promote the Ummah's prowess and glory could only be considered to have the highest regard for economic wealth. If we thoroughly examine the Qur'anic verses and Prophetic Traditions dealing with property and wealth, believing them to be the mainstay of human society's activities and the solution to its problems, we find ample supporting evidence that property and wealth have an important status according to the Shariʿah.

Indeed, zakah on economic property is the third pillar of Islam, its implementation the emblem of the true Muslim and its absence that of the hypocrite – as in God's statements:

> Behold, your only helper shall be God, and His Apostle, and those who have attained faith – those who are constant in prayer, and render the purifying dues (zakah). (5:55)

> And woe unto those who ascribe divinity to aught beside Him, [and] those who do not spend in charity (zakah): for it is they, they who [thus] deny the truth of the life to come. (41:6–7)[1]

These verses are a clear indication of the importance of wealth to the well-being of the community in both its acquisition and its expenditure.

Thus, reminding human beings of His favors and bounties, God says: "God grants abundant sustenance, or gives it in scant measure, to whichever He wills of His creatures" (29:62); "Are they, then, not aware that it is God Who grants abundant sustenance, or gives it in scant measure, unto whomever He wills?" (30:37). On many occasions, describing those who assist others with their wealth, He says in both a laudatory and motivating tone:

> This Divine Writ – let there be no doubt about it – is [meant to be] a guidance for all the God-conscious who believe in [the existence of] that which is beyond the reach of human perception, who are constant in prayer, and who spend on others out of what We provide for them as sustenance. (2:2–3)

> O You who have attained faith! Spend [in Our way] out of what We have granted you as sustenance ere there come a Day when there will be no bargaining, no friendship, and no intercession. (2:254)

God again says:

> Alluring to man is the enjoyment of worldly desires through women, children, heaped-up treasures of gold and silver, thoroughbred horses, cattle, and lands. All this may be enjoyed in the life of this world – but the most beautiful of all objectives is with God. (3:14)

> and to whom I have granted resources cast. (74:12)

> and He Who made you heirs to their lands, their houses, and their goods. (33:27)

> [O you who believe!] God has promised you many war gains, which you shall yet achieve. (48:20)

> He knows that in time there will be among you sick people, and others

who will go about the land in search of God's bounty [that is, journeying for the sake of trade]. (73:20)

[However,] you will be committing no sin if [during the pilgrimage] you seek to obtain any bounty from your Sustainer [that is, by trading while in the state of *iḥrām* during the Hajj season]. (2:198)

Furthermore, He says: "[Thus, part of such wealth shall be given] to the poor among those who have forsaken the domain of evil: those who have been driven from their homelands and their possessions, seeking favor with God and [His] goodly acceptance" (59:8). Pointing out the importance of economic wealth for fulfilling the community's needs and solving its problems God says: "and strive hard in God's cause with your possessions and your lives" (9:41); "And spend [freely] in God's cause, and let not your own hands throw you into destruction" (2:195).

On the other hand, numerous Traditions have been narrated in which the Prophet is reported to have said:

No doubt this wealth is sweet and green. Blessed is the wealth of a Muslim, from which he gives to the poor, the orphans, and needy travellers.[2]

This worldly wealth is [like] green and sweet [fruit], and whoever takes it without greed, God will bless it for him, but whoever takes it with greed, God will not bless it for him, and he will be like the one who eats but is never satisfied.[3]

The rich are in fact the poor [little rewarded] on the Day of Resurrection, except him to whom God gives wealth which he gives [in charity] to his right, left, in front, and behind, and does good deeds with it.[4]

What made Ibn Jamīl refuse to give zakah, though he had been a poor man, and was made wealthy by God and His Apostle?[5]

It is also narrated in the *Ṣaḥīḥ* of Muslim that Abū Hurayrah reported:

> The poor amongst the emigrants came to the Messenger of God (may peace be upon him) and said: "The possessors of great wealth (*ahl al-duthūr*) have obtained the highest ranks and the lasting bliss." He (the Prophet) said: "How is that?" They said: "They pray as we pray, and they observe the fast as we observe the fast, and they give charity but we do not give charity, and they set slaves free but we do not set slaves free." Upon this the Messenger of God (may peace be upon him) said: "Shall I not teach you something by which you will catch up with those who have preceded you, and overtake those who come after you, only those who do as you do being more excellent than you?" They said: "Yes, Messenger of God." He said: "Extol God, declare His Greatness, and praise Him thirty-three times after every prayer." Abū Ṣāliḥ said: "The poor amongst the emigrants returned to the Messenger of God (may peace be upon him) saying: 'Our brethren, the possessors of property, have heard what we have done and they did the same.' So the Messenger of God said: 'This is God's Grace, which He gives to whom He wishes.'"[6]

In another Tradition, the Prophet is also reported to have said: "Every day two angels come down from Heaven and one of them says, 'O God! Compensate every person who spends in Your Cause,' and the other [angel] says, 'O God! Destroy every miser'."[7] Thus, spending is encouraged by the promise that what one spends will be compensated, whereas one is warned against miserliness, with the threat that what one abstains from spending will be destroyed. Moreover, it is reported that when Kaᶜb ibn Mālik said: "As a part (sign) of my repentance [for remaining behind and not participating in the battle of Tabūk],[8] I would like to give up all my property in the cause of God and His Apostle", the Prophet said to him, "Keep some of your wealth, for it is good for you."[9] He is also reported to have said to Saᶜd ibn Abī Waqqāṣ when he wanted to will all his property in charity: "No... It is better for you to leave your inheritors wealthy than to leave them poor and begging from others. Whatever you spend for God's sake will be considered a charitable deed, even the handful of food you put in your wife's mouth."[10]

Without citing further from the abundant textual proofs in the Shariʿah sources regarding this subject, I must point out here that the extensive quotations cited above are meant to dispel the doubts entertained by many scholars about the importance of wealth in the Shariʿah. It is erroneously believed by them that wealth and property are despised, if not altogether rejected in Islam. However, the spiritual nature of the Shariʿah highlights psychological virtues and moral perfection in contrast with the evil motives that mostly occur to corrupt rich people, causing them to misuse the Provider's (God's) blessing. This characteristic has prevented the Shariʿah sources from explicitly encouraging people to acquire wealth and property and expounding the virtues of that pursuit.

The reason for this is to avoid adding the religious exhortation to human beings' natural impulse to acquire wealth, an impulse which has been highlighted by the Qur'an as in the following verses:

> Alluring to man is the enjoyment of worldly desires through women, children, heaped-up treasures of gold and silver, thoroughbred horses, cattle, and lands. All this may be enjoyed in the life of this world – but the most beauteous of all goals is with God. (3:14)

> But nay, nay, [O men, consider all that you do and fail to do:] you are not generous toward the orphan, you do not urge one another to feed the needy, you devour the inheritance [of others] with great greed, and you love wealth with a boundless love! (89:17–20)

Clearly, combining the instinctive wish to acquire wealth with the external encouragement to do so increases people's cupidity and greed and drives them into temptation and wild competition, thus deflecting them from pursuing other more important courses of human perfection. Thus, God says:

> Your worldly goods and your children are but a trial and a temptation. (64:15)

> And know that your worldly goods and your children are but a trial and a temptation, and that with God there is a tremendous reward. (8:28)[11]

> For, it is neither your riches nor your children that can bring you nearer to Us: only he who attains faith and does what is right and just [comes near unto Us]. (34:37)

In an authentic Tradition, the Prophet is also reported to have said:

> By God, I am not afraid that you will become poor, but I am afraid that worldly wealth will be given to you in abundance as it was given to those [nations] before you. You will start competing with one another for it as the previous nations competed for it, and then it will divert you [from good] as it diverted them.[12]

He thus compared the condemned type of competition to that of previous nations, that is, the type of competition whereby people would totally devote themselves to the pursuit of material wealth instead of competing for virtues and moral values. Indeed, such ferocious competition for worldly wealth might even cause people to disprove many values and qualities of human spiritual and moral perfection for the sake of acquiring and accumulating wealth.

Therefore, the Shariʿah has contented itself with simply not forbidding human beings to acquire wealth by legitimate means and with showing the various aspects of good and evil that might ensue from the different ways of spending it. The aim is to use the tools of desire and fear to persuade people to spend their money wisely and avoid misusing it. Similarly, the Shariʿah has been satisfied with not wronging people by depriving them of the virtues and gains ensuing from their wealth when they use it for beneficial purposes. Thus, God says in the Qur'an:

> And when you have performed your acts of worship, [continue to] bear God in mind as you would bear your own fathers in mind – nay, with a

> yet keener remembrance! For there are people who [merely] pray, "O our Sustainer! Give us in this world" – and these shall not partake in the blessings of the life to come. But there are among them those who pray, "O our Sustainer! Grant us good in this world and good in the life to come, and keep us safe from suffering through the fire:" it is these that shall have their portion [of happiness] in return for what they have earned. And God is swift in reckoning. (2:200–202)

> But as for all who lay up (*yaknizūn*) treasures of gold and silver and do not spend them for the sake of God – give them the tidings of grievous suffering [in the life to come]. (9:34)

Regarding zakah, which is mentioned in this verse, the Prophet is reported to have said: "Whatever reaches a quantity on which zakah is payable (*niṣāb*) is not a treasure (*kanz*) when the zakah is paid."[13] Furthermore, we read in the Qur'an: "[But as for you, O believers,] never shall you attain true piety unless you spend on others out of what you cherish yourselves; and whatever you spend – verily, God has full knowledge thereof" (3:92).

Because of this, the Prophet's Companions, during the reign of the third caliph ʿUthmān ibn ʿAffān, rejected the view of Abū Dharr, who preached that people should refrain from acquiring wealth and warned them that the wealth they accumulated would be a curse for them in the life to come. He used to proclaim this view in the streets of Damascus, saying: "Announce to those who accumulate gold and silver [that they will suffer] a grievous chastisement, for their foreheads, sides, and backs will be burnt by hell fire."[14] Then, he would quote the Qur'anic verse 9:34 mentioned in the above paragraph. Muʿāwiyyah ibn Abī Sufyān, the then governor of Shām (Syria), objected to this view by arguing that the verse referred to the followers of previous revelations (*Ahl al-Kitāb*), not to [Muslims], and that any wealth that reached the *niṣāb* was not a treasure (*kanz*) when the zakah was paid. However, Abū Dharr continued to proclaim his view to the extent that Muʿāwiyyah had to complain about him to ʿUthmān, who summoned him to Madinah. There, people swarmed into Abū Dharr's presence and he felt compelled to withdraw to the small city of Rabadhah, east of Madinah.[15] Furthermore, it is an established fact among our scholars that the preservation of wealth is one of the fundamental and universal principles of the Shariʿah, falling into the *ḍarūrī* category. It is also quite clear from their statements that the systems used for increasing and circulating wealth in the community constitute most of what belongs to the *ḥājī* category, such as sale, hire, and *salam*. We have already mentioned the general rule regarding the preservation and increase of wealth in our discussion of the categories of *maṣlaḥah* intended by Islamic legislation. We shall now elaborate on what was covered only briefly.

KINDS OF WEALTH AND PROPERTY

We mentioned earlier that one of the primary objectives of the Shariʿah concerning the community's wealth is to ensure its preservation and growth. Since that wealth consists of an aggregate, it is protected by establishing appropriate rules for its management both at the public and private levels. In fact, the protection of the community's wealth as an aggregate depends on the protection of its particular components consisting of individual property and wealth. Likewise, we find that most of the economic legislation in the Shariʿah is concerned with the protection of the individuals' wealth and private property. This is because the benefits and utility of private property lead to the general public good of the community. In other words, the wealth owned by the individuals benefits both its respective owners and the whole community, for its utility is not restricted to the immediate beneficiaries handling them. This has indeed been indicated by the following verse in which God says: "And do not entrust to those who are weak of judgment (*sufahā'*) your wealth and property (*amwalakum*), which God has made a means of support for you" (4:5).[16] Here, the command is addressed to the community as a whole or to those of it who are in authority. In it, the wealth has been attributed to other than its real owners, because its owners here are the legally incompetent (*sufahā'*), to whom it should not be entrusted. The phrase: "which God has made a means of support for you", further underscores the attribution of wealth to the community and clarifies its purpose, for it describes that wealth as being used for the support and good of the whole community.

Likewise, the wealth circulating among the community can be considered both as a whole and in detail. When considered as a whole, it is the right of the community as a whole, thus enabling the community to live in comfort and be independent of others. It is therefore one of the Shariʿah objectives to regulate the management of wealth. This is to ensure its just distribution in the community as far as possible and to provide all the appropriate means for its growth both in itself and in substitutes, regardless of whether the immediate beneficiaries are individuals, or small or large groups of people. When examined in detail, it is considered by virtue of the fact that each component is the right of the party owning or handling it, whether individuals or groups of people specified or unspecified, or the right of the party to whom it is transferred from its owner. Wealth can be further classified into what belongs to specific individuals or groups and what is earmarked for the interest of unspecified social categories of the community.

The first category consists of the private property of specific owners, while the second consists of what is known in the Shariʿah legal terminology as community property (*māl al-muslimīn*) or the property of the public treasury with its various resources and expenses. The second category originated at the time of the Prophet and comprised items such as the revenues of zakah, the camels earmarked for the transportation of fighters in God's cause, and the armors for them to wear in battle. Thus, it is reported that the Prophet said: "But it is unfair of you to demand a zakah from Khālid, for he is keeping his armor for God's cause."[17] It also includes what has been endowed for the benefit of all Muslims. It is thus reported that when the Prophet said: "Who will buy the well of Rūmah[18] [and endow it for the general welfare of Muslims] so that he may use it as the other Muslims without any privilege", ʿUthmān bought it and endowed it for the good of all Muslims.[19]

To gain deeper insight into this important topic, which only a few scholars of the Shariʿah have covered in some detail, I regard it my duty to treat it thoroughly with special emphasis on its basis. Thus, I would say, the community's possessions and property constitute its wealth, and wealth is what people both as individuals and groups use directly or indirectly to acquire what is beneficial and useful or reject what is harmful, under all circumstances, at all times, and for different purposes. By the expression "under all circumstances, at all times, and for different purposes" we mean that only when they are suitable for use for long periods do possessions count as real wealth, thus excluding flowers and fruit for they do not constitute real wealth, though trading in them is an accessory to wealth. The phrase "directly or indirectly" is meant to pinpoint the fact that making use of one's property can be direct to satisfy one's needs or indirect by exchanging it with someone else to benefit from its replacement.

Wealth is defined as consisting of five simultaneous characteristics: (1) it can be hoarded (*iddikhār*); (2) it is a desirable acquisition; (3) it can be circulated (*tadāwul*); (4) it can be measured (*miqdār*); and (5) it must be acquired (*muktasab*).

Let us now elaborate on these characteristics. A long storage life is required for the following reason. Useful, but perishable goods must be used quickly, even if there is no need of them, whereas they are often inaccessible when the need for them arises. That wealth is a desirable acquisition is a characteristic derived from its utmost usefulness. Likewise, cattle, cereals, and trees are wealth for villagers; gold, silver, jewels, and precious antiques constitute wealth for city dwellers; and cattle and their hair and wool as well as water pools, pastureland, and hunting tools constitute wealth for the Bedouin and rural people.[20] That wealth can be circulated, that is, exchanged, flows from its high desirability and demand for it. Exchange can be the transfer of the property itself from the ownership (*ḥawz*) of one person to the hands of someone else. It can also mean consideration (*iʿtibār*), examples being liability contracts (*ʿuqūd al-dhimam*) like *salam* sales, *ḥawālah* (endorsement; transfer of debt), sales according to a catalog or list of contents (*barnāmij*), and the exchange of bank notes.[21]

Measurability is required because anything lacking that quality cannot be possessed in a particular quantity. Things that are not measurable cannot be stored and do not therefore constitute wealth. Examples are sea, sand, rivers, and forests. However, rivers and forests might be seen as sources of wealth because they provide fertility and manufacturing power. Seas have not been regarded as wealth in the technical language [of the Muslim jurists], although they facilitate the movement of both people and goods for the nations who have access to them rather than those who have not. By contrast minerals have been considered a kind of wealth even though they are not quantified. The amount extracted is usually limited by the high cost entailed.

Finally, the last property of wealth, namely, its acquisition, means that it must have been gained by its owner with real effort. Therefore wealth cannot include sand in a desert region or grass in a forest region.

Now, you should know that economic wealth constitutes an important aspect of the balance of power between different nations and peoples in their quest for control over the world. A nation's strength, sovereignty, self-sufficiency, and independence are proportionate to its economic wealth compared with other nations.

OWNING AND EARNING

There are two ways for the community and its members to create wealth: owning (*tamalluk*) and earning (*takassub*). These two ways have already been mentioned in general terms in chapter 33. Owning is the basis of wealth formation by humans. It consists of possessing anything from which they can gain what will satisfy their needs, whether from their produce or their substitutes, namely, the price of these items. The most important principle of owning consists of exclusive possession. Indeed, it has been one of the basic principles of human civilization that humans would strive to obtain their needs for securing their sustenance and safety. They would thus hunt for their food, pick fruit, cut logs for fire, and build a house for shelter against heat and cold. They would also seek to control nearby water sources to avoid the danger of thirst, possess a horse and equip themselves with weapons for self-defence. They would furthermore acquire nice clothes and precious jewels for their dress and their adornment.

To this end, humans have always been prepared to suffer the sweat of toil and the loneliness of emigration. So, they compete for all that is permissible for human beings; they redirect streams to their land before someone else does so, etc. In so doing, they endure all kinds of fatigue and make every possible physical and mental effort. In this pursuit, they strive to increase their possessions as much as possible and store what exceeds their immediate needs as a reserve to draw upon should misfortune befall them. Their fear of being deprived of these things as a result of their own inability to acquire them or the scarcity or disappearance of resources serves to intensify their desire to stockpile them.

Acquisition and stockpiling have been considered the basis of ownership and property, and human beings saw that their efforts gave them the exclusive right to whatever they could possess as a result. Accordingly, if one group tried to grab the possessions of another group, then the latter would consider that sheer aggression and injustice and their anger and resistance would be aroused. As people's minds became imbibed with the sense of justice and love for it, they respected one another's possessions and sanctioned their rights to them. Thus, everyone saw that he or she was entitled to dispose of his or her possessions independently. Therefore, God related in the Qur'an that the people of Madyan were astonished at prophet Shuʿayb's[22] attempt to put restrictions on their economic dealings, which was why they rejected and mocked him:

> They said: "O Shuʿayb! Does your [habit of] praying compel you to demand of us that we give up all that our forefathers were accustomed to worship, or that we refrain from doing whatever we please with our possessions? Behold, [you would have us believe that] you are indeed the only clement, the only right-minded man!" (11:87)

In fact, Islam has considered this meaning the basis of property and ownership. Thus, the Prophet is reported to have said in a hadith: "If anyone revives a dead land, it belongs to him, and the unjust root has no right."[23] Then, from the consideration of ownership originating from one's exclusive right to one's possessions together with the consideration of one's labor in such possessions, the Shariʿah has identified the following factors as the only means to acquisition and property (*tamalluk*):

1. Exclusive possession of something to which no one else has the right, such as cultivating barren land (*iḥyā' al-mawāt*);
2. Working on a piece of land with its proprietor, such as *mughārasah*;[24] and
3. Exchanging one item for another, such as sale, and transferring an item from its owner to someone else, such as donation and inheritance.

Likewise, ownership means people's ability in the eyes of the Shariʿah to utilize something (*ʿayn*) or a benefit (*manfaʿah*) by making use of it directly, by exchanging it, or by giving it freely to someone else, thus excluding all obviated disposition.[25] The rule in the Shariʿah with regard to human beings' wealth and possessions is that mature free people have absolute freedom to dispose of them as they wish. Only when the owner is legally incompetent to undertake that authority or disposition can this rule be suspended. This legal incompetence may be due to youth, mental incapacity (that is, insanity and mental retardation affecting one's handling of financial matters), bankruptcy because of indebtedness, loss of one's freedom, or legal limitation of one's control over all or part of one's wealth. The last form of incompetence relates to the donating of more than the third of one's property by someone who is dangerously ill. It also includes disposing of a property that is conditional upon its owner's death, such as bequests. It also consists of a donation of more than the third of her wealth by a married woman living with her husband.

Earning (*takassub*) consists of exerting oneself to gain what would help to satisfy one's needs, whether by physical labor or by mutual consent with others. It depends on three primary factors (*uṣūl*): land (*arḍ*), labor (*ʿamal*), and financial capital (*ra's al-māl*).

Land occupies the foremost place among these three factors. When we use the term land here, we mean everything to which human labor can be applied on the planet Earth, including seas and oceans, rivers, minerals, water springs, etc, though land in the sense of ground and mainland is the first and most readily accessible source of wealth. This is because land in this sense is the source of trees, grain, and pasturage as well as water springs. Hence, God says:

> And after that, the earth: wide has He spread its expanse, and has caused its waters to come out of it, and its pastures.[26] (79:30–31)

> He it is Who has made the earth easy to live upon:[27] go about, then, in all its regions, and partake the sustenance which He provides: but [always bear in mind that] to Him you shall be resurrected. (67:15)

> He it is Who has created for you all that is on earth. (2:29)

> Let man, then, consider [the sources of] his food: [how it is] that We pour down water, pouring it down abundantly; and then We cleave the earth [with new growth], cleaving it asunder, and thereupon We cause grain to grow out of it, and vines and edible plants, olive trees and date-palms, gardens thick with foliage, and fruits and herbage, for you and for your animals to enjoy.[28] (80:24–32)

Of course, land varies in its fertility. Thus, its most fertile areas are the richest, for which reason desert sands are of lesser economic and financial value.

On the other hand, labor is the means of extracting most of the earth's bounties. It is also the means of creating wealth from such businesses as hire, trade, etc. The basis of labor is mental soundness and physical vigor. Mental soundness is the condition for proper management of the means of wealth, while physical strength is the condition for its implementation, such as the use of machines and animals. Labor includes such things as sowing, planting, and traveling to import foodstuffs and goods. Therefore God reminds us of this favor in the following verses: "He it is who enables you to travel on land and sea" (10:22); "He knows that in time there will be among you sick people, and others who will go about the land in search of God's bounty" (73:20).

Labor might be undertaken by the acquirer of wealth with a view to ownership (*tamalluk*), such as logging and reviving barren land (*iḥyā' al-mawāt*), or with a view to earning, such as exchanging one's property for an item of higher value. Someone other than the owner of the wealth might also undertake labor. This consists of the work performed by one person on someone else's property so as to rescue a portion of it in exchange for one's labor, such as hire in physical labor.

Financial capital enables the continuation of labor to increase one's wealth. It consists of savings that are spent in a way that produces profit. Indeed, financial capital has been considered among the basic sources of wealth, for it is essential for the continuation of work. If financial capital is lacking, laborers might be unable to continue their work and thus their earnings would come to an end. Obviously, means of work, such as engines, steam-driven machines, electrical equipment, and even animals used for packing and plowing, would constitute part of capital.

With that knowledge, you should now realize that people's financial transactions are based upon either ownership, such as buying residential property and foodstuff for consumption, or earnings, such as buying land and olive trees for cultivation. To the latter belong all types of partnership contracts, such as *commenda* (*qirāḍ*) and the land tenures of *muzāraʿah*, *mughārasah*, and *musāqāh*. It also includes the different types of hire contracts such as hiring oneself, animals, machines, ships, trains, etc.

36

Maqāṣid al-Shariʿah: Financial Transactions (II)

THE NATURE OF WEALTH

The objectives of the Shariʿah concerning all kinds of economic wealth can be summarized under five headings: marketability (*rawāj*); transparency (*wuḍūḥ*); preservation (*ḥifẓ*); durability (*thabāt*); and equity (*ʿadl*) in handling it. Marketability implies the fair circulation of wealth in the hands of as many people as possible. It thus constitutes one great objective of the Shariʿah, clearly attested to by its encouragement of financial activity and its requirement to document the handing over of property from one person to another.

Concerning marketability, the Qur'an says: "He knows that in time there will be among you sick people, *and others who will go about the land in search of God's bounty*" (73:20). In the same context, it is reported that the Prophet said: "Whenever a Muslim plants a tree, he earns the reward of charity, for what is eaten from it is charity; what is taken from it, what the beasts eat from it, what the birds eat from it is charity for him."[1] It is also reported that ʿAbd Allāh ibn ʿUmar said: "No death, after martyrdom in the cause of God, is more attractive to me than to die while doing business."[2] This is because the Qur'an has mentioned trade together with fighting in God's cause: "and others who will go about the land in search of God's bounty, and others who will fight in God's cause" (73:20). In *Muwaṭṭa'*, it is narrated that ʿUmar ibn al-Khaṭṭāb said: "Trade with the property of orphans and then it will not be eroded by zakah."[3]

Indeed, the implication (*ishārah*) of the [italicized part of the] following verse clearly indicates the importance of trade in the sight of the Shariʿah:

> And be not loath to write down every contractual provision, be it small or great, together with the time at which it falls due; this is more equitable in the sight of God, more reliable as evidence, and more likely to prevent you from having doubts [later]. *If, however, [the transaction] concerns ready merchandise which you transfer directly to one another, you will incur no sin if you do not write it down.* (2:282)

Out of keen concern for removing any obstacles to trade, it has thus allowed the recording of the transaction to be disregarded [if it concerns ready merchandise]. A further indication of Islam's encouragement of trade is its abolition of the prohibition thereof by the Arabs in their marketplaces, Majannah, Dhū al-Majāz, and ʿUkāẓ, during the pilgrimage season before the advent of the Qur'an. They used to say of anyone trading during the first ten days of Dhū al-Ḥijjah: "He is a trader (*dājj*), not a pilgrim (*ḥājj*)."[4] Islam abolished this tradition in the following verse: "[However,] you will be committing no sin if you seek to obtain any bounty from your Sustainer" (2:198), that is, during the pilgrimage.[5]

There are numerous textual proofs legalizing and encouraging the documentation [of transactions]. Most prominent is the following verse:

> O you who have attained faith! Whenever you give or take credit[6] for a stated term, set it down in writing. Let a scribe write it down equitably between you; and no scribe shall refuse to write as God has taught him: thus shall he write. Let him who contracts the debt dictate; and let him be conscious of God, his Sustainer, and not weaken anything of his undertaking. If he who contracts the debt is weak in mind or body, or, is not able to dictate himself, then let him who watches over his interests dictate equitably. Call upon two of your men to act as witnesses;

> and if two men are not available, then a man and two women from among those who are acceptable to you as witnesses, so that if one of them should make a mistake, the other could remind her. The witnesses must not refuse [to give evidence] whenever they are called upon. Do not be loath to write down every contractual provision, be it small or great, together with the time at which it falls due; this is more equitable in the sight of God, more reliable as evidence, and more likely to prevent you from having doubts [later]. If, however, [the transaction] concerns ready merchandise that you transfer directly to one another, you will incur no sin if you do not write it down. Have witnesses whenever you trade with one another, but neither scribe nor witness must suffer harm; for if you do [them harm], behold, it will be sinful conduct on your part. Remain conscious of God, since it is God who teaches you [herewith] – and God has full knowledge of everything. (2:282)[7]

Of the same purport is the practice of God's Apostle, as we shall see in our discussion of the objectives of judgments and testimonies.

To achieve the purpose of marketability, contracts relating to the various kinds of dealings have been instituted to regulate the transfer of financial rights (*ḥuqūq māliyyah*), whether in exchange for something else or gratis, which constitutes part of the *ḥājī* category of *maṣāliḥ*, as indicated previously. These contracts have been considered binding because of their formulae, that is, the statements indicating the mutual consent of the contracting parties. Certain conditions are required in them for the benefit of both parties. Once a contract has satisfied those conditions, it is valid and produces its legal effect, for the rule is that a contract is binding owing to the existence of its formula.

To facilitate marketability, certain contracts containing a measure of ambiguity (*gharar*) have been allowed such as *mughārasah, salam, muzāraʿah* and *qirāḍ*. Indeed, some of our scholars have defined these contracts as exemptions because they constitute exceptions from the rule of ambiguity (*gharar*),[8] even though they do not consist of an alteration of a *ḥukm* from difficulty to ease for a specific excuse. In describing them as exemptions, they had in mind one or the other of two things: either alteration of rules has a more general meaning than changing a rule after it has been instituted, or that it means changing something which, if confirmed, will run counter to the established rules.

To achieve the purpose of marketability, the rule in the Shariʿah is that financial contracts are binding rather than optional, unless otherwise stipulated, according to God's words: "O you who have attained faith! Be true to your covenants!" (5:1), as has been argued by Qarāfī in his discussion of Rule Number 196 in his book *al-Furūq*.[9] There is no disagreement among jurists over contracts that are binding only after the commencement of the work contracted rather than by their conclusion – namely, *juʿāl*[10] and *qirāḍ*, although there is some disagreement over *mughārasah* and *muzāraʿah*. The reason for this is that the jurists have taken into account the workers' excuse. It means that the workers in these contracts might finish the job quickly out of desire for the return [they expect from it], and then they realize their inability to carry out the work required of them. Accordingly, the real benefit and purpose of a contract lie in its being binding, although this characteristic is defective in these four kinds of contracts owing to accidental impediment, contrary to what has been argued by Qarāfī in Rule Number 209.[11]

One of the meanings of circulation intended by the Shariʿah is the transfer of wealth in the community among as many hands as possible without causing any harm to those who have acquired it lawfully. This transfer is effected by trade as well as compensation given to the workers from the owners' properties. In fact, facilitating the circulation of wealth between all the community's members and preventing it from remaining in the hands of one person or just moving from one specific person to another constitutes an important objective of the Shariʿah that has been clearly indicated in the following Qur'anic statement dealing with the distribution of the spoils of war: "Whatever [spoils taken] from the people of those villages God has turned over to His Apostle – [all of it] belongs to God and the Apostle, the near of kin [of deceased believers], the orphans, the needy, and the wayfarer, so that it may not be [a benefit] going round and round (*dūlah*) among such of you as may [already] be rich" (59:7). The idea of wealth "going round and round" refers to its transfer from one person to another. The verse thus means that the circulation of the wealth ensuing from the spoils, and all wealth for that matter, should not be confined to a few people, such as, for example, transferring it from the hands of the father to those of his eldest son or from one person to his friend.[12]

In fact, the Shariʿah has managed to achieve this objective in an admirably simple way. It has taken full account of people's right to use their property and enjoy its benefits by not confiscating it in such a way as would cause harm to them. In this, it has considered that part of human nature which makes people selfish when it comes to giving their property away. Likewise, in its treatment of the question of wealth, it has looked at it on two levels: during the life of its owner and after the owner's death.

On the first level, the Shariʿah has acknowledged the exclusive right of people to their wealth and has allowed them to use it as they wish during their lifetime. By so doing, it aims at encouraging people to make the effort to earn and save money. In this way, the Shariʿah hopes to achieve its purpose of increasing the community's general wealth and removing any impediments to its progress. Accordingly, no one has any right to another person's wealth and property, except those specified by God, such as zakah in its different forms and the fifth share of spoils.

On the second level the Shariʿah has established a set of rules covering the just distribution of a deceased's estate. It considers that a person would have satisfied his/her desires and interest pertaining to his/her life and property during his/her life and that his/her attachment to it after death is insignificant except as a matter of idle curiosity (*fuḍūl*). It also considers that knowing that one's wealth and property will be divided after one's death does not actually discourage a person from working hard to earn and increase his/her wealth. Therefore, Islam has legislated the distribution of wealth after its owner's death. Accordingly, it has abolished the old practice during the age of pagan ignorance (*Jāhiliyyah*), whereby people would bequest their property to the most loved or famous among their community, either to seek their favor or as a means to express their pride in them. Then, Islam enjoined people to bequeath to their next of kin according to God's statement in the following verse: "It is ordained for you, when death approaches any of you and he is leaving behind much wealth, to make bequests in favor of his parents and [other] near of kin in accordance with what is fair:[13] this is binding on all who are conscious of God" (2:180). Thereafter, this provision concerning bequest was abrogated by laying down the decisive rules of inheritance that have been detailed in the Qur'an and Sunnah,[14] according to which one is not allowed to dispose of one's property after one's death apart from a bequest of one-third of it to non-heirs. Thus, the Shariʿah has achieved its purpose regarding the distribution of wealth in a wise and acceptable manner by transferring it to its owner's next of kin, for this is not contrary to human nature. Besides, these provisions help to preserve the deceased person's wealth within his/her clan or tribe. Since the whole community is comprised of clans and tribes, the Shariʿah thus achieves its ultimate purpose of preserving the wealth within the wider community.

Furthermore, contrary to the practice during the period of pagan ignorance (*Jāhiliyyah*), according to which women were excluded from inheritance, the Shariʿah has not deprived relatives on the maternal side from a share in the property of the deceased person. How could it be otherwise when the Qur'an has called such a share an obligation (*farīḍah*) and stressed compliance with it at the beginning of the passage on inheritance by saying: "Concerning [the inheritance of] your children, God enjoins [this] upon you" (4:11), in the middle by stating: "As for your parents and your children – you know not which of them is more deserving of benefit from you: [therefore this] ordinance from God" (4:11) and at the end by saying: "These are the bounds set by God" (4:13).

One of the means of the distribution of wealth is that part of it must be used to maintain one's spouse(s) and relatives. This has not been left to the whim of the family guardian. Rather, the *Sharʿ* has ordained him to spend his wealth in a reasonable manner. This constitutes part of what has been expressed in the following verses of the Qur'an:

This Divine Writ – let there be no doubt about it – is [meant to be] a guidance for all the God-conscious who believe in [the existence of] that which is beyond the reach of human perception, and are constant in prayer, *and spend on others out of what We provide for them as sustenance.*[15] (2:2–3)

And neither allow your hand to remain shackled to your neck, nor stretch it out to the utmost limit [of your capacity], lest you find yourself blamed [by your dependents], or even destitute. (17:29)

and who, whenever they spend on others, are neither wasteful nor niggardly but [remember that] there is always a just mean between those [two extremes]. (25:67)

Another way of using one's wealth is to spend it on luxuries. This indeed constitutes the most important means of enabling the middle and lower classes of the community to benefit from the wealth of the upper class. It also helps in promoting the talents of craftspeople and artists and encourages them to produce artefacts of first-class workmanship and exquisite taste. This type of spending is mentioned in the following verses:

O Children of Adam! Beautify yourselves for every act of worship, and eat and drink [freely], but do not waste: verily, He does not love the wasteful! Say: "Who is there to forbid the beauty which God has brought forth for His creatures, and the good things from among the means of sustenance?" Say: "They are [lawful] in the life of this world to all who have attained faith – to be theirs alone on Resurrection Day". Thus clearly do We spell out these messages unto people of [innate] knowledge![16] (7:31–32)

However, the Shariʿah has not actively encouraged this method of using wealth. It has rather confined itself to the motivation for it that is ingrained in human nature, as we have already pointed out in chapter 35. It has thus aimed at avoiding that incitement to spend on luxuries, which draws individuals down the road of wastefulness to financial ruin. Of course, any deficiency in one sector of the overall wealth of the community might create a financial upheaval for all its members.

Another important means of circulating wealth is facilitating transactions as much as possible by highlighting their benefits over the minor harm that they might cause. For this reason, the Shariʿah does not require for the validity of sale contracts that the two items of exchange (*ʿiwaḍayn*) be available at the same time, thus avoiding the risk of bankruptcy that might result from that. Similarly, labor-based transactions, such as *mughārasah* and *musāqāh*, and sales based on a catalog have been sanctioned, whereas the harm that they might entail has been minimized. All these measures aim at facilitating exchanges so that people's needs are easily satisfied. This has been clearly indicated in the following Qur'anic passage in which God says: "If, however, [the transaction] concerns ready merchandise which you transfer directly to one another, you will incur no sin if you do not write it down" (2:282).

Valuable items (*mutamawwilāt*) vary greatly in their circulation and marketability according to their category. Easy circulation and marketability are based on four requirements: ease of transportation; suitability for long storage; high demand; and suitability for division into smaller units. Thus, grains such as wheat and barley are more easily marketable than dates, raisins, and dried figs. They are also easier to transport, can be stored for a longer period, are in greater demand, and more easily divided. In contrast, fruits are lower on the scale of all these properties. Dairy produce and meat are lower still. Honey, cooking oil, and butter are on a similar level with regard to storage and transportation, but differ in their level of demand. However, cattle and livestock are in greater demand and are easier to transport but are less suitable for division and long storage. Land and real estate are lower on the scale of all these properties except demand, which is higher, and preservation, for they are less subject to risk.

One of the most important conventions of humankind regarding the economic aspect of human civilization is the institution of money in the form of gold and silver coins (*naqdayn*) as substitutes for their exchanges. In their natural transactions, people used to barter, thus trading certain goods for other goods, the demand for which was based on their utility and individuals' current needs. The more primitive their life style, the less people used gold and silver currencies in their transactions. That was why Muslim jurists classified populations into people of gold and silver and people of cattle. It would have been appropriate if they had also considered in their classification people of cereals and fruits, such as the Aws, the Khazraj, and Thaqīf, for people who used to depend on these commodities for their transactions were numerous among the Arabs both before and after the advent of Islam.

No doubt, money-based transactions are easier than barter in all respects, especially in the division of value and the exchange of large quantities and commodities that cannot be easily bartered, such as land and real estate. However, in the case of pressing necessity, such as during times of siege, drought, and famine, money may be of no use to its possessors. Hence, money is a good medium of exchange under people's normal circumstances, that is, peace, affluence, and abundance.

One important advantage of money-based transactions that is clearly manifested is the possibility to distinguish between the seller and the buyer. Hence, the party providing money is the buyer, while the party providing the merchandise is the seller. Furthermore, money is usually in higher demand than supply, contrary to other commodities that are subject to both supply and demand. Only rarely is money a subject of supply, such as in the case of the owners of capital, who allocate part of their money for others to use, as in *salam, qirāḍ*, and the sale of banknotes.

Many of the transactions that took place during the Prophet's time were in the form of barter. There are many prohibitions against selling items for items because barter usually entails ambiguity (*gharar*) and unfairness (*taghābun*). Moreover, it is difficult to determine the value of the substitutes owing to the wide variation in their properties, such as the difference between the varieties of dates and wheat regarding their freshness, quality, and ripeness.

Furthermore, the fact that a transaction might compel one or both of its parties to accept uncertainty would put the needy party in a difficult position to satisfy his needs. Meanwhile, the other party might be tempted to exploit this situation and impose his terms on his counterpart. Thus, uncertainty and unfairness are usually part of barter, and therefore the Shariʿah has permitted it where it is unavoidable, while forbidding what exceeds the limits of necessity. Is it not apparent that it has allowed *juzāf,* sales of items that can be measured and weighed, but not of gold and silver coins?

Accordingly, it has been narrated by Rāfiʿ ibn Khadīj in the Tradition concerning the prohibition of land rent that people used "to rent the land with the yield of a specific delimited portion of it to be given to the landlord. Sometimes the vegetation of that portion was affected by blight etc., while the rest remained safe, and vice versa, so the Prophet forbade this practice. At that time gold and silver were not used [for renting the land]."[17] Bukhārī mentioned that al-Layth ibn Saʿd commented on this, saying: "If those who have discernment for distinguishing what is legal from what is illegal looked into what has been forbidden concerning this matter, they would not permit it, for it is surrounded by risk."[18] In a Tradition attributed to al-Barā' ibn ʿĀzib and Zayd ibn Arqam, it is reported that they said: "We were traders in the time of God's Apostle and we asked God's Apostle about money exchange. He replied, 'If it is from hand to hand, there is no harm in it; but if it is selling on credit, it is not permissible.'"[19] This means that the Prophet did not forbid excess in monetary exchange as in exchanging food for its own kind. The reason I presume, is the absence of uncertainty for it is possible to determine easily the value of dinars and dirhams. It is also narrated in Mālik's *Muwaṭṭa'* from Abū Saʿīd al-Khuḍrī and Abū Hurayrah that,

> God's Messenger, may God bless him and grant him peace, appointed a man as an agent in Khaybar, and he brought him some excellent dates. The Messenger of God, may God bless him and grant him peace, said to him, "Are all the dates of Khaybar like this?" He said, "No. By God, Messenger of God! We take a *ṣāʿ* of this kind for two *ṣāʿs* or two *ṣāʿs* for three." The Messenger of God, may God bless him and grant him peace, said, "Do not do that. Sell the assorted ones for dirhams and then buy the good ones with the dirhams."[20]

It becomes clear from all this that to increase money-based transactions as a means of encouraging circulation [of commodities and wealth] constitutes one of the Shariʿah objectives. Thus, it is reported in Abū Dāwūd's *Sunan* that ʿAbd Allāh ibn Masʿūd narrated that "God's Apostle forbade breaking the coins of the Muslims current among them except for some defect."[21] I consider the wisdom of the Prophet's prohibition for men to use gold and silver jewellry was only to prevent the decrease in the circulation of gold and silver coins owing to the high demand for these two metals, resulting in their scarcity.

Concerning the legality of the documentation [of dealings], we read God's statements in the Qur'an:

> And have witnesses whenever you trade with one another; O you who have attained faith! Whenever you give or take credit for a stated term, set it down in writing. (2:282)

> And if you are on a journey and cannot find a scribe, pledges [may be taken] in hand: but if you trust one another, then let him who is trusted fulfill his trust, and let him be conscious of God, his Sustainer. (2:283)

The aim of requiring transparency in wealth and property (*wuḍūḥ al-amwāl*) is to avoid harm and disputes as much as possible, for which reason pledges and documentation have been prescribed. The protection of wealth and property is based on God's statement:

> O you who have attained faith! Do not devour one another's possessions wrongfully not even by way of trade based on mutual agreement – and do not destroy one another. (4:29)

It is also based on the Prophet's Sayings:

> No doubt, your blood and your properties are sacred to one another like the sanctity of this day of yours, in this month [Dhū al-Ḥijjah] of yours, in this town [Makkah] of yours.[22]

> No Muslim's property should be allowed to be taken from him without his own accord.[23]

> Whoever is killed while protecting his property then he is a martyr.[24]

These are all clear references to the importance of the protection and protector of property and an indication of the great sin of its aggressor. If this is true of the protection of the individuals' properties (*māl al-afrād*), the protection of the community's property (*māl al-ummah*) is even more important.

Accordingly, it is the duty of the community's rulers and those in charge of its public interests to pay special attention to the protection of its public wealth, whether this wealth is exchanged with other nations or kept in the hands of the community. Of the first aspect mention can be made of the legislation regulating the Muslim community's trade with other nations and specifying how each party's goods and property is to imported into the other party's land. It also includes enacting the regulations governing trade with countries that are at war with the Muslim community. To this belongs also the need to specify the kinds of taxes to be levied on non-Muslim subjects living under Muslim rule (*ahl al-dhimmah*) and on subjects from countries warring against Muslims for the goods that they import into Muslim lands. It also includes the rules on poll tax and land tax. Of the second aspect, reference can be made to the regulation of markets and the monopoly of goods. This also includes the efficient management of the different zakah accounts (*maṣārif*) and public endowments (*awqāf ʿāmmah*).

Likewise, it is incumbent on anyone entrusted with any kind of wealth to protect it in accordance with God's command in the Qur'an:

> And do not entrust to those who are weak of judgment your possessions which God has assigned to you for support (*qawāman*); but let them have their sustenance therefrom, and clothe them, and speak unto them in a kindly way. (4:5)

> And test the orphans [in your charge] until they reach a marriageable age; then, if you find them to be mature of mind, hand over to them their possessions; and do not consume them by wasteful spending, and in haste, ere they grow up. (4:6)

It is equally the duty of everyone to respect property, for which reason the Shariʿah has prescribed compensation for damage to property simply by assessing the damage, regardless of whether or not it was intended, for intention has no effect in such a situation. The documentation of properties is required for their owners in a format to prevent all kinds of risk and dispute.

The purpose of the Shariʿah in imposing this rule is based on the following considerations.

First, that the owner, whether an individual or a group, should have the exclusive right to what has been earned lawfully so that this right is not subject to any kind of delay or risk. Therefore, God says, "And have witnesses whenever you trade with one another" (2:282). Accordingly, no one should be deprived of his/her exclusive right to his/her property except for the sake of a public interest (*maṣlaḥah ʿāmmah*). Thus, as quoted previously, ʿUmar ibn al-Khaṭṭāb said: "By Him in Whose Hand my life is! Were it not for the animals [in my custody] which I give to be ridden for striving in God's Cause, I would not have turned even a span of their land into a *ḥimā*."[25]

That is why rules governing the validity and validation of contracts and the fulfillment of stipulations have been instituted. That is also why the Shariʿah has decided on the revocation of vitiated contracts owing to their conflicting with the Shariʿah's purpose or because they violate someone else's right. It was on this account that the Prophet said to the person who asked him about selling ripe dates for dry ones: "Do ripe dates shrink when they become dry? When he was told that they did, he forbade that."[26] In fact, the Prophet's question "Do ripe dates shrink" is not a real one. It is rather an allusion to the invalidity of such a sale. This is clearly expressed in his prohibition of selling fruit before it ripens, saying: "If God spoils the fruit, what right would one have to take one's brother's (that is, other people's) money?"[27]

The same can be said regarding the Shariʿah objective for earning (*iktisāb*), the rule for which is that liabilities (*iltizāmāt*) and conditions are binding. Thus we read in the following Prophetic Tradition: "Muslims are bound by their conditions, except a condition that makes the lawful unlawful and the unlawful lawful."[28] Furthermore, we read God's command in the Qur'an: "O you who have attained faith! Whenever you give or take credit for a stated term, set it down in writing" (2:282).

Second, the property owner should be free to dispose of what is owned or earned in such a way as would not cause considerable harm to others or violate the rules of the Shariʿah. Therefore, a legally incompetent person (*safīh*) is banned from dealing with his/her wealth, the owner of a property is not allowed to deal with his/her property in such a way as would cause harm to his/her neighbor, and usurious transactions have been forbidden owing to their evil consequences at both the private and public levels.

Third, no property should be taken from its owner without his consent. Thus, it is reported in a Prophetic Tradition that "the unjust root has no right".[29] If the owner's property involves someone else's right and he refuses to discharge it, he must be obligated to do so. Accordingly, the judge has been given the power to sell a person's property and to adjudicate on the basis of maturity (*istiḥqāq*) [in order to settle others' rights]. It is also on account of this purpose that, if someone disposes of a real estate out of semblance (*shubhah*) of ownership, he is given the right over its returns until the date for handing it over to its real owner is pronounced by the court.

As confirmation of this purpose, the Shariʿah has recognized the ownership and properties as they existed during the pre-Islamic era of pagan ignorance (*Jāhiliyyah*) both in their original hands and those to whom they were transferred. Thus, God's Messenger said: "Any house or land that has been divided in the *Jāhiliyyah*, it is according to the division of the *Jāhiliyyah*. Any house or land that has not been divided before the coming of Islam is divided according to Islam."[30]

Fourth, the last consideration is that of justice, meaning that wealth and property should not have been acquired wrongfully and unjustly. That is to say, it must be acquired by personal effort on the basis of a substitute given to the original owner, by donation, or by inheritance. An important aspect of justice in relation to wealth consists equally of the protection of the public interests and the prevention of public misfortune. This concerns specifically the categories of wealth bearing on the vital needs of large social groups, such as food and defence. Even though these categories of wealth might be of private property, their owners are not absolutely free to dispose of them as they wish, in contrast to other types of wealth.

It is in this light that we can understand the reason for the prohibition of consuming the meat of donkeys during the battle of Khaybar, in the sense that donkey meat was not prohibited for itself (*dhātī*) but for something incidental (*ʿaraḍī*) to it. This was the opinion of many scholars, who maintained that the grounds for the prohibition was that donkeys were the means of equipment and transportation during that battle. In this connection, it is also reported in *Ṣaḥīḥ al-Bukhārī* that ʿAbd Allāh ibn ʿUmar said, "Some people used to go ahead to meet the caravan and buy food from them. God's Apostle forbade them to sell it till it had been carried to the market."[31]

Therefore, it is simply appropriate that hoarding food and thereby raising prices should be prevented. Hence, as reported in *Muwaṭṭa'*, ʿUmar ibn al-Khaṭṭāb said: "There is no hoarding in our market, and men who have excess gold in their hands should not buy up one of God's provisions which he has sent to our courtyard and then hoard it up against us. Someone who brings imported goods with great fatigue to himself in the summer and winter, that person is the guest of ʿUmar. Let him sell what God wills and keep what God wills."[32]

VALIDITY AND INVALIDITY

It is in accordance with the purpose of the Shariʿah pertaining to financial transactions that the rules governing the validity (*ṣiḥḥah*) and invalidity (*fasād*) of contracts related to ownership and acquisition have been legislated. Likewise, valid contracts are those which meet the requirements of the Shariʿah and fulfill its true purpose in the creation thereof. Invalid contracts, on the contrary, are contracts that do not meet some of those requirements, thus failing to realize the purpose of the Shariʿah.

However, certain defects might be tolerated for the sake of giving priority to the purpose (*maṣlaḥah*) of confirming certain types of contracts, such as invalid sales owing to certain omissions (*mufawwitāt*) that are expounded in the works of jurisprudence. For this reason, the eighth-century great scholar and chief mufti of Granada, Abū Saʿīd ibn Lubb, sanctioned certain transactions practiced by the people, so far as there was some support for them – even if it was weak – from among the views of the jurists, despite the fact that they were invalidated in the Mālikī School.

37

Maqāṣid al-Shariʿah: Labor-Based Transactions

You may now have realized from the previous discussion that the Shariʿah objective in the different kinds of financial transactions is the creation of wealth for both the individual and the community. It has already been mentioned that wealth consists principally of things of monetary value (*mutamawwilāt*) and labor. Thus, labor constitutes one of the basic elements of wealth and is the means to the utilization of the other two.

In this chapter we mean by labor a particular kind, namely the effort applied by someone without capital to someone else's capital to earn part of its profit. Now, it so happens that those who are capable of labor and production include many who do not have any capital enabling them to carry out productive labor or lack sufficient capital matching their productive potential. It also happens that many owners of capital are unable to use it in accordance with its productive capacity, especially those whose wealth was a gift or an inheritance. As a result, two fundamentals of wealth – that is, capital and labor – are very likely to be prevented from being put to productive use in many cases. This indeed constitutes a great loss for the workers, the owners of capital, and the entire society.

To overcome this situation, right-thinking people have been guided to discover ways of combining capital and skilled labor to benefit both parties. Thus, it has been a higher objective of Islamic legislation not to prevent either of the two parties from following the best method of achieving this objective in a just manner, while tolerating some incompatibility with the rules governing transactions based on exchanges (*muʿāwaḍāt*).

Labor-based transactions consist mainly of *ijārah* (hire), *musāqāh* (sharecropping), *mughārasah* (orchard sharecropping), *qirāḍ* (commenda), *juʿl* (wages) and *muzāraʿah* (cultivation partnership). Except for *mughārasah*, all these transactions consist of contracts entailing the workers' physical and mental labor and requiring them to spend part of their lives on them. However, although *mughārasah* entails some contribution from the workers by providing, for example, the seedlings, it is minimal compared with their required input of labor. This applies equally to *musāqāh* in that the workers might also be required to contribute by providing some of the equipment for the job, such as buying bails or preparing the reservoirs needed for irrigation.

The contracts based on these transactions are not free from some degree of ambiguity (*gharar*), owing to the difficulty of accurately assessing the amount of work required and the amount of profit for the workers from their labor and for the investors from their capital. Nevertheless, the Shariʿah has ignored all these types of risk, believing that greater harm would result from depriving so many people from the great benefits of work.

Similarly, these contracts are not immune to certain harm that might befall the workers in many cases, such as when they participate in *musāqāh* or *muzāraʿah* but the trees do not bear fruit, or when they work in *juʿl* but the stipulated benefit does not materialize, or when they work in *qirāḍ* but no profit is made. Thus, the workers would have spent much of their time and suffered much hardship in fulfilling these contracts for nothing. Yet, the Shariʿah has again ignored these consequences because it considers that to remain unemployed is indeed more harmful for laborers than facing failure in one case or another.

In these contracts, the workers are most likely eager to finish the job as quickly as possible owing to their pressing need to earn their livelihood and their physical labor is the only means of doing so. Therefore, we often see the situation where they have committed themselves to work beyond their capacity because they cannot afford to do otherwise. Therefore, if the investors who employ them compel them to accept stringent terms and conditions, they will either be deprived of earning by their labor or simply accept the contract and then fail to fulfill it. Hence, disputes will arise. Similarly, this situation of the workers might also tempt the investors to exploit the workers' need for work by violating their rights so as to increase output and maximize profits.

Likewise, it has been the purpose of the Shariʿah in all these types of contracts to protect the workers' rights by stipulating specific conditions so that their work is not wasted or undervalued. Therefore there is no excuse for the investors to impose strict conditions on them, since there are different ways available for the investors to make use of their money. They have the choice of investing it or simply keeping it and spending it on their needs. In contrast, the workers will remain unemployed if they are deprived of the assistance of the investors.

However, there is no room for believing that the Shariʿah has allowed the investor's money to be taken by the workers unjustly. Rather, it has intended only to protect their rights from being violated, for this is the correct path to justice and benefits both parties – workers and investors. I have examined the sources of the Sunnah dealing with the types of these labor-based transactions despite the scarcity of Prophetic Traditions relating to them and studied the views of the early scholars, especially those of Madinah, concerning them. From this inquiry, I have found that the Shariʿah's objectives in this respect are based on eight principles.

(1) It is the aim of the Shariʿah to increase labor-based contracts, and ignoring the element of risk implies this. If it were not for the need for these contracts, the Shariʿah would not have condoned in them what it has not condoned in financial transactions for both contracted parties. Likewise, these transactions belong to the *ḥājī* category of *maṣāliḥ*.

It was in this spirit that the *Anṣār* offered half of the produce of their date-palm gardens in exchange for working in them. It was also in this spirit that God's Messenger made a deal with the Jewish community of Khaybar that they attend to the date palms for half of the produce after the land of Khaybar had become Muslim public property following military conquest (*fatḥ ʿunwah*). Most of the scholars of Islam have agreed on the legitimacy of *musāqāh* and *muzāraʿah*. The Mālikī jurists have validated *mughārasah*, whereas the Ḥanafīs and Shāfiʿīs have disregarded it.[1]

That is why we have highlighted the weakness of the view restricting the validity of *musāqāh* to date palms and vineyards and preferred the view upholding the lawfulness of this type of transaction in all kinds of tree and crop cultivation over that confining it to trees. That is also why we have sanctioned the practice of the people of Andalusia using endowment land on the basis of *mughārasah*.

(2) The Shariʿah allows risk that is common in similar transactions. This is in fact a corollary of the first principle, which I have already discussed at the beginning of this chapter. It means that risk is a characteristic of these contracts, and I do not believe that the Shariʿah has not accepted risk in contracts other than those of human labor. However, it must be remembered that the risk accepted here refers only to what is difficult to assess, such as the amount of work and its duration and the different conditions affecting its performance, namely hot or cold weather.

However, there must be a clear specification of what can be accurately assessed. Examples are the kind of work [in *ijārah*], the level of wages [in *juʿl*], the amount of capital [in *qirāḍ*], and the percentage to be given to its executor from the profit accruing from it, and the portion of the yield to be given to the worker [in *musāqāh* and *mughārasah*].

(3) The third principle consists of shunning anything that overburdens the worker in such contracts.[2] This aims at preventing the investors from simply seeking to maximize their profits by exploiting the need of the workers to earn their livelihood by entering into these contracts. Therefore, the jurists stated that no condition should be imposed on the workers in *musāqāh* that requires from them more

than their physical labor, unless it is something negligible, such as repairing the hedges or reservoirs of the farm. Nor is it allowed to impose on these workers any expenses, such as those of the farm livestock or its guards. As far as *mughārasah* is concerned, no condition should be imposed on the workers requiring them, for example, to clear woodland or build a fence around the area to be planted. On the other hand, if a condition is stipulated on the landlord, this is allowed, binding, and must be executed.

Similarly, our scholars maintained with regard to *muzāraᶜah* that if the landlord gives a tilled land to the peasant (*muzāriᶜ*) and stipulates that the latter must return it tilled at the end of the period of the *muzāraᶜah*, this is unlawful. The reason is that after tilling his land, the landlord needs someone to cultivate it. Even if the land is not tilled, the worker will not accept the transaction. So requiring him to leave it tilled when the *muzāraᶜah* is completed amounts to coercion.

(4) The fourth principle is that these contracts are not considered binding by verbal expression. In our [Mālikīs] view, they are optional until the commencement of work. This view is unanimous in the School regarding *juᶜl* and *qirāḍ*, while it is the majority view as far as *mughārasah* and *muzāraᶜah* are concerned. The jurists have excluded from this rule *musāqāh*, whose contract they consider binding by its conclusion.3 This is because they considered that if it were not binding until the commencement of work, this would result in much harm to the trees and crop.

However, I personally believe that all contracts entailing physical labor should not be considered binding by verbal conclusion. Since this reverts to the notion of option for the worker, it would be appropriate that in these contracts a specific time must be fixed for the worker to commence the work, just as in an optional sale (*bayᶜ al-khiyār*), so as to prevent any harm to the investor. Likewise, a date should be fixed for commencing the work in any of these contracts to avoid wasting the investor's time.

(5) In these contracts, it is permissible to stipulate giving the workers extra benefits beyond what they receive in lieu of their labor

to the exclusion of the investor. Thus, our scholars stated that the workers in *musāqāh* may stipulate on the owner of the orchard that a portion of barren land be given to them to use for their own benefit. At the same time, they were clear that such a stipulation is not permissible for the landlord; if any such condition is imposed for the benefit of the latter, it entails the revocation of the contract.[4]

(6) The sixth principle consists of paying the workers their due immediately upon completion of work, without any delay. This is because the workers are most likely in need of using the return for their work, as they mostly do not have savings on which to live. Thus, the Prophet said in a *ḥadīth qudsī*, "God said, 'I will oppose three types of people on the Day of Resurrection' and among these He mentioned 'one who employs a laborer, has the whole job completed by him, but does not pay him for his labor.'"[5]

This applies to both delaying the payment of the worker's wages and not paying it at all, with the second, of course, being more serious. Likewise, it has been considered God's right, for which reason He said: "I will oppose three types of people", that is, on behalf of the holder of that right. This is high praise of the right and a clear deterrent from making light of it. In a Tradition narrated by ʿAbd Allāh ibn ʿUmar, Jābir ibn ʿAbd Allāh, and Anas ibn Mālik, the Prophet said: "Give the employee his wage before his sweat dries."[6]

(7) The seventh principle consists of providing the worker with the means necessary to complete the work, for he must not be forced to complete it by himself. Accordingly, the jurists stated regarding the worker in *musāqah* that if he is unable to complete the work, another worker should be employed so that there is no loss to the garden's owner, even if the second worker is less trustworthy than the first. If no replacement for the worker can be found, then it is permissible for the owner to sell the part of fruit allocated to the worker when it is ripe in order to hire someone to complete the work and pay the balance to the first worker. Furthermore, the Mālikīs even maintained that the worker in *mughārasah* can sell his right to the work to a replacement employee and this is indeed one of the pearls of Mālikī jurisprudence.

(8) The eighth principle consists of shunning all kinds of conditions and contracts that resemble slave labor, such as requiring employees to work the whole or a very long period of their lives for the same employer, so that they have no way out. Therefore, our scholars invalidated *musāqāh* for trees that continue to bear fruit throughout the year, such as banana trees and alfalfa. This applies also to the kinds of trees that take a long time before starting to bear fruit, such as palm shoots and olive seedlings. In this connection, the scholars of Tunisia (Africa) were of the view that the pollination of barren trees, like the coarse old olive trees on Mount Wuslāt near the city of Kairouan (Qayrawān), falls under *mughārasah* rather than *musāqāh*.

In my view, it is rather better to fix a period for the *musāqāh* for the kinds of trees bearing fruit continually, like banana trees, during which the worker can gain benefit, than simply invalidating it altogether. This is because, as we have already seen in the first principle, it is an objective of the Shariʿah to promote and increase these transactions. Accordingly, there should be no doubt that the kind of *muzāraʿah* known in Tunisia as *sharikat al-khammās*,[7] on which most of the *muzāraʿah* contracts used to be based, contradicts the purpose of the Shariʿah, no matter how much its proponents might emphasize its necessity.

38

Maqāṣid al-Shariʿah: Gifts and Donations

Gift and donation contracts are based on the notion of mutual help (*muwāsāt*) among the members of society. Since it reinforces citizenship, *muwāsāt* serves the higher objectives of the *ḥājī* category of *maṣlaḥah* and embodies a noble Islamic virtue. With it are achieved help for the destitute, the enrichment of the poor, and the realization of so many benefits for the Muslims.

In this book we do not intend to discuss all kinds of gifts and donations that well-off people generously put in the hands of beggars or in the hands of relatives and loved ones out of kindness and courtesy, whether as daily charities or occasional and seasonal presents. These donations do not constitute rights that are sought by those entitled to them. They rather belong to the general expenses that have become part and parcel of people's customary personal conduct. They have also become part of the religious exhortations and thus revert to acts of piety (*qurubāt*).

Accordingly, what we mean here are those donations and gifts that are intended to invest the recipient with ownership or transfer of property (*tamlīk*), enrichment (*ighnā'*), and the establishment of crucial welfare institutions (*maṣāliḥ*) that represent the kinds of wealth for which people usually compete and for the exclusive possession of which contenders often quarrel. Alms (*ṣadaqah*), gifts (*hibah*), and commodity loans (*ʿāriyah*) might fall under the first meaning of expenses just as they might belong to the second meaning when the donation consists of yield (*rīᶜ*), a real estate (*ᶜaqār*), or a large amount of money. Likewise, they serve the purpose of enrichment and transfer of property, whether the beneficiaries are specific individuals, specific categories of people, or the public interest benefiting the whole community. Examples are donations made to assist students, the poor, the sick, or sages and hermits, and donations toward the cost of building fortresses and harbors and equipping soldiers. These donations might begin as acts of piety, to which one is motivated by a feeling of generosity and a wish to do good. Then, one might decide to commit oneself to these practices to the extent that they become rights that have to be transferred from the donor to the recipients.

In like manner, donations and gifts in this sense fall under the Shariᶜah rules (*aḥkām*) governing rights that are frequently the subject of dispute between people, whether over acquiring and preserving them or extracting and protecting them. A dispute may arise as a result of regret and retraction by the donor or the reluctance of his or her inheritors or guardian to make the donation. It might also be due to the transgression by those to whom the donation is made, over what they are entitled to receive.

Because of these contingent elements that often affect donations and gifts in the sense intended here, they are dealt with on the basis of the rules and principles governing rights as well as in the light of the Shariᶜah objectives. The sources of the Shariᶜah contain numerous explanations of the purposes of the Shariᶜah regarding donation and gift contracts. Our thorough study of those sources has enabled us to identify the following main principles of the Shariᶜah in this respect.

(1) The first principle is to increase donations and gifts in view of their public and private benefits. Because human greed is a major obstacle to the abundance of these acts, the Shariᶜah has taken special care to encourage people and stimulate their interest in gifts and donations by classifying them as acts whose reward for the donor does not cease even after death. Thus, it is reported in an authentic Tradition: "When a man dies, his acts come to an end, except three,

recurring charity, or knowledge [by which people] benefit, or a pious son, who prays for him [i.e. for the deceased]."[1]

During the Prophet's time, there were numerous cases of repeated charity (*ṣadaqāt jāriyyah*) and endowments (*awqāf*) that were made by either him or his Companions. Mention can be made here of ʿUmar ibn al-Khaṭṭāb's[2] and Abū Ṭalḥah al-Anṣārī's[3] charities, which they made upon the Prophet's advice. Mention can also be made of ʿUthmān ibn Affan's charity which he made when he heard the Prophet saying: "Who will buy the well of Rūmah[4] [and endow it for the general welfare of the people] so that he may use it like the other Muslims without any privilege," ʿUthmān bought it and endowed it for the welfare of all Muslims.[5] Lastly, we can mention Saʿd ibn ʿUbādah's charity, which consisted of a garden called al-Makhraf.[6]

These charities were endowments intended to benefit all the Muslims according to specific terms and detailed conditions. This removes any doubt that one of the Shariʿah objectives is to increase this kind of contracts. So, how can a person like Judge Shurayḥ say that endowments are not allowed? Therefore, when he heard of Shurayḥ's view, Mālik ibn Anas commented:

> May God's mercy be upon Shurayḥ! He said what he said in his own country [Kūfah], but he did not come to Madinah to see the legacy of outstanding personalities from among the Prophet's wives, his Companions and the Successors and the endowments that they had created from their wealth. And here are the charities of God's Apostle *(ṢAAS)* consisting of seven gardens! A man should speak only of what he has full knowledge of.[7]

(2) The second principle is that donations must be made voluntarily and should not be accompanied by any hesitation. This is because they are acts of kindness (*maʿrūf*) and generosity consisting of giving away a portion of one's valued property without any immediate replacement. Thus, the intent of the donor must sincerely be to benefit society in general and to aspire to an ample reward from God. Accordingly, it is the Lawgiver's purpose that endowers should

make suitable provision so that endowments do not result in harm and grief. If giving charity results in harm, it will cause people to fear doing good, for good must not result in evil, as indicated by God's words in the following verse: "No human being shall be burdened with more than he is well able to bear: neither shall a mother be made to suffer because of her child, nor, because of his child, he who has begotten it. And the same duty rests upon the [father's] heir" (2:233).[8] Likewise, the sense of option as understood regarding donations is more specific than that expounded by the jurists in respect of exchanges (*muʿāwaḍāt*). This means that the time allowed for considering an endowment contract binding after the decision to create it has been made is more flexible than that allowed for exchange contracts.

The evidence for these rules is based on numerous indicants from the Sunnah as well as statements by the scholars of the Ummah. Thus, we read in the following authentic Tradition:

> That you should give charity [when you are] healthy and miserly, one haunted by the fear of poverty, hoping to become rich (charity in that mental and physical state is the best). Nor should you defer [charity to the time] when you are about to die and will be saying: "This is for so and so, and this is for so and so." Lo, it has already come into [the possession of so and so].[9]

This is a situation that requires serious reflection and resolution and does not allow for procrastination until one's death becomes imminent. Reflection and resolution is confirmed by either possession (*taḥwīz*) or witness (*ishhād*).

Indeed, the stipulation of possession in donations and gifts is aimed at achieving this purpose, because, in contrast with exchange contracts, endowment contracts become binding only after the recipient has taken possession of the donated property. Therefore, if the endower dies before the recipient takes possession of the donated property, the donation is annulled and it reverts to the rule of bequests. In this regard, it is reported in *Muwaṭṭa'* that ʿĀ'ishah said:

Abū Bakr al-Ṣiddīq gave me palm trees, whose produce was twenty *awsuq*, from his property at al-Ghābah. When he was dying, he said, "By God, little daughter, there is no one I would prefer to be wealthy after I die than you. There is no one it is more difficult for me to see poor after I die than you. I gave you palm-trees, whose produce is twenty *awsuq*. Had you harvested them and taken possession of them, they would have been yours, but today they are the property of the heirs, who are your two brothers and your two sisters, so divide it according to the Book of God."

ʿĀ'ishah continued,

I said, "My father! By God, even if it had been more, I would have left it. There is only Asmā'. Who is my other sister?" Abū Bakr replied, "What is in the womb of Khārijah. I think that it is going to be a girl."[10]

A witness can be a substitute for possession to validate the contract, which is the view held by Mālik. I believe this is based on the Tradition narrated by al-Nuʿmān ibn Bashīr:

He said that his father Bashīr made a gift to him. However, ʿAmrah bint Rawāḥah, Bashīr's wife, did not agree with that unless the Prophet *(ṢAAS)* bore witness to it. So Bashīr brought al-Nuʿmān to the Messenger of God *(ṢAAS)* and said, "I have made a gift to this son of mine." The Messenger of God *(ṢAAS)* said, "Have you given each of your children the same as this?" He said, "No." The Messenger of God *(ṢAAS)* then ordered him to take the gift back.[11]

This report clearly proves that the lady did not consider the donation to be valid until it had been witnessed. It also shows that it was customary for those people to require donations to be witnessed. That was why ʿAmrah demanded that the Prophet should bear witness to the case in question.

It is a known fact that the donor might fear the delay of possession by the recipient of the donated property, and therefore he would resort to the testimony of the verbal creation of the donation and then follow it with the transfer of property. In our view, this is sufficient to establish the validity of the gift. According to the Mālikīs, the recipient likewise becomes the owner of the property given by the donor and therefore has the right to demand its possession. Many scholars, including al-Shāfiʿī and Abū Ḥanīfah, held the view that possession was a necessary condition for the validity of a gift contract and that as long as the recipient had not taken possession, it did not become binding on the donor.[12] This view aims at easing the situation for the benefactors until their verbal promise of an endowment is followed by its implementation. The Ḥanafīs have maintained that it is permitted to retract one's gift even after the recipient has taken possession of it, except in seven cases, which reverts to the same purpose.[13]

Aḥmad ibn Ḥanbal, Abū Thawr, and Dāwūd al-Ẓāhirī are among those who hold that verbal contracts of donation are valid and binding. Their view, which is also attributed to Abū Yūsuf, the companion of Abū Ḥanīfah, was to construe them in the same way as other kinds of contracts. Therefore, they overlooked the element of kindness and benefaction (*maʿrūf*) in these contracts. The reason is to avoid restricting acts of charity and causing benefactors to abstain from them, thus leading to the demise of so many benefits.

I do believe the reason for giving the father the right of retraction of a gift from the son is that parents usually make donations to their children with less reflection and out of affection and compassion for them, while at the same time entertaining no doubt that their children's wealth is also theirs. Likewise, should the father regret his decision, the Shariʿah has given him the option of retracting the gift. Moreover, there is here a consideration of the sense of fatherhood so that the child does not become a cause of constriction and constraint for the father. The mother too has the right of retraction if the father is alive, according to many juristic details in fiqh books. In this connection, Bukhārī narrated that Mālik ibn Anas explained the meaning of *ʿariyah* as being "the donation of a date-palm by one person [from his grove] to another person; then owing to the donor's being harmed by the recipient's grove, it has been allowed for the donor to buy the palm-tree for dates."[14]

From this we realize that the Shariʿah is very much concerned to protect benefactors from any harm that might befall them as a result of their good deeds, so that people are not deterred from doing good.

(3) The third principle is that tolerance and flexibility should be applied to the means of validating donation contracts according to the wishes of donors. Donating property is difficult for human beings, and therefore its motive must be religious liberality and noble morality. However, the donor's good motive may be confused by many evil thoughts, the most powerful of which is what God has mentioned in the following verse: "Satan threatens you with the prospect of poverty and bids you to be niggardly, whereas God promises you His forgiveness and bounty; and God is Infinite, All-Knowing," (2:268). Since the first principle clarifies that it is the Shariʿah objective to encourage donations and gifts, tolerance and flexibility in their validation strengthen that purpose.

Therefore, the Shariʿah has allowed making the gift conditional upon the donor's death through wills and testaments, even though this contradicts the rule regarding the disposal of property, for one can only dispose of one's property during one's lifetime. Thus, the donors' stipulations are to be implemented according to the type of donations, whether they are general, or specific, temporary or permanent. Any other conditions must also be observed provided they do not contravene a higher objective of the Shariʿah, which aims at reconciling its objectives where they differ. Although this might result in the omission of some aspects of a particular objective, that is negligible in comparison.

It is the dominant view among the masters of Mālik's School that stipulations regarding endowments, gifts, and charities are binding, such as the retraction of a charity (*ṣadaqah*) or a gift (*hibah*). Also binding is the stipulation by the donor or almsgiver that the item given must not be donated or sold. In fact, the leading scholars of the School differed over this according to five opinions that have been fully investigated by Ibn Rāshid of Qafsī[15] in his book *al-Fā'iq*. Of those five views he preferred the one that stipulations are binding and that charities and gifts are similar to endowments in this respect.[16]

In fact, the principle that we have established here sheds sufficient light upon his preference which differs from exchanges (*muʿāwaḍāt*). As far as the non-stipulation of possession is concerned, we shall deal with it in what follows.

(4) The fourth principle is that the act of donating must not lead to the violation and loss of the rights of others, such as heirs and creditors. During the pre-Islamic age of pagan ignorance (*Jāhiliyyah*) bequests used to replace inheritance and people tended to use them as a means of depriving even their next of kin in order to give their property to the notables and leaders of the tribe for the sake of enhancing their reputation. In this respect, Ismāʿīl ibn Isḥāq said that the people of that period never gave wives and daughters the inheritance rights that Islam has given them, nor did they have any definite rules of inheritance that could be observed.

Likewise, when God prescribed bequest for the parents and the next of kin and then instituted the rules of inheritance, the image of the bequests of the *Jāhiliyyah* was still lingering in people's minds. Therefore, bequests were restricted to non-heirs and to no more than one-third of one's property, as has been clearly expressed in the Tradition concerning Saʿd ibn Abī Waqqāṣ, in which the Prophet is reported to have told him: "[Bequeath] a third, and a third is a lot. Leaving your heirs rich is better than leaving them poor to beg from people."[17] We have already mentioned Abū Bakr's words to ʿĀ'ishah, "but today they are the property of the heirs".

This shows that many people use bequests and donations to alter inheritance or harm creditors, while thinking the former absolves them from the sin of the latter, for they have substituted one good purpose (*maʿrūf*) for another. Therefore, it has been an important aspect of the blocking of means in this respect to keep the forms of donation free of manipulation. Thus, witness to the donation has been considered insufficient and unconvincing to prevent these suspicions, since the donor and recipient might agree on an arrangement to deprive the heirs and creditors of their rights, while keeping the subject of donation under the control of the donor. Accordingly, the recipient taking possession of the donated property has another effect besides that mentioned in the second principle. It also becomes clear that Mālik's view on the invalidity of endowments made for male children to the exclusion of female children is supported by stronger evidence. Moreover, these endowments belong to the customs of the period of pagan ignorance, although it has been the practice among Mālikī jurists to allow them, albeit with disapproval, based on another opinion from Mālik, reported by al-Mughīrah. Accordingly, a seriously ill person is forbidden to make donations rather than exchanges by sale or otherwise. This is because a sale entails compensation, in contrast to donation in which suspicion arises concerning the donor's intent.

39

Maqāṣid al-Shariʿah: Judgeship and Testimony

Our thorough study of the statements (*aqwāl*) and dispositions (*taṣarrufāt*) of the Shariʿah gives us the necessary knowledge that it is one of its objectives that the Muslim community should have rulers who run its public affairs, administer justice, and implement the Shariʿah rules in its ranks. This is because the Islamic Shariʿah, being a code governing people's inter-relationships and entitlement to specified rights, was sent down only so that these purposes might be achieved. Otherwise, this would not happen, for rights are prone to violation and usurpation owing to people's wrath or desire as much as they are prone to misunderstanding, ignorance, and neglect.

Indeed, anyone instituting a code and system, or sending an envoy, or ordering the execution of a certain act will always anticipate while doing so one situation or another where certain obstacles might prevent the achievement of what is intended by that. Likewise, one would take the necessary precautions to deal with that situation. Hence, it is only natural that one of the highest objectives of the Shariʿah, after conveying it, should be to establish its authority, implement its rules, and promote its supremacy. That is why it is obligatory to have a group of scholars whose task is to convey and establish the Shariʿah, as ordained by God in the following verse:

> With all this, it is not desirable that all of the believers take the field [in time of war]. From within every group in their midst, some shall refrain

> from going to war, and shall devote themselves [instead] to acquiring a deeper knowledge of the Faith (*al-dīn*), and [thus be able to] teach their home-coming brethren, so that these [too] might guard themselves against evil. (9:122)[1]

Similarly, it is reported that the Prophet told the delegation of Banū Layth when they came to him: "Return to your people, stay with them and teach them."[2]

Furthermore, it is an obligation to institute rulers to take care of the matters related to it and appoint a special body to assist those rulers in implementing its injunctions. Likewise, establishing the state and government is a corollary of the Shariʿah teachings so that there does not come a time when its rules are suspended. This has indeed been indicated in the following verse, in which God says:

> Indeed, [even aforetime] did we send forth Our apostles with all the evidence of [this] truth; and through them We bestowed Revelation from on high, and [thus gave you] a balance [with which to weigh right and wrong], so that men might behave with equity; and We bestowed [upon you] from on high [the ability to use] iron, in which there is awesome power as well as [a source of] benefits for man. (57:25)[3]

In fact, there are many verses to this effect and the Prophet's statements and acts in this respect were repeated (*tawātur*). It was a habitual practice of his to send governors and judges to remote regions. He himself undertook the task of judging between people in Madinah, the metropolis of Islam.

Moreover, the many statements and addresses (*khiṭābāt*) of the Qur'an framed in the plural form are a discourse to the community as a whole regarding policies that can be implemented only by a group of people invested with the necessary authority to do so by their fellow citizens.[4] It is not, however, our aim in this book to expound the relevant arguments on this topic, for it belongs to the disciplines of *uṣūl al-dīn* and the Shariʿah political science (*ʿilm al-siyāsah al-sharʿiyyah*).

One of the important means of preparing the ground for the

establishment of the Shariʿah, which is also one of its major objectives, is to spread its knowledge and increase the number of its scholars. This constitutes a collective duty (*farḍ kifāyah*) on the entire Muslim community, as this will help to satisfy its needs, depending on the expansion of their land and greatness of their countries. God has thus entrusted the Ummah with His Book, which contains the greatest and noblest teachings consisting of both fundamental principles and elaborate rules. On several occasions, the Prophet ordered those Muslims in his presence to convey the knowledge of the Shariʿah that they received from him to those who were absent. He further exhorted anyone listening to his Sayings to convey them as accurately as one would have heard them without any alteration.[5]

Consequently, the early generations of the ummah took it upon themselves to increase the number of the Qur'an *maṣāḥif* and distribute them in the different regions of the Muslim world, and to compile the Traditions of the Prophet that were transmitted by trustworthy narrators. An equally important task that followed this consisted of the compilation and systematization of the opinions of the scholars of Islam, which has come to be known as fiqh. From all this emerged and crystalized the characteristics of the conveyers of the Shariʿah.

Now, to ensure the implementation of any legal system (Shariʿah), the people should be deeply imbued with a sense of its sanctity. In fact, people's conviction of the soundness of the law enables their willing obedience. Of all legal systems (*sharā'iʿ*), the Islamic Shariʿah is the most revered by its followers, for its infallibility has been firmly established on the basis of Revelation. Therefore, the scholars of the Muslim community have always sought to trace all the laws and rules that they expound to the indicants of the Qur'an and Sunnah. Thus, God says in the Qur'an: "But nay, by your Sustainer! They do not [really] believe unless they make you [O Prophet] a judge of all on which they disagree among themselves, and then find in their hearts no bar to an acceptance of your decision and give themselves up [to it] in utter self-surrender" (4:65).[6] Of course, this Qur'anic statement is specifically about the rule and judgment of the Prophet. However, it implies varying degrees of authority and obedience for those who rank below his standing in proportion to the proximity of their rule and judgment to that of the Prophet. Therefore, our scholars have preferred the view that the judge has to describe in detail the evidence supporting his verdict to achieve, as far as possible, the removal of insecurity in the implementation of the Shariʿah rulings.

We are not here going to deal with the Shariʿah objectives of conveying its teachings and safeguarding its message, nor to delve into the conditions for caliphs, rulers, governors, influential people (*ahl al-ḥall wa al-ʿaqd*), and military commanders, who all have a share in the establishment of the Shariʿah, for this is also beyond our purpose in this book. Our inquiry shall concentrate on the Shariʿah objectives for the category of people responsible for implementing its rules designed to deliver rights to their true claimants according to its established fundamental principles and specific rules. Our discussion here will therefore be focused on judges, their advisors (*ahl al-shūrā*), their aides and anything that influences their verdicts, namely proofs (*bayyināt*) and judicial procedures.

In this connection, Qarāfī has shown that no one appointed to any office – from the caliphate down to guardianship – is allowed to act in that capacity unless it is to promote a benefit (*maṣlaḥah*) or prevent evil (*mafsadah*). Imams and rulers should therefore excuse themselves from anything that does not require the greatest effort. This means that what is outweighed (*marjūḥ*) is not the best and that adopting it is the easy way out.[7] To what he said, I should add the following. When Jābir ibn ʿAbd Allāh gave his pledge of allegiance to God's Apostle, the Prophet stipulated that he should "be sincere and true to every Muslim."[8] Furthermore, Qarāfī mentioned, "In every investiture, priority must be given to the person who is more qualified and more suitable to the respective office over the one who is less so."[9] To this effect he adduced clear-cut evidence, which we need not cite here. Generally speaking, the Shariʿah objectives for the whole judiciary are that it should include everything that helps to reveal the truth (*ḥuqūq*) and eliminate untruth (*bāṭil*), whether it is manifest or hidden. This has been understood from the Tradition narrated in *Muwaṭṭa'* in which the Prophet said:

> I am but a man to whom you bring your disputes. Perhaps one of you is more eloquent in his proof than the other, so I give judgment according to what I have heard from him. Whatever I decide for him which is part of the right of his brother, he must not take any of it, for I am granting him a portion of the Fire.[10]

This tradition clearly shows that there are different ways of arriving at the truth. It also shows that the best procedure to be followed by the judge is that enabling him to discover the truth, which the judge can decide only from the body of evidence available to him. Lastly, this Tradition clearly shows that litigants are required to produce proof of their rights and that trickery is indeed a transgression that will lead only to perdition and Hellfire. It is also reported in *Muwaṭṭa'* "that two men brought a dispute to God's Messenger *(ṢAAS)*. One of them said, 'Messenger of God! Judge between us by the Book of God!' The other said (and he was the wiser of the two), 'Yes, Messenger of God. Judge between us by the Book of God and give me permission to speak.' He said, 'Speak'."[11]

In the same context, al-Tirmidhī and Abū Dāwūd reported from ʿAlī ibn Abī Ṭālib that when the Prophet sent him to the Yemen as a judge, he told him:

> When two litigants sit in front of you, do not decide till you hear what the other has to say as you heard what the first had to say; for it is best that you should have a clear idea of the best decision.[12]

Accordingly, it is the duty of the judge to investigate as fully as possible all the pieces of evidence leading to the truth, even if this results in the protection of only certain rights over others, for safeguarding some rights is better than losing them all. In this connection, the Prophet related the following story:

> Two women quarreled about a child, each asserting that the child was hers. So they both took the case to David, who judged that the child be given to the older lady, although being older has no influence on extracting the truth. David did not compel either of the two ladies to

> confess, though he was sure that one of them was a liar. Maybe he did not consider coercion a means of confession. However, Solomon resorted to coercion to extract a confession in judging between the two ladies when they brought the case to him.[13]

The Muslim jurists through the ages have not ceased to add to the judicial procedures [laid down in the Qur'an and Sunnah] many new rules almost totally unknown to their predecessors. The best judicial procedures formulated by Muslim scholars and of which I am aware are those developed by the scholars of Andalus, as detailed in the books on *nawāzil* (judicial cases) and *tawthīq* (documentation). Of course, the most important element in the judicial system is the judge himself, for the integrity of everything else in this system depends on the judge's integrity. It has already become obvious that the Shariʿah purpose in the institution of judges is to deliver rights to their genuine claimants.

This depends on a number of conditions such as independence of opinion, knowledge, freedom from others' influence, and righteousness (*ʿadālah*). Independence of opinion requires reason and rationality (*ʿaql*), obligation (*taklīf*), intelligence (*fiṭnah*), and soundness in mind and body (*salāmat al-ḥawās*). Thus, we read the Prophet's Saying: "A judge must not judge in a state of anger."[14]

A judge must also have knowledge of the Shariʿah ordinances to be applied to the kind of cases under his jurisdiction. Hence, it is reported:

> When the Apostle of God *(ṢAAS)* intended to send Muʿadh ibn Jabal to the Yemen, he asked: "How will you judge when the occasion of deciding a case arises?" He replied: "I shall judge in accordance with God's Book." He asked: "[What will you do] if you do not find any guidance in God's Book?" He replied: "[I shall act] in accordance with the Sunnah of God's Apostle *(ṢAAS)*." He asked: "[What will you do] if you do not find any guidance in the Sunnah of the Apostle of God *(ṢAAS)* and in God's Book?" He replied: "I shall do my best to form an opinion and I shall spare no effort." The Apostle of God *(ṢAAS)* then patted him on the chest and said: "Praise be to God, Who has helped

the messenger of the Apostle of God to find something which pleases the Apostle of God."[15]

To this effect, Mālik said: "I do not believe that the qualities required for judgeship can today be found in one person. If only two of them are found in any man, the one with both knowledge and piety should be appointed to this office."[16] Therefore, the person appointed as judge must be the best of those qualified for this office, and the more knowledgeable he is, the better choice he becomes.

There is disagreement among the jurists over whether the judge must be a *mujtahid*, that is, one whose scholarly authority and attainment of the level of ijtihad have been acknowledged by the scholars of his time. I personally believe that a scholar who is a follower (*muqallid*) of a school of the established *mujtahids* and who knows the Shariᶜah indicants is no less qualified for the office of judge than a *mujtahid*. This is especially so since Muslims have become followers of established schools whose scholarly standing is beyond dispute.[17]

Therefore, there must not be any argument about the fact that the *muqallid* jurist's jurisdiction is specifically valid for the school followed by the people for whom he is appointed judge. If it happens that in a region there is more than one school, appointment of judges can be made depending on the number of the schools that people follow. This is to ensure people's confidence in the judgments made, which gains their respect for the Shariᶜah and obedience to its rules dealt with earlier, although this situation creates disunity. This is only a means of following the most appropriate body of juristic opinions of the different scholars, since other more convincing ways acceptable to the different categories of the Ummah have yet to be evolved.

The judge must be able to call to mind the Shariᶜah ordinances governing the different issues that most frequently occur, and must be capable of finding out easily and quickly, if need be, the rules governing the unusual issues. He must also be fully familiar with the works of jurisprudence, which must be easily accessible to him, and well equipped with the means enabling him to make use of them. For this reason, Ibn al-Qāsim said that someone who is not a *faqīh* must not be appointed as judge. In the same vein, Aṣbagh, Ashhab, Muṭarrif, and Ibn al-Mājishūn held the view that the judge must not be a traditionalist (*ṣāḥib ḥadīth*) without any knowledge of fiqh, or a *faqīh* with no knowledge of the Traditions.[18] Similarly, Ibn Rāshid recounted in his book *al-Fā'iq* that the chief judge of Egypt, Nafīs al-Dīn ibn Shukr,[19] told him that it was permissible to appoint to the office of judge anyone capable of knowing how to identify the issues in their possible sources, supporting this statement with the view that it is not necessary for a *mujtahid* to memorize the verses of the Qur'an pertaining to legal ordinances (*ayāt al-aḥkām*). Ibn Rāshid then commented: "It is obvious that this entails much difficulty for litigants, as it will delay the judgment of their cases while waiting for them to be understood by the judge. Furthermore, it opens the door to appointing incompetent and ignorant people to the office of judge."[20]

What Ibn Rāshid said is indeed the truth; a *mujtahid* scholar is not in fact required to judge between people. However, when he is appointed judge, the conditions required for him are stricter than for the *mujtahid* generally. Ibn Rāshid's view that this is a means of appointing ignorant people is also sound, for the capacity to acquire juristic knowledge is something that cannot be easily defined and only scholars can judge it. Furthermore, we know that when dictators want to appoint an ignorant person to the office of judge, they assert that though he is not an authoritative scholar, he is capable of deriving the juristic knowledge from the relevant sources (although that is untrue), or maybe, even if he is capable he does not make the necessary effort to do so. Hence, there should be no doubt about the requirement for the judge to be able to call to mind the relevant juridical material.

One further condition that in fact reverts to that of knowledge consists of the capacity to understand the intent and terminology of the jurists. In this respect, Ibn ʿAbd al-Barr said in his book *al-Kāfī*: "As far as I know, there is no disagreement between the scholars of Madinah and elsewhere that only someone who is trustworthy in terms of soundness of faith, goodness of character, capacity of understanding, and knowledge should be appointed to the office of judge."[21] A judge also needs the ability to comprehend the proofs relating to the different issues and their underlying rationales (*ᶜilal*). This is the most important way of discerning dubious cases, hence the scholars' statement that a *faqīh* with no knowledge of the traditions is not suitable as a judge.

Freedom from other people's influence is an aspect of the general condition of freedom that the jurists stipulated for the judge. There has been confusion among jurists regarding the justification (*taᶜlīl*) for this stipulation. However, their failure to understand the reason for it clearly shows us that the subject of the justification is normally taken for granted. I suggest that the rationale behind the stipulation of freedom is that the lack of it (*ᶜubūdiyyah*) makes one behave in a way that will please the person to whom one is subservient. Likewise, a slave judge will be under the influence of his master in whatever judgments he makes on the cases brought to him. This means that the judge must be free from anything that puts him under the influence of others, for bondage takes different forms.

Thus, we read in the Prophet's hadith: "Wretched and doomed to perish is the slave of the dinar, dirham, *qaṭīfah* (velvet), and *khamīṣah* (a garment), for if he is given [them], he is pleased; otherwise he is dissatisfied."[22] Thus, the items mentioned are considered causes of the lack of freedom. Therefore, our scholars are agreed on the prohibition of bribery according to God's words: "And do not devour one another's possessions wrongfully, and neither use it as bait for judges" (2:188).[23]

Accordingly, it becomes clear why Ashhab said that it is necessary for the judge to make little of political rulers, in the sense of ignoring their interference in the court cases under his jurisdiction and to apply the law strictly to them as well as to their relatives. It does not mean violating the rights of the rulers in the general obedience due to their legitimate authority.

Integrity (*ᶜadālah*) consists of the caution (*wāziᶜ*) that prevents the judge from judging unjustly and from failing to examine thoroughly the pleas of litigants. This is because administering justice (*qaḍā'*) is a position of trust, which God has mentioned in association with the rights to be rendered to their owners: "Behold, God bids you to deliver all with which you have been entrusted (*amānāt*) to those who are entitled to them, and whenever you judge between people, to judge with justice" (4:58).[24] Hence, our scholars are of the view that *ʿadālah* is a condition for validating the appointment to the office of judge.[25]

The Muslim scholars have also discussed the question of the removal of judges from office, though they have not reached a firm decision. Their caution is based on two factors: considering judges to be the representatives of the ruler on the one hand, and the need to preserve the respect for the office of judge in the sight of the people on the other. This issue is more concerned with the judge's freedom from other people's influence, for his removal tarnishes his image and the prospect of it weakens his rigor and seriousness if his faith and integrity are defective. Therefore, al-Māzarī held the view that if the judge's knowledge and integrity are beyond doubt and no one has questioned his standing, he must not be dismissed simply because of complaints against him, and those complaints should be investigated confidentially.[26]

However, there are conflicting opinions regarding the removal of a judge from office because his integrity has not been confirmed. According to Ashhab, he must be removed, while others have maintained that he must not.[27] The upholders of the latter view argue that it has not been recorded that ʿUmar ever removed a judge, although he dismissed governors and commanders merely because of complaints, namely Saʿd ibn Abī Waqqāṣ, Khālid ibn al-Walīd, and Shuraḥbīl. I would add to this: nor has it been recorded that the Prophet and Abū Bakr ever removed a judge.

One of our erudite scholars, and I think it was Ibn ʿArafah, said that the removal of a judge would undermine public respect for the judgeship. Nevertheless, after the time of the Predecessors, it became accepted that the holder of the office of judge had the right to remain in it permanently. This custom derived from the weakness of the rulers in both knowledge and integrity who had the authority to appoint the judges. Some of the Hafsid sultans[28] established the practice whereby a judge cannot remain in office for more than three years, which is gravely erroneous. This is because the main purpose of judgeship is to achieve *maṣlaḥah* and dismissal from office should only be for the sake of avoiding *mafsadah*, since rulers must bear *masāliḥ* in mind in all their actions, as has been explained by Qarāfī in his book *al-Furūq*.[29] Accordingly, it is one of the great purposes (*maṣāliḥ*) of the Shariʿah to preserve public respect for the Shariʿah-related offices and enable their holders to perform their tasks without being subjected to fear or disparagement.

The conditions that are required for court advisors (*rijāl shūrā al-qaḍā'*) are similar to those for judges, except that they must be more knowledgeable.

Let us now move on to another topic that we promised to cover toward the end of our discussion of the specification of the different categories of rights. We mentioned there that certain rights might be entrusted to someone other than their original holders. We should say here that it is of the nature of rights to be managed by their original holders. However, this might be impracticable or impossible, such as in the different kinds of tenures (*wilāyāt*) and mandates (*wakālāt*), for rulers might not be able to attend themselves to all the matters that fall under their jurisdiction because they are too numerous or too remote, or because the officers concerned are required to attend to more important things. There are narrations that indicate that the Prophet used to delegate some tasks to some of his Companions.

This also applies to contracts in which someone is entrusted with managing the rights of the original holder. Although this engagement might not be due to impracticality or impossibility for the holder of the rights, their management by him or her might put him or her at risk. Thus, rights entrusted in this way might be purely the entitlement of someone other than the person entrusted with their management, like the rights of minors with regard to their parents and guardians, the rights of women with regard to their guardians in matters of marriage.

They might also be a combination of rights belonging to both the person entrusted with their management and someone else, like the rights of spouses in relation to each other, the rights of kinship between parents and children, the rights of partners vis-à-vis one another as in shared properties, trade, and businesses of the kind of *muḍārabah*, common estates (*irtiwāk*), and manufacturing.

To facilitate the most efficient management of businesses (*aʿmāl*) and the realization of their benefits, the Shariʿah has entrusted one of the parties concerned with the task of looking after those rights, bearing in mind their varied characters and their recurrent use by all the parties regardless of time, space, and circumstances. Likewise, priority in the distribution and management of shared rights has been given to one of the parties entitled to them rather than to an outsider or putting them under the supervision of an appropriate authority.

Accordingly, the Shariʿah has considered the guardian of certain rights more entitled to managing them than the others. Examples are giving the custody of young children to the mother and that of adolescents to the father; giving the right of supervision of the family to the husband rather than the wife, and the right to manage the affairs of the household to the wife instead of the husband; giving the right of handling the businesses of *qirāḍ*, *mighārasah*, *musāqāh*, and *muzāraʿah* to the worker rather than the owner of capital, land, or trees.

Certain forms of trusteeship might be based on the authority of the Shariʿah, whether as a legal principle, as in the parents' rights over their children's property, or judicial verdict, such as appointing a manager (*nāẓir*) for endowments (*waqf*). In other forms, the holder of the right him or herself might create the trusteeships, such as procuration and partnerships like *qirāḍ* and *musāqāh*, and the guardianship of parents over their children. Anyone entrusted with the management of a specific right must make every lawful effort to achieve a benefit from it. One must not behave arbitrarily or wastefully in managing what one has been entrusted with.

Thus, addressing husbands God says: "And consort with your wives in a goodly manner" (4:19). Addressing executors (*awṣiyā'*), He says: "And if you share their lives, [remember that] they are your brethren" (2:220).[30] As Qarāfī has expressed it,

> Anyone holding any office from the caliphate down to testaments (*waṣiyyah*) can act only to realize a benefit (*jalb maṣlaḥah*) or to prevent an evil (*darᶜ mafsadah*)... [Rulers and judges] in their capacities must not act in ways that lead to outweighing *mafsadah* or simply to realize an outweighed or equivalent *maṣlaḥah*, or in a way that neither produces a benefit nor wards off an evil. It is for this reason that al-Shāfiᶜī, may God be pleased with him, said that a *waṣīy* (custodian) must not exchange a quantity [of the property of the minor under his guardianship] for an equivalent quantity of its kind, for this does not produce any benefit.[31]

Should any unexpected failings be noticed in the conduct of the guardian of these rights, the matter must be brought to court. The judge can decide to put the respective parties under the supervision of a trustee (*amīn*). Examples are putting both spouses under the supervision of male and female trustees in a dispute over mutual harassment, appointing a superintendent for an endowment which has been mismanaged by its beneficiaries, employing temporary auditors to investigate guardians (*awṣiyā'*) and endowment caretakers. Meanwhile, the disputed rights are to be put under the supervision of reliable trustees.When the mismanagement of rights by their guardians becomes disastrously widespread, it is the duty of the judiciary to put an end to these abuses. In this respect, and in conjunction with his commentary on the Qur'anic verse: "And test the orphans [in your charge] until they reach a marriageable age, then, if you find them to be mature of mind, hand over to them their possessions" (4:6), the Andalusian scholar Shaikh Ibn ᶜAṭiyyah says the following:

> A group [of jurists] said: "Handing over the property to the person in custody by his executor (*waṣīy*) should be brought to the notice of the ruler (*sulṭān*) and the mental maturity [of the person in custody] must be proven to him; otherwise the guardian must be someone trusted by the ruler in these matters." Another group maintained that the whole matter should be left to the discretion and consideration of the guardian and need not be brought to the notice of the ruler. In our view,

the truth of the matter in relation to the guardians of our time is that bringing the matter to the notice of the ruler and proving the maturity of the person(s) concerned cannot be dispensed with. This is because connivance and collusion have been noticed as one of the recurrent attitudes of executors, thus asserting the mental maturity or sobriety of the persons in their custody.[32]

Ibn ʿAṭiyyah upheld this view despite the fact that the verse authorizes the guardians to decide whether the orphans in their custody have reached mental maturity. His view has become the basis of juristic and judicial practice in Tunisia during the recent period.[33] Nevertheless, its implementation depends on the evaluation of the prevailing general circumstances of society, not on that of unusual cases.

To complete our discussion, there remains the question of delivering rights to their claimants as quickly as possible, which is so important an objective. Unnecessary delay beyond the time required to establish them leads to many evil consequences. One example is the deprivation of people from benefiting from their rights, which is extremely harmful. Another example is enabling the ineligible claimant to benefit from someone else's property, which is a great injustice against the eligible claimant. The Qur'an has alluded to these examples in the following verse: "with intent that you may eat up wrongfully and knowingly, anything that by right belongs to others" (2:188).

A third evil consequence is the prolongation of dispute between the eligible and ineligible parties, which results in discord and disorder in society. If there is doubt about the litigants' claims to a disputed right and it is difficult to decide between them, the result is a very negative situation of indecision and hesitation to make a judgment. This opens the door to a continual dispute between the litigants, whereby they will continue to publicize their dubious claims. Consequently, this will lead to the great evil of the undermining of Islamic brotherhood between the members of society.

Lastly, a delay by the judiciary will cause judges to be treated with suspicion. Their slowness in passing judgment will be seen as a deliberate attempt to wear down the eligible party so that he abandons pursuing his/her right, thus leaving it to the ineligible party, who will wrongfully make use of it. Likewise, the sense of respect for the judiciary will vanish from people's minds, which would result in serious evil for society.

This is the intellectual justification of the matter at hand. In addition, there is ample evidence to this effect that can be culled from the conduct and actions of the Prophet and his Companions. It is reported in many authentic traditions that the Prophet used to judge between litigants in the same hearing and would not unnecessarily defer them to future hearings. Likewise, he judged between al-Zubayr and a man from the *Anṣār* concerning a water stream in Ḥarrah in the suburbs of Madinah,[34] he judged between Kaᶜb ibn Mālik and ᶜAbd Allāh ibn Abī Ḥadrad concerning a debt on the latter for the former whereby he suggested to Kaᶜb to deduct half of the debt, etc.

It is also reported in Bukhārī's *Ṣaḥīḥ* that the Prophet sent Abū Mūsā al-Ashᶜarī to the Yemen as governor and judge and then followed him with Muᶜādh ibn Jabal. When Muᶜādh came and saw a chained man with Abū Mūsā, he asked what was wrong with the man. He was told that the man had committed a crime. So, Muᶜādh refused to sit down unless the penalty of God and His Apostle was implemented on the man.[35] Similarly, in a memo to Abū Mūsā al-Ashᶜarī, who was the judge of Basra, ᶜUmar ibn al-Khaṭṭāb is reported to have written the following: "adjudicate when you have understood and execute when you have adjudicated."[36] He thus made adjudication consequential upon understanding without any delay by the use of the apodosis clause that implies its occurrence as a result of the fulfillment of its conditional clause. Furthermore, he ordered him to carry out his sentence once passed. All this is meant to expedite the delivery of rights to their genuine claimants.

My statement "delaying the delivery of rights to their lawful claimants more than the time required to establish them" was meant to emphasize the notion of "delivering rights to their claimants as quickly as possible." This is to caution against the wrong attitude of many weak scholars and hypocritical judges who would concern themselves only with how many judgments they pass out of pride. However, their judgments lack the necessary conditions for the correct means of finding the truth. It so happens that when these judgments are subjected to scrutiny, they prove totally unsound and prone to refutation. Accelerating judgment between litigants cannot therefore be commended for its own sake if the judgment does not put an end to the dispute and the litigants are not convinced of its being sound and just. That is why ʿUmar said, "Adjudicate when you have understood."

During the Prophet's time and the years immediately following it, judicial procedures (*murāfaʿāt*) were indeed simple. Most people at that time were pious, truthful, and obedient to the rulers. A person violating the limits of the Shariʿah would willingly come forward to seek the implementation of its rules on him/her, such as the case of Māʿiz al-Aslami. Thus, if people were called for justice before the Prophet or the caliphs after him, they would mostly not waver in replying truthfully to whatever questions they were asked. If they denied anything, it was usually owing to some doubt about the accusations made against them. In this connection, Muslim, Abū Dāwūd and Tirmidhī reported that a man from Hadramawt and another one from Kindah came to the Prophet. The man from Hadramawt declared that the father of the man from Kindah had usurped his land. The man from Kindah contended that the land was his and that he had inherited it from his father. The Prophet asked the man from Hadramawt if he had any evidence to support his claim. He replied in the negative and demanded that the man from Kindah swear that he did not know that his father had taken the land by force from him. At this juncture, the man from Kindah refrained from taking an oath.[37] Neither Muslim nor Abū Dāwūd mentioned what judgment the Prophet passed on the two men. Yet, it is most probable that he decided that the land should be given to the man from the Hadramawt, basing his judgment on the abstention by the man from Kindah from swearing or maybe because of his very oath.

Afterwards, people gradually became bolder in violating the rights of others, and therefore they invented different kinds of tricks. False testimony (*shahādat al-zūr*) appeared for the first time in Islam toward the end of ʿUmar's reign. People then deemed it allowable to spite one's adversary and to provoke hostility and evil. Thus, they would conceal the truth in court cases (*nawāzil*) so as to obstruct the law from being implemented. They would even dupe the new and inexperienced judges by bringing to them old cases that had already been adjudicated by previous judges. Therefore, to curb these evil practices and establish the truth, judges and scholars undertook to develop the appropriate rules for settling disputes. One of the tasks that was given their attention was to investigate the status of witnesses. In this connection, the Mālikī scholars upheld the view that an oath should not be required from the defendant unless it was proven that there had been frequent dealings (*khulṭah*) between him and the plaintiff or that he was not trustworthy, that is, he was suspect.[38] Likewise, ʿUmar ibn ʿAbd al-ʿAzīz said, "People incur as many court cases as the iniquity they perpetrate."[39] To this were added detailed rules and methods that abound in the books on court cases (*nawāzil*) and to which the Mālikī scholars can rightly pride themselves on having made an important contribution.

In the past, Muslim judges compiled registers in which they recorded the cases, terms (*ājāl*), pieces of evidence, etc., they decided upon. These registers served as aide-mémoires to the judge and to his successors so that they would build on the work of their predecessors lest previously judged cases be brought again to the court. Most probably, these records would have been made in the presence of two reliable witnesses. Of the best ways followed in this respect was the writing down of verdicts with the testimony of just notaries. It is true that many of the procedures introduced by the scholars are responsible for the prolonged handling of judicial cases. However, this is necessary to put an end to the delay caused by the quibbles and tricks used by the litigants to keep the matter in dispute wrongfully in their hands.

One of the most appropriate ways to accelerate the fair judgment of cases and deliver rights to their lawful claimants is to specify the juristic school and its juridical doctrine on the basis of which verdicts will be made. Furthermore, one of the best procedures that have been established in Mālikī jurisprudence consists of holding the item in dispute (*al-muddaʿā fīh*) once evidence has been established and it is only a matter of pronouncing the verdict, which is called *ʿuqlah* (lit. shackle or impediment). This is derived from Mālik's statement in *Muwaṭṭa'* that constituted the basis for judicial practice in the school according to the rule that the yield [of the disputed item] belongs to the claimant until the date his right is established, not when the verdict is pronounced.[40] Holding the item in dispute thus serves a twofold purpose. First, it halts the harm by the erring party in persisting in his inequity before enabling the rightful party to be granted his right. Second, it hastens the delivery of the right to its owner once the verdict is decided. This measure is further justified by the fact that many perverse people would resort to hiding the item in dispute when the judgment is pronounced to dispossess them of it or to assign it to someone else who would claim to be the lawful owner, thus causing difficulty and distress to the party for whom the case is decided by preventing the decision from being implemented.

Now, the purpose of the Shariʿah for witnesses (*shuhūd*) is to inform of what establishes rights.[41] Therefore, witnesses are supposed to be truthful in their testimony. This depends on their reluctance to tell lies. This type of self-restraint (*wāziʿ*) might be: religious, that is, righteousness (*ʿadālah*), or moral, that is, magnanimity (*murū'ah*). The meaning of righteousness and integrity or *ʿadālah* varies only in accordance with the different views of the scholars in considering certain types of behavior as signs of weakness in a person's religiousness (*diyānah*), provided that their disagreement is substantial. It also varies according to the predominance of some juristic views over others amongst the people concerning whom testimony is to be given.

It is possible that certain influences would affect the level of self-restraint, such as intense love or intense hatred, which indeed weakens one's righteousness and integrity. Similarly, the family relationship (*qarābah*) can be influential. Accordingly, the qualities of witnesses must be scrutinized inasmuch as people's *ʿadālah* is weakened. However, some aspects of magnanimity are not subject to variation, for they emanate from a deeper level of human psychological makeup. Certain other aspects may vary according to people's customs and culture. These aspects must not be of real importance in relation to the knowledge of *Maqāṣid al-Shariʿah* (*ʿilm al-maqāṣid*), as has been stated [by the jurists] concerning walking barefoot in a society where people do not do so or eating in the street among people who disapprove of that. Indeed, this allows for ample tolerance.

The purpose concerning rights established by testimony is to preserve them and grant them as required. This requires registering the testimony of the witnesses, especially when the right is of a type that remains in use over a period in which the witnesses cease to exist. Therefore, documentation has been ordained in the Shariʿah by God's words: "O you who have attained faith! Whenever you give or take credit for a stated term, set it down in writing. And let a scribe write it down equitably between you; and no scribe shall refuse to write as God has taught him: thus shall he write" (2:282). Indeed, this verse lays down a great principle for the documentation of rights that has been implemented since the time of Revelation. Likewise, it has been the continual practice of Muslims everywhere to write down the confirmation of all kinds of transactions, such as descriptions of properties and donations, etc.

40

Maqāṣid al-Shariʿah: Penalties

I have shown in chapter 19 that all the dispositions of the Shariʿah center on reforming the condition of the community in all its affairs. There I stated in a general way that the deterrent, punishment, and fixed penalties (*ḥudūd*) instituted by the Shariʿah are exclusively meant to rectify people's conditions. We must now elaborate the Shariʿah purposes concerning the different types of punishment consisting of *qiṣāṣ* (*lex talionis*, just retaliation), *ḥudūd*, and *taʿzīr* (discretionary penalties). This is because one of the higher objectives of the Shariʿah is to preserve the social order of the community and it is only by blocking all sources of discord and aggression that this objective can be achieved.

The blocking of these sources itself is a fair policy only when it is based on the infallible Shariʿah and implemented by a legitimate authority. Otherwise, people's repulsion of evil will result in much more evil, as implied by the following verse: "Hence, if anyone has been slain wrongfully, We have empowered the defender of his rights [to exact a just retribution]; but even so, let him not exceed the bounds of equity in [retributive] killing"(17:33).[1] Thus, God also says:

> Hence, judge between the followers of earlier revelation in accordance with what God has bestowed from on high, and do not follow their errant views; and beware of them, lest they tempt you from anything

which God has bestowed from on high upon you. And if they turn away [from His commandments], then know that it is but God's will [thus] to afflict them for some of their sins: for, behold, a great many people are iniquitous indeed. Do they, perchance, desire [to be ruled by] the law of pagan ignorance? But for people who have inner certainty, who could be a better Lawgiver than God? (5:49–50)

Although it is said that these verses were revealed on a specific occasion, their content and import clearly indicate disapproval of and threat for anyone entertaining a longing for the conditions [of pagan ignorance]. It was one aspect of the rule of pagan ignorance that the victim would take revenge by himself, as expressed by the poet, al-Shamaydhar al-Ḥārithī:

We are not like those whom you used to strike with swords,
So that we submit to oppression or resort to a judge;
Nay, the verdict of the sword reigns supreme among us,
And only when the sword is satisfied do we become satisfied.[2]

Thus, the aim of the Shariʿah with regard to the legislation of fixed penalties (*ḥudūd*), just retribution (*qiṣāṣ*), discretionary penalties (*taʿzīr*) and injury compensation (*urūsh*[3] *al-jināyāt*) is to achieve the following three objectives: to reform the criminal, to satisfy the victim, and to deter the imitator of criminals.

(1) The first objective, that is, reformation, refers to the highest objective of the Shariʿah, which is bringing reform (*iṣlāḥ*) to every aspect of the daily lives of individuals comprising a society. This we discussed in chapter 12 on the all-purpose principle of Islamic legislation. Thus, God says: "Now as for the man who steals and the woman who steals, cut off the hand of each of them in requital for what they have done, as a deterrent ordained by God: for God is Almighty, Wise"[4] (5:38). Punishing the criminal aims at removing from his soul the evil that incites him to commit crime. This evil mostly becomes more deeply rooted in the criminal when the idea of committing a crime is translated into practice. That is why God has

followed the implementation of the *ḥadd* with the phrase: "But as for him who repents after having thus done wrong, and makes amends, behold, God will accept his repentance" (5:39).

Ḥudūd constitute the maximum possible sentences, for they have been instituted for the most serious crimes. By intensifying these prescribed penalties, the aim of the Shariʿah is to deter people and remove evil from the offender. Accordingly, when it is proven that a crime has been committed by mistake, the *ḥadd* punishment is waived. Similarly, if there is the slightest doubt or uncertainty (*shubuhah*) that could be used in favor of the offender, then the matter is considered on the same level as a mistake, in the sense that *ḥudūd* do not apply. Furthermore, if it is revealed that the unintentional offense has been committed owing to extreme negligence to take the necessary precautions, the negligent person shall receive the appropriate disciplinary treatment.

(2) When seeking satisfaction for the victim, we must remember that it is part of human nature to harbor rancor against aggressors and anger against those who wrong us in error. These feelings often push people to take vengeance against their aggressors in a way that always transgresses the bounds of justice. This is because vengeance bursts out of a passionate anger that usually affects people's rational thinking and blinds them to the light of justice. Thus, when the victim or his relatives and defenders (*awliyā'*) are capable of retaliating, they will soon do so; otherwise, they will conceal their wrath, thus awaiting the first opportunity for revenge. It is against this that God has cautioned us by saying: "but even so, let him not exceed the bounds of equity in [retributive] killing" (17:33). Under these circumstances, revenge and crime will never end and the social order of the community will never settle on peace and stability. Therefore, it has been the purpose of the Shariʿah to undertake the task of satisfying the victim and putting an end to the age-old practice of vengeance and counter-vengeance. Hence, the Prophet said during the Farewell Pilgrimage (*Ḥajjat al-Wadāʿ*): "Abolished are also the blood-feuds of the period of pagan ignorance (*Jāhiliyyah*)."[5]

Likewise, the purpose of giving the victim fair satisfaction takes into account the inclination for revenge that is rooted in human nature. Accordingly, the Shariʿah has given the relatives of a murder victim (*qatīl*) the right of guiding the convicted offender (*qātil*), under the supervision of the judge, by a rope in his hand to the place where just retribution will be inflicted on him, which is known as *qawad* (retaliation). This is meant to satisfy them to the same extent if they were to take justice into their own hands.

The satisfaction of the victim is more important in the Shariʿah than the reformation of the offender. Therefore, it carries greater weight when it is not possible to achieve both at the same time. An example is *qiṣāṣ*, where the reformation of the criminal cannot be achieved, so priority is given to the satisfaction of the victim or his relatives. For this, there is no point in the well-known disagreement amongst the scholars over the question of consent by the heirs entitled to exact *qiṣāṣ* (*awliyā' al-dam*) to a pardon and blood money instead of inflicting retaliation, if the offender's wealth is sufficient for that. In this respect, Ashhab's view that the murderer must be forced to pay the blood money is more tenable, contrary to Ibn al-Qāsim's opinion.[6] That is why they agreed that if some of the relatives of the victim forgive the offender, *qiṣāṣ* is then cancelled. These factors, of course, do not apply to killing in brigandage (*ḥirābah*) and assassination (*ghīlah*), as we shall point out shortly.

(3) The third purpose, deterring imitators, is implied by God's saying in the Qur'an: "As for the adulteress and adulterer – flog each of them with a hundred stripes, and let not compassion for them keep you from [carrying out] this law of God, if you [truly] believe in God and the Last Day; and let a group of the believers witness their chastisement" (24:2). Thus, Ibn al-ʿArabī said in his book *Aḥkām al-Qur'an*: "The real interpretation of this is that the execution of the *ḥadd* deters the one on whom it is implemented, and those who attend and witness it will learn a lesson from it and be deterred by it. Its story will then be on everybody's lips, thus warning those who come after."[7] It thus reverts to the purpose of reforming the community as a whole. This is because the execution of punishment according to established rules discourages perverse people and also

criminals from satisfying their devilish desires by committing crimes. Likewise, anything that acts as a deterrent constitutes a punishment. However, deterring the general public [other than the offender] must not transgress the limits of justice. Therefore, it has been an aspect of the wisdom of the Shariʿah that has laid down the punishment of the offender as a deterrent to others without violating justice. Hence, the Shariʿah policy in instituting *ḥudūd*, *qiṣāṣ*, and other types of penalties is meant to deter people from taking criminals as models.

Nevertheless, a pardon (*ʿafw*) by the victim under certain circumstances does not defeat the purpose of deterrence, for it only rarely happens, and therefore it cannot be taken as the main reason for the offender to commit a crime. Consequently we find that the Shariʿah does not take into consideration forgiveness in the crimes that do not affect the right of a specific party, such as theft, the consumption of intoxicants, and adultery, because these offences are a violation of the very essence of legislation itself, and so too is brigandage (*ḥirābah*). As regards assassination, no pardon by the relatives of the victim is accepted, owing to its hideousness. However, the repentance of the brigand (*muḥārib*) before his arrest has been accepted out of concern for peace and security and as a means of encouraging his companions to follow his good example.[8]

Conclusion

Thus, I have fulfilled my great purpose to formulate these discourses on *Maqāṣid al-Sharīʿah*. I hope that they will be of help to jurists, as well as to seekers of profound knowledge, to raise their thinking and perception to loftier heights and to strengthen their resolve to pursue and achieve the higher objectives of *Maqāṣid al-Sharīʿah*. For indeed, making things easier and accessible rests only with God, the Helper in good intentions. And he who dives deep will surely reap the most precious rewards.

The fair copy [of this book] was completed on 18 Jumāda I, 1360 [1941], at my home in Mars Jarrāḥ, known as al-ʿAbdalliyyah.

MUHAMMAD AL-TAHIR IBN ASHUR

NOTES

PREFACE

1. Abū al-Maʿālī ʿAbd al-Malik ibn Abī Muḥammad ʿAbd Allāh ibn Yūsuf al-Juwaynī, known as Imām al-Ḥaramayn, was born in 419/1028 in a small village called Juwayn near Nishapur in northern Iran. A great Shāfiʿī jurist and Ashʿarī theologian, al-Juwaynī had a lasting impact on the development of *uṣūl al-fiqh* (Islamic legal theory) and *Ashʿarī kalām* (theology). He was a close collaborator with the strong Seljuk Prime Minister Niẓām al-Mulk, who appointed him Professor of Shafiʿite jurisprudence at the Niẓāmiyyah School established by him in Baghdad. Al-Juwaynī left many outstanding works that remained unchallenged sources for the subsequent generations of students of Islamic theology and legal theory. They include, among others, *al-Shāmil fi Uṣūl al-Dīn, Kitāb al-Irshād ilā Qawāṭiʿ al-'Adillah fī Uṣūl al-Iʿtiqād* (in theology), *Kitāb al-Talkhīṣ fī Uṣūl al-Fiqh, al-Burhān fī Uṣūl al-Fiqh* (in legal theory). He died in 478/1085.
2. Abū al-Maʿālī al-Juwaynī, *al-Burhān fī Uṣūl al-Fiqh*, ed. ʿAbd al-ʿAẓīm al-Dīb (Cairo: Dār al-Wafā, 1412/1992), vol. 1, p.79.
3. His full name is Abū ʿAbd Allah Muḥammad ibn ʿAlī ibn ʿUmar ibn Muḥammad al-Tamīmī al-Māzarī. He was born in the city of Mazarah in Sicily in 453 AH. Most probably, he migrated to Tunisia in 464 AH after the island had completely fallen under the control of the Normans. In Tunisia, he studied with some of the most authoritative Mālikī scholars of his time, especially Abū al-Hasan ʿAlī ibn Muḥammad al-Rabʿī al-Lakhmī (d. 478 AH) and Abū Muḥammad ʿAbd al-Ḥamīd Ibn al-Ṣā'igh (d. 486 AH). Like most great scholars in the Islamic tradition, al-Māzarī studied, besides *tafsīr*, hadith, fiqh and *uṣūl al-fiqh*, theology and philosophy as well as mathematics and medicine. This endowed him with breadth of vision and analytic mind in dealing with juristic issues.

   In his juristic thinking, he combined the traditionalist approach of the jurists of the Malikite School of Kairouan with the rationalistic and argumentative approach of the Malikites of Baghdad. In Islamic jurisprudence, both *uṣūl* and *furūʿ*, al-Māzarī had a special penchant for issues of a greater level of juristic difference (*khilāf ʿālī*) in his quest for the higher objectives of the Shariʿah. In addition to his commentary on al-Juwaynī's *Burhān* (see note 5), he produced many valuable works in different fields of Islamic scholarship. They include, among others, *Sharḥ al-Talqīn* (a commentary on the *Talqīn*, a compendium on Mālikī jurisprudence by the great Mālikī jurist of Baghdad, al-Qāḍī Abū Muḥammad ʿAbd al-Wahhāb who died in 422 AH), *al-Muʿlim bi-Fawā'id Muslim* (a partial commentary in three volumes on the famous Hadith collection of the great traditionalist Muslim ibn al-Ḥajjāj (d. 261 AH). Al-Māzarī died at the age of 83 in 536/1141 in the coastal city of Mahdia and was buried in the nearby town of Monastir, where his grave is still preserved as a venerated shrine for many Tunisian Muslims.

4. Juwaynī, *Burhān*, p.78.
5. Al-Māzarī's commentary on *al-Burhān,* entitled *Īḍāḥ al-Maḥṣūl min Burhān al-Uṣūl*, from which the author made this quote has been edited by Ammar Talbi (Beirut: Dār al-Gharb al-Islāmī, 2001) based on the only known surviving manuscript in Ibn Ashur's collection. Unfortunately, many folios of this manuscript are missing or unintelligible, including the major parts of the chapter from which the quote was taken; this has made it difficult to document it accurately.
6. Shihāb al-Dīn Aḥmad ibn Idrīs al-Qarāfī al-Ṣanhājī. Born in 626/1229 in the small village of Qarāfah near Cairo, al-Qarāfī studied with the most outstanding scholars of his time, especially ʿIzz al-Dīn ibn ʿAbd al-Salām. He was the most authoritative Malikī jurist of his time in Egypt. Al-Qarāfī was an energetic and prolific writer, whose writings covered many disciplines, such as theology, jurisprudence, anti-Christian polemics, Arabic language sciences, Qur'anic interpretation, etc. His voluminous book *al-Dhakhīrah* is a major source of Mālikī juristic doctrines, in which he applied a comparative approach. His book *al-Furūq* is a pioneering work in codifying the juristic rules and maxims. In addition, he wrote many books on *uṣūl al-fiqh*, such as *Tanqīḥ al-Fuṣūl, Nafā'is al-Uṣūl fi Sharḥ al-Maḥṣūl.* He died in 684/1285.
7. Abū ʿAbd Allāh Muḥammad ibn ʿUmar ibn al-Ḥusayn Fakhr al-Dīn al-Rāzī was born in Rayy in 544/1149. He was known by various titles testifying to the high status he attained during his life, such as Abū al-Faḍl, Abū al-Maʿālī, Ibn al-Khaṭīb, al-Imām, etc. His father, Ḍiyā' al-Dīn, was himself an outstanding scholar of his time. Fakhr al-Dīn was brought up in the

Shāfiʿite School of jurisprudence and belonged the Ashʿarite School of *kalām*-philosophy. Following the tradition of classical Islamic scholarship, al-Rāzī spent many years traveling to various parts of the Muslim world in search of knowledge. During his journeys, he engaged in intellectual debates with representatives of opposing schools, especially the Muʿtazilites. His scholarship was indeed encyclopedic, as proved by the diversity and extensiveness of his extant works covering most of the traditional Islamic disciplines.

Among his works were the following: *Mafātīḥ al-Ghayb* (Qur'anic exegesis), *al-Maḥṣūl fī ʿIlm al-Uṣūl* (Islamic legal theory or *uṣūl al-fiqh*), *al-Maṭālib al-ʿĀliyyah mina al-ʿIlm al-Ilāhī* and *al-Mabāḥith al-Mashriqiyyah* (theology and philosophy). One outstanding feature of al-Rāzī's intellectual legacy was an attempt to synthesize Ashʿarite and Muʿtazilite doctrines as well as theology and philosophy. Al-Rāzī died in Herat in 606/1209. For more on his life and works see, Yasin Ceylan, *Theology and Tafsīr in the Major works of Fakhr al-Dīn al-Rāzī* (Kuala Lumpur: International Institute of Islamic Thought and Civilization [ISTAC], 1996); and Roger Arnaldez, *Fakhr al-Dīn al-Rāzī: Commentateur du Coran et philosophe* (Paris: Librairie Philosophique J. Vrin, 2002.)

8. Shams al-Dīn Abū al-Ḥasan ʿAlī ibn Ismāʿīl ibn ʿAlī ibn ʿAṭiyah was born in 557 AH and died in 618 AH. He was a jurist, legal theorist (*uṣūlī)* and Qur'an commentator. His works include *al-Taḥqīq wa al-Bayān fī Sharḥ al-Burhān* (in *uṣūl al-fiqh*) and *Safīnat al-Najāt* (a commentary on al-Ghazālī's *Iḥyā' ʿUlūm al-Dīn*).
9. Shihāb al-Dīn al-Qarāfī, *Nafā'is al-Uṣūl fī Sharḥ al-Maḥṣūl* (9 vols.), ed., ʿĀdil Aḥmad ʿAbd al-Mawjūd and ʿAlī Muḥammad Muʿawwaḍ (Riyad: Maktabat Mustaphā al-Bāz, 1995), vol. 3, pp.1247–1248.
10. His full name is Abū al-Ḥusayn Muḥammad ibn ʿAlī ibn al-Ṭayyib al-Baṣrī. He was a great erudite Muʿtazilite theologian and legal theorist of the Basrian School. He was born in Basra and lived in Baghdad until his death in 436/1044. He produced a number of important works on *ʿilm al-kalām* and *uṣūl al-fiqh*. They include, among others, *Sharḥ al-ʿUmad* (a commentary on al-Qāḍī ʿAbd al-Jabbār's *al-ʿUmad* in *uṣūl al-fiqh*), *al-Muʿtamad fī Uṣūl al-Fiqh, Taṣṣaffuḥ al-'Adillah* and *Ghurar al-'Adillah* (both in *ʿilm al-kalām*).
11. The question of temporal duration of accidents (*aʿrāḍ*), to which conflicting solutions were suggested, constituted one of the much-debated issues in the epistemological and cosmological doctrines of *ʿilm al-kalām* or Islamic theology. For further details of the theory of accidents and its place in *kalām*-philosophy, see, Alnoor Dhanani, *The Physical Theory of Kalām:*

Atoms, Space, and Void in Baṣrian Muʿtazilī Cosmology (Leiden: E.J. Brill, 1994), pp.38–54. Abū al-Ḥasan al-Ashʿarī and many of his followers were of the view that accidents do not exist for more than one moment. See in this regard, Abū Bakr Muḥammad ibn al-Ḥasan ibn Fūrak, *Mujarrad Maqālāt al-Sheikh Abī al-Ḥasan al-Ashʿarī*, ed., Daniel Gimaret (Beirut: Dār El-Mashraq, 1987), pp.12–13.

12. The notion of vacuum or void (*khalā'*) is one of the most important concepts in ancient and medieval philosophical and theological thought. It is specifically linked to the concept of being, time, space and motion. In the ancient atomism developed by philosophers like Democritus of Abdera and Leucippus of Miletus in the 5th century BC in their natural philosophy, the basic idea was that if you could look at matter on a smaller and smaller scale ultimately you would see individual *atoms* – objects that could not be divided further. Everything was made up of these atoms, which moved around in a *void* or *vacuum*. It is a kind of empty space in which the combination (*ijtimāʿ*), separation (*iftirāq*), and movement (*ḥarakah* or *intiqāl*) of the atoms can take place. Most Muslim *kalām* scholars in constructing their cosmological doctrines employed this notion of void.

13. Qarāfī, *Nafā'is al-Uṣūl*, vol. 1, pp.161–162 where the view attributed to Abū al-Ḥusayn and Qarāfī's comment on it can be found. However, I have not been able to locate the view attributed to Abū al-Ḥusayn al-Baṣrī in *Sharḥ al-ʿUmad*. All that is mentioned in the discussion of correctness and falsehood (*al-taṣwīb wa al-takhṭi'ah*) in ijtihad, is that "truth" in the principles of the religion and in the principles of jurisprudence is one. It means the fundamental tenets of faith and the universal predicates upon which are based the legal rulings as well as the general principles of ethics, are not affected by differences in time, people, or circumstances. As for those particular rulings based on the achievement of variable interests for those who are morally responsible (*mukallafīn*), he is of the view that there is right and wrong.

    Al-Baṣrī, however – at least as appears from the context and outward meaning of his words – is not referring to the principles of jurisprudence in the sense of the methods and universal rules of deduction and juristic argumentation, according to Qarāfī, as the author has mentioned. See, Abū al-Ḥusayn al-Baṣrī, *Sharḥ al-ʿUmad* (2 vols.), ed., ʿAbd al-Ḥamīd ibn ʿAlī Abū Zunayd (Cairo: al-Maṭbaʿah al-Salafiyyah, 1410 AH), vol. 2, pp.235–318. See also by the same author, *al-Muʿtamad fī Uṣūl al-Fiqh*, ed., Muhammad Hamidullah et al. (Damascus: Institut Français de Damas, 1965), vol. 2, pp.948–990.

14. Abū Isḥāq Ibrāhīm ibn Mūsā ibn Muḥammad al-Lakhmī al-Shāṭibī grew

up in Granada (or Gharnāṭah in Muslim Spain or al-Andalus) and acquired his entire training in this city, which was the capital of the Naṣrī kingdom. In his youth, al-Shāṭibī witnessed the reign of Sulṭān Muḥammad V al-Ghanī Bi'llāh, which was a very eventful period in the history of Granada. During al-Shāṭibī's life, Granada became a centre of attraction for scholars from all parts of North Africa, such as the eminent Ibn Khaldūn. This gave him the chance to study with the most outstanding scholars of his time, especially those with a clear penchant towards ijtihad and the rejection of *taqlīd*. This was clearly reflected in his special interest in the study of *uṣūl al-fiqh* resuling in his magnum opus *al-Muwāfaqāt,* whose main focus is the methodology and philosophy of Islamic Law, in particular, the higher objectives of the Shariᶜah, (*maqāṣid al-Shariᶜah*). In addition to this book, he left another important work entitled *Kitāb al-Iᶜtiṣām*. Al-Shāṭibī died on 8 Shaᶜbān 790/1388.

15. See the words of al-Shāṭibī and his arguments that the principles of jurisprudence are categorical in, *al-Muwāfaqāt fī Uṣūl al-Shariᶜah*, ed., ᶜAbd Allāh Drāz (Beirut: Dār al-Maᶜrifah, 1996), vol. 1/1, pp.29–33.
16. The author refers here to the tradition known in Tunisia for many centuries, i.e. the celebration of sessions of Hadith studies during the month of Ramadan in mosques and religious schools. The origin of "these sessions is that benefactors and those interested in religious knowledge and the noble Hadith, from among those who sponsor the building of mosques and religious schools and others, inaugurate in these Islamic colleges sessions for the study of Hadith which are delivered by scholars. The returns of the endowment by sponsors used to serve as financial assistance to these scholars. Most of these Hadith lessons deal with The *Ṣaḥīḥ of Bukhārī*. Sponsors may confine these lessons to mere reading of the traditions (*riwāyah*), as one discovers upon consulting the archival documents of these institutions." See for more details, "al-Akhtām bi-Tūnis," *al-Majallah al-Zaytūniyyah*, part 1, vol. 3, pp.118–123. Dār al-Gharb al-Islāmī in Beirut has published all the issues of this magazine in five volumes. See also, Muḥammad ibn al-Khūjah (General), *Tārīkh Maᶜālim al-Tawḥīd fī al-Qadīm wa al-Jadīd* (Tunis: al-Maṭbaᶜah al-Tūnisiyyah, 1358/1927), pp.337–349.
17. This is not a statement by scholars as the author's words might imply, but a famous Prophetic tradition that became a legal maxim. See Imām Mālik ibn Anas, *Muwaṭṭa'*, ed., Aḥmad Ratib Amrush (Beirut: Dār al-Nafā'is, 1414/1994), 'Aqḍiyah', hadith 1426, p.529.
18. Abū al-Walīd Muḥammad ibn Aḥmad Ibn Rushd, *al-Muqaddimāt al-Mumahhidāt*, ed., Muḥammad Ḥajjī (Beirut: Dār al-Gharb al-Islāmī,

1408/1988), vol. 2, p.309; Abd al-Bāqī ibn Yūsuf al-Zurqānī, *Sharḥ Muwaṭṭa'* (Cairo: al-Maktabah al-Tijāriyyah al-Kubrā, 1959), vol. 4, p.204.

19. See, for example, Mālik ibn Anas, *Muwaṭṭa'*, ed., Ahmad Ratib Amrush (Beirut: Dār al-Nafā'is, 1414/1994), 'Ṣiyām,' p.204. There are, in fact, many Prophetic traditions referring to Islam's characteristic of easiness. See, for example, Abū ʿAbd Allāh Muḥammad ibn Ismāʿīl al-Bukhārī, *Ṣaḥīḥ*, 'Īmān,' hadith 39, pp.9–10.
20. Mālik, *Muwaṭṭa'*, 'Nikāḥ,' hadiths 1100–1101, p.355; Bukhārī, *Ṣaḥīḥ* (Riyadh: Darussam, 1419/1999), 'Buyūʿ,' hadiths 2139–2140, p.343; Muslim, *Ṣaḥīḥ* (Beirut: Dār al-Kutub al-ʿIlmiyyah, 1421/2001), 'Nikāḥ,' hadiths 1412–1414, pp.526–527; 'Buyūʿ,' hadith 1514, p.585.
21. Mālik, *Muwaṭṭa'*, 'Nikāḥ,' p.355.
22. His full name is Abū Muḥammad al-ʿIzz or ʿIzz al-Dīn ʿAbd al-ʿAzīz ibn ʿAbd al-Salām ibn Abī al-Qāsim al-Sulamī. He was born in Damascus in 577 or 578 AH and died in 660 AH. He studied with a number of eminent scholars such as Ibn ʿAsākir and Sayf al-Dīn al-Āmidī. A prominent Shāfiʿī jurist of his time with a clear mystic inclination, Ibn ʿAbd al-Salām came into conflict with the Mamluk sultans of his era in both Damascus and Cairo and was imprisoned and persecuted because of his denouncing their injustices and transgression of the Shariʿah. His works cover various areas of Islamic scholarship, such as Qur'an interpretation, jurisprudence both at the methodological and substantial levels, etc. He devoted his well-known book *al-Qawāʿid al-Kubrā* (also known as *Qawāʿid al-Aḥkām fī Ṣāliḥ al-Anām*) to the study and elucidation of the different aspects of *maṣāliḥ* and *mafāsid* considered by the Shariʿah rules and injunctions.
23. What is meant here is al-Shāṭibī's book *al-Muwāfaqāt fī Uṣūl al-Shariʿah*. According to al-Shāṭibī in the Introduction, its original title was *al-Taʿrīf bi-Asrār al-Taklīf*, but he changed it to *al-Muwāfaqāt* following a dream by one of his friends. See, the Introduction to *Muwāfaqāt*, vol. 1/1, p.25.
24. There are Muslim scholars who studied the different aspects of the Shariʿah with to discover the different objectives intended by its various rules and injunctions. Examples are al-Ghazālī (*Shifā' al-Ghalīl and Iḥyā' ʿUlūm al-Dīn*), al-Rāghib al-Aṣfahānī (*al-Dharīʿah ilā Makārim al-Shariʿah*), al-Āmidī (*al-Iḥkām fī Uṣūl al-Aḥkām*), Muḥammad ibn ʿAbd al-Raḥmān al-Bukhārī (*Maḥāsin al-Islām*), and Ibn Qayyim al-Jawziyyah (*Miftāḥ Dār al-Saʿādah and Iʿlām Muwaqqiʿīn*).
25. In Islamic jurisprudence, the term *diyānah* has been used to refer to the spiritual internal aspects of religiosity and religious life concerning specifically the individual's personal relationship with God, so as to distinguish

them from what constitutes an objective body of laws and rules regulating external human conduct. Ibn Ashur is here stressing that differentiation, whereby only the second aspect entails judicial interference. The word *diyānah* thus differs from *dīn* with its comprehensive meaning encompassing both aspects.

26. The first edition, published by Maktabat al-Istiqāmah in 1366/1946 in Tunis, refers to the title *Uṣūl Niẓām al-Ijtimāᶜ fī al-Islām* [Principles of Human Association in Islam]. Subsequent editions in Tunisia and Algeria give the title mentioned here. However, when the book was published by al-Sharikah al-Tūnisiyyah li al-Tawazīᶜ (Tunisia), it came out under a slightly different title: *Uṣūl al-Niẓām al-Ijtimāᶜī fī al-Islām* [Principles of the Social Order in Islam]. It is not clear whether these differences are the responsibility of the author or the publishers.

PART I: ESTABLISHING *MAQĀṢID AL-SHARIᶜAH*

PREFATORY NOTE

1. Shāṭibī, *Muwāfaqāt*, vol. 2/2, p. 323.

2: THE JURISTS' NEED TO KNOW *MAQĀṢID AL-SHARIᶜAH*

1. In Islamic legal theory and jurisprudence, *naql sharᶜī* means the transfer of a word or an expression, known as *manqūl* (polysem), from its original lexical meaning to another one which is a matter of convention established by the Lawgiver (*al-Shāriᶜ*).
2. I mean by *ilghā'* abrogation (*naskh*) or giving a preference (*tarjīḥ*) of one indicant to another or, alternatively, the realization of the unsoundness (*fasād*) of ijtihad outcome. By *tanqīḥ* I mean things like specification (*takhṣīṣ*) and qualification (*taqyīd*). – Author.
3. The author refers here to the rational modes of ijtihad transcending the narrow techniques of analogical reasoning (*qiyās*). Of those modes he will particularly elaborate on the rule of *maṣlaḥah mursalah*, which constitutes what he calls *qiyās kullī*.
4. On the meaning and scope of *maṣlaḥah mursalah*, see Abū Isḥāq Ibrāhim ibn Mūsā al-Shāṭibī, *Kitāb al-Iᶜtiṣām* (hereinafter *Iᶜtiṣām*), ed. Khālid ᶜAbd al-Fattāḥ Shibl Abū Sulaymān (Beirut: Dār al-Fikr, 1416/1996), vol. 2,

pp.78–94. See also, Najm al-Dīn al-Ṭūfī, *Sharḥ Mukhtaṣar al-Rawḍah*, ed. Abd Allah Abd al-Muhsin al-Turki (Beirut: Mu'assassat al-Risālah, 1419/1998), vol. 3, pp.204–217; Wael B. Hallaq, *A History of Islamic Legal Theories* (Cambridge: Cambridge University Press, 1999), pp.112–230.

5. For the meaning of *munāsib* and *munāsabah*, see the author's note 18 below in this chapter.
6. Shāṭibī, *Iᶜtiṣām*, pp.95–113.
7. Abū Umayyah Shurayḥ ibn al-Ḥarth ibn Qays al-Kindī, known as Justice Shurayḥ (Shurayḥ al-Qāḍī). A trustworthy traditionalist, an eminent jurist, and a man of vast knowledge of Arabic literature and poetry, he held the office of judge during the rule of ᶜUmar ibn al-Khaṭṭāb, ᶜUthmān ibn ᶜAffān, ᶜAlī ibn Abī Ṭālib, and Muᶜāwiyah ibn Abī Sufyān. He died in 78 AH.
8. Al-Qāḍī ᶜIyāḍ, *Tartīb al-Madārik*, ed. Aḥmad Bakīr Maḥmūd (Beirut: Dār Maktabat al-Ḥayāt & Tripoli, Libya: Dār Maktabat al-Fikr, 1387/1967), vol. 1/1, pp.221–222.
9. The hadith about the option to cancel a sale at the time of the agreement as narrated by Mālik goes as follows: ᶜAbd Allāh ibn ᶜUmar reported that God's Apostle *(ṢAAS)* said: "Both parties in a business transaction have the right of withdrawal as long as they have not separated, except in the transaction called *khiyār*." See, *Muwaṭṭa'*, 'Buyūᶜ', hadith 1363, p.466. It is also narrated with the same wording in Bukhārī, *Ṣaḥīḥ*, 'Buyūᶜ', hadith 2111, p.339; Muslim, *Ṣaḥīḥ*, 'Buyūᶜ', hadith 1531, p.590.
10. Mālik ibn Anas, *Muwaṭṭa'*, p.466. See the author's comment on this tradition and his criticism of its misinterpretation by previous scholars in Muhammad al-Tahir ibn Ashur, *Kashf al-Mughaṭṭā mina al-Maᶜānī wa al-Alfāẓ al-Wāqiᶜah fī Muwaṭṭa'* (Tunis: al-Sharikah al-Tūnisiyyah lī al-Tawzīᶜ, Algiers: al-Sharikah al-Waṭaniyyah lī al-Nashr wa al-Tawzīᶜ, 1976), pp.280–281.
11. Shihāb al-Dīn Aḥmad ibn Idrīs Qarāfī, *al-Dhakhīrah fī Furūᶜ al-Mālikiyyah* (hereinafter Dhakhīrah), ed. Abū Isḥāq Aḥmad ᶜAbd al-Raḥmān (Beirut: Dār al-Kutub al-ᶜIlmiyyah, 1422/2001), vol. 4, pp.251–254; *Kitāb al-Furūq* (hereinafter *Furūq*), ed. Muhammad Aḥmad Sarrāj & ᶜAlī Jumᶜah Muḥammad (Cairo: Dār al-Salām, 1421/2001), vol. 3, pp.1059–1063.
12. See the many versions of this tradition in Bukhārī, *Ṣaḥīḥ*, 'ᶜIlm', hadith 126, p.27; Hajj, hadiths 1583–1586, p.257; *Aḥādīth al-Anbiyā'*, hadith 3368, p.564; *Tafsīr al-Qur'an*, hadith 4484, p.762; *Tamannī*, hadith 7243, p.1247. ᶜAbd Allāh ibn ᶜUmar's statement is found in hadith 1583.
13. His real name was ᶜAbd Allāh ibn Qays, but he was, and continues to be known as Abū Mūsā al-Ashᶜarī. He left his native land, the Yemen, for Makkah immediately after hearing that a Prophet had appeared there. At Makkah, he stayed in the company of the Prophet from whom he gained

knowledge and guidance. He returned to his country to propagate the Word of God and spread the mission of His Apostle. We have no further news of him for more than a decade. Then, just after the end of the Khaybar expedition he came to the Prophet in Madinah. His arrival there coincided with that of Jaʿfar ibn Abī Ṭālib and other Muslims from Abyssinia. This time Abū Mūsā came with more than fifty people from the Yemen, all of whom had accepted Islam. Abū Mūsā al-Ashʿarī was of outstanding qualities that manifested themsleves brilliantly in the service of Islam, both during the Prophet's time and afterwards. He excelled as *faqīh*, military commander and judge.

14. Abū Saʿīd Saʿd ibn Mālik ibn Sinān al-Khudrī al-Khazrajī al-Anṣārī. He was born 10 years before the Hijrah in 74 AH. He narrated many of the Prophet's Traditions as well as statements and opinions of the four caliphs and other Companions. Abū Saʿīd al-Khudrī was one of the most knowledgeable and intelligent Companions in relation to the juristic interpretation and understanding of the Shariʿah sources. A number of the Prophet's Companions, such as ʿAbd Allāh ibn ʿAbbās (the Prophet's cousin), ʿAbd Allāh ibn ʿUmar ibn al-Khaṭṭāb, Jābir ibn ʿAbd Allāh and Abū Umāmah, narrated from him. Owing to his youth, the Prophet did not allow him to participate in the Battle of Uḥud, in which his father was killed.
15. See the details of this incident in Bukhārī, *Ṣaḥīḥ*, 'Isti'dhān', hadith 6245, p.1087; Muslim, *Ṣaḥīḥ*, 'Adāb', hadith 2153, pp.852–853.
16. Mālik, *Muwaṭṭa'*, 'Zakah', hadith 618, p.188. See also, al-Māwardī, *The Ordinances of Government*, trans. Wafaa H. Wahba (Reading, Berks., UK: Garnet Publishing, 2000), p.159.
17. Clearly, this requires circularity (*dawr*), especially since the author has made – in his subsequent exposition of the methods of knowing the objectives of the Shariʿah – the thematic inference (*istiqrā'*) of the effective causes of commands (*ʿilal al-aḥkām*) the utmost method for determining these objectives. So how can one assert here that the affirmation of causes is needed to know the same objectives? It is perhaps in anticipation of such an objection that the author does not speak with unquestionable conviction, but rather with conjecture and probability.
18. Suitability (*munāsabah*) is a meaning (*maʿnā*) in a person's act that necessitates obligating (*wujūb*), prohibiting (*taḥrīm*) or permitting (*idhn*) that act. This meaning is an apparent and constant attribute (*waṣf*) deemed by the mind (*ʿaql*) that the *ḥukm* on it fits the purpose (*maqṣad*) of the Shariʿah in that *ḥukm*. The purpose of the Shariʿah consists either of the realization of benefit (*maṣlaḥah*) or the repulsion of harm (*mafsadah*). An example of such an attribute is just retaliation (*qiṣāṣ*) against the murderer who kills intentionally, which suits the purpose (*maqṣad*) of the Shariʿah. The purpose of the rule of

qiṣāṣ is to requite the aggressor what he himself has committed, and also to deter those who have not committed this crime from doing likewise. Another example is the consumption of wine. Intoxication causes serious harm and therefore intoxicants must be prohibited.

The *mujtahid's* derivation of this suitable attribute is known as *takhrīj al-manāṭ*. As for *tanqīḥ al-manāṭ* (the emendation and refinement of the *ratio legis*), it consists of excluding (*ilghā'*) some of the attributes or states of the act from being the underlying cause (*ʿillah*) of the *ḥukm*, and considering what has not been excluded as the basis or ground (*manāṭ*) of that *ḥukm*. An example of this is the Saying of the Prophet: "Whoever frees a bondsman, who is jointly owned with other partners, should estimate the value of what is owned by these partners and then pay them their shares, for the bondsman to be completely free. If he cannot pay his partners, then the bondsman is free but only partly" (Bukhārī, *Ṣaḥīḥ*, 'Sharikah', *Bāb* 47; 'ʿItq', hadiths 2522–2523, 2/3: p.165; 'Aymān', *Bāb* 12; 'Aḥkām', *Bāb* 14). The word "bondsman" in this hadith might imply that emancipation applies only to male slaves. However, it is a matter of consensus (ijmaʿ) that this applies also to female slaves by virtue of *tanqīḥ al-manāṭ*. As for *ilghā' al-fāriq*, it is one of the methods of emendation and refinement of the *ratio legis* (*tanqīḥ al-manāṭ*) as in this example – Author.

19. Abū ʿAbd al-Raḥmān Aḥmad ibn Shuʿayb al-Nasā'ī, *Sunan* (Istanbul: Dār al-Dawah, 1413/1992), 'Ṭalāq', *Bāb* 7 (vol. 6, p.144); *Bāb* 72 (vol. 6, p.210); Aḥmad ibn Ḥanbal, Musnad (Beirut: al-Maktab al-Islāmī, 1405/1985), vol. 6, p.373 & 417. Judging the report of Fāṭimah bint Qays as inaccurate, ʿUmar argued his view based on the following Qur'anic verses: "Do not expel them from their homes [i.e. during the waiting-period]; and neither shall they [be made to] leave unless they become openly guilty of immoral conduct", "[Hence,] let the women [who are undergoing a waiting-period] live in the same manner as you live yourselves, in accordance with your means; and do not harass them with a view to making their lives a misery" (65: 1 & 6).
20. Bukhārī, *Ṣaḥīḥ*, 'Janā'iz', hadith 1288, p.206.

3: METHODS OF ESTABLISHING *MAQĀṢID AL-SHARIʿAH*

1. Mālik ibn Anas, *Muwaṭṭa'*, 'Nikāḥ', hadith 1110, p.359.
2. See Qarāfī's discussion of the different views on this issue in his *Dhakhīrah*, vol. 4, pp.156–158.
3. This is a reference to ʿĪsā al-Ghubrīnī, one of the students of Shaikh Muhammad ibn ʿArafah. He said this on the occasion of an incident in which a brother cashed, on behalf of his sister, the value of a jointly owned property

and then declared that he had given her her share of it. – Author.

Ibn ʿArafah is Abū ʿAbd Allāh Muhammad ibn ʿArafah al-Wirghimī, the descendant of a family from the town of Wirghimah in Southern Tunisia. He was born in Tunis in 716 AH and died in Jumada II, 803 AH. He was buried in al-Jallāz cemetery in the city of Tunis. He was known for his mastery of all the branches of sciences known in his time and became an established authority. He wrote many works on Qur'anic exegesis, jurisprudence, legal theory, theology and logic. He led the prayers and was the deliverer of the Friday sermon in the Zaytūnah-Grand Mosque for fifty years. It also seems that there was some rivalry and competition as well as enmity between him and his contemporary and countryman, Ibn Khaldūn.

As for al-Ghubrīnī, his full name is Abū Mahdī ʿĪsā ibn Aḥmad ibn Muḥammad al-Ghubrīnī al-Tūnisī. He studied under Ibn ʿArafah and was appointed to the office of chief judge in Tunis, in addition to being the deliverer of the Friday sermon at the Zaytūnah mosque. He died in either 813 or 815 AH.

4. Mālik ibn Anas, *Muwaṭṭa'*, 'Buyūʿ', hadith 1312, p.429.
5. Ibid, p.278; see also, Bukhārī, *Ṣaḥīḥ*, 'Buyūʿ', hadith 2117, p.340; 'Istiqrāḍ', hadith 2407, p.387; 'Khuṣūmāt', hadith 2414, p.388; 'Ḥiyal', hadith 6964, pp.1200–1201; Muslim, *Ṣaḥīḥ*, 'Buyūʿ', hadith 1533, p.591.
6. Bukhārī, *Ṣaḥīḥ*, 'Buyūʿ', hadith, 2139, p.343 and 2165, p.346; 'Nikāḥ', hadith 5142, p.920; Mālik ibn Anas, *Muwaṭṭa'*, 'Buyūʿ', hadiths, 1378–1379, p.476; Muslim, *Ṣaḥīḥ*, 'Buyūʿ', hadith 1515, p.585. This tradition reads as follows: "Do not let one of you bid against the other."
7. Muslim, *Ṣaḥīḥ*, 'Musāqāh', hadith 1605, p.624.
8. The author has omitted this phrase from the quotation.
9. Ibn Rushd, *Muqaddimāt*, vol. 2, pp.417–418.
10. See the narration of this incident with a different wording than that mentioned by the author in Bukhārī, *Ṣaḥīḥ*, 'al-ʿAmal fī al-Ṣalāh', hadith 1211, p.193.
11. Strictly speaking, the Zahirites are the followers of Abū Sulaymān Dāwūd ibn ʿAlī ibn Khalaf al-Iṣfahānī, who died in 270 AH in Baghdad. Dāwūd is considered to have attempted to build a system that would supplement that developed by al-Shāfiʿī. Amongst the scholars who tried to systematize Dāwūd's views was the Andalusian Abū Muḥammad ʿAlī ibn Ḥazm (d. 456/1064). According to Ibn Khaldūn, the Zahirites "restricted the sources of the law to the texts and the general consensus. They considered obvious analogy and causality suggested by the texts as resting in the texts themselves, because a text that indicates a *ratio legis* [*ʿillah*] permits a legal decision for all the cases covered by such a kind of reasoning." Ibn Khaldūn, *The Muqaddimah*, trans. Franz Rosenthal (London: Routledge & Kegan Paul, 1967), vol. 3, pp.4–5. For a comprehensive study of the Zahirite doctrines and methodol-

ogy, see Ignaz Goldziher, *The Ẓāhirīs: Their Doctrine and their History*, English trans. Wolfegang Behn (Leiden: E. J. Brill, 1971).

12. In its literal meaning, the word *bāṭiniyyah* means esotericism. In Islamic intellectual and religious history, this term has become especially synonymous with to the name of the Ismaʿili sect or Ismaʿilis, an offshoot of the Shiʿite Muslims. Used as a name, the term Bāṭinīs or Bāṭiniyyah specifically refers to this sect whose followers believe in the existence of a continual esoteric chain of infallible persons through whom the "true and inner knowledge" of Islam is transmitted. As a general term, the word *bāṭiniyyah* refers to all kinds of esoteric interpretation of the scriptural sources of Islam, which would disregard all apparent meanings and language-bound connotations.
13. Shāṭibī, *Muwāfaqāt*, vol. 1/2, pp.666–673.

4: EVALUATION OF THE PREDECESSORS' METHODS

1. The term *Salaf* as used by Ibn Ashur in this and similar contexts refers in the first place to the generation of the Prophet's Companions (*Ṣaḥābah*) and might also refer to that of the Followers (*Tābiʿūn*), that is the generation immediately succeeding that of the Companions.
2. I.e., the next chapter and the chapter on the definitive and probable goals of the Shariʿah.
3. Bukhārī, *Ṣaḥīḥ*, 'al-Ḥarth wa al-Muzāraʿah', hadith 2340, p.376; Muslim, *Ṣaḥīḥ*, 'Buyūʿ', hadith 1536 (88–96), pp.597–598.
4. *Arbiʿā'* (sing. *rabīʿ*) are streams or small rivers. In the hadith there is an indication that they used to rent land for a portion of the owned river's water. [Author].
5. Bukhārī, *Ṣaḥīḥ*, 'al-Ḥarth wa al-Muzāraʿah', hadith 2344, pp.376–377.
6. Ibid, hadiths 2343 & 2345, pp.376–377; Muslim, *Ṣaḥīḥ*, 'Buyūʿ', hadith 1547 (106–112), pp.599–600.
7. Bukhārī, *Ṣaḥīḥ*, 'al-Ḥarth wa al-Muzāraʿah', hadith 2342, p.376.
8. *Wasq*, a dry measure equivalent to sixty *ṣāʿs* (one *ṣāʿ* is equivalent to 51/3 pounds). A *wasq* also means a camel-load, a wagonload or a shipload.
9. Bukhārī, *Ṣaḥīḥ*, 'al-Ḥarth wa al-Muzāraʿah', hadith 2339, p.376; Muslim, *Ṣaḥīḥ*, 'Buyūʿ', hadith 1548 (113–114), p.600 and hadith 1500 (120–123), pp.601–602.
10. Mālik ibn Anas, *Muwaṭṭa'*, 'Buyūʿ", hadith 1315, p.430.
11. Muhammad ibn Muslim ibn Shihāb al-Zuhrī died in 124 AH. Ibn Shihāb al-Zuhrī received his first education from Saʿīd ibn al-Musayyib, who taught him for eight years. He was also taught by ʿUbayd Alāh ibn ʿAbd Allāh ibn ʿUtbah, who was one of the seven leading jurists of the time. Ibn Shihāb al-Zuhrī was

the son of Muslim ibn Shihāb, who supported ʿAbd Allāh ibn al-Zubayr, who fought against the Umayyads for many years. Al-Zuhrī is one of the greatest authorities on Hadith.

12. Saʿīd ibn al-Musayyib ibn Ḥazn ibn Abī Wahb was born in 13 AH and died in 94 AH. A notable of the tribe of Banū Makhzūm, he was the foremost in Traditions, jurisprudence and the Qur'anic interpretation among the generation succeeding the Companions, the *Tābiʿūn*. He narrated from his father, ʿUthmān ibn ʿAffān, ʿAlī ibn Abī Ṭālib, and other Companions.
13. Mālik ibn Anas, *Muwaṭṭa'*, 'Buyūʿ', hadith 1315, p.430. Cf. Muslim, *Ṣaḥīḥ*, 'Buyūʿ', hadith 1547 (115–117), p.601.
14. Abū Ḥārith al-Layth ibn Saʿd al-Fihrī al-Miṣrī (d. 175 AH) was an excellent *faqīh* and leading scholar of Egypt. He was the Successor of the Successors. Mālik, who had corresponded and argued with him, said that he was one of the people of knowledge.
15. Bukhārī, *Ṣaḥīḥ*, 'al-Ḥarth wa al-Muzāraʿah', hadith 2346/2347, p.377.
16. Bukhārī, *Ṣaḥīḥ*, 'Maghāzī', hadith 4012/4013, p.677; Mālik, *Muwaṭṭa'*, 'Kirā' al-Arḍ', pp.501–502.
17. Bukhārī, *Ṣaḥīḥ*, 'al-Ḥarth wa al-Muzāraʿah', hadith 2327, pp.373–374; Muslim, *Ṣaḥīḥ*, 'Buyūʿ', hadith 1547 (116–117), p.601.
18. Bukhārī, *Ṣaḥīḥ*, 'al-Maghāzī', hadith 4391, pp.744–745.
19. Mālik ibn Anas, *Muwaṭṭa'*, 'Buyūʿ', hadith 1363, p.466; see also a number of versions of the same tradition in Bukhārī, 'Buyūʿ', hadiths 2107 and 2113, pp.338–339; Muslim, *Ṣaḥīḥ*, 'Buyūʿ, hadith 1524(23–28), pp.587–588.
20. Abū Bakr Muḥammad ibn ʿAbd Allāh ibn Muḥammad ibn al-ʿArabī was born in 468 AH in Sevilla, died in Marrakech in 543 AH and was buried in Fez. During his journey to the Mashreq (Islamic East) in pursuit of knowledge, he met al-Ghazālī while in his mystical seclusion in Jerusalem. As a prominent Mālikī jurist, he held the post of judge (*qāḍī*) in his home town. He was a multi-faceted scholar and a prolific writer. His works cover many disciplines of Islamic scholarship such as Prophetic Traditions, Qur'anic exegesis, jurisprudence, theology, history, etc.
21. The tradition regarding the purchase of animals whose udders are tied up to withhold the milk has been reported in slightly different versions. One of them, on the authority of Abū Hurayrah, reads as follows: "He who has bought a goat with its udder tied up should go back with it, milk it, and, if he is satisfied with its milk, he should retain it, otherwise he should return it along with a *ṣāʿ* of dates." Reports on the cattle whose milk is withheld for days (*muṣarrāh*) can be found in Bukhārī, *Ṣaḥīḥ*, 'Buyūʿ', hadiths 2148–2151, pp.344–345; Muslim, *Ṣaḥīḥ*, 'Buyūʿ', hadiths 1525(23–28), pp.587–588.
22. The phrase *al-kharāj bi al-ḍamān* occurs literally in a Prophetic tradition on

the authority of ʿĀ'ishah. Like another famous statement by the Prophet i.e. *Lā ḍarara wa lā ḍirār*, it has become one of the established juridical maxims governing sales in Islamic jurisprudence, although the authenticity of the tradition in which it occurs has been disputed by the traditionalists. Its meaning can be expressed as follows. The revenue derived from the thing purchased is the property of the purchaser because of the responsibility he has borne for it. If one purchases something and makes use of it, thus deducing a revenue from it, and then discovers in it a defect that the seller concealed from him, he has a right to return it and to claim a full refund from its original owner. However, the revenue that he derived from it is his lawful property, because he has been responsible for it, and if it had perished, part of his property would have perished.

See on the meaning and scope of this maxim, Jalāl al-Dīn ʿAbd al-Raḥmān al-Suyūṭī, *al-Ashbāh wa al-Naẓā'ir fī Qawāʿid wa Furūʿ Fiqh al-Shāfiʿiyyah*, ed. Khālid ʿAbd al-Fattāḥ Shibl Marʿashlī (Beirut: Dār al-Fikr, n.d.), pp.175–176; Zayn al-ʿĀbibīn ibn Ibrāhīm ibn Nujaym, *al-Ashbāh wa al-Naẓā'ir* (Beirut: Dār al-Kutub al-ʿIlmiyyah, 1400/1980), p.175; ʿAlī Ḥaydar, *Sharḥ Majallat al-Aḥkām al-ʿAdliyyah*, trans. Fahmī al-Ḥusaynī (Beirut: Dār al-ʿIlm li'l-Malāyīn, n.d.), vol. 1, pp.78–79; Aḥmad al-Zarqā, *Sharḥ al-Qawāʿid al-Fiqhiyyah*, ed. ʿAbd al-Sattār Abū Ghuddah (Beirut: Dār al-Gharb al-Islāmī, 1403/1983), p.361; *The Mejelle*, trans. C. R. Tyser et al. (Kuala Lumpur: The Other Press, n.d.), p.14.

23. Shāṭibī, *Muwāfaqāt*, vol. 2/3, pp.21–22.
24. Mālik ibn Anas, *Muwaṭṭa'*, 'Hajj', hadith 722, p.224.
25. See Bukhārī, *Ṣaḥīḥ*, 'Janā'iz', hadiths 1265, 1268, pp.202–203.

5: INSUFFICIENCY OF THE LITERAL METHODOLOGY

1. On the meaning of *naṣṣ* see, Mohamed M. Yunis Ali, *Medieval Islamic Pragmatics: Sunni Legal Theorists' Models of Textual Communication* (Richmond, Surrey, UK: Curzon Press, 2000), pp.128–132 and *passim*; Sukrija Husejn Ramiz, *Language and the Interpretation of Islamic Law* (Cambridge, UK: The Islamic Texts Society, 2003), pp.73–75.
2. Al-Qāḍī ʿIyāḍ, *Madārik*, vol. 1, p.96; Qarāfī, *Sharḥ Tanqīḥ al-Fuṣūl* (Beirut: Dār al-Fikr, 1424/2004), p.354.
3. Cf. Qarāfī, Ibid. and *Dhakhīrah*, vol. 1, p.149.
4. Shāṭibī, *Iʿtiṣām*, vol. 1, p.153.
5. Bukhārī, *Ṣaḥīḥ*, 'Kafālah', hadith 2294, p.366; also 'Adab', hadith 6083, p.1061 and '*Iʿtiṣām*', hadith 7340, p.1262.
6. Narrated by Aḥmad, Tabarānī, Ibn Ḥibbān and Abū Dāwūd. – Author. See

Muslim, *Ṣaḥīḥ*, 'Faḍā'il al-Ṣaḥabāh', hadith 2530 (by Jubayr ibn Muṭʿim), p.982; Aḥmad ibn Ḥanbal, *Musnad*, vol. 2, pp.180, 205, 207, 213 & 215; vol. 3, p.162 and vol. 5, p.61; Sulaymān ibn Aḥmad al-Ṭabarānī, *al-Muʿjam al-Kabīr*, ed. Ḥamdī ʿAbd al-Majīd al-Salafī (Baghdad: Ministry of Awqāf, n.d.), vol. 2, p.143 (no. 1580), p.149 (no. 1597) and vol. 11, p.281 (no. 11740); Muḥammad ibn Ḥibbān, *Ṣaḥīḥ Ibn Ḥibbān*, ed. Shuʿayb al-Arnā'ūṭ (Beirut: Mu'assassat al-Risālah, 1993), vol. 7, pp.26 and 453 (Ibn ʿAbbās).

6: THE PROPHET'S INTENT OF LEGISLATION

1. In fact, long before al-Qarāfī, Ibn Qutaybah (213/828–276/889) had concerned himself with this issue. He clearly stated that the Prophet's statements and actions comprised three types: (1) What had been revealed to him by the Angel Gabriel; (2) what God allowed him to institute based on his personal judgement, depending on the cases presented to him; (3) what he would issue as a matter of discipline for his followers so that if they follow it they become more virtuous, otherwise there is no harm on them. Abū Muḥammad ʿAbd Allāh ibn Muslim ibn Qutaybah, *Ta'wīl Mukhtalif al-Ḥadīth*, ed. Muhammad Abd al-Rahim (Beirut: Dār al-Fikr, 1415/1995), pp.180–183.
   After Qarāfī, this issue was taken up by the eminent Ḥanbalī scholar Ibn Qayyim al-Jawziyyah, especially in his book *Zād al-Maʿād fī Hadyi Khayr al-ʿIbād*, ed. Shuayb al-Arna'ut et al. (Beirut: Mu'assassat al-Risālah, 1405/1985), vol. 3, pp.489–490. The Indian scholar Shāh Walī Allāh al-Dahlawī also dealt with this issue on similar lines in his seminal work *Ḥujjat Allah al-Balīghah*. [Shāh Walī Allāh of Delhi, *The Conclusive Argument from God*, trans. Marcia K. Hermansen (Leiden: E.J. Brill, 1996), vol. 1, pp.373–375.]
   Nowadays, following Ibn Ashur who dealt with it in detail in the present chapter, this issue is still a matter of serious debate among contemporary Muslim scholars. The crux of the whole debate centers on determining in the Prophetic Traditions what is of permanent legislative value and what is contextual and does not therefore carry any legislative connotation. See, for example, Yusuf al-Qaradawi, *Kayfa Nataʿāmalu maʿa al-Sunnah: Maʿālim wa Ḍawābiṭ* (Herndon, VA: International Institute of Islamic Thought [IIIT], 1411/1990) and Muhammad Mahdi Shams al-Din, *al-Ijtihād wa al-Tajdīd fī al-Fiqh al-Islāmī* (Beirut: al-Mu'assassah al-Dawliyyah, 1419/1999), pp.86–87 and *al-Ijtihad wa al-Taqlīd: Baḥth Fiqhī Istidlālī Muqārin* (Beirut: al-Mu'assassah al-Dawliyyah, 1419/1998), pp.168–175.
   A summary of the historical debate on this issue has been provided by Yusuf al-Qaradawi, in 'al-Jānib al-Ḥaḍārī fī al-Sunnah al-Nabawiyyah,' *(al-Sunnah al-Nabawiyyah wa Manhajuhā fī Binā' al-Maʿrifah wa al-Ḥaḍārah*, proceed-

ings of a conference jointly organized by IIIT and al-Majmaʿ al-Malakī li-Buḥūth al-Ḥaḍārah al-Islāmiyyah, Amman: 15–19 Dhū al-Qiʿdah 1409 /19–23 June 1989), vol. 2, pp.976–1029.

2. Bukhārī, *Ṣaḥīḥ*, 'al-Ḥarth wa al-Muzāraʿah', hadith 2335, p.375. Bukhārī mentioned, ʿUrwah said: "ʿUmar gave the same verdict in his Caliphate." See also, *Muwaṭṭa'*, 'Aqḍiyyah', hadith, 1422, p.528. Mālik said, "That is what is done in our community."

3. See a detailed discussion of the jurists' different views on this issue in al-Māwardī, *The Ordinances of Government*, pp.194–197.

4. Bukhārī, *Ṣaḥīḥ*, 'Nafaqāt', hadith 5364, 958; Muslim, *Ṣaḥīḥ*, 'Aqḍiyah', hadith 1714, p.680.

5. Narrated by Mālik in his *Muwaṭṭa'* and the authenticated traditionalists. – Author. This tradition was reported by Abū Qatādah al-Anṣārī al-Salamī, the knight of God's Messenger. The Prophet stated this after the battle of Ḥunayn. See also, Bukhārī, *Ṣaḥīḥ*, 'Maghāzī', hadith 4321, pp.730–731; Mālik ibn Anas, *Muwaṭṭa'*, 'Jihad', hadith 981, pp.301–302, with the wording: "Whoever kills a person and has proof that he has done so, his spoils are his"; Muslim, *Ṣaḥīḥ*, 'Jihad', hadith 1751, pp.694–695.

6. Qarāfī, *Furūq*, vol. 1, pp.349–350.

7. Bukhārī, *Ṣaḥīḥ*, 'Ṭalāq', hadith 5283, p.944.

8. See the long reports of the Prophet's sermon during his last pilgrimage in Muslim, *Ṣaḥīḥ*, 'Hajj', hadith 1218, pp.454–457; ʿAbd al-Malik ibn Hishām, *al-Sīrah al-Nabawiyyah*, ed. Mustapha al-Saqqā et al. (Damascus/Beirut: Dār al-Khayr, 1417/1996), vol. 2/4, pp.188–192

9. Muslim, *Ṣaḥīḥ*, 'Hajj', hadith 1297, p.483; Adū Dāwūd, *Sunan*, 'Manāsik', hadith 310, vol. 1, pp.495–496.

10. Bukhārī, *Ṣaḥīḥ*, 'ʿIlm', hadith 104–105, pp.23–24; Hajj', hadith 1739, p.280; 'Maghāzī', hadith 4295, p.727; Muslim, *Ṣaḥīḥ*, 'Hajj', hadith 1354, p.506.

11. Mālik ibn Anas, *Muwaṭṭa'*, 'Hajj', hadith 951, pp.290–291. Cf. Bukhārī, *Ṣaḥīḥ*, 'Hajj', hadiths 1734–1737, pp.280–281; Muslim, *Ṣaḥīḥ*, 'Hajj', hadith 1306 (327–333)–1307, pp.486–487.

12. Bukhārī, *Ṣaḥīḥ*, 'Musāqāh', hadith 2361, p.379. Bukhārī narrated different versions of this report in many places. See also, Muslim, *Ṣaḥīḥ*, 'Faḍā'il', hadith 2357, p.920.

13. Muslim, *Ṣaḥīḥ*, 'Īmān', hadiths 223–224, p.69. This tradition as reported by Wā'il reads as follows: "A man from Ḥadramawt and a man from Kindah came to the Prophet *(ṢAAS)*. The man from Ḥadramawt said to the Prophet *(ṢAAS)*: 'O Messenger, this person has taken over some land of mine which had belonged to my father.' The man from Kindah replied: 'It is my land, I have it in my possession, I cultivate it and he has no right over it [...]'."

14. Bukhārī, *Ṣaḥīḥ*, 'Ṣulḥ', hadith 2695/2696, p.440; Mālik ibn Anas, *Muwaṭṭa'*, 'Ḥudūd', hadith 1497, p.591.
15. This great jurist and traditionalist of Cordoba was born in 404 and died in 497 AH. His book *Aqḍiyat Rasūl Allāh (ṢAAS)* (The Judicial Verdicts of God's Messenger peace and blessings of God be upon him) was published in different editions in Ḥalab (Aleppo), Beirut, and al-Qasīm. His other books include *Nawāzil al-Aḥkām al-Nabawiyyah*. He taught many able students such as the great Mālikī jurist and judge (grandfather of the jurist-philosopher Ibn Rushd or in Latin Averroes) Abū al-Walīd ibn Rushd, author of *al-Bayān wa al-Taḥṣīl* – a major reference of Mālikī juristic doctrines.
16. See the different versions of this report in Bukhārī, *Ṣaḥīḥ*, 'Ṭalāq', hadiths 5273–5277, p.943; Mālik ibn Anas, *Muwaṭṭa'*, 'Ṭalāq', hadith 1190, pp.384–385.
17. See several reports on this question in Bukhārī, *Ṣaḥīḥ*, 'Īmān', hadith 53, pp.12–13 and hadith 87, pp.20–21; 'Ashribah' hadiths 5594–5596, p.993; Muslim, *Ṣaḥīḥ*, 'Īmān', hadith 17, pp.31–32; 'Ashribah', hadith 2000, p.796.
18. See, in this respect, a detailed discussion of the juristic views of the major classical schools in Ibn Rushd, *The Distinguished Jurist's Primer* (Bidāyat al-Mujtahid wa Nihāyat al-Muqtaṣid), trans. Imran Ahsan Khan Nyazee (Reading Berks, UK: Garnet Publishing, 2003), vol. 2, pp.307–316. See also, Ibn Naqib al-Misri, *Reliance of the Traveller*, trans. Nuh Ha Mim Keller, (Belttsville, MD: Amana Publications, 1994), pp.432–434.
19. See reports on the prohibition of eating donkey meat in Bukhārī, *Ṣaḥīḥ*, 'Maghāzī', hadith 4216, p.716; 'Nikāḥ', 5115, p.915, 'al-Dhabā'iḥ wa al-Ṣayd', hadiths 5520–5529, pp.983–984; 'Ḥiyal', hadith 6961, p.1200; Muslim, *Ṣaḥīḥ*, 'al-Ṣayd wa al-Dhabā'iḥ', hadiths 1407–1940, pp.771–773. For an exposition of the different views on the underlying reasons of the prohibition see Aḥmad ibn ʿAlī ibn Ḥajar al-ʿAsqalānī, *Fatḥ al-Bārī bi-Sharḥ Ṣaḥīḥ al-Bukhārī* (Riyadh/Amman: International Ideas Home), vol. 3, pp.2459–2461.
20. See a summary of the scholars' different interpretations of this tradition in Ibn Ḥajar al-ʿAsqalānī, *Fatḥ al-Bārī*, vol. 2, pp.1486–1487.
21. For further juristic details on this issue, see al-Māwardī, *The Ordinances of Government*, pp.154–157; Ibn Rushd, *The Jurist's Primer*, vol. 1, pp.474–476.
22. I mean by legislation (*tashrīʿ*) what a Prophetic statement or action may apparently suggest as prescription (*wujūb*) or proscription (*taḥrīm*), its real intent is something else. Otherwise, guidance and instruction do also connote a certain measure of enacted legality (*mashrūʿiyyah*), as we have already mentioned towards the end of the Preface. – Author.

23. Bukhārī, *Ṣaḥīḥ*, 'Īmān', hadith 30, p.8; also "ʿItq', hadith 2545, p.411; Muslim, *Ṣaḥīḥ*, 'Aymān', hadith 1661, p.652.
24. Al-Ḥarrah, a vast land surrounding Madinah. – Author.
25. See the details of this incident in Bukhārī, *Ṣaḥīḥ*, 'Ṣulḥ', hadith 2708, p.442; Muslim, *Ṣaḥīḥ*, 'Faḍā'il', hadith 2357, p.920.
26. Bukhārī, *Ṣaḥīḥ*, 'Ṣulḥ', hadith 2706, p.442; Bukhārī, *Ṣaḥīḥ*, 'Hibah', hadiths 2621–2623, p.424; Muslim, *Ṣaḥīḥ*, 'Musāqāh', hadith 1558, p.606.
27. Mālik ibn Anas, *Muwaṭṭa'*, 'Zakah', hadith 625, p.190; Muslim, *Ṣaḥīḥ*, 'Hibāt', hadith 1622, p.631
28. Mālik ibn Anas, *Muwaṭṭa'*, 'Zakah', hadith 626, pp.190–191: "Mālik was asked about whether a man who gave some *ṣadaqah*, and then found it being offered back to him for sale by someone other than the man to whom he had given it, could buy it or not, and he said: 'I would prefer him to leave it'."
29. Mālik ibn Anas, *al-Mudawwanah al-Kubrā* (Birut: Dār al-Fikr, n.d.), vol. 4, p.349. Mālik said: "One should not buy one's *ṣadaqah* either from the person to whom one has given it or from anyone else."
30. Muḥammad ibn Ibrāhīm ibn Ziyād Ibn al-Mawwāz was born in Alexandria in 180 and died in 269 AH. Throughout the 4th century, his famous compendium known as *Kitāb Ibn al-Mawwāz* or *al-Mawwāziyyah* was the most important work containing the most delicate propositions and issues of Maliki juristic doctrines. For more detail, see Miklosh Muranyi, *Dirāsāt fī al-Fiqh al-Mālikī*, trans. Said Buhayri et al. (Beirut: Dār al-Gharb al-Islāmī, 1409/1988), pp.149–153.
31. See Ibn al-Mawwāz's view in Sulaymān ibn Khalaf al-Bājī, *al-Muntaqā: Sharḥ Muwaṭṭa'* (Cairo: Maṭbaʿat al-Saʿādah, 1331 AH [offset edn. Dār al-Kitāb al-ʿArabī, Beirut]), vol. 2, p.181.
32. Mālik ibn Anas, *Muwaṭṭa'*, 'al-ʿItāqah wa al-Walā'', hadith 1473, p.555; Bukhārī, *Ṣaḥīḥ*, 'Ṣalāh', hadiths 456, p.79; 'Buyūʿ', 2155 and 2168, pp.345 and 346–347; 'Mukātib', hadith 2560, p.413, etc.; Muslim, *Ṣaḥīḥ*, "ʿItq', hadiths 1504–1505, pp.580–582.
33. The complete story of Barīrah is reported in Bukhārī, *Ṣaḥīḥ*, 'Shurūṭ', 2729, pp.446–447, as follows: "ʿĀ'ishah said, 'Barīrah came to me and said, "My people (masters) have written the contract for my emancipation for nine *Awaq* of gold to be paid in yearly instalments, one *awqiyyah* per year; so help me".' ʿĀ'ishah said (to her), 'If your masters agree, I will pay them the whole sum provided the *walā'* will be for me.' Barīrah went to her masters and told them about it, but they refused the offer and she returned from them while God's Apostle was sitting. She said, 'I presented the offer to them, but they refused unless the *walā'* would be for them.' When the Prophet heard that and ʿĀ'ishah told him about it, he said to her, 'Buy Barīrah and let them stipulate

that her *walā'* will be for them, as the *walā'* is for the manumitted.' ʿĀ'ishah did so. After that God's Apostle got up amidst the people, glorified and praised Allah and said, 'What is wrong with some people who stipulate things which are not in Gods Laws? Any condition that is not in God's Laws is invalid even if there were a hundred such conditions. God's Rules are the most valid and God's Conditions are the most solid. The *walā'* is for the manumitted'." It is also mentioned in "ʿItq' (hadith 2536, 2/3: 169) that ʿĀ'ishah said: "bought Barīrah but her masters put the condition that her *walā'* would be for them. I told the Prophet about it. He said (to me), 'Manumit her as her *walā'* will be for the one who pays the price'. So, I manumitted her. The Prophet called Barīrah and gave her the option of either staying with her husband or leaving him. She said, 'Even if he gave me so much money, I would not stay with him', and so she preferred her freedom to her husband."

See also many versions of this report with slight differences in wording in *Muwaṭṭa'*, 'al-ʿItaqa wa al-walā'', pp.555–556.

34. See the arguments and counter-arguments concerning the interpretation of the phrase "take her and stipulate *walā'* for yourself" in ʿAbd al-Bāqī ibn Yūsuf al-Zarqānī, *Sharḥ Muwaṭṭa' Mālik* (Cairo: Maṭbaʿat al-Istiqāmah, 1373/1954), vol. 4, pp.91–93; Muḥammad Zakariyā al-Anṣārī al-Kāndahlawī, *Awjaz al-Masālik Ilā Muwaṭṭa' al-Imām Mālik* (Beirut: Dār al-Fikr, 1400/1980), vol. 10, p.38.

35. Bukhārī, *Ṣaḥīḥ*, 'Buyūʿ', hadith 2193, p.350. See also many reports about the same issue in Muslim, *Ṣaḥīḥ*, 'Buyūʿ', hadiths 1534–1538, pp.591–593; Abū Dāwūd, *Sunan*, ed. Muḥammad Muḥyī al-Dīn ʿAbd al-Ḥamīd (Beirut: Dār al-Fikr, n.d.), 'Buyūʿ', hadith 3372, vol.32, p.253. According to Ibn Ḥajar al-ʿAsqalānī, jurists held three different views of understanding of this report. Ibn Abī Laylā and al-Thawrī held that it meant absolute prohibition and consensus on that. Yazīd ibn Abī Ḥabīb held the opposite view that the hadith meant absolute permission. Between these extremes, there are varying qualified juristic positions. Ibn Ḥajar, *Fatḥ al-Bārī*, vol. 1, p.1172; Ibn Rushd, *The Jurist's Primer*, vol. 2, pp.169–170.

36. The expression "Then do not do that" means "Do not give a present to one of your children to the exclusion of the others." See the reports of this Tradition in Bukhārī, *Ṣaḥīḥ*, 'Shahādāt', hadith 2650, p.429, 'Hibah', hadith 2586, p.418; Mālik ibn Anas, *Muwaṭṭa'*, 'Aqḍiyah', hadith 1433, p.533; Muslim, *Ṣaḥīḥ*, 'Hibāt', hadith 1623 (9–12), pp.631–632.

37. Mālik ibn Anas, *Muwaṭṭa'*, 'Aqḍiyah', p.535.

38. Bukhārī, *Ṣaḥīḥ*, 'Shahādāt', hadith 2650, p.429; Muslim, *Ṣaḥīḥ*, 'Hibāt', hadith 1623 (14–19), pp.632–633.

39. Yusuf ibn Abd Allah ibn Abd al-Barr, *al-Tamhīd limā fī Muwaṭṭa' mina al-*

Ma^cānī wa al-Asānīd (Rabat: Ministry of Awqāf, 1441), vol. 7, pp.223–243; Abd al-Baqi ibn Yusuf al-Zarqani, *Sharḥ Muwaṭṭa' Mālik* (Cairo: Maṭba^cat al-Istiqāmah, 1373/1954), vol. 3, p.320.

40. Muslim, *Ṣaḥīḥ*, 'Ṭalāq', hadith 1480, p.567.

41. The full version of this tradition reads as follows: "My companions are like stars, whomever you follow, you will be rightly guided". Although it has been narrated through more than one chain, its authenticity is dubious. Concerning it, al-Bayhaqī said: "[Though] its text is widespread (*mashhūr*), its chains of transmission are weak." See, al-Mullā ^cAlī al-Qārī, *Sharḥ al-Shifā'*, ed. Ḥasanayn Muḥammad Makhlūf, (Cairo: Maktabat Ibn Taymia, n.d.), vol. 3, pp.689–690. The late great traditionalist al-Albānī even confirmed its fabrication: Muḥammad Nāṣir al-Dīn al-Albānī, *Silsilat al-Aḥādīth al-Ḍa^cīfah wa al-Mawḍū^cah* (Beirut: al-Maktab al-Islāmī, 1398), vol. 1, pp.78–85, hadiths 58–62.

    However, there are authentic reports that carry a close meaning to this one, like the following narrated by the Companion Abū Burdah [Muslim, *Ṣaḥīḥ*, 'Faḍā'il al-Ṣaḥābah', hadith 2531(207), p.982]: "Abū Burdah reported on the authority of his father: We offered the sunset prayer along with God's Apostle (may peace be upon him). We then said: If we sit (along with God's Messenger) and observe night prayer with him it would be very good, so we sat down and he came to us and said: 'You are still sitting here.' I said: 'God's Messenger, we observed evening prayer with you, then we said: Let us sit down and observe night prayer along with you,' whereupon he said: 'You have done well' or 'you have done right.' He then lifted his head towards the sky, and it often happened that as he lifted his head towards the sky, he said: 'The stars are a source of security for the sky and when the stars disappear there comes to the sky (i.e. it meets the same fate) as it has been promised (it would plunge into darkness). And I am a source of safety and security to my Companions and when I go away, there will fall to the lot (of my Companions) as they have been promised, and my Companions are a source of security for the Ummah, and as they go, there will fall to the lot of my Ummah as (its people) have been promised'."

42. *Mudda* is an old unit of dry or liquid measure equal to eight gallons (36.4 litres).

43. Bukhārī, *Ṣaḥīḥ*, 'Faḍā'il Aṣḥāb al-Nabīy *(ṢAAS)*', hadith 3673, p.617.

44. This is part of a long tradition narrated by Bukhārī, *Ṣaḥīḥ*, 'Manāqib al-Anṣār', hadith 3936, pp.664–665; Muslim, *Ṣaḥīḥ*, 'Faḍā'il al-Ṣaḥābah', hadith 2540 (221–222), pp.985–986.

45. Bukhārī, *Ṣaḥīḥ*, 'Janā'iz', 1239, p.198 and 'Libās', hadith 5849, p.1031.

46. Abū Dāwūd, *Sunan*, 'Libās', hadiths 4044–4046, vol.4, p.47; the word "prostrating" is not mentioned in the version narrated by Abū Dāwūd. See also,

Muslim, *Ṣaḥīḥ*, 'al-Libās wa al-Zīnah', hadith 2078, p.828.

47. Bukhārī, *Ṣaḥīḥ*, 'Shufʿah', hadith 2258, p.359.
48. Bukhārī, *Ṣaḥīḥ*, 'Shufʿah', hadith 2257, p.359.
49. Mālik ibn Anas, *Muwaṭṭa'*, 'Aqḍiyah', hadith 1427, p.529. See also, Bukhārī, *Ṣaḥīḥ*, 'Maẓālim', 2463, p.397; Muslim, *Ṣaḥīḥ*, 'Musāqāh', hadith 1609, p.625 (with different wording).
50. See a detailed discussion of the different on this issue in Sulayman ibn Khalaf al-Baji, *al-Muntaqā Sharḥ Muwaṭṭa'* (Beirut: Dār al-Kitāb al-ʿArabī, n.d., an offset of the Cairo ed. by Maṭbaʿat al-Saʿādah, 1331 AH), vol. 6, p.43.
51. It has been already documented.
52. See this report in slightly different wording in Muslim, *Ṣaḥīḥ*, 'Zakah', hadith No. 991, p.357.
53. See chapter 35 in Part III.
54. Mālik ibn Anas, *Muwaṭṭa'*, 'Salah', hadith 287, pp.93–94; Bukhārī, *Ṣaḥīḥ*, 'Adhān', hadith 644, p.106; Muslim, *Ṣaḥīḥ*, 'al-Masājid wa Mawāḍiʿ al-Ṣalāh', hadith 651, p.236–237.
55. Bukhārī, *Ṣaḥīḥ*, 'Adab', hadith 6016, p.1052. It is also reported with a slightly different wording by Muslim, *Ṣaḥīḥ*, 'Īmān', hadith 46, p.41.
56. Known by the three names mentioned by the author, al-Muḥaṣṣab is situated between Makkah and Minā.
57. The author has combined the words of both ʿĀ'ishah and ʿAbd Allāh ibn ʿAbbās that are in Bukhārī, *Ṣaḥīḥ*, 'Hajj', hadiths 1765 (ʿĀ'ishah) and 1766 (Ibn ʿAbbās), p.284. ʿĀ'ishah said: "It [al-Abṭaḥ] was simply a place where the Prophet *(ṢAAS)* used to camp so that it might be easier for him to leave for Madinah." Ibn ʿAbbās said: "Staying at al-Muḥaṣṣab [another name for al-Abṭaḥ] is not one of the ceremonies [of Hajj], but al-Muḥaṣṣab is a place where God's Apostle camped (during his *Ḥajjat al-Wadāʿ*)." The apparent purport of Mālik's statement in *Muwaṭṭa'* (p.279) is the opposite of what the author has mentioned. Mālik said: "No one should go beyond al-Muʿarras when coming back until one has prayed there; and if one happens to go past it outside the time of prayers, let one none the less stop and pray, one's prayer would be valid. One should pray as much as one wishes, this is because I heard that God's Messenger, blessings and peace be upon him, stopped there, and that ʿAbd Allāh ibn ʿUmar also stopped his camel there."
58. This is a reference to the report by ʿĀ'ishah in Bukhārī, *Ṣaḥīḥ*, 'Adhān', hadith 626, p.103 and 'Tahajjud', hadith 1160, p.185; Muslim, *Ṣaḥīḥ*, 'Ṣalāt al-Musāfirīn', hadith 736 (121–122), p.267.
59. Ibn Hishām, *al-Sīrah al-Nabawiyyah* (Cairo: Muṣṭafa al-Bābī al-Ḥalabī, 1955), vol. 2, p.303; Muḥammad ibn ʿAbd Allāh al-Ḥākim al-Naysābūrī, *al-Mustadrak* (Beirut: Dār al-Maʿrifah, 1407/1987), vol. 3, pp.426–427;

Aḥmad ibn ʿAlī Ibn Ḥajar, *al-Iṣābah fi Tamyīz al-Ṣaḥābah* (Cairo: Mawlāy ʿAbd al-Ḥafīdh, 1328 AH), vol. 1, p.427.

60. *Al-ʿUtbiyyah*, also known as *al-Mustakhrajah min al-Samāʿāt*, is a fiqh compendium compiled by Muḥammad ibn Aḥmad ibn ʿAbd al-'Azīz al-Umawī al-ʿUtbī (d. 255 AH). Al-ʿUtbī gathered in this book all what the students of Mālik and also what the students of Ibn al-Qāsim heard from him. For further details about this book, its sources, narrators, and extant manuscripts, see Muranyi, *Dirāsāt fī Maṣādir al-Fiqh al-Mālikī*, pp.110–139. The text of this book is included in Abū al-Walīd ibn Rushd (d. 520 AH), *al-Bayān wa al-Taḥṣīl* (which is a valuable commentary on it) (Beirut: Dār al-Gharb al-Islāmī,), 22 vols.

61. Ibn Rushd, *al-Bayān wa al-Taḥṣīl*, vol. 7, p.236. Muslim [*Ṣaḥīḥ*, 'Faḍā'il', hadiths 2361–2363, pp.922–923] has reported three versions of this Prophetic Tradition under the subtitle (*Bāb*): "It is obligatory to follow the Prophet (may peace be upon him) in all matters pertaining to religion, but one is free to act on one's own opinion in matters which pertain to technical skill." No. 2362 where narrated from Rāfiʿ ibn Khadīj, reads as follows:
"Rāfiʿ ibn Khadīj reported that God's Messenger (may peace be upon him) came to Madinah, where the people had been grafting the trees. He said: 'What are you doing?' They said: 'We are grafting them,' whereupon he said: 'It may perhaps be good for you if you do not do that,' so they abandoned this practice (and the datepalms) began to yield less fruit. They mentioned it (to the Prophet), whereupon he said: 'I am a human being, so when I command you about a thing pertaining to religion, do accept it, and when I command you about something based on my personal opinion, keep it in mind that I am a human being'."

62. The complete version of this Tradition reads as follows: "God has appointed for everyone who has a right what is due to him, and no bequest must be made to an heir." Narrated by a number of Companions, this Tradition has been reported by Abū Dāwūd, *Sunan*, 'Waṣāyā', hadith 2670, vol. 3, pp.290–292; Tirmidhī, *Sunan*, 'Waṣāyā', hadith 2120, vol. 4, p.433; Abū ʿAbd Allāh Muḥammad ibn Yazīd ibn Mājah, *Sunan*, ed. M. M. al-Azami (Riyadh: Sharikat al-Ṭibāʿah al-ʿArabiyyah, 1404/1984), 'Waṣāyā', 2746, vol. 2, p.117; Aḥmad ibn Ḥanbal, *Musnad*, vol. 4, pp.186–187, 238–239 and vol. 5, p.267.
In all its versions, this Tradition is very clear about the illegality of a bequest to an heir. However, one might invoke the following Qur'anic verse in support of its lawfulness "It is ordained for you, when death approaches any of you and he is leaving behind much wealth, to make bequests in favour of his parents and [other] near of kin in accordance with what is fair." (2:180) To this,

Mālik would reply that this verse was abrogated. "What came down about the division of the fixed shares of inheritance in the Book of God, the Mighty, the Exalted, abrogated it", thus referring to verses 11–13 of *Surah al-Nisā'* (4). He then added: "The established Sunnah with us [the Madinah scholars], in which there is no dispute, is that it is not permitted for a testator to make a bequest (in addition to the fixed share) in favour of an heir, unless the other heirs permit him. If some of them permit him and others refuse, he is allowed to diminish the share of those who have given their permission. Those who refuse take their full share of the inheritance." *Muwaṭṭa'*, 'Aqḍiyah', p.543.

63. Bukhārī, *Ṣaḥīḥ*, 'Jihad', hadith 3053, pp.504–505; 'Jizyah', hadith 3168, p.528; 'Maghāzī', hadith 4431, p.754; Muslim, *Ṣaḥīḥ*, 'Waṣiyyah', hadith 1637, p.640; '*Iʿtiṣām*', hadith 7366, pp. 1266-1267,
64. See the full version of this tradition in *Muwaṭṭa'*, 'Aqḍiyah', hadith 1452, p.541; Bukhārī, *Ṣaḥīḥ*, 'Waṣāyā', hadith 2742, p.452; Ibn Mājah, *Sunan*, 'Waṣāyā', hadith 2740, vol. 2, p.116.
65. See details of the different views on this issue in ʿAbd al-Razzāq al-Ṣanʿānī, *al-Muṣannaf*, ed. Ḥabīb al-Raḥmān al-Aʿẓamī (Deoband: al-Majlis al-Islāmī bi al-Hind, 1403 AH), vol. 9, pp.68–69; Abū Muḥammad ʿAlī Ibn Ḥazm, *al-Muḥallā bi al-Āthār*, ed. Abd al-Ghaffar Sulayman al-Bandarani (Beirut: Dār al-Kutub al-ʿIlmiyyah, 1408/1988), vol. 8, pp.356–362

7: CERTAIN AND PROBABLE *MAQĀṢID AL-SHARĪʿAH*

1. See many versions of this tradition in Ibn Mājah, *Sunan*, 'Man Ballagha ʿIlman', hadiths 234–235, vol. 1, pp.499–50; Bukhārī, *Ṣaḥīḥ*, 'ʿIlm', hadith 1741, pp.281; 'Aḍāḥī', hadith 5550, p.987; and 'Fitan', hadiths 7078 and 7447, pp.1219–1220 and 1283 respectively.
2. al-Juwaynī, *Burhān*, vol. 1, p.78.
3. The author is paraphrasing the text of al-Juwaynī; see the latter's exact words in *Burhān*, vol. 1, p.78.
4. Unfortunately, the only available manuscript from which Talbi has edited al-Māzarī's commentary, *Burhān al-Uṣūl min Īḍāḥ al-Maḥṣūl*, is missing more than 12 folios, for instance, the Introduction which would contain Ibn Ashur's quotation.
5. al-Juwaynī, *Burhān*, vol. 1, p.79.
6. Qarāfī, *Nafā'is al-Uṣūl*, vol. 3, pp.1247–1248.
7. al-Shāṭibī, *Muwāfaqāt*, vol. 1/1, pp.29–30.
8. Abū Muḥammad ʿIzz al-Dīn Ibn ʿAbd al-Salām al-Sulamī, *al-Qawāʿid al-Kubrā* (also known as *Qawāʿid al-Aḥkām fī Iṣlāḥ al-Anām*), ed. Nazih

Hammad et al. (Damascus: Dār al-Qalam, 1421/2000), vol. 2, pp.314–315.

9. Literally, "deceived" or "defrauded yourselves [in this respect]": "an allusion to the idea prevalent among the early Muslims, before the revelation of this verse, that during the period of fasting all sexual intercourse should be avoided, even at night-time, when eating and drinking are allowed (Rāzī). The above verse removed this misconception". Muhammad Asad, *The Message of the Qur'an* (Gibraltar: Dar al-Andalus, 1984), p.39, note 159.
10. Literally, "and seek that which God has ordained for you": an obvious stress on the God-willed nature of sexual life. Ibid. p.40.
11. Aḥmad ibn Ḥanbal, *Musnad*, vol. 1, p.236 and vol. 5, p.266; Bukhārī, *al-Adab al-Mufrad*, ed. Kamal Y. al-Hut (Beirut: ʿĀlam al-Kutub, 1405/1985), hadith 287, p.109; Ṭabarānī, *al-Muʿjam al-Kabīr*, hadith 7868, vol. 8, p.216.
12. Bukhārī, *Ṣaḥīḥ*, 'Tahajjud', hadith 1151, p.184; Muslim, *Ṣaḥīḥ*, 'Ṣalāt al-Musāfirīn', hadith 782, p.283; al-Ḥasan ibn Masʿūd al-Baghawī, *Sharḥ al-Sunnah* (Beirut: Dār al-Maʿrifah, 1987), vol. 4, p.40.
13. Nasā'ī, *Sunan*, 'Īmān', hadith 5034, vol. 8, p.121; Bukhārī, *Ṣaḥīḥ*, 'Īmān, 1/1', p.128; Aḥmad ibn Ḥanbal, *Musnad*, vol. 5, p.69.
14. Bukhārī, *Ṣaḥīḥ*, 'Maghāzī', hadiths 4341/4342 and 4344/4345, pp.735–756.
15. Bukhārī, *Ṣaḥīḥ*, 'Wuḍū'', hadith 220, p.41; Abū Dāwūd, *Sunan*, 'Ṭahārah', hadith 380, vol. 1, p.264.
16. al-Shāṭibī, *Muwāfaqāt*, vol. 3/3, pp.14–15.
17. It is established in *ʿilm al-ḥikmah* (epistemology) that the discipline farthest from doubt and the closest to certainty is that in which rules and formulas do not contradict one another, such as calculus (*ḥisāb*). Then comes mathematics by virtue of the small likelihood of inconsistency in its propositions. Then follows physics (*ʿilm al-ṭabīʿah*), because even when the researcher succeeds in establishing a scientific proposition consisting of a particular natural law, the possibility of another natural law contradicting it cannot be excluded. Lastly, we have philosophy and psychology. – Author.

8: RATIONALISED & NON-RATIONALISED SHARIʿAH INJUNCTIONS

1. Ibn Mājah, *Sunan*, 'Ashribah', hadiths 3434–3436, vol. 2, p.257; Abū Dāwūd, *Sunan*, 'Ashribah', hadith 3681, 2/3: 327; Tirmidhī, *Sunan*, 'Ashribah', hadith 1865, vol. 2/4, p.292; ʿAlī ibn ʿUmar al-Dāraquṭnī, *Sunan*, ed. Abd Allah Hashim Yamani (Cairo: Dār al-Maḥāsin, 1386/1966), 'Ashribah', vol. 2/4, p. 250, 254 & 262.
2. *Taḥqīq al-manāt* is the process of confirming the existence of the basis or *ʿillah* (of the rule) in the particular cases falling under it. –Author,

3. Bukhārī, *Ṣaḥīḥ*, 'Ṣawm', p.314.
4. Mālik ibn Anas, *Muwaṭṭa'*, 'Farā'iḍ', hadith 1092, p.349.
5. The six types in question are gold, silver, wheat, barley, dates, and salt. They have been mentioned together in a tradition narrated by ʿUbādah ibn al-Ṣāmit in which the Prophet said:
"Gold is to be paid for with gold, raw and coined, silver with silver, raw and coined (in equal weight), wheat with wheat in equal measure, barley with barley in equal measure, dates with dates in equal measure, salt with salt in equal measure; if anyone gives more or asks more, he has dealt in usury. However, there is no harm in selling gold for silver and silver (for gold), in unequal weight, payment being made on the spot. Do not sell them if they are to be paid for later. There is no harm in selling wheat for barley and barley (for wheat) in unequal measure, payment being made on the spot. If the payment is to be made later, then do not sell them."
Abū Dāwūd, *Sunan*, ed. Muhammad Muhyi al-Din ʿAd al-Hamid (Beirut: al-Maktabah al-ʿAṣriyyah, 1416/1995), 'Buyūʿ', hadith, 3349, vol. 3, p.248; Ibn Mājah, *Sunan*, 'Tijārāt', hadiths 2272–2275, vol. 2, p.25. For a detailed discussion of the jurists' views on the underlying cause(s) of the prohibition of excess and delay in these species, see Ibn Rushd, *The Distinguished Jurist's Primer*, vol. 2, pp.158–163.
6. ʿAbd al-Razzāq ibn Hammām al-Ṣanʿānī, *Muṣannaf*, ed. Habib al-Rahman al-Azami (Beirut: al-Maktab al-Islāmī, 1403/1983), hadith 17182; Abū Bakr Ibn Abī Shaybah, *al-Muṣannaf*, ed. Ahmad al-Nadwi (Lucknow: al-Dār al-Salafiyyah, 1403/1983), hadith 344, vol. 9, p.140; Aḥmad ibn Ḥanbal, *Musnad*, vol. 4, p.275; Dāraquṭnī, vol. 3, p.106; Abū Aḥmad ʿAbd Allāh ibn ʿAdīy in *al-Kāmil fī Ḍuʿafā' al-Rijāl* (Beirut: Dār al-Fikr, 1405/1985), vol. 2, p.42 (and considered it as weak); Aḥmad ibn al-Ḥusayn al-Bayhaqī, *al-Sunan al-Kubrā* (Hyderabad-Deccan: Dā'irat al-Maʿārif al-ʿUthmāniyyah, 1335 H), vol. 8, p.42; and Jamāl al-Dīn Abū Muḥammad ʿAbd Allāh ibn Yūsuf al-Zaylaʿī, *Naṣb al-Rāyhah* (Cairo: Dār al-Ma'mūn, 1357 H), vol. 4, p.333.
7. See Abū Muḥammad ʿAlī ibn Aḥmad Ibn Ḥazm, *al-Iḥkām fi Uṣūl al-Aḥkām* (Beirut: Dār al-Kutub al-ʿIlmiyyah, 1405/1985), vol. 2, pp.195–232; see also ʿAbd al-Majīd Turkī, *Munāẓarāt fī Uṣūl al-Shariʿah* (Beirut: Dār al-Gharb al-Islāmī, 1994), pp.342–463.
8. Abū Bakr ibn al-ʿArabī, *ʿĀriḍat al-Aḥwadhī ʿAlā Sharḥ Ṣaḥīḥ al-Tirmidhī* (Cairo: Maṭbaʿat al-Ṣāwī, 1353/1934), vol. 10, p.112.
9. The doctrine of *ʿawl* in inheritance is a method of reduction, by which fractional shares not amounting to a whole are allocated. In other words, *ʿawl* is a method of adjustment that is "used in cases where the estate is not enough to give everyone their full shares, and proportionately distributes the deficit to all

the heirs in an equitable way." Al-Misri, *Reliance of the Traveller*, p.497. According to Ibn Rushd, "the majority of the Companions upheld ʿ*awl* as did the jurists of different regions, except Ibn ʿAbbās". Ibn Rushd, *The Distinguished Jurist's Primer*, vol. 2, p.422.

10. Aḥmad ibn al-Ḥusayn al-Bayhaqī, *al-Sunan al-Kubrā* (Hyderabad-Deccan: Dā'irat al-Maʿārif al-ʿUthmāniyyah, 1335 AH), vol. 6, p.253; Qarāfī, *Dhakhīrah*, vol. 10, p.206; Aḥmad ibn ʿAlī ibn Ḥajar, *al-Talkhīṣ al-Ḥabīr*, ed. Abd Allah Hashim al-Yamani (Beirut: Dār al-Maʿrifah, n.d.), vol. 3, p.90.
11. ʿ*Aṣabah*, agnate or universal heir, is "someone who takes the remaining estate, if any, after heirs deserving obligatory shares have taken them. When there are no such heirs, the universal heir takes all." Al-Misri, *Reliance of the Traveller*, p.499.
12. Ibn Rushd, *The Distinguished Jurist's Primer*, vol. 2, p.422; Muhammad Mustafa Shalabi, *Aḥkām al-Mawārīth Bayna al-Fiqh wa al-Qānūn* (Beirut: Dār al-Nahḍah al-ʿArabiyyah, 1978), pp.256–257.
13. Bukhārī, *Ṣaḥīḥ* 'Ḥarth wa muzāraʿah', hadiths 2330 & 2343, p.374 & 376; also the report of Ibn ʿAbbās in Ibn Mājah, *Sunan*, 'Aḥkām', hadith 2489, vol. 2, p.76.
14. According to Mālik, *muzābanah* consisted of selling fresh dates for dried dates, while *muḥāqalah* consisted of buying unharvested wheat in exchange for threshed wheat and renting land in exchange for wheat. He also explained *muzābanah* as buying something whose number, weight, and measure is not known with something whose number, weight, or measure is known. *Muwaṭṭa'*, 'Buyūʿ', hadith 1315, p.430.
15. Bukhārī, *Ṣaḥīḥ*, 'al-Ḥarth wa al-Muzāraʿah', hadith 2327, pp.373–374.
16. Bukhārī, *Ṣaḥīḥ*, 'al-Ḥarth wa al-Muzāraʿah', hadith 2346/2347, p.377.
17. Shāṭibī, *al-Muwāfaqāt*, vol. 1/2: pp.585–602.
18. Ibn Rushd, *The Distinguished Jurist's Primer*, vol. 2, pp.158–163.

PART II: ON THE GENERAL OBJECTIVES OF ISLAMIC LEGISLATION

9: THE DETERMINANT CHARACTERISTIC OF *MAQĀṢID AL-SHARĪʿAH*

1. We do not mean by the term "real" here its meaning in philosophy, namely that which has a real and external existence of its own, as opposed to what exists only nominally. What we rather mean are the mentally posited realities (*iʿtibāriyyāt*) that consist of ideas and meanings that exist in the mind, but whose existence is contingent upon the existence of one or two essences

(*ḥaqīqah*). This term also includes relational things (*umūr nisbiyyah*), such as time and space, and attributions (*umūr iḍāfiyyah*), such as fatherhood (*ubuwwah*) and sonhood (*bunuwwah*). – Author.

2. Al-Shamaydhar al-Ḥārithī was a courageous poet cavalier from the tribe of Banū al-Ḥārith ibn Kaʿb.
3. Aḥmad ibn Muḥammad al-Marzūqī, *Sharḥ Dīwān al-Ḥamāsah*, ed. ʿAbd al-Salām Hārūn (Cairo: Maṭbaʿat Lajnat al-Ta'līf wa al-Tarjamah wa al-Nashr, 1387/1967), vol. 1, p.125.
4. Sawwār ibn al-Muḍarrab al-Saʿdī was one of four famous poets from Oman who lived in the early Islamic period until the end of the first Ibāḍī (Khārijī) Imamate in 134 H. He launched his attacks against the Umayyad rule from Kūfah during its governorship by al-Ḥajjāj ibn Yūsuf al-Thaqafī who sought to kill him, but Sawwār was able to escape al-Ḥajjāj's forces. The other three poets were Māzin ibn Ghaḍūbah al-Ṭā'ī, Kaʿb ibn Maʿdān al-Ashqarī and Thābit ibn Kaʿb al-ʿAtkī.
5. Marzūqī, *Sharḥ Dīwān al-Ḥamāsah*, vol. 1, p.132.
6. The term *taʿzīr* refers to the category of crimes and penalties that are not textually specified in the scriptural sources of the Shariʿah, but are enacted by the legislature in the form of laws, acts, or regulations. "Discretion to legislate in this regard is left entirely to the authorities provided that legislation should conform with the requirements of society and its proper functioning, and should defend its interests, maintain social order and preserve other common interests of society within the limits of the basic Islamic legal principles." Gaafer M. Abd-Elrahim, 'The Concept of Punishment in Islamic Law in Relation to Contemporary Legal Trends', (Ph.D. dissertation, Faculty of Union Graduate School, Cincinnati, OH, 1987), pp.162–163.
7. *Kafā'ah* is the doctrine of equality or proportionality of status in marriage that makes the husband and wife suitable for each other. Its major aspects include religion, physical beauty, lineage, freedom, economic wealth, and social status. For other views of these aspects of *kafā'ah*, see Ibn Rushd, *The Distinguished Jurist's Primer*, vol. 2, pp.17–19; Qarāfī, *Dhakhīrah*, vol. 4, pp.22–26.
8. See, for example the Qur'an, 2:190.
9. The grounds for this provision consist of both Qur'anic and Prophetic evidence. In the Qur'an, we read in the following verse the italicized phrase: "Forbidden to you are your mothers, and your daughters, and your sisters, and your aunts - paternal and maternal, and a brother's daughters, and a sister's daughters; *and your milk-mothers, and your milk-sisters*; and the mothers of your wives; and your step-daughters – who are your foster children – born of your wives with whom you have consummated your marriage; but if

you have not consummated your marriage, you will incur no sin [by marrying their daughters]; and [forbidden to you are] the spouses of the sons who have sprung from your loins; and [you are forbidden] to have two sisters [as your wives] at the same time – but what is past is past: for, behold, God is indeed Much-Forgiving, a Dispenser of Grace" (4:23).

As for the Sunnah, the Prophet is reported to have said: "What is forbidden (*ḥarām*) by birth is forbidden by suckling." See, Bukhārī, *Ṣaḥīḥ*, 'Nikāḥ', hadith 5099, p.912; Mālik ibn Anas, *Muwaṭṭa'*, 'Raḍā'', hadith 1287; Muslim, 'Raḍā'', hadith 1444(1–2), p.544. The issue is discussed in more detail in chapter 34, pp.258–261.

10. Slightly different versions of this tradition can be found in Aḥmad ibn Ḥanbal, *Musnad*, vol. 3, p.129 and vol. 4, p.421. See details of the different versions in Abd al-Rauf ibn Ali al-Manawi, *Fayḍ al-Qadīr* (Beirut: Dār al-Maʿrifah, 1972), vol. 4, pp.51–512.

For further discussion, see al-Mawardi, *The Ordinances of Government*, pp.405. The necessity of this condition was disputed by some prominent classical scholars even before Ibn Khaldūn reinterpreted it in his doctrine of social cohesion or *ʿaṣabiyyah*. For example, Imām al-Ḥaramayn al-Juwaynī said , "none of the purposes of *imāmah* depends on belonging to a specific descent or ancestry." Imām al-Ḥaramayn al-Juwaynī, al-Ghayyāthī (known also as *Ghayyāth al-Umam fī Iltiyāth al-Ẓulam*), ed. Khalil al-Mansur (Beirut: Dār al-Kutub al-ʿIlmiyyah, 1417/1997), p.140. Cf. his *A Guide to Conclusive Proofs of the Principles of Belief* [*Kitāb al-Irshād ilā Qawāṭiʿ al-'Adilla fī Uṣūl al-Iʿtiqād*], trans. Paul E. Walker (Reading, Berks, UK: Garnet Publishing, 2000), p.235; Ibn Khaldūn, *The Muqaddimah*, vol. 1, pp.396–402.

11. *Iʿtibārāt* consist of the meanings and ideas (*maʿānī*) that have a specific reality of their own they exist only in the mind of rational human beings such that the mind cannot avoid perceiving them, for they are related to real things (*ḥaqā'iq*). However, their existence is contingent upon one particular reality, such as time and space, or two realities, such as fatherhood and childhood. – Author.

12. Although jurists disagreed on the lawfulness of eating dogfish and water hog, they are lawful according to the following tradition. The Qur'an says: "Lawful to you is all water-game, and what the sea brings forth" (*al-Mā'idah*, 5:96). The Prophet is also reported to have said: "In sea water is purity, and that which is dead in it is *ḥalāl*." See, Mālik ibn Anas, *Muwaṭṭa'*, 'Ṭahārah', hadith 40, p.26 and 'Ṣayd', hadith 1068, p.332; Abū Dāwūd, *Sunan*, ed. Muhammad Muhyi al-Din Abd al-Hamid (Beirut: al-Maktabah al-ʿAṣriyyah, 1416/1995), 'Ṭahārah', hadith 83, vol. 1, p.21; Tirmidhī, *Sunan*, ed. Ahmad Muhammad Shakir (Cairo: Dār al-Ḥadīth, 1419/1999), 'Ṭahārah', hadith

69, vol. 1, p.162. This, it seems, is the reason why Mālik, as mentioned by his disciple Ibn al-Qāsim in *al-Mudawwanah*, used to say, "You call it sea pig!" whenever he was asked about water hog. Ahmad ibn Muhammad al-Shinqiti, (Cairo: Maṭbaʿat al-Madanī, 1392/1972), vol. 1, p.154; Muhammad Zakariya al-Kandahlawi, *Awjaz al-Masālik ilā Muwaṭṭa' al-Imām Mālik*, ed. Taqiy al-Din al-Nadwi (Damascus: Dār al-Qalam, 1424/2003), vol. 10, pp.101–102.

13. Mālik ibn Anas, *Muwaṭṭa'*, 'Ḥajj', hadith 845, p.260; Bukhārī, *Ṣaḥīḥ*, 'Ḥajj', hadith 1690, p.273; 'Waṣāyā', hadiths 2754–2755, p.455 and 'Adab', hadiths 6159–6160, pp.1073–1074; Muslim, *Ṣaḥīḥ*, 'Ḥajj', hadith 1322, p.492.
14. Mālik ibn Anas, *Muwaṭṭa'*, hadith 722, 'Ḥajj', p.224.
15. Bukhārī, *Ṣaḥīḥ*, 'Janā'iz', hadiths 1265–1267, pp.202–203; Muslim, *Ṣaḥīḥ*, 'Hajj', hadith 1206 (93–103), pp.445–446. *Talbiyyah* or chanting *Labbayk* consists of saying in Hajj: "Ever at Your service O God, ever at Your service. Ever at Your service, You have no partner, ever at Your service. Verily, all praise, blessings, and dominion are Yours. You have no partner."
16. This was the view of the Mālikīs and Hanifites. Muhammad ibn Ali al-Shawkani, *Nayl al-Awṭār min Asrār Muntaqā al-Akhbār* (Beirut: Dār Ibn Ḥazm, 1421/2000), p.742. Cf. Zarqānī, *Sharḥ Muwaṭṭa'*, vol. 2, p.233 and Bājī, *al-Muntaqā*, vol. 2, p.200.
17. This is part of a tradition, whose exact wording according to Mālik's narration reads as follows: "By He in Whose hand my self is! From each of you who is wounded in the way of God – and God knows best who is wounded in His way, when the Day of Rising comes, blood will gush forth from his wound. It will be the color of blood, but its scent will be that of musk", *Muwaṭṭa'*, 'Jihad', hadith 912, p.306. See also, Bukhārī, *Ṣaḥīḥ*, 'al-Jihad wa al-Siyar', hadith 2803, p.464; Muslim, *Ṣaḥīḥ*, 'Imārah', hadith 1876, pp.750–751. Regarding the Prophet's recommendation not to wash the body of the martyr, see, for example, Bukhārī, *Ṣaḥīḥ*, 'Janā'iz', hadiths 1343 and 1346, pp.214–215.
18. *Tayammum* or dry ablution is a dispensation to perform the prayer or similar act without lifting one's minor or major impurity, by the use of earth instead of water for one's ablution.

10: GROUNDING *MAQĀṢID AL-SHARĪʿAH* ON *FIṬRAH*

1. Abū Saʿīd Nāṣir al-Dīn ʿAbd Allāh ibn ʿUmar ibn Muḥammad al-Bayḍāwī was born in the city of Bayda (Farsi: Dar Isfīd) in Iran, where his father was chief judge, in the time of the Atabek ruler, Abū Bakr ibn Saʿd (1226–1260). He

himself became judge in Shīrāz, and died in Tabrīz in 685/1286. His chief work is the commentary on the Qur'an entitled *Anwār al-Tanzīl wa Asār al-Ta'wīl* [The Lights of Revelation and the Secrets of Interpretation]. This work is in the main a digest of the great Muʿtazilite commentary *al-Kashshāf* of Zamakhsharī with omissions and additional notes. Like Zamakhsharī's *Kashshāf*, many super-commentaries have been written on al-Bayḍāwī's work. Al-Bayḍāwī was also the author of several theological treatises.

2. According to al-Rāzī, the phrase "And so, set thy face steadfastly towards the [one ever-true] religion, turning away from all that is false (*ḥanīfan*)," means "stick to the God-given nature consisting of monotheism (*tawḥīd*) on which God has created the human beings." As for the phrase "not to allow any change to corrupt what God has created [*Lā tabdīla li-khalqi Allāh*]", "it means that the oneness of God (*waḥdāniyyah*) is deeply and unalterably rooted in them so that when you ask them about who has created the heavens and the earth, they will answer that it is God. However, innate faith (*īmān fiṭrī*) is not sufficient." Fakhr al-Dīn al-Rāzī, *al-Tafsīr al-Kabīr* or *Mafātīḥ al-Ghayb* (Beirut: Dār al-Kutub al-ʿIlmiyyah, 1990), vol. 13/25, p.105.
The author's representation of al-Bayḍāwī's interpretation of the verse is rather inaccurate. In fact, it is more in line with what Ibn Ashur is advocating here. See al-Qāḍī Nāṣir al-Dīn Abū Saʿīd ʿAbd Allāh al-Bayḍāwī, *Tafsīr al-Bayḍāwī*, entitled *Anwār al-Tanzīl wa Asrār al-Ta'wīl*, ed. Abd al-Qadir Irfan al-Ashsha Hassunah (Beirut: Dār al-Fikr, 1416/1996), vol. 4, 335.

3. Reference is here made to the following hadith narrated by Abū Hurayrah: "One day while the Prophet was sitting in the company of some people, a man came and asked, 'What is faith?' God's Apostle replied, 'Faith is to believe in God, His angels, (the) meeting with Him, His Apostles, and to believe in Resurrection.' Then he [the man] further asked, 'What is Islam?' God's Apostle replied, 'To worship God Alone and none else, to offer prayers correctly, to pay the compulsory charity (zakah) and to observe fasts during the month of Ramadan.' Then he further asked, 'What is *iḥsān* (perfection)?' God's Apostle replied, 'To worship God as if you see Him, and if you cannot achieve this state of devotion, then you must consider that He is looking at you.' Then he further asked, 'When will the Hour be established?' God's Apostle replied, 'The answerer has no better knowledge than the questioner. But I will inform you about its portents: 1) When a slave (lady) gives birth to her master, 2) When the shepherds of black camels start boasting and competing with others in the construction of higher buildings. And the Hour is one of five things which nobody knows except God.' The Prophet then recited: 'Verily, with God (Alone) is the knowledge of the Hour...' (31:34) Then that man left and the Prophet asked his Companions to call him back, but they

could not see him. Then the Prophet said, 'That was Gabriel, who came to teach the people their religion.'" Abū ʿAbd Allāh [al-Bukhārī] said: "He (the Prophet) considered all that a part of faith." Bukhārī, *Ṣaḥīḥ*, '*Īmān*', hadith 50, p.12; 'Tafsīr', hadith 4777, p.839.

4. The important point for the legal theorists (*uṣūliyyūn*) is the occurrence of a general expression (*ʿumūm*) in conjunction with a particular cause. They maintain that if a general expression has been associated in the sequence of the discourse with a specific cause, this does entail the specification (*takhṣīṣ*) of its general meaning. – Author.
   For further details, see Abū Bakr Muḥammad ibn al-Ṭayyib al-Bāqillānī, *al-Taqrīb wa al-Irshād 'al-Ṣaghīr'*, ed. ʿAbd al-Ḥamīd ibn ʿAlī Abū Zunayd (Beirut: Mu'assassat al-Risālah, 1418/1998), vol. 3, pp.284–300; Abū al-Ḥusayn al-Baṣrī, *Kitāb al-Muʿtamad Fī Uṣūl al-Fiqh*, vol. 1, pp.311–312; Sayf al-Dīn al-Āmidī, *al-Iḥkām Fī Uṣūl al-Aḥkām*, ed. Ibrāhīm al-ʿAjūz (Beirut: Dār al-Kutub al-ʿIlmiyyah [n. d.]), vol. 1, pp.534–535 and *Muntahā al-Sūl fī ʿIlm al-Uṣūl*, ed. Aḥmad Farīd al-Mazīdī (Beirut: Dār al-Kutub al-ʿIlmiyyah, 2003/1424), pp.150–151; Shihāb al-Dīn al-Qarāfī, *Sharḥ Tanqīḥ al-Fuṣūl* (Beirut: Dār al-Fikr, 1424/2004), pp.169–175; Najm al-Dīn al-Ṭūfī, *Sharh Mukhtaṣar al-Rawḍah*, ed. ʿAbd Allāh ibn ʿAbd al-Muḥsin al-Turkī (Beirut: Mu'assassat al-Risālah, 1419/1998), vol. 2, pp.501–508.
5. Al-Qāḍī Abū Muḥammad ʿAbd al-Ḥaqq ibn Ghālib ibn ʿAbd al-Raḥmān Ibn ʿAṭiyah was born in Gharnāṭah (Granada) in 481 AH and died in Lūrgah (Lorca) in 542/1148. He was an eminent Qur'an commentator and renowned jurist with a sound knowledge of the Traditions (*Ḥadīth*). – Author.
6. Abū al-Qāsīm Maḥmūd ibn ʿUmar al-Zamakhsharī (467/1070–539/1144) was a Persian-born Muslim scholar, whose exegetic work *al-Kashshāf*, 'The Discoverer of Truth', stands out as one of the major works of *tafsīr bi al-ra'y*. Based on the Muʿtazilite rationalist approach and considered to be the standard work of Muʿtazilite *tafsīr*, Zamakhsharī's writings place much emphasis on Arabic grammar and lexicography as a means of interpretation with less attention given to transmitted reports and traditions. This exegetic work has been the subject of many commentaries and glossaries by eminent scholars, who were mostly Ashʿarites.
7. Abū Muḥammad Makkī ibn Abī Ṭālib al-Qaysī was born in the historic Islamic city of al-Qayrawān (Kairouan) in 355/966 at a time when it was being destabilized by the attacks of the apostate Berber tribes and the ascending ʿUbaydī (Fatimid) forces. He traveled many times to Egypt, the Ḥijāz (Makkah and Madinah), and Syria in pursuit of knowledge.
   In Kairouan, he studied jurisprudence with Muḥammad ibn Abī Zayd, an authority in Mālikī doctrines in the whole Maghreb, and Abū al-Ḥasan al-

Qābusī, another authority in Qur'an readings (*qirā'āt*) and Ḥadīth. In 393 he left for Cordoba where he settled for the rest of his life and became one of its foremost scholars. He died in 437/1045 at the age of eighty-two. Makkī's main focus was the Qur'an and the disciplines enabling one to read it correctly and interpret it soundly. His numerous works include, among others, *al-Tabṣirah fī al-Qirā'āt*, *al-Kashf ʿan Wujūh al-Qirā'āt al-Sabʿ wa ʿIlaluhā wa Ḥujajuhā* (both on Qur'anic readings) and *al-Hidāyah ilā Bulūgh al-Nihāyah* (Qur'an commentary).

8. Ibn ʿAṭiyyah, *al-Muḥarrar al-Wajīz fi Tafsīr al-Kitāb al-ʿAzīz*, ed. Abd al-Slam Abd al-Shafi Muhammad (Beirut: Dār al-Kutub al-ʿIlmiyyah, 1413/1993), vol. 4, p.336.
9. Maḥmūd ibn ʿUmar al-Zamakhsharī, *al-Kashshāf ʿan Ḥaqā'iq Ghawāmiḍ al-Tanzīl wa ʿUyūn al-Aqāwīl fī Wujūh al-Ta'wīl*, ed. Muhammad Abd al-Salam Shahin (Beirut: Dār al-Kutub al-ʿIlmiyyah, 1415/1995), vol. 3, pp.463–64.
10. See the author's elaboration on this issue in *Tafsīr al-Taḥrīr wa al-Tanwīr*, vol. 10/21, pp.91–92.
11. Abū ʿAlī al-Ḥusayn ibn ʿAbd Allāh ibn Sīnā (Avicenna) was born in 980 AC in Kharmaithen (near Bukhārā), Central Asia (now Uzbekistan) and died in June 1037 in Hamadan, Persia (now Iran). Ibn Sīnā is often known by his Latin name of Avicenna. We know many details of his life, for he wrote an autobiography that has been supplemented with material from a biography written by one of his students, Abū ʿUbayd al-Jūzjānī. The course of Ibn Sīnā's life was dominated by the period of great political instability through which he lived. The Samanid dynasty, which ruled at that time, controlled Transoxania and Khorasan from about 900. Bukhārā was their capital and it, together with Samarkand, were the cultural centers of the empire. However, from the middle of the 10th century, the power of the Samanids began to weaken.

    By the time Ibn Sīnā was born, Nūḥ ibn Manṣūr was the Sultan in Bukhārā although he was struggling to retain control of the empire. Ibn Sīnā's father was the governor of a village in one of Nūḥ ibn Manṣūr's estates. He was educated by his father, whose home was a meeting place for men of learning in the area. Ibn Sīnā was a remarkable child, with a memory and an ability to learn which amazed the scholars who met in his father's home. By the age of 10 he had memorized the Qur'an and most of the Arabic poetry which he had read. When he reached the age of 13, he began to study medicine and he mastered it by the age of 16 when he began to treat patients. He also studied logic and metaphysics, receiving instruction from some of the best teachers of his day, in all areas he continued his studies on his own. In his autobiography, Ibn Sīnā stresses that he was more or less self-taught, although at crucial times in his life he received help.

Together with al-Fārābī, Ibn Sīnā's legacy lies mainly in philosophical studies and medicine. His works include, among others, *al-Shifā'*, *al-Najāt*, and *al-Ishārāt wa al-Tanbīhāt* in philosophy and logic and *al-Qānūn fī al-Ṭibb* in medicine.

12. Thus it is in the original. If this is not a distortion, it is clear that he means by imaginary what is mentally posited (*iʿtibārī*) rather than what is perceived by the imaginative faculty (*al-quwwah al-wāhimah*). – Author.
13. Ibn Sīnā, *Kitāb al-Najāt fī al-Ḥikmah al-Manṭiqiyyah wa al-Ṭabīʿiyyah wa al-Ilāhiyyh*, ed. Majid Fakhri (Beirut: Dār al-Āfāq al-Jadīdah, 1405/1985), p.99.
14. See the author's more elaborate interpretation of these verses in *Tafsīr al-Taḥrīr wa al-Tanwīr*, vol. 15, pp.422–429.
15. Diogenes of Sinope (412–323 BC) was chief among the school known as the Cynics, though possibly not representative of it. He is said to have carried the principles of the sect to an extreme of asceticism. It was said of Diogenes that throughout his life he searched with a lantern in the daylight for an honest man. And though Diogenes apparently did not find an honest man, he had, in the process, exposed the vanity and selfishness of human beings.
The school of the Cynics, was founded by Antisthenes (444–370 BC) who had been a pupil of Socrates and teacher of Diogenes. It was marked by an ostentatious contempt for ease, wealth, and the enjoyments of life. Diogenes, on coming to Athens from his native lands, Sinope, came as a rake and spendthrift. After falling under the spell of Antisthenes, Diogenes became at once an austere ascetic, his clothing of the coarsest, his food the plainest, and his bed the bare ground. At length he found himself a permanent residence in a tub.
An interesting story is the one where the young Alexander the Great (356–323 BC) met Diogenes, then a very old man. The powerful young conqueror, being solicitous of the old philosopher, asked what, if anything, he could do for him. Diogenes replied, "Stand out of my sunshine."
16. Mālik ibn Anas, *Muwaṭṭa'*, 'Jāmiʿ', hadith 1636, p.651; Bukhārī, *Ṣaḥīḥ*, 'Īmān', hadith 24, p.7 and 'Adab', hadith 6118, p.1066.
17. For further details of the meaning of *fiṭrah* and its cognitive and psycho-sociological implications, see Muhammad Hussayn al-Tabataba'i, *al-Mīzān fī Tafsīr al-Qur'an* (Beirut: Mu'assassat al-Aʿlamī, 1411/1991), vol. 16, pp.183–197; Muhammad Asad, *The Message of the Qur'an* (Gibraltar: Dar al-Andalus, 1984), p.621, note 27 and also his note 139 to *sūrah al-Aʿrāf*, 7:172, p.230.
18. In this connection it is narrated on the authority of ʿAbd al-Raḥmān ibn Abī Bakrah that his father said: "We were in the company of the Messenger of God (may peace be upon him) that he observed: 'Should I not inform you about the most grievous of the grave sins?' (The Prophet) repeated it three times, and

then said: 'Associating anyone with God, disobedience to parents, false testimony or false utterance.'" Muslim, *Ṣaḥīḥ*, 'Īmān', hadiths 143–145, p.53.

19. *Tarahhub*, *rahbāniyyah* or *tabattul* is to lead a monastic ascetic life. Dārimī reported that ʿĀ'ishah, the Prophet's wife, said: "God's Apostle forbade monastic asceticism and hermitage." Dārimī also reported that Saʿd ibn Abī Waqqāṣ narrated, "God's Apostle *(ṢAAS)* said to ʿUthmān ibn Maḍʿūn who had avoided having sexual intercourse with women: 'I have not been sent with any monastic asceticism (*rahbāniyyah*). Are you shunning my way?' He [ʿUthmān] said: 'No, O Messenger of God!' Then, God's Apostle said: 'It is part of my way that I pray and sleep, fast and eat, and marry and divorce. He who shuns my way is not my follower. O ʿUthmān! Your wife has a right over you, and your body has a right over you.'" ʿAbd Allāh ibn ʿAbd al-Raḥmān al-Dārimī, *Musnad/Sunan*, ed. Hussayn Salim al-Darani (Beirut: Dār Ibn Ḥazm, 1421/2000), 'Nikāḥ', hadith 2210, vol. 3, pp.1386–1387.

20. Samurah ibn Jundub narrated that the Prophet had said: "He who kills his slave shall be killed, he who amputates his slave shall be amputated and he who castrates his slave shall be castrated." Aḥmad ibn Shuʿayb al-Nasā'ī, *al-Sunan al-Kubrā*, ed. Hassan Abd al-Munim Shalabi (Beirut: Mu'assassat al-Risālah, 1421/2001), 'Qasāmah', hadiths 6912–6914, vol. 6, pp.331–332. ʿAbd Allāh ibn Masʿūd also narrated that the following: "We used to fight in battles in the company of the Prophet and we had no wives with us. So we said, 'O God's Apostle! Shall we have ourselves castrated?' The Prophet forbade us to do that and recited to us: 'O you who believe! Do not make unlawful the good things which God has made lawful for you, but commit no transgression (5:87)'." Bukhārī, *Ṣaḥīḥ*, 'Nikāḥ', hadiths 5071 & 5075, pp.907–908. According to Ibn Ḥajar, there is no disagreement that the castration of human beings is categorically prohibited for it involves a number of evils. Among those evils, he mentioned masochism, self-mutilation that might cause death, destruction of one's manhood, alteration of God's creation, and ingratitude for His mercy and bounty that consist of creating man in such a form for a great purpose in the world. Ibn Ḥajar al-ʿAsqalānī, *Fatḥ al-Bārī*, vol. 2, p.2239.

21. Ibn Mājah, *Sunan*, 'Diyyāt [Section entitled: If someone tortures his slave, the latter must be freed]', hadiths 2679–2680, vol. 2, p.894. Other traditions concerning the good treatment of slaves have already been cited.

22. See different versions in this regard in Nasā'ī, *Sunan*, 'Ḍaḥāyā', Section 41, vol. 7, p.239; Dārimī, *Sunan*, 'Aḍāḥī', hadiths 1979–1981, vol. 2, p.408. In one of the versions, ʿAbd Allāh ibn ʿAmr ibn al-ʿĀṣ narrated: "God's Apostle cursed anyone who tortured an animal."

11: MAGNANIMITY OF THE SHARIʿAH

1. See many versions of this Tradition in Abū Jaʿfar Muḥammad ibn Jarīr al-Ṭabarī, *Jāmiʿ al-Bayān fī Ta'wīl Āyi al-Qur'an* (Beirut: Dār al-Kutub al-ʿIlmiyyah, 1992), vol. 1, pp.389–390. This Tradition refers to the Qur'anic account of the Israelites (2:67–71). Asad, *The Message of the Qur'an*, p.15, note 55. Some scholars of Ḥadīth, such as Ibn Kathīr, have expressed reservations in attributing this Tradition to the Prophet himself. In the best of cases, they say, it is a comment by Abū Hurayrah, its narrator, on the story of the Israelites. Ismāʿīl ibn ʿUmar ibn Kathīr, *al-Bidāyah wa al-Nihāyah* (Cairo: Maṭbaʿat al-Saʿādah, 1351/1355 AH), vol. 1, p.194.
2. Bukhārī, *Ṣaḥīḥ*, 'Tafsīr', hadith 4487, p.763.
3. See the author's detailed discussion of the meaning and scope of *wasaṭṭiyyah* and its intellectual, spiritual, ritual, and social implications in *Tafsīr al-Taḥrīr wa al-Tanwīr*, vol. 2, pp.15–22.
4. This meaning is so familiar in understanding the purport of the term *wasaṭ* that the famous poet Abū Tammām said:
It used to be itself the middlemost (wasaṭan) protected thing
And it has now been so beset by mishaps
That it has been pushed out to the periphery. – Author.
5. Abū ʿAbd Allāh Muṭarrif ibn ʿAbd Allāh ibn al-Shikhkhīr al-Tābiʿī was a highly respected and influential scholar and traditionalist of the second class (*ṭabaqah*) of the Successors in Basra. Among other Companions of the Prophet, he narrated from his father ʿAbd Allāh, ʿAlī ibn Abī Ṭālib, ʿAmmār ibn Yāsir, ʿImrān ibn al-Ḥuṣayn, and ʿĀ'ishah. He is reported to have said concerning the question of predestination, "One must not climb and throw oneself and then say: 'God has preordained me to fall.' Rather, one must act carefully and do one's level best. Then if anything befalls him, he should realize that it has been predetermined." He died in 95/713.
6. Muḥammad ibn ʿAbd al-Raḥmān al-Sakhāwī, *al-Maqāṣid al-Ḥasanah*, ed. Abd Allah ibn al-Siddiq al-Ghammari (Beirut: Dār al-Kutub al-ʿIlmiyyah, 1407/1987), no. 455, p.205.
7. It has been reported by Ibn Abī Shaybah, *Muṣannaf*, vol. 13, p.479; al-ʿAjlūnī, *Kashf al-Khafā'* (Beirut: Dār Iḥyā' al-Turāth al-ʿArabī, 1351 AH), vol. 1, p.391; Sakhāwī, *Maqāṣid*, no. 455, p.205.
8. Bukhārī, *Ṣaḥīḥ*, 'Buyūʿ', hadith 2076, p.333. See also Ibn Mājah, *Sunan*, 'Tijārāt', hadith 2221, vol. 2, p.12.
9. The Tradition referred to by the author reads as follows: "God loves the one who is lenient in buying, selling, and in settling his debt." Abd al-Ra'uf ibn Ali al-Manawi, *Fayḍ al-Qadīr bi-Sharḥ al-Jāmiʿ al-Ṣaghīr* (Beirut: Dār al-Maʿrifah, 1972, hadith 1885), vol. 2, p.294; and *al-Tysīr bi-Sharḥ al-Jāmiʿ*

al-Ṣaghīr (Riyadh: Maktabat al-Imām al-Shāfiʿī, 1408/1988), vol. 1, p.271.

10. Reported by Ibn Abī Shaybah and Bukhārī in his *Ṣaḥīḥ* as *muʿallaq* and in his *al-Adab al-Mufrad* as *musnad*. – Author.
See Bukhārī, *Ṣaḥīḥ*, 'Īmān', p.9; *al-Adab al-Mufrad*, hadith 288, p.109 (on the authority of Ibn ʿAbbās); Aḥmad ibn Ḥanbal, *Musnad*, vol. 1, p.236, Muḥammad Nāṣir al-Dīn al-Albānī, *Silsilat al-Aḥādīth al-Ṣaḥīḥah* (Beirut: al-Maktab al-Islāmī, 1403/1983), hadith 881, vol.2, pp.569–570.
11. Bukhārī, *Ṣaḥīḥ*, '*Īmān*', hadith 39, pp.9–10.
12. Aḥmad ibn Ḥanbal, *Musnad*, vol. 1, p.236 and vol. 5, p.266; Bukhārī, *al-Adab al-Mufrad*, hadith 287, p.109; Ṭabarānī, *al-Muʿjam al-Kabīr*, hadith 7868, vol. 8, p.216.
13. Bukhārī, *Ṣaḥīḥ*, 'Maghāzī', hadith 4342 and 4344/4345, pp.735–736; Muslim, *Ṣaḥīḥ*, 'al-Jihad wa al-Siyar', hadiths 1733, p.689. In all the versions of the Tradition in question, the two men sent by the Prophet to the Yemen were ʿAlī ibn Abī Ṭālib and Abū Mūsā al-Ashʿarī rather than Muʿādh.
14. This is part of a long hadith in Bukhārī, *Ṣaḥīḥ*, 'Wuḍū'', hadith 220, p.41 and 'Adab', hadith 6128, p.1068.
15. Bukhārī, *Ṣaḥīḥ*, 'Ḥudūd', hadith 6786, p.1170. The full and exact text of this Tradition reads as follows: "Whenever the Prophet was given an option between two things, he used to select the easier of the two as long as it was not sinful; but if it was sinful, he would keep away from it. By God, he never took revenge for himself concerning any matter that was presented to him, but when God's Limits were transgressed, he would take revenge for God's Sake."
16. Shāṭibī, *Muwāfaqāt*, vol. 1/1, p.302.
17. Abū Hurayrah narrated that Prophet said, "There are five things from the *fiṭrah*: cutting the nails, trimming the moustache, removing the hair from the armpit, shaving the pubic region, and circumcision." Bukhārī, *Ṣaḥīḥ*, 'Libās', hadiths 5889 & 5891, p.1036; Mālik ibn Anas, *Muwaṭṭa'*, 'Jāmiʿ', hadith 1666, p.660.

12: THE GENERAL OBJECTIVES OF ISLAMIC LEGISLATION

1. "Shuʿayb is said to be identical with Jethro, the father-in-law of Moses, also called in the Bible Reú-el (Exodus ii, 18), meaning "Faithful to God". The region of Madyan – the Midian of the Bible – extended from the present-day Gulf of Aqabah westwards deep into the Sinai Peninsula and to the mountains of Moab east of the Dead Sea; its inhabitants were Arabs of the Amorite group of tribes." Asad, *The Message of the Qur'an*, p.216, note 67.
2. The Nabataean tribe of Thamūd descended from the tribe of ʿĀd and is often referred to in pre-Islamic poetry as the "Second ʿĀd." Apart from Arabian

sources, a series of older references, not of Arabian origin, confirm the historical existence of the name and people of Thamūd. Thus the inscription of Sargon of the year 715 BC mentions the Thamūd among the people of eastern and central Arabia subjected by the Assyrians. We also find the Thamudaei, Thamudenes mentioned in Aristo, Ptolemy, and Pliny. At the time of which the Qur'an speaks, the Thamūd were settled in the northernmost Hejaz, near the borders of Syria. Rock-inscriptions attributed to them are still extant in the region of al-Ḥijr. As in the case of the ʿĀdite prophet Hūd – and the prophet Shuʿayb spoken of in verses 85–93 of *Sūrah al-Aʿrāf* – Ṣāliḥ is called the "brother" of the tribe because he belonged to it. Ibid., p.214, note 56.

3. *Īmā'* is one of the methods for confirming the occasioning factors (*ʿillah*) of the Shariʿah commands. It is usually discussed in conjunction with analogical reasoning (*qiyās*). For more detail, see Ahmad Hasan, *Analogical Reasoning in Islamic Jurisprudence* (Islamabad: Islamic Research Institute, 1986), pp.235–249 and *passim*.
4. See the author's elaboration on the question of rights in Part III, Chapter 33.
5. This is part of a long hadith in Bukhārī, *Ṣaḥīḥ*, 'Īmān', hadith 25, p.7. It reads as follows: "Both lawful and unlawful things are evident, yet in between them there are doubtful (suspect) things and most people have no knowledge of them. So whoever saves himself from these suspect things saves his religion and his honor. Whoever indulges in these suspect things is like a shepherd who grazes (his animals) near the *ḥimā* (private pasture) of someone else and at any moment he is likely to trespass on it. (O people!) Beware! Every king has a *ḥimā* and the *ḥimā* of God on the earth is His forbidden things (*maḥārimuh*). Beware..."
6. In conjunction with his analysis of the causes that led to the decline of Muslim education in his book *Alaysa al-Ṣubḥ bi-Qarīb: al-Taʿlīm al-ʿArabī al-Islāmī Dirāsah Tārīkhiyyah wa Ārā' Iṣlāḥiyyah* (Tunis: al-Sharikah al-Tūnisiyyah li-Funūn al-Rasm, 1988, pp.129–130), the author attributed this statement to the Louis-Gabriel-Ambroise, Vicomte de Bonald. French statesman, writer, and philosopher, de Bonald was born at Monna, near Millau, in Rouergue (Aveyron) October 2, 1754. He died at Paris, November 23, 1840. He was educated at the College of Juilly; joined the King's Musketeers, returned to his own province in 1776, was elected mayor of Millau in 1785, and in 1790 was chosen member of the departmental Assembly for Aveyron. His first work, *Théorie du pouvoir politique et religieux* (1797), was suppressed in France by order of the Directory. His works include, among others, *Essai analytique sur les lois naturelles de l'ordre social* (1800), *Du divorce* (1801), *La législation primitive* (1802), *Réflexions sur l'intérêt général de l'Europe* (1815), *Recherches philosophiques sur les premiers objets des connaissances morales*

(1818), *Mélanges littéraires, politiques et philosophiques* (1819) and *Démonstration philosophique du principe constitutif des sociétés* (1827).

7. Muslim, *Saḥīḥ*, 'Īmān', hadith 38, pp.39–40.
8. For the author's detailed discussion of these aspects, see his book Us l al-Nizām al-Ijtimāʿā fī al-Islām, ed. Mohamed El-Tahir El-Mesawi (Amman: Dār al-Nafā'is, 1421/2001), pp.45–97.

13: THE MEANING OF *MAṢLAḤAH AND MAFSADAH*

1. Abū ʿAmr Jamāl al-Dīn ʿUthmān ibn al-Ḥājib was born in 570/1174 and died in 646/1249. He lived in Cairo and Damascus. He was a great Mālikī jurist and jurisconsult (mufti) as well as an authority on Arabic lexicography and grammar.
2. ʿAḍud al-Dīn ʿAbd al-Raḥmān al-Ījī was born in 700/1301 in the small town of Īj nearby Shīrāz and died during his imprisonment in its military fortress in 756/1355. He was an outstanding legal theorist, linguist and Ashʿarī theologian. After Fakhr al-Dīn al-Rāzī, Ashʿarite theology is continued chiefly in a series of manuals eclectically dependent upon the great writers of the past. The most famous of these, al-Ījī's *al-Mawāqif fī Uṣūl al-Dīn*, has continued to serve as a textbook on theology to the present day. Among the various commentaries written on it, the most important and widely used is that of al-Sharīf ʿAlī ibn Muḥammad al-Jurjānī (d. 816/1413), and together with this text the *Mawāqif* has gone through a large number of printed editions since the early nineteenth century. Besides the *Mawāqif* his works include *al-ʿAqā'id al-ʿAḍudiyyah, Sharḥ al-Mukhtaṣar* (in *uṣūl al-fiqh*) and a commentary on the Qur'an.
3. ʿAḍud al-Dīn ʿAbd al-Raḥmān al-Ījī, *Sharḥ al-ʿAḍud* (a commentary on Ibn al-Ḥājib's *uṣūl* work *Mukhtaṣar al-Muntahā al-Uṣūlī*), ed. Fadi Nasif et al. (Beirut: Dār al-Kutub al-ʿIlmiyyah, 1421/2000), p.320.
4. ʿAḍud al-Dīn ʿAbd al-Raḥmān ibn Aḥmad al-Ījī, *al-Mawāqif fī ʿIlm al-Kalām* (Beirut: ʿĀlam al-Kutub, n. d.), p.324; also *Sharḥ al-Mawāqif* (a commentary on al-Ījī's *al-Mawāqif* by al-Sharīf ʿAlī ibn Muḥammad al-Jurjānī), ed. Mahmud Umar al-Dimyati (Beirut: Dār al-Kutub al-ʿIlmiyyah, 1419/1998), vol. 4/8, p.203.
5. See Shāṭibī's discussion of the meaning and categories of *maṣlaḥah* in *Muwāfaqāt*, vol. 1/2, pp.339–365. Cf. Abū Ḥāmid al-Ghazālī, *Mustaṣfā min Ilm al-'Usul*, ed. Muhammad Sulayman al-Ashqar (Beirut: Mu'assassat al-Risālah, 1417/1997), vol. 1, pp.414–422.
6. For a comprehensive discussion of the place and meaning of the concept of *maṣlaḥah* in Islamic legal theory and juristic thought, see Muhammad Saʿid

Ramadan al-Buti, *Ḍawābiṭ al-Maṣlaḥah fī al-Shariʿah al-Islāmiyyah* (Beirut: Mu'assassat al-Risālah, 1422/2001) and Ihsan Abdul-Wajid Bagby, 'Utility in Classical Islamic Law: The Concept of *Maṣlaḥah* in Classical *Uṣūl al-Fiqh*' (Ph.D dissertation University of Michigan, 1986.)

7. See Ījī, *Sharḥ al-ʿAḍud*, p.324.
8. See juristic details on *ḥajr* or interdiction and its conditions and to whom it applies in Ibn Rushd, *The Distinguished Jurist's Primer*, vol. 2, pp.334–340.
9. This is known as *ʿāqilah* (clan supporting wergild) and it means a group of people responsible for paying the blood money on behalf of the offender. As the author has pointed out, these people are usually agnates or all the relations on the paternal side, but the term was also applied to the divan of a soldier.
10. So much so that the Arab poet Zuhayr [ibn Abī Sulmā] said (Author):
    Wounds used to be healed by hundreds [of she-camels from the offender]
    But now it is those who are not offenders who furnish this blood money.
    See the verse in Yaḥyā ibn ʿAlī al-Tabrīzī, *Sharḥ al-Qaṣā'id al-ʿAshr*, ed. Abd al-Salam al-Hufi (Beirut: Dār al-Kutub al-ʿIlmiyyah, 1405/1985), p.138.
11. Likewise, in Islam the prohibition of euthanasia or so-called mercy-killing envisages a higher and universal objective consisting of the protection of human life and the establishment of its sanctity in people's psyche and culture.
12. ʿIzz al-Dīn ibn ʿAbd al-Salām, *Qawāʿid*, vol. 1, pp.9–10.
13. Ibid. p.9.
14. Shāṭibī, *Muwāfaqāt*, 1/1, p.340.
15. Nero was the Roman emperor from 54 to 68 AC. He is remembered most for his perverse mentality and his persecution of Christians. Nero was born in Antium in 37 AC to Agrippina the Younger and Gnaeus Domitius Anenobarbus, a great-grandson of Augustus. He was raised by his mother and they were poor, but that changed when Agrippina married her uncle, the emperor Claudius. Agrippina persuaded Claudius to adopt Nero and in 50 AC he became the probable heir to the throne, even ahead of Claudius's own son! In 54 AC Agrippina murdered Claudius and Nero became ruler at the age of 17. At first Nero's mother had a great deal of authority within his reign. However, Nero grew resentful of her power and Agrippina was removed from the palace in 55. At this time, two of Nero's men, the Praetorian Prefect Burrus and his tutor Seneca, took over and ruled the empire successfully. Biographers cite that up until 59 Nero was known for his generosity and mildness. During this period he forbade capital punishment and contests entailing bloodshed in the circus. He even reduced taxes. This side of the emperor disappeared when he ordered the murder of his mother, who was accused of treason in 59.
    One of the most famous events of his reign was the fire of Rome in 64 AD; Nero was in Antium when the fire started in the Circus Maximus. The fire spread

and raged furiously over Rome for nine days. When Nero returned, he started to rebuild the city, which caused some to suspect him of planning the fire to make room for a new city built in his honor. His reign began disintegrating when the Senate became unimpressed with him and his unfulfilled promises and turned against him. A group of these senators banded together in 65 to form the Pisonian Conspiracy, whose aim was to murder Nero and replace him with C. Calpurnius Piso. Eventually they were discovered and punished severely with the number of executions increasing daily. One of these victims was Seneca.

Nero was obsessed with Greece and Greek culture, frequently traveling there and participating in poetry, singing, and games as well as orgies and parties. In 68, after an extensive time there, a food shortage and unrest brought him back to Rome. After his return there were many uprisings against him. One was led by Vindex, the governor of Gallia Lugaunensis, and this spurred on many others who wanted to see the tyrannical Nero removed. Rome was on a whole tired of Nero, for he was more interested in his own self-seeking life of pleasure than in ruling the most powerful empire in the world. Nero's reign finally came to an end in 68 AC when he committed suicide with the help of his secretary, Epaphroditus. He is said to have muttered before his death, "What an artist dies in me!"

16. In my statement "that it cannot be substituted by something else both in terms of the acquisition of benefit or incurring of harm", there is a generalization of meaning that calls for further elaboration. The phrase "it cannot" means that when the *mujtahid* probes the different degrees of *maṣlaḥah* or *mafsadah* with a view to seeing whether the one or the other is pure or mixed with its opposite or whether it conflicts with its opposite, his search ends with the conclusion that neither of these possibilities applies. [That is, the occurrence of *maṣlaḥah* or *mafsadah* is absolute and pure and is not contradicted.] As for the phrase "replaced", it refers to the *mujtahid's* conviction of the existence of an attribute of the act other than the one that has appeared at first. This means that there is an irrevocable relationship between the act and its attribute that cannot be attenuated, be it beneficial or harmful. My saying "with something else" means that no other attribute of the same genre of benefit or harm can replace the attribute already established.

Furthermore, my statement that "the harm resulting from this action is irremediable" means that there are no situations in which the negative harmful attributes of an act are associated with other attributes that would reduce their evil and harm or annul it altogether. Thus, we assert that the evil attributes of the action are constant and permanent and that only in very rare cases would they be inoperative. Such cases are not to be taken into consideration by the

Lawgiver, just like all irregular attributes, such as the slow or fast intoxication of wine drinkers, whether they drink it neat or mixed with something else. Likewise, the occurrence of such irregular cases are no justification for tolerating the neglect of the established attribute of the act and its effect because its harm and evil might be attenuated or compensated in some rare situations or in relation to some rare individuals. What really matters for the grounding of the Shariʿah rules is what is prevalent and preponderant. Hence, we must not hesitate to disregard what ʿUmārah ibn al-Walīd ibn al-Mughīrah, addressing his wife who stipulated he stop drinking wine in order to marry him, said in apology to her after he breached his promise [Abū al-Faraj ʿAlī ibn al-Ḥasan al-Aṣfahānī, *al-Aghānī* (Beirut: Dār Iḥyā' al-Turāth al-ʿArabī, n. d.), vol. 17, p.72]:

Don't you rejoice that when they were overcome by inebriation,
I came out of it sound and suffering no loss;
Clear as if I have never been one of them;
Discordance is indeed not acceptable in respect of noble deeds.

This is the case of a rare person, if, of course, he is sincere in his claim. Rare cases such as this cannot invalidate the universal purport of the Shariʿah rule.– Author. In the original Arabic, this elaboration constitutes part of the main text and not a note. However, since it comes as a long parenthetical clause, we deemed it better to put it as a note in order to preserve the smooth flow of the text.

17. See on this and the next page the two reports and Mālik's comment on them.
18. Mālik ibn Anas, *Muwaṭṭa'*, 'Nikāḥ', hadiths 1100–1101, p.355.
19. Mālik ibn Anas, *Muwaṭṭa'*, 'Buyūʿ', hadiths 1378–1379, p.476.
20. ʿIzz al-Dīn ibn ʿAbd al-Salām, *Qawāʿid*, vol. 1, pp.13–14.
21. Ibid., pp.7–8.
22. ʿIzz al-Dīn ibn ʿAbd al-Salām, *Qawāʿid*, vol. 2, pp.314–315.
23. Ibid., pp.79–80.
24. Muslim, *Ṣaḥīḥ*, 'Imārah', hadith 1847, pp.740–741.
25. Bukhārī, *Ṣaḥīḥ*, 'Faḍā'il al-Qur'an', hadith 4986, p.894.
26. It is narrated on the authority of Abū Hurayrah (Bukhārī, *Ṣaḥīḥ*, 'Waṣāyā', hadith 2766, p.458; 'Ṭibb', hadith 6857, p.1182) that the Prophet said: "Avoid the seven great destructive sins." The people enquire, "O God's Apostle! What are they? "He said, 'To associate others in worship along with God, to practise sorcery, to kill the life which God has forbidden except for a just cause (according to Islamic Law), to take *ribā* (usury), to take an orphan's wealth, to turn tail to the enemy and flee from the battlefield at the time of fighting, and to accuse chaste women, who never even think of anything touching chastity and are good believers.'"

In another tradition on the authority of ʿAbd al-Raḥmān ibn Abī Bakrah (Muslim, *Ṣaḥīḥ*, 'Iman', hadiths 143–146, pp.53–54), it is narrated that his father said: "We were in the company of the Messenger of God *(ṢAAS)* when he observed: 'Should I not inform you about the most grievous of the grave sins?' The Prophet repeated it three times, and then said: 'Associating anyone with God, disobedience to parents, false testimony or false utterance.' The Prophet was reclining, then he sat up, and he repeated it so many times that we wished him to be silent."

27. According to the view of most Muslim jurists, Sunnis as well as Shiʿites, the punishment of a married adulterer and adulteress is stoning to death (*rajm*). However, this view has been disputed on both scriptural and rational grounds. See for this, Abd-Elrahim, *The Concept of Punishment in Islamic Law*, pp.171–175.
28. See Ibn Rushd, *The Distinguished Jurist's Primer*, vol. 2, pp.547–552.
29. Narrated ʿAbd Allāh ibn ʿAbbās: The Prophet *(ṢAAS)* said: "If you find anyone doing as Lot's people did [i.e. has sexual intercourse with another man], punish the one who does it, and the one to whom it is done." Abū ʿAbd Allāh al-Ḥākim al-Naysābūrī, *al-Mustadrak*, ed. Mustafa Abd al-Qadir Ata (Beirut: Dār al-Kutub al-ʿIlmiyyah, 1990), hadith 847, vol. 4, p.394; al-Tirmidhī, *Sunan*, ed. Ahmad Muhammad Shakir (Beirut: Dār Iḥyā' al-Turāth al-ʿArabī, n.d.), 'Ḥudūd', hadith 1456, vol.4, p.57; Abū Dāwūd, *Sunan*, ed. Muḥammad Muhyi al-Din Abd al-Hamid (Beirut: Dār al-Fikr, n.d.), 'Ḥudūd', hadith 4462, vol. 4, p.158.

   After discussing the textual evidence on the unlawfulness of homosexuality, the great Zaydite jurist of the Yemen al-Shawkānī said the following: "How deserving is indeed the committer of such a crime and perpetrator of such a horrible vice of being given such a punishment as would make him a warning lesson to those who think. How deserving is he indeed of being punished in such a way as would break the evil desires of such people who are rebellious against nature." Muḥammad ʿAlī al-Shawkānī, *Nayl al-Awṭār*, p.1480.

14: THE PURSUIT OF *MAṢĀLIḤ* IN THE SHARIʿAH

1. Abū al-ʿAlā' Aḥmad ibn ʿAbd Allāh ibn Sulaymān at-Tannūkhī al-Maʿarrī (363/973–449/1057) was born in a small town known as Maʿarrat al-Nuʿmān in Syria. He was a great poet and man of letters. Amongst his poetic works are: *al-Luzūmiyyāt* and *Saqṭ al-Zand*. His prose work consists mainly of *Risālat al-Ghufrān*, which is an imaginative journey in the Hereafter. Al-Maʿarrī used to call himself the prisoner of the two prisons (*rahīn al-maḥbisayn*): one was natural, consisting of his loss of sight, and the other was social, consisting of

his seclusion in his house and isolation from people.

2. This verse is narrated seperately and is not make part of al-Maʿarrī's collections (*Dīwān*) of *al-Luzūmiyyāt* and *Saqṭ al-Zand*, for he said it when he was at death's door. It tallies with other verses of his in which he denounces marriage and procreation. See in this regard, Mahmud Shukri al-Alusi, *Rūḥ al-Maʿānī* (Beirut: Dār al-Fikr, 1398/1978), vol. 15, p.61.
3. Bukhārī, *Ṣaḥīḥ*, 'Tahajjud', hadith 1153, p.184.
4. His full name was Ṣubaygh ibn ʿAsal, from Iraq. The reason why ʿUmar took this measure with him was because of his raising of confusing and derailing questions amongst the populace.
5. Mālik ibn Anas, *Muwaṭṭa'*, 'Buyūʿ', hadiths 1344–1345, pp.451–452.
6. Abū Muḥammad Ṭalḥah ibn ʿUbayd Allāh was from the tribe of Quraysh. He was among the first five people who embraced Islam at the hands of Abū Bakr al-Ṣiddīq. He was one of the ten Companions who were promised Paradise and one of the six Companions appointed by ʿUmar ibn al-Khaṭṭāb to conduct the consultation for the selection of his successor. He fought with the Prophet in the battle of Uḥud until he lost his hand. He was killed during the Battle of the Camel in 36 AH by Marwān ibn al-Ḥakam. See Ibn Ḥajar al-ʿAsqalānī, *Iṣābah*, vol. 2, p.22; *Fatḥ al-Bārī*, vol. 2, p.1684.
7. Bukhārī attributed this statement to Abū Ṭalḥah Zayd ibn Sahl al-Anṣārī rather than Ṭalḥah ibn ʿUbayd Allāh. *Ṣaḥīḥ*, 'Maghāzī', hadith 4064, p.687; Ibn Ḥajar, *Fatḥ al-Bārī*, vol. 2, p.1800. For the reports concerning Ṭalḥah ibn ʿUbayd Allāh, see Bukhārī, *Ṣaḥīḥ*, 'Maghāzī', hadiths 4060–4063, p.687; and *Fatḥ al-Bārī*, vol. 2, p.1799.
8. Ibn ʿAbd al-Salām, *Qawāʿid*, vol. 1, pp.8, 129–130, 136–163 and *passim*.
9. See the discussion of two similar hypothetical cases in Ghazālī, *Mustaṣfā*, vol. 1, pp.420–422.
10. This is based on al-Shāṭibī's discussion of this question in the fifth proposition of the second section of 'Kitāb al-Maqāṣid' – Author. See *al-Muwāfaqāt*, vol. 1/2, pp.628–642.

15: CATEGORIES OF *MAṢLAḤAH* INTENDED BY ISLAMIC LEGISLATION

1. The earliest classification of the Shariʿah objectives according to their necessity for human existence is that made by Imām al-Ḥaramayn al-Juwaynī in conjunction with his discussion of the types of the underlying reasons for (*ʿilal*) the Shariʿah commands and the varieties of *qiyās* (*Burhān*, vol. 2, pp.602–604). It constituted a framework for subsequent *uṣūl al-fiqh* scholars, who only refined and elaborated it without altering its basic structure.
2. Describing the intertribal strife and warfare that had prevailed amongst the

Arabs during the pagan era of ignorance, the poet Zuhayr said: the verse is in his *Muᶜallaqah* (ode):

You two came too late for the rescue of the tribes of ᶜAbs and Dhubyān When the war between them had become so furious and they had destroyed one another. – Author.

See Yaḥyā ibn ᶜAlī al-Tabrīzī, *Sharḥ al-Qaṣā'id al-ᶜAshr*, p.136; Aḥmad ibn Muḥammad ibn al-Naḥḥās, *Sharḥ al-Qaṣā'id al-Mshhūrāt al-Mawsūmāt bi al-Muᶜallaqāt* (Beirut: Dār al-Kutub al-ᶜIlmiyyah, 1405/1985), vol. 1, p.105. Although the author originally cited this verse in the body of the text, we deemed it more appropriate to transfer it to the notes.

3. Ghazālī, *Mustaṣfā*, vol. 1, p.417; Abū Zakariyā Yaḥyā ibn Mūsā al-Rahūnī, *Tuḥfat al-Mas'ūl fī Sharḥ Mukhtaṣar Muntahā al-Sūl* (being a commentary on Ibn al-Ḥājib's *Mukhtaṣar Muntahā al-Sūl*), ed. Yusuf al-Akhdhar al-Qayyim (Dubai: Dār al-Buḥūth li al-Dirāsāt al-Islāmiyyah wa Iḥyā' al-Turāth, 1422/2002), vol. 4, p.102; Qarāfī, *Sharḥ Tanqīḥ al-Fuṣūl*, p.304 and *Dhakhīrah*, vol. 1, p.126; Shāṭibī, *Muwāfaqāt*, vol. 1/2, p.326.
4. Najm al-Dīn Abū al-Rabīᶜ Sulaymān ibn ᶜAbd al-Qawīyy al-Ṭūfī, from Ṭūfā, a village on the outskirts of Baghdad. He was born in 675 AH. He was an eminent Ḥanbalī jurist and legal theorist, whose views and theological affiliation have raised controversy. He is mostly cited for having upheld that the consideration of *maṣlahah* overrides the textual sources of the Shariᶜah. Some biographical sources have descriped him as a Shiᶜite. Al-Ṭūfī died in 716 AH in Jerusalem. Most of his extant works that cover many disciplines of classical Islamic scholarship are yet to be edited and published. His *Sharḥ Mukhtaṣar al-Rawḍah* is one of the most authoritative works on *uṣūl al-fiqh*. For Ṭūfī's view on the components of the *ḍarūriyyāt*, see *Sharḥ Mukhtaṣar al-Rawḍah*, ed. Abd Allah Abd al-Muhsin al-Turki (Beirut: Mu'assassat al-Risālah, 1419/1998), vol. 3, p.209.
5. Ghazālī, *Mustaṣfā*, vol. 1, pp.417–421.
6. Shāṭibī, *Muwāfaqāt*, vol. 1/1, pp.34–39; see also vol. 2/3, pp.5–14.
7. Along with this verse we can mention the following verses: "Say: 'Come, let me convey to you what God has [really] forbidden to you: Do not ascribe divinity, in any way, to anyone besides Him; and [do not offend against but, rather,] do good unto your parents; and do not kill your children for fear of poverty – [for] it is We who shall provide sustenance for you as well as for them; and do not commit any shameful deeds, be they open or secret; and do not take any human being's life –[the life] which God has declared to be sacred – otherwise than in [the pursuit of] justice: this has He enjoined upon you so that you might use your reason; and do not touch the substance of an orphan – save to improve it – before he comes of age. And [in all your dealings] give full

measure and weight, with equity: [however,] We do not burden any human being with more than he is well able to bear; and when you voice an opinion, be just, even though it be [against] one near of kin And [always] observe your bond with God: this has He enjoined upon you, so that you might keep it in mind' " (6:151–152). See also, (17:23–33).

8. Bukhārī, *Ṣaḥīḥ*, 'Īmān', hadith 18, p.6; 'Manāqib al-Anṣār', hadiths 3892–3893, p.654; 'Tafsīr', hadith 4894, p.868, etc.
9. Shāṭibī, *al-Muwāfaqāt*, vol. 1/1, pp.324–325.
10. In this and other similar contexts in both this and other works of his, Ibn Ashur uses the term 'world' (*ʿālam*) to mean society. We have preserved his usage, for it reflects one important feature of his thought.
11. This plague took place in 17 AH and claimed so many lives that it halted the march of the Muslim army into the Shām. Muḥammad ibn Jarīr Abū Jaʿfar al-Ṭabarī, *Tārīkh al-Rusul wa al-Mulūk*, ed. Muhammad Abu al-Fadl Ibrahim (Beirut: Dār al-Fikr, 1399 AH), vol. 5, pp.3530–3531; ʿAlī ibn Muḥammad ʿIzz al-Dīn ibn al-Athīr, *al-Kāmil fī al-Tārīkh* (Beirut: Dār al-Kitāb al-ʿArabī, n.d.), vol. 2, p.236.
12. According to the Qur'an, two things characterized the immoral conduct of the Canaanite people of the prophet Lūṭ (Lot): highway robbery and homosexuality that they used to practice openly. Thus, the interpretation alluded to by the author consists of the fact that the expression "and thus go against the way of nature" (*wa taqṭaʿūna al-sabīl*) means the "the cutting of the natural way of procreation by sexually associating with men and abstaining from women." Ibn ʿAṭiyyah, *al-Muḥarrar al-Wajīz*, vol. 4, pp.314–315. This interpretation is also upheld by Zamakhsharī, Rāzī, and Baghawī (Asad, *The Message of the Qur'an*, p.610, note 24).
13. Hysterectomy is the surgical removal of the uterus; tubal ligation is the surgical procedure commonly known as "tying the tubes". These procedures might be used for genuine medical reasons to protect the woman's health. They might also be used merely to avoid the trouble of rearing children by women not concerned about motherhood. While in the first case such procedures may be permissable or even mandatory in the Shariʿah, as they lead to the protection of life, in the second case they are totally forbidden as they undermine one of the fundamental objectives of the Shariʿah consisting of the preservation of mankind through procreation.
14. *Ḥāshiyat al-Banānī ʿalā Jamʿ al-Jawāmiʿ*, vol. 2, pp.432–433.
15. Shāṭibī, *Muwāfaqāt*, vol. 1/1, pp 326.
16. See a detailed discussion of the juristic views of share-cropping in Ibn Rushd, *The Distinguished Jurist's Primer*, vol. 2, pp.293–300.
17. The eighty-lashes penalty for slander has been prescribed in the following

verse: "And as for those who accuse chaste women [of adultery], and then are unable to provide four witnesses [in support of their accusation], flog them with eighty stripes; and ever after refuse to accept from them any testimony – since it is they, they that are truly depraved" (24:4).

"By obvious implication, this injunction applies also to cases where a woman accuses a man of illicit sexual intercourse, and is subsequently unable to prove her accusation legally. The severity of the punishment to be meted out in such cases, as well as the requirement of four witnesses – instead of the two that Islamic Law regards as sufficient in all other criminal and civil suits – is based on the imperative necessity of preventing slander and off-hand accusations. As laid down in several authentic sayings of the Prophet, the evidence of the four witnesses must be direct, and not merely circumstantial: in other words, it is not sufficient for them to have witnessed a situation which made it evident that sexual intercourse was taking place: they must have witnessed the sexual act as such, and must be able to prove this to the entire satisfaction of the judicial authority (Rāzī, summing up the views of the greatest exponents of Islamic Law). Since such a complete evidence is extremely difficult, if not impossible, to obtain, it is obvious that the purpose of the above Qur'anic injunction is to preclude, in practice, all third-party accusations relating to illicit sexual intercourse – for, 'man has been created weak' (4:28) – and to make a proof of adultery dependent on a voluntary, faith-inspired confession of the guilty parties themselves." Muhammad Asad, *The Message of the Qur'an*, pp.533–534, note 7.

18. See the author's discussion of the question of temporary marriage in chapter 34 of Part III.
19. The customs (*khiṣāl*) of *fiṭrah* consist of what has been described in the following tradition. Abū Hurayrah said, "There are five things from the *fiṭrah*: cutting the nails, trimming the moustache, removing the hair from the armpit, shaving the pubic region, and circumcision." Mālik ibn Anas, *Muwaṭṭa'*, 'Jāmi'', hadith 1666, p.660; Bukhārī, 'Libās', hadiths 5889–5891, p.1036.
20. Ghazālī, *Mustaṣfā*, vol. 1, p.417.
21. The author has devoted chapter 24 to this important topic of the prohibition of evasive legal means (*sadd al-dharā'i'*).
22. See Juwaynī, *Burhān*, vol. 2, pp.602–610 and Ghazālī, *Mustaṣfā*, vol. 1, pp.420–432.
23. Zayd ibn Thābit ibn al-Dhaḥḥāk (Abū Khārijah) was born in Madinah eleven years before the Hijra (in 611 AC) but was raised in Makkah. His father was killed when he was 6 years old, and at the age of 11 he emigrated to Madinah, at approximately the same time as the Prophet in 622 AC. Zayd and his family were among the first *Anṣārs* (helpers) to accept Islam, when members of his

clan embraced the faith and swore allegiance to the Prophet in 1 AH. Not yet 13, Zayd personally appealed to the Prophet to let him join the Muslim army, which was preparing for the Battle of Badr (2 AH) against the Makkan pagans. On account of his youth, the Prophet refused his request and sent him home, much to the distress of his mother, al-Nawār bint Mālik. A couple of years later, he again attempted to enlist in the Muslim army preparing for the Battle of Uhud (3 AH) with a group of other teenagers, some of whom were admitted to the ranks, but the Messenger again rejected Zayd owing to his youth and inexperience. Maybe the Prophet foresaw the heavy burden history would later place on the shoulders of this young man!

Twice rejected for military service, Zayd continued his efforts to work for the cause of Islam. Though young in age, he was academically inclined and was also gifted in languages. He could read and write (a rare accomplishment at that time). He excelled in Arabic and distinguished himself in the recitation of the Qur'an. For these reasons, the Prophet selected him as his Chief Scribe of the Qur'an (*kātib al-nabiyy*), despite his youth. It has been reported that the Prophet requested Zayd to learn Hebrew and Syriac to assist him with diplomatic letters and correspondence, later sent to neighboring heads of state, inviting them to Islam. Then, in his early twenties, Zayd became an exponent of the Qur'an and one of those who had memorized the existing Revelation as taught by the Prophet himself. Ḥadīth records also state that Zayd had the unique distinction of witnessing the Prophet's recitation before the angel Jibrīl during the last Ramadan.

Zayd ibn Thābit played a key role in the collection of the written Qur'an. The first Caliph, Abū Bakr, commissioned him for this task upon a suggestion by ʿUmar ibn al-Khaṭṭāb in the wake of the Battle of Yamāmah (12 AH) in which many *ḥuffāẓ* (memorizers of the Qur'an), 70 according to some reports, were killed. ʿUthmān ibn ʿAffān, the third Caliph, recommissioned Zayd as head of a committee entrusted with the task of preparing copies of the Qur'an. The work of this committee resulted in what has come to be known as "*ʿUthmān's Muṣḥaf*" (Uthmani Codex).

In addition to this vital task, Zayd ibn Thābit was a jurist who was highly respected for his scholarship by fellow Companions during the first century AH. According to hadith historians, Zayd related 92 traditions. When he died in 45/665, Abū Hurayrah said: "The scholar of this nation has died today; may God make Ibn ʿAbbās his successor."

24. The war of Yamāmah was the first internal challenge to the first Caliph, Abū Bakr. As soon as the news of the death of the Prophet Muhammad spread beyond the environs of Madinah, false prophets appeared in many parts of the country. The most famous among them were Musaylamah in Yamāmah,

Ṭulayḥah al-Asadī in Najd, Luqayṭ ibn Mālik in Oman, and al-Aswad ʿAnsī in the Yemen. Some of them wanted the government of Madinah to share its authority with them, and some others wanted "autonomy" in their territories. Abū Bakr sent Muslim troops, which suppressed them and put an end to the civil war which they had tried to provoke.

25. See the story of the collection of the Qur'an in Bukhārī, *Ṣaḥīḥ*, 'Tafsīr al-Qur'an', hadith 4679, p.804; 'Faḍā'il al-Qur'an', hadiths 4986–4987, pp.894–895; 'Aḥkām', hadith 7191, pp.1238–1239; 'Tawḥīd', hadith 7425, p.1277. See also Aḥmad ibn Ḥanbal, *al-Musnad*, vol. 1, p.13; Tirmidhī, *Sunan*, 'Tafsīr Sūrat al-Tawbah', *Bāb* 18. See in English, Muhammad A. Draz, *Introduction to the Qur'an*, trans. Ayeshah Abdel-Haleem (London & New York: I.B. Tauris, 2000), pp.15–24. For a recent comprehensive and critical treatment of the issues pertaining to the compilation of the Qur'an in comparison with the Old and New Testaments, see M.M. Al-Azami, *The History of the Qur'anic Text from Revelation to Compilation* (Leicester: UK Islamic Academy, 2003).

26. Literally, *dīwān* means a register. The first register was instituted by ʿUmar ibn al-Khaṭṭāb; this *dīwān* listed the soldiers and notables who received a pension from the state. Under the Umayyads, *diwāns* were created for the assessment and collection of land taxes, for correspondence, for the post office, and for expenditure. Originally these *dīwāns* were recorded in local languages, but under ʿAbd al-Malik ibn Marwān they were gradually Arabized. The Abbasids elaborated the *dīwān* system established by the Umayyads and provided for a central bureaucracy headed by an administrative secretary, the *wazīr*.

27. The term *sawād* refers to the Iraqi countryside under Khosrau's rule, which Muslims conquered in the reign of ʿUmar ibn al-Khaṭṭāb. It was called "black land" (*arḍ al-sawād*) owing to its being darkened by thick vegetation and trees. ʿUmar refused to divide it between the soldiers who participated in conquering it on both doctrinal and practical grounds. For more details on its topography and the juristic debate caused by ʿUmar's policy concerning it, see al-Māwardī, *The Ordinances of Government*, pp.189–193.

28. This statement by ʿUmar ibn ʿAbd al-ʿAzīz has already been documented.

29. Abū Muḥammad ʿAbd Allāh ibn Abī Zayd al-Qyrawānī was born in 310 AH and died in 386 AH. He lived in the old Islamic city of Qayrawān (Kairouan), the capital of the Aghlabid dynasty (184/800–296/908) and the seat of Islamic learning in North Africa for many centuries. He was an authority on many branches of Islamic scholarship such as Qur'an exegesis, fiqh and *uṣūl al-fiqh*, and *ʿilm al-kalām*. His authority on Mālikī jurisprudence was such that he was recognized as Mālik Junior (*Mālik al-Ṣaghīr*). Biographers attribute to him over twenty-five books in different disciplines.

30. The early doctrinal view keeping that dogs in urban areas is forbidden was based on the following Tradition. It is reported on the authority of ʿAbd Allāh ibn ʿUmar that the Prophet said: "Whoever acquires a dog other than a sheep-dog or hunting dog, will have two *qīrāt* deducted from the reward of his good deeds every day." Mālik ibn Anas, *Muwaṭṭa'*, 'Jāmiʿ', hadiths 1764–1765, p.688; Bukhārī, *Ṣaḥīḥ*, 'Dhabā'iḥ & Ṣayd', hadiths 5480–5482, p.976; Muslim, *Ṣaḥīḥ*, hadiths 1574–1576, pp.611–612.
However, later jurists upheld the lawfulness of acquiring watchdogs in urban areas during times of fear and insecurity based on the view of Ibn Abī Zayd mentioned by the author. See in this regard, Ali ibn Abd al-Salam al-Tasuli, *al-Bahjah fī Sharḥ al-Tuḥfah* (Beirut: Dār al-Maʿrifah, 1397/1977), vol. 2, p.46.
31. Ahmad ibn Muhammad Zarruq, *Sharḥ Risālat ibn Abī Zayd al-Qayrawānī* (Beirut: Dār al-Fikr, 1402/1982), vol. 2, pp.413–414; *Tasūlī, al-Bahjah fī Sharḥ al-Tuḥfah*, vol. 2, p.46; Ali ibn Khalaf al-Manufi, *Kifāyat al-Ālib al-Rabbānī ʿAlā Risālat ibn Abī Zayd al-Qayrawānī*, ed. Ahmad Hamdi Imam (Cairo: Maktabat al-Madanī, 1407/1987), vol. 4, pp.441–442.
32. Bukhārī, *Ṣaḥīḥ*, 'Aḥkām', hadith 7158, pp.1231–1232; Muslim, *Ṣaḥīḥ*, 'Aqḍiyyah', hadith 1717, p.681; Abū Dāwūd, *Sunan*, ed. Muhammad Muhyi al-Din Abd al-Hamid (Ṣaydā/Beirut: al-Maktabah al-ʿAṣriyyah, n.d.), 'Aqḍiyah', hadith 3588, vol. 3, p.382;
33. This is the second hemistich of a verse of poetry.

16: UNIVERSALITY OF THE ISLAMIC SHARIʿAH

1. See the complete text of the Tradition in Bukhārī, *Ṣaḥīḥ*, 'Tayammum', hadith 335, p.58; Dārimī, *Sunan*, ed. Fawwaz Ahmad Zamarli et al. (Beirut: Dār al-Rayyān & Dār al-Kitāb al-ʿArabī, 1407/1987), 'Siyar', hadith 2467, vol. 2, p.244.
2. It was for this reason that Arab Christians were most reluctant to accept Islam, for they saw themselves as the followers of the right religion. For the same reason, the Jews in Madinah resolutely stuck to their religion except for very few individuals who embraced Islam. – Author.
3. Dhī Qār, also know as Yawm Qurāqir, Yawn al-Jibāyāt, Yawm Dhāt al-ʿAjram, and Yawm Baṭḥā' Dhī Qār, was one of the fiercest battles between the Arabs and Persians in the pre-Islamic period. It was fought by a well, known as Dhī Qār, which belonged to the Bakr ibn Wā'il tribe, not far from the present location of the city of Kufah. This battle took place during the reign over the Lakhmid kingdom of Ḥīrah (southern Iraq and northern Arabia) by Iyyās ibn Qubayṣah ibn Abī ʿAfrā' ibn al-Nuʿmān ibn Ḥayyah al-Ṭā'ī (605–614 AC), an Arab client-king of Persia, between the Arabs and the Persians. The immediate

reason for this battle is said to have been the claim made by Chosroe for the possessions of al-Nuʿmān ibn al-Mundhir, whom he had killed. Since the people of Bakr ibn Wā'il, to whom al-Numan's possessions had been entrusted, rejected the claim, Chosroe sent a huge army to punish the rebellious tribe and extract the claimed possessions. This provoked other Arab tribes and the battle turned out to be a serious defeat for the Persian imperial army and a resounding victory for the Arabs.

Yawm Ḥalīmah refers to the battle that took place in 554 AC between the Lakhmid king al-Mundhir (Greek: Almundarus) ibn Mā' al-Samā' and the Ghassanid king of Syria al-Ḥārith (Greek: Arethas) ibn Jabalah (also known as al-Ḥārith ibn Abī Shammar), a vassal king of the Byzantine empire. According to al-Kalbī, it is called the Day of Ḥalīmah because when al-Ḥārith ibn Abī Shammar was training the army he sent to fight al-Mundhir, Ḥalīmah, the daughter of al-Ḥārith, perfumed all the soldiers and provided them with winding-sheets. However, a stronger view upheld by annalists (like Abū ʿUbaydah Maʿmar ibn al-Muthannā [d. 209 AH]) and historians (like Ibn al-Athīr) is that the name Ḥalīmah rather refers to a place that is also known as Dhāt al-Ḥiyār.

Since the Lakhmids were allied to the Persians and the Ghassanids were the allies of the Byzantines, the Battle of Ḥalīmah can be seen as a war by proxy between the two great empires, as pointed out by the author.

4. Bukhārī, *Ṣaḥīḥ*, 'Ilm', hadith 105, pp.23–24; 'Ḥajj', hadiths 1739–1742, pp.280–281; 'Maghazi', hadith 4406, p.747; 'Hudud', hadith 6785, p.1170; 'Fitan', hadith 7078, pp.1219–1220; 'Tawhid', hadith 7447, p.1283; Muslim, *Ṣaḥīḥ*, 'Qasamah', hadith 1679, pp.663–664; Dārimī, *Sunan*, 'Manāsik', hadith 1916, vol. 2, p.92. It is also in Tirmidhī (*Tafsīr al-Qur'an*) and Ibn Mājah (*Manāsik and Fitan*).
5. Abū Dāwūd, *Sunan*, 'Ashribah', hadith 3681, vol. 2/3, p.327; Nasā'ī, *Sunan*, 'Ashribah', hadith 5607, vol. IV/8, p.300; Tirmidhī, *Sunan*, 'Ashribah', hadith 1865, vol. 2/4, p.292.
6. For a comprehensive discussion of the problems of unqualified and qualified words and statements and the ways of solving them, see Muhammad Fathi al-Durayni, *al-Manāhij al-Uṣūliyyah fī al-Ijtihād bi al-Ra'y fī al-Tashrīʿ al-Islāmī* (Beirut: Mu'assassat al-Risālah, 1418/1997), pp.519–543.
7. Muslim, *Ṣaḥīḥ*, 'Zuhd', hadith 3004, p.1145.
8. Bukhārī, *Ṣaḥīḥ*, 'ʿIlm', hadith 112, 24; 'Luqaṭah', hadith 2434, pp.391–392; 'Diyāt', hadith 6880, p.1185; Muslim, *Ṣaḥīḥ*, 'Ḥajj', hadith 1355, p.506.
9. See a detailed discussion and exposition of issues of solitary reports (*akhbār āḥād*) by al-Layth ibn Saʿd in a long letter to Mālik ibn Anas, cited verbatim in Ibn Qayyim al-Jawziyyah, *Iʿlām Muwaqqiʿīn ʿan Rabb al-ʿĀlamīn*, ed.

Muhammad Abd al-Salam Ibrahim (Beirut: Dār al-Kutub al-ʿIlmiyyah, 1411/1991), vol. 2/3, pp.69–73. See also, al-Imām Muḥammad ibn Idrīs al-Shāfiʿī, *al-Risālah fī Uṣūl al-Fiqh*, trans. Majid Khadduri (Cambridge, UK: The Islamic Texts Society, 1997), pp.246–284; Bernard G. Weiss, *The Search for God's Law: Islamic Jurisprudence in the Writings of Saif al-Dīn al-Āmidī* (Salt Lake City, UT: University of Utah Press, 1992), pp.291–328.

10. For an exposition of Mālik's view on this issue, see Abū Bakr Muḥammad ibn ʿAbd Allāh ibn al-ʿArabī, *Aḥkām al-Qur'an*, ed. Ali Muhammad Bijawi (Beirut: Dār al-Jīl, 1407/1987), vol. 1, p.206.
11. Bukhārī, *Ṣaḥīḥ*, 'Libās', hadiths 5931–5948, pp.1040–1042; Muslim, *Ṣaḥīḥ*, 'Libās', hadith 2125, p.845; Tirmidhī, *Sunan*, 'Libās', hadith 1759, vol. 4, p.236; Ibn Mājah, *Sunan*, 'Nikāḥ', hadith 1996, vol. 3, p.367.
12. The author did not, however, maintain this view in his interpretation of the verse quoted here. Cf. his *Tafsīr al-Taḥrīr wa al-Tanwīr*, vol. 11/22, pp.106–107.
13. Dāraquṭnī, *Sunan*, 'Ashribah', hadith 104, vol. 2/4, p.298. The complete version of this Tradition is cited by the author in Chapter "Alteration and Confirmation in the Shariʿah."
14. Abū Bakr ibn Muḥammad ibn ʿAmr ibn Ḥazm was a man of knowledge, with an outstanding mastery of history. He served both as judge and governor of Madinah. When he died in the year 120 AH, he was more than 80 years old.
15. It is narrated by Bukhārī (*Ṣaḥīḥ*, "ʿIlm', Bāb 34, p.22) that ʿUmar ibn ʿAbd al-ʿAzīz wrote to Abū Bakr ibn Ḥazm, "Look for the knowledge of Hadith and have it written down, for I am afraid that religious knowledge will vanish and the learned men will pass away (die). Do not accept anything save the Sayings (hadiths) of the Prophet. Circulate knowledge and teach the ignorant, for knowledge does not vanish except when it is kept secret (to oneself)."
16. *Mawāqīt* (sing. *mīqāt*) are the places where the *iḥrām* (i.e., intention to start the Ḥajj as well as wearing the Ḥajj attire) is to be formulated. For more details, see Ibn Rushd, *The Distinguished Jurist's Primer*, vol. 1, pp.381–384.
17. See a detailed discussion of the different views on the renting of land in Ibn Rushd, *The Distinguished Jurist's Primer*, vol. 2, pp.264–267.
18. *Bayʿ al-wafā'* was introduced and formulated by Ḥanafī jurists of Transoxiana during the 5th century AH. It has been expressed in different terms in other juristic schools, such as *bayʿ al-ʿuhdah* (the Mālikīs), *bayʿ al-ṭāʿah* (the Ḥanbalīs), *bayʿ al-rajā'* (the Zaydīs), and *bayʿ al-khiyār* (the Imāmīs).

    It is defined as "a contract meant to ensure the payment of debt and to make ...". Shaikh al-Islam Abū ʿAbd Allāh Muḥammad Bayram II (d. 1247 H), "al-Wafā' bi mā Yataʿallaqu bi-Bayʿ al-Wafā'", ed. and ann. Muhammad al-Habib ibn al-Khujah, *Majallat Majma*ᶜ *al-Fiqh al-Islāmī*, no.7, vol. 3, 1412/1992, pp.187–306. See also, *The Mejelle*, English translation of *Majallat al-Aḥkām al-*ᶜ*Adliyyah* (a compendium of Islamic civil law according to the Ḥanafī school), (Kuala Lumpur: The Other Press, n.d.), pp.58–59; Mustafa Ahmad al-Zarqa, ᶜ*Aqd al-Bay*ᶜ (Damascus: Dār al-Qalam, 1420/1999), pp.155–165.

19. "The absence of any 'hardship' in the religion of Islam is due to several factors: (1) it is free of any dogma or mystical proposition which might make the Qur'anic doctrine difficult to understand or might even conflict with man's innate reason; (2) it avoids all complicated ritual or system of taboos which would impose undue restriction on man's everyday life; (3) it rejects all self-mortification and exaggerated asceticism, which must unavoidably conflict with man's true nature ; and (4) it takes fully into account the fact that 'man has been created weak'." Asad, *The Message of the Qur'an*, pp.517–518

20. This saying has already been documented.

21. Bukhārī, *Ṣaḥīḥ*, 'Iᶜtiṣām', hadith 7289, p.1254; Muslim, *Ṣaḥīḥ*, 'Faḍā'il', hadith 2358, pp.920–921. On the issue of the 'silence of the Lawgiver' (*sukūt al-Shāri*ᶜ) and its juristic significance and implications, see Nuᶜman Jughaym, *Ṭuruq al-Kashf* ᶜ*an Maqāṣid al-Shāri*ᶜ (Amman: Dār al-Nafā'is, 1422/2002), pp.187–213.

22. Abū Bakr Abd Allah ibn Muḥammad ibn Abī Shaybah, *al-Muṣannaf*, ed. Kamal Yusuf al-Hut (Riyadh: Maktabat al-Rushd, 1409), hadith 22716, vol. 4, p.518; Aḥmad ibn Muḥammad ibn Salāmah ibn ᶜAbd al-Malik Abū Jaᶜfar al-Ṭaḥāwī, *Sharḥ Ma*ᶜ*ānī al-Āthār*, ed. Muhammad Zuhri al-Najjar (Beirut: Dār al-Kutub al-ᶜIlmiyyah, 1399), vol. 4, p.123.
Similar reports are also available in Bukhārī, *Ṣaḥīḥ*, 'Shufᶜah', hadith 2258, p.359; 'Ḥiyal', hadiths 6977–6981, pp.1203–1204; Abū Dāwūd Sulaymān ibn al-Ashᶜath, *Sunan*, ed. Muḥammad Muḥyī al-Dīn ᶜAbd al-Ḥamīid (Beirut: Dār al-Fikr al-ᶜArabī, n. d.), 'Ijārah', hadith 3517, vol. 3, p.186; Aḥmad ibn al-Ḥusyan ibn ᶜAlī Abū Bakr al-Bayhaqī, *al-Sunan al-Kubrā*, ed. Muḥammad ᶜAbd al-Qādir ᶜAṭā (Makkah al-Mukarramah: Maktabat Dār al-Bāz, 1414/1994), hadith 11361, vol. 6, p.106; Sulaymān ibn Aḥmad ibn Ayyūb Abū al-Qāsim al-Ṭabarānī, *al-Mu*ᶜ*jam al-Kabīr*, ed. Ḥamdī ibn ᶜAbd al-Majīd al-Salafī (Mosul: Maktabat al-ᶜUlūm wa al-Ḥikam, 1408/1988), hadith 6803, vol. 7, p.196.

23. In this respect, two traditions have been narrated, one on the authority of Jābir ibn ᶜAbd Allāh and the other on the authority of ᶜAlī ibn Abī Ṭālib and ᶜAbd Allāh ibn ᶜAbbās, according to which the Prophet judged a case on the basis of pre-emption for a neighbor. Nasā'ī, *Sunan*, ed. Abd al-Fattah Abu Ghuddah (Aleppo: Maktab al-Maṭbūᶜāt al-Islāmiyyah, 1406/1986), hadith 4705

(Jabir), vol. 7, p.321; Ibn Abī Shaybah, *Muṣannaf*, ed. Kamal Yusuf al-Hut (Riyadh: Maktabat al-Rushd, 1409 AH), hadith 22716 (ʿAlī & ʿAbd Allāh), vol. 4, p.518.

See a detailed discussion of the different views with their respective evidence in Ibn Rushd, *The Distinguished Jurist's Primer*, vol. 2, pp.307–316; Badr al-Dīn Abū Muḥammad Maḥmūd ibn Aḥmad al-ʿAynī, *ʿUmdat al-Qārī Sharḥ Ṣaḥīḥ al-Bukhārī* (Beirut: Dār Iḥyā' al-Turāth al-ʿArabī, n. d.), vol. 12, p.21.

24. Muhammad ibn Muhammad al-Raʿi, *Intiṣār al-Faqīr al-Sālik* (Beirut: Dār al-Gharb al-Islāmī, 1981), p.186.

17: EQUALITY IN THE SHARIʿAH

1. Aḥmad ibn Ḥanbal, *al-Musnad*, vol. 4, p.158 and vol. 5, p.411; Abd al-Rauf ibn ʿAli al-Manawi, *Fayḍ al-Qadīr bi-Sharḥ al-Jāmiʿ al-Ṣaghīr* (Beirut: Dār al-Maʿrifah, 1972), hadith 6368, vol. 5, p.37.

2. See a more detailed discussion of this issue by the author in his *Uṣūl al-Niẓām al-Ijtimāʿī fī al-Islām*, pp.156–162.

   Muslim legal theorists (*uṣūliyyūn*) dealt with this issue in their discussion of the subject *ʿumūm*. See for example, Abū Muḥammad ʿAlī ibn Aḥmad ibn Saʿīd Ibn Ḥazm, *al-Iḥkām fī Uṣūl al-Aḥkām*, ed. Muhammad Muhammad Tamir (Beirut: Dār al-Kutub al-ʿIlmiyyah, 1424/2004), vol. 1, pp.408–414; al-Qarāfī, *Sharḥ Tanqīḥ al-Fuṣūl*, pp.156–157; Najm al-Dīn al-Ṭūfī, *Sharh Mukhtaṣar al-Rawḍah*, vol. 2, pp.514–5523; Badr al-Dīn Muḥammad ibn Bahādar ibn ʿAbd Allāh al-Zarkashī, *al-Baḥr al-Muḥīṭ Fī Uṣūl al-Fiqh*, ed. Muhammad Muhammad Tamir (Beirut: Dār al-Kutub al-ʿIlmiyyah, 1421/2000), vol. 2, pp.331–336; Muḥammad ibn ʿAlī al-Shawkānī, *Irshād al-Fuḥūl Ilā Taḥqīq al-Ḥaqq Min ʿIlm al-Uṣūl*, ed. Muhammad Subhi ibn Hasan Hallaq (Damascus/Beirut: Dār Ibn Kathīr, 1421/2000), pp.435–439; Bernard G. Weiss, *The Search For God's Law*, pp.437–438.

3. This is verse 12 of Surah 60, which reads as follows: "O Prophet! Whenever believing women come to you to pledge their allegiance to you, [pledging] that [henceforth] they will not ascribe divinity, in any way, to aught but God, will not steal, will not commit adultery, will not kill their children, will not indulge in slander, falsely creating it from nothing, and will not disobey you in anything [that you declare to be] right – then accept their pledge of allegiance, and pray to God to forgive them their [past] sins: for, behold, God is Much-Forgiving, a Dispenser of Grace."

4. This is based on the Prophet's saying reported by Bukhārī (*Ṣaḥīḥ*, 'Farā'iḍ', hadith 6764, p.1167) on the authority of Usāmah ibn Zayd: "A Muslim cannot be the heir of a disbeliever, nor can a disbeliever be the heir of a Muslim."

The juristic agreement on this issue does not, however, rise to the level of universal consensus (ijmaʿ) as the author's expression might imply. At best, it is a majority view. Among the scholars who contested it were Ibn Taymiyyah and his disciples Shams al-Dīn Abū ʿAbd Allāh Muḥammad ibn Abī Bakr Ibn Qayyim al-Jawziyyah. The latter devoted to this question a lengthy and detailed discussion in his book *Aḥkām Ahl al-Dhimmah*, ed. Subhi al-Salih (Beirut: Dār al-ʿIlm li al-Malāyīn, 1994), vol. 2, pp.462–474. Recently, the renowned scholar Yusuf al-Qaradawi has strongly supported the position of the two Hanbalī jurists in a fatwa that he issued in response to a question from a British Muslim concerning the lawfulness of inheriting from his Christian parents. See his *Fī Fiqh al-Aqalliyāt al-Muslimah* (Cairo: Dār al-Shurūq, 1422/2001), pp.126–131.

5. Abū Dāwūd Sulaymān ibn al-Ashʿath, *Sunan* (Istanbul: Dār al-Daʿwah, 1413/1992), 'Jihad', hadith 2751, vol. 3, p.183.

6. This juridical provision is based on the Tradition narrated by ʿAbd Allāh ibn ʿAmr ibn al-ʿĀṣ (Abū Dāwūd, *Sunan*, 'Jihad', hadith 2751, vol. 3, p.183) that the Apostle of God said: "Muslims are equal in respect of blood. The lowest of them is entitled to give protection (*dhimmah*) on behalf of them, and the one residing far away may give protection on behalf of them. They are like one hand against all those who are outside the community. Those who have quick mounts should return them to those who have slow mounts, and those who came out along with a detachment (should return to) those who are stationed. A believer shall not be killed for an unbeliever, nor a confederate within the term of confederation with him."

   However, as the author has pointed out, there is disagreement amongst the jurists in this regard as well as on the acceptance of the testimony of non-Muslim subjects (*Dhimmīs*) and unrighteous (*fāsiq*) people. See further details on these two issues in al-Māwardī, *The Ordinances of Government*, pp.251–252; Ibn Rushd, *The Distinguished Jurist's Primer*, vol. 2, pp.483–484 and 556–557; al-Shawkānī, *Nayl al-Awṭār*, pp.1406–1411; Ibn Ashur, *Tafsīr al-Taḥrīr wa al-Tanwīr*, vol. 2, p.140 and vol. 4/7, pp.95–97.

7. This is part of a long directive that the Prophet used to address to the leaders of expeditions against the Arab polytheists. Its exact wording runs as follows: "If they (Arab polytheists) accept the *dhimmah* contract (*ʿaqd al-dhimmah*), then inform them that they have the same rights and duties as Muslims." ʿAlā' al-Dīn Abū Bakr al-Kāsānī, *Badā'iʿ al-Ṣanā'iʿ fī Tartīb al-Sharā'iʿ* (Cairo: Sharikat al-Maṭbūʿāt al-ʿIlmiyyah, 1327 AH), vol. 7, p.100. See also, Abd al-Karim Zaydan, *Aḥkām al-Dhimmiyyīn wa al-Musta'manīn* (Beirut: Mu'assasat al-Risālah, 1988), vol. 2, p.70.

8. The view of the jurists regarding the illegibility of woman for the office of the

supreme leader (imamate) is mainly based on a isolated Tradition reported by Abū Bakrah. He said, "During the battle of the Camel [between ʿAlī and ʿĀ'ishah], God benefited me with a Word (I heard from the Prophet). When the Prophet heard the news that the people of Persia had made the daughter of Khosroe their Queen (ruler), he said, 'Never will succeed such a nation as makes a woman their ruler'." Bukhārī, *Ṣaḥīḥ*, 'Maghāzī', hadith 4425, p.753 and 'Fitan', hadith 7099, p.1224.

This issue in particular and women's participation in politics in general have been the subject of heated debate of the last few decades, especially as much criticism has been levied against Islam on account of this and other related issues. See a succint discussion of the conflicting views and their respective arguments in Rached al-Ghannushi, *al-Ḥurriyyāt al-ʿĀmmah fī al-Dawlah al-Islāmiyyah* (Beirut: Markaz Dirāsāt al-Wiḥdah al-ʿArabiyyah, 1993), pp.128–133.

9. Summing up the classical position of Muslim jurists on women's eligibility to judgeship, al-Māwardī said: "Women, although judgements may take their testimony into consideration, are not qualified to hold major government positions. According to Abū Ḥanīfah, women may pass judgement in areas where their testimonies are valid, but not in areas where their testimonies are not acceptable. Ibn Jarīr al-Ṭabarī departed from the consensus by making women eligible to hold judgeships under all circumstances, but there is no strength in a view that meets with unanimous rejection, in addition to God's own words: 'Men are in charge of women, for God has preferred in bounty one of them over the other' (Qur'an 4:34)." Al-Māwardī, *The Ordinances of Government*, p.72.

10. According to the majority of Muslim jurists, *ḥaḍānah* or custody belongs to the mother if she is divorced by the husband and the child is still of tender age. This majority view has been based upon the following Tradition, according to which the Prophet is reported to have said: "He who causes separation between a mother and her child, God will cause a separation between him and his loved ones on the Day of Judgement." Ibn Rushd, *The Distinguished Jurist's Primer*, vol. 2, p.66.

11. This is by virtue of the following Qur'anic provision: "And call upon two of your men to act as witnesses; and if two men are not available, then a man and two women from among such as are acceptable to you as witnesses, so that if one of them should make a mistake, the other could remind her." (2:282).

"The stipulation that two women may be substituted for one male witness does not imply any reflection on woman's moral and intellectual capacities: it is obviously due to the fact that, as a rule, women are less familiar with business procedures than men and, therefore, more liable to commit mistakes in this respect." Asad, *The Message of the Qur'an*, p.63, note 273. See a detailed exposition of the different juristic views on the validity and scope of women's testimony independently or with male witnesses in Ibn Rushd, *The Distinguished Jurist's Primer*, vol. 2, pp. 558–560; Abd al-Ghani al-Maydani, *al-Lubāb fī Sharḥ al-Kitāb* (Beirut: al-Maktabah al-ʿIlmiyyah, 1400/1980), vol. 4, p. 54.

12. The author is here merely reiterating the classical view of Muslim jurists concerning the Qurayshite descent as one of the conditions for the office of the caliphate. However, the validity of this condition has been disputed by a number of eminent jurists and scholars, such as Imām al-Ḥaramayn Abū al-Maʿālī al-Juwaynī and Ibn Khaldūn. For al-Juwaynī, *al-Ghayāthī*, (Beirut: Dār al-Kutub al-ʿIlmiyyah, 1417/1997, p.140), the Qurayshite descent (*al-nasab al-Qurayshī*) is unnecessary on the grounds that "nothing of the purposes (*maqāṣid*) of the imamate depends on belonging to a specific descent or ancestry", for we know that the purpose of investing someone with the office of the imam is to insure "the orderly running (*intiẓām*) of the affairs of Muslims and Islam."

In the same vein, Ibn Khaldūn discussed the condition of the Qurayshite descent and reformulated it in his theory on group feeling and social cohesion. After stating the alleged consensus on it among the jurists, he said: "We shall now discuss the wisdom of making descent a condition of the imamate, so that the correct facts underlying all those opinions will be recognized. We say: All religious laws must have (specific) purposes and significant meanings of their own, on account of which they were made. If we, now, investigate the wisdom of Qurashite descent as a condition (of the imamate) and the purpose which the lawgiver (Muhammad) had in mind, (we shall find that) in this connection he did not only think of the blessing that lies in direct relationship with the Prophet, as is generally (assumed). Such direct relationship exists (in the case of Qurayshite descent), and it is a blessing. However, it is known that the religious law has not as its purpose to provide blessings. Therefore, if (a specific) descent be made a condition (of the imamate), there must be a (public) interest which was the purpose behind making it into law. If we probe into the matter and analyze it, we find that the (public) interest is nothing else but regard for group feeling. (Group feeling) gives protection and helps people to press their claims. The existence of (group feeling) frees the incumbent in the position (of imam) from opposition and division. The Muslim community accepts him and his family, and he can establish friendly terms with them."

He then went on to say: "The Quraysh were able to assume the responsibility of doing away with (division) and preventing people from (splitting up). Therefore, Qurayshite descent was made a condition of the institution of (the imamate). The Quraysh represented the strongest (available) group feeling.... Thus, all the other Arabs obeyed them." Ibn Khadūn, *The Muqaddimah*, vol. 1, pp.399–400.

13. Muslim, *Ṣaḥīḥ*, 'Jihad', hadith 1780, vol. 3, pp.1406 and 1408.

18: FREEDOM IN THE SHARIᶜAH

1. ᶜAlī ibn Ḥusām al-Dīn ibn ᶜAbd al-Malik al-Muttaqī al-Hindī, *Muntakhab Kanz al-ᶜUmmāl fī Sunan al-Aqwāl wa al-Afᶜāl* (Beirut: Dār Iḥyā' al-Turāth al-ᶜArabī, 1410/1990), vol. 4, p.577.
2. This juridical norm stating that *al-Shāriᶜ mutashawwif li al-ḥurriyyah* has been mainly formulated by the jurists in conjunction with their discussion of the Shariᶜah provisions governing marriage between free men and female slaves. See for example, Shams al-Dīn Muḥammad ibn al-Khaṭīb al-Shirbīnī, *Mughnī al-Muḥtāj ilā Maᶜrifat Alfāẓ al-Minhāj*, ed. Jawbali al-Shafiᶜi (Beirut: Dār al-Fikr, 1419/1998), 'Nikāḥ', vol. 3, p.239.
   It can be inferred from numerous legal provisions (*aḥkām*) stipulated by the Shariᶜah on different occasions that all have the united aim of promoting the manumission and emancipation of slaves. The author has cited a number of these provisions throughout the present chapter.
3. In the same vein, the eminent poet-philosopher Muhammad Iqbal wrote in 1909: "The Prophet of Islam, being a link between the ancient and modern world, declared the principle of equality and though, like every wise reformer, he slightly conceded to the social conditions around him in retaining the name of slavery, he quietly took away the whole spirit of this institution... The democratic ideal of perfect equality, which had found the most uncompromising expression in the Prophet's life, could only be brought home to an extremely aristocratic people by a very cautious handling of the situation." *Thoughts and Reflections of Iqbal*, ed. and annot. by Syed Abdul Vahid (Lahore: Shaikh Muhammad Ashraf, 1992), p.39. See also a very pertinent discussion of the issue of slavery as tackled by Islam in Marcel A. Boisard, *Humanism in Islam* (Kuala Lumpur: Islamic Book Trust, 2003), pp.77–82.
4. The justification given here by the author is untenable. For one, the reason why people embraced the belief system of Islam, submitted to the laws of the Shariᶜah and belonged to its community could by no means be the fear of being enslaved by the Arab Muslims during the early Islamic conquests. Otherwise, we should expect many people to have renounced Islam following the military and political decline of Muslim power in the world.
5. Ṣafwān ibn Umayyah ibn Khalaf was a deadly enemy of Islam. His father Umayyah was killed during the battle of Badr, while his mother Nājiyah bint

al-Walīd ibn al-Mughīrah embraced Islam. When Makkah was liberated from the pagan forces of the Quraysh, Ṣafwān ran away to Jeddah with the intention of going to Yemen. ʿUmayr ibn Wahb, a close friend of Ṣafwān, who had converted to Islam after showing deep hatred and enmity against its Messenger, came to the Prophet and told him about Ṣafwān. The Prophet gave him his turban and said, "This is a sign of amnesty." ʿUmayr went to Ṣafwān with the turban and told him that he had no cause to run away, for his safety had been guaranteed. When he came to see the Prophet, he said, "Have you given me safety?" The Prophet said, "Yes, it is true." Later, he too became a Muslim and distinguished himself in the service of Islam (Ibn Hishām, *al-Sīrah al-Nabawiyyah*, vol. 2/4, p.47). Ṣafwān died in the same year as ʿUthmān ibn ʿAffān (35/656).

6. Ibn Hishām, *al-Sīrah al-Nabawiyyah*, vol. 2/4, p. 67.
7. Al-Nābighah al-Dhubyānī was a pre-Islamic Arab poet who lived in the fifth century AC. He flourished at the court of the princes of Ḥīrah, especially during the reign of al-Nuʿmān ibn al-Mundhir III.
8. Al-Nābighah al-Dhubyānī, *Dīwān*, ed. Muhammad al-Tahir ibn Ashur (Tunis: al-Sharikah al-Tūnisiyyah li al-Tawzīʿ, 1976), p.115.
9. According to Marcel Boisard, thanks to Islam's fundamental view of the human being as a creature dignified by God, his Creator, the status of slaves in Islamic society was never that of a "thing" of the Roman law. "No discredit soiled his status. Contrary to medieval Christianity, Muslim doctrine, strongly impregnated by Qur'anic prescriptions, was not influenced by the theories from Greek antiquity, especially those of Aristotle, concerning slavery." Boisard, *Humanism in Islam*, p.79.
10. Solon was the Lawmaker of Athens. He died in 559 BC. He is usually remembered as one of the Seven Wise Men of Greece, also called Sophoi. This term is traditionally used to describe a group of ancient Greek sages of the 7th and 6th centuries BC, drawn from among the outstanding politicians and political philosophers. The first listing of them was by Plato in his *Protagoras*. Although these listings differed widely, they usually included Thales of Miletus, a philosopher, and Solon, lawgiver of Athens, who are most prominently remembered. Others, hardly known now, were Pittacus of Mitylene, Bias of Priene, Myson the Chenian, Cleobulus the Lindian, and Chilon of Sparta.
11. See more details in Franz Rosenthal, *The Muslim Concept of Freedom Prior to the Nineteenth Century* (Leiden: E. J. Brill, 1960).
12. The Qur'anic account concerning Joseph's fate after he had been abandoned by his brothers runs as follows: "And there came a caravan; and they sent forth their drawer of water, and he let down his bucket into the well – [and when he

saw Joseph] he exclaimed: 'Oh, what a lucky find, this boy!' And they hid him with a view to selling him: but God had full knowledge of all that they were doing. And they sold him for a paltry price – a mere few silver coins: thus low did they value him" (12:19–20). Cf. the Biblical account in Genesis, 37:12–36 and 39:1–6.

13. In its approach to the problem of slavery, Islam adopted a "system [that] has a double characteristic: reduction of access to servitude and expansion of the way toward liberty." Boisard, *Humanism in Islam*, p.79. See more elaboration on this aspect in Ibn Ashur, *Tafsīr al-Taḥrīr wa al-Tanwīr*, vol. 3/5, pp.158–159.

14. According to the following verse:
"And it is not conceivable that a believer should slay another believer, unless it be by mistake. And upon him who has slain a believer by mistake there is the duty of freeing a believing soul from bondage and paying an indemnity to the victim's relations, unless they forgo it by way of charity. Now if the slain, while himself a believer, belonged to a people who are at war with you, [the penance shall be confined to] the freeing of a believing soul from bondage; whereas, if he belonged to a people to whom you are bound by a covenant, [it shall consist of] an indemnity to be paid to his relations in addition to the freeing of a believing soul from bondage. And he who does not have the wherewithal shall fast [instead] for two consecutive months. [This is] the atonement ordained by God: and God is indeed All-Knowing, Wise" (4:92).

15. Bukhārī, 'Ṣawm', hadith 1936, p.311; 'Hibah', hadith 2600, pp.420–421; 'Nafaqāt', hadith 5368, p.959.

16. Injurious comparison or *ẓihār* is the act of declaring one's wife to be as unlawful to one as one's mother, a practice that was a commonplace amongst the pre-Islamic Arabs. The Qur'an clearly condemned and abolished it. See verses 33:4 and 58:2–4.

17. By virtue of God's saying in the following verse:
"God will not take you to task for oaths which you may have uttered without thought, but He will take you to task for oaths which you have sworn in earnest. Thus, the breaking of an oath must be atoned for by feeding ten needy persons with more or less the same food as you are wont to give to your own families, or by clothing them, or by freeing a human being from bondage; and he who has not the wherewithal shall fast for three days [instead]. This shall be the atonement for your oaths whenever you have sworn [and broken them]. But be mindful of your oaths! Thus God makes clear unto you His messages, so that you might have cause to be grateful" (5:89).

18. Bukhārī, *Ṣaḥīḥ*, 'ʿIṭq', hadith 2521, p.407.

19. For more details concerning the treatment of the issue of slavery in classical

Islamic jurisprudence, see Ibn Rushd, *The Distinguished Jurist's Primer*, vol. 2, pp.443–474.

20. Bukhārī, *Ṣaḥīḥ*, 'ʿIṭq', hadith 2518, p.407; Muslim, *Ṣaḥīḥ*, 'Īmān', hadith 136, p.52.
21. Bukhārī, *Ṣaḥīḥ*, 'ʿIlm', hadith 97, p.22.
22. Bukhārī, *Ṣaḥīḥ*, 'Īmān', hadith 30, p.8; Muslim, *Ṣaḥīḥ*, 'Aymān', hadith 1661, p.652.
23. Ibn Mājah, *Sunan*, 'Diyyāt', hadiths 2679–2680, vol. 2, p.894.
24. Bukhārī, *Ṣaḥīḥ*, 'ʿItq', hadith 2552, p.412.
25. Ibn Ashur, *Uṣūl al-Niẓām al-Ijtimāʿī fī al-Islām*, pp.159–178.
26. Muslim, *Ṣaḥīḥ*, '*Īmān*', hadith 78, p.42; Tirmidhī, *Sunan* (Istanbul: Dār al-Daʿwah, 1413/1993), 'Fitan', hadith 2172, vol. 4, pp.469–470; Abū Dāwūd, *Sunan*, 'Malāḥim', hadith 4340, vol. 4, p.511.
27. Abū Dāwūd, *Sunan*, 'ʿIlm', hadith 3660, vol. 2/3, p.322.
28. Abū Jaʿfar Muḥammad ibn Jarīr al-Ṭabarī, *Dhuyūl Tārīkh al-Ṭabarī* (volume 11 of his *Tārīkh al-Rusul wa al-Mulūk*, ed. Muhammad Abu al-Fadl Ibrahim (Cairo: Dār al-Maʿārif, n. d.), pp.659–660. See also al-Qāḍī ʿIyāḍ ibn Mūsā al-Yaḥṣubī, *Madārik*, ed. Ahmad Bakir Mahmud (Beirut: Dār Maktabat al-Ḥayāt; Tripoli (Libya): Dār Maktabat al-Fikr, 1387/1967), vol. 1, pp.191–193.
29. According to Abū Ḥanīfah, al-Shāfiʿī and Aḥmad ibn Ḥanbal, she is absolutely free to deal with all her property in whatever way she likes. ʿAbd Allāh ibn Aḥmad ibn Qudāmah, *al-Mughnī*, ed. Abd Allah al-Turki et al. (Cairo: Dār Hajar, 1406/1986), vol. 4, pp.513–514. This view is based on the following Prophetic Traditions on the authority of Jābir ibn ʿAbd Allāh and Zaynab (ʿAbd Allah's wife). Jābir's report reads as follows: "O women! Give charity… So [women] went on giving away from their jewels, thus putting their earrings and finger rings in Bilāl's cloth." Muḥammad ibn ʿAlī Ibn Daqīq al-ʿĪd, *Iḥkām al-Aḥkām Sharḥ ʿUmdat al-Aḥkām* (Cairo: Idārat al-Maṭbaʿah al-Munīriyyah, 1340), vol. 2, pp.129–130. Zaynab's report, reads as follows: "O women! Give charity, even if from your jewels," Muslim, *Ṣaḥīḥ*, 'Zakāh', hadith 1000, p.360.

    Differently from this view, the Mālikīs maintained that once married, a woman could not dispose of more than one-third of her property without the consent of her husband. See details in Ahmad ibn Muhammad al-Dirdir, *al-Sharḥ al-Ṣaghīr* (Beirut: Dār al-Maʿrifah, 1398/1987), vol. 3, p.402.
30. See the full story of this incident in ʿAlī ibn Ḥusām al-Dīn al-Muttaqī al-Hindī, *Kanz al-ʿUmmāl fī Sunan al-Aqwāl wa al-Afʿāl* (Beirut: Dār Iḥyā' al-Turāth al-ʿArabī, 1410/1990), vol. 4, p.420; Muḥammad Yūsuf al-Kāndahlawī, *Ḥayāt al-Ṣaḥābah*, ed. Nayif al-Abbas et. al (Damascus: Dār al-Qalam, 1388/1968), vol. 2, p.97.

31. See in this respect Ibn Rushd, *The Distinguished Jurist's Primer*, vol. 2, pp.286–287.
32. *Qirāḍ* or *muḍārabah* is a partnership contract based on the sharing of profit. It consists of "the giving of wealth [*māl*] by one person to another so that he may trade with it (in return) for a defined ration of the profit that the worker (*ʿāmil*) earns, that is, a part that is agreed upon by both." Ibn Rushd, *The Distinguished Jurist's Primer*, vol. 2, p.284.

19: ALTERATION & CONFIRMATION OBJECTIVES IN THE SHARIʿAH

1. This is based on the following Qur'anic verse: "And if any of you die and leave wives behind, they shall undergo, without remarrying, a waiting-period of four months and ten days; whereupon, when they have reached the end of their waiting-term, there shall be no sin in whatever they may do with their persons in a lawful manner. And God is aware of all that you do" (2:234).
2. Zaynab bint Abū Salamah was the daughter of ʿAbd Allāh ibn ʿAbd al-Asad ibn Hilāl, known as Abū Salamah, and Hind bint Abū Umayyah ibn al-Mughīrah, known as Umm Salamah. Her father Abū Salamah participated in the battle of Badr with the Prophet. He died of wounds suffered on the day of Uḥud. In addition to Zaynab, Hind bore to ʿAbd Allāh ibnʿUmar, Salamah and Durrah. After the death of her husband Abū Salamah, Umm Salamah was married to the Prophet in the year 3/624. Her son Salamah married the daughter of Ḥamzah ibn ʿAbd al-Muṭṭalib.
3. Mālik explained, "*Taftaḍḍu* means to rub her skin with it [i.e. the animal] in the same way as with a healing charm." *Muwaṭṭa'*, 'Ṭalāq', hadith 1265, pp.409–410.
4. The meaning of the Qur'anic term *maʿrūf* is inclusive of all that is agreeable to humankind's original nature and acceptable by sound reason, thus consisting of what is right and good. The term *munkar*, refers to all that is disagreeable to human nature and unacceptable by reason, thus standing for all that is false and evil. Acknowledging them is part of humankind's inborn disposition. Ibn Ashur, *Tafsīr al-Taḥrīr wa al-Tanwīr*, vol. 2/4, pp.36–52 and vol. 5/9, p.135.
5. Mālik explained, "*Ghīlah* is when a man has intercourse with his wife while she is nursing her child," *Muwaṭṭa'*, 'Raḍāʿ', hadith 1288, p.418; Muslim, *Ṣaḥīḥ*, 'Nikāḥ', hadith 1442, p.542.
6. Read in its totality, the verse refers "to the many severe rituals and obligations laid down in Mosaic Law, as well as to the tendency towards asceticism evident in the teachings of the Gospels. Thus the Qur'an implies that those "burdens and shackles" [*iṣr* and *aghlāl*], intended as means of spiritual discipline for particular communities and particular stages of man's development,

will become unnecessary as soon as God's message to man shall have achieved its final, universal character in the teachings of the Last Prophet, Muhammad." Asad, *The Message of the Qur'an*, p.226, note 125.

7. The terms *baḥīrah* and *sā'ibah* have occurred in verse 103 of *Sūrat al-Mā'idah* together with two other terms (i.e., *wāṣilah* and *ḥām*) to denote "certain categories of domestic animals which the pre-Islamic Arabs used to dedicate to their various deities by setting them free to pasture and prohibiting their use or slaughter. They were selected mainly on the basis of the number, sex and sequence of their offspring; but the lexicographers and commentators are by no means unanimous in their attempts at definition. For this reason – as well as because of their inherent complexity – the above four terms cannot be translated into any other language; consequently, I [Muhammad Asad] am rendering them in the text as 'certain kinds of cattle marked out by superstition and set aside from the use of man': this being, in the consensus of all authorities, the common denominator of the four categories. It is obvious that their mention at this place [5: 103] (as well as, by implication, in 6: 138–139 and 143–144) serves as an illustration of the arbitrary invention of certain supposedly "religious" obligations and prohibitions." Asad, *The Message of the Qur'an*, p.166, note 124.
8. Bukhārī, *Ṣaḥīḥ*, 'Adab', hadith 5992, p.1049; Muslim, *Ṣaḥīḥ*, 'Īmān', hadith 123, p.64.
9. As described by ʿĀ'ishah, the wife of the Prophet (Bukhārī), among the types of sexual relationship practiced in the pre-Islamic period was the one known as *nikāḥ al-istibḍāʿ* (wife-lending). "A man would say to his wife after she had become clear from her period, 'Send for so-and-so and have sexual relations with him.' Her husband would then keep away from her and would not sleep with her till she became pregnant by the other man with whom she was sleeping. When her pregnancy became evident, her husband would sleep with her if he wished. Her husband did so (i.e., let his wife sleep with another man) so that he might have a child of noble lineage". (See the full text of ʿĀ'ishah's report in chapter 34 on the objectives of the rules concerning the family.)
10. This tradition has already been documented.
11. Mālik ibn Anas, *Muwaṭṭa'*, 'Aqḍiyah', hadith 1430, p.530.
12. The Prophet's statement was an answer to Usāma ibn Zayd's question on the day of the conquest of Makkah: "O God's Apostle! Where will we encamp tomorrow?" Bukhārī, *Ṣaḥīḥ*, 'Maghāzī', hadith 4282, p.725.

20: SHARIʿAH IS ABOUT ESSENCES & REAL ATTRIBUTES

1. I have used the term genera to refer to obligation (*wujūb*), unlawfulness

(*ḥurmah*), validity (*ṣiḥḥah*), vitiation (*fasād*), and invalidity (*buṭlān*), as well as *ghurm*, sanction and reward and similar things related to the consequences of actions. – Author.

2. Abū Bakr Muhammad ibn Abd Allah Ibn al-ʿArabī, *al-Qabas ʿalā Muwaṭṭa'*, ed. Muḥammad ʿAbd Allāh Walad Karīm (Beirut: Dār al-Gharb al-Islāmī, 1992), vol. 3, pp. 1171–1172.
3. As explained by ʿAbd Allāh ibn ʿAbbās, the great Companion and cousin of the Prophet, *shighār* "is to marry the daughter of a man and marry one's daughter to that man (at the same time) without a dower (in both cases); or to marry a man's sister and marry one's own sister to the same man without dower." Bukhārī, *Ṣaḥīḥ*, 'Ḥiyal', hadith 6960, p.1200; Muslim, *Ṣaḥīḥ*, 'Nikāḥ', hadiths 1415–1417, p.527. As it appears from Ibn ʿAbbās's explanation, the reason for the prohibition of *shighār* marriage is the absence of dower, which makes it look like a form of barter.
4. The real meaning for which sorcery has been considered as the second grave sin next to associating with God has been expressed in the following Prophetic saying narrated by Abū Hurayrah:

   "The Prophet said, 'Avoid the seven great destructive sins.' The people enquired, 'O God's Apostle! What are they?' He said, 'To join others in worship along with God, to practice sorcery, to kill the life which God has forbidden except for a just cause, to eat up *ribā* (usury), to eat up an orphan's wealth, to give back to the enemy and fleeing from the battlefield at the time of fighting, and to accuse, chaste women, who never even think of anything touching chastity and are good believers.'" [Bukhārī, *Ṣaḥīḥ* 'Waṣāyā', hadith 2766, p.458; 'Ḥudūd', hadith 6857, p.1182; Muslim, *Ṣaḥīḥ* '*Īmān*', hadith 145, p.53.]

   This is because one of the most important meanings of sorcery at that time consisted of worshipping the jinn and straying from monotheism (*tawḥīd*) and belief in God's apostles and revealed true religion. This meaning is far from people's wrong perception today that sorcery consists of such magic arts as palmistry and talismans or such strange practices of charlatans that are meant for mere amusement and entertainment. – Author.

   According to Ibn Ashur, sorcery can be traced back to three basic principles: 1- The first principle consists of subduing people through the use of deceiving and frightening things deriving from the sorcerer's psychological influence and the conjured person's psychological weakness as well as from previous accidents experienced and believed by the latter in such a way that when the sorcerer targets him/her, he/she falls under his spell. This principle has been pointed out in the following Qur'anic verse in respect of Pharaoh's magicians: "And when they threw down [their staffs], they cast a spell upon the people's eyes, and struck them with awe" (7:116). 2- The second principle consists of using special effects pertaining to the characters of animal and mineral bodies. This derives from the natural characteristics of things, with varying degrees of influence. It includes such characteristics as the effect of mercury and effects of certain drugs that affect the mind either positively or negatively or cause languor in the body and doping in the nerves. This has been pointed out in the following verse in conjunction with the Qur'an account of the Pharaoh's magicians: "And [now] throw that [staff] which is in thy right hand – it shall swallow up all that they have wrought: [for] they have wrought only a sorcerer's artifice, and the sorcerer can never come to any good, whatever he may aim at!" (20:69). 3- The third principle pertains to charlatanism and the use of surreptitious, swift and undulating movements in such a way as would make immobile things appear to be moving. This aspect is pointed out by the following verse: "And lo! by virtue of their sorcery, their [magic] ropes and staffs seemed to him to be moving rapidly" (20:66).

As he further explains, all the above-mentioned three principles operate in conjunction with acts exerted on the bewitched person and in direct relation to him/her and affect him/her in accordance with his/her psychic susceptibility to their influence and in so far as he/she is unaware of them. Taken in their totality, they constitute the meaning of sorcery described in 2:102.

Thus, sorcery has always been associated with evil-mindedness, perverse beliefs, evil deeds and terrifying intimidation of people. For all this, all true religions have condemned every attempt at magic and sorcery and considered it an act of apostasy and disobedience to God as it consists of a belief in the influence of false gods and the jinn attributed to them in old religious beliefs. It is also specifically for this that Muslim jurists, especially Mālik ibn Anas, have strongly emphasized the punishment of sorcerers and considered sorcery as a manifestation of its practitioner's unsound and perverted faith. Ibn Ashur, *Tafsīr al-Taḥrīr wa al-Tanwīr*, vol. 1, pp.633–638.

5. *ʿUmrā muʿaqqabah* is a life-grant to a person and to his children.
6. Jābir ibn ʿAbd Allāh reported God's Messenger as saying: "He who confers a life-grant upon a person, it becomes his possession and that of his descendants, for he surrendered his right in that by his declaration. (This property) now belongs to one to whom this lifelong grant has been made, and to his descendants." Yaḥyā mentioned at the beginning of his narration: "Whoever is given a life grant, then it belongs to him and his descendants." Muslim, *Ṣaḥīḥ*, 'Hibāt', hadith 1625–1626, pp.633–35; Bukhārī, *Ṣaḥīḥ*, 'Hibah', hadiths 2625–2626, p.424.
7. Narrated by Ahmad and Ibn Abī Shaybah. – Author. See also Bukhārī, *Ṣaḥīḥ*, 'Ashribah', hadith 5590, p.992; Abū Dāwūd, *Sunan*, 'Ashribah', hadiths

3688–3689, vol. 3, p.329: "Some of my people will assuredly drink wine calling it by another name"; Ibn Mājah, *Sunan*, 'Ashribah', hadith 3427–3428, vol. 2, p.256; Abū Bakr ibn Abī Shaybah, *al-Muṣannaf*, ed. Ahmad al-Nadwi (Bombay: al-Dār al-Salafiyyah, 1403/1983), hadith 381, vol. 1, p.107; Aḥmad ibn Ḥanbal, *Musnad*, vol. 5, p.318.

According to Bukhārī, the Prophet said: "From among my followers there will be some people who will consider lawful illegal sexual intercourse, the wearing of silk, the consumption of intoxicants ..., as lawful, (calling them by fictious names). There will be some people who will stay near the side of a mountain. In the evening their shepherd will come to them with their sheep and ask them for something, but they will say to him, 'Return to us tomorrow.' God will destroy them during the night ...."

8. Bukhārī, *Ṣaḥīḥ*, 'Ashribah', hadiths 5593–5596, p.993; Mālik, *Muwaṭṭa'*, 'Ashribah', hadiths 1534–1535, p.608; Muslim, *Ṣaḥīḥ*, 'Īmān', hadith 23, p.31.

21: ANALOGICAL REASONING BASED ON EFFECTIVE CAUSES

1. This was the great exegete al-Zamakhsharī in his interpretation of the following verse: "Behold, God does not disdain to propound a parable of a gnat, or of something [even] less than that. Now, as for those who have attained faith, they know that it is the truth from their Sustainer – whereas those who are bent on denying the truth say, 'What could God mean by this parable?'" (2:26). – Author.

   See Maḥmūd ibn ʿUmar al-Zamakhsharī, *al-Kashshāf ʿan Ḥaqā'iq Ghawāmiḍ al-Tanzīl*, ed. Muhammad Abd al-Salam Abd al-Shafi (Beirut: Dār al-Kutub al-ʿIlmiyyah, 1415/1995), vol. 1, p.116.
2. These three levels consist of the *ʿilal*, *maqāṣid qarībah*, and *maqāṣid ʿāliyah* mentioned by the author in the preceding paragraph.
3. The terms *sabab* (cause), *sharṭ* (condition) and *māniʿ* (impediment) refer to the three components of the *ḥukm waḍʿī* (declaratory law). Declaratory law does not create an obligation; it rather facilitates the operation of the *ḥukm taklīfī* (normative or defining law) that is the obligation-creating rule. In its technical meaning, *sabab* is what the Lawgiver has determined to be the identifier of a legal rule so that its existence means the presence of the *ḥukm* or normative law, while its absence means the absence of the rule. *Sharṭ*, refers to the existence of facts that constitute a necessary condition for a *ḥukm*. Lastly, *māniʿ* is a condition or set of facts whose existence prevent the *ḥukm* from being applied even if the reason is found and the condition is met. In other words, it is a factor whose existence indicates the negation of the *ḥukm* or its *sabab*. Imran

Ahsan Khan Nyazee, *Islamic Jurisprudence* (Islamabad: International Institute of Islamic Thought & Islamic Research Institute, 2000), pp.74–76.

4. See in this regard, Abū al-Ḥussayn al-Baṣrī, *Kitāb al-Muʿtamad fī Uṣūl al-Fiqh*, vol. 2, pp.794–796; Ahmad Hasan, *Analogical Reasoning in Islamic Jurisprudence*, pp.66–67.
5. Mālik ibn Anas, *Muwaṭṭa'*, 'Farā'iḍ', hadith 1088, p.346.
6. Ibid., hadith 1087.

22: MANIPULATION TO MAKE THE UNLAWFUL APPEAR LAWFUL

1. Bukhārī, *Ṣaḥīḥ*, 'Adhān', hadith 783, p.127.
2. Mālik ibn Anas, *Muwaṭṭa'*, 'Wuqūt al-Ṣalāh', hadiths 24–25, pp.19–21.
3. Shāṭibī, *Muwāfaqāt*, vol. 1/2, pp.655–656.
4. See Bukhārī, *Ṣaḥīḥ*, 'Ḥiyal', hadiths 6953–6981, pp.1199–1204.
5. Shāṭibī, *Muwāfaqāt*, vol. 1/2, p.660.
6. Ibid., p.613.
7. Ibid., p.615.
8. This is part of a long tradition narrated by Abū Hurayrah (Muslim, *Ṣaḥīḥ*, 'Imārah', hadith 1905, pp.759–760):

   "I heard the Messenger of God say: The first man [whose case] will be decided on the Day of Judgment will be one who died a martyr. He shall be brought [before the Judgment Seat]. God will make him recount His blessings [that is, the blessings which He had bestowed upon him] and he will recount them [and admit having enjoyed them in his life]. [Then] God will say: 'What did you do [to requite these blessings]? He will say: 'I fought for You until I died as a martyr.' God will say: 'You have told a lie. You fought so that you might be called "a brave warrior." And you were called so.' [Then] orders will be passed against him and he will be dragged with his face down and cast into Hell. Then will be brought forward a man who acquired knowledge, imparted it [to others], and recited the Qur'an. He will be brought and God will make him recount His blessings and he will recount them [and admit having enjoyed them in his lifetime]. Then will God ask: 'What did you do [to requite these blessings]?' He will say: 'I acquired knowledge, disseminated it, and recited the Qur'an, seeking Your pleasure.' God will say: 'You have told a lie. You acquired knowledge so that you might be called "a scholar;" you recited the Qur'an so that it might be said: "He is a *Qārī*" and such has been said.' Then orders will be passed against him and he shall be dragged with his face down and cast into the Fire. Then will be brought a man whom God had made abundantly rich and had granted every kind of wealth. He will be brought and God will make him recount His blessings. He will recount them and [admit having enjoyed them in his lifetime]. God will [then] ask: 'What have you done [to requite these blessings]?' He will say: 'I spent money in every cause in which You wished that it should be spent.' God will say: 'You are lying. You did [so] that it might be said about [you]: "He is a generous fellow" and so it was said.' Then will God pass orders and he will be dragged with his face down and thrown into Hell."

9. Shāṭibī, *Muwāfaqāt*, vol. 1/2, pp.656–660.
10. *Khulᶜ* or redemption is a transaction in which the wife undertakes payment to the husband for obtaining her divorce. In other words, it is a type of divorce initiated by the wife consisting of release for payment from her. See further details in Ibn Rushd, *The Distinguished Jurist's Primer*, vol. 2, pp.79–84; Ahmad ibn Naquib al-Misri, *Reliance of the Traveller*, trans. Nuh Ha Mim Keller (Beslville, MD: Amana Publications, 1997), pp.562–563.
11. Gold and silver constituted the official money used in economic transactions. Now they are replaced with banknotes and other types of money.
12. Wiping one's footgear or leather socks (*al-masḥ ᶜalā al-khuffayn*) with wet hands is a dispensation that can replace washing the feet as part of the ablutions before prayers. The footgear Muslims use for this is ankle-high leather socks that zip up and are worn inside the shoes. For further details see Ibn Naquib al-Misri, *Reliance of the Traveller*, pp.67–70.
13. Muḥammad ibn Aḥmad ibn ᶜUmar al-Shāshī died in 507/1115.
14. Abū Bakr ibn al-ᶜArabī, *al-ᶜAwāṣim mina al-Qawāṣim*, ed. Ammar Talbi (Doha: Dār al-Thaqāfah, 1413/1992), p.373.
15. Mālik ibn Anas, *Muwaṭṭa'*, 'Ṭalāq', hadiths 1242–1243, p.403.
16. The hadith was narrated by ᶜAlī ibn Abī Ṭālib, Abū Hurayrah and ᶜUqbah ibn ᶜĀmir and reads as follows: "The curse of God is upon the *muḥallil* and upon the person for whom he is making her [i.e. the divorced wife] permissible." Tirmidhī, *Sunan*, 'Nikāḥ', hadith 1943, vol. 5, p.44. It has also been narrated by Muslim, *Ṣaḥīḥ*, 'Nikāḥ', hadith 1433, pp.537–538, and Dārimī (*Sunan*, ed. Fawwaz Ahmad Zamarli et al. (Cairo: Dār al-Rayyān & Beirut: Dār al-Kitāb al-ᶜArabī, 1407/1987), 'Nikāḥ', hadith 2258, vol. 2, p.211.
17. The *muḥallil* is the man who marries an irrevocably divorced woman on the condition that he will make her permissible for her first husband (*muḥallal*). For further details, see Ibn Rushd, *The Distinguished Jurist's Primer*, vol. 2, pp.104–105.
18. Bukhārī, *Ṣaḥīḥ*, 'Musāqāh', hadith 2353, p.378 and 'Ḥiyal', hadith 6962, p.1200; Mālik ibn Anas, *Muwaṭṭa'*, 'Aqḍiyah', hadith 1424, p.528.
19. By the expression "our view", the author refers to the Mālikī position concerning the non-obligatory nature of charity. See on this, Qarāfī, *Dhakhīrah*, vol. 5, p.355.

20. Bukhārī, *Ṣaḥīḥ*, 'Nikāḥ', hadith 5121, p.915; Muslim, *Ṣaḥīḥ*, 'Radā'', hadith 1425, p.530.
21. According to Muhammad Asad, there is another important aspect to the story of Joseph at this very point of its procession:
 It "is a further illustration of the basic doctrine that 'judgment [as to what is to happen] rests with none but God' (verse 67 of the same *surah*).
 Joseph had wanted to keep Benjamin with himself, but under the law of Egypt he could not do this without the consent of his half-brothers, who were the legal guardians of their minor brother; and they – bound as they were with the solemn promise given to their father – would certainly not have agreed to Benjamin's remaining behind.
 The only other alternative open to Joseph was to disclose his identity to them; but since he was not yet prepared to go so far, he was obliged to allow Benjamin to depart with his brothers. The accidental discovery of his gift, entirely unexpected by Joseph changed everything: for now Benjamin appeared to be guilty of theft, and under the law of the land Joseph was entitled to claim him as his slave, and thus to keep him in his house.
 The words, 'In this way did We contrive for Joseph [the attainment of his heart's desire],' referring to the incident of the cup, indicate that its final outcome was neither planned nor even foreseen by Joseph."
 Asad, *The Message of the Qur'an*, op.cit., p.349, note 77.

23: PROHIBITION OF EVASIVE LEGAL MEANS

1. Al-Qāḍī Abū Muḥammad ʿAbd al-Wahhāb ibn ʿAlī ibn Naṣr al-Baghdādī was born in 363 AH and died in 421 AH. An outstanding traditionalist and jurist, al-Qāḍī ʿAbd al-Wahhāb had studied with some of the most eminent scholars of Baghdad, like Abū Bakr al-Abharī, Ibn al-Qaṣṣār, and Abū Bakr al-Bāqillānī. Amongst his students were great scholars like al-Māzarī. He produced major works in Mālikī jurisprudence. They include, among others, *al-Mukhtaṣar, al-Maʿūnah, Sharḥ al-Risālah, al-Mumahhad, al-Inṣāf, Sharḥ al-Mudawwanah,* and *al-Talqīn*.
2. In documenting this quotation, the author relied on a manuscript copy of al-Māzarī's commentary of al-Qāḍī ʿAbd al-Wahhāb's *Talqīn*. He referred to the beginning of the chapter on deferred sales (*buyūʿ al-ājāl*). Unfortunately, only the first three volumes dealing with ritual ablution (*ṭahārah*) and prayer (*ṣalāh*) have so far been edited by Shaikh Mukhtar al-Sallami and published by Dār al-Gharb al-Islāmī (Beirut, 1997).

3. Qarāfī, *Furūq*, vol. 2, pp.450–451; *Sharḥ Tanqīḥ al-Fuṣūl*, p.353; *al-Dhakhīrah*, vol. 1, pp.147–148.
4. Concerning this, ʿAbd Allāh ibn ʿUmar narrated that the Prophet said: "He who buys foodstuff should not sell it till he has received it." Mālik ibn Anas, *Muwaṭṭa'*, 'Buyūʿ', hadiths 1329–1330, p.442; Bukhārī, *Ṣaḥīḥ*, 'Buyūʿ', hadith 2133, p.342; Muslim, *Ṣaḥīḥ*, 'Buyūʿ', hadith 1525, p.588.
5. The term *qiyās jalī* can be translated as perspicuous or patent analogy. It consists of *a fortiori* arguments in analogical reasoning in which the new case (*farʿ*), though unspecified by the Shariʿah texts, comes under the meaning of these texts. In other words, it is an analogy in which the effective cause (*ʿillah*) is more obvious in the new case than in the original case (*aṣl*). As for the term *qiyās khafī*, it can be translated as concealed or latent analogy. It involves a process whereby the *mujtahid* does not readily find the effective cause of the *ḥukm*, but infers it from the texts by resorting to a number of methods. It can also be defined as an analogy in which the effective cause is less obvious in the new case than in the original case.

   See more details on the different views on the meaning, scope and validity of these and other variants of *qiyās* in Ahmad Hasan, *Analogical Reasoning in Islamic Jurisprudence*, pp.79–91; Wael B. Hallaq, *A History of Islamic Legal Theories*, pp.96-104.
6. See Mālik's comments in this respect in *Muwaṭṭa'*, 'Buyūʿ', pp.460–461 and 468–469. See further details on the same issue in Ibn Rushd, *The Distinguished Jurist's Primer*, vol. 2, pp.171–179; Qarāfī, *Sharḥ Tanqīḥ al-Fuṣūl*, p.353.
7. Qarāfī, *Furūq*, vol. 3, p.1056; *Sharḥ Tanqīḥ al-Fuṣūl*, p.356.
8. Qarāfī, *Sharḥ Tanqīḥ al-Fuṣūl*, p.353; also *Furūq*, vol. 2, 451.
9. Muslim, *Ṣaḥīḥ*, 'Ṣiyām', hadith 1104, p.399; Bukhārī, *Ṣaḥīḥ*, 'Tamannī', hadith 7241, p.1247.
10. Muslim, *Ṣaḥīḥ*, 'ʿIlm', hadith 2670, p.1029.
11. *Waraʿ* devolves upon seeking to attain certainty in things in which high probability is sufficient, such as trying to determine the direction of the Qiblah by resorting to astronomical methods that are not required of us, or continuing to fast during the month of Ramadan after sunset to ascertain the validity of breaking fast and starting to fast a long while before dawn. More serious than this is to avoid brushing one's teeth while fasting, fasting on the day of fast breaking (*ʿĪd al-Fiṭr*) if the new moon of the month [of Shawwāl] is seen only late at night. Certain aspects of *waraʿ* belong to evil-whispering, such as the excessive use of water for ablution and bathing (ghusl), associating something permissible with what is obligatory or forbidden, or performing a prescribed act more than what is actually required by the Lawgiver, like fasting by some-

one who is seriously ill. Such an attitude is sometimes even taken by some *mujtahidīn*, like adopting the view that one's prayer is invalid if a donkey passes before one while at prayer. – Author.

24: PRECISION AND DETERMINATION IN ISLAMIC LEGISLATION

1. *Khiyār al-majlis* or "the option to cancel at the time of the agreement" means the right of the buyer and seller to nullify the agreement at any time before they part company.
2. "By pagan ignorance (*Jāhiliyyah*) is meant here not merely the time before the advent of the Prophet Muhammad but, in general, a state of affairs characterized by a lack of moral perception and a submission of all personal and communal concerns to the criterion of "expediency" alone: that is, exclusively to the consideration as to whether a particular aim or action is useful or damaging (in the short-term, practical sense of these words) to the interests of the person concerned or of the community to which he belongs. Inasmuch as this 'law of expediency' is fundamentally opposed to the concepts of morality preached by every higher religion, it is described in the Qur'an as 'the law (*ḥukm*) of pagan ignorance'." Asad, *The Message of the Qur'an*, p.154, note 71.
3. *Rajʿah* or *ṭalāq rajʿī* is the divorce in which "the husband possesses the right over the wife's return, without there being a choice for her in the matter." Ibn Rushd, *The Distinguished Jurist's Primer*, vol. 2, p.71.
4. Abū Isḥāq Ismāʿīl ibn Isḥāq ibn Isāmʿīl ibn Muḥammad ibn Zayd al-Azadī was born in 200 AH in Basra and died in 282 AH in Baghdad. He was a great Mālikī jurist who was also counted among the leading scholars of Qur'anic readings (*qirā'āt*) and Arabic language. A descendant of a notable family of established tradition of scholarship, Ismāʿīl ibn Isḥāq was crucial in the spread and consolidation of Mālikī jurisprudence in Iraq thanks to his authoritative scholarship and many students. His works include, among others, *Muwaṭṭa'*, *Aḥkām al-Qur'ān*, *al-Mabsūṭ*, *al-Uṣūl*, *Kitāb al-Farā'iḍ*, and *al-Iḥtijāj bi al-Qur'ān*.
5. The term *takāyul* refers to the practice current among the Arabs of the pre-Islamic period of pagan ignorance (*Jāhiliyyah*) concerning the implementation of retribution for homicide. It consisted of the following: if a person from a tribe killed someone from another tribe who was of a higher social status than the murderer, the claimants of the murdered person would require that retribution be exacted not from the person who committed the murder, but from someone who is of an equal status to the victim. Thus, they believed the value of a person's blood is equivalent to his/her social status determined

by descent, wealth, nobility, etc. Ibn Ashur, *Tafsīr al-Taḥrīr wa al-Tanwīr*, vol. 2, p.136.

6. Bukhārī, *Ṣaḥīḥ*, 'Nikāḥ', hadith 5081, p.909.
7. That is, when they have ripened.
8. See Mālik's comment in this respect on hadiths 1111–1113, *Muwaṭṭa'*, p.359. For more juristic detail, see Ibn Rushd, *The Distinguished Jurist's Primer*, vol. 2, pp.25–26; Qarāfī, *al-Dhakhīrah*, vol. 4, pp.160–162.
9. See a detailed discussion of this issue in Ibn Rushd, *The Distinguished Jurist's Primer*, vol. 2, pp.538–540.
10. Ibid., pp.22–23.
11. *Īlā'*, vow of continence or forswearing, means that the husband swears he will not have sexual intercourse with his wife, either for an unrestricted period or for more than four months. In this sense, *īlā'* or forswearing one's wife is unlawful. However, a husband is not considered to have sworn his wife when he forswears sexual intercourse for four months or less, or when he is impotent.
12. This is usually discussed under the topic of option of defects in marriage that deals with defects for which marriages are rescinded. The one-year period mentioned by the author pertains to the husband's impotency. See Ibn Rushd, *The Distinguished Jurist's Primer*, vol. 2, pp.58–60.
13. This is the view of Mālik ibn Anas. See further details on this issue in Shams al-Dīn Abū ʿAbd Allāh Muḥammad ibn Abī Bakr Ibn Qayyim al-Jawziyyah, *Zād al-Maʿād Fī Hady Khayr al-ʿIbād* (Beirut: Dār Ibn Ḥazm, 1420/1999), pp.1044–1049.
14. See an elaborate discussion of these issues by the author in Part III of this book.
15. See details in this respect in Ibn Rushd, *The Distinguished Jurist's Primer*, vol. 2, pp.540–542.

25: RIGOR & MERCY IN ENFORCING & OBSERVING ISLAMIC LEGISLATION

1. Bukhārī, *Ṣaḥīḥ*, 'Ṣulḥ', hadith 2697, p.440; Muslim, *Ṣaḥīḥ*', 'Aqḍiyah', hadith 1718, p.682.
2. Mālik ibn Anas, *Muwaṭṭa'*, 'al-ʿAtāqah wa al-Walā'', hadith 1473, p.555; Bukhārī, *Ṣaḥīḥ*, 'Ṣalāh', hadith 456, p.79; 'Shurūṭ', hadith 2729, pp.446–447; Muslim, *Ṣaḥīḥ*, 'ʿItq', hadith 1504 (6, 8), p.580.
3. This is a translation of the expression *al-maʿdūm sharʿan ka al-maʿdūm ḥissan*. See further details on this rule in Aḥmad ibn Yaḥyā al-Wansharīsī, *Īḍāḥ al-Masālik ilā Qawāʿid al-Imām Mālik*, ed. Ahmad al-Khattabi (Rabat: Ministry of Awqāf, 1400/1980), pp.138–140.
4. See details on the different positions of the legal theorists concerning this rule

in Abū al-Ḥusayn al-Baṣrī, *Muʿtamad*, vol. 1, pp.183–200; al-Āmidī, *al-Iḥkām*, vol. 1, pp.407–411; Qarāfī, *Sharḥ Tanqīḥ al-Fuṣūl*, pp.138–140; al-Ḥāfiḍ al-ʿAlā'ī, *Taḥqīq al-Murād fī ann al-Nahy Yaqtaḍī al-Fasād*, ed. Ibrahim al-Salqini (Damascus: Maṭbaʿat Zayd ibn Thābit, 1395/1975).

5. In his commentary on this verse, the author points out that the term balance (*mīzān)* is used metaphorically to symbolize the realization of justice between people as human affairs can run properly only by the implementation of justice. This meaning has been further consolidated and deepened by the indication of the purpose for which the apostles were sent and revelation made to them, namely that human beings "might behave with equity (*qisṭ*)." For him, the use of the term *qisṭ* is meant to denote justice in a more comprehensive and universal sense than that implied by the term balance, for the latter might refer specifically to judicial justice between litigants. Thus, the ultimate purpose of revelation is to establish justice in all human affairs according to the requirements of the truth (*ḥaqq*). The bestowal of iron is a reference to God's inspiration for human beings to make use of this earthly metal for their different purposes. The indication that iron contains both awesome power and benefits for man is meant "to bring to the audience's awareness and consideration God's deeper wisdom in creating iron and inspiring [human beings with] the use of it and to point out that the benefits and awesome power inherent in it should be employed properly" for the sake of justice. Ibn Ashur, *Tafsīr al-Taḥrīr wa al-Tanwīr*, vol. 13/27, pp.416–417.

Commenting on the same verse, Muhammad Asad has the following to say: "Side by side with enabling man to discriminate between right and wrong (which is the innermost purpose of all divine revelation), God has endowed man with the ability to convert to his use the natural resources of his earthly environment. An outstanding symbol of this ability is man's skill, unique among all animated beings, in making tools; and the primary material for all-tool making – and indeed, for all human technology – is iron: the one metal which is found abundantly on earth, and which can be utilized for beneficial as well as destructive ends. The 'awesome power' (*ba's shadīd*) inherent in iron manifests itself not merely in the manufacture of weapons of war but also, more subtly, in man's ever-growing tendency to foster the development of an increasingly complicated technology which places the machine in the foreground of all human existence and which, by its inherent – almost irresistible – dynamism, gradually estranges man from all inner connection with nature. This process of growing mechanization, so evident in our modern life, jeopardizes the very structure of human society and, thus, contributes to a gradual dissolution of all moral and spiritual perceptions epitomized in the concept of 'divine guidance'. It is to warn man of this danger that the Qur'an stresses –

symbolically and metonymically – the potential evil (*ba's*) of 'iron' if it is put to wrong use: in other words, the danger of man's allowing his technological ingenuity to run wild and thus to overwhelm his spiritual consciousness and, ultimately, to destroy all possibility of individual and social happiness." Asad, *The Message of the Qur'an*, p.841, note 42.

6. This statement attributed to the third caliph ʿUthmān ibn ʿAffān has been reported in various, yet quite similar, versions. See Yūsuf ibn ʿAbd Allāh ibn ʿAbd al-Barr, *al-Tamhīd limā fī Muwaṭṭa' mina al-Asānīd* (Rabat: Ministry of Awqāf, 1411 AH), vol. 1, p.118; Ibn Rushd, *al-Bayān wa al-Taḥṣīl*, vol. 17, p.59.
7. Qarāfī, *Furūq*, vol. 4, pp.1165–1179.
8. This juridical norm (*qāʿidah fiqhiyyah*) reads as follows: *al-mashaqqah tajlib al-taysīr*. It means that whenever there is hardship facing the human subjects (*mukallafūn*) in implementing the prescriptions and proscriptions of the Shariʿah, the latter resorts to specific measures to relieve them from it. See details on this norm in Zarqa, *Sharḥ al-Qawāʿid al-Fiqhiyyah*, pp.105–110.

26: PUBLIC AND INDIVIDUAL LICENSE

1. Shāṭibī, *Muwāfaqāt*, vol. 1/1, pp.273–286, 301303.
2. It should be pointed out, however, that Imām al-Ḥaramayn al-Juwaynī addressed the question of collective necessity and strongly criticized the jurists for confining themselves to *rukhṣah* at the level of the individual. He went so far as to describe the jurists' position in this respect as incoherent and confused. See his *Ghiyāthī*, pp.218–225.
3. *Salam* is a contract permitting advance payment for goods to be supplied or produced. See further details on its validity and the different juristic views pertaining to it in Ibn Rushd, *The Distinguished Jurist's Primer*, vol. 2, pp.240–249.
4. *Mughārasah* is a type of land tenure or a contract in which the landlord gives his land to someone to plant fruit trees. On the different juristic views concerning the validity of this transaction and its relationship with types of land-based dealings, see Ziaul Haque, *Landlord and Peasant in Early Islam* (Islamabad: Islamic Research Institute, 1984), pp.311–346.
5. According to Ibn Rushd, "The majority of the jurists – Mālik, al-Shāfiʿī, al-Thawrī, Abū Yūsuf and Muḥammad ibn al-Ḥasan, the disciples of Abū Ḥanīfa, Aḥmad, and Dāwūd – are in favour of its [*musāqah's*] permissibility. It is for them an exemption, based on sunna, from the prohibition of the sale of uncertain things and from uncertain *ijāra*." *The Distinguished Jurist's Primer*, vol. 2, p.291.

6. Shāṭibī, *Muwāfaqāt*, vol. 1/1, pp.268–270.
7. Abū al-Qāsim Muḥammad ibn Sirāj died in 848 AH in Granada. He was its grand mufti and chief judge as well as the leading scholar of Mālikī jurisprudence in it. He travelled to Telemcen and Tunis, where he met eminent scholars. Among his teachers was the famous Abū Saʿīd ibn Lubb (d. 782 AH) who was also Shāṭibī's teacher. His students include, among others, Abū ʿAmr ibn Manẓūr (see following note) and Abū Abd ʿAllāh al-Mawwāq (d. 897/1491). His works include, among others, *Sharḥ al-Mukhtaṣar*. His fatwas have been compiled, edited, and published by Muhammad Abu al-Ajfan under the title *Fatāwā Qāḍī al-Jamāʿah Abī al-Qāsim ibn Sirāj* (Abu Dhabi: al-Majmaʿ al-Thaqāfī, 1420/2000).
8. Abū ʿAmr or ʿUmar Muḥammad ibn Muḥammad ibn Muḥammad ibn Manẓūr died in 887 AH in Granada at a very old age. He was judge of the community for many years. A number of his fatwas have been preserved in al-Wansharīsī's *Miʿyār*.
9. See their fatwas in *al-Miʿyār* of al-Wansharīsī. – Author. Al-Wansharīsī, *Miʿyār*, vol. 5, pp.37–38 (Ibn Manẓūr) and vol. 7, pp.140 & 153 (Ibn Sirāj; also his *Fatāwā*, p.165).
10. Abū ʿAbd Allāh Muḥammad ibn Ḥasan Nāṣir al-Dīn al-Laqqānī was born in 873 AH and died in 958 AH. He was an eminent jurist and rose to the level of scholarly authority in Egypt after the death of his brother, Shams al-Dīn. He studied with many outstanding scholars, such as Aḥmad Zarrūq, al-Nūr al-Sanhūrī, and al-Burhān al-Laqqānī. He had many prominent students, such as the famous biographer Aḥmad Bāb of Timbuktu (Mali).
11. Hoarding of *awqāf* property (*iḥkar al-awqāf*) is a tenancy, according to which the *waqf* land remains in the hands of the tenant, known as the hoarder (*muḥtakir*), as long as he pays the rental. See further details in Zuhdī Yakan, *al-Awqāf fī al-Shariʿah wa al-Qānūn* (Beirut: Dār al-Nahḍah al-ʿArabiyyah, 1388 AH), pp.102–104 & 121–124.
12. ʿIzz al-Dīn ibn ʿAbd al-Salām, *Qawāʿid*, vol. 2, pp.313–314.

27: *WĀZIʿ*: ITS MEANING AND VARIETIES

1. This notion has been expressed by the pre-Islamic Arab poet ʿAmr ū ibn Kulthūm in the following verse:
   They [i.e. wives] feed our horses and say
   You are not our husbands if you do not protect us. – Author.
   This is the ninety-second verse of his ode (*muʿallaqah*). Tabrīzī, *Sharḥ al-Qaṣā'id al-ʿAshr*, p.27. Originally, the author quoted this verse in the main text, but we deemed it more appropriate to transfer it to an endnote. ʿAmrū ibn

Kulthūm, was a pre-Islamic Arab poet who flourished in the 6th century AC and whose *qaṣīdah* (ode) is one of the seven that comprise the celebrated anthology of pre-Islamic verse *al-Muʿallaqāt* http://www.britannica.com/needmore. Little is known of his life; he became chief of the tribe of Taghlib in Mesopotamia at an early age and, according to tradition, killed ʿAmr ibn Hind, the Arab king of al-Ḥīrah, c. 568 AC. ʿAmrū ibn Kulthūm lived to a very advanced age and was a highly respected person.

2. See also the Qur'an: 6:151 and 81:8–9.
3. He refers here to verse [No. 75] of the pre-Islamic Arab poet Ṭarafah ibn al-ʿAbd (*Dīwān*) in which he said:
And the injustice inflicted by relatives is more painful
For a person than the effect of a sharpened sword.
Author. – Tabrīzī, *Sharḥ al-Qaṣā'id al-ʿAshr*, p.115. Ṭarafah ibn al-ʿAbd was from Bahrain, and lived from 543 to 569 AC.
4. Rāzī, *al-Tafsīr al-Kabīr*, vol. 5/10, p.19.
5. Abū ʿAlī Muḥammad ibn ʿAbd al-Wahhāb al-Jubbā'ī was born in 235 AC and died in 303 AC. He was one of the most celebrated scholars of the Muʿtazilite. Born at Jubbā in Khuzistān, he attended the school at Basra of Abū Yaʿqūb Yūsuf al-Shaḥḥām who at that time occupied the Chair of Abū al-Hudhayl al-ʿAllāf. He succeeded al-Shaḥḥām, and it can be said that he was able to add a final brilliance to the tradition of the masters, while at times he refreshed and opened the way to new solutions.
He thus holds a place in the line of the Basra Muʿtazilah who, especially over the question of the human action, differ from the Baghdad Muʿtazilah. In Basra itself, he was particularly at variance with al-Naẓẓām and al-Jāḥiẓ, but he also differed from the two lines of thought of al-Aṣamm and ʿAbbād, although these were closer to his own.
Al-Jubbā'ī had two pupils who later became celebrated: his son Abū Hāshim and Abū al-Ḥasan al-Ashʿarī who, after breaking away, was to devote himself to refuting Muʿtazilism and to become the founder of the new theological school of Ashʿarism.
6. Bukhārī, *Ṣaḥīḥ*, 'Hibah', hadith no. 2622, p.424.
7. See Yūsuf ibn ʿAbd Allāh ibn ʿAbd al-Barr, *al-Tamhīd limā fī Muwaṭṭa' mina al-Asānīd* (Rabat: Ministry of Awqāf, 1411), vol. 1, p.118; Ibn Rushd, *al-Bayān wa al-Taḥṣīl*, vol. 17, p.59.
8. Ibn ʿAṭiyah, ʿAbd al-Ḥaqq, 481 to 546 AH, was born and lived in Granada. He was a jurist, a Qur'an commentator and a judge. – Author.
9. Ibn ʿAṭiyyah, *al-Muḥarrar al-Wajīz*, vol. 2, p.11.
10. Ibn al-ʿArabī, *Aḥkām al-Qur'an*, ed. Muhammad Ali al-Bijawi (Beirut: Dār al-Jīl, 1407/1987), vol. 1, p.187.

11. The *Ḥisbah* is a religious institution under the authority of the state that appoints people to take responsibility for enjoining what is right, whenever people start to neglect it, and forbidding what is wrong, whenever people start to engage in it. The purpose of this is to safeguard society from deviance, protect the faith, and ensure the welfare of the people in both religious and worldly matters according to the Law of God. God has made it obligatory upon all Muslims to enjoin good and forbid wrongdoing to the extent of their knowledge and abilities. Thus, He says in the Qur'an, "Let there arise from you a group calling to all that is good, enjoining what is right and forbidding what is wrong. It is these who are successful" (3:104).
The *Ḥisbah* is organized to safeguard the limits of God from being violated, protect people's honor, and ensure public safety. It also includes monitoring the marketplace, craftsmanship, and manufacturing concerns to make sure that the laws of Islam are upheld by these entities. It must also ensure that quality standards are maintained. The *Ḥisbah* carries out these duties in conjunction with the appropriate government agencies and other relevant establishments.

28: THE MERCIFUL NATURE OF THE SHARIᶜAH

1. The late Muhammad Asad has a broader view than the legalistic interpretation of this and other similar verses advanced by most of the Qur'an commentators, including Ibn Ashur, for he attempts to embrace the entire historical experience of the Jews characterized by "humiliation and suffering." Thus, he comments on the verse in question: "Most of the commentators assume that this refers to the severe dietary restrictions imposed on the Jews, which are alluded to in 3:93 and 6:146. Since, however, 3:93 clearly states that these restrictions and prohibitions were a punishment for evil deeds committed 'before the Torah was bestowed from on high', while the verse we are now discussing relates to their sinful behaviour in later times, we must conclude that the punishment spoken of here has another meaning: namely, the age-long deprivation of the Jewish people of the many "good things of life" which other nations enjoy – in other words, the humiliation and suffering which they have had to undergo throughout most of their recorded history, and particularly after the time of Jesus. It is on the basis of this interpretation that I have rendered the expression *ḥarramnā ᶜalayhim* (lit. "We forbade them") as 'We denied to them'." *The Message of the Qur'an*, p.135, note 174.
2. The Shariᶜah's gradual approach to the prohibition of intoxicants is clearly epitomized in the following Qur'anic verses stated in the chronological sequence of their revelation.

(1) "They will ask you about intoxicants and gambling. Say: 'In both there is a great evil as well as some benefit for men; but the evil which they cause is greater than the benefit which they bring.' And they will ask you about what they should spend [in God's cause]. Say: 'What you can spare.' In this way God makes clear to you His messages, so that you might reflect on this world and on the life to come..." (2:219–220).

(2) "O you who have attained faith! Do not attempt to pray while you are in a state of intoxication [but wait] until you know what you are saying; nor yet [while you are] in a state requiring total ablution, until you have bathed – except if you are travelling [and are unable to do so]. But if you are ill, or are travelling, or have just satisfied a want of nature, or have cohabited with a woman, and can find no water – then take resort to pure dust, passing [it] lightly over your face and your hands. Behold, God is indeed an absolver of sins, Much-Forgiving." (4:43).

(3) "O you who have attained to faith! Intoxicants, gambling, idolatrous practices, and the divining arts are but loathsome evil of Satan's doing: shun it, then, so that you might attain a happy state" (5:90).

3. This provision falls under the general legal maxim that, "Damage or harm must be removed (*al-ḍarar yuzāl*)". For more details of the meaning, scope and application of this maxim, see ʿAbd al-Wahhāb ibn ʿAlī Tāj al-Dīn al-Subkī, *al-Ashbāh wa al-Naẓā'ir*, ed. Adil Abd al-Mawjud & Ali Muʿawwad (Beirut: Dār al-Kutub al-ʿIlmiyyah, 1411/1991), vol. 1, p.41; Ahmad al-Zarqa, *Sharḥ al-Qawāʿid al-Fiqhiyyah*, ed. Mustapha al-Zarqa & ʿAbd al-Fattah Abu Ghuddah (Beirut: Dār al-Gharb al-Islāmī, 1403/1983), p.120.

4. Yaḥyā ibn Yaḥyā al-Laythī died in 234/848 in Cordoba. His father Yaḥyā was from the tribe of Maṣmūdah in Tangier. He travelled to the Hujaz in pursuit of knowledge and studied *Muwaṭṭa'* under Mālik during the last year of Mālik's life. His transmission therefore represents the text as Mālik was teaching it at the end of his life. It is by far the best-known transmission and is the one that is generally meant when reference is made to *Muwaṭṭa'*. Yaḥyā is mainly responsible for the spread of the Mālikī School in Andalusia and he was nicknamed by Mālik "the Sage of Andalusia."

5. Ibn Rushd, *al-Bayān wa al-Taḥṣīl*, vol. 9, p.417; Muḥammad ibn Abī Bakr ibn Qayyim al-Jawziyyah, *Zād al-Maʿād fī Hady Khayr al-ʿIbād*, ed. Shuʿayb al-Arna'ut et al. (Beirut: Mu'assassat al-Risālah, 1405/1985), vol. 3, p.572.

6. Ibn Rushd, *al-Bayān wa al-Taḥṣīl*, vol. 9, pp.416–417.

7. Abū ʿAbd Allāh 'Abd al-Raḥman Ibn al-Qāsim al-ʿUtaqī (d. 191/806) was Mālik's foremost disciple. He was one of Mālik's companions who had a tremendous influence in recording his school since he was the source for Saḥnūn in his record of the teaching of Mālik. Ibn al-Qāsim has the same posi-

tion as Muḥammad ibn al-Ḥasan al-Shaybānī has in the school of Abū Ḥanīfah. There is a close correspondence between the two men. Both of them transmitted the school and made free use of ijtihad. Ibn al-Qāsim had opinions that differed from those of his teacher, Mālik. Ibn ʿAbd al-Barr of Cordoba (368–463) – a major hadith master of the Mālikī School, said of him, "He was a *faqīh* dominated by opinion. He was a righteous, poor, steadfast man." Ibn al-Qāsim died in 191 AH at the age of 63 in Egypt.

8. See in this regard, Ibn Rushd, *al-Bayān wa al-Taḥṣīl*, vol. 9, pp.416–417.
9. Ibn al-ʿArabī, *Aḥkām al-Qur'ān*, vol. 1, p.215 (verse 235).
10. ʿAlī ibn Abī Ṭālib and ʿAbd Allāh ibn Masʿūd amongst the Prophet's Companions upheld this view. It was also the view of Abū Ḥanīfah, Sufyān al-Thawrī, and al-Shāfiʿī. Muḥammad ibn Aḥmad al-Qurṭubī, *al-Jāmiʿ li-Aḥkām al-Qur'ān*, ed. Ahmad ʿAbd al-ʿAlim al-Barduni (Beirut: Dār Ihyā' al-Turāth al-ʿArabī, n. d.), vol. 3, pp.193–195; Ibn ʿAṭiyyah, *al-Muḥarrar al-Wajīz*, vol. 1, pp.317–318; Ibn Ashur, *Tafsīr al-Taḥrīr wa al-Tanwīr*, vol. 2, p.455.
11. This provision is based on the Prophetic Tradition reported by Abū Dāwūd and al-Nasā'ī, in which the Prophet said: "He who corrupts someone else's wife or slave is not one of us." See further details in *al-Mawsūʿah al-Fiqhiyyah al-Kuweitiyyah* (Ministry of Awqāf and Islamic Affairs, 1412/1992, vol. 5, p.291).
12. Bukhārī, *Ṣaḥīḥ*, 'Ṣawm', hadith 1965, p.316; also Muslim, *Ṣaḥīḥ*, 'Ṣiyām', hadith 1103, p.398; Mālik ibn Anas, *Muwaṭṭa'*, 'Ṣiyām', hadiths 672–673, pp.203–204.

29: THE SHARIʿAH'S AIM IN AVOIDING ELABORATION

1. *Liʿān* or *mulāʿanah* is usually translated as imprecation. It is the process followed when the husband accuses his wife of unlawful sexual intercourse for which he cannot produce four witnesses as required by the Qur'an in the following verse: "And as for those who accuse their own wives [of adultery], but have no witnesses except themselves, let each of these [accusers] call on God four times to witness that he is indeed telling the truth, and the fifth time, that God's curse be upon him if he is telling a lie. But [as for the wife, all] chastisement shall be averted from her by her calling on God four times to witness that he is telling a lie, and the fifth [time], that God's curse be upon her if he is telling the truth." (24:6–9)
2. Mālik ibn Anas, *Muwaṭṭa'*, 'Ṭalāq', hadith 1194, p.386; Bukhārī, *Ṣaḥīḥ*, 'Ṭalāq', hadith 5308, pp.948–949; Muslim, *Ṣaḥīḥ* 'Liʿān', hadith 1492, p.594.

3. Bukhārī, *Ṣaḥīḥ*, 'Iᶜtiṣām', hadith 7289, p.1254.
4. Bukhārī, *Ṣaḥīḥ*, 'Ṣalāt al-Tarāwīḥ', hadith 2012, p.322.
5. This tradition has already been documented in the chapter on the universality of the Shariᶜah.
6. Muḥammad ibn Aḥmad al-Qurṭubī, *al-Jāmiᶜ li-Aḥkām al-Qur'an*, ed. Ahmad Abd al-Alim al-Barduni (Beirut: Dār Iḥyā' al-Turāth al-ᶜArabī, n.d.), vol. 3, p.40. The questions referred to by Ibn ᶜAbbās are in the surahs of *al-Baqarah*, 2:189, 215, 217, 219, 220 and 222; *al-Mā'idah*, 5:4; *al-Aᶜrāf*, 7:187; *al-Anfāl*, 8:1; *al-Iṣrā'*, 17:85; *al-Kahf*, 18:83; *Ṭā Hā*, 20:105 and *al-Nāziᶜāt*, 79:44.
7. Ibn al-ᶜArabī, *al-ᶜAwāṣim mina al-Qāwāṣim*, p.255.
8. The fundamentals of inheritance have been laid down in the following verses: "(7) Men shall have a share in what parents and kinsfolk leave behind, and women shall have a share in what parents and kinsfolk leave behind, whether it be little or much – a share ordained [by God]. (8) And when [other] near of kin and orphans and needy persons are present at the distribution [of inheritance], give them something thereof for their sustenance, and speak unto them in a kindly way. (9) And let them stand in awe [of God], those [legal heirs] – who, if they [themselves] had to leave behind weak offspring, would feel fear on their account – and let them remain conscious of God, and let them speak [to the poor] in a just manner. (10) Behold, those who sinfully devour the possessions of orphans but fill their bellies with fire: for [in the life to come] they will have to endure a blazing flame! (11) Concerning [the inheritance of] your children, God enjoins [this] upon you: The male shall have the equal of two females' share; but if there are more than two females, they shall have two-thirds of what [their parents] leave behind; and if there is only one, she shall have one-half thereof. And as for the parents [of the deceased], each of them shall have one-sixth of what he leaves behind, in the event of his having [left] a child; but if he has left no child and his parents are his [only] heirs, then his mother shall have one-third, and if he has brothers and sisters, then his mother shall have one-sixth after [the deduction of] any bequest he may have made, or anv debt [he may have incurred]. As for your parents and your children – you know not which of them is more deserving of benefit from you: (therefore this) ordinance from God. Verily, God is All-Knowing, Wise. (12) And you shall inherit one-half of what your wives leave behind, provided they have left no child; but if they have left a child, then you shall have one-quarter of what they leave behind, after [the deduction of] any bequest they may have made, or any debt [they may have incurred]. And your widows shall have one-quarter of what you leave behind, provided you have left no child; but if you have left a child, then they shall have one-eighth of what you leave behind, after [the deduction of] any bequest you may have made, or any debt [you may have

incurred]. And if a man or a woman has no heir in the direct line, but has a brother or a sister, then each of these two shall inherit one-sixth; but if there are more than two, then they shall share in one-third [of the inheritance], after [the deduction of] any bequest that may have been made, or any debt [that may have been incurred], neither of which having been intended to harm [the heirs]. [This is] an injunction from God: and God is All-Knowing, Forbearing. (13) These are the bounds set by God. And whoever pays heed unto God and His Apostle, him will He bring into gardens, through which running waters flow, therein to abide: and this is a triumph supreme. (14) And whoever rebels against God and His Apostle and transgresses His bounds, him will He commit unto fire, therein to abide; and shameful suffering awaits him." (4:7–14).

9. Dāraquṭnī, *Sunan*, hadith 13, vol. 2/4, pp.152–153. The exact version of this tradition can be translated as follows: "God has given every person his share [of inheritance]..."

10. See a detailed discussion of this rule in Badr al-Dīn al-Zarkashī, *al-Baḥr al-Muḥīṭṭfī Uṣūl al-Fiqh*, ed. Muhammad Muhammad Tamir (Beirut: Dār al-Kutub al-ʿIlmiyyah, 1421/2000), vol. 4, pp.322–325.

11. For a detailed discussion of this and other related issues concerning ends and means in the Shariʿah injunctions, see Ibn ʿAbd al-Salām, *Qawāʿid*, vol. 2, pp.7–9; Qarāfī, *al-Furūq*, vol. 2, pp.450–453.

30: THE SHARIʿAH'S AIM IN BUILDING A SOLID & STABLE SOCIAL ORDER

1. It is important to note that the author dealt with the question of the socio-political order and public interest in an elaborate way in part 2 of his book, *Uṣūl al Niẓām al-Ijtimāʿī fī al-Islām*.

31: THE NECESSITY OF IJTIHAD

1. According to Muhammad Asad, the verses refer "to the conditions prevailing at Medina at the time of the Prophet's hijrah. The two Arab tribes of Medina – Al-Aws and Khazraj – were, in pre-Islamic times, permanently at war with one another; and out of the three Jewish tribes living there – the Banū Qaynuqāʿ, Banū Naḍīr and Banū Qurayẓah – the first-named two were allied with Khazraj, while the third was allied with Al-Aws. Thus, in the course of their warfare, Jew would kill Jew in alliance with pagans ('aiding one another in sin and hatred'): a twofold crime from the viewpoint of Mosaic Law. Nevertheless, they would subsequently ransom their mutual captives in obedience to that very same Law – and it is this glaring inconsistency to which the

Qur'an alludes in the next sentence [: Do you, then, believe in some parts of the divine writ and deny the truth of other parts? What, then, could be the reward of those among you who do such things but ignominy in the life of this world and, on the Day of Resurrection, commitment to most grievous suffering? For God is not unmindful of what you do]." *The Message of the Qur'an*, p.18, note 69.

2. The author refers here to the Qur'anic account of the story of the cow mentioned in 2:67–71. See his comment on these verses and interpretation of their import bearing on the obstinacy and stubbornness of the children of Israel with regard to God's commandments brought to them by the prophet Moses in Ibn Ashur, *Tafsīr al-Taḥrīr wa al-Tanwīr*, vol. 1, pp.546–562.

It is also appropriate to quote here Asad's comment on the significance of this story. As he put it, the story brings to light the Jews' "obstinate desire to obtain closer and closer definitions of the simple commandment revealed to them through Moses [that it] had made it almost impossible for them to fulfil it." In his commentary on this passage Ṭabarī quotes the following remark of Ibn ʿAbbās: "If [in the first instance] they had sacrificed any cow chosen by themselves, they would have fulfilled their duty; but they made it complicated for themselves, and so God made it complicated for them." A similar view has been expressed, in the same context, by Zamakhsharī. It would appear that the moral of this story points to an important problem of all (and, therefore, also of Islamic) religious jurisprudence: namely, the inadvisability of trying to elicit additional details in respect of any religious law that had originally been given in general terms – for, the more numerous and multiform such details become, the more complicated and rigid becomes the law. This point has been acutely grasped by Rashīd Riḍā', who says in his commentary on the above Qur'anic passage (see *Manār I*, 345f.): "Its lesson is that one should not pursue one's [legal] inquiries in such a way as to make laws more complicated.... This was how the early generations [of Muslims] visualized the problem. They did not make things complicated for themselves – and so, for them, the religious law (*dīn*) was natural, simple and liberal in its straightforwardness. But those who came later added to it [certain other] injunctions which they had deduced by means of their own reasoning (ijtihad); and they multiplied those [additional] injunctions to such an extent that the religious law became a heavy burden on the community." For the sociological reason why the genuine ordinances of Islamic Law – that is, those which have been prima facie laid down as such in the Qur'an and the teachings of the Prophet – are almost always devoid of details, I would refer the reader to my book *State and Government in Islam* (pp.11 ff. and *passim*). The importance of this problem, illustrated in the above story of the cow – and correctly grasped by the Prophet's Companions –

explains why this surah has been entitled The "Cow", *The Message of the Qur'an*, pp.15–16, note 55.

3. The most sinful are the scholars versed in the knowledge of the Shariᶜah, who simply live for themselves in isolation from the people. The next most sinful are the ordinary people who do not seek knowledge from the scholars and who even turn their backs on competent scholars when they teach them. The third most sinful are the rulers who do not urge competent scholars to carry out the duty of ijtihad. – Author.
4. See for example Abū Bakr Muḥammad ibn Aḥmad ibn Abī Sahl al-Sarakhsī, *Uṣūl al-Sarakhsī*, ed. Rafīq al-ᶜAjm (Beirut: Dār al-Maᶜrifah, 1418/1997), vol. 2, p.125; al-Ṭūfī, *Sharḥ Mukhtaṣar al-Rawḍah*, vol. 3, pp.259–260.
5. Qarāfī, *Sharḥ Tanqīḥ al-Fuṣūl*, p.268.
6. The establishment of a number of international institutions and bodies such as the Islamic Fiqh Council (al-Majmaᶜ al-Fiqhī al-Islāmī, 1398/1978) of the Muslim World League and The Islamic Fiqh Academy affiliated to the OIC (1408/1987) can be mentioned as an attempt to actualize the suggestion made by the author in the mid-1940s.

PART III: *MAQĀṢID AL-SHARIᶜAH*: HUMAN DEALINGS (*MUᶜĀMALĀT*)

32: ENDS AND MEANS IN TRANSACTIONS

1. Qarāfī, *Sharḥ Tanqīḥ al-Fuṣūl*, p.353; *Furūq*, vol. 2, pp.450–451.
2. Ibn ᶜAbd al-Salām, *Qawāᶜid*, vol. 1, pp.74–75.
3. This refers to the following Tradition narrated by Bukhārī and Muslim on the authority of Abū Hurayrah: "God's Apostle was asked, 'What is the best deed?' He replied, 'To believe in God and His Apostle [Muhammad].' The questioner then asked, 'What is the next (best)?' He replied, 'To participate in Jihad in God's Cause.' The questioner again asked, 'What is the next (best)?' He replied, 'To perform Hajj [Pilgrimage to Makkah] *mabrūr* [which is accepted by God, is performed with the intention of seeking God's pleasure only and not to show off, without committing a sin, and in accordance with the Traditions of the Prophet]'." Bukhārī, *Ṣaḥīḥ*, 'Īmān', hadith 26, p.5; Muslim, *Ṣaḥīḥ*, 'Īmān', hadith 136, p.52.
4. Ibn ᶜAbd al-Salām, *al-Qawāᶜid*, vol. 1, p.75.
5. This refers to the prescriptive rules pertaining to human acts, namely, *wājib* (obligatory), *mandūb* (recommended), *muḥarram* (forbidden), *makrūh* (abominable), and *mubāḥ* (permissible).

6. It is appropriate to note here that Shāṭibī structured part 2 of his book (i.e. *Kitāb al-Maqāṣid*) that deals mainly with the question of *maqāṣid* around these two major themes under the titles of *qaṣd al-Shāriʿ* and *qaṣd al-Mukallaf*. See *al-Muwāfaqāt*, vol. 1/2, pp.321–685.
7. *ʿĀriyyah* (plural: *ʿarāyā*) is the fruit left on the trees by the owner of an orchard for the consumption of the poor. The sale of *ʿāriyyah* is the exchange of dry dates for fresh dates still on the tree. This transaction is permitted as an exemption from the provisions of *ribā* and *salam*. See further details in Ibn Rushd, *The Distinguished Jurist's Primer*, vol. 2, pp.260–264.
8. *Waqf khāṣṣ* is a special endowment whose utility is entailed to the children of its creator. – Author.
9. Ibn ʿAbd al-Salām, *Qawāʿid*, vol. 1, pp.219–221 and *passim*; Qarāfī, *Furūq*, vol. 1, pp.269–270. See also Nyazee, *Islamic Jurisprudence*, pp.92–97.
10. Bukhārī, *Ṣaḥīḥ*, 'Jihad', hadith 2856, p.472; 'Libās', hadith 5967, pp.1044–1045; 'Isti'dhān', hadith 6267, p.1091; 'Riqaq', hadith 6500, pp.1126–1127; 'Tawḥīd', hadith 7373, pp.1268–1269; Muslim, *Ṣaḥīḥ*, 'Īmān', hadith 48–51, pp.36–37.
11. This is the view of Mālik ibn Anas and al-Layth ibn Saʿd, for whom forgiveness does not preclude punishment altogether. This view is also attributed to ʿUmar ibn al-Khaṭṭāb. See Ibn Rushd, *The Distinguished Jurist's Primer*, vol. 2, p.489; Muhammad Arafah al-Dasuqi, *Ḥāshiyah* on *al-Sharḥ al-Kabīr* of Aḥmad ibn Muḥammad al-Dirdīr (Beirut: Dār al-Fikr, n.d.), vol. 4, p.287.
12. For more details on the rules and conditions of pledge (*rahn*), see Ibn Rushd, *The Distinguished Jurist's Primer*, vol. 2, pp.325–333.
13. Qarāfī, *Furūq*, vol. 1, p.452; Ibn ʿAbd al-Salām, *Qawāʿid*, vol. 1, p.168, 175.
14. See Ibn Rushd, *The Distinguished Jurist's Primer*, vol. 2, pp.53–54.
15. Ibid., pp.66–67.

33: PRINCIPLES AND CATEGORIES OF RIGHTS IN THE SHARIʿAH

1. See the author's profound and elaborate discussion of the theological bearing of this verse regarding the meaning and scope of *Maṣlaḥah Tafsīr al-Taḥrīr wa al-Tanwīr*, vol. 1/1, pp.380–381.
2. This is an insertion of part of the following Qur'anic verse: "But excepted shall be the truly helpless – be they men or women or children – who cannot bring forth any strength and have not been shown the right way" (4:98).
3. *Ḥimā* is an enclosed piece of land for the pasturage of the state horses.
4. Mālik ibn Anas, *Muwaṭṭa'*, 'Jāmiʿ', hadith 1842, pp.707–708; Bukhārī, *Ṣaḥīḥ*, 'Jihad', hadith 3059, p.506.
5. Al-Qāḍī Abū Muḥammad ʿAbd al-Wahhāb ibn ʿAlī, *al-Ishrāf*, ed. al-Habib

ibn Tahir (Beirut: Dār Ibn Ḥazm, 1420/1999), vol. 2, pp.761–762; see also his *al-Maᶜūnah ᶜAlā Madhhab ᶜĀlim al-Madinah*, ed. Khamish Abd al-Haqq (Makkah al-Mukarramah: Maktabat Nizār al-Bāz), 1415, vol. 2, p.885 and vol. 4, pp.141–142.

6. That is, Islam has based its legislation for inheritance on the real and natural considerations of parentage (*ubuwwah*) and sonhood (*bunuwwah*), which are not subject to variation. Ibn Ashur, *Tafsīr al-Taḥrīr wa al-Tanwīr*, vol. 34, p.262.
7. On the meaning, subject-matter, kinds, methods and basis of *qismah* (division of property and goods), see Ibn Rushd, *The Distinguished Jurist's Primer*, vol. 2, pp.317–324; al-Shaybānī, *Tabyīn al-Masālik*, vol. 4, pp.152–153; Aḥmad ibn Muḥammad al-Dirdīr, *al-Sharḥ al-Ṣaghīr* on the margin of al-Ṣāwī's *Bulghat al-Sālik* (Beirut: Dār al-Maᶜrifah, 1398/1978), vol. 3, pp.759–771.
8. Bukhārī, *Ṣaḥīḥ*, 'Adhān', hadith 615, p.102. The hadith reads as follows: "If the people knew the reward for pronouncing the *adhan* [the call to prayer], for standing in the first row [in congregational prayers], and found no other way to acquire that except by drawing lots, and if they knew the reward of the *Ẓuhr* prayer [in the early stage of its stated time], they would race for it [go early], and if they knew the reward of *ᶜIshā'* and *Fajr* prayers in congregation, they would come to offer them, even if they had to crawl."
9. Mālik ibn Anas, *Muwaṭṭa'*, 'Qasāmah', hadith 1591, pp.633–634; Bukhārī, *Ṣaḥīḥ*, 'Adab', hadith 6142/6143, pp.1070–1071; 'Aḥkām', hadith 7192, p.1239; Muslim, *Ṣaḥīḥ*, 'Qasāmah', hadith 1669, p.657. Ḥuwayyiṣah and Muḥayyiṣah were the sons of Masᶜūd ibn Kaᶜb ibn ᶜĀmir from the Anṣār. Muḥayyiṣah was younger than Ḥuwayyiṣah. He embraced Islam before him and participated in the battles of *Uḥud*, *al-Khandaq* (the Ditch), and other major events.
10. Aḥmad ibn Ḥanbal, *Musnad*, vol. 1, pp.220 & 225.
11. Reference here is made to the tradition narrated by Mujāhid that Umm Salamah asked the Prophet: "O Messenger of God! Why do men fight in God's cause and we [women] do not and we are given only half of what is given to men in inheritance? Then, the verse was revealed." Ṭabarī, *Jāmiᶜ al-Bayān fī Ta'wīl Āyi al-Qur'an* (Beirut: Dār al-Kutub al-ᶜIlmiyyah, 1412/1992), vol. 4, p.49; Ibn Qayyim al-Jawziyyah, *Iᶜlām Muwaqqiᶜīn*, vol. 2/4, p.298.
12. Regarding the conditions covering the appointment of judges, al-Māwardī has provided a succinct summary of the different views of the jurists concerning woman's eligibility to the office of judgeship. He said: "Although judgments may take their testimony into consideration, women are not qualified to hold major government positions." According to Abū Ḥanīfa, women may pass judgment in areas where their testimonies are valid, but not in areas

where their testimonies are not acceptable. Ibn Jarīr al-Ṭabarī departed from the consensus by making women eligible to hold judgeships under all circumstances, but there is no strength in a view that meets with unanimous rejection, in addition to God's own words: "Men are in charge of women, for God has preferred in bounty one of them over the other" (Qur'an 4:34); that is, in mind and judgement, so that it is improper for them to take precedence over men. Al-Māwardī, *The Ordinances of Government*, p.72.
However, an increasing number of scholars and thinkers have contested this view on Islamic grounds.

34: *MAQĀṢID AL SHARIʿAH*: FAMILY

1. Bukhārī, *Ṣaḥīḥ*, 'Nikāḥ', hadith 5127, p.917.
2. Fornication (*sifāḥ*) is a temporary illegal sexual (*zinā*) relationship without commitment. Cohabitation (*mukhādanah*) is a permanent and committed illegal sexual relationship. – Author.
3. Imru' al-Qays ibn Ḥujr ibn al-Ḥārith (500–540 AC) was a famous poet of the pre-Islamic era (*Jāhiliyyah*). He was from the Kahtanite tribe of Kinda and the author of the first Ode (*Muʿallaqah*). Al-Malik al-Ḍillīl was his nickname. Imru'ū al-Qays belonged to a family with a long tradition of rule and he himself became king.
4. Tabrīzī, *Sharḥ al-Qaṣā'id al-ʿAshr*, p.37.
5. His name was Abū ʿAbd Allāh Saḥīm ibn Wathīl. He was an eloquent slave poet from Abyssinia. He was bought by Banū al-Ḥasḥās, one of the clans of the tribe of Banū al-Najjār from the Khazraj. He was killed in 40/660 because of his rhapsodizing about women, especially his master's sister and daughter.
6. This is the second verse of a poem, in which the poet describes how he used to seduce the tribe's girls and persuade them to surrender themselves to him without any resistance. Muḥammad ibn Shākir al-Kutubī, *Fawāt al-Wafayāt*, ed. Ihsan Abbas (Beirut: Dār Ṣādir, n.d.), vol. 1, p.239; ʿAbd al-Qādir ibn ʿUmar al-Baghdādī, *Khizānat al-Adab wa Lubb Lubāb Lisān al-ʿArab*, ed. Abd al-Salam Harun (Cairo: al-Khānjī, 1409/1989), vol. 2, pp.102–106 and *Sharḥ Abyāt al-Mughnī*, ed. Abd al-Aziz Rabah et al. (Damascus: Dār al-Ma'mūn, 1980), vol. 2, pp.340–342.
7. See more elaboration by the author on this verse in Ibn Ashur, *Tafsīr al-Taḥrīr wa al-Tanwīr*, vol. 10/21, pp.71–72.
8. See Hammudah Abd al-Ati, *The Family Structure in Islam* (Indianapolis, IN: American Trust Publications, 1977), pp.70–76.
9. Emphasizing the importance and solemnity of the marriage contract and highlighting the difference between it and all other human dealings, Qarāfī (*Furūq*,

vol. 3, p.931) said the following: "And so marriage (*nikāḥ*) is of a solemn significance and occupies a sublime place. This is because it is the means to the preservation of the dignified human species, which has been raised above all creatures. It is also because marriage is the only way to chastity, that blocks all avenues of evil, corruption, and confusion of descent. Thirdly, it is because marriage is the path to real love, tenderness, and companionship [between man and woman]."

10. See an exposition of the different views on this issue in Abd al-Ghaniy al-Maydani, *al-Lubāb fī Sharḥ al-Kitāb* (Beirut: Dār al-Kutub al-ʿIlmiyyah, 1400/1980), vol. 3, p.8.
11. For the sake of clarifying the author's argument, we have preferred a literal rendering of the term *'ujūr* which has otherwise been translated as dowers by a number of scholars like Yusuf Ali, Pickthall, and Asad.
12. See, for example, Ibn Rushd, *The Distinguished Jurist's Primer*, vol. 2, p.8; Yaḥyā ibn Sharaf al-Nawawī, *Sharḥ Ṣaḥīḥ Muslim* (Beirut: Dār Iḥyā' al-Turāth al-ʿArabī, n.d.), vol. 9, p.202; Qarāfī, *Furūq*, vol. 3, p.927; Abū ʿAbd Allāh Muḥammad al-Anṣārī al-Raṣṣāʿ, *Sharḥ Ḥudūd ibn ʿArafah*, ed. Muhammad Abu al-Ajfan & al-Tāhir al-Mamuri (Beirut: Dār al-Gharb al-Islāmī, 1993), vol. 1, p.326.
    For a detailed sociological and anthropological discussion of the issue of dower and its significance in Islam, see Abd al-Ati, *The Family Structure in Islam*, pp.62–70.
13. The expression "what is being conveyed unto you in this Divine writ about orphan women" refers to the following verse already quoted by the author: "And if you have reason to fear that you might not act equitably towards orphans, then marry from among [other] women such as are lawful to you – [even] two, or three, or four" (4:3).
14. Bukhārī, *Ṣaḥīḥ*, 'Tafsīr', hadith 4574, pp.780–781.
15. Thus, ʿAntarah said: "Oh! Eve snatched by whom lawful for she has become, forbidden to me she has become, I wish she were not." He meant that she married and, therefore, he was not allowed to get to her out of magnanimity. [Author]. Tabrīzī, *Sharḥ al-Qaṣā'id al-ʿAshr*, Verse 59, "Muʿallaqah", p.243.
16. In making the argument about the sense of moral protection in marriage, the author has clearly resorted to a semantic analysis of the primary signification of the root verb *ḥṣn* denoting strength, fortification, immunity, protection, inaccessibility, trust, etc. See E.W.Lane, *Arabic-English Lexicon* (Cambridge, UK: Islamic Texts Society, 1984), vol. 1, pp.586–587.
17. Mālik ibn Anas, *Muwaṭṭa'*, 'Nikāḥ', hadith 1140, p.369; Bukhārī, *Ṣaḥīḥ*, 'Nikāḥ', hadiths 5115–5119, p.915.
18. More so, this is view of the *Imāmīs* (also known as Twelver Shiʿa), followers of

Imam Jaʿfar al-Ṣādiq (702–765) ibn Muhammad al-Bāqir are by far the largest of all Shiite groups even though their Imams never gained political power like the Imams of the Ismailis and Zaidis. They recognize a line of twelve successive Imams, the last of whom they believe to remain alive to this day, despite his having gone into occultation in 874 AC. The Imāmī School has been the official and majority *madhhab* of Iran since the early 16th century AC, and is also strongly represented throughout the Middle East and Asia, especially in Iraq, Lebanon, India, and Pakistan.

19. For a detailed discussion of this issue, see Abd al-Ati, *The Family Structure in Islam*, pp.103–109; Arthur Gribetz, *Strange Bedfellows: Mutʿat al-Nisā' and Mutʿat al-Ḥajj* (Berlin: Klaus Schwarz Verlag, 1994), pp.9–21. See also Ibn Rushd, *The Distinguished Jurist's Primer*, vol. 2, pp 67–68, and Muḥammad ibn ʿAlī ibn Muḥammad al-Shawkānī, *Nayl al-Awṭār*, pp.1264–1267.
20. See on this issue Ibn Rushd, *The Distinguished Jurist's Primer*, vol. 2, pp.475–477. It is worth noting here that once a slave woman has borne a child to her master, her status automatically changes from slavery to freedom and her children are born free. Like many other provisions of the Shariʿah addressing the problem of slavery, which was the norm at the advent of Islam, this constituted an integral part of the global humane approach of the Shariʿah to remove all sources of slavery.
21. Mālik ibn Anas, *Muwaṭṭa'*, 'Raḍāʿ', hadith 1287, p.417; Bukhārī, *Ṣaḥīḥ*, 'Shahādāt', hadith 2645, p.428.
22. Rāzī said this in his commentary on verse 23 of *Sūrah al-Nisā'*: "Forbidden to you are your mothers, and your daughters, and your sisters, and your aunts paternal and maternal, and a brother's daughters, and a sister's daughters; and your milk-mothers, and your milk-sisters; and the mothers of your wives; and your step-daughters – who are your foster-children – born of your wives with whom you have consummated your marriage; but if you have not consummated your marriage, you will incur no sin [by marrying their daughters]; and [forbidden to you are] the spouses of the sons who have sprung from your loins; and [you are forbidden] to have two sisters [as your wives] at one and the same time – but what is past is past: for, behold, God is indeed Much-Forgiving, a Dispenser of Grace", *al-Tafsīr al-Kabīr*, vol. 5/10, p.22.
23. Ibn Ashur, *Tafsīr, al-Taḥrīr wa al-Tanwīr*, vol.3/4, pp.295–296.
24. This has been clearly instituted in the following Qur'anic verse in the wider context of Islam's legislation for social intercourse between Muslims and People of the Book. Thus, we read in the Qur'an:

    "Today, all the good things of life have been made lawful to you. And the food of those who were vouchsafed revelation previously is lawful to you, and your food is lawful to them. And [lawful to you are], in wedlock, women from among those who believe [in this divine writ], and, in wedlock, women from among those who have been vouchsafed revelation before your time provided that you give them their dowers, taking them in honest wedlock, not in fornication, nor as mistresses" (5:5).

Commenting on this Qur'anic provision allowing Muslim men to marry women from the followers of other revealed religions, Muhammad Asad has the following to say: "Whereas Muslim men are allowed to marry women from among the followers of another revealed religion, Muslim women may not marry non-Muslims: the reason being that Islam enjoins reverence of all the prophets, while the followers of other religions reject some of them – e.g., the Prophet Muhammad or, as is the case with the Jews, both Muhammad and Jesus. Thus, while a non-Muslim woman who marries a Muslim can be sure that – despite all doctrinal differences – the prophets of her faith will be mentioned with utmost respect in her Muslim environment, a Muslim woman who would marry a non-Muslim would always be exposed to an abuse of him whom she regards as God's Apostle." Asad, *The Message of the Qur'an*, p.142, note 14.

25. The obligation to provide maintenance for one's parents, children and next of kin is enjoined upon the Muslim regardless of whether or not they are Muslim. See, for example, Bukhārī, *Ṣaḥīḥ*, 'Zakah', hadiths 1461 and 1466–1467, pp.236–238; 'Hibah', hadith 2592, p.419 and 2620, p.424, 'al-Jizyah wa al-Muwādaʿah', hadith 3183, p.530; 'Adab', hadith 5978, p.1047; Muslim, *Ṣaḥīḥ*, 'Zakah', hadiths 998–1003, pp.360–361.

In this respect, the Shafiʿi jurist Ibn Naqib al-Misri says: "It is obligatory for one to support the persons listed below, whether one is male or female, whether one has money in excess of one's own living expenses and (if male,) those of one's wife." Then he mentioned the following persons: (1) one's father, father's father, and on up; (2), one's mother, grandmother (from either parent's side) and on up (making no difference what their religion is); and (3) one's children, male and female, their children, and on down. *Reliance of the Traveller*, pp.547–548.

26. On the jurists' views concerning the obligation to provide maintenance for one's grandparents and grandchildren, see the following works: Muḥammad ibn Aḥmad al-Shaybānī al-Shinqīṭī, *Tabyīn al-Masālik* (Beirut: Dār al-Gharb al-Islāmī), vol. 3, p.244; Muhammad ibn Ahmad al-Shirbini, *al-Iqnāʿ fī Ḥall Alfāẓ Abī Shujāʿ* (Beirut: Dār al-Maʿrifah, n.d), vol. 2, p.140; Muhammad ibn Ahmad al-Ayni, *al-Bināyah fī Sharḥ al-Hidāyah* (Beirut: Dār al-Fikr, 1400/1980), vol. 4, p.906.

27. See further elaboration by author on this aspect in *Tafsīr al-Taḥrīr wa al-Tanwīr*, vol. 3/4, pp.247–250 and 255–267.

28. This has been laid down in the following Qur'anic phrase: "and [you are forbidden] to have two sisters [as your wives] at one and the same time" (4:23).
29. Bukhārī, *Ṣaḥīḥ*, 'Shurūṭ', hadith 2721, p.445; Muslim, *Ṣaḥīḥ*, 'Nikāḥ', hadith 1418, p.527; Abū Dāwūd, *Sunan*, 'Nikāḥ', hadith 2639, vol. 2, p.604; Tirmidhī, *Sunan*, 'Nikāḥ', hadith 1127, vol. 3, p.434; Aḥmad ibn Ḥanbal, *Musnad*, vol. 4, p.144.
30. For further details on Saʿīd ibn al-Musayyab's view and those agreeing with him, such as ʿAṭā' ibn Abī Rabāḥ, al-Shaʿbī, al-Zuhrī, Qatādah, al-Ḥasan al-Baṣrī, and Muḥammad ibn Sīrīn, see Hamad ibn Muhammad al-Hattabi, *Alām al-Ḥadīth fī Sharḥ Ṣaḥīḥ al-Bukhārī*, ed. Muhammad ibn Sʿad al-Suʿud (Makkah: Jāmiʿat Umm al-Qurā, 1409/1988), vol. 3, p.1980; Muhammad Rawas Qalʿaji, *Mawsūʿat Fiqh Ibrāhīm al-Nakhʿī* (Makkah: Jāmiʿat Umm al-Qurā, 1399/1980), vol. 2, p.677.
31. Mālik said in this regard, "The custom among us [i.e. the jurists of Madinah] is that when a man marries a woman, and he makes a condition in the marriage contract that he will not marry a second wife or take a concubine (*tasarrur*), it means nothing unless there is an oath of divorce or release attached to it. The oath is obligatory and is required from him." *Muwaṭṭa'*, 'Nikāḥ', p.360. See further details in Ibn al-ʿArabī, *al-Qabas ʿAlā Muwaṭṭa'*, ed. Muhammad Abd al-Karim Weld Karim (Beirut: Dār al-Gharb al-Islāmī, 1992), vol. 2, pp.698–701.
32. This is what has been confirmed in the report concerning Ḍamḍam al-Fazārī, according to which the Prophet explicitly forbade him from disowning a child by relying on his dissimilarity from him, as narrated in the authentic collections of Bukhārī and Muslim. – Author.

    Thus, it is reported by Abū Hurayrah: "A man [from Banū Fazārah] came to the Prophet and said, 'O God's Apostle! A black child has been born to me.' The Prophet asked him, 'Have you any camels?' The man said, 'Yes.' The Prophet asked him, 'What color are they?' The man replied, 'Red.' The Prophet said, 'Is there a dusky one among them?' The man replied, 'Yes.' The Prophet said, 'where did it come from?' He said, 'May be it is because of heredity.' The Prophet said, 'May be your latest son has this color because of heredity'." Bukhārī, *Ṣaḥīḥ*, 'Ṭalāq', hadith 5305, p.948; 'Ḥudūd', hadith 6847, p.1180 and 'Iʿtiṣām', hadith 7314, p.1259; Muslim, *Ṣaḥīḥ*, 'Liʿān', hadith 1500 (18–20), p.578.
33. Zayd was captured as a child of eight years of age during a raid, which was the norm before Islam. Ḥakīm ibn Ḥizām bought him for his aunt Khadījah bint Khuwaylid. After she married Muhammad, Khadījah gave Zayd to him. At some point, Zayd's real family found out where he was and went to Muhammad to demand Zayd's return. Zayd was given a choice and he chose

to stay with Muhammad, and it was after this that Zayd was adopted and became known as Zayd ibn (son of) Muhammad. All this took place before the Revelation came to the Prophet.

As for Sālim, he was a slave of Persian origin to a certain Fāṭimah bint Yaʿār, a lady from Madinah. When he accepted Islam, a lady from the Anṣār by the name of Sā'ibah manumitted him. Then he was adopted as a son by a Muslim, who was formerly a leading nobleman of the Quraysh, Abū Ḥudhayfah ibn ʿUtbah.

When the verse of the Qur'an was revealed abolishing adoption, people like Zayd and Sālim had to change their names. Zayd, who had been known as Zayd ibn Muhammad, had to be called after his own natural father. Henceforth he was known as Zayd ibn Ḥārithah. Sālim, however, did not know the name of his father. Indeed, he did not know who his father was. However, he remained under the protection of Abū Ḥudhayfah and so came to be known as Sālim Mawlā Abī Ḥudhayfah. Zayd is said to have been the first male to have embraced Islam and believed in the Apostleship of the Prophet Muhammad. In the year 8 AH the Prophet appointed him commander of the Muslim army during the battle of Mu'tah, in which he was killed.

35: *MAQĀṢID AL-SHARIʿAH*: FINANCIAL TRANSACTIONS (I)

1. Qur'anic verses relating to this are numerous, such as "They will answer [on the Day of Judgment]: 'We were not among those who prayed, and neither did we feed the needy'" (74:43–44). – Author.
2. The comparison of wealth to a green and sweet fruit is based on a parable made by the Prophet before this, as narrated by Abū Saʿīd al-Khudrī that God's Messenger said: "The things I am afraid of most for your sake [concerning what will befall you after me] is the pleasures and splendors of the world and its beauties which will be disclosed to you." Somebody said, "O God's Apostle! Can the good bring forth evil?" The Prophet remained silent for a while. It was said to that person, "What is wrong with you? You are talking to the Prophet *(ṢAAS)* whereas he is not talking to you." Then we noticed that he was being inspired divinely. Then the Prophet wiped away his sweat and said, "Where is the questioner?" It seemed as if the Prophet liked his question. Then he said, "Good never brings forth evil. Indeed, it is like what grows on the banks of a stream, which either kills or makes the animals sick, except if an animal eats its fill of the *khaḍirah* (a kind of vegetable) and then faces the sun, and then defecates and urinates and grazes again. No doubt this wealth is sweet and green..." Bukhārī, *Ṣaḥīḥ*, 'Zakah', hadith 1465, p.237; Muslim, *Ṣaḥīḥ*, 'Zakah', hadith 1035, p.371.

3. Bukhārī, *Ṣaḥīḥ*, 'Riqāq', hadith 6441, p.1117; Muslim, *Ṣaḥīḥ*, 'Zakah', hadith 995, p.359.
4. Bukhārī, *Ṣaḥīḥ*, 'Riqāq', hadith 6444, p.1118; Aḥmad ibn Ḥanbal, *Musnad*, vol. 2, p.358, 391, 525 and vol. 5, p.181.
5. Bukhārī, *Ṣaḥīḥ*, 'Zakah', hadith 1468, p.238; Muslim, *Ṣaḥīḥ*, 'Zakah', hadith 983, p.352.
6. Muslim, *Ṣaḥīḥ*, 'Masājid', hadith 595, pp.218–219; Bukhārī, *Ṣaḥīḥ*, 'Adhān', hadith 843, pp.136–137; 'Daᶜawāt', hadith 6329, p.1101; Aḥmad ibn Ḥanbal, *Musnad*, vol. 5, pp.167–168.
7. Bukhārī, *Ṣaḥīḥ*, 'Zakah', hadith 1442, p.233; Muslim, *Ṣaḥīḥ*, 'Zakah', hadith 1010, p.363.
8. This incident, which besides Kaᶜb ibn Mālik included Marārah ibn al-Rabīᶜ and Hilāl ibn Umayyah, has been recorded by the Qur'an in the following verses:

   Indeed, God has turned in His Mercy to the Prophet, as well as to those who have forsaken the domain of evil and those who have sheltered and succored the Faith – [all] those who followed him in the hour of distress, when the hearts of some of the other believers had well-nigh swerved from faith. And once again: He has turned in His Mercy – for, behold, He is Compassionate towards them, a Dispenser of Grace. And [He turned in His Mercy, too,] toward the three [groups of believers] who had fallen prey to corruption, until in the end – after the earth, despite all its vastness, had become [too] narrow for them and their souls had become [utterly] constricted – they came to know with certainty that there is no refuge from God other than [a return] to Him; and thereupon He turned again to them in His Mercy, so that they might repent: for, verily, God Alone is an acceptor of repentance, a Dispenser of Grace. (9:117–118).

9. Bukhārī, *Ṣaḥīḥ*, 'Zakah', *Bāb* 18, p.230; 'Waṣāyā', hadith 2757, p.456 and 'Tafsīr', hadith 4676, p.803.
10. Bukhārī, *Ṣaḥīḥ*, 'Waṣāyā', hadith 2742, p.452; Muslim, *Ṣaḥīḥ*, 'Waṣiyyah', hadith 1628, pp.636–637.
11. To make the author's argument here clearer it seems appropriate to quote Asad's comment on this verse, which will also serve to clarify the purport of the other verses. He says: "Inasmuch as love of worldly goods and a desire to protect one's family may lead a person to transgression (and, thus, to a betrayal of the moral values postulated in God's message), they are described as *fitnah* – which, in this context, is best rendered by the two words 'trial and temptation'. This reminder connects with verse 25 above, 'beware of that temptation to evil which does not befall only those who are bent on denying the truth,' since it is acquisitiveness and a desire to confer benefits on one's own family which often tempt an otherwise good person to offend against the

rights of his fellow-men. It is to be borne in mind that, contrary to the New Testament, the Qur'ān does not postulate a contempt for worldly attachments as a prerequisite of righteousness: it only demands of man that he should not allow these attachments to deflect him from the pursuit of moral verities." *The Message of the Qur'an*, p.242, Note 28.

12. Bukhārī, *Ṣaḥīḥ*, 'Riqāq', hadith 6425, p.1115; Tirmidhī, *Sunan*, 'Ṣifat al-Qiyāmah', hadith 2426, vol. 4, p.640; Ibn Mājah, *Sunan*, 'Fitan', hadith 3997, vol. 2, pp.1324–1325; Aḥmad ibn Ḥanbal, *Musnad*, vol. 4, p.137 & 327.
13. Bukhārī, *Ṣaḥīḥ*, 'Zakah', *Bāb* 4, pp.226–227; Ibn Mājah, *Sunan*, 'Zakah', vol. 1, pp.569–570; Abū Dāwūd, *Sunan*, 'Zakah', hadith 1564, vol. 2, p.95.; Al-Bayhaqī, *Sunan*, vol. 4, pp.82–83.
14. Bukhārī, *Ṣaḥīḥ*, 'Zakah', hadith 1407, pp.227.
15. The story of Abū Dharr's withdrawal to the city of al-Rabadhah is reported by Bukhārī (*Ṣaḥīḥ*, 'Zakah', hadith 1406, pp.226–227). Zayd ibn Wahb narrated the following: "I passed by a place called al-Rabadhah and by chance I met Abū Dharr and asked him, 'What has brought you to this place?' He said, 'I was in Shām and differed with Muʿāwiyah on the meaning of [the following verses of the Qur'an]. "They who hoard up gold and silver and spend them not in the way of God" (9:34). Muʿāwiyah said, "This verse is revealed regarding the people of the scriptures." I said, "It was revealed regarding us and also the people of the scriptures." So, we had a quarrel and Muʿāwiyah sent a complaint about me to ʿUthmān. ʿUthmān wrote to me to come to Madinah, and I came to Madinah. Many people came to me as if they had not seen me before. So I told this to ʿUthmān who said to me, "You may depart and live nearby if you wish." That was the reason for my being here, for even if an Ethiopian had been nominated as my ruler, I would have obeyed him.'" See also Muslim, *Ṣaḥīḥ*, 'Zakah', hadith 992, p.358.
16. We have adopted here 'Abdullah Yusuf Ali's translation of the verse in order to convey the point argued by the author. An alternative rendering of it is the following one by Muhammad Asad: "And do not entrust to those who are weak of judgment the possessions which God has placed in your charge for [their] support; but let them have their sustenance therefrom, and clothe them, and speak to them in a kindly way."

    According to the author, it is possible that the term *sufahā'* is a specific reference to orphan children, for minority is mostly associated with weakness of judgement (*safah*), thus it is necessary to prevent them from disposing of their possessions on their own. It is also possible, and this is a much richer connotation that is more in line with the spirit of Qur'anic legislation, that it means weakness of judgement in an absolute way, whether it is due to minority or mental retardation, thus including grown-up people. As for the attribution of possessions to the plurality addressed by the phrase "O Mankind (*al-nās*)" in the beginning of the surah, it is a clear indication that the wealth circulating in people's hands is only apparently the exclusive property and right of its owners. When examined more carefully, it is revealed that such wealth includes rights of the whole society, since what belongs to the individuals actually benefits the society at large in various ways. For Ibn Ashur, this is a very important clue to the Qur'anic conception of private and public wealth. Ibn Ashur, *Tafsīr al-Taḥrīr wa al-Tanwīr*, vol. 3/4, p.234–235.

17. Bukhārī, *Ṣaḥīḥ*, 'Zakah', hadith 1468, p.238; Muslim, 'Zakah', hadith 983, p.352; Aḥmad ibn Ḥanbal, *Musnad*, vol. 2, p.322.
18. Rūmah was a well-known well in Madinah.
19. Bukhārī, *Ṣaḥīḥ*, 'Musāqāh/I', p.378; al-Tirmidhī, *Sunan*, 'Manāqib', hadith 3703; al-Nasā'ī, *Sunan*, 'Waqf al-Masājid', hadith 3608, vol. 6, p.235.
20. From this we understand the variation in Arab language concerning the connotation of the word *māl*. Likewise, the owners of camels call them *māl*, such in ʿUmar's statement, "Were it not for the animals [*māl*] (in my custody) which I give to be ridden for striving in God's Cause". Similarly, palm cultivators consider palm-trees wealth, as in the report about Abū Ṭalḥah that he had the greatest amount of property (*māl*) in palm-trees among the *Anṣār* in Madinah and that the dearest of his properties to him was *Bayruḥā'*, which was in front of the mosque. When the verse "You will not obtain righteousness until you spend what you love" (3:92) was revealed, Abū Ṭalḥah went to the Messenger of God and said, "Messenger of God, the Blessed, the Exalted, has said, 'You will not obtain righteousness until you spend what you love.' The property (*māl*) which I love the best is *Bayruḥā'*. It is *ṣadaqah* for God's sake. I hope for its good and for it to be stored with God. Place it wherever you wish, Messenger of God." The Prophet said, "Well done! That is property (*māl*) which is profitable! That is property which is profitable". [Mālik ibn Anas, *Muwaṭṭa'*, 'Jāmiʿ', hadith 1828, pp.703–704]. Also, people possessing gold and silver call them *māl*. – Author.
    For more details on this aspect, see Nazih Kamal Hammad, *Muʿjam al-Muṣṭalaḥāt al-Iqtiṣādiyyah fī Lughat al-Fuqahā'* (Herndon VA: International Institute of Islamic Thought, 1410/1995), p.238.
21. *Banque* is a French term derived from the medieval Latin word *banco* that originally refered to a place where a person would sit to write or simply to rest. It then was used to mean the place used by the money changer. Later, the meaning of this term was extended to refer to the building where a group of people worked in money changing, orders for payment (*ḥawālāt*) and bills of exchange (*safātij*). – Author.

22. "Shu'ayb is said to be identical with Jethro, the father-in-law of Moses, also called in the Bible Reú-el (Exodus ii, 18), meaning 'faithful to God'. The region of Madyan – the Midian of the Bible – extended from the present-day Gulf of Aqabah westwards deep into the Sinai Peninsula and to the mountains of Moab east of the Dead Sea; its inhabitants were Arabs of the Amorite group of tribes." Asad, *The Message of the Qur'an*, p.216, note 67.
23. Mālik ibn Anas, *Muwaṭṭa'*, 'Aqḍiyah', hadith 1421, p.528. In his commentary on the hadith, Mālik said: "The unjust root is whatever is taken or planted unlawfully."
24. *Mughārasah* is a kind of land tenure or contract in which the landlord gives his barren land to someone to plant fruit trees in it. On the different juristic positions concerning the validity of this transaction and its relationship with other types of land-based dealings, see Ziaul Haque, *Landlord and Peasant in Early Islam* (Islamabad: Islamic Research Institute, 1984), pp.311–346.
25. This definition is taken from Ibn al-Shāṭ's commentary on Qarāfī's *Furūq* with some modification. – Author.
    The exact words of Abū al-Qāsim ibn al-Shāṭ read as follows: "The correct definition of ownership is that it is man's capacity whether by himself or by delegating someone else to make use of a thing (*'ayn*) or benefit (*manfa'ah*) and to take the substitute of a thing (*'ayn*) or benefit (*manfa'ah*)." See *Furūq*, vol. 3, p.1009, note No. 6.
26. "The term "pasture" (*mar'ā*) connotes here, metonymically, all herbal produce suitable for consumption by man or animal (Rāzī)." Muhammad Asad, *The Message of the Qur'an*, p.928, note 14.
27. "Lit., 'who has made the earth submissive (*dhalūlan*) to you': i.e., yielding to the intelligence with which He has endowed man." Asad, *The Message of the Qur'an*, p.881, note 14.
28. "The implication is that man ought to be grateful for all this God-given bounty, but as a rule is not: and this connects with the subsequent evocation of the Day of Resurrection, already hinted at in the reference to the recurring phenomenon of life-renewal." Asad, *The Message of the Qur'an*, p.931, note 9.

36: *MAQĀṢID AL-SHARI'AH*: FINANCIAL TRANSACTIONS (II)

1. Bukhārī, *Ṣaḥīḥ*, 'al-Ḥarth wa al-Muzāra'ah', hadith 2320, p.372; Muslim, *Ṣaḥīḥ*, 'Musāqāh', hadith 1553, p.604; al-Ḥasan ibn Mas'ūd al-Baghawī, *Mafātīḥ al-Sunnah* (Beirut: Dār al-Ma'rifah, 1987), 'Zakah', hadith 1344, vol. 1, p.47; Dārimī, *Sunan*, 'Buyū'', hadith 2613, vol. 2, p.580; Tirmidhī, *Sunan*, 'Aḥkām', hadith 1388, vol. 3, p.666; Aḥmad ibn Ḥanbal, *Musnad*, vol. 3, p.147, 192, 229 and 243.

2. There are numerous reports, including Traditions attributed to the Prophet, emphasizing this meaning. See, for example, Ibn ʿAṭiyah, *al-Muḥarrar al-Wajīz*, vol. 5, p.391; Muḥammad ibn Ahmad al-Qurṭubī, *al-Jāmiʿ li-Aḥkām al-Qur'an*, ed. Aḥmad ʿAbd al-ʿAlīm al-Bardūnī (Beirut: Dār Iḥyā' al-Turāth al-ʿArabī, n.d.), vol. 19, pp.55–56.
3. According to the scholars of Traditions, this is a statement by ʿUmar. However, some people attribute to the Prophet a Tradition in this regard, in which he is reported to have said: "Seek trade with orphans' property so that zakah will not erode it." They also attribute to him the Tradition: "Oh! Whoever assumes custody of an orphan who has a property should trade with it and not leave it to be eroded by zakah." Yet, all such reports are based on weak transmission chains. – Author.
   See ʿUmar's statement, in Mālik ibn Anas, *Muwaṭṭa'*, 'Zakah', hadith 588, p.167. In the same context, Mālik narrated that ʿĀ'ishah, the wife of the Prophet, used to give the property of the orphans that were in her house to whoever would use it to trade with on their behalf. Commenting on this issue, Mālik said, "There is no harm in using the property of orphans to trade with on their behalf if their gurdian has given permission. Furthermore, I do not think that he is under any liability." Ibid., pp.167–168.
4. See on the detailed meaning of the term *dājj*, Abū al-Faḍl Jamāl al-Dīn Muḥammad ibn Mukarram ibn Manẓūr, *Lisān al-ʿArab* (Beirut: Dār Ṣādir, 1410/1990), vol. 2, pp.263–264.
5. In this regard, Ibn ʿAbbās narrated: "ʿUkāẓ, Majannah, and Dhū al-Majāz were the markets of the people during the pre-Islamic period of ignorance. When the people embraced Islam, they disliked doing trading there till the following verse was revealed: 'There is no harm for you if you seek the bounty of your Lord [during Hajj by trading, etc] (2:198)'." Bukhārī, *Ṣaḥīḥ*, 'Hajj', hadith 1770, p.285; 'Buyūʿ', hadith 2050 and 298 (pp.329 & 337) and 'Tafsīr', hadith 4519, p.768. See further detail on the occasion and context of the revelation of this verse in Ibn ʿAṭiyah, *al-Muḥarrar al-Wajīz*, vol. 1, pp.274–275; Ibn Ashur, *Tafsīr al-Taḥrīr wa al-Tanwīr*, vol. 2, pp.237–38.
   Commenting on this verse, Muhammad Asad quotes Muhammad Abduh, who pointed out (in *al-Manār*) "that the endeavour 'to obtain any bounty from your Sustainer' implies God-consciousness and, therefore, constitutes a kind of worship provided, of course, that this endeavour does not conflict with any other, more prominent religious requirement." *The Message of the Qur'an*, p.43, note 181.
6. "The above phrase embraces any transaction on the basis of credit, be it an outright loan or a commercial deal. It relates (as the grammatical form *tadāyantum* shows) to both the giver and taker of credit." Muhammad Asad, *The Message of the Qur'an*, p.62, note 269.

7. Known as *āyat al-dayn* or *al-mudāyanah*, this verse is the longest verse in the Qur'an, and it happens also to be in the longest surah. It lays down detailed rules concerning the authentication and documentation of people's financial transactions. According to the author, the verse highlights a very important fact of human society, namely mutual borrowing (*tadāyun*) as a crucial means of promoting financial transactions and economic growth in the different fields of economic activity, especially agriculture, industry, and trade. Implying that the community, in general, consists of both creditors and debtors, it has provided the necessary provisions that ensure confidence and stability in people's dealings by preventing all causes of dispute and disorder by the authentication and documentation of the rights of the different parties. Ibn Ashur, *Tafsīr al-Taḥrir wa al-Tanwīr*, vol. 3/3, pp.98–100.
8. The rule of ambiguity (*gharar*) is the prohibition of transactions which include uncertainty and risk for one or more of the parties involved. This uncertainty might be the result of a number of things, such as lack of knowledge of the subject-matter, failure to determine its price or its attributes and characteristics, failure to determine the contract, lack of knowledge about the existence of the commodity, the impossibility of delivery, etc. See more detail in Ibn Rushd, *The Distinguished Jurist's Primer*, vol. 2, pp.179–192.
9. Qarāfī, *Furūq*, vol. 3, pp.1059–1063.
10. *Juʿāl* is hire "in which the acquisition of benefits is probable, like the stipulation of recovery (of the patient) in the case of the doctor, proficiency in the case of the teacher." Ibn Rushd, *The Distinguished Jurist's Primer*, vol. 2, p.282.
11. Qarāfī, *Furūq*, vol. 4, p.1128.
12. Cf. Ibn Ashur, *Tafsīr al-Taḥrir wa al-Tanwīr*, vol. 13/28, p.85.
13. "The word *khayr* occurring in this sentence denotes "much wealth" and not simply "property": and this explains the injunction that one who leaves much wealth behind should make bequests to particularly deserving members of his family in addition to – and preceding the distribution of – the legally-fixed shares mentioned in 4:11–13. This interpretation of *khayr* is supported by sayings of ʿĀ'ishah and ʿAlī ibn Abī Ṭālib, both of them referring to this particular verse." Asad, *The Message of the Qur'an*, p.38, note 152.
14. The principal verses spelling out the legal shares of inheritance due to the next of kin read as follows:

    Concerning [the inheritance of] your children, God enjoins [this] upon you: The male shall have the equal of two females' share; but if there are more than two females, they shall have two-thirds of what [their parents] leave behind; and if there is only one, she shall have one-half thereof. As for the parents [of the deceased], each of them shall have one-sixth of what he leaves behind, in the event of his having [left] a child; but if he has left no child and his parents are his [only] heirs, then his mother shall have one-third, and if he has brothers and sisters, then his mother shall have one-sixth after [the deduction of] any bequest he may have made, or any debt [he may have incurred]. As for your parents and your children – you know not which of them is more deserving of benefit from you: [therefore this] ordinance from God. Verily, God is All-Knowing, Wise. You shall inherit one-half of what your wives leave behind, provided they have left no child; but if they have left a child, then you shall have one-quarter of what they leave behind, after [the deduction of] any bequest they may have made, or any debt [they may have incurred]. Your widows shall have one-quarter of what you leave behind, provided you have left no child; but if you have left a child, then they shall have one-eighth of what you leave behind, after [the deduction of] any bequest you may have made, or any debt [you may have incurred]. If a man or a woman has no heir in the direct line, but has a brother or a sister, then each of these two shall inherit one-sixth; but if there are more than two, then they shall share in one-third [of the inheritance], after [the deduction of] any bequest that may have been made, or any debt [that may have been incurred], neither of which having been intended to harm [the heirs]. [This is] an injunction from God: and God is All-Knowing, Forbearing. These are the bounds set by God. And whoever pays heed unto God and His Apostle, him will He bring into gardens through which running waters flow, therein to abide: and this is a triumph supreme. (4:11–13).

15. "*Ar-rizq* ("provision of sustenance") applies to all that may be of benefit to man, whether it be concrete (like food, property, offspring, etc.) or abstract (like knowledge, piety, etc.). The "spending on others" is mentioned here in one breath with God-consciousness and prayer because it is precisely in such selfless acts that true piety comes to its full fruition. It should be borne in mind that the verb *anfaqa* (lit. "he spent") is always used in the Qur'an to denote spending freely on, or as a gift to, others, whatever the motive may be." Asad, *The Message of the Qur'an*, p.4, note 4.
    The phrase "and spend on others out of what We provide for them as sustenance" occurs on a number of occasions in the Qur'an, namely, 22:35; 28:54; 32:16, and 42:38.
16. "By declaring that all good and beautiful things of life – i.e., those which are not expressly prohibited – are lawful to the believers, the Qur'an condemns, by implication, all forms of life-denying asceticism, world-renunciation and self-mortification. While, in the life of this world, the good things are shared by believers and unbelievers alike, they will be denied to the latter in the hereafter." Asad, *The Message of the Qur'an*, p.207, note 24.
17. Bukhārī, *Ṣaḥīḥ*, 'al-Ḥarth wa al-Muzāraʿah', hadith 2327, pp.373–374.
18. Ibid., p.377.
19. Ibid., 'Buyūʿ', hadith 2060/2061, p.331.

20. Mālik ibn Anas, *Muwaṭṭa'*, 'Buyūᶜ', hadith 1312, p.429.
21. Abū Dāwūd, *Sunan*, ed. Izzat Ubayd al-Daᶜas (Damascus: Dār al-Ḥadīth, 1971), 'Buyūᶜ', hadith 3449, vol. 3, p.730; Ibn Mājah, *Sunan*, 'Abwāb al-Tijārāt', hadith 2283, vol. 2, p.29; Aḥmad ibn Ḥanbal, *Musnad*, vol. 3, p.419.
22. Bukhārī, *Ṣaḥīḥ*, 'Hajj', hadith 1741, pp.280–281. In another slightly different version (Nos. 1739 & 1442), the hadith reads as follows: "No doubt! Your blood, your properties, and your honor are sacred to one another like the sanctity of this day of yours, in this town of yours, in this month of yours." See also Muslim, *Ṣaḥīḥ*, 'Hajj', hadith 1218, pp.454–456.
23. Aḥmad ibn Ḥanbal, *Musnad*, vol. 5, p.72; Dāraquṭnī, *Sunan*, vol. 3, p.26; Abū Aḥmad ibn al-Ḥusayn ibn ᶜAlī al-Bayhaqī, *al-Sunan al-Kubrā* (Beirut: Dār al-Fikr al-ᶜArabī, n.d.), vol. 6, p.100 and vol. 8, p.182; Muḥammad Nāṣir al-Dīn al-Albānī, *Irwā' al-Ghalīl fī Takhrīj Aḥādīth al-Sabīl* (Beirut: al-Maktab al-Islāmī, 1403/1983), vol. 5, pp.179–282.
24. Bukhārī, *Ṣaḥīḥ*, 'Maẓālim', hadith 2480, p.401; Muslim, *Ṣaḥīḥ*, 'Īmān', hadith 226, p.70.
25. Mālik ibn Anas, *Muwaṭṭa'*, 'Jāmiᶜ', hadith 1842, pp.707–708; Bukhārī, *Ṣaḥīḥ*, 'Jihad', hadith 3059, p.506.
26. Mālik ibn Anas, *Muwaṭṭa'*, 'Buyūᶜ', hadith 1320, pp.428–429; Abū Dāwūd, *Sunan*, 'Buyūᶜ', hadith 3359; Tirmidhī, *Sunan*, 'Buyūᶜ', hadith 1225, vol. 3, p.528; Nasā'ī, *Sunan*, 'Buyūᶜ', hadith 4545, vol. 7, pp.268–269.
27. Ibn Ḥibbān, *al-Iḥsān bi-Taqrīb Ṣaḥīḥ Ibn Ḥibbān*, ed. Shuᶜayb al-Arna'ut (Beirut: Mu'assassat al-Risālah, 1991), hadith 4990, vol. 11, p.365; al-Ḥākim, *al-Mustadrak*, vol. 2, p.38. It is also in Bukhārī, *Ṣaḥīḥ*, 'Buyūᶜ', hadiths 2197–2198, p.350; Muslim, *Ṣaḥīḥ*, 'Musāqāh', hadiths 1554–1555, p.605.
28. Portions of this Tradition can be found in Bukhārī, *Ṣaḥīḥ*, 'Ijārah/14', p.363; Tirmidhī, *Sunan*, 'Aḥkām', hadith 1352, vol. 3, p.634; al-Ḥākim, *al-Mustadrak*, vol. 4, p.101; Abū Dāwūd, *Sunan*, 'Aqḍiyah', hadith 3592, vol. 4, p.19. For a full account of this Tradition and its authenticity, see al-Albānī, *Irwā' al-Ghalīl*, vol. 5, pp.132–146.
29. This is part of a Prophetic Saying concerning the cultivation of barren land. Its full text reads as follows: "If anyone brings barren land into cultivation, it belongs to him, and the unjust root has no right". As Mālik explained, "The unjust root is whatever is dug, taken or planted unlawfully." *Muwaṭṭa'*, 'Aqḍiyah', hadith 1421, p.528; Bukhārī, *Ṣaḥīḥ*, 'al-Ḥarth wa al-Muzāraᶜah/15', p.370.
30. Mālik ibn Anas, *Muwaṭṭa'*, 'Aqḍiyah', hadith 1430, p.530.
31. Bukhārī, *Ṣaḥīḥ*, 'Buyūᶜ', hadiths 2166–2167, p.346.
32. Mālik ibn Anas, *Muwaṭṭa'*, 'Buyūᶜ', hadith 1344, p.451.

37: *MAQĀṢID AL-SHARIʿAH*: LABOR-BASED TRANSACTIONS

1. For a comprehensive study and detailed analysis of juristic views concerning these and other related topics, see Ziaul Haque, *Landlord and Peasant in Early Islam.*
2. In this respect, Mālik said, "The Sunnah about what is permitted to an owner of a garden in sharecropping is that he can stipulate to the sharecropper the maintenance of the walls, cleaning the spring, dredging the irrigation canals, pollinating the palms, pruning branches, harvesting the fruit and so on, provided that the sharecropper has a share of the fruit fixed by mutual agreement. However, the owner cannot stipulate the beginning of new work that the agent will have to undertake, such as digging a well, bringing its water to the surface, instigating new planting, or building a cistern whose cost is great. That is as if the owner of the garden said to a certain man, 'Build me a house here, or dig me a well, or make a spring flow for me, or do some work for me for half the fruit of this garden of mine,' before the fruit of the garden is ripe and it is lawful to sell it. This is the sale of fruit before it is clearly ready. The Messenger of God, may God bless him and grant him peace, forbade fruit to be sold before it was clearly ready." Mālik ibn Anas, *Muwaṭṭa'*, p.496.
3. Ibn Rushd, *Muqaddimāt*, vol. 2, p, 552; Raṣṣāʿ, *Sharḥ Ḥudūd Ibn ʿArafah*, vol. 2, p.508.
4. Mālik said in this regard, "If a sharecropper waters the palms and among them there is some uncultivated land, whatever he cultivates in the uncultivated land is his." He added, "If the landowner makes a condition that he will cultivate the uncultivated land for himself, that is not good because the sharecropper does the watering for the landowner and so he improves the property [without any return for himself]." *Muwaṭṭa'*, p.495.
5. Bukhārī, *Ṣaḥīḥ*, 'Buyūʿ', hadith 2227, p.355; 'Ijārah', hadith 2270, pp.361–362.
6. It was reported by Ibn Mājah on the authority of Ibn ʿUmar, by Ṭabarānī in his *Awsaṭ* on the authority of Jābir and by al-Ḥakīm al-Tirmidhī in his *Nawādir al-Uṣūl* on the authority of Anas. Though all its transmission chains are individually weak, they do, however, reinforce one another. – Author.
   Muḥammad ibn ʿAlī ibn al-Ḥasan Abū ʿAbd Allāh al-Tirmidhī, *Nawādir al-Uṣūl Fī Aḥādīth al-Rasūl*, ed. ʿAbd al-Raḥmān ʿUmayrah (Beirut: Dār al-Jīl, 1412/1992), vol. 1, p.116; Ibn Mājah, *Sunan*, ed. Mahmud Muhammad Nassar (Beirut: Dār al-Kutub al-ʿIlmiyyah, 1419/1998), hadith 2443, vol. 3, p.172.
7. *Khammās* is the worker in *muzāraʿah* for one-fifth of the produce. – Author.

38: *MAQĀṢID AL-SHARIʿAH*: GIFTS & DONATIONS

1. Muslim, *Ṣaḥīḥ*, 'Waṣiyyah', hadith 1631, p.638; Dārimī, *Sunan*, ed. Fawwaz Ahmad Zamerli et al. (Cairo/Beirut: Dār al-Rayyān & Dār al-Kitāb al-ʿArabī, 1407/1987), 'Muqaddimah', *Bāb* 46, vol. 1, p.148.
2. ʿAbd Allāh ibn ʿUmar narrated that when ʿUmar acquired a piece of land in Khaybar, he came to the Prophet, saying, "I have acquired a piece of land, better than any that I have ever had. So what do you advise me regarding it?" The Prophet said, "If you wish, you can keep it as an endowment to be used for charitable purposes." So, ʿUmar gave the land as charity [that is, as an endowment] on the condition that the land would be neither sold nor given as a present, nor bequeathed, [and its yield] would be used for the poor, the kinsmen, the emancipation of slaves, Jihad, and for guests and travelers; its administrator could take a reasonable proportion of its crop, and he also could feed his friends without intending to be wealthy by its means. Bukhārī, *Ṣaḥīḥ*, 'Waṣāyā', hadith 2772, p.459.
3. In this respect, Anas ibn Mālik narrated the following: "Abū Ṭalḥah had more property of date-palm trees gardens than any other amongst the Anṣār in Madinah. The dearest them to him was *Bayruḥā'* garden, which was in front of the Mosque of the Prophet. God's Apostle used to go there and drink its nice water." Anas added, "When these verses were revealed: 'By no means shall you attain righteousness unless You spend [in charity] of that which you love.' (3:92), Abū Ṭalḥah said to God's Apostle, 'O God's Apostle! God, the Blessed, the Superior says: "By no means shall you attain righteousness, unless you spend [in charity] of that which you love", and no doubt, *Bayruḥā'* garden is the dearest of all my property to me. So I want to give it in charity in God's Cause. I expect its reward from Allah. O God's Apostle! Spend it where God makes you think it feasible.' To that God's Apostle said, 'Bravo! It is useful property. I have heard what you have said (O Abū Ṭalḥah), and I think it would be proper if you gave it to your kith and kin.' Abū Ṭalḥah said, 'I will do so, O God's Apostle.' Then Abū Ṭalḥah distributed that garden amongst his relatives and his cousins." Bukhārī, *Ṣaḥīḥ*, 'Zakah', hadith 1461, pp.236–237; Muslim, *Ṣaḥīḥ*, 'Zakah', hadith 998, p.360.
4. Rūmah was a famous well in Madinah.
5. Bukhārī, *Ṣaḥīḥ*, 'Muasāqāh/I', p.378; Tirmidhī, *Sunan*, 'Manāqib', hadith 3703; al-Nasā'ī, *Sunan*, 'Waqf al-Masājid', hadith 3608, vol. 6, p.235.
6. Narrated Ibn ʿAbbās: "The mother of Saʿd bin ʿUbādah died in his absence. He said, 'O God's Apostle! My mother died in my absence; will it be of any benefit for her if I give *ṣadaqah* on her behalf?' The Prophet said, 'Yes,' Saʿd said, 'I make you a witness that I gave my garden called al-Makhraf in charity on her behalf.' Bukhārī, *Ṣaḥīḥ*, 'Waṣāyā', hadith 2756, pp.455–456.

7. Ibn Rushd, *Muqaddimāt*, vol. 2, p.418; al-Qāḍī ʿIyāḍ, *Tartīb al-Madārik*, vol. 2, p.120. See a similar statement by Mālik on *waqf* in Fakhr al-Dīn al-Rāzī, *Manāqib al-Imām al-Shāfiʿī*, ed. Ahmad Hijazi al-Saqqa (Beirut: Dār al-Jīl, 1413/1993), pp.48–49.
8. See the author's comment on this phrase of the verse in Ibn Ashur, *Tafsīr al-Taḥrīr wa al-Tanwīr*, vol. 2, pp.431–434.
9. The hadith begins as follows: "Abū Hurayrah reported that there came a person to the Messenger of God *(ṢAAS)* and said: 'Messenger of God, which charity is the best?' Upon this the Prophet said: 'That...'." Bukhārī, *Ṣaḥīḥ*, 'Zakah', hadith 1419, p.229; 'Waṣāyā', hadith 2748, p.453; Muslim, *Ṣaḥīḥ*, 'Zakah', hadith 1032, p.370.
10. Mālik ibn Anas, *Muwaṭṭa'*, 'Aqḍiyah', hadith 1434, p.533. Khārijah was the wife of Abū Bakr's 'brother' from the *Anṣār*.
11. Bukhārī, *Ṣaḥīḥ*, 'Hibah', hadiths 2586–2587, p.418; Muslim, *Ṣaḥīḥ*, 'Hibat', hadiths 1623–1624, p.631–633; Mālik ibn Anas, *Muwaṭṭa'*, 'Aqḍiyah', hadith 1433, p.533.
12. Ibn Rushd, *The Distinguished Jurist's Primer*, vol. 2, pp.399–400; Raṣṣāʿ, *Sharḥ Ḥudūd ibn ʿArafah*, vol. 2, pp.544–546.
13. According to the Ḥanafī jurists, the seven cases in which it is permitted to retract one's gift are:
(1) Any increment in the item donated that necessitates an increase in its value; (2) the death of one party of the contract; (3) receipt by the donor of compensation for the gift, even if it is from a third party; (4) that the gifted item is no longer in the possession of the recipient; (5) marital relationship prior to, not after, the gift is made; (6) kinship prohibiting marriage; and (7) destruction of the corpus (*ʿayn*) donated. See further details in Kāsānī, *Badā'iʿ al-Ṣanā'iʿ*, vol. 6, pp.128–129; Fakhr al-Dīn ʿUthmān ibn ʿAlī Zaylaʿī, *Tabyīn al-Ḥaqā'iq Sharḥ Kanz al-Daqā'iq* (Beirut: Dār al-Maʿrifah, n.d.), vol. 5, pp.98–101.
14. Bukhārī, *Ṣaḥīḥ*, 'Buyūʿ', *Bāb* 84, p.349.
15. Abū ʿAbd Allāh Muḥammad ibn ʿAbd Allāh ibn Rāshid al-Bakrī al-Qafsī was a leading jurist and legal theorist from Tunisia. He travelled to the Mashriq (East) where he studied with some of its outstanding scholars, such as Shams al-Dīn al-Aṣfahānī, Ibn al-Munayyir (d. 683/1284) and Ibn Daqīq al-ʿĪd (d. 702/1302). Among his students were Ibn Marzūq al-Jadd (d. 781/1379) and ʿAfīf al-Dīn al-Yāfiʿī al-Miṣrī (d. 768/1366). His works include, among others, *al-Shihāb al-Thāqib Sharḥ ibn al-Ḥājib* (in fiqh), *al-Mudhahhab fī Ḍabṭ Qawāʿid al-Madhhab*, *al-Fā'iq fī al-Aḥkām wa al-Wathā'iq*, and *Nukhbat al-Wāṣil fī Sharḥ al-Ḥāṣil*.
16. Ibn Rushd, *al-Bayān wa al-Taḥṣīl*, vol. 17, pp.540–542; Muhammad ibn

ʿAbd al-Rahman al-Hattab, *Mawāhib al-Jalīl li-Sharḥ Mukhtaṣar Khalīl* (Beirut: Dār al-Fikr, 1398/1978), vol. 6, p.50.

17. This Tradition has already been documented in chapter 6 of Part I.

39: *MAQĀṢID AL-SHARIʿAH*: JUDGESHIP & TESTIMONY

1. To understand the full import of this verse, it would be appropriate to quote Muhammad Asad's comment on it. He said:
"Although the above injunction mentions specifically religious knowledge, it has a positive bearing on every kind of knowledge – and this in view of the fact that the Qur'an does not draw any dividing-line between the spiritual and the worldly concerns of life but, rather, regards them as different aspects of one and the same reality. In many of its verses, the Qur'an calls upon the believer to observe all nature and to discern God's creative activity in its manifold phenomena and "laws", as well as to mediate upon the lessons of history with a view to gaining a deeper insight into man's motivations and the innermost springs of his behaviour: and, thus, the Qur'an itself is characterized as addressed to "those who think".
In short, intellectual activity as such is postulated as a valid way to a better understanding of God's will and – if pursued with moral consciousness – as a valid method of worshipping God. This Qur'anic principle has been emphasized in many well-authenticated sayings of the Prophet, for instance, 'Striving after knowledge is a sacred duty (*farīḍah*) for every man and woman who has surrendered himself or herself to God (*muslim wa muslimah*)' (Ibn Mājah); or, 'The superiority (*faḍl*) of a learned man over a [mere] worshipper [i.e., one who merely prays, fasts, etc.] is like the superiority of the full moon over all the stars' (Tirmidhī, Abū Dā'ūd, Ibn Mājah, Ibn Ḥanbal, Dārimī). Consequently, the obligation of the believers to 'devote themselves to acquiring a deeper knowledge of the Faith' (*li-yatafagqahū fī al-dīn*) and to impart its results to their fellow-believers relates to every branch of knowledge as well as to its practical application." *The Message of the Qur'an*, p.285, note 162.
2. Narrated by Mālik ibn al-Ḥuwayrith who was from the Banū Layth ibn ʿAbd Manāf ibn Kinānah. – Author. Bukhārī, *Ṣaḥīḥ*, "ʿIlm', *Bāb* 25, p.20.
3. See on the connotation of iron in relation to revelation, Taqīy al-Dīn Aḥmad Ibn Taymiah, *al-Siyāsah al-Sharʿiyyah fī Iṣlāḥ al-Rāʿī wa al-Raʿiyyah*, ed. Muhammad Ayman ibn Hasan al-Shabrawi (Beirut: Dār al-Kutub al-ʿIlmiyyah, 1421/2000), pp.32–33.
4. Of this kind of Qur'anic discourse, mention can be made of the following verses: "And if you have reason to fear that a breach might occur between a [married] couple, appoint an arbiter from among his people and an arbiter

from among her people; if they both want to set things right, God may bring about their reconciliation. Behold, God is indeed All-Knowing, Aware" (4:35); "Hence, if two groups of believers fall to fighting, make peace between them; but then, if one of the two [groups] goes on acting wrongfully towards the other, fight against the one that acts wrongfully until it reverts to God's commandment" (49:9). See also my book entitled *Naqd ʿIlmī li-Kitāb al-Islām wa Uṣūl al-Ḥukm* [Cairo: al-Maṭbaʿah al-Salafiyyah, 1344 AH]. – Author.

This book was written as a rebuttal of Ali Abd al-Raziq's thesis consisting in negating Islam's concern with politics and governance. This thesis was expounded in a book by the title *al-Islām wa Uṣūl al-Ḥukm* [Islam and the Principles of Governance], first published in Cairo in 1925, soon after the abolition of the Caliphate by Kamal Atatürk in 1924.

5. See in this regard, reports in Bukhārī, *Ṣaḥīḥ*, 'ʿIlm', hadiths 104–114, pp.23–24; 'Aḥādīth al-Anbiyā'', hadith 3461, p.582.
6. "This verse lays down in an unequivocal manner the obligation of every Muslim to submit to the ordinances which the Prophet, under divine inspiration, promulgated with a view to exemplifying the message of the Qur'an and enabling the believers to apply it to actual situations. These ordinances constitute what is described as the sunnah (lit. "way") of the Prophet Muhammad, and have (whenever they are authenticated beyond any possibility of doubt) full legal force side by side with the Qur'an." Asad, *The Message of the Qur'an*, p.117, note 84.
7. Qarāfī, *Furūq*, vol. 4, 1165.
8. This is part of a Tradition narrated by Jarīr ibn ʿAbd Allāh in which he said: "I went to the Prophet and said, 'I give my pledge of allegiance to you for Islam.' The Prophet added the condition for me 'to be sincere and true to every Muslim'. So I gave my pledge to him for this." (Bukhārī, *Ṣaḥīḥ*, 'Īmān', hadith 58, p.13). It also narrated by Tamīm al-Dārī that the Prophet said: "Religion (*al-dīn*) consists of sincerity and goodwill." Upon this we said: "For whom?" He replied: "For God, His Book, His Messenger and for the leaders and the general Muslims." Muslim, *Ṣaḥīḥ*, 'Īmān', hadith 95, p.44.
9. Qarāfī, *Furūq*, vol. 2, p.601.
10. Mālik ibn Anas, *Muwaṭṭa'*, 'Aqḍiyah', hadith 1397, p.509.
11. Ibid., 'Ḥudūd', hadith 1497, p.591.
12. Abū Dāwūd, *Sunan* (Istanbul: Dār al-Daʿwah, 1413/1992), 'Qaḍā'', hadith 3582, vol. 4, p.11; Tirmidhī, *Sunan* (Istanbul: Dār al-Daʿwah, 1413/1992), 'Aḥkām', hadith 1331, vol. 3, p.618.
13. The full version of the story reads as follows: "There were two women, each of whom had a child with her. A wolf came and took away the child of one of

them, whereupon the other said, 'It has taken your child.' The first said, 'But it has taken your child.' So they both took the case to David, who judged that the living child be given to the elder lady. So both of them went to Solomon, the son of David, and informed him [of the case]. He said, 'Bring me a knife so as to cut the child into two pieces and divide it between them.' The younger lady said, 'May God be merciful to you! Don't do that, for it is her [i.e. the other lady's] child.' So he gave the child to the younger lady." Bukhārī, *Ṣaḥīḥ*, 'Aḥādīth al-Anbiyā'', hadith 3427, pp.576–577; 'Farā'iḍ,' hadith 6769, p.1167; Muslim, *Ṣaḥīḥ*, 'Aqdiyah', hadith 1720, p.682.

14. This tradition has already been documented in chapter 15. The purport of this tradition is that when a judge acts under the effect of anger, he most probably does not make a sound and just judgement of the case brought to him.
15. Tirmidhī, *Sunan* (Istanbul edition), 'Aḥkām', hadith 1327, vol. 4, p.616; Abū Dāwūd, *Sunan*, ed. Muhammad Muhyi al-Din Abd al-Hamid, 'Aqḍiyah', hadith 3592, vol. 3, p.303.
16. Ibn Rushd, *Muqaddimāt*, vol. 2, pp.259–260; Qarāfī, *Dhakhīrah*, vol. 8, p.16.
17. Cf. Qarāfī, *Dhakhīrah*, vol. 8, p.13.
18. Ibn Rushd, *Muqaddimāt*, vol. 2, p.260; Qarāfī, *Dhakhīrah*, vol. 8, p.16; Burhān al-Dīn Abū al-Wafā' Ibrāhīm ibn al-Imām Shams al-Dīn Ibn Farḥūn al-Mālikī, *Tabṣirat al-Ḥukkām Fī Uṣūl al-Aqḍiyah wa Manāhij al-Aḥkām* [hereinafter *Tabṣirah*], ed. Jamal Marᶜishli (Beirut: Dār al-Kutub al-ᶜIlmiyyah, 1416/1995), vol. 1, p.24.
19. Nafīs al-Dīn Hibat Allāh ibn Shukr (605–680 AH) was Egypt's Mālikī chief judge.
20. The author quoted Ibn Rāshid from a manuscript of his book *al-Fā'iq*, which is yet to be edited and published.
21. Ibn ᶜAbd al-Barr, *al-Kāfī fī Fiqh Ahl al-Madīnah*, vol. 2, p.275.
22. Bukhārī, *Ṣaḥīḥ*, 'Jihad', hadith 2886–2887, p.477; 'Riqāq', hadith 6435, p.1117.
23. See the author's elaboration of the economic and juridical connotations of this verse in Ibn Ashur, *Tafsīr al-Taḥrīr wa al-Tanwīr*, vol. 2, pp.186–193.
24. "I.e., in the judicial sense, as well as in the sense of judging other people's motives, attitudes and behaviour. – The term *amānah* (pl. *amānāt*) denotes anything one has been entrusted with, be it in the physical or moral sense." Asad, *The Message of the Qur'an*, p.115, note 75.
25. Ibn Rushd, *Muqaddimāt*, vol. 2, pp.258–259; Ibn Farḥūn, *Tabṣirah*, vol. 1, p.21.
26. Cf. Qarāfī, *Dhakhīrah*, vol. 8, p.119.
27. Ibn Rushd, *Muqaddimāt*, vol. 2, p.259.

28. The Hafsid dynasty in Tunisia was founded by Abū Zakariyā Yaḥyā (the Almohad governor of Gabes and then of Tunis) in1229. He captured Constantine and Bougie (now in present-day Algeria) in 1230 and annexed Tripolitania (Lybia) in 1234, and Algiers in 1235. The rule of the Hafsids continued until 1574 when they were toppled by the Ottomans who captured Tunis and annexed it to the Sublime Porte in Constantinople.
29. Qarāfī, *Furūq*, vol. 4, *Farq* 223, p.1165.
30. "The implication is that if one shares the life of an orphan in his charge, one is permitted to benefit by such an association – for instance, through a business partnership – provided this does not damage the orphan's interests in any way", Asad, *The Message of the Qur'an*, p.48, note 206.
31. Qarāfī, *Furūq*, vol. 4, p.1165. See also *Dhakhīrah*, vol. 8, p.37.
32. Ibn ʿAtiyah, *al-Muḥarrar al-Wajīz*, vol. 2, p.11. For a detailed discussion of this issue, see Shihāb al-Dīn al-Qarāfī, *al-Iḥkām fī Tamyīz al-Fatāwā ʿan al-Aḥkām* (Beirut: Dār al-Anwār, 1983), vol. 2, pp.151–161.
33. In the late 19th and early 20th centuries.
34. It has already been documented in chapter 6.
35. Bukhārī, *Ṣaḥīḥ*, 'Aḥkām', hadith 7157, p.1231.
36. The part of ʿUmar's memo quoted here has been reported in slightly different wordings by many sources. See for example, Dāraquṭnī, *Sunan*, ed. ʿAbd Allāh Hāshim al-Yamānī (Cairo: Dār al-Maḥāsin, 1386/1966), 'al-Aqḍiyah wa al-Aḥkām', vol. 4, p.206; Bayhaqī, *al-Sunan al-Kubrā* (Hyderabad, Deccan: Dā'irat al-Maʿārif al-ʿUthmāniyyah, 1335 AH), pp.135 & 150; *Maʿrifat al-Sunan wa al-Āthār*, ed. ʿAbd al-Muʿṭī Qalʿajī (Aleppo: Dār al-Waʿy, 1411/1991), vol. 14, p.240; Ibn Rushd, *Muqaddimāt*, vol. 2, p.268; Qarāfī, *Dhakhīrah*, vol. 8, p.61; Ibn Qayyim al-Jawziyyah, *Iʿlām Muwaqqiʿīn ʿan Rabb al-ʿĀlamīn*, ed. Muḥammad ʿAbd al-Salām Ibrāhīm (Beirut: Dār al-Kutub al-ʿIlmiyyah, 1411/1991), vol. 1/1, pp.67–68; Ibn Farḥūn, *Tabṣirah*, vol. 1, p.25. See a full translation of this memo in Māwardī, *The Ordinances of Government*, pp.80–81.
37. See the story of this case with some differences from what has been mentioned by the author here in Muslim, *Ṣaḥīḥ*, 'Īmān', hadith 139, p.69; Abū Dāwūd, *Sunan*, ed. Muḥammad Muḥyī al-Dīn ʿAbd al-Ḥamīd (Beirut: Dār al-Fikr, n.d.), 'Aqḍiyah', hadiths 3622–3623, vol. 3, p.312; Tirmidhī, *Sunan*, ed. Mustapha Muaḥmmad Ḥusayn al-Dhahabī (Cairo: Dār al-Ḥadīth, 1419/1999), 'Aḥkām', hadith 1340, vol. 3, p.403; Aḥmad ibn Ḥanbal, *Musnad*, vol. 1, pp.460–461 & vol. 4, p.192; Nūr al-Dīn ʿAlī ibn Abī Bakr ibn Sulaymān al-Haythamī, *Majmaʿ al-Zawā'id wa Manbaʿ al-Fawā'id*, ed. Muḥammad ʿAbd al-Qādir Aḥmad ʿAṭā (Beirut: Dār al-Kutub al-ʿIlmiyyah,

1422/2001), 'al-Aymān wa al-Nudhūr', hadiths 6902–6904, vol. 4, pp.227–228.

38. See in this regard Mālik ibn Anas, *Muwaṭṭa'*, 'Aḍiyah', pp.514–515; Abū al-Shitā' al-Sunhājī, *Mawāhib al-Khallāq ʿAlā Sharḥ al-Tāwdī li-Lāmiyat al-Zaqqāq* (Rabat: Maktabat al-Umniyah, 1375/1955), vol. 1, p.168; Aḥmad ibn Muḥammad ibn al-Ṣiddīq, *Masālik al-Dilālah fī Sharḥ Matn al-Risālah* (Cairo: Dār al-ʿAhd al-Jadīd, 1374/1954), p.203; Ibn Farḥūn, *Tabṣirah*, vol. 1, 258.

39. This statement has already been documented in the author's preface.

40. Mālik's statement to which the author is referring here was made in conjunction with his comment on the cases in which pre-emption (*shufaʿah*) is not possible. Thus, Yaḥyā ibn Yaḥyā al-Laythī related: "Mālik referred to a man who bought some land that remained in his possession for some time. Then, a man came who realized that he had a share of that land by inheritance. Mālik said, 'If the man's right of inheritance is established, he also has a right of pre-emption. If the land has produced a crop, the crop belongs to the buyer until the day when the right of the other is established, because he would have tended what was planted against being destroyed or being carried away by a flood.'" *Muwaṭṭa'*, p.507.

41. By this I refer to the two kinds of testimony, namely *istirʿā'* and *taḥammul*. – Author.

    Istirʿā' testimony is to bear witness according to what one personally knows about someone else's circumstances, such as poverty or opulence, freedom or slavery, etc. *Taḥammul* (testimony), refers to bearing witness based on what has been dictated to one by those concerning whom one testifies, such as a sale contract between two parties or a marriage contract between a man and a woman, etc. Muhammad al-ʿAziz Juʿayyit, *al-Ṭarīqah al-Marḍiyyah fī al-Ijrā'āt al-Sharʿiyyah ʿalā Madhhab al-Mālikiyyah* (Tunis: Maktabat al-Istiqāmah, n.d.), p.149.

40: *MAQĀṢID AL-SHARIʿAH*: PENALTIES

1. "This refers to the legal punishment for homicide, termed *qiṣāṣ* ("just retribution") and explained in 2:178 and the corresponding notes. In the present context, the term wall ("protector" or "defender of [one's] rights") is usually taken to mean the heir or next of kin of the victim; Zamakhsharī, however, observes that it may also apply to the government (*al-sulṭān*): an interpretation which is obviously based on the concept of the government as the "protector" or "defender of the rights" of all its citizens. Thus, the defender of

the victim's rights (in this case, a court of justice) is not only not entitled to impose a capital sentence on any but the actual murderer or murderers, but may also, if the case warrants it, concede mitigating circumstances and refrain from capital punishment altogether." Asad, *The Message of the Qur'an*, p.423, notes 39 and 40.

2. Ahmad ibn Muhammad al-Marzuqi, *Sharḥ Dīwān al-Ḥamāsah*, ed, ʿAbd al-Salam Harun (Cairo: Maṭbaʿat Lajnat al-Ta'līf wa al-Tarjamah wa al-Nashr, 1387/1967), vol. 1, p.125.
3. *Urūsh* (sing. *arsh*) consist of financial penalties to be paid for injuries.
4. "The extreme severity of this Qur'anic punishment can be understood only if one bears in mind the fundamental principle of Islamic Law that no duty (*taklīf*) is ever imposed on man without his being granted a corresponding right (*ḥaqq*); and the term "duty" also comprises, in this context, liability to punishment. Now, among the inalienable rights of every member of the Islamic society – Muslim and non-Muslim alike – is the right to protection (in every sense of the word) by the community as a whole. As is evident from innumerable Qur'anic ordinances as well as the Prophet's injunctions forthcoming from authentic Traditions, every citizen is entitled to a share in the community's economic resources and, thus, to the enjoyment of social security: in other words, he or she must be assured of an equitable standard of living commensurate with the resources at the disposal of the community. For, although the Qur'an makes it clear that human life cannot be expressed in terms of physical existence alone – the ultimate values of life being spiritual in nature – the believers are not entitled to look upon spiritual truths and values as something that could be divorced from the physical and social factors of human existence.

In short, Islam envisages and demands a society that provides not only for the spiritual needs of man, but for his bodily and intellectual needs as well. It follows, therefore, that – in order to be truly Islamic – a society (or state) must be so constituted that every individual, man and woman, may enjoy that minimum of material well-being and security without which there can be no human dignity, no real freedom and, in the last resort, no spiritual progress: for, there can be no real happiness and strength in a society that permits some of its members to suffer undeserved want while others have more than they need. If the whole society suffers privations owing to circumstances beyond its control (as happened, for instance, to the Muslim community in the early days of Islam), such shared privations may become a source of spiritual strength and, through it, of future greatness. But if the available resources of a community are so unevenly distributed that certain groups within it live in affluence while the majority of the people are forced to use up all their energies in search of their daily bread, poverty becomes the most dangerous enemy of spiritual progress, and occasionally drives whole communities away from God-consciousness and into the arms of soul-destroying materialism. It was undoubtedly this that the Prophet had in mind when he uttered the warning words (quoted by Al-Suyūṭī in *al-Jāmiʿ al-Ṣaghīr*), "Poverty may well turn into a denial of the truth (*kufr*)."

Consequently, the social legislation of Islam aims at a state of affairs in which every man, woman and child has (a) enough to eat and wear, (b) an adequate home, (c) equal opportunities and facilities for education, and (d) free medical care in health and in sickness. A corollary of these rights is the right to productive and remunerative work while of working age and in good health, and a provision (by the community or the state) of adequate nourishment, shelter, etc. in cases of disability resulting from illness, widowhood, enforced unemployment, old age, or under-age. As already mentioned, the communal obligation to create such a comprehensive social security scheme has been laid down in many Qur'anic verses, and has been amplified and explained by a great number of the Prophet's commandments. It was the second Caliph, ʿUmar ibn al-Khaṭṭāb, who began to translate these ordinances into a concrete administrative scheme (see Ibn Sʿad, *Ṭabaqāt* III/3, 213–217); but after his premature death, his successors had neither the vision nor the statesmanship to continue his unfinished work.

It is against the background of this social-security scheme envisaged by Islam that the Qur'an imposes the severe sentence of hand-cutting as a deterrent punishment for robbery. Since, under the circumstances outlined above, "temptation" cannot be admitted as a justifiable excuse, and since, in the last resort, the entire socio-economic system of Islam is based on the faith of its adherents, its balance is extremely delicate and in need of constant, strictly-enforced protection. In a community in which everyone is assured of full security and social justice, any attempt on the part of an individual to achieve an easy, unjustified gain at the expense of other members of the community must be considered an attack against the system as a whole, and must be punished as such: and, therefore, the above ordinance which lays down that the hand of the thief shall be cut off.

One must, however, always bear in mind the principle mentioned at the beginning of this note: namely, the absolute interdependence between man's rights and corresponding duties (including liability to punishment). In a community or state which neglects or is unable to provide complete social security for all its members, the temptation to enrich oneself by illegal means often becomes irresistible – and, consequently, theft cannot and should not be punished as severely as it should be punished in a state in which social security is a reality in the full sense of the word. If the society is unable to fulfil its duties with regard to every one of its members, it has no right to invoke the full sanction of criminal law (*ḥadd*) against the individual transgressor, but must confine itself to milder forms of administrative punishment. (It was in correct appreciation of this principle that the great Caliph ʿUmar waived the *ḥadd* of hand-cutting in a period of famine which afflicted Arabia during his reign.) To sum up, one may safely conclude that the cutting-off of a hand in punishment for theft is applicable only within the context of an already existing, fully functioning social security scheme, and in no other circumstances." Asad, *The Message of the Qur'an*, pp.149–150, note 48.

5. This is part of the Prophet's sermon that he gave at Mount ʿArafah during his last pilgrimage. See Muslim, *Ṣaḥīḥ*, 'Hajj', hadith 1218, p.456.
6. See a detailed discussion in this regard in Ibn Rushd (Grandfather), *al-Bayān wa al-Taḥṣīl*, vol. 15, p.446 and *Muqaddimāt*, vol. 3, pp.288–289; Ibn Rushd (Grandson), *The Distinguished Jurist's Primer*, vol. 2, pp.486–488.
7. Abū Bakr Ibn al-ʿArabī, *Aḥkām al-Qur'an*, ed. Ali Muhammad al-Bijawi (Cairo: Dār Iḥyā' al-Kutub al-ʿArabiyyah, 1377/1958), vol. 3, p.1315.
8. See a detailed discussion of this issue in Ibn Rushd, *The Distinguished Jurist's Primer*, vol. 2, pp.549–551. For a comprehensive treatment of the philosophy, aims, and categories of sanctions in the Shariʿah, see Gaafer M. Abd-Elrahim, *The Concept of Punishment in Islamic Law*.

BIBLIOGRAPHY

ʿAbd al-Wahhāb, Baghdādī al-Qāḍī Abū Muḥammad ibn ʿAlī ibn Naṣr al-, *Sharḥ al-Talqīn*, (ed.) Mukhtar al-Sallami (Beirut: Dār al-Gharb al-Islāmī, 1997).

ʿAbd al-Wahhāb, al-Qāḍī Abū Muḥammad ʿAbd al-Wahhāb ibn ʿAlī, *al-Ishrāf*, (ed.), al-Habib ibn Tahir (Beirut: Dār Ibn Ḥazm, 1420/1999).

——, *al-Maʿūnah ʿalā Madhhab ʿĀlim al-Madīnah*, (ed.), Khamish Abd al-Haqq (Makkah al-Mukarramah: Maktabat Nizār al-Bāz, 1415 AH).

Abd-Elrahim, Gaʿafer M., "The Concept of Punishment in Islamic Law in Relation to Contemporary Legal Trends," Ph.D. dissertation, Faculty of Union Graduate School, Cincinnati, OH, 1987.

Abū Dāwūd, Sulaymān ibn al-Ashʿath, *Sunan*, (ed.), Muhammad Muhyi al-Din Abd al-Hamid (Beirut: Dār al-Fikr al-ʿArabī, n.d.)

——, *Sunan* (Istanbul: Dār al-Daʿwah, 1413/1992).

——, *Sunan*, (ed.), Izzat Ubayd al-Daʿas, Damascus: Dār al-Ḥadīth, 1971.

——, *Sunan*, (ed.), Muhammad Muhyi al-Din Abd al-Hamid (Ṣaydā/Beirut: al-Maktabah al-ʿAṣriyyah, n.d.)

——, *Sunan*, (ed.), Muhammad Muhyi al-Din Abd al-Hamid (Beirut: al-Maktabah al-ʿAṣriyyah, 1416/1995).

Abū al-Ḥusayn Muslim ibn al-Ḥajjāj, *Ṣaḥīḥ* (Beirut: Dār al-Kutub al-ʿIlmiyyah, 1421/2001).

Aḥmad ibn Ḥanbal, *al-Musnad* (Beirut: al-Maktab al-Islāmī, 1405/1985).

Aḥmad ibn Muhammad Zarruq, *Sharḥ Risālat ibn Abī Zayd al-Qayrawānī* (Beirut: Dār al-Fikr, 1402/1982).

ʿAlā'ī, al-Ḥāfiẓ al-, *Taḥqīq al-Murād fī ann al-Nahy Yaqtaḍī al-Fasād*, (ed.), Ibrahim al-Salqini (Damascus: Maṭbaʿat Zayd ibn Thābit, 1395/1975).

Albānī, Muḥammad Nāṣir al-Dīn al-, *Irwā' al-Ghalīl fī Takhrīj Aḥādīth al-Sabīl* (Beirut: al-Maktab al-Islāmī, 1403/1983).

——, *Silsilat al-Aḥādīth al-Ḍaʿīfah wa al-Mawḍūʿah* (Beirut: al-Maktab al-Islāmī, 1398 AH).

——, *Silsilat al-Aḥādīth al-Ṣaḥīḥah* (Beirut: al-Maktab al-Islāmī, 1403/1983).

Ali, Abdullah Yusuf, *The Holy Qur'ān*, Arabic original with English translation and Selected Commentaries (Kuala Lumpur: Saba Islamic Media, 1998).

Ali, Mohamed M. Yunis, *Medieval Islamic Pragmatics: Sunni Legal Theorists' Models of Textual Communication* (Richmond, Surrey (UK): Curzon Press, 2000).

Alusi, Mahmud Shukri al-, *Rūḥ al-Maʿānī* (Beirut: Dār al-Fikr, 1398/1978.)

Āmidī, Sayf al-Dīn al-, *al-Iḥkām fī Uṣūl al-Aḥkām*, (ed.), Ibrahim al-Ajuz (Beirut: Dār al-Kutub al-ʿIlmiyyah, n.d.)

——, *Muntahā al-Sūl Fī ʿIlm al-Uṣūl*, ed., Ahmad Farid al-Mazidi (Beirut: Dār al-Kutub al-ʿIlmiyyah, 2003/1424).

Arnaldez, Roger, *Fakhr al-Dīn al-Rāzī: Commentateur du Coran et Philosophe* (Paris: Librairie Philosophique J. Vrin, 2002).

Asad, Muhammad, *The Message of the Qur'an* (Gibraltar: Dar al-Andalus, 1984).

Aṣbahānī, Abū al-Faraj ʿAlī ibn al-Ḥasan al-, *al-Aghānī* (Beirut: Dār Iḥyā' al-Turāth al-ʿArabī, n.d.)

ʿAsqalānī, Aḥmad ibn ʿAlī ibn Ḥajar al-, *Fatḥ al-Bārī bi-Sharḥ Ṣaḥīḥ al-Bukhārī* (Riyadh/Amman: International Ideas Home, n.d.)

——, *al-Iṣābah fi Tamyīz al-Ṣaḥābah* (Cairo: Mawlāy ʿAbd al-Ḥafīdh, 1328 AH).

Ati, Hammudah Abd al-, *The Family Structure in Islam* (Indianapolis, IN: American Trust Publications, 1977).

ʿAynī, Badr al-Dīn Abū Muḥammad Maḥmūd ibn Aḥmad al-, *ʿUmdat al-Qārī Sharḥ Ṣaḥīḥ al-Bukhārī* (Beirut: Dār Iḥyā' al-Turāth al-ʿArabī, n.d.)

——, *al-Bināyah fī Sharḥ al-Hidāyah* (Beirut: Dār al-Fikr, 1400/1980.)

Al-Azami, M. M., *The History of the Qur'ānic Text from Revelation to Compilation* (Leicester, UK: UK Islamic Academy, 2003).

Bagby, Ihsan Abdul-Wajid, "Utility in Classical Islamic Law: The Concept of *Maṣlaḥah* in Classical *Uṣūl al-Fiqh*," unpublished Ph.D. dissertation, University of Michigan, 1986.

Baghawī, al-Ḥasan ibn Masʿūd al-, *Mafātīḥ al-Sunnah* (Beirut: Dār al-Maʿrifah, 1987).

Baghdādī, ʿAbd al-Qādir ibn ʿUmar al-, *Khizānat al-Adab wa Lubb Lubāb Lisān al-ʿArab*, (ed.) Abd al-Salam Harun (Cairo: al-Khānjī, 1409/1989).

——, *Sharḥ Abyāt al-Mughnī*, (ed.), Abd al-Aziz Rabah et al. (Damascus: Dār al-Ma'mūn, 1980).

Bājī, Sulaymān ibn Khalaf al-, *al-Muntaqā: Sharā Muwaṭṭa'* (Cairo: Maṭbaʿat al-Saʿādah, 1331 AH); offset (Beirut: Dār al-Kitāb al-ʿArabī).

Bāqillānī, Abū Bakr Muḥammad ibn al-Ṭayyib al-, *al-Taqrīb wa al-Irshād al-Ṣaghīr'*, (ed.), Abd al-Hamid ibn Ali Abu Zunayd (Beirut: Mu'assassat al-Risālah, 1418/1998).

Baṣrī, Abū al-Ḥusayn al-, Sharḥ al-ʿUmad, ed. Abd al-Hamid ibn Ali Abu Zunayd, Cairo: al-Maṭbaʿah al-Salafiyyah, 1410 AH.

——, *al-Muʿtamad fī Uṣūl al-Fiqh*, (ed.), Muhammad Hamidullah et al. (Damascus: Institut Francais de Damas, 1964–1965).

Bayḍāwī, al-Qāḍī Nāṣir al-Dīn Abū Saʿīd ʿAbd Allāh al-, *Tafsīr al-Bayḍāwī* or *Anwār al-Tanzīl wa Asrār al-Ta'wīl*, (ed.), Abd al-Qadir Irfan al-Ashsha Hassunah (Beirut: Dār al-Fikr, 1416/1996).

Bayhaqī, Aḥmad ibn al-Ḥusayn al-, *al-Sunan al-Kubrā* (Hyderabad, Dacca: Dā'irat al-Maʿārif al-ʿUthmāniyyah, 1335 AH).

——, *al-Sunan al-Kubrā*, (ed.), Muhammad Abd al-Qadir Ata (Makkah al-Mukarramah: Maktabat Dār al-Bāz, 1414/1994).

——, *Maʿrifat al-Sunan wa al-Āthār*, (ed.) Abd al-Muti Qalʿaji (Aleppo: Dār al-Waʿy, 1411/1991).

Bayram II, Shaikh al-Islam Abū ʿAbd Allāh Muḥammad, "*al-Wafā' bi mā Yataʿallaqu bi-Bayʿ al-Wafā'*", (ed.), and annot., Muhammad al-Habib ibn al-Khujah, *Majallat Majmaʿ al-Fiqh al-Islāmī*, No.7, vol. 3, 1412/1992.

Boisard, Marcel A., *Humanism in Islam* (Kuala Lumpur: Islamic Book Trust, 2003).

Bukhārī, Abū ʿAbd Allāh al-, *al-Adab al-Mufrad*, (ed.), Kamal Y. al-Hut (Beirut: ʿĀlam al-Kutub, 1405/1985).

——, *Ṣaḥīḥ*, Riyadh: Darussalam, 1419/1999.

Buti, Muhammad Saʿid Ramadan al-, *Ḍawābiṭ al-Maṣlaḥah fī al-Sharīʿah al-Islāmiyyah* (Beirut: Mu'assassat al-Risālah, 1422/2001).

Ceylan, Yasin, *Theology and Tafsir in the Major works of Fakhr al-Din al-Razi* (Kuala Lumpur: International Institute of Islamic Thought and Civilization, [ISTAC], 1996).

Dāraquṭnī, ʿAlī ibn ʿUmar al-, *Sunan*, (ed.), Abd Allah Hashim Yamani (Cairo: Dār al-Maḥāsin, 1386/1966).

Dārimī, ʿAbd Allāh ibn ʿAbd al-Raḥmān al-, *Musnad/Sunan*, (ed.), Hussayn Salim al-Darani (Beirut: Dār Ibn Ḥazm, 1421/2000).

——, *Sunan*, (ed.), Fawwaz Ahmad Zamarli et al. (Beirut: Dār al-Rayyān & Dār al-Kitāb al-ʿArabī, 1407/1987).

Dasuqi, Muhammad Arafah al-, *Ḥāshiyah* on *al-Sharḥ al-Kabīr* of Aḥmad ibn Muḥammad al-Dirdīr (Beirut: Dār al-Fikr, n.d.)

Dhanani, Alnoor, *The Physical Theory of Kalam: Atoms, Space, and Void in Basrian Muʿtazili Cosmology* (Leiden, The Netherlands: E.J. Brill, 1994).

Dhubyānī, al-Nābighah al-, *Dīwān*, (ed.), Muhammad al-Tahir Ibn Ashur, (Tunis: al-Sharikah al-Tūnusiyyah li al-Tawzīʿ, 1976).

Dirdir, Ahmad ibn Muhammad al-, *al-Sharḥ al-Ṣaghīr* (Beirut: Dār al-Maʿrifah, 1398/1987).

Draz, Muhammad A., *Introduction to the Qur'ān*, trans. Ayeshah Abdel-Haleem (London & New York: I. B. Tauris, 2000).

Duraynī, Muḥammad Fatḥī al-, *al-Manāhij al-Uṣūliyyah fī al-Ijtihād bi al-Ra'y fī al-Tashrīʿal-Islāmī* (Beirut: Mu'assassat al-Risālah, 1418/1997).

Ghannushi, Rached al-, *al-Ḥurriyyāt al-ʿĀmmah fī al-Dawlah al-Islāmiyyah* (Beirut: Markaz Dirāsāt al-Wiḥdah al-ʿArabiyyah, 1993).

Ghazālī, Abū Ḥāmid al-, *al-Mustaṣfā Min ʿIlm al-Uṣūl*, (ed.), Muhammad Sulayman al-Ashqar (Beirut: Mu'assassat al-Risālah, 1417/1997).

Goldziher, Ignaz, *The Zahiris: Their Doctrine and their History*, trans. from the German by Wolfgang Behn (Leiden, The Netherlands: E. J. Brill, 1971).

Gribetz, Arthur, *Strange Bedfellows: Mutʿat al-Nisā' and Mutʿat al-Ḥajj* (Berlin: Klaus Schwarz Verlag, 1994).

Hallaq, Wael B., *A History of Islamic Legal Theories* (Cambridge, UK: Cambridge University Press, 1999).

Hammad, Nazih Kamal, *Muʿjam al-Muṣṭalaḥāt al-Iqtiṣādiyyah fī Lughat al-Fuqahā'* (Herndon, VA: International Institute of Islamic Thought, 1410/1995).

Hasan, Ahmad, *Analogical Reasoning in Islamic Jurisprudence* (Islamabad, Pakistan: Islamic Research Institute, 1986).

Hattab, Muhammad ibn Abd al-Rahman al-, *Mawāhib al-Jalīl li-Sharḥ Mukhtaṣar Khalīl* (Beirut: Dār al-Fikr, 1398/1978).

Ḥaṭṭābī, Ḥamad ibn Muḥammad al-, *Alām al-Ḥadīth fī Sharḥ Ṣaḥīḥ al-Bukhārī*, (ed.), Muḥammad ibn Sᶜad Āl Suᶜūd (Makkah: Jāmiᶜat Umm al-Qurā, 1409/1988).

Haydar, Ali, *Sharḥ Majallat al-Aḥkām al-ᶜAdliyyah*, trans. from Osmanli Turkish by Fahmi al-Husayni (Beirut: Dār al-ᶜIlm li'l-Malāyīn, n.d.)

Haythamī, Nūr al-Dīn ᶜAlī ibn Abī Bakr ibn Sulaymān al-, *Majmaᶜ al-Zawā'id wa Manbaᶜ al-Fawā'id*, (ed.), Muhammad Abd al-Qadir Ahmad Ata (Beirut: Dār al-Kutub al-ᶜIlmiyyah, 1422/2001).

Hindī, ᶜAlī ibn Ḥusām al-Dīn al-Muttaqī al-, *Kanz al-ᶜUmmāl fī Sunan al-Aqwāl wa al-Afᶜāl* (Beirut: Dār Iḥyā' al-Turāth al-ᶜArabī, 1410/1990).

Ibn Abd al-Barr, Yusuf ibn Abd Allāh, *al-Tamhīd Limā fī Muwaṭṭa' mina al-Asānīd* (Rabat: Ministry of Awqāf, 1411 AH).

Ibn Abī Shaybah, Abū Bakr ᶜAbd Allāh ibn Muḥammad, *al-Muṣannaf*, (ed.), Kamal Yusuf al-Hut (Riyadh: Maktabat al-Rushd, 1409).

——, *al-Muṣannaf*, (ed.), Ahmad al-Nadwi (Bombay, India: al-Dār al-Salafiyyah, 1403/1983).

——, *Muṣannaf*, (ed.), Kamal Yusuf al-Hut (Riyadh: Maktabat al-Rushd, 1409 AH).

Ibn Adiy, Abu Ahmad Abd Allah, *al-Kāmil fī Ḍuᶜafā' al-Rijāl* (Beirut: Dār al-Fikr, 1405/1985).

Ibn al-ᶜArabī, Abū Bakr, *Aḥkām al-Qur'ān*, (ed.), Ali Muhammad al-Bijawi (Beirut: Dār al-Jīl, 1407/1987).

——, *al-Qabas ᶜalā Muwaṭṭa'*, (ed.), Muhammad Abd Allah Walad Karim (Beirut: Dār al-Gharb al-Islāmī, 1992).

——, *ᶜĀriḍat al-Aḥwadhī ᶜalā Sharḥ Ṣaḥīḥ al-Tirmidhī* (Cairo: Maṭbaᶜat al-Ṣāwī, 1353/1934).

——, *Aḥkām al-Qur'ān*, (ed.), Ali Muhammad al-Bijawi (Cairo: Dār Iḥyā' al-Kutub al-ᶜArabiyyah, 1377/1958).

——, *al-ᶜAwāṣim mina al-Qawāṣim*, (ed.), Ammar Talbi (Doha: Dār al-Thaqāfah, 1413/1992).

Ibn Ashur, Muhammad al-Tahir, *Alaysa al-Ṣubḥ bi-Qarīb: al-Taᶜlīm al-ᶜArabī al-Islāmī Dirāsah Tārīkhiyyah wa Ārā' Iṣlāḥiyyah* (Tunis: al-Sharikah al-Tūnisiyyah li-Funūn al-Rasm, 1988).

——, *Kashf al-Mughaṭṭā mina al-Maᶜānī wa al-Alfāẓ al-Wāqiᶜah fī Muwaṭṭā* (Tunis: al-Sharikah al-Tūnisiyyah lī al-Tawzīᶜ; Algiers: al-Sharikah al-Waṭaniyyah lī al-Nashr wa al-Tawzīᶜ, 1976).

——, *Naqd ᶜIlmī li-Kitāb al-Islām wa Uṣūl al-Ḥukm* (Cairo: al-Maṭbaᶜah al-Salafiyyah, 1344 AH).

——, *Tafsīr al-Taḥrīr wa al-Tanwīr* (Tunis: Maison Souhnoun, 1997).

——, *Usūl al-Nizām al-Ijtimāᶜī Fī al-Islām*, ed. Mohamed El-Tahir El-Mesawi (Amman: Dār al-Nafā'is, 1421/2001).

Ibn al-Athīr, ᶜAlī ibn Muḥammad ᶜIzz al-Dīn, *al-Kāmil fī al-Tārīkh* (Beirut: Dār al-Kitāb al-ᶜArabī, n.d.)

Ibn Atiyyah, Abd al-Haqq, *al-Muḥarrar al-Wajīz fi Tafsīr al-Kitāb al-ᶜAzīz*, (ed.), Abd al-Salam Abd al-Shafi Muhammad (Beirut: Dār al-Kutub al-ᶜIlmiyyah, 1413/1993).

Ibn Daqīq al-ᶜĪd, Muḥammad ibn ᶜAlī, *Iḥkām al-Aḥkām Sharḥ ᶜUmdat al-Aḥkām* (Cairo: Idārat al-Maṭbaᶜah al-Munīriyyah, 1340 AH).

Ibn Farḥūn, Burhān al-Dīn Abū al-Wafā' Ibrāhīm ibn al-Imām Shams al-Dīn, *Tabṣirat al-Ḥukkām fī Uṣūl al-Aqḍiyah wa Manāhij al-Aḥkām*, (ed.), Jamal Marᶜishli (Beirut: Dār al-Kutub al-ᶜIlmiyyah, 1416/1995).

Ibn Fūrak, Abū Bakr Muḥammad ibn al-Ḥasan, *Mujarrad Maqālāt al-Shaikh*

Abī al-Ḥasan al-Ashʿarī, (ed.), Daniel Gimaret (Beirut: Dār El-Machreq, 1987).

Ibn Ḥajar, Aḥmad ibn ʿAlī, *Maqāṣid al-Sharīʿati al-Islāmiyyah,* (ed.), Mohammed El-Tahir El-Mesawi (Amman: Dār al-Nafā'is, 1421/2000).

——, *al-Talkhīṣ al-Ḥabīr*, (ed.), Abd Allah Hashim al-Yamani (Beirut: Dār al-Maʿrifah, n.d.)

Ibn Ḥazm, Abū Muḥammad ʿAlī, *al-Iḥkām fī Uṣūl al-Aḥkām*, (ed.) Muhammad Muhammad Tamir (Beirut: Dār al-Kutub al-ʿIlmiyyah, 1424/2004).

——, *al-Muḥallā bi al-Āthār*, (ed.), Abd al-Ghaffar Sulayman al-Bandarani (Beirut: Dār al-Kutub al-ʿIlmiyyah, 1408/1988).

Ibn Ḥibbān, Muḥammad, *Ṣaḥīḥ Ibn Ḥibbān*, (ed.), Shuʿayb al-Arna'ut (Beirut: Mu'assassat al-Risālah, 1993).

Ibn Hishām, ʿAbd al-Malik, *al-Sīrah al-Nabawiyyah* (Cairo: ʿĪsā Bābī al-Ḥalabī, 1955).

——, *al-Sīrah al-Nabawiyyah*, (ed.), Mustafa al-Saqqa et al. (Damascus: Dār al-Khayr, 1417/1996).

Ibn Kathīr, Ismāʿīl ibn ʿUmar, *al-Bidāyah wa al-Nihāyah* (Cairo: 1351/1355 AH).

Ibn Khaldūn, *The Muqaddimah*, trans., Franz Rosenthal (London: Routledge & Kegan Paul, 1967).

Ibn al-Khujah, General Muhammad, *Tārīkh Maʿālim al-Tawḥīd Fī al-Qadīm wa al-Jadīd* (Tunis: al-Maṭbaʿah al-Tūnisiyyah, 1358/1927).

Ibn Mājah Abū ʿAbd Allāh Muḥammad ibn Yazīd, *Sunan*, (ed.), M. M. al-Azami (Riyadh: Sharikat al-Ṭibāʿah al-ʿArabiyyah, 1404/1984).

——, *Sunan*, (ed.), Mahmud Muhammad Nassar (Beirut: Dār al-Kutub al-ʿIlmiyyah, 1419/1998).

Ibn Manẓūr, Abū al-Faḍl Jamāl al-Dīn Muḥammad ibn Mukarram, *Lisān al-ʿArab* (Beirut: Dār Ṣādir, 1410/1990).

Ibn Nujaym, Zayn al-ʿĀbidīn ibn Ibrāhīm, *al-Ashbāh wa al-Naẓā'ir* (Beirut: Dār al-Kutub al-ʿIlmiyyah, 1400/1980).

Ibn Qayyim al-Jawziyyah, Shams al-Dīn Abū ʿAbd Allāh Muḥammad ibn Abī Bakr, *Iʿlām Muwaqqiʿīn ʿan Rabb al-ʿĀlamīn*, (ed.), Muhammad Abd al-Salam Ibrahim (Beirut: Dār al-Kutub al-ʿIlmiyyah, 1411/1991).

——, *Zād al-Maʿād Fī Hady Khayr al-ʿIbād*, (ed.) Shuʿayb al-Arna'ut et al (Beirut: Mu'assassat al-Risālah, 1405/1985).

——, *Zād al-Maʿād fī Hady Khayr al-ʿIbād* (Beirut: Dār Ibn Ḥazm, 1420/1999).

Ibn Qudāmah, ʿAbd Allāh ibn Aḥmad, *al-Mughnī*, (ed.), Abd Allah al-Turki et al. (Cairo: Dār Hajar, 1406/1986).

Ibn Qutaybah, Abū Muḥammad ʿAbd Allāh ibn Muslim, *Ta'wīl Mukhtalif al-Ḥadīth*, (ed.), Muhammad Abd al-Rahim (Beirut: Dār al-Fikr, 1415/1995).

Ibn Rushd, Abū al-Walīd (the Grandfather), *al-Bayān wa al-Taḥṣīl*, (ed.), Muhammad Hajji et al. (Beirut: Dār al-Gharb al-Islāmī, 1408/1988).

——, *al-Muqaddimāt al-Mumahhidāt*, (ed.), Muhammad Hajji (Beirut: Dār al-Gharb al-Islāmī, 1408/1988).

Ibn Rushd, Abū al-Walīd (the Grandson), *The Distinguished Jurist's Primer* (*Bidāyat al-Mujtahid wa Nihayat al-Muqtasid*), trans., Imran Ahsan Khan Nyazee (Reading, Berks, UK: Garnet Publishing, 2003).

Ibn Sīnā, Abū ʿAlī al-Ḥusayn, *Kitāb al-Najāt Fī al-Ḥikmah al-Manṭiqiyyah wa al-Ṭabīʿiyyah wa al-Ilāhiyyh*, (ed.), Majid Fakhri (Beirut: Dār al-Āfāq al-Jadīdah, 1405/1985).

Ibn Sirāj, Abū al-Qāsim Muḥammad, *Fatāwā Qāḍī al-Jamāʿah Abī al-Qāsim ibn Sirāj*, (ed.), Muhammad Abu al-Ajfan (Abu Dhabi: al-Majmaʿ al-Thaqāfī, 1420/2000).

Ibn Taymiah, Taqīy al-Dīn Aḥmad, *al-Siyāsah al-Sharʿiyyah fī Iṣlāḥ al-Rāʿī wa al-Raʿiyyah*, (ed.) Muhammad Ayman ibn Hasan al-Shabrawi (Beirut: Dār al-Kutub al-ʿIlmiyyah, 1421/2000).

Ījī, ʿAḍud al-Dīn ʿAbd al-Raḥmān al-, *Sharḥ al-ʿAḍud* (a commentary on Ibn al-Ḥājib's *uṣūl* work *Mukhtaṣar al-Muntahā al-Uṣūlī*), (ed.), Fadi Nasif et al. (Beirut: Dār al-Kutub al-ʿIlmiyyah, 1421/2000).

——, *al-Mawāqif fī ʿIlm al-Kalām* (Beirut: ʿĀlam al-Kutub, n.d.)

Imām Mālik ibn Anas, *al-Mudawwanah al-Kubrā* (Beirut: Dār al-Fikr, n.d.)

——, *Muwaṭṭa'*, (ed.), Ahmad Ratib Amrush (Beirut: Dār al-Nafā'is, 1414/1994).

Iqbal, Muhammad, *Thoughts and Reflections of Iqbal*, (ed.), and annot., Syed Abdul Wahid (Lahore: Shaikh Muhammad Ashraf, 1992).

Juʿayyiṭ, Muḥammad al-ʿAzīz, *al-Ṭarīqah al-Marḍiyyah fī al-Ijrā'āt al-Sharʿiyyah ʿalā Madhhab al-Mālikiyyah* (Tunis: Maktabat al-Istiqāmah, n.d.)

Jughaym, Numan, *Ṭuruq al-Kashf ʿan Maqāṣid al-Shāriʿ* (Amman: Dār al-Nafā'is, 1422/2002).

Jurjānī, al-Sharīf ʿAlī ibn Muḥammad al-, *Sharḥ al-Mawāqif* (a commentary on al-Ījī's *Mawāqif*), (ed.), Mahmud Umar al-Dimyati (Beirut: Dār al-Kutub al-ʿIlmiyyah, 1419/1998).

Juwaynī, Abū al-Maʿālī al-, *al-Burhān fī Uṣūl al-Fiqh*, (ed.), Abd al-Azim al-Dib (Cairo: Dār al-Wafā, 1412/1992).

——, *al-Ghayāthī* (Beirut: Dār al-Kutub al-ʿIlmiyyah, 1417/1997).

——, *A Guide to Conclusive Proofs of the Principles of Belief* [*Kitāb al-Irshād ilā Qawāṭiʿ al-'Adilla fī Uṣūl al-Iʿtiqād*], trans., Paul E. Walker (Reading, UK: Garnet Publishing, 2000).

Kāndahlawī, Muḥammad Yūsuf al-, *Ḥayāt al-Ṣaḥābah*, (ed.), Nayif al-Abbas et al. (Damascus: Dār al-Qalam, 1388/1968).

Kāndahlawī, Muḥammad Zakariyā al-, *Awjaz al-Masālik ilā Muwaṭṭa' al-Imām Mālik*, (ed.), Taqiy al-Din al-Nadwi (Damascus: Dār al-Qalam, 1424/2003).

——, *Awjaz al-Masālik ilā Muwaṭṭa' al-Imām Mālik* (Beirut: Dār al-Fikr, 1400/1980).

Kāsānī, ʿAlā' al-Dīn Abū Bakr al-, *Badā'iʿ al-Ṣanā'iʿ fī Tartīb al-Sharā'iʿ* (Cairo: Sharikat al-Maṭbūʿāt al-ʿIlmiyyah, 1327 AH).

Kutubi, Muhammad ibn Shakir al-, *Fawāt al-Wafayāt*, (ed.), Ihsan Abbas, (Beirut: Dār Ṣādir, n.d.)

Lane, E. W., *Arabic–English Lexicon* (Cambridge, UK: Islamic Texts Society, 1984).

Al-Majallah al-Zaytūniyyah (Beirut: Dār al-Gharb al-Islāmī).

Manufi, Ali ibn Khalaf al-, *Kifāyat al-Ṭālib al-Rabbānī ʿalā Risālat Ibn Abī Zayd al-Qayrawānī*, (ed.), Ahmad Hamdi Imam (Cairo: Maktabat al-Madanī, 1407/1987).

Manāwī, ʿAbd al-Ra'ūf ibn ʿAlī al-, *al-Tysīr bi-Sharḥ al-Jāmiʿ al-Ṣaghīr* (Riyadh: Maktabat al-Imām al-Shāfiʿī, 1408/1988).

——, *Fayḍ al-Qadīr bi-Sharḥ al-Jāmiʿ al-Ṣaghīr* (Beirut: Dār al-Maʿrifah, 1972).

Marzūqī, Aḥmad ibn Muḥammad al-, *Sharḥ Dīwān al-Ḥamāsah*, (ed.), Abd al-Salam Harun (Cairo: Maṭbaʿat Lajnat al-Ta'līf wa al-Tarjamah wa al-Nashr, 1387/1967).

Al-Mawsūʿah al-Fiqhiyyah al-Kuwaitiyyah (Kuwait: Ministry of Awqāf and Islamic Affairs, 1412/1992).

Māwardī, al-, *The Ordinances of Government*, trans., Wafaa H. Wahba (Reading, Berks, UK: Garnet Publishing, 2000).

Maydani, Abd al-Ghani al-, *al-Lubāb fī Sharḥ al-Kitāb* (Beirut: al-Maktabah al-ʿIlmiyyah, 1400/1980).

Māzarī, Abū ʿAbd Allah Muḥammad ibn ʿAlī ibn ʿUmar ibn Muḥammad al-, *Īḍāḥ al-Maḥṣūl min Burhān al-Uṣūl*, (ed.), Ammar Talbi (Beirut: Dār al-Gharb al-Islāmī, 2001).

——, *al-Muʿlim bi-Fawā'id Muslim*, (ed.), Muhammad al-Shadhuli al-Nayfar (Beirut: Dār al-Gharb al-Islāmī, 1992).

Misri, Ahmad ibn Naqib al-, *Reliance of the Traveller*, trans., Nuh Ha Mim Keller (Beltsville, MD: Amana Publications, 1997).

Muranyi, Miklos, *Dirāsāt fī al-Fiqh al-Mālikī*, trans. from the German by Saʿid Bhiri et al. (Beirut: Dār al-Gharb al-Islāmī, 1409/1988).

Naḥḥās, Aḥmad ibn Muḥammad ibn al-, *Sharḥ al-Qaṣā'id al-Mashhūrāt al-Mawsumāt bi al-Muʿallaqāt* (Beirut: Dār al-Kutub al-ʿIlmiyyah, 1405/1985).

Nasā'īʿ, *Sunan*, (ed.), Abd al-Fattah Abu Ghuddah (Aleppo, Syria: Maktab al-Maṭbūʿāt al-Islāmiyyah, 1406/1986).

Nasā'ī, Abū ʿAbd al-Raḥmān Aḥmad ibn Shuʿayb al-, *Sunan* (Istanbul: Dār al-Daʿwah, 1413/1992).

——, *al-Sunan al-Kubrā*, (ed.), Hassan Abd al-Munʿim Shalabi (Beirut: Mu'assassat al-Risālah, 1421/2001).

Nawawī, Yaḥyā ibn Sharaf al-, *Sharḥ Ṣaḥīḥ Muslim* (Beirut: Dār Iḥyā' al-Turāth al-ʿArabī, n.d.)

Naysābūrī, Abū ʿAbd Allāh al-Ḥākim al-, *al-Mustadrak* (Beirut: Dār al-Maʿrifah, 1407/1987).

——, *al-Mustadrak*, (ed.), Mustafa Abd al-Qadir Ata (Beirut: Dār al-Kutub al-ʿIlmiyyah, 1990).

Nyazee, Imran Ahsan Khan, *Islamic Jurisprudence* (Islamabad, Pakistan: International Institute of Islamic Thought & Islamic Research Institute, 2000).

Pickthall, Muhammad Marmaduke, *The Noble Qur'ān*, Arabic original with English translation (Kuala Lumpur: Islamic Book Trust, 2001).

Qalaji, Muhammad Rawas, *Mawsūʿat Fiqh Ibrāhīm al-Nakhʿī* (Makkah: Jāmiʿat Umm al-Qurā, 1399/1980).

Qari, al-Mulla Ali al-, *Sharḥ al-Shifā'*, (ed.), Hasanayn Muhammad Makhluf (Cairo: Maktabat Ibn Taymia, n.d.)

Qaradawi, Yusuf al-, 'al-Jānib al-Ḥaḍārī fī al-Sunnah al-Nabawiyyah', in *al-Sunnah al-Nabawiyyah wa Manhajuhā fī Binā' al-Maʿrifah wa al-Ḥaḍārah*, proceedings of a symposium organized by IIIT and al-Majmaʿ al-Malakī li-Buḥūth al-Ḥaḍārah al-Islāmiyyah, Amman: 15–19 Dhū al-Qiʿdah 1409/ 19–23 June 1989.

——, *Fī Fiqh al-Aqalliyāt al-Muslimah* (Cairo: Dār al-Shurūq, 1422/2001).

——, *Kayfa Nataʿāmalu Maʿa al-Sunnah: Maʿālim wa Ḍawābiṭ* (Herndon, VA: International Institute of Islamic Thought [IIIT], 1411/1990).

Qarāfī, Shihāb al-Dīn Aḥmad ibn Idrīs al-, *al-Dhakhīrah fī Furūʿ al-Mālikiyyah*, ed. Abu Ishaq Ahmad Abd al-Rahman (Beirut: Dār al-Kutub al-ʿIlmiyyah, 1422/2001).

——, *Kitāb al-Furūq*, (ed.), Muhammad Ahmad Sarraj & Ali Jumah Muhammad (Cairo: Dār al-Salām, 1421/2001).

——, *al-Iḥkām fī Tamyīz al-Fatāwā ʿan al-Aḥkām* (Beirut: Dār al-Anwār, 1983).

——, *Sharḥ Tanqīḥ al-Fuṣūl* (Beirut: Dār al-Fikr, 1424/2004).

——, *Nafā'is al-Uṣūl fī Sharḥ al-Maḥṣūl*, (ed.), Adil Ahmad Abd al-Mawjud and Ali Muhammad Muʿawwad (Riyadh: Maktabat Mustaphā al-Bāz, 1995).

Qaysī, Abū Muḥammad Makkī ibn Abī Ṭālib al-, *al-Kashf ʿan Wujūh al-Qirā'āt al-Sabʿ*, (ed.), Muḥyī al-Dīn Ramaḍān (Beirut: Mu'assassat al-Risālah, 1418/1997).

Qurṭubī, Muḥammad ibn Aḥmad al-, *al-Jāmiʿ li-Aḥkām al-Qur'ān*, (ed.), Ahmad Abd al-Alim al-Barduni (Beirut: Dār Ihyā' al-Turāth al-ʿArabī, n.d.)

Rahūnī, Abū Zakariyā' Yaḥyā ibn Mūsā al-, *Tuḥfat al-Mas'ūl fī Sharḥ Mukhtaṣar Muntahā al-Sūl* (a commentary on Ibn al-Ḥājib's *Mukhtaṣar Muntahā al-Sūl*), (ed.), Yusuf al-Akhdhar al-Qayyim (Dubai: Dār al-Buḥūth li al-Dirāsāt al-Islāmiyyah wa Iḥyā' al-Turāth, 1422/2002).

Raʿi, Muhammad ibn Muhammad al-, *Intiṣār al-Faqīr al-Sālik* (Beirut: Dār al-Gharb al-Islāmī, 1981).

Ramic, Sukrija Husejn, *Language and the Interpretation of Islamic Law* (Cambridge, UK: The Islamic Texts Society, 2003).

Raṣṣāʿ, Abū ʿAbd Allāh Muḥammad al-Anṣārī al-, *Sharḥ Ḥudūd Ibn ʿArafah*, (ed.), Muhammad Abu al-Ajfan & al-Tahir al-Mamuri (Beirut: Dār al-Gharb al-Islāmī, 1993).

Rāzī, Fakhr al-Dīn al-, *al-Tafsīr al-Kabīr or Mafātīḥ al-Ghayb* (Beirut: Dār al-Kutub al-ʿIlmiyyah, 1990).

Rosenthal, Franz, *The Muslim Concept of Freedom Prior to the Nineteenth Century* (Leiden, The Netherlands: E. J. Brill, 1960).

Sakhāwī, Muḥammad ibn ʿAbd al-Raḥmān al-, *al-Maqāṣid al-Ḥasanah*, (ed.), Abd Allah ibn al-Siddiq al-Ghammari (Beirut: Dār al-Kutub al-ʿIlmiyyah, 1407/1987).

Ṣanʿānī, ʿAbd al-Razzāq al-, *al-Muṣannaf*, (ed.), Habib al-Rahman al-Azami (Deoband: al-Majlis al-Islāmī bi al-Hind, 1403 AH).

——, *Muṣannaf*, (ed.), Habib al-Rahman al-Azami (Beirut: al-Maktab al-Islāmī, 1403/1983).

Sarakhsī, Abū Bakr Muḥammad ibn Aḥmad ibn Abī Sahl al-, *Uṣūl al-Sarakhsī*, (ed.), Rafiq al-Ajm (Beirut: Dār al-Maʿrifah, 1418/1997).

Shāfiʿī, al-Imām Muḥammad ibn Idrīs al-, *al-Risālah fī Uṣūl al-Fiqh*, trans., Majid Khadduri (Cambridge, UK: The Islamic Texts Society, 1997).

Shah Wali Allah of Delhi, *The Conclusive Argument from God*, trans., Marcia K. Hermansen (Leiden, The Netherlands: E.J. Brill, 1996).

Shalabi, Muhammad Mustafa, *Aḥkām al-Mawārīth bayna al-Fiqh wa al-Qānūn* (Beirut: Dār al-Nahḍah al-ʿArabiyyah, 1978).

Shams al-Din, Muhammad Mahdi, *al-Ijtihād wa al-Tajdīd Fī al-Fiqh al-Islāmī* (Beirut: al-Mu'assassah al-Dawliyyah, 1419/1999).

——, *al-Ijtihād wa al-Taqlīd: Baḥth Fiqhī Istidlālī Muqārin* (Beirut: al-Mu'assassah al-Dawliyyah, 1419/1998).

Shāṭibī, Abū Isḥāq Ibrāhīm ibn Mūsā ibn Muḥammad al-Lakhmī al-, *al-Muwāfaqāt fī Uṣūl al-Sharīʿah*, (ed.), Abd Allah Draz (Beirut: Dār al-Maʿrifah, 1996).

——, *Kitāb al-Iʿtiṣām*, (ed.), Khalid Abd al-Fattah Shibl Abu Sulayman (Beirut: Dār al-Fikr, 1416/1996).

Shawkānī, Muḥammad ʿAlī al-, *Nayl al-Awṭār* (Beirut: Dār ibn Ḥazm, 1421/2000).

——, *Irshād al-Fuḥūl ilā Taḥqīq al-Ḥaqq min ʿIlm al-Uṣūl*, (ed.), Muhammad Subhi ibn Hasan Hallaq (Damascus/Beirut: Dār Ibn Kathīr, 1421/2000).

Shinqīṭī, Aḥmad ibn Muḥammad al-, *Aḍwā' al-Bayān* (Cairo: Maṭbaʿat al-Madanī, 1392/1972).

Shinqīṭī, Muḥammad ibn Aḥmad al-Shaybānī al-, *Tabyīn al-Masālik* (Beirut: Dār al-Gharb al-Islāmī).

Shirbīnī, Muḥammad ibn Aḥmad al-, *al-Iqnāʿ fī Ḥall Alfāẓ Abī Shujāʿ* (Beirut: Dār al-Maʿrifah, n.d.)

——, *Mughnī al-Muḥtāj ilā Maʿrifat Alfāẓ al-Minhāj*, (ed.), Jawbalī al-Shāfiʿī (Beirut: Dār al-Fikr, 1419/1998).

Siddiq, Ahmad ibn Muhammad ibn al-, *Masālik al-Dilālah fī Sharḥ Matn al-Risālah* (Cairo: Dār al-ʿAhd al-Jadīd, 1374/1954).

Subkī, ʿAbd al-Wahhāb ibn ʿAlī Tāj al-Dīn al-, *al-Ashbāh wa al-Naẓā'ir*, (ed.), Adil Abd al-Mawjud and Ali Muʿawwad (Beirut: Dār al-Kutub al-ʿIlmiyyah, 1411/1991).

Sulamī, Abū Muhammad ʿIzz al-Dīn Ibn ʿAbd al-Salām al-, *al-Qawāʿid al-Kubrā* (also known as *Qawāʿid al-Aḥkām fī Iṣlāḥ al-Anām*), (ed.), Nazih Hammad et al. (Damascus: Dār al-Qalam, 1421/2000).

Sunhājī, Abū al-Shitā' al-, *Mawāhib al-Khallāq ʿalā Sharḥ al-Tāwdī li-Lāmiyat al-Zaqqāq* (Rabat: Maktabat al-Umniyah, 1375/1955).

Suyūṭī, Jalāl al-Dīn ʿAbd al-Raḥmān al-, *al-Ashbāh wa al-Naẓā'ir fī Qawāʿid wa Furūʿ Fiqh al-Shāfiʿiyyah*, (ed.), Khalid Abd al-Fattah Shibl Marashli, (Beirut: Dār al-Fikr, n.d.)

Ṭabarānī, Sulaymān ibn Aḥmad al-, *al-Muʿjam al-Kabīr*, (ed.), Hamdi Abd al-Majid al-Salafi (Baghdad: Ministry of Awqāf, n.d.)

——, *al-Muʿjam al-Kabīr*, (ed.), Hamdi Abd al-Majid al-Salafi (Mosul, Iraq: Maktabat al-ʿUlūm wa al-Ḥikam, 1408/1988).

Ṭabarī, Abū Jaʿfar Muḥammad ibn Jarīr al-, *Dhuyūl Tārīkh al-Ṭabarī* (volume 11 of his *Tārīkh al-Rusul wa al-Mulūk*), (ed.), Muhammad Abu al-Fadl Ibrahim (Cairo: Dār al-Maʿārif, n.d.)

——, *Jāmiʿ al-Bayān fī Ta'wīl Āyi al-Qur'ān* (Beirut: Dār al-Kutub al-ʿIlmiyyah, 1992).

——, *Tārīkh al-Rusul wa al-Mulūk*, (ed.), Muhammad Abu al-Fadl Ibrahim (Beirut: Dār al-Fikr, 1399 AH).

Ṭabāṭabā'ī, Muḥammad Ḥussayn al-, *al-Mīzān fī Tafsīr al-Qur'ān* (Beirut: Mu'assassat al-Aʿlamī, 1411/1991).

Tabrīzī, Yaḥyā ibn ʿAlī al-, *Sharḥ al-Qaṣā'id al-ʿAshr*, (ed.), Abd al-Salam al-Hufi (Beirut: Dār al-Kutub al-ʿIlmiyyah, 1405/1985).

Taḥāwī, Aḥmad ibn Muḥammad ibn Salāmah ibn ʿAbd al-Malik Abū Jaʿfar al, *Sharḥ Maʿānī al-Āthār*, (ed.), Muhammad Zuhri al-Najjar (Beirut: Dār al-Kutub al-ʿIlmiyyah, 1399 AH).

Tasūlī, ʿAlī ibn ʿAbd al-Salām al-, *al-Bahjah fī Sharḥ al-Tuḥfah* (Beirut: Dār al-Maʿrifah, 1397/1977).

The Mejelle, English translation of *Majallat al-Aḥkām al-ʿAdliyyah* (a compendium of Islamic civil law according to the Ḥanafī school), (Kuala Lumpur: The Other Press, n.d.)

Tirmidhī, Muḥammad ibn ʿAlī ibn al-Ḥasan Abū ʿAbd Allāh al-, *Nawādir al-Uṣūl fī Aḥādīth al-Rasūl*, (ed.), Abd al-Rahman Umayrah (Beirut: Dār al-Jīl, 1412/1992).

Tirmidhī, Muḥammad ibn ʿĪsā al-, *Sunan*, (ed.), Ahmad Muhammad Shakir (Cairo: Dār al-Ḥadīth, 1419/1999).

——, *Sunan*, (ed.), Mustapha Muhammad Husayn al-Dhahabi (Cairo: Dār al-Ḥadīth, 1419/1999).

——, *Sunan* (Istanbul: Dār al-Daʿwah, 1413/1993).

Ṭūfī, Najm al-Dīn Abū al-Rabīʿ Sulaymān ibn ʿAbd al-Qawīy al-, *Sharḥ Mukhtaṣar al-Rawḍah*, (ed.), Abd Allah Abd al-Muhsin al-Turki (Beirut: Mu'assassat al-Risālah, 1419/1998).

Turkī, ʿAbd al-Majīd, *Munāẓarāt fī Uṣūl al-Sharīʿah* (Beirut: Dār al-Gharb al-Islāmī, 1994).

Wansharīsī, Aḥmad ibn Yaḥyā al-, *Īḍāḥ al-Masālik ilā Qawāʿid al-Imām Mālik*, (ed.), Ahmad al-Khattabi (Rabat: Ministry of Awqāf, 1400/1980).

Weiss, Bernard G., *The Search for God's Law: Islamic Jurisprudence in the Writings of Sayf al-Dīn al-Āmidī* (Salt Lake City, UT: University of Utah Press, 1992).

Yaḥṣubī, al-Qāḍī ʿIyāḍ al-, *Tartīb al-Madārik*, (ed.), Aḥmad Bakīr Maḥmūd (Beirut: Dār Maktabat al-Ḥayāt & Tripoli [Libya]: Dār Maktabat al-Fikr, 1387/1967).

Yakan, Zuhdi, *al-Awqāf Fī al-Sharīʿah wa al-Qānūn* (Beirut: Dār al-Nahḍah al-ʿArabiyyah, 1388 AH).

Zamakhsharī, Maḥmūd ibn ʿUmar al-, *al-Kashshāf ʿan Ḥaqā'iq Ghawāmiḍ al-Tanzīl wa ʿUyūn al-Aqāwīl fī Wujūh al-Ta'wīl*, (ed.), Muhammad Abd al-Salam Shahin (Beirut: Dār al-Kutub al-ʿIlmiyyah, 1415/1995).

Zarkashī, Badr al-Dīn Muḥammad ibn Bahādar ibn ʿAbd Allāh al-, *al-Baḥr al-Muḥīṭ fī Uṣūl al-Fiqh*, (ed.), Muhammad Muhammad Tamir (Beirut: Dār al-Kutub al-ʿIlmiyyah, 1421/2000).

Zarqa, Ahmad al-, *Sharḥ al-Qawāʿid al-Fiqhiyyah*, (ed.), Abd al-Sattar Abu Ghuddah (Beirut: Dār al-Gharb al-Islāmī, 1403/1983).

Zarqa, Mustafa Ahmad al-, *ʿAqd al-Bayʿ* (Damascus: Dār al-Qalam, 1420/1999).

Zaydan, Abd al-Karim, *Aḥkām al-Dhimmiyyīn wa al-Musta'manīn* (Beirut: Mu'assasat al-Risālah, 1988).

Zaylaʿī, Fakhr al-Dīn ʿUthmān ibn ʿAlī al-, *Tabyīn al-Ḥaqā'iq Sharḥ Kanz al-Daqā'iq* (Beirut: Dār al-Maʿrifah, n.d.)

Zaylaʿī, Jamāl al-Dīn Abū Muḥammad ʿAbd Allāh ibn Yūsuf al-, *Naṣb al-Rāyah li Aḥādith al-Hidāyah* (Cairo: Dār al-Ma'mūn, 1357 AH).

Ziaul Haque, *Landlord and Peasant in Early Islam* (Islamabad, Pakistan: Islamic Research Institute, 1984).

Zurqānī, Abd al-Bāqī ibn Yūsuf al-, *Sharḥ Muwaṭṭa'* (Cairo: al-Maktabah al-Tijāriyyah al-Kubrā, 1959).

——, *Sharḥ Muwaṭṭa' Mālik* (Cairo: Maṭbaʿat al-Istiqāmah, 1373/1954).

GLOSSARY OF TERMS

ᶜAzīmah: This term indicates the binding force of a Shariᶜah rule without consideration of mitigating hardship.

Ḍarūrah: Necessity. A situation that requires the mitigation of a rule.

Ḍarūriyyāt (sing. *ḍarūrī*): The things that are vital and indispensable for life and existence and constitute the ultimate higher objectives (*maqāṣid*) of Islamic Law. They occupy the highest position in the hierarchical order of Islamic values.

Dharīᶜah (plur. *dharā'iᶜ*): Means to an end. It may also be called *wasīlah*.

Fatwa (plur. *fatāwā*): A formal legal opinion issued by a *muftī* (jurisconsult) based on a question posed to him by an inquiring person (called *mustaftī*).

Fiṭrah: The original God-given nature of man.

Gharar: Uncertainty or risk involved in a transaction.

Ḥabs: Trust. It is synonymous with the term *waqf*.

The definitions in this glossary are drawn from the following sources: Ibn Rushd, *Distinguished Jurist's Primer* (*Bidāyat al-Mujtahid*), trans. Imran Ahsan Khan Nyazee (Reading: Garnet Publishing Limited, 2003); Imran Ahsan Khan Nyazee, *Islamic Jurisprudence* (Islamabad: International Institute of Islamic Thought & Islamic Research Institute, 2000); Sano Koutoub Moustapha, *Muᶜjam Muṣṭalaḥāt Uṣūl al-Fiqh, Arabī-Inkilīzī* (Concordance of Jurisprudence Fundamentals Terminology), (Syria, Damascus: Dār al-Fikr, 2000); Muhammad Rawwās Qalᶜanjī, *Muᶜjam Lughat al-Fuqahā'*, Arabic-English-French (Beirut: Dār al-Nafā'is, 1996), and Wael B, Hallaq, *A History of Islamic Legal Theories: An Introduction to Sunnī Uṣūl al-Fiqh* (Cambridge, UK: Cambridge University Press, 1997).

Ḥadd (plur. *Ḥudūd*): Limit, bound. In the Islamic penal code, the term *Ḥadd* refers to the set of punishments that have been enunciated and determined in the Shariʿah textual sources (i.e., the Qur'an and Sunnah of the Prophet) both in terms of their nature, scope and quantity.

Ḥājiyyāt: Necessary things whose realization is intended by the Shariʿah for the purpose of removing hardship from human life. Next to the *ḍarūriyyāt* that constitute indispensable objectives of Islamic law and whose neglect cause severe harm to human life and existence, the *Ḥājiyyāt* are needed for maintaing an orderly society properly governed by the law.

Ḥikmah: Wisdom. In Islamic jurisprudence, the term *ḥikmah* refers to the wise purpose or objective for which a Shariʿah command has been instituted, which revolves around bringing good to human beings and/or preventing harm from them. It may be used unterchangeably with the term *maṣlaḥah*.

Ḥiyal (sing. *ḥīlah*): Tricks, stratagems, artifices. This term refers to legal devices used to exploit that which is legitimate for an illegitimate purpose or end; or, that which appears to be legitimate but is not.

Ḥukm: Rule, injunction, prescription.

Ḥukm Sharʿī: Technically, this term refers to communication from God, the Almighty, pertaining to the acts of human agents (*mukallafūn*) through a demand or option (*ḥukm taklīfī*), or through a declaration (*ḥukm waḍʿī*).

Ḥukm Taklīfī: The obligation-creating rule. The primary rule of the legal system. According to the majority of legal theorists, the *ḥukm ṭaklīfī* consists of *wājib* (obligatory act), *mandūb* (recommended act), *ḥarām* (prohibited act), *makrūh* (disapproved act), and *mubāḥ* (permitted act).

Ḥukm Waḍʿī: The declaratory rule. A secondary rule of the legal system that facilitates the operation of the primary rules. It includes *sabab* (cause), *sharṭ* (condition) and *māniʿ* (obstacle or impediment).

Ḥuqūq (sing. *ḥaqq*): Rights, entitlements.

Ḥuqūq al-ʿAbd: The rights of man.

Ḥuqūq Allah: The rights of God.

Ijārah: Hire. Rent.

Ijtihad: Independent reasoning. Technically, this term refers to the effort exerted by a qualified jurist (*faqīh/mujtahid*) to arrive at the meaning intended by the Lawgiver in the textual sources of Islamic Law and apply it to its subject-matters in the real life of human beings.

ʿIllah: *Ratio legis*, cause, reason, rationale. Considered to be the most important pillar of *qiyās*, *ʿillah* is defined as being the attribute or quality in a human act that constitutes the ground or basis of a Shariʿah rule.

Istiṣlāḥ: The act or process of reasoning on the basis of *maṣlaḥah*.

Jibillah: The natural state according to which God has created man.

Al-Kulliyyāt al-Khamsah: This term refers to the five universal and most general higher objectives (*maqāṣid*) for the preservation and promotion of which the Shariʿah commands and rules have been promulgated. They constitute what is indispensable (*ḍarūrī*), for human life and existence. They consist of the protection of religious faith (*ḥifẓ al-dīn*), the protection of human life (*ḥifẓ al-nafs*), the protection of intellect (*ḥifẓ al-ʿaql*), the protection of progeny (*ḥifẓ al-nasl*) and the protection of property (*ḥifẓ al-māl*).

Kulliyyāt (plur. *kullī*, meaning universal): The universal things constituting the ultimate higher objectives of Islamic Law.

Liʿān: Oath of condemnation, imprecation. Disavowal of paternity by mutual oath of both spouses. This oath is resorted to by the husband in refutation of an accusation or *qadhf* by his wife, anf by the wife in refutation of an accusation of adultery by her husband.

Mafsadah: Evil, harm. It is the opposite of *maṣlahah*.

Manāṭ: Basis, ground. This term is used synonymously with the term *ʿillah*.

Maṣlaḥah: Interest, benefit, something good.

Maslaḥah Mursalah: Interest or benefit that has not been regulated or qualified by a specific text and is based on a general principle of the Shariʿah or its spirit.

Muʿallal: A Shariʿah rule whose *ʿillah* can be known either textually or by rational methods that are detailed by legal theorists under the heading of *masālik al-ʿillah* (methods of establishing the effective cause) in conjunction with the discussion on *qiyās*.

Muʿāmalāt: Social dealings, transactions.

Muḥallil: A man who weds a woman who has been irrevocably divorced (*mabtūtah*) with the intention of divorcing her so that her previous husband can marry her again. This type of marriage contract is called *nikāḥ al-tāḥlīl* and is prohibited in the Shariʿah.

Munāsabah: Appropriateness, suitability. In the technical language of the legal theorists (*uṣūliyyūn*), it is a meaning in a person's act that necessitates the obligation, prohibition or permission of that act. Such a meaning is an apparent and constant attribute (*waṣf*) deemed by reason to constitute the basis of the Shariʿah rule or command, as it is suitable (*munāsib*) to the purpose of the Lawgiver in instituting that *ḥukm*. The purpose of the Lawgiver consists of realizing benefit (*maṣlaḥah*) or preventing harm (*mafsadah*) or of achieving both goals at the same time.

Nikāḥ al-Muḥallil: It is a marriage contract in which a man marries an irrevocably divorced woman with the intention of divorcing her so that she can remarry her previous husband.

Nikāḥ al-Shighār: This is a form of marriage in which one man gives his female ward in marriage to another man on the condition that the other man will give his ward in marriage to the first, without there being any dower except the body of the woman in exchange for that of the other. Such a contract is not allowed in the Shariʿah.

Qaṭʿ: Certainty based on conclusive textual or rational evidence.

Qaṭʿī: Definitive. A legal proof is considered as *qaṭʿī* when it is conclusive and denotes certainty.

Qiyās: Analogy, syllogism. In Islamic jurisprudence, *qiyās* or analogical reasoning consists of extending the rule of a specific case (called *aṣl*) established by the Shariʿah textual sources to a new case awaiting legal decision on the basis of a common underlying cause (*ʿillah*).

Qiyās Kullī: A kind of anology in which the hold of individual texts and specific cases is released and reasoning proceeds in line with a general principle or set of general principles derived from the Shariʿah texts considered collectively. It is also called *qiyās mursal*.

Rukhṣah (plur. *rukhaṣ*): Exemption, lisence. It represents the mitigation of a rule by substituting for it a more lenient one, due to some hardship.

Sadd al-Dharā'iʿ: As a jurisprudential rule, the term *sadd al-dharā'iʿ* means the prohibition of evasive legal means, that is, blocking the lawful means to an unlawful end.

Shariʿah: Way, water spring, watering place, Law. In Qur'anic use, the term shariʿah denotes the whole of the Divine teachings pertaining to matters of belief and conduct. In the teminology of the jurists, it refers to the body of legal commands instituted by the Qur'an and Prophetic sayings.

Taʿabbud/taʿabbudī: Devotion or worship. It refers to the commands or rulings in Islamic Law for which one cannot provide an explantion through human reason, such as the number of *rakʿahs* in prayer.

Tabarruʿ: Donation.

Taḥayyul: Manipualtion, tricking, use of artifice.

Taḥqīq al-Manāṭ: The confirmation of the existence of the *ʿillah* in the new case (*farʿ*) to which a rule is to be extended through *qiyās*.

Taḥsinīyyāt: Embellishments, improvements. In the hierarchical order of the Shariʿah objectives, the *taḥsinīyyāt* come next to the *ḥājiyyāt* and refer to those aspects of Islamic Law that bring comfort amd ease in human life. They are not needed to such an extent that without them the law becomes inoperable or deficient and relinquishing them is not detrimental to the *ḍarūriyyāt* or the *ḥājiyyāt*. They are meant to improve the general character of the Shariʿah.

Takhrīj al-Manāṭ: The *mujtahid's* derivation of the suitable attribute for the *ḥukm* (or *ʿillah*) is known as *takhrīj al-manāṭ*.

Taʿlīl: Causation, rationalisation.The act of identifying the effective cause or underlying reason (*ʿillah*) of a Shariʿah command.

Tanqīḥ al-Manāṭ: Emendation and refinement of the effective cause (*ʿillah*) by excluding (*ilghāʾ*) some of the attributes or states of the act from being the effective cause or *ratio legis* (*ʿillah*) of the command.

Tawātur Maʿnawī: Thematic recurrence of reports.

Waqf: Trust, endowment.

Wāziʿ: Restraining force.

GENERAL INDEX

TRANSLATOR'S NOTE

Since it first appeared in 1946 Ibn Ashur's *Maqāṣid al-Sharīʿah* has undergone a series of publications both in Tunisia and Algeria. This translation is based on my own critical and annotated edition of the work published in 1421/2001 by Dār al-Nafā'is, Amman, Jordan.

To produce an edition worthy of today's rigorous academic standards, work on the translation has entailed documenting as many as possible of the original's references and cross references (familiar mainly to students of Islamic legal theory and Law only); providing a more up-to-date bibliography based on the most recent editions of the sources referred to by the author; and providing biographical information on the many scholars mentioned throughout the text etc. I have also used the phrase "Author" in the endnotes to distinguish the author's notes from my own. However, out of consideration for the requirements of an English-speaking readership, some of the notes that appear in my Arabic edition of the book have been omitted in this edition, whilst others not in the Arabic have been added. The level of material arrangement has also been improved for the sake of clarity. Qur'anic references have mainly been taken from Muhammad Asad's, *The Message of the Qur'an*.

Due to the high intellectual value of the book and its significance for the development of Islamic thought in modern times and seeing the increasing interest in the study of *Maqāṣid al-Sharīʿah* I have tried as fully as possible to produce an accurate and academically sound edition of the work whilst capturing as closely as possible the character of the original, and hope that it will benefit all readers both specialist and non-specialist alike.

Mohamed El-Tahir El-Mesawi
Kuala Lumpur, 25 Safar 1427 / 25 March 2006